Also by Chris Fujiwara

Jacques Tourneur: The Cinema of Nightfall

Defining Moments in Movies

THE WORLD AND ITS DOUBLE

THE WORLD AND ITS DOUBLE

The Life and Work of Otto Preminger

CHRIS FUJIWARA

ff

faber and faber

First published in the United States in 2008
by Faber and Faber, Inc.
An affiliate of Farrar, Straus and Giroux, LLC
18 West 18th Street, New York 10011

First published in the United Kingdom in 2008
by Faber and Faber Limited
3 Queen Square London WC1N 3AU

Designed by Jonathan D. Lippincott
Printed in the United States of America

A CIP record for this book is available from the British Library

ISBN 978-0-571-22370-1

2   4   6   8   10   9   7   5   3   1

For my mother

If you're interested in me, too bad for you.

—Otto Preminger

Contents

Introduction

These days, one reads mostly of two Otto Premingers. The first exists in history books as an important figure in the struggles against film censorship and the anti-Communist blacklist. The second exists for film buffs, as a great director of "film noir."

Rarely does one read of a Preminger who interests me more, and who was once even celebrated: a master of mise-en-scène and a symbol of cinematic fascination. In Preminger, fascination—the movement toward and into something—is in constant tension with its opposite: withdrawal from something, neutrality, detachment. A simultaneous push-pull generates the fantastic energy of his films, their subtle, spiraling rhythms, their veiled and discreet pathos, their intellectual weight and urgency. The present book was born out of a deepening involvement with this dual movement and a desire to trace its workings.

Preminger was a famous theater director in Vienna before he established himself as a film director in the United States, and his films show a theatrical orientation: a bias toward fluid staging and the long take ("If it were possible, I would do the whole of the film in one shot," he once said), toward a mise-en-scène in which multiple characters are in view at the same time, toward dialogue and the text.[1] Just as strong as the drive toward a unified stream of time in Preminger's films is the pull of the reality of actual locations, with their nonnegotiable demands on placing and maneuvering actors, the camera, and sound equipment. So strong is this pull that the location might be said to represent for Preminger's cinema an overcoming of the theater.

As a historical figure, Preminger might now be called the victim of a certain irony. The director who best represents the essential of classical cinema (a term I shall reconsider here and there in this book), he also predicted and was responsible for creating much of the landscape of current cinema—a cinema that is, however, in many ways a betrayal of the kind of adult entertainment he wanted to bring to the screen. Perhaps Preminger anticipated this betrayal, too, and surpassed it in his late films, through a course far more radical and more destructive than was taken by merely commercial directors.

The succession of disparate projects in Preminger's career—so daunting to anyone who tries to see the work as a whole—makes apparent a will to reinvent himself, to avoid being defined as the director of a single film or a single kind of film, to not be limited by what he had done before. This will is visible not only in his work as an independent producer-director from 1953 to 1979, though of course it is plainer there, but also in his work as a contract producer-director at Twentieth Century-Fox in the 1940s. "I have only one principle," Preminger said, "which is that there are no principles, and only one rule, which is that there are no rules. I am a man who lives from day to day, and who loves living, and that's all. I don't want someone to put me in a little box and tell me, you are like this or like that. You won't succeed. I want to reserve the right to change completely between nine in the morning and six at night, and to be a different man each day of the week."[2]

A crucial aspect of Preminger's deeply personal "impersonality" is control. He presents himself as someone who dominates his materials, his story, and his actors and who invites the audience to share his elation over this mastery, to identify with him in surveying the world of the film and floating above it, in modifying perspectives, moving in closer or backing away. The great freedom of movement in Preminger's films is communicated also to his characters: again and again, his work provides rueful, cynical, tragic, and triumphant testimony to the freedom of humanity.

An important part of Preminger's image was the character of the dictatorial, bullying, Teutonic director who terrified and humiliated actors. This was indeed a role, one that Preminger—who was also known to the public for playing Nazis in films—put on deliberately, partly to limn a memorable and entertaining public image, and partly to secure the conditions he felt necessary for making his films. "I can be patient and nice," Preminger once remarked, "but when I'm like that it takes me so much longer to get what I want."[3] Helga Cranston, who edited *Saint*

Joan and *Bonjour Tristesse*, noted that Preminger "liked to keep up the tension, and he also liked the idea that people were afraid of him. He once said to me, 'You know, maybe you think I'm exaggerating, but I know that I can't get 100 percent of what I want, so I'm trying to aim for 80 percent, with the hope of getting 60.' I think that he was badgering people to give him more than they were able to with the hope that it would somehow approach what he wanted in the first place."[4]

Many who concede his brilliance as a producer and even his skill with the camera have claimed that Preminger was not a good director of actors. No doubt both the evidence on the screen and the testimony of his coworkers plainly show that Preminger was not an "actor's director" in the ways that George Cukor, Jean Renoir, Elia Kazan, or John Cassavetes were (to cite four very different examples of directors for whom a collaborative and improvisatory practice was not only a working principle but an aesthetic tenet). Yet Preminger's films abound in excellent performances. He preferred a natural and direct kind of acting that was simply the projection of the actor's own nature through the filter of the character. He once told an actor who was having trouble in a scene, "It's so simple. Just visualize yourself in the situation, and say the line."[5] When it works, it works. No film is better acted than *The Moon Is Blue* or *Anatomy of a Murder*.

Although many actors believed that Preminger was the kind of director who had the whole film planned in his head before he started shooting, evidence reveals that this was true only in a broad sense and that decisions of where to place the camera and when to cut were made—much of the time—during the rehearsal of the scene, and not before. Obviously, there are exceptions: the close-ups of Akiva and Barak facing each other across prison bars in *Exodus* could have been, and were, anticipated at the writing stage. In general, as Preminger said, "I never prepare any shots . . . I visualize things: I know how I'm going to do it. But when I rehearse with actors I often change my idea because I like the film to come out of a rehearsal, out of a live contact, rather than to design it in advance and have it set. This is a question of system . . . I try to use the camera to make the point of the scene; that is about the only principle I can tell you, so it always works out differently."[6]

Preminger once told an interviewer that he had trained himself *as much as possible* to forget, when directing, that he was also the producer.

He was a perfectionist—but a relative perfectionist, not a pure perfectionist. He was capable of calling for twenty takes of a scene if he thought the performances could be improved, but he was satisfied with what some would regard as technical flaws: the shadow of the camera equipment is so omnipresent in his independent productions as to be almost a directorial signature, whether the cameraman was Sam Leavitt or Leon Shamroy. On the other hand, Preminger insisted that the screenplay be spoken as written, and he was not one to tolerate actors' taking minor liberties with dialogue: this was one area where he thought perfection was easily enough achievable that nothing short of it was to be countenanced.

I have stated earlier that Preminger was a classical director, and now I would like to qualify that remark. The particular meaning I want the word "classicism" to have in this book, though it may be unfamiliar, is central to my view of what makes Preminger a great filmmaker. His classicism lies in a conviction that the world of the film is real, but that that world must be conquered and verified. This verification, the action of the filmmaker, is of no less importance than the reality to which it is applied: it is a relentless quest, a testing of surfaces, a drive to crush, excoriate, penetrate—in any case, at least, to move on, as at the end of *Exodus* the trucks of the Haganah soldiers move on to fight the next battle somewhere else, and at the end of *Anatomy of a Murder* the vindicated defendant and his wife have already moved on to avoid paying their attorney.

This drive both defines Preminger's classicism and marks the inadequacy of that term. For in his negativity there is a striking modernity, which has kept its mystery. Here, too, is part of the enduring fascination of Preminger's cinema.

THE WORLD AND
ITS DOUBLE

1
Breaking the Lightning

Otto Preminger's father, Markus Preminger, was born on January 15, 1877, in Czernowitz, the capital of Bukovina, then part of the Austrian Empire, and now in Ukraine (where it is called Chernivtsi). "His parents were poor devout Jews," wrote Otto in his autobiography. "His father, an intelligent man, a Talmudic scholar, wanted him to have a first-rate education."[1] Markus completed his training as a lawyer in 1901, graduating cum laude, and subsequently served in Czernowitz as an investigating judge on the National Court and as a prosecutor in political criminal cases. "By the end of the [nineteenth] century an articulate educated class dominated the city's Jewry, German-speaking and modern in its outlook," William O. McCagg, Jr., wrote. Jews not only made up some 30 percent of the population of Czernowitz but also constituted the majority of the German-speaking population of Bukovina. "Even within Zionism there was a clear pattern of middle-class Jewish desire to save and abet the dying old Habsburg state," according to McCagg.[2] Perhaps these facts help account for Markus's firm loyalty to the Austrian state and, decades later, his failure to foresee, until it was no longer in doubt, that Austria, too, would fall to the barbarism that had overtaken Germany.

In 1903 Markus married Josepha Fränkel (born on March 11, probably in either 1883 or 1884), the daughter of Abraham Fränkel, who ran a lumber business in Poland, and his wife, Eugenia. Markus and Josepha's first son, Otto Ludwig, was born on December 5, 1905. That date and his place of birth have been matters of controversy. As Otto put it, "One set of documents lists Vienna as my birthplace but another set, equally valid-looking, places my birth at my great-grandfather's farm some distance away. One records that I was born on the fifth of December, 1906, the other exactly one year earlier."[3] Preminger preferred to use the later date, but 1905 was the year given in the registration forms for minorities (*Meldezettel für Unterparteien*) he filed in 1925 and 1933. The 1925 form gives Wiznitz, Romania (in 1905, part of Bukovina), as his place of birth; the 1933 form, Rozniatow, Poland (in 1905, part of Galicia). Rolf Aurich, who researched Preminger's origins, speculates that Preminger may have actually been born in Czernowitz and notes that in any case, "it is certain that he was not born in Vienna."[4] The farm Preminger mentions, which belonged to his mother's father's parents, was probably located in Wiznitz; it may also have been in Rozniatow, or even in Roznow, Poland (part of Galicia in 1905), which is mentioned as Preminger's birthplace on another Viennese registration form. During Otto's childhood, his family spent several summers at that farm. Official documents from Preminger's first decade in the United States generally give his date and place of birth as December 5, 1905, Wiznitz, Romania.

When the First World War broke out, the Russian Army confronted Austria, and the Preminger family (by now augmented by the birth of a second son, Ingo, on February 25, 1911) were forced to move, first to Vienna for a short time in 1914, then to Graz, capital of the province of Styria, where Markus served as first lieutenant auditor of the Thalerhof internment camp. At Graz, nine-year-old Otto became the victim of an anti-Semitic assault. On his way home from school, he was waylaid in a recessed doorway by a group of older boys who beat him and "called [him] names [he] had never heard before." Returning home with his face bloody and his clothes torn, he told his parents that he had slipped and fallen, though they realized the truth at once, as Otto would learn only later.[5] The incident was apparently never discussed openly among the family; Ingo had never heard of it until it was related to him by Otto's first biographer, Willi Frischauer.[6] But as Ingo also said, "When you went to school, as a Jew, in those days, you learned about anti-Semitism. First day you're in school. When you're six years old, you know what it means to be a Jew."[7] In 1912, another Viennese, Arthur Schnitzler, wrote, "It was not possible, especially not for a Jew in public life, to ignore the fact that he was a Jew; nobody else was doing so, not the Gentiles and even less the Jews. You had the choice of being counted as insensitive, obtrusive and fresh; or of being oversensitive, shy and suffering from feelings of persecution."[8]

Markus Preminger knew "a little bit" of Hebrew, Ingo recalled, and went to synagogue once a year, on Yom Kippur, but otherwise the Premingers observed no religious traditions. Markus's attitude toward Zionism was favorable, said Ingo, "but he wasn't interested in going to Israel or anything like that."

In the spring of 1915 Markus Preminger was transferred to Vienna as legal adviser to the military court. Markus's politics apparently suited him for this position. According to Ingo, "He was not very interested in politics, but he was rather conservative." (He did, however, vote Social Democratic, as did almost all Viennese Jews.) The family lived in the 8th district, in what Ingo later remembered as "a nice little apartment" in the Strozzigasse. Later, as Markus's fortunes advanced, the family moved to a better apartment in 9, Mahlerstrasse. The Premingers would eventually occupy an apartment in the Ringstrasse, across from the university, though that was not until 1926 or so.

In Vienna, Otto first attended the Piaristengymnasium, a Catholic school, starting in the 1915–16 school year. During those same months Otto's father won prominence prosecuting leaders of the Czech independence movement, including Karel Kramář, Václav Klofáč, and Edvard Beneš. In 1918 Markus retired from public service and opened a private practice in which he became very successful.

Meanwhile, Otto Preminger had developed a precocious interest in the arts. "When I was nine, eleven years old, I wrote poetry," he later recalled.[9] His burgeoning interest in theater, opera, and literature benefited from his being diagnosed with a heart murmur, which excluded him from the physical sports in which most of his peers spent their hours. (On the other hand, he was "very non-musical," according to Ingo.) Otto's taste ran toward the classics. He frequently missed classes in order to spend his days reading plays in the National Library. He had a good memory, which he exercised by reciting Shakespeare and Goethe to his maternal grandfather. At age fourteen or so, during one of his father's evening salons, Otto drew aside the famous actress Leopoldine Konstantin, on whom he had developed a crush, to give her a private recitation of Schiller's *Das Lied von der Glocke*, with its epigraph, "*Vivas voco / Mortuos plango / Fulgura frango*" (I call the living / I mourn the dead / I break the lightning).

Otto rapidly acquired experience acting in public, playing Lysander in an open-air production of A *Midsummer Night's Dream* at the Burggarten in 1922. In 1923, he took a decisive step by making contact with the famous director Max Reinhardt. The Austrian-born Reinhardt, then fifty, had from an early age been based mainly in Berlin, where he achieved renown. Lately he had announced plans to open a theater in Vienna. The Theater in der Josefstadt, as it was called, was purchased for Reinhardt by financier, industrialist, and patron of the arts Camillo Castiglioni, a rabbi's son who made his fortune in Vienna after the war. Then more than a century old, the dilapidated theater, located, in Gottfried Reinhardt's words, "in one of the seedier quarters of then impoverished Vienna on the verge of revolt"[10]—and only a few steps away from the Piaristengymnasium, where Otto passed his final exams on June 21—was beautifully restored in rococo style, with no expense being spared ("Unlimited funding was exactly the budget that suited [Reinhardt] best," quipped Preminger).[11]

In later years, Max Reinhardt's willingness to accept the inexperienced Preminger as an apprentice actor would not be forgotten by the younger director. "That was one of the reasons he always made a point of seeing young actors," Erik Preminger recalled about his father. "Anybody who called for an appointment with him was given five minutes with him. He set aside an hour every week, five minutes per appointment, and would see, literally, anybody who called and wanted to see him."[12]

The inaugural production of Reinhardt's new theater was Carlo Goldoni's eighteenth-century comedy *Il Servitore di due padroni* (*Der Diener zweier Herren* [*The Servant of Two Masters*]). Preminger was one of several costumed stagehands who performed set changes before the eyes of the audience and in tempo with the music.

By now Preminger had decided that he would make the theater his career. This news inspired little joy in his father, who, however, promised to support his son in whatever he did, as long as Otto finished his formal studies. Otto enrolled in the law program at the University of Vienna. Studying at home and benefiting from private tutors hired by his father, Otto eventually passed his exams and became a doctor of law in 1928.

In the first season at the Theater in der Josefstadt, Reinhardt gave Preminger only small parts. In April 1925, however, Reinhardt cast the young actor as Lysander in A *Midsummer Night's Dream*. Around the same time, Preminger studied in Reinhardt's course at the Viennese

Academy of Music and Performing Arts and apparently impressed the master enough for Reinhardt to make him an assistant both in his seminar at the Schönbrunn Palace and at the Salzburg Festival, where Reinhardt revived his famous production of the pantomine-spectacle *Das Mirakel* (*The Miracle*).

So many contradictory things have been claimed about Max Reinhardt that it is now difficult for nonspecialists to come to an appreciation of his capital role in European theater (and film). Part of the problem is that he was an eclecticist. Samuel L. Leiter wrote, "Unlike those contemporaries of his who specialized in a narrow range of theatrical approaches, Reinhardt felt that each play was a separate entity with its own inherent style and that the director's task was to discover and then transmit this style through the production. The play always came first, not the director."[13] In this eclecticism, Preminger followed Reinhardt. In interviews, Preminger was in the habit of denying that he had a style, insisting that each subject proposes its own terms: "I want to do every single film the way I feel at that moment."[14]

For Preminger, reflecting in 1973 on the older director, "Reinhardt's way of directing was a kind of very happy, Renaissance way of directing. He loved to show the actor what to do." Above all, in Preminger's view, Reinhardt "was truly an actor's director. He was most effective when he liked an actor, and perhaps *only* when he liked him . . . If he felt the slightest resistance in the actor, he let him go his own way. He told him a few things, of course. But if he felt that the actor really wanted to be directed by him, then his imagination, the variety of advice, the way he worked the actor in the scene and *for* the scene, was just fantastic. I don't think any director ever had that gift. Maybe it was because he was an actor originally." Asked whether he had learned from Reinhardt, Preminger answered, "I adored him and I admired him. I did not really learn detail from him. That is to say, I did not imitate him, but nobody who watched him direct and became a director could escape his influence."[15]

Preminger and Reinhardt shared certain traits: a taste for disappearing behind, or becoming immersed within, the work at hand; an equally pronounced taste for grandeur of scale and duration. Both were praised for their ability with crowd scenes. If Preminger's films bear traces of Reinhardt's style and techniques, they are most likely to be found in Preminger's deliberately theatrical films, such as *The Man with the*

Golden Arm and *Porgy and Bess*, or in certain scenes of *The Cardinal*. It should also be said that Preminger belonged to the cinematic tradition of Murnau, who also worked under Reinhardt and who became, in the 1920s, the primary exponent of a kind of filmmaking in which the reality of bodies in space, transformed by the camera lens, takes on a double existence, both physical and spiritual, and in which tension and meaning are directly embodied in the interplay of physical forces and resistances. Such cinema has its origins, partly, in the realist/illusionist theater of Reinhardt, and it survives in the realism of Preminger. Alexander Bakshy wrote that in a Reinhardt performance, "the effect of unity is . . . based not so much on an illusion of reality of the play enacted, as, if I may say so, on an illusion of 'reality of onlooking.' "[16] This striking formulation illuminates the dynamic of participation that the Murnau tradition would explore, and it hints at the special kind of distanciation that would be Preminger's distinctive contribution to this tradition.

In 1925 Preminger left Reinhardt to perform in Prague, Zurich, and Aussig, Czechoslovakia. In Prague, where his father was still infamous for his prosecution of Czechoslovakia's heroes, he appeared at the Neues Deutsches Landestheater under the stage name of Otto Pretori. It was during this period that Preminger began to lose his hair. His father, too, had gone bald early in life, "but that was no consolation for an aspiring leading man."[17] Otto learned to live with the affliction and later to pride himself on it. "Bald men, haven't you noticed, are much nicer," he told New York journalist Eileen Creelman in 1943. "Of course. They must be. They have no vanity. They never look in the mirror at themselves. Baldness takes away their conceit. That makes them more attractive."[18] Baldness dashed Preminger's hopes of becoming a romantic leading man, although he continued acting. In late 1925 and early 1926 he worked at the Stadttheater in Aussig, acting in several plays and making what was apparently his professional directorial debut with Franz Grillparzer's nineteenth-century comedy *Weh dem, der lugt* (Woe to Him Who Lies), which premiered on December 23, 1925. The *Aussiger Tagblatt* thought the production of *Weh dem, der lugt* "unified, fresh . . . and full of life."[19]

In 1926 and early 1927 Preminger acted at the Zurich Schauspielhaus, and in 1927 he returned to Vienna, where he entered into a partnership with the German actor Rolf Jahn, who had raised enough capital to buy and renovate the former Modernes Theater. December 20 saw the inaugural production of the new theater, renamed Die Komödie. According to Preminger, the opening night was a disaster. (The play was Chekhov's *The Cherry Orchard*.) In March 1928 Preminger and Die Komödie had greater success with *Der letzte Schleier*, a courtroom drama by G. W. Wheatley that held the stage for 132 performances. Preminger split up with Jahn in June 1929 after a number of clashes between the two partners, including a dispute about the potential of Marlene Dietrich, whom Preminger wanted to hire only to be overruled by Jahn. Ingo Preminger summed up the experience of Die Komödie: "There was nothing in that theater that was interesting."

In October 1929 Preminger and actor Jakob Feldhammer became codirectors of another new theater, the Neues Wiener Schauspielhaus (formerly the Volksoper). Its inaugural performance, Preminger's production of Frank Wedekind's *König Nicolo*, took place on November 5; and three days later, Preminger's production of Siegfried Geyer's *Die Sachertorte* opened to much acclaim. According to W. E. Yates, the theater "offered a programme of light comedy and contemporary drama."[20] In February 1930 Preminger scored a coup by importing German actor Oskar Homolka to star under his direction in a play based on Josef von Sternberg's film *Underworld*. Later that year, Preminger broke up with Feldhammer, citing "various internal conflicts, mostly of an artistic nature."[21]

At Camillo Castiglioni's suggestion, Max Reinhardt hired Preminger to direct at the Theater in der Josefstadt, which was in financial trouble. Preminger's directorial debut at Reinhardt's theater was another courtroom drama, Max Alsberg and Otto Ernst Hesse's *Voruntersuchung*, which premiered on January 20, 1931, and was a great success. Preminger's work at the Josefstadt attracted much favorable notice. In the August 18, 1931, *Neue freie Presse*, Paul Wertheimer praised him as "perhaps the strongest and at the same time subtlest of the young Viennese directors." His direction of *Reporter*, the German version of Ben Hecht and Charles MacArthur's *The Front Page*, "gave the piece an unheard-of drive, a guaranteed true American tempo," wrote another critic. For still another, Preminger's direction of A. A. Milne's *Michael and Mary* created "by the most discreet means, with the eloquence of silent gestures and unspoken words . . . an atmosphere in which the plot unwinds near reality."[22] Preminger's taste for material during the early 1930s already points toward his later work—above all the predilection for American subjects, for trial scenes, and for examinations of institutions, such as Sidney Kingsley's *Men in White*, a study of the workings of a hospital.

Ingo thought that Otto as a director during that period "was good. I think he was competent. I must tell you frankly, he and I never saw eye to eye as far as directing was concerned. He was very strict. He worked on the script, and that script, every word had to be observed, every comma had to be observed. I favor a freer way of directing, where there's input from everybody." Asked whether success changed Otto's personality, Ingo replied, "No, he was all his life the same guy. He was brusque, but also very friendly, very loyal. He loved people or hated people. He sometimes was given to furious outbreaks."

In 1931, financier Heinrich Haas gave Preminger the opportunity to direct his first film: *Die grosse Liebe*, a sentimental story about a down-and-out war veteran whom the mother of a missing soldier mistakes for her son. While preparing the film, Preminger described the story to a journalist as "a sort of folk play [*Volksstuck*]" in which Vienna would be represented not by such usual symbols as wine taverns, the Prater, and Viennese *Burgmusik*, "but rather through the character of the people and the atmosphere that swirls around them. We are striving for lively and credible figures."[23] Well-known stars Attila Hörbiger (with whom Preminger frequently worked in the theater) and Hansi Niese took the lead roles, and Adrienne Gessner, who would shortly become a fixture at the Josefstadt, played the ingenue.

A journalist for *Mein Film* visited Preminger at home during a typical preproduction day. After a lengthy round of phone calls, Preminger worked on the script with scenarist Siegfried Bernfeld and on the sets with art director (and cowriter) Artur Berger and art director Emil Stepanek. "I am myself a long-time interested moviegoer," said Preminger. "I am particularly attracted to directing sound film, because that form of art is not anchored in any tradition, and the creative imagination, now receptive to new results and realizations, allows so much freedom of movement and latitude."[24] Preminger shot the film in September and October of 1931.

Preminger later preferred to forget *Die grosse Liebe*. Though no masterpiece, the film has points of interest. Its most striking qualities are the looseness of its construction and the warm generosity it shows toward its main characters. The acting is good, if sometimes a little effect-conscious and over-deliberate. The scene in which the hero's companions are reduced to depressed silence by the spectacle of the mother embracing her rediscovered "son" has exactly the mood of the scene in *The Front Page* (which Preminger had recently staged) in which the cynical newsmen are momentarily chastened by the visit of Molly, the girl-friend of the condemned Earl Williams.

Preminger's career did not suffer from *Die grosse Liebe*, which opened in Vienna in December 1931 and in Berlin the following March, but neither did the film create any heightened impetus or new opportunities for him to work in cinema. Despite his claim of a longtime prior interest in cinema, it does not appear that he was strongly drawn to the medium. "Before becoming a filmmaker," he was asked in 1961, "did you go to the cinema?" "No," Preminger replied. "I went only to the theater. Of the cinema of that time, I know nothing, except perhaps Garbo and Dietrich."[25] Undoubtedly Preminger saw far more opportunities in the Austrian theater than in Austria's cinema, which had long lagged behind that of Germany and was still going through a difficult conversion to sound when he made *Die grosse Liebe*. Within two years of the release of that film, indirect and direct pressures from Nazi Germany would further alter conditions for Austrian cinema (which was dependent on the German market), so that even if Preminger still cherished any hopes for a second try at filmmaking, his chances to realize them would be all but nonexistent.[26]

Ingo recalled that Otto first met Marion Mill (born Magda Deutsch), a Hungarian-born nightclub performer, while interviewing actresses for parts in a road company. According to Ingo, his brother asked him to see Mill perform in a new show. Ingo reported back that Mill was "terrible," but Otto interviewed her and hired her anyway. "She had absolutely no acting talent," said Ingo. "But she would impress people with her personality. She was very amusing." Otto, in his autobiography, claims that he first met Mill in 1931, when she came to his office at the Josefstadt to ask for his legal advice in settling a contract dispute with the management of a revue in which she was performing, but in fact, Mill had acted for Preminger in 1929 in his production of *Die Sachertorte* at the Neues Wiener Schauspielhaus.

"All that I experienced before I met Otto counted for nothing," she wrote in her autobiography. "I was fascinated by his learning, which sur-passed that of any man I had known. He knew all of Goethe, and all of Shakespeare and all the Roman Law by heart, and could quote them at length. He was the most widely-read man I had ever known. He was what few learned men are, exceedingly witty. His finesse in conversation was as great as his finesse in directing; and this was so great that Rein-hardt—the great Professor Reinhardt—listened to him and usually gave him his way." Otto and Marion married on her birthday, August 3, prob-ably in 1931 (though his autobiography says 1932). Right after the wed-ding, her new husband hurried back to rehearsals for a new play. "In this experience on my wedding day I was having a foretaste of what our mar-ried life was to be," wrote Marion.[27]

After Reinhardt stepped down as managing director of the Josefstadt, Preminger was named his successor in July 1933. (He also, probably at the same time, took over as head of the Reinhardt Seminar at Schön-brunn, where he had been teaching.) By now Preminger was well estab-lished in Vienna as a purveyor of urbane entertainment. Otto kept somewhat aloof from the cultural avant-garde of Vienna, unlike Ingo, who frequently attended Karl Kraus's public readings. "Otto was not a guy who liked people who were fighting the order," said Ingo. "He later became more of a revolutionary himself, but he was more traditional in those days. He didn't respect Kraus like I did."

After his first season as manager of the Josefstadt, Preminger said, he received an offer from the Austrian minister of education, Kurt von Schuschnigg, to become the director of Vienna's Burgtheater, the state theater of Austria. On being told that as "a mere formality," his accep-tance of the post would require him to convert to Catholicism, Prem-inger declined the offer, as he later said, "without hesitation . . . My refusal to convert most likely saved my life. If I had accepted I would not have been a free agent two years later when Joseph Schenck invited me to Hollywood. I would have been in Vienna when Hitler invaded Austria in 1938 and would have met the same fate as many of my friends. Because, for Hitler, converted or not a Jew remained a Jew."[28]

Preminger later said, seemingly reluctant to use the word, "I always felt very—well, very *assimilated* in Austria."[29] Yet according to Ingo, Otto "never had a liking of Vienna and the Viennese, the way people talk about them." The events of 1933 hardened Otto's attitude, Ingo recalled. "He held Vienna responsible for Hitler, which is only partly so. Because many people in Vienna didn't like Hitler, even non-Jews. But every Viennese, every Austrian to him was a Nazi." With Hitler's rise to power in Germany, "Otto was immediately very pessimistic and predicted the fall of Austria right away. That's why, in 1935, he left. He begged us all to leave. My father said, 'I was in the Austrian army; I was a district attorney; I, they will never touch.' "

Historian Bruce F. Pauley noted that "Jews were . . . gradually eased out of various aspects of Austria's cultural life after 1934 . . . At the state theaters only Jewish actors with international reputations were able to perform, although at private theaters there remained both Jewish actors and directors . . . Austrian films were produced without Jews so that they could be shown in Nazi Germany."[30]

In April 1935, while rehearsing Ralph Benatzky's *Der König mit dem Regenschirm* (The King with the Umbrella), Preminger received word that Joseph M. Schenck, chairman of the recently formed Twentieth Century-Fox, was visiting Vienna and wished to meet him in his hotel. Preminger's friend Julius Steger, a Vienna-born director who had worked in America, served as interpreter between the two. Schenck was aware of Preminger's work and reputation and wanted to bring him to Hollywood to direct. Preminger accepted the offer. Said Ingo, "A lot of people thought he was crazy. He was at the top of the heap in Vienna." Nevertheless, Otto wanted out of Vienna and saw Schenck's offer as his chance.

Learning of Preminger's plans, Broadway producer Gilbert Miller, on a visit to Vienna, asked Preminger to come to New York to direct the Broadway production of Edward Wooll's *Libel!*, a courtroom mystery whose Vienna premiere Preminger had directed with success in 1934 (as *Sensationsprozess*). Preminger, who since Schenck's invitation had been taking private English lessons with a university student, accepted.

Preminger's last stage production in Vienna was *Die erste Legion*, the German version of American playwright Emmet Lavery's *The First Legion*, a play set in a Jesuit monastery. (It was filmed in Hollywood in 1951 by Douglas Sirk.) The great Albert Bassermann starred. Chancellor von Schuschnigg was in attendance on the play's opening night, October 8, 1935, as was the head of the Catholic Church in Vienna, Cardinal Theodor Innitzer, whom, twenty-eight years later, Preminger would make a character in *The Cardinal*.

A few days after the premiere, Preminger left for Paris (in the company of Sam Spiegel, with whose help Preminger managed to smuggle some Austrian banknotes across the border) and then reached Le Havre, where, on October 16, he boarded the SS *Normandie*. Preminger would often speak of October 21, the date of his arrival in New York (under alien registration number 5630884), as his second birthday. For the rest of his life, New York would be his main home. "This is a city no one born here can really appreciate. One must come from another place to know how wonderful this city can be."[31]

2

It's the Artistic Side That's Questionable

The morning after arriving in New York, Preminger began rehearsing *Libel!* with a cast of transplanted Britishers led by Colin Clive as an M.P. accused of stealing the identity of a man with whom he had been held as a German prisoner of war. Though far from having mastered English, Preminger coped with his chore. "If I could not understand what an actor said during rehearsals I knew he was addressing me because the lines were not in the play. My only remaining problem was to figure out what he wanted."[1] Apparently Gilbert Miller overlooked Preminger's linguistic insufficiencies; he seems to have seen his new protégé as a valuable expert in spectacle. While *Libel!* was still in rehearsals, Miller turned to Preminger for help with staging a crowd scene in Miller's production of *Victoria Regina* (in which Vincent Price costarred).

Libel! premiered on December 2 in Philadelphia and, after a two-week run there, came to Henry Miller's Theatre in New York. Edith J. R. Isaacs of *Theatre Arts* praised Preminger's ability to bring to the static courtroom setting "an unceasing flow of necessary and contributing movement, without a single concerted activity or any theatrical display. It is quite a remarkable achievement in focusing and harnessing stage movement."[2] The play was a success (150 performances), though Preminger had no time to savor it; joined by Marion, who had followed him to New York, he was soon off to Los Angeles.

Preminger arrived in Los Angeles on the Super Chief on January 3, 1936, and took up residence at the Beverly Wilshire Hotel, where he would stay for the next two years. He got into the papers the next day (no doubt with the help of Twentieth Century-Fox's publicity department), informing the *Los Angeles Examiner* that with its abundance of underemployed talent, the city should take the lead in creating a national theater. Preminger was taken under the wing of Darryl F. Zanuck, head of production at Twentieth Century-Fox. The first project for which Zanuck considered Preminger was a film version of *Libel!* On January 10, 1936, the *Los Angeles Times* announced that Preminger would codirect the film—a sign of Zanuck's reservations about his new talent. On January 28, the same paper reported that Preminger was preparing *Libel!* The film never materialized.

Meanwhile, Preminger attended parties (including a surprise dinner for Ernst Lubitsch in August) and, at Zanuck's behest, observed the production of *Sing, Baby, Sing,* a musical with Alice Faye, Adolphe Menjou, and Gregory Ratoff. (Ratoff, one of Zanuck's "court jesters" and a jack-of-all-trades at the studio, would become a friend of Preminger's.) The director, Sidney Lanfield, became irritated with the apprentice's constant presence at his elbow, suspecting perhaps that Zanuck intended to replace him with the younger director. On April 23 Preminger wrote Ferdinand Bruckner (whose play *Die Marquise von O* Preminger had staged in 1933), "Two things are exceptional here: the unique beauty of this country and the unimaginable organization of the film industry. It is difficult to describe what I find so fabulous about this organization; it is the unimaginable, hushed harmony of thousands of little gears; a technical perfection to the minutest detail, and all this without hullabaloo or pathos. It's the artistic side that's questionable. Only a few persons can actually produce what they really want. Whether I will be counted among those remains to be seen. I am learning a lot and have already learned a great deal. But everything here is different in atmosphere and taste than in Europe. The task at hand is to make what we love and want to produce, in such a way that it nevertheless meets with success."[3]

Marion threw herself into Hollywood's social scene. "Soon she developed a passion for parties," said Otto. "They were perhaps a substitute for the theatrical career she had given up . . . We began to go our separate ways, though we did not notice it for a while."[4] In June, Preminger's name was linked with two projects, *Rings on Her Fingers* and *Love Flight*. The latter was a remake of a Spanish-language film, *Las fronteras del amor*, which Frank Strayer had directed for Fox in 1934. Drawn from an original story by Bernice Mason, the plot concerns a famous opera singer who, tired of the arduous performance schedule and silly publicity stunts arranged by his manager, goes into hiding and falls in love with a socialite. Zanuck envisioned *Love Flight* as a quickie vehicle for the renowned baritone Lawrence Tibbett, whom Zanuck had under contract and wanted to get rid of. "There's no chance he'll ever be a success in films so you go ahead and practice on him," Zanuck told Preminger, who duly worked on the script throughout June and July with writers Frances Hyland and Saul Elkins and associate producer John Stone. Production started in mid-August—the same month when Preminger filed his Declaration of Intention to renounce his Austrian citizenship and become a U.S. citizen—and, as far as is known, went smoothly, despite Tibbett's refusal to deviate from his contractual daily quitting time of five o'clock.[5] Shooting ended on September 15, to the satisfaction of Zanuck, who, before the film's release, signed Preminger to a one-year contract as director at $1,000 per week, starting October 6.

Renamed *Under Your Spell* after one of the songs Arthur Schwartz and Howard Dietz wrote for the picture, the first American film by Otto Ludwig Preminger (as he was billed in the titles) opened on November 6. Reviewers had praise for Tibbett's singing, but Preminger's direction went over less well, *Variety* calling it "spotty, not overcoming any of the story's shortcomings."[6] In the meantime, Preminger moved on to *Love Is News* and then (after star Loretta Young objected, thinking him unsuited to an essentially American story) to the Wallace Beery vehicle *The Lost Nancy Steele*, an assignment that proved troublesome. On November 8 *The New York Times* noted "indications that [Beery] will refuse to appear in" the film. Preminger later recalled that the star failed to show up for their first scheduled meeting and that Gregory Ratoff, serving as Zanuck's emissary, mournfully broke the news that Beery "says he won't make a film with a director whose name he can't pronounce."[7]

Preminger neglected to mention that he shot for four days on *Nancy Steele*, in which, in the event, Victor McLaglen took over for Beery as Dannie, an Irish American who, opposed to the United States entering World War I, kidnaps the baby daughter of a munitions magnate. On November 28, production was halted. According to Nunnally Johnson, who served as the film's producer, Zanuck summoned him to his office to talk about the picture and complained about the pace of the direction. "It not only looks slow in the rushes, but he's taking too long with all the stuff he's shooting. Wasting money. I can't have it. The budget won't stand it." Johnson disagreed with Zanuck about Preminger's work and declined to fire the director—but of this task Zanuck proved instantly capable. Preminger's footage was scrapped, and the film was restarted with a new director (George Marshall) and a new title, *Nancy Steele Is Missing!*[8]

Whatever the nature of Preminger's difficulties with *Nancy Steele*, they were apparently not held against him. *Rings on Her Fingers*, again with Nunnally Johnson producing, was reconfirmed as his next project. This film failed to materialize. Preminger tried to initiate a film on Émile Zola and the Dreyfus case, only to be told by a producer, "You couldn't bribe the American people to look at such a picture." Subsequently Warners made *The Life of Emile Zola*, which, in 1938, Preminger assigned the number 8 slot on a list published in a newspaper series called My Ten Favorite Pictures. His enthusiasm for the film is surprising in view of his antipathy for its director, William Dieterle. (Even more surprising is the appearance of the Wallace Beery vehicle *Viva Villa!* as number 3.) For the record, here is the full list:

1. *The Gold Rush*
2. *The Birth of a Nation*
3. *Viva Villa!*
4. *Lady for a Day*
5. *It Happened One Night*
6. *Sous les toits de Paris*
7. *Mr. Deeds Goes to Town*
8. *The Life of Emile Zola*
9. *Snow White and the Seven Dwarfs*
10. *La grande illusion*[9]

Preminger found himself assigned to *Danger—Love at Work*, a screwball comedy written by James Edward Grant and Ben Markson in transparent imitation of two 1936 hits, George S. Kaufman and Moss Hart's Broadway farce *You Can't Take It with You* (which Frank Capra would film for Columbia in 1938) and Gregory La Cava's film *My Man Godfrey*. Zanuck saw the script of *Danger—Love at Work* as a vehicle for contractee Simone Simon, whose English had a strong French accent, and despite misgivings, Preminger dutifully started production in late May 1937 with Simon as South Carolina belle Antoinette "Toni" Pemberton.

The first few days' rushes persuaded Zanuck of his error, and Simon was replaced with Ann Sothern, with whom Preminger recommenced the film and finished it in early July. In August, a new prologue in the office of a law firm was written and shot, rather clumsily. The film received good reviews, a typical one from *Time* calling it "unpretentious, well-paced, and often very funny."[10]

The two films that resulted from Preminger's first stay in Hollywood may be dealt with briefly. *Under Your Spell*, marginally the more interesting of the two, contains a good deal of camera movement along with Preminger's first screen courtroom scene (the case involves the heroine's attempt to prevent the hero from leaving the country, citing his contractual obligation to sing at her party). The grandiloquent crane work suggests directorial muscle flexing of a kind that Preminger would later eschew (and would, indeed, criticize in the work of his colleague, John Brahm, whom he accused of seeking to manufacture a "style").

Even less Premingerian, and less capably directed, *Danger—Love at Work* moves quickly but has nowhere to go. A less frenetic pace might have made the film less irritating, but given the material, it is hard to quarrel with Preminger's decision to get through the thing as quickly as possible. Ann Sothern does her vigorous best, but since she has a hard enough time making her character likable, it's unsurprising that she fails to erase memories of Carole Lombard in *My Man Godfrey*. The eccentricities of the Pemberton family (whose members include John Carradine as a self-described "post-surrealist" painter) are largely annoying rather than funny, while saucer-eyed Jack Haley as the lawyer hero fails to make an attractive case for normality.

During the summer of 1937, Preminger's parents visited him. He begged his father to apply for immigration visas, but Markus refused, still confident that he had nothing to fear from the Nazis.

On September 7, 1937, Preminger signed a new $1,250-a-week contract as director for Twentieth Century-Fox. The start date was supposed to be the day after he finished work on his next project, *Shanghai Deadline*; the date was later amended to October 11. "My status was changing from an untried employee to a favorite," Preminger noted; he began receiving regular invitations to Zanuck's dinners. In November, Preminger was entrusted with the direction of a major production of Robert Louis Stevenson's *Kidnapped*. This prestigious assignment turned into a disaster that brought an abrupt end to the first phase of Preminger's Hollywood career.

For the explanation of what went wrong, we have only Preminger's account. He claimed that his first instinct was to turn down *Kidnapped*. "I considered myself a literate man but I hadn't even heard in Vienna about the writer or his book. The whole idea of Scotland, the Highlands, was something foreign to me—except I knew the Scottish wore kilts. Even my English at that time was not far enough advanced for me to be able to read the book." Gregory Ratoff advised him to stay the course: "This is Zanuck's biggest picture . . . If you turn it down they won't talk to you. You just have to do it."[11]

Preminger started production in early January 1938, with Warner Baxter and Freddie Bartholomew in the leads and Gregg Toland as cameraman. According to Preminger, Zanuck was in New York at the start of production, and by the time he returned to Hollywood, there were several days' rushes for him to see. (Production schedules in the Fox legal files indicate that Preminger shot for at least a week and possibly for as long as three weeks.) "He didn't like what I had done," said Preminger, "and I don't blame him. I think it wasn't very good. We got into a fight about a scene with a dog. I don't remember the details any more, but I know that Zanuck claimed there was a scene in the script which I said wasn't in the script, and we got into a tremendous shouting match. I was right, it wasn't in the script. But he got so mad that he threw me out and assigned another director."[12] The new director was Alfred L. Werker, under whom *Kidnapped* got under way again on January 24. Whether any of Preminger's footage remains in the final film cannot be known.

Preminger's shouting match with Zanuck—a man at whom no one shouted—meant that he was no longer given assignments at Twentieth Century-Fox, even though his contract still had nine months to run. Neither was he eligible for work at any other studio. Shut out of film projects, Preminger spent his time studying English at UCLA, reading books, and contemplating possible vehicles for a return to stage direction.

3

Cues for Passion

His Hollywood career seemingly over, Preminger returned to New York, where he and Marion occupied a room at the Ambassador Hotel. They later moved to the St. Regis on Fifth Avenue and Fifty-fifth Street. This would remain Preminger's address until 1941; in later years, he would still maintain ties to the place. Even though he had little money and no certain prospects, "it did not occur to me to try a more modest style of living."[1] He tried to line up work as a theatrical producer-director. He renewed old contacts. Grete Mosheim, formerly a leading actress in Reinhardt's ensemble, held a Sunday salon in her home on Central Park South, which Preminger frequently attended along with Reinhardt (who had immigrated to America in the same year as Preminger, 1935) and actors Lili Darvas, Oskar Karlweis, and Walter Slezak.[2]

On the morning of March 12, 1938, German troops crossed the border into Austria. The following day, Hitler announced the Anschluss—the annexation of Austria by Germany. Anticipating the worst, Ingo Preminger, now a practicing attorney, had already relocated his two-year-old daughter, Eve, to Switzerland. On the day of the Anschluss, Ingo and his wife drove to the train station and boarded a train to Czechoslovakia. At the border, he flushed his money down a toilet. From Prague, he and his wife went to Zurich, where they joined Ingo and Otto's parents, who had escaped from Vienna with the aid of the chief of police, Michael Skubl, an old friend of Markus's. According to Ingo, Markus had money in a Swiss bank. "They managed all kinds of ways of taking money out. So they were very lucky."[3]

They all reached New York in 1938. Initially, they were able to get only visitors' visas, and they faced the prospect of having to leave the United States when the visas expired. Otto Preminger was fond of recounting that Tallulah Bankhead, a casual acquaintance of his, learned of his family's problem and introduced him to her father, who was Speaker of the House of Representatives, and her uncle, a senator from Alabama, and that with the help of the two legislators his parents, his brother, and his brother's family were able to obtain permanent-resident status. Eventually they obtained immigrant visas.[4] "I loved America," said Ingo. "So did Otto."[5]

Later, Otto would sponsor other refugees. In a selective service questionnaire Preminger filed in May 1941, he noted that he was supporting Martin Berliner, who had come to New York on Preminger's affidavit. Berliner had acted at the Josefstadt for Preminger and had appeared in a small part in *Die grosse Liebe*.[6] Preminger would help in other ways. "During the war and long after," recalled actor Leon Askin, "he sent monthly checks to an elderly Viennese actor, the checks arriving as regularly as Social Security checks."[7]

In New York in 1938, the first production Preminger was able to mount closed out of town in the fall: Lewis Meltzer's *Yankee Fable*, a farce set during the American Revolution, starring Ina Claire, who, according to Preminger, "could not remember her lines."[8] The struggling director fared better with the revival of Sutton Vane's play *Outward Bound*, concerning a group of passengers on an ocean liner who come to realize that they have died and are making their final journey. Producer William Brady saw the play as a vehicle for the comeback of the legendary Laurette Taylor, whose career had been blighted by alcoholism. Given the touchy assignment of directing the play, Preminger at first found his star "constrained and unhappy . . . reserved and suspicious in the extreme." His efforts to prove to the actress that he had faith in her boosted her self-confidence, and "from that time on," her daughter, Marguerite Courtney, wrote, "Laurette was at every rehearsal, keenly interested, friendly, enthusiastic. Preminger let her give suggestions freely, took her to lunch, discussed scenes, actors, production details, large and small. In every possible way he tried to promote the sense of her importance to the production, of his complete confidence in all matters. She throve on it."[9] Bramwell Fletcher, an actor in the production as well as one of its coproducers, found in Preminger "an amazing faculty for handling actors."[10] Preminger, for his part, later looked back on Taylor as "an actress who was as great as any actress that ever lived . . . a genius. You could only learn by directing her."[11] *Outward Bound* opened on December 22, 1938, and became a hit. The next month, President Roosevelt summoned the production to Washington for a command performance, to be followed by supper at the White House, where the director and the star were seated at Roosevelt's table. The president's personality "left an indelible memory" on Preminger, who felt that Roosevelt trusted and liked him.[12]

Preminger's success with Taylor led straight to his next directing job, a new comedy by Catherine Turney and Jerry Horwin called *My Dear Children*, which John Barrymore had become interested in. At a birthday party for Barrymore in New York in February 1940, the actor discussed the play with producers Richard Aldrich and Richard Myers; Preminger was also there. Contracts were signed the next day. *My Dear Children* went into rehearsals, during which Barrymore seized on opportunities to improve the script (the story concerned an aging actor who helps sort out the romantic problems of his three grown daughters) and to turn a work "which had been originally written with quite an amount of pathos . . . into a screamingly funny farce." The play opened in Princeton on March 24, 1939, with Albert Einstein in attendance, to an "overwhelmingly thunderous reception." On opening night, Barrymore's antics set the tone for what would become a lengthy run: as the stage manager prompted him from the wings, the actor replied in full voice, to the audience's merriment, "Just a little louder, darling, I couldn't hear you."[13]

Barrymore's tour of *My Dear Children* became a smash. Spectators returned night after night to see what the actor would come up with next, "for he rarely gave the same show twice—to the discomfort of the actors who had to play with him."[14] Dorothy McGuire, playing one of the three daughters, quit after Omaha, saying, "I had a great admiration for John Barrymore when we started, but I cannot watch this man make a fool of himself."[15] Preminger, who had stayed in New York, rejoined the touring company somewhere in America and was appalled by the spectacle of Barrymore obliging the audience, playing "a drunken clown" in a performance that "lasted approximately forever."[16] Barrymore would wisecrack, curse, greet friends whom he spotted in the audience, react to the audience's sneezes and to noises from the street, and stop the play to tell anecdotes about his past. Preminger told the actor he thought his behavior "beneath human dignity." One evening, Barrymore's ad libs caused Preminger to get up and pace the aisle in anguish, and Barrymore shouted from the stage, "For Pete's sake, Otto, go back and sit down. We'll get through it somehow." Among those who admired Barrymore's performances was Orson Welles, who, after seeing the show in Chicago, reported that if he had a child, he would make him watch every performance. "Then I'd tell him he knew everything there was to know about acting."[17]

That kind of performance made the director irrelevant, and, when *My Dear Children* reached New York in January 1940, none of the reviews mentioned Preminger's name. By then he had launched, again for Aldrich and Myers, another hit, in which his contribution did not go unnoticed. Clare Boothe's *Margin for Error* is a comedy-mystery to which Boothe adds a large dose of anti-Nazi propaganda by making the murder victim a German consul in an unnamed American city, to whose protection a Jewish policeman is assigned. Preminger, who worked with Boothe on revising the script, also stepped into the part of the Consul after the actor originally cast in the role, Rudolf Forster (a Reinhardt veteran from Berlin and Vienna), abruptly decided to repatriate to Germany. Preminger's casting was something of a last resort and an inspiration of Boothe's: twelve actors tested for the part and were found wanting before Boothe persuaded Preminger that the line readings he was giving the aspirants were so good that he should play the part himself. *Margin for Error* opened in Princeton on October 14, 1939, and on November 3 it reached New York, where the reviewers were more impressed with Preminger's acting than with the play. Despite their reservations, the play ran for 264 performances.

The description of the Consul in Boothe's text is a good sketch of the cliché figure that, thanks to his success in the role, would help shape Preminger's public persona. The Consul is "the type of German who makes caricaturists' lives easy and pro-German propaganda difficult . . . Something of a sadist, and a good deal of a glutton, he fancies himself as a bon-vivant and man of the world."[18] Preminger thought the key to Baumer's character was his disabused nature. "If people like this monster—and I've been told they actually do—it is because I play him so as to make them feel his cynicism, his utter disbelief in Nazi claptrap."[19] In contrast, the most memorable villains in Preminger's films would be idealists, alienated from others and rendered monstrous by their own conviction.

In November 1939 Preminger was appointed assistant professor of play production at Yale for the academic year 1939–40, with a salary of $3,000. He had looked around for a teaching job in April 1938, a few months after the debacle of *Kidnapped*, and in May 1939 he met with Allardyce Nicoll, head of the Yale School of Drama. That September, Nicoll asked him for references. A flurry of distinguished testimonials came in. Gilbert Miller noted that at the Reinhardt Seminar at Schönbrunn, Preminger "gave ample proof of his ability as a teacher, especially in the discovery and development of young talent." Bruno Frank, a German émigré writer who would later work on the script of *A Royal Scandal*, wrote that he saw some twenty of the productions staged at the Josefstadt under Preminger's management, "all of them, without exception, showing high artistic qualities, and a good many attaining perfection." Screenwriter Samson Raphaelson, with whom Preminger had worked on an aborted adaptation of *The King with the Umbrella*, praised his "astonishing grasp of our language and our ways of thinking. He is a man of culture as well as a practical man of the theatre, and where do you find people like that? Very rarely in the theatre!" Max Gordon, Laurette Taylor, and Thornton Wilder also sent testimonials.[20]

The need to give priority to his professional theatrical career meant that Preminger never had, during the two years he was to teach at Yale, a very full experience of academic life in the United States. (Once, Nicoll sent him a memo: "I know that at the end of last session both the students and the Faculty were very much disturbed by the fact that you had missed so many classes or had changed their hours.") His experience at Yale led him to believe that, as he later said, "universities are not the place to teach acting or directing. You should teach there the history, the theory of acting, the theory of the theater. The real craft . . . you can't teach this as an academic thing."[21]

During the 1940 fall semester, Preminger had his first two Broadway flops. The first was Lynn Starling and Howard J. Green's *Beverly Hills*, a satire on Hollywood wheeling and dealing. According to Brooks Atkinson, the production boasted "the most elegant dramatic stage setting of the Autumn. Spending money recklessly, [Preminger] has bought the smartest clothes in town and dressed some stunning actresses in them . . . Possibly Mr. Preminger has made *Beverly Hills* more unbearable than necessary by dwelling exclusively on the spuriousness of the characters."[22] It opened on November 7, 1940, and lasted twenty-eight performances. *Cue for Passion*, a mystery by Edward Chodorov and H. S. Kraft, evaporated even more quickly, running a mere twelve performances after its December 19, 1940, opening. Like *Beverly Hills*, the play was an exposé of the poisonous private lives of people prominent in the culture industry. Preminger's next play was another failure: called *The More the Merrier* (and bearing no relation to George Stevens's 1943 film), it concerned a group of tourists snowbound in a Colorado castle and featured, among other slapstick attractions, a corpse outfitted with roller skates. Interviewed during rehearsals for the play, Preminger said he was pleased to be working on a farce. "In Vienna I was all the time associated with comedy and farce productions, but here I have a reputation for deadpan theater which I should like to correct. My particular affection in the light-theater field lies not so much with outright farce as it does with normal and everyday people caught up in comedy situations."[23] *The More the Merrier* opened on September 15, 1941, and closed after sixteen performances.

With *In Time to Come*, an episodic chronicle of Woodrow Wilson's failed efforts on behalf of the League of Nations from 1918 to 1921, Preminger fared better—at least as far as the critics were concerned. Brooks Atkinson declared the play "profoundly sobering and impressive . . . [Writers Howard Koch and John Huston] have unfolded a great tragedy of ideals." Richard Watts, Jr., praised the "straightforward, reportorial narrative style" of the play. On the other hand, Richard Lockridge noted that Wilson was "austere and detached" in the play as in real life, and that "it is hard to make such men into the heroes of drama." A comment by John Mason Brown indicates a link between *In Time to Come* and Preminger's major film work: in the scene in which Wilson confronts his chief nemesis, Republican senator Henry Cabot Lodge, "two irreconcilable men and viewpoints are allowed to confront one another with admirable impartiality." The play opened on December 28, 1941, and closed after forty performances. Preminger concluded, "Nobody was in the mood to see a play about peace when we had just entered World War II."[24]

4

Second Apprenticeship

In 1941, Ernst Lubitsch, who had just signed a contract with Twentieth Century-Fox, told his new employers that he was interested in *Margin for Error*. The studio undertook to buy the film rights. On April 10, 1941, Paul Kohner, Lubitsch's agent, wrote Preminger that he "could be in a position to get you the same part you created on stage." Preminger wrote back on April 15, "I would love to play the part in *Margin for Error* on the screen, particularly for Lubitsch, because I think I will not only make a hit as an actor but will also learn a lot from Lubitsch as a director."[1] Lubitsch eventually decided not to do *Margin for Error* after all, a decision for which all lovers of cinema must be deeply grateful, for it meant that instead he made *To Be or Not to Be*. In early 1942 Nunnally Johnson offered Preminger another Nazi part: Gestapo officer Major Diessen in *The Pied Piper*, which Johnson was producing at Fox with Irving Pichel directing. Preminger signed a contract on March 5 for $2,500 a week with a two-week guarantee. Clearly, the shouting match between Zanuck and Preminger over *Kidnapped* had not completely hardened Zanuck against his former protégé, although Zanuck did not take the step of welcoming Preminger back personally. Preminger did his scenes for *The Pied Piper* in late April.

The Hollywood to which Preminger returned in 1942 was a different place from the one he had left in 1938. One difference lay in the increased population of European—especially German and Austrian—refugees. As Gottfried Reinhardt, Max's son, wrote, "Half of European and four-fifths of the German-speaking civilization moved into this Californian coastal strip . . . It was the mass migration of a thrown-together elite unprecedented in history, the volume and force of which is hard to grasp even now, only forty years later."[2] The Premingers were intimate with or at least acquainted with some of the most illustrious members of this elite (Marion Mill Preminger later recalled meeting Thomas Mann and Franz Werfel at dinner at Lion Feuchtwanger's house),[3] not a few of whose members found work in the movies. The Clover Club, a casino on Sunset Boulevard, was popular among European exiles. Gottfried Reinhardt recalled, "There, one evening, being the only non-Hungarian at the roulette table except me, the agglutinative language got on Otto Preminger's nerves and he brought his fist down on the green baize, shouting: 'Goddamnit, guys, you're in America! Speak German!' "[4]

During production of *The Pied Piper*, Preminger found time to do a screen test at Warner Bros. for the part of Strasser, the German officer in *Casablanca*. The part went instead to Conrad Veidt, but little time passed before Preminger was offered another Nazi role, that of the master spy Fauscheim in the Bob Hope comedy *They Got Me Covered*, which David Butler directed for Samuel Goldwyn Productions in the summer of 1942. "It was a most profitable assignment," Preminger recalled, "because it went on forever and most of it was cut out."[5]

The wheel turning full circle, Twentieth Century-Fox offered Preminger the part of the Nazi Consul, Baumer, in the film of *Margin for Error*. Preminger said he would be interested in playing Baumer, but he also wanted to direct the film. Told by his agent, Charles Feldman, that it was out of the question, Preminger went to see William Goetz, Zanuck's longtime executive assistant (and Louis B. Mayer's son-in-law). Goetz had, on April 29, assumed charge of production at Fox, replacing Zanuck, who had accepted a commission to supervise training and combat films for the U.S. Army Signal Corps. (*The Pied Piper* was one of the last films to go into production before Zanuck's departure.) As Preminger told it, "On the spur of the moment, I made [Goetz] a reckless offer. I would direct the film without pay, taking only my salary as an actor. If, at the end of one week, my work wasn't satisfactory he could replace me as director. I would continue as actor and cooperate fully with the new director." The next day, Goetz told Preminger that his terms were acceptable. Though not a few of Preminger's stories are unreliable, this one can be confirmed. On August 2 he signed a contract to act in *Margin for Error* at $2,000 a week, with a four-week guarantee, and to direct the picture without compensation. For this unusual arrangement, Preminger asked for and obtained waivers from the Screen Directors Guild and the

Screen Actors Guild. Ralph Dietrich, "a nice man with very little experience," in Preminger's words, was assigned as the producer.[6]

Dissatisfied with Lillie Hayward's script, Preminger asked the studio to pay for a rewrite, but Dietrich denied his request. Without telling Dietrich, Preminger worked at home with Samuel Fuller on a rewrite. "He paid me out of his own pocket. He paid me cash, every week," said Fuller, who also remembered that Preminger was then involved in "a top-secret affair" with Hedy Lamarr (whom Preminger had met in Vienna when he was teaching at the Reinhardt Seminar).[7] "We rewrote my scenes with Milton Berle, who played the Jewish policeman, and changed many others," said Preminger.[8]

Production started on September 30. Preminger recalled that he spent his trial week as director "fighting to keep my nerves under control." At the end of the week, Goetz told Preminger to keep directing.[9] Vienna-born Carl Esmond, who played Max, the Consul's secretary, found Preminger less typically Viennese than "Teutonic." "The only discussion I had with Preminger was about the accent. Because Preminger thought he had a much better accent than I had in English. And I said, 'No, you haven't.' . . . But I was fine with him, even afterwards."[10] *Margin for Error* wrapped in November and was released in February 1943. *Variety*'s reviewer complained of Preminger's "heavy hand" as director,[11] but other reviews were more favorable, and the film did well enough to augur well for Preminger's future in Hollywood.

An experimental mixing of comedy and drama—a combination that would continue to tempt Preminger—*Margin for Error* doesn't quite work, but it is unique: earnest and empty, surprising and eerie in its hollowness. Cunningly, the film manages to convey its unsavory sexual theme—Baumer is blackmailing his disaffected wife, Sophie (Joan Bennett), for sex—by keeping Sophie offscreen for long periods as if she were a dirty secret, allowing her only brief, awkward appearances, and then disposing of her quickly, as if afraid she might blurt out or expose through her physical presence too much about herself and the plot.

All the characters are in different senses hostages to something: they can act only within the extremely small range of choice (margin for error) left them by the higher causes and allegiances to which they are subject. Even Baumer reveals himself as an irredeemably stupid man (and not a wily, malignant egotist) when the goading of police officer

Moe (Berle) causes him to blurt out, "Hitler is a genius!" Preminger shows the characters as specimens, as very small. Moe's courtship of the maid Frieda is treated with a clinical lack of sympathy for the characters, who are defined in terms of their economic behavior (in a drugstore, Frieda, told she has won a prize, asks for a tube of lipstick that costs more than the value of the prize; Moe makes up the difference with unconcealed reluctance). In one of the most resonant sequences of the film (a sequence that, in keeping with the rest of the film, is still only hollowly resonant), various people listen to a radio broadcast of a speech by Hitler (with simultaneous English translation). Two figures appear in medium shot at opposite ends of the room, their backs to the camera, in a composition dominated by a big swastika on the wall in the background. The faceless people scarcely exist except as bodies over which Hitler's speech is played, and they are necessary as such: there must be bodies to hear the speech, to make it resonate. The sequence of the Hitler speech has the immense, chasmic quality that one associates with Preminger and that reappears in the scene in *Exodus* of Barak's announcement of the United Nations vote to partition Palestine. (One might also compare *The Cardinal*, another film in which Hitler is a voice from offscreen.) The seamless movement of *Margin for Error*—the interaction of socially "higher" and "lower" worlds controlled by mise-en-scène and cutting—prefigures such later films as *In Harm's Way* and *Hurry Sundown*, with their displacement of interest among characters at various social levels.

Margin for Error pleased Goetz enough that he signed Preminger to a one-year contract "as a producer, director, writer, and/or actor" starting November 19, 1942, at $1,750 per week. In December, Preminger was assigned to direct the film version of another anti-Nazi play, Maxwell Anderson's *Candle in the Wind*, but this project does not seem to have engaged him for very long. Soon he was embarked instead on a chronicle of the rise of Nazism as told from the point of view of William Dodd, the U.S. ambassador to Germany from 1933 to 1939. The film would be based on Dodd's diary (published in 1941) and on the 1939 book *Through Embassy Eyes*, an account of the same period by the ambassador's daughter, Martha Dodd. Writer Michael Kanin may have first suggested the book to Preminger.[12] In early 1943 Preminger commissioned Martha Dodd and Fay Kanin, Michael's wife, to do a treatment, and then, in June, he hired Ring Lardner, Jr., who had been Michael Kanin's writing partner on the Oscar-winning script of *Woman of the Year*, to write the screenplay. Preminger and Lardner got along well and formed a long-lasting friendship. According to Lardner, "Otto's knowledge of matters Germanic enabled him to contribute a good deal to my research, which went speedily."[13] Anticipating by more than a year a Hollywood trend that would start officially with Louis de Rochemont and Henry Hathaway's *The House on 92nd Street* (1945), Preminger conceived *Ambassador Dodd's Diary* as a semidocumentary: the film would incorporate newsreel footage of the Reichstag fire and other events.[14]

While Preminger was preparing *Ambassador Dodd's Diary*, Zanuck, who had received permission to revert to inactive status on May 31, resumed control of production at the studio. Instead of practically living at the studio, as had been his custom before his departure, Zanuck summoned producers and directors to his Santa Monica beach house to confer with them. Soon it became Preminger's turn to undergo this ritual. "We had not spoken to each other since the incident on *Kidnapped*. Whenever we had seen each other at parties, he just turned the other way." He found Zanuck sitting beside the pool in his garden, wearing swim trunks. Without rising or turning around, Zanuck said curtly, "You keep working on these three properties, two of which we'll keep. You can produce them, but you will never direct again as long as I am here at Fox."[15]

The Dodd project was fated to be the third, aborted project. It stalled around August 1943, when Preminger tested and hired Harry Carey and Dorothy Gish in the roles of Dodd and his wife. After that, Preminger turned his attention to the two projects Zanuck let him continue with: *Laura* and the film that would eventually be called *In the Meantime, Darling*. Though his status at Fox was uncertain, his standing in the United States became stronger. On August 27, 1943, Preminger was issued Certificate of Naturalization #5570073, granting him U.S. citizenship.

In October or November, Zanuck added to Preminger's plate by assigning him to take over *All Out Arlene*, a romantic comedy with a patriotic theme, from Ernst Lubitsch, who was recuperating from the heart attack he suffered on September 1. Henry and Phoebe Ephron, Lubitsch's writers on the project, had been warned by Gilbert Miller that they wouldn't like Preminger, and they didn't. Henry Ephron wrote, "His manner of working was madness. If one of us came up with an amusing line, he would never laugh. He would simply nod his head and say, 'That's funny.' But he never smiled, he never chuckled and there was never any encouraging laughter. It was hardly an inspiring atmosphere to work in. Where was that wonderful free Lubitsch laugh that filled you with enthusiasm and made you try harder and be even funnier?"[16] The Ephrons wouldn't be the last to feel that Preminger was no Lubitsch. Preminger didn't like the Ephrons' work on *All Out Arlene* any more than they liked him, and he sought to interest Lardner in doing a rewrite; for whatever reason, the film was never made.

Lardner would find that working on multiple projects at once was Preminger's standard operating procedure. "Inevitably, problems with the current project took precedence over the future one, and he would draft the writer of the latter to help him out with the former."[17] With Preminger fighting the battles of *Laura*, it may be doubted whether he was able to devote much energy to pushing *Ambassador Dodd's Diary*, which now bore the optimistic title *Now It Can Be Told*. After Zanuck's hugely expensive personal production of *Wilson* was released to disastrous box office, Zanuck declared a moratorium on films dealing with history or public affairs, and *Dodd* was canceled. Years later, asked about *Ambassador Dodd's Diary*, Preminger replied simply, "Zanuck was afraid of it."[18] His trepidation may have had something to do with the left-wing politics of Martha Dodd.

"A comedy, but with something else," as Preminger later described it (pointing to his heart "with a sober gesture," in the words of Jacques Rivette),[19] set in a crowded hotel reserved for married army officers and their wives, *In the Meantime, Darling* started as a treatment called *Paris, Tenn.* by future blacklistee Michael Uris. As the first film Preminger both produced and directed, *In the Meantime, Darling* can be considered a personal project. Of the qualities that recommended Uris's treatment to Preminger, no doubt the most salient were its topicality, its 100 percent American nature, its emphasis on a female protagonist, and its theme of collective activity. A first draft by Uris and Arthur Kober was finished by July 9, 1943. Sticking to his vow to keep Preminger out of the director's chair, Zanuck assigned Archie Mayo to direct the film, which, by August 2, became known as *Army Wife*. The script went through further revisions before going into production as *I Married a Soldier* on December 20, 1943. By then, Zanuck had released Mayo from the project and given permission for Preminger to direct—an opportunity Preminger had probably courted, just as he sought to direct *Laura*. In later years, understandably, he had little to say about the less prestigious film and the circumstances of his assuming its direction. Perhaps Zanuck's experiences with Preminger in preparing *Laura* had restored his confidence in the director. In any case, with its modest budget and its cast of newcomers and character actors, Zanuck risked little in confiding the direction of *I Married a Soldier* to Preminger.

The film was the first for both Frank Latimore and Gale Robbins, and the first in which Jeanne Crain received top billing. Among the younger actors getting on-camera practice in minor parts were Glenn Langan, then being groomed for a stardom that would never come, and future director Blake Edwards, who later recalled being "chewed out" by Preminger and responding in kind.[20] Another actor, Stanley Prager, became the hero, or the victim, of a legendary Preminger anecdote. During shooting, the actor froze and became unable to continue with a scene. Preminger seized Prager by the shoulders, shook him violently, and, with his face about two inches away from the actor's, shouted, "Relax! Relax! Relax!"

As shooting continued into January 1944, the script underwent extensive changes. A *Los Angeles Examiner* item dated February 4 hints that the production was troubled: having gone through three title changes, it was being referred to around the lot as *What Next?* After the film was finished, more script revisions were ordered. Filmed in late March, by which time the title had become *In the Meantime, Darling*, the retakes were largely designed to enhance Jeanne Crain's presence in the film. The script had already received more than its share of objections from Joseph Breen's Production Code Administration (PCA). Breen advised the filmmakers that a scene in the script showing the newlyweds Maggie (Crain) and Danny (Latimore) in bed together would be deleted by British Board of Film Censors, and he recommended taking protection shots.[21] In the final film, the couple do appear in bed together. This was almost the only aspect of the film Preminger later cared to remember: "There was much excitement because for the first time in films, the Code permitted us to show married people sleeping in the same bed."[22]

Preminger also related an unpleasant incident involving Eugene Pallette, cast as Maggie's wealthy father. Preminger had become aware that Pallette "was an admirer of Hitler and [was] convinced that Germany would win the war." At one point, the script called for Pallette to enter the kitchen and sit down next to Clarence Muse, playing the hotel's handyman. Pallette told Preminger, "You're out of your mind. I won't sit next to a nigger." Preminger had Pallette fired from the picture and written out of the remaining scenes.[23]

Released in September 1944 to lukewarm reviews, the minor work that resulted from all this commotion is uneven, but it improves on Preminger's previous films in several respects. The screenplay of *In the Meantime, Darling* is built on circumstances that allow Preminger to emphasize the equivalence of individuals within a group, anticipating his large-scale works of the 1960s. One striking shot shows Preminger organizing disparate movements within a single take: as Maggie leaves through a door at the back of the set, the camera picks up Lieutenant Larkin (Glenn Langan) walking into the parlor and sitting down to join a card game. The location exteriors of the hotel give the film a certain gritty authenticity, especially in the final sequence, with its unsentimental visual shock of army trucks swarming around the solitary and forlorn building.

Maggie's alienation gives the story a Premingerian flavor. The scene in which Maggie waits for Jerry (Jane Randolph) in the latter's private parlor and roams around handling and looking at various objects (discovering that Jerry's husband was killed in action) is thematically close to the scene of Mark exploring Laura's apartment in *Laura*. In this scene and throughout the film, Preminger and Jeanne Crain manage to make us feel that Maggie's progressive integration into the group at the Craig Hotel (and thus into the larger group, of which the group at the Craig are a microcosm, of Americans sacrificing their private comforts for a great cause) is a matter of importance. For the first time in a Preminger film, we are in the presence of a figure with a soul, flickering however dimly.

5

If You Can Find Something Different

In 1943, buoyed by Otto's improved prospects, the Premingers bought a house at 333 Bel Air Road. In her autobiography, *All I Want Is Everything*, Marion devotes six pages of a chapter titled "The Monotony of Excitement" to describing this house, with its salon furnished with French Empire pieces, a "gray salon" decorated with "a small exquisite Renoir," a dining room "which, at that time, was the only dining-room in America with two tables—one for the host, one for the hostess," a complicated communications system including twenty telephones, and a master bedroom filled with rare books and decorated with "two magnificent watercolors of dancers by Rodin."[1] According to Otto Preminger, "not a single room or piece of furniture is recognizable" from her account.[2] The detail of the communications system does, however, ring true. Otto's later attachment to gadgetry is well attested.

Marion developed a flair for entertaining and, in Otto's words, "made a career of parties, which not only bored me but also conflicted with my need to rise early in the morning and go to work."[3] The couple were seen less and less together. According to Otto, Marion accepted her husband's affairs with other women, although she does not write about this aspect of their marriage in her autobiography. Marion's "greatest comfort and inspiration" came from her close friendship with interior decorator Elsie de Wolfe, Lady Mendl.[4] Lady Mendl had attracted, according to Otto, "an assortment of refugee Europeans of such right-wing leanings that I referred to them jokingly as 'the FBI set.' I was sure that some of them were Nazi agents . . . We were invited to all the parties the Mendls gave, and they entertained frequently. I found the affairs boring."[5]

It was at one of these parties that Preminger met the famous stripper Gypsy Rose Lee, with whom he had a brief affair in early 1944. One day,

Preminger recounted later, he phoned Lee to be told that she had gone to New York. "It was so abrupt, I thought perhaps I had done something. When I was next in New York, I tried to call her again. This time her secretary answered and told me she was in the hospital. When I reached her there, she said, 'Congratulations. This morning we had a son.'" She turned down his offer of support: "I don't need your money. I have money of my own. Erik is going to be *my* son. He's not even to know that you're his father." Instead, Lee attributed the child's paternity to her estranged husband, Alexander Kirkland. At first Otto was permitted to visit Erik whenever he was in New York, but after Lee remarried, his visits caused tension with her new husband, and "she told me not to come anymore."[6] It was not until Erik was twenty-two that he and Otto would meet again and acknowledge each other as father and son.

The affair with Gypsy Rose Lee took place during the troublesome preproduction of the film that would be Preminger's breakthrough in Hollywood. Asked by Peter Bogdanovich, "What particularly interested you about *Laura*?" Preminger replied, "The gimmick. You see, a suspense picture depends mainly on finding a new gimmick. There are very few new plots. If you can find something different, as in this case, where a girl you thought was dead automatically becomes a murder suspect by walking into her own apartment—that helps."[7]

Vera Caspary's *Laura* was published as a serial in *Collier's* magazine in October and November of 1942 before appearing in book form in early 1943. Preminger persuaded—"practically forced," he said in one interview—Zanuck to acquire *Laura*.[8] Caspary was offered, but turned down, the chance to write the screenplay; instead, Philip Lewis and George Bricker worked on adapting the novel before Jay Dratler was assigned to the project. Dratler's first-draft continuity script, dated October 30, 1943, follows the book in using, in succession, three different narrators: first Waldo Lydecker, a famous New York columnist; then Mark McPherson, the police detective assigned to investigate the murder of Waldo's protégée, advertising executive Laura Hunt; and finally Laura herself, who turns out to be still alive, a fashion model named Diane Redfern having been killed in her stead (by a disfiguring gunshot, making identification difficult). In Dratler's script, much of the voice-over commentary merely spells out reactions and feelings—in particular, Mark's romantic obsession with the supposedly dead Laura—that the audience would have had no difficulty inferring from dialogue and directly presented action. At the denouement, which would cause months of headaches for Preminger, Zanuck, and several writers, the jealous and insane Waldo, who killed Diane mistaking her for Laura, tries again to kill Laura but is stopped by the police and arrested.

After, at Preminger's invitation, Vera Caspary had read the first-draft script, the novelist asked Preminger, "Why don't you give her the character she has in the book?" He replied, "In the book, Laura has no character . . . Laura has no sex." Their discussion concluded with Caspary's saying, "Perhaps you don't know anything about love, Mr. Preminger."[9] She would not be the last person to whom this possibility would occur.

On November 1, Zanuck sent Preminger and Bryan Foy—to whose B-picture unit the project had first been relegated, but where it would not stay long—a memo criticizing Dratler's script, which, "as a dialogue job," he found "very ordinary." The main female role posed, in Zanuck's view, the biggest problem: "Laura is a mess. She is neither interesting nor attractive, and I doubt if any first-rate actress would play her . . . She does no thinking in the picture at all. She has no decisions to make." Zanuck planned to cast Monty Woolley as Waldo and wanted the character's lines "punched up with more sarcastic humor and ironic, sadistic wisecracks." Zanuck recommended downplaying the love angle—a suggestion that Preminger would resist—and criticized Laura's voice-over narration, which he thought pointless. That this narration would survive three revisions of the screenplay means that Preminger argued in favor of it and persuaded Zanuck to let him try it. Only with the April 18, 1944, final shooting script would Laura's narration be jettisoned. On the other hand, Mark's narration was still envisioned all through production and was recorded by Dana Andrews, only to be discarded in postproduction. As for Mark himself, "There ought to be more of Cagney about him . . . There was a good thing in the book, which you have eliminated here, and that was the point that fashionable Park Avenue murders were not Mark's dish. He was a guy who dealt with gangs like the Dutch Schultz racketeers, and he hated the idea of being mixed up with these people." As we'll see, Preminger allowed the film's first director, Rouben Mamoulian, to portray Mark in a way that directly violated Zanuck's instructions.[10]

To polish the script, Preminger called on Ring Lardner, Jr., whose most momentous contribution may have been the addition of a scene (later rewritten) in which Mark brings Laura to police headquarters for interrogation. A final script dated November 29, bearing the names of both Dratler and Lardner, was submitted to Joseph Breen's Production Code Administration, which voiced the same objections it had raised to the October 30 script: the characters drink too much; the filmmakers should avoid implying that either Laura and Waldo, or Diane and Shelby Carpenter (Laura's weak-willed fiancé), have had sex; and a line by Laura's maid, Bessie, about wiping off the glasses in Laura's apartment makes too explicit a recommendation of a method by which potential criminals in the audience might avoid incriminating themselves. Breen also asked that a line spoken by Mark to Waldo in the first sequence— "You like your men better if they're not a hundred percent"—be rephrased, "since as written, it has the unacceptable flavor of a possible pathological sex angle so far as Waldo is concerned." (The line was eventually dropped.) Caspary's novel had planted further hints of homosexuality in Waldo—hints that the film mostly suppresses.

The search was on for a director and a cast. Holding firm to his refusal to let Preminger direct *Laura*, Zanuck offered the film to John Brahm, Walter Lang, and Lewis Milestone, all of whom turned it down. On February 24, 1944, *The Hollywood Reporter* announced that Irving Cummings would direct *Laura*, but, in Preminger's words, "The man who finally accepted the script was Rouben Mamoulian. He also didn't like it, as it turned out, but he wanted the money. When he found out that I was not particularly in Zanuck's good graces, he started to ignore me. He began to design the sets with the art department without asking me. He started to rewrite the script, which I stopped. I said, 'You accepted the script, you've got to do it.' I had no hopes of directing it, however. I was just resigned to the fact that I would sit out my contract and at least produce this film which I liked."[11]

On March 20, 1944, Zanuck wrote a memo to Preminger, Mamoulian, and Samuel Hoffenstein, the writer now assigned to the project. (Preminger later praised Hoffenstein and credited him with having "practically created the character of Waldo Lydecker for Clifton Webb.")[12] Though pleased with the January 25 revised final script, Zanuck still thought that "the character of Laura herself is flat and uninspired . . . Laura should come into the story like a breath of spring, like something out of this world." Zanuck strongly objected to two lines in which Waldo implies that Laura feels sexual desire: "With you a lean, strong body is the measure of the man" and "It's the same obvious pattern—the muscular man." The two lines (which both have their origin in Caspary's novel) remained, substantially, in all subsequent revisions of the script, down to the finished film. We can assume that Preminger held out for this aspect of the characterization of Laura (and of Waldo); composer David Raksin's recollection that Preminger considered Laura "a whore" offers support for this assumption.

Though Jennifer Jones (who under an agreement with David O. Selznick was contracted to make one film a year for Fox) was announced for the part, it went to studio contract player Gene Tierney, who approached the role with misgivings. "In truth," she later wrote, "only Otto Preminger had absolute faith in the project."[13] Zanuck had mentally cast Reginald Gardiner as Shelby, but in the event, Vincent Price finally played Shelby—with a combination of unctuousness, ruthlessness, and narcissism that was, no doubt, better than anything Gardiner, basically a comic actor, would have brought to the role. Judith Anderson was cast as Anne Treadwell, Laura's aunt, and though Zanuck had wanted John Hodiak to play Mark (George Raft was also apparently considered at one stage), Preminger preferred, and got, Dana Andrews, who would become one of the actors most closely associated with the director. In the four films in which Andrews played leading roles for Preminger, Andrews defined at once a character type, an acting style, and a way of observing character that are constitutive of the Preminger universe.

Zanuck now wanted Laird Cregar (well established in villainous roles), rather than Monty Woolley, as Waldo, but Preminger objected: "You must have a man who either is unknown or has never played heavies before. Otherwise, the audience will know right away, and there will be no chance to suspect Gene Tierney."[14] Preminger's insistence on misdirecting suspicion onto Laura is interesting in view of the fact that in the finished film, the possibility that Laura is guilty seems at most a formality (a sense well conveyed in Mark's line, "I was ninety-nine percent certain about you, but I had to get rid of that one percent doubt"). The originally filmed ending, in which Laura retrieves the murder weapon from the secret compartment in the clock, testifies to Preminger's continuing desire to make the audience believe that Laura is guilty ("Her behavior seems to offer unmistakable evidence that she is the guilty one," notes the script in its May 29, 1944, revision). Perhaps this desire lies at the heart of Vera Caspary's claim that Preminger wanted to turn *Laura* into "a conventional detective story."[15] In insisting that the audience regard Laura as a suspect, Preminger proves his fidelity to his original feeling for the project, to the "gimmick" that, more than anything else, attracted him to Caspary's story: "a girl you thought was dead automatically becomes a murder suspect by walking into her own apartment."

Preminger fought to cast Clifton Webb as Waldo. A well-known stage star, Webb was persona non grata at Fox; Zanuck thought the actor's effete manner would get him laughed off the screen in the Midwest. Over casting director Rufus LeMaire's objections, Preminger persuaded Zanuck to let him shoot a test with Webb. The test won Zanuck over, and Webb was hired for *Laura*. "I wanted him for the part, because he was new," said Preminger. "Also, at that time, when a picture supposedly took place in New York, it would still have that Los Angeles feeling. People didn't really bother to capture that kind of big-town sophistication. Clifton was ideal for it, as today it's easy to see."[16] The "New York" aspect of the film, to which Webb's persona is indeed essential, is one of the most distinctive elements that Preminger contributed to *Laura*. (At a private screening of an early cut of the film, columnist Walter Winchell showed his appreciation by laughing at the dialogue, "which made Zanuck furious because he hated the film," said Preminger, adding, "it must be said that Winchell is from New York, and the film is very New York, whereas Zanuck hated New York, he wouldn't even go to spend two days there.")[17]

Shooting began under Mamoulian's direction on April 27 and was scheduled to finish on June 16. As Preminger told it, "Mamoulian started to direct the picture, and he ignored me completely. He didn't even let me come on the stage, said I made him nervous because I was also a director." Preminger thought that Mamoulian "just didn't understand the picture. For instance, he put Judith Anderson in long, waving robes—almost like a period play. But this was all meant to be very crisp and contemporary, like New York." At Preminger's urging, Lew Schreiber, Zanuck's right-hand man, sent the rushes of *Laura* to his boss, who was then out of town. "They were so bad you couldn't believe it," said Preminger. Zanuck blamed everything on Preminger, telling him,

"You should have stayed in New York or in Vienna, where you belong." (If Zanuck really told Preminger that he should have stayed in Vienna, the crack was worse than unkind.) On Zanuck's return, he summoned Preminger and Mamoulian to his office, where Preminger impressed Zanuck by talking through the scenes the way he thought they should be done. Zanuck told Mamoulian, "Well, I think he's right. Try again tomorrow. I'll give you another chance."[18]

A revised shooting schedule, dated May 3, called for retakes in the opening sequence of Mark visiting Waldo's apartment and the first sequence in Anne Treadwell's apartment, both of which had already been shot during the first week. The schedule was revised again on Friday, May 12, with Mamoulian still listed as director. Then on Monday, May 15, Louella Parsons reported in the *Los Angeles Examiner* that "Rouben Mamoulian has asked to be released from directing *Laura*, and Otto Preminger, the producer of this much discussed movie, will direct the picture himself. The trouble is a difference of opinion of the psychological treatment of the story and character. The two men could not see eye to eye, and so Mamoulian stepped out."

In 1958 Dana Andrews recounted the behind-the-scenes machinations that led to Mamoulian's departure. According to the actor, both Preminger and Mamoulian had told him to play Mark McPherson as a college-educated criminologist. "I think Mr. Preminger wanted to be different, in this respect—to blaze a trail." When Zanuck returned from out of town, "a great commotion was heard. He saw the rushes of what had been shot, and suddenly in the middle of the afternoon the picture was stopped, and the director and the producer were over with Mr. Zanuck. And the word came to us that they were going to take Mamoulian off the picture." Andrews was summoned to Zanuck's office to find the executive in conference with Preminger and Mamoulian. Zanuck told the men that he wanted Andrews to play his role in the customary hard-boiled manner—"like Pat O'Brien." Whereupon Preminger declared, "Why, that's what I was telling Rouben." Enraged, Mamoulian exclaimed, "That's a lie. You did not! You explained to me that you wanted this man played in the other way." Andrews bowed out of the meeting, and found, the next morning, that Preminger had been assigned to take over as director. "This was designing and it was ambitious," Andrews concluded, "but he did a wonderful job."[19]

Preminger's version involved a lunch he attended with Zanuck and about eighteen members of the upper echelons at Fox, where, abruptly, Zanuck turned to him and asked, "Do you think we should take Mamoulian off the picture?" Without hesitating, Preminger said yes. As they were on their way back from the dining room to the administration building, Zanuck told Preminger offhandedly, "Monday you can start directing *Laura*."[20]

Arriving on the set on Monday morning, May 15, Preminger found the atmosphere chilly. Cameraman Lucien Ballard, he said, "ignored me completely. While we were getting ready to shoot he would read a paper and smoke a cigar as if he was a guest on the set."[21] The actors, except for Clifton Webb, were hostile. Dana Andrews later said that Mamoulian's removal "upset everybody in the picture, because we were very fond of Rouben . . . Judith Anderson practically refused to act. She made her appearance, technically, but wouldn't take Mr. Preminger's direction."[22] According to Preminger, Anderson, deliberately mispronouncing his name with the hard German *g* instead of the soft American one he had adopted, challenged him to show her how to play the part. He replied, "That is exactly what I am going to do, and you will do it exactly like this. Then I will take you to see the rushes tomorrow, and you will be the first one to agree that I was right. I'll show you both scenes: the way you did it before, and the way you're going to do it now." The projection of the rushes, Preminger said, convinced Anderson and the others that his approach was correct. "I had no more difficulties, and we had a wonderful time."[23]

Anderson's own account was less rosy. "We were all on edge and very tense," she recalled. "Preminger's direction was Germanic in approach. He saw the picture his way. There was a change of everything, and conflicts about everything. I much preferred Mamoulian's direction. It would have been a happier experience if he had been directing."[24] Vincent Price commented insightfully on the difference the change in directors made to *Laura*: "What Otto added to the film—and none of us could figure it out at first—was the ability to give each one of the characters an underlying sense of evil. Nobody in that picture is normal. Mamoulian hadn't done that; he was a very good director and a nice man, but he had no concept about these kind of upper class scum people. Otto gave our characters a feeling of evil underneath this sophistication, a facade these high society people had. And it worked. When you saw the picture you realized these characters were essentially very, very evil—yet with their high society veneer, you'd never guess."[25]

Consolidating his control, Preminger replaced Lucien Ballard with Joseph LaShelle, who had shot—"beautifully," as Preminger recalled— the test with Clifton Webb. For *Laura*, Preminger and LaShelle worked out a style making extensive use of camera movement, even in situations where it would have been normal to cut, for example in going from room to room or from medium shot to close-up.[26] According to Tierney, LaShelle was slow. "He would take ages to light a scene. Every time I heard him say, 'No, no, it's not right,' I could feel my teeth clench, and I knew there went another hour or two of waiting for the lights to be reset."[27]

Preminger replaced Mamoulian's costume designer with Bonnie Cashin, with whom he had previously worked on *In the Meantime, Darling*. (On May 24, the Breen Office approved stills of Judith Anderson's changed wardrobe.) Preminger scrapped some of Mamoulian's sets and, in doing so, got rid of the portrait of Laura that had been commissioned from Azadia Newman, Mamoulian's wife. Preminger substituted a photograph of Tierney by studio photographer Frank Polony, enlarged and brushed with paint. This image, which introduces and closes the film and reappears prominently throughout, may be taken as Preminger's trademark, a sign of his will to dominate the film.

According to Tierney, "Preminger . . . drove himself, and us, so hard! He was simply tireless. When the rest of the cast seemed ready to drop from exhaustion, Otto would still muster as much vigor as when the day began."[28] Visiting the set, Vera Caspary saw Preminger direct a scene of Waldo and Laura at Sardi's. "It was not only brilliantly theatrical but true. Preminger had re-created the world of *Laura*, not only the appearance of the restaurant, but the sense of gossip and phony charm. Every actor, every extra, every crew member was with it. The little world of Preminger's creation had become real."[29]

A revised schedule dated Monday, May 22, had Preminger starting the week with retakes of the sequence in which Mark, Waldo, and Shelby visit Laura's apartment, then continuing on the same set with the sequence revolving around the bottle of cheap Scotch whose presence in the apartment arouses Mark's suspicions. New revised schedules were made on June 2 and June 13. The picture's finish date was extended to

June 27. Zanuck told Preminger to use as much of Mamoulian's footage as possible, but Preminger kept sneaking more and more retakes into the schedule, confiding to LaShelle, "We're not going to leave any scene at all of Mamoulian's in this picture."[30] Preminger later said, "We threw out everything Mamoulian had directed."[31] Vincent Price confirmed this: "We reshot every single scene that Rouben Mamoulian had done."[32] Lucien Ballard's claim that he and Mamoulian shot 75 percent of the film, after which Preminger "had it easy, because Mamoulian had set every scene (Preminger used his basics, and refilmed just a little)" is contradicted by the available records, and Mamoulian himself affirmed, according to Jacques Lourcelles, that none of his footage survives in the film.[33]

The ending of the film is a subject of confusion—not because of Mamoulian's possible authorship, since it is certain that he was off the picture before it was filmed. In the ending as Preminger first shot it, Laura finds the gun hidden in her clock and, realizing that Waldo killed Diane, goes to his apartment to urge him to flee. Laura returns to her apartment, stalked by Waldo. He is about to kill her when Mark arrives; in a struggle, Waldo's gun goes off, shattering the clock. As Waldo is led away (making a parting shot about the "disgustingly earthy relationship" Laura can look forward to with Mark), the camera pans to the clock, and Waldo is heard saying, "You're all I'll be thinking of—till Time stands still—for me. Goodbye, Laura."

According to Preminger's well-known account of the screening of his first cut of *Laura* for Zanuck, the latter, when it was over, declared, "We missed the bus on this one." Zanuck called in Jerome Cady to do a new ending, which, Preminger claimed, featured "a narration by Gene Tierney which negated everything that had happened in the picture. She was to say it was not true—it had all been in Clifton Webb's imagination." Preminger reluctantly filmed the ending, and a new cut was screened for Zanuck; columnist Walter Winchell, a friend of both Zanuck and Preminger, was present. After the screening, Winchell praised the film, calling it "big time," but criticized the ending. Zanuck turned to Preminger and said, "Do you want to have your old ending back?" So Preminger restored his film to its earlier and now definitive form.[34]

The extant script material contradicts Preminger's account. Laura's voice-over narration existed in the earlier versions of the script but was discarded in the final shooting script of April 18, 1944, and was not subsequently restored. The ending that appears in the film, with a few minor differences and one major one, was the new ending written in July by Jerome Cady and filmed over several days, ending July 20. Preminger's recollection of a narration by Laura that "negated everything that had happened in the picture" doubtless refers to the passage in Cady's revision in which Laura, telling Mark about her first meeting with Waldo, contradicts Waldo's account (which was shown in flashback earlier in the film). She explains, "He dramatizes everything. To him, I, like everything else, am only half real. The other half exists only in his own mind . . . Once he writes something, he believes it." This passage was presumably shot and included in the cut that was screened for Winchell, who probably criticized it, whereupon Zanuck allowed Preminger to delete it. In the final film, the omission is covered by a cutaway to Waldo in the stairs, which is somewhat jarring, since it implies that Waldo, whom we have previously seen pausing in the stairs, has remained there, exposed to potential discovery, for several minutes.

Composer David Raksin, assigned to the film after its completion (and probably after the completion of the final cut, following the July retakes), was unaware of any controversy concerning the ending, although, like everyone at Fox, he was aware of *Laura*'s reputation as a troubled production. Raksin attended an executives' screening of the film, at the end of which Zanuck told Preminger that he wanted to shorten or delete the scene of Mark walking around Laura's apartment (the very scene Zanuck had wanted to expand in his November 1, 1943, notes on the script). Raksin, then still a relative newcomer, got up the nerve to object. "Mr. Zanuck, if you do that, people will not understand that the detective is falling in love with Laura. I think music in this case can really tip the balance, [helping the audience to] understand what [Mark] is thinking." Zanuck let Raksin proceed.[35]

For the theme mentioned in the dialogue as Laura's favorite tune and heard at several points in the picture, Preminger wanted to use Duke Ellington's "Sophisticated Lady." (He had also considered George Gershwin's "Summertime," from *Porgy and Bess*, but Ira Gershwin refused to let Preminger use the song. In Caspary's novel, Laura is fond of Jerome Kern's "Smoke Gets in Your Eyes.") Raksin objected that the song was too well known and that it carried associations applicable neither to the film nor to the character of Laura. When Preminger insisted, Raksin asked (as he recalled):

> "Mr. Preminger, can it be that you have some notion of who that girl really is, and that you tie it to the title of the song?" He looked at me as if I were a stupid idiot and said, "Well, she's a whore." I said, "Mr. Preminger, by whose definition?" He turned to [Alfred] Newman [head of Fox's music department] and said, "Where did you find this fellow?" Newman said: "Why don't you listen to what he's saying, Otto? You never know what this guy will come up with." So Preminger said, "This is Friday. You come in with something better we like by Monday, or we use 'Sophisticated Lady.' " So Monday I wound up with "Laura," and Newman and I played it for Preminger, and he liked it.[36]

The score was recorded on September 12. To enhance the scene of Laura's return, Raksin used a special effect of tape-recorded chords played back over off-center capstans to produce a quaver. (He named this effect the "Len-a-tone," after his friend, sound technician Harry Leonard, who had hit on the device as a way of artificially aging Gregory Peck's voice for scenes in *The Keys of the Kingdom*.) The effect would become something of a Raksin trademark, recurring in his scores for Preminger's *Fallen Angel*, Nicholas Ray's *Bigger Than Life*, and Vincente Minnelli's *Two Weeks in Another Town*, among other films.

Released on October 11 in New York, *Laura* became a moderate hit for Fox, though not a blockbuster, earning $2 million in domestic rentals, against production costs of $1,020,000.[37] (In the long term, the film assuredly became a major moneymaker.) Raksin's "Laura" became a hit (and a jazz standard), and Tierney, Webb, and Andrews all became top stars. *Laura* was nominated for Academy Awards in five categories: director (Preminger), supporting actor (Webb), screenplay (Dratler, Hoffenstein, and Reinhardt), black-and-white cinematography (LaShelle), and black-and-white interior decoration (art directors Leland Fuller and Lyle Wheeler and set decorator Thomas Little). On March 15, 1945, only LaShelle, among the *Laura* contingent, took home an Oscar: Leo McCarey won as Best Director for *Going My Way*, which was also named Best Picture. Nevertheless, *Laura* became a Hollywood classic and defined the Preminger mystique for generations of filmgoers.

Laura opens by introducing us to a world of glass, of fragile and precious objects on display, a closed world (Waldo's apartment) within another closed world (Manhattan, which Waldo, who narrates the scene, imagines dead). Everything is suspended; there is a sense of waiting ("I had him wait," says Waldo in voice-over as the panning camera reveals Mark), but a waiting for nothing, without anticipation. Since Laura is already dead, no future is indicated; there will be nothing but a melancholy return into the past.

"I noticed that his attention was fixed upon my clock." Waldo's narration announces the importance of the clock, with which the film, the inner film (framed by the images of Laura's portrait under the opening and ending titles), will close. The clock is linked to Laura and to her death: Waldo's voice-over specifies that "there was only one other in existence—and that was in Laura's apartment, in the very room where she was murdered." The duplication of the clock suggests that, in *Laura*, there are two times. The first is a stalled, dead time, from which nothing new can emerge: the time of Waldo's apartment, of the dead and abandoned New York, of a narrative that takes place under the sign of death and inside a circle that has already closed or whose closing the narrative traces (a process represented in the lines from Ernest Dowson that Waldo recites in his last radio broadcast: "Out of a misty dream / Our path emerges for a while, then closes / Within a dream"). The second is a time of change, from which the new constantly emerges, in flight from a past that it desires to renounce and betray. It is fitting that the apparitions of Laura in the flashbacks are characterized by a light rhythm and a rapid tempo, that she is seen dancing in the flashbacks, that they link her to music, and that when she returns, we should suddenly hear the sound of a clock ticking.

The film will seem to take place within the first time. Waldo's voice-over already signifies an allegiance to death and the past. This voice-over ends, however, in mid-film. Waldo will go on to narrate, for Mark's benefit, Laura's rise, but the opening scene will be the only one in which a voice-over is heard that is nondiegetic—not spoken in a situation represented within the narrative. Thus the closure implied by Waldo's voice-over is an illusion: the film never reaches the place where his narrative closes, never confirms the claim he makes to mastery; despite Waldo, time has not stopped, and the film will show the inexorability of its flight into the future.

On the other hand, this flight can only take place off camera, as the final shot of the film shows: first Laura, then Mark, leave the frame in the direction of Waldo's dying voice while the camera tracks forward to the smashed face of the clock. The film reaches, then, a formal, though not a narrative, closure: Waldo's voice-over accompanies both the beginning and the end (at the end, the voice—"goodbye, my love"—might more properly be called a voice-off, but in terms of a purely material description, the distinction is nonexistent). Waldo's clock, seen at the beginning of the film, is doubled by its duplicate in Laura's apartment. The death of Waldo is the death of the film, which survives him only in two images of frozen and inanimate objects: the clock whose time has stopped forever, and then the portrait again, with "The End" superimposed on it.

The clock becomes, like Diane Redfern, a surrogate Laura—its face, like Diane's, destroyed so that Laura's might be spared. Diane dies someone else's death under someone else's name (in the book, even her "own" name is an assumed one)—she dies the death of contingency, accident, irrelevance: an inappropriate, meaningless death. She dies so that Laura can live on and be reborn in the time of the new.

The time in which the new can emerge belongs to Mark and Laura. This is the myth of the film as a love story, of Laura's awakening from a "bad dream" (Mark's phrase), "out of a misty dream" (Dowson's) to a kind of reality. In order to reach this reality, we, with the characters, must pass through several stages of illusion. The great scene in which Mark brings Laura to police headquarters marks an effort to dispel illusion, the bad illusion (of the corrupt world represented by Shelby and Anne, and of Laura as someone who belongs to that world). The scene is marked by violation: Mark floods Laura's face with harsh light, which causes her visible pain. The strain and effort of the scene accompany a rebirth. The glamorous close-ups of Gene Tierney, inserted in the scene somewhat arbitrarily and with some dissonance, are appropriate because they manifest transcendence: the creation of another image of Laura to contrast with the images of Waldo and the painter Jacoby.

It must be said that this new image is not fully inhabited by Laura herself—that, in some sense, Laura doesn't exist, even when she is, finally, stripped to essentials and freed from the world that deforms her. This is the great problem of *Laura*. Zanuck had worried about the character's nonexistence throughout the preparation of the script, and Gene Tierney perhaps sensed it: "I never felt my own performance was much more than adequate. I am pleased that audiences still identify me with Laura, as opposed to not being identified at all. Their tributes, I believe, are for the *character*—the dreamlike Laura—rather than any gifts I brought to the role."[38] Tierney recognizes here her own absence in the film and the truth that the character exists less through herself, less as a performance, than through the desires of others (of the audience and of the male characters in the film) that conjure her "dreamlike" presence. (Baudelaire, in the dedication to *Les Paradis artificiels*, wrote, "Woman is fatally suggestive; she lives out of another life than her own; she lives spiritually in the imaginations that she haunts and fecundates."[39]

Instead of claiming (as Caspary's novel tries to do but arguably fails) that Laura exists other than as a series of appearances, Preminger's film highlights that mode of existence—not only through the emphasis on her portrait but also through the elaborate montage that shows her rise to success in her career and in New York society. In this flashback, Laura is occasionally shown speaking, but her voice is never heard; the sound track carries only Waldo's narration and Raksin's score—homages to and discourses on Laura. (The insistence of Waldo's voice and the erasure of Laura's are emphasized in the shot in which Laura listens as Waldo reads his column to her.) Meanwhile, the camera repeatedly tracks toward Laura's face, drawn over and over again toward her beauty in a compulsive movement that is matched by Laura's inexhaustible willingness to turn toward or approach the camera.

Laura as *created*: this is what the portrait means, and this is the image that viewers carry from the film, giving the character an imaginary life from which Gene Tierney herself felt alienated. The created Laura is a frozen, timeless, inaccessible image—which even Waldo criticizes in observing that the artist Jacoby, in painting the portrait, failed to capture the vibrancy and warmth of the living model. Vibrancy and warmth must be subtracted from the woman so that the painting may stand for the timelessness of man's desire. In his final radio broadcast, Waldo says, "Love is eternal . . . Love is stronger than life. It reaches beyond the dark shadow of death." Love's immortality (in contrast to the "disgustingly

earthy relationship" that Waldo predicts for Laura with Mark) is figured
in the portrait, a timelessness that captures Mark's imagination, luring
him repeatedly back to the apartment ("you're here often enough to pay
rent," Waldo chides), and that depends on and demands the death of the
real Laura.

A certain deficiency in Laura herself does not weaken the film; on
the contrary, her failure to exist completely becomes an important element in the film's texture. Outside the imaginations of Waldo and Jacoby, Laura is simple and prosaic. It may be felt that the film gives no
special emphasis to the tension between their images of her and Laura
as she is for herself. The film can be seen as another version of the type
of gothic story in which the heroine struggles against a role she is forced
to play—a Premingerian version, in which the struggle is acted out almost invisibly and inaudibly but can be inferred from the evidence given
by the film.

If Laura has some autonomous existence and is not merely the creation of men (Waldo, Jacoby, Preminger), it lies in her recognizing and
separating herself from the corruption and depravity around her. ("For
the first time in ages I know what I am doing," she says to Waldo, rejecting him for Mark.) During the superb scene of the party for Laura's "res-
urrection," she receives two successive shocks that reveal to her the true
nature of the people around her. First, Shelby says that he intended to
hide the shotgun in order to protect her—meaning that he believes
Laura killed Diane. Second, in Laura's bedroom, Anne says that she
"thought of" killing Laura. Seated at her dresser, Laura lowers her eyes
and turns, dejectedly, toward the mirror, then stubs out her cigarette in
the ashtray, gets up, and leaves the room. Her ambiguous attitude
(mournful acceptance?) departs crucially from the shooting script,
which describes her as "profoundly shaken." In the film as Preminger directed it, her composure shows both worldliness and an acceptance of
the impossibility of finding an appropriate way to battle such depravity
as has been exposed to her. This attitude makes the bedroom scene a
central moment in Preminger's work.

Bewildering as they are in their diversity, Laura remains transparent
in each of her apparitions; Mark, not Laura, becomes the film's main object of investigation. It is Mark who, more than anyone, undergoes the
pressure of the camera's persistent, prowling interrogations, and his are

the reactions that we watch for most persistently throughout this film, in which so much depends on eliciting and assessing reactions (as in the scenes in which Mark offers the suspects a drink from the bottle of cheap Scotch, which he thought out of place in Laura's elegant liquor cabinet, or the scene in which he astonishes Waldo with the sight of Laura alive).

When Waldo, aware that Mark has put in a bid for the portrait, taunts Mark, casting aspersions on what he supposes to be the plebeian nature of Mark's romantic imaginings, Mark frowns and slaps his pinball puzzle against his knee. These signs of distress signify distress only indirectly: what they indicate first is the effort to avoid showing distress. Several moments in the film foreground a certain style—as crucial to the film as LaShelle's hard-edged black and white and the relentless physicality of the camera movement—of half-suppressed response in Dana Andrews's performance. When Waldo, offscreen, rises from the bathtub, Mark looks at him with a tiny smirk. When Laura tells him that she has decided not to marry Shelby, Mark flashes the hint of a pleased smile. The strain of Mark's effort, elsewhere in the film, to repress his emotions makes this smile an epiphany. (The same emphasis on unspoken reactions, with the—of course illusory—sense that the camera is merely witnessing them without their having been produced for the camera, occurs in moments involving other characters, as when the cop-hating Bessie is thrown off guard by Mark's humanizing, "Go ahead and spit if that makes you feel any better.")

By suppressing Mark's voice-over narration, Preminger unifies the experience of time in the film. The decision to eliminate the narration was probably Zanuck's rather than Preminger's, but whoever was responsible, it was one of the most momentous artistic decisions made on *Laura*, transforming the film and establishing the direction of Preminger's future work (which is devoid of voice-over narration, with the conspicuous exception of *Bonjour Tristesse* and more fleeting ones in a few other films). In *Laura*, Mark's voice-over would have introduced posterity and the transcendent into the experience of time, turning it into a closed, self-contained story, as Waldo's voice-over does at the beginning of the film. Instead, Preminger insists on a continuous stream of things happening in the present, on the openness of this stream, and on preserving the viewer's wavering externality to Mark, who is thus presented as immanent to the diegesis and deprived of the freedom to move outside it—deprived, that is, of the temporal freedom of the film viewer. And by virtue of our partial empathy with Mark, through the medium of the camera that stands in for us, we give up our own temporal freedom. *Laura* becomes a film of action rather than of reflection; or rather, the camera itself becomes the element, or the subject, of reflection. The camera is what reflects, thinks, responds, and reckons; the film never violates the law by which we are held apart from the characters.

The visual style that Preminger develops for *Laura* enables him to exploit a property of photographic cinema so basic that in discussing most films, it may, without loss, escape consideration: the inability of the camera to be in more than one place at one time. Because of the mobility of the camera in *Laura*, we are aware of offscreen space as not just, or even primarily, space, but as *place*: a place previously visited, to which we might return. This awareness becomes acute in the famous scene of Laura's return. As Mark sleeps in the armchair beneath the portrait, the camera tracks back. We hear the sound of a door opening. A palpable delay occurs before we are shown—by a cut—the place from which the sound emanates, a place occupied by Laura. At first she's unaware of Mark's presence; as the shot progresses, she sees him offscreen and walks toward him, switching on the light beside her portrait, the camera meanwhile retreating before her so that Mark, in the armchair, becomes visible at the right of the frame.

The sound of the door opening, which we hear over the shot of Mark and the portrait, creates an exquisite suspense that is tightly linked to our sense of the apartment as a concrete place. This sense is already strong in the shot because Mark is unconscious: by falling asleep, he frees us from his point of view, in which we have begun to feel trapped, but as yet we we are given nothing to do with our freedom other than to admire a set that has already been established. Yet this reestablishment of the apartment as a place, effected by the backward movement of the camera, is nothing less than the reestablishment of a world: the world in which Laura was alive, before the murder. This world is almost a sensate being; it receives impressions. The sound of the door is heard by no one (since Mark is asleep), so it's as if the apartment itself were hearing the sound, as it has many times before (every time she came home).

Even after Preminger and the writers made the basic decision to represent Laura's return as happening outside Mark's consciousness, it was still possible to show her return so as to suggest that it is being seen, in some sense, as Mark would see it, to depict it in the colors of his emotions. Such an "expressionistic" approach might have visualized the door's opening and Laura's gradual coming into view in the doorway: the time of these processes would have correlated with the mounting excitement of the perceiver, whose presence the gradual emergence of Laura into the frame would have strongly implied. The lighting could have emphasized the psychology of the perceiver by having Laura, at the same time that she comes through the door, also come from darkness to light, having her walk into a spotlight, for example, for a star close-up that would respond in the most unambiguous manner to the desires of the audience. Preminger and LaShelle rigorously refuse such an approach. After the cut, Laura is simply there in the shot: we don't see her come in. The lighting is bright and even: a mundane, normal lighting, and Laura is shown full figure, not in close-up.

It is thus a world that establishes itself, a world momentarily emptied of consciousness. When the camera tracks back from Mark in the armchair and reaches medium distance, it's as if this world were holding its breath. The psychology suggested is only remotely that of Mark; perhaps it is informed by Mark's consciousness, since we, too, by now, want Laura, want her alive, but the dominant point of view is that of reality itself—the room's point of view.

The world of *Laura* is even, and evenly viewed; integral, and integrally viewed: it has no outside. The camera's progress through this world is an interrogation of surfaces, and we feel it as a pressure that sometimes relaxes, sometimes tightens. It would be inaccurate to consider the camera and the world of appearances as two bands proceeding in the same general direction; rather, the camera, which explores this world, also creates it. The visible world of the film is itself an encounter between two bodies, one that presses, another that resists. This resistance of the world is the key to Preminger's work. The world wasn't made for the camera; it has preexisted and will exist after the camera's moment. Photographing the world may be a struggle, a battle, an operation (as we will sense more and more in Preminger's all-location films from *Anatomy of a Murder* on); but even in the most controlled circumstances (*Laura* is shot almost entirely in the studio), Preminger insists that the act of making cinema should involve violation, disturbance, a complication that brings duration and risk into play.

The camera is neither the neutral recorder of what transpires before it nor an agent in complete empathy with the characters. Like Dana Andrews's Mark, Preminger's camera achieves its most characteristic effects by hiding behind a mask of indifference. The camera refuses to show that it is moved (another way of saying this: the camera refuses to tell us that *we* should be moved), but the urgency of its movements proves an emotional intelligence.

6

The Lubitsch Touch

In April 1944, while *Laura* was still in preproduction, Preminger received a directorial assignment that must have seemed an ambiguous indicator of his standing at Fox. Ernst Lubitsch had been preparing *The Czarina*, an adaptation of a play by that title by Lajos Biro and Melchior Lengyel, which Lubitsch had filmed in 1924 as *Forbidden Paradise*, with Pola Negri as Catherine the Great. Lubitsch had suffered a massive heart attack in September 1943 and was under doctors' orders not to submit himself to the rigors of directing. *The Czarina* was the first film under a revised Fox contract for Lubitsch's services as producer. The assignment to direct the film went to Preminger, who had been linked with the older director at least since 1941, when Fox bought *Margin for Error* for Lubitsch. The two men had come to know each other: Preminger's Bel Air house was just down the block from Lubitsch's, and both were regulars at the Sunday afternoon kaffeeklatsches of another near neighbor, writer-producer Walter Reisch.

Preminger may have seen *The Czarina* as a further chance to prove his versatility to Zanuck. Maybe he saw in it, perversely, an opportunity to set himself apart from Hollywood's preeminent German-Austrian director. Preminger recalled later, "Someone said I was quite brave, in a way, because everyone talked about the 'Lubitsch touch.' I don't worry about these things. I am not brave. I don't think about it. It is part of my philosophy not to worry about what other people think of me." Though Preminger claimed, years later, to have "admired and loved" Lubitsch, his films give little evidence of having been marked by Lubitsch's style.[1] Preminger would work in Lubitsch's shadow twice again (completing the direction of Lubitsch's last film, *That Lady in Ermine*, and remaking Oscar Wilde's *Lady Windermere's Fan*, which Lubitsch had filmed with great success). All three of Preminger's "Lubitsch" films, as Andrew Sarris has pointed out, mark Preminger's difference from Lubitsch rather than his similarity: "As Lubitsch was the unobtrusive cutting of the twenties and thirties, Preminger is the camera movement and long takes of the fifties and sixties. If Lubitsch summed up his time, Preminger was ahead of it in his Fox period."[2]

Preminger collaborated with Lubitsch on the casting of *The Czarina*. Tallulah Bankhead, fresh from her success in Alfred Hitchcock's *Lifeboat*, would play Catherine. Lubitsch tried, according to Preminger, to replace Bankhead with Greta Garbo, who had told her *Ninotchka* director that she would return from retirement to appear in *The Czarina*, but Preminger remained loyal to Bankhead, threatening to resign from the film if she were replaced. Zanuck ruled in favor of Bankhead, whom the front office judged better box office than Garbo.[3] The other main roles went to Anne Baxter, Charles Coburn, and resident Fox juvenile William Eythe, while the supporting cast was stocked with such colorful character actors as Vincent Price, Sig Ruman, Mischa Auer, Vladimir Sokoloff, Mikhail Rasumny, and (in a typically Lubitschian piece of unconventional casting) Grady Sutton.

Shooting started in September 1944. Contemporary press releases indicated a division of responsibility between the two directors: Lubitsch rehearsed the actors, after which Preminger took over, staging the scenes for the camera and rolling the camera. Bankhead recalled that Preminger "was actually directing us during the whole thing, and Lubitsch would come down to see the takes."[4] According to Vincent Price, "Otto had the sense of humor of a guillotine. [Lubitsch] had to sit on the soundstage every day to watch a humorless Otto Preminger murder the comedy. He made it very pedestrian."[5] Coming from Price, who *liked* Preminger, the statement must be given a certain weight. Preminger recalled, "I had many difficulties, friendly difficulties, with [Lubitsch] because I directed it differently than he would have. In other words, I didn't try to make it a Lubitsch film. When I felt I was going too much into his style, I tried to avoid it."[6] The film marked Preminger's first collaboration with director of photography Arthur Miller, "a humorous little man" whom he later praised as one of the two best cameramen he worked with, along with Leon Shamroy. Preminger would work with Miller on only one subsequent film (*Whirlpool*).[7]

The long-standing friendship between Preminger and Bankhead did not suffer from their professional collaboration. The star told John Kobal in 1964, "All this talk about Otto Preminger being such a tyrant . . . he was the kindest person in the world I ever worked with and one of my dearest friends, so I've never seen that side of him. I really mean it. In spite of what you may have heard, you know."[8]

Elsewhere on the Fox lot, Preminger's friend Gregory Ratoff was directing *Where Do We Go from Here?*, a musical fantasy with songs by Kurt Weill and Ira Gershwin. Preminger did a day's work on the film, playing the monocled commanding officer of Hessian troops fighting George Washington near Valley Forge. In his one scene, Preminger's general interrogates the time-traveling hero (Fred MacMurray), whom his troops have captured: the prisoner claims to be a German, but the general catches him in a lie about his relatives and sentences him to execution.

The Czarina wrapped on November 25. An added sequence was shot in mid-January 1945. By then, Zanuck had decided to change the title of the film, fearing that the word "czarina" would baffle American audiences.[9] Retitled *A Royal Scandal*, the film was released in April 1945 to mixed reviews. (In Britain the film was released as *Czarina*.) Bankhead recalled that Preminger didn't want credit for the film, but he is indeed the credited director, although the main title reads "Ernst Lubitsch's *A Royal Scandal*."[10]

A sex comedy set against a background of court intrigue, *A Royal Scandal* feels more like Lubitsch than Preminger, with its constant irony and innuendo; its lofty attitude toward history, politics, and setting ("Everybody in Russia's going to be happy," exults Catherine's idealistic paramour, Alexei, but he's disavowed by the film: this is Lubitsch's Russian *To Be or Not to Be*); its blend of the conventional and the mockingly subversive. Even the actors' line readings are Lubitschian, as is, of course, the dialogue—to such an extent that it is hard to imagine how the film, which is clearly second-tier Lubitsch, might have been improved had Lubitsch directed it personally.

Although it's hard to determine the specific contribution of Preminger to *A Royal Scandal*, there is little to suggest that Preminger, despite being free to do the film "his way," saw his function on the film as going beyond fulfilling a design created by Lubitsch. Preminger himself said that he was "nothing more than the hand that realizes as best as it can the thought of the true author."[11] In *A Royal Scandal*, Preminger acts not as a creator, but as a technician: he is concerned with the mechanics of mise-en-scène, not with its soul. As problematic as this distinction is, it is hard to avoid in the case of *A Royal Scandal*. (As we will see, the case with *That Lady in Ermine*, on which Preminger again took over direction of a film that Lubitsch had conceived and prepared, is somewhat different.)

Visually, the film is very stately, with large sets, elaborate decor, slow rhythms, and several fairly long takes (but none that runs to nine minutes, although Bankhead recalled doing a single take of that length).[12] Nothing allows us to assume that the film's visual style should be attributed to Preminger and its dialogue and acting to Lubitsch. Abstracting visual style from screenplay and performance is a delicate business; in any "classical" film, whatever its level of brilliance, the three together constitute a unity—and Preminger and Lubitsch, despite the vast differences between them, are both masters of that classicism in which film comes very close to theater (the offscreen sigh of the fainting Catherine functions very much as an "offstage" sigh).

The film seems to have been made consciously as a diversion, a burlesque, making the unifying presence of a big star into a thematic motif. (For Lubitsch, the magnitude of the star was an important element of conceptual humor—thus his preference for Garbo, whom it is hard to imagine, however, as Catherine.) Thus, *A Royal Scandal* is a voluntarily minor film, making no pretense to the profundity and consistency of *Ninotchka*, *To Be or Not to Be*, *Heaven Can Wait*, or Lubitsch's next film, *Cluny Brown*. To be sure, *A Royal Scandal* has a serious theme—aging—and at least in potential the film is a feminine equivalent of *Heaven Can Wait*. Yet the film never gives us the sense that Catherine's experiences lead her to a realistic acceptance of the loss of her youth. She remains throughout a comic character, deprived of self-insight.

Bankhead gives a delicious comic performance, and Charles Coburn, Vincent Price (despite his terrible French accent), and Sig Ruman are fine. The weakness of William Eythe in the key part of Alexei is a major liability. Lacking comic flair, he is bland and unimpressive, a second- or third-string Henry Fonda, too physically slight to be convincing turning over tables (twice) in heroic rages. The part called for Joel McCrea,

Gary Cooper, or maybe John Wayne—any of whom would have offered Bankhead a physical and moral resistance that would have heightened the comedy of the film, whereas Eythe's passivity and vapidity reduce Alexei to an unreal object created by Catherine's lust. But McCrea, Cooper, and Wayne were under contract at other studios, Fonda was in the navy, and probably none of the leading men Fox had under contract in 1944 would have been ideal in the part. (The studio's lack of a strong and diverse stable of stars tended to restrict its movies, as Preminger would find in coping again and again with such limited talents as Eythe, Cornel Wilde, and Jeanne Crain.)

As Anna, Alexei's fiancée and Catherine's lady-in-waiting, Anne Baxter inhabits the film rather unhappily, but this is more interesting than Eythe's mere deficiency. It's because of Baxter that *A Royal Scandal* feels at all close to the preoccupations and predilections of Preminger. With the scene in which Catherine tries to get Anna to take a vacation, and Anna insists on staying on, the film leaves the realm of Lubitschian comedy and enters that of Premingerian tragicomedy: each woman assumes a mask, and each is conscious of both the other's insincerity and the other's awareness of *her* insincerity (a structure that in *Advise & Consent* will be labeled as the "Washington D.C. lie"). In this scene, Anna becomes a Preminger heroine: a person committed to a ruse, which she carries out with defiance, pride, and uncertainty.

Preminger appears to have responded to the plight of Anna, a powerless woman using guile in a desperate struggle against a despot who is also her rival. Anna's resistance and intelligence engage him in a way that the outrageous comic monster who is Bankhead's Catherine does not. Anna is conceived realistically, that is, politically (in terms of her relations with others in her sphere); Catherine, on the other hand, creates her own laws and her own universe. While Catherine is a heroine of the absolute, Anna dwells in the relative.

The unreality of Catherine was the basis for Preminger's main objection to the film and the main lesson he took from it. At a preview of *A Royal Scandal* outside Los Angeles, the audience laughed in all the right places, but Preminger noticed that people seemed subdued after the show. Driving home together from the preview, Lubitsch and Zanuck were elated, but Preminger was pessimistic. "We have a big hit," said Zanuck; "you heard how they laughed." "They laughed," Preminger

agreed, "but they hated themselves for laughing."[13] As Preminger predicted, *A Royal Scandal* was not a success. (It earned domestic rentals of
$1.5 million, against production costs of $1.755 million.)[14] Analyzing the
audience's response, Preminger found evidence of a growing maturity:
"The era of 'the Lubitsch touch' was coming to an end. It was a change
that Zanuck was not yet prepared to understand . . . Audiences wanted
more than the chance to laugh. They wanted to see characters on the
screen who behaved consistently."[15]

The last of Preminger's early, immature films—though made after he
had already entered the mature phase of his work with *Laura*—*A Royal
Scandal* represents, for Preminger, the bankruptcy of the pleasure principle, no longer sufficient to assure the ability of a film to win a newly
sophisticated and critical audience. Preminger, as his criticism of *A
Royal Scandal* implies, by now had come to see himself as the champion
of the reality principle, and his direction of Anne Baxter suggests an internal criticism of the film from this point of view. He would later offer a
more developed corrective to (his vision of) Lubitsch, not just in the very
different types of comedy represented by *The Fan, The Moon Is Blue,
Skidoo,* and *Such Good Friends,* but in the mode of realistic tragicomedy
that encompasses *Daisy Kenyon, Bonjour Tristesse,* and *Anatomy of a
Murder.*

7

Obsession

After finishing *A Royal Scandal*, Preminger spent some time, though probably not much, preparing one of the most unlikely projects he would ever be associated with: a Technicolor musical version of O. Henry's "The Gift of the Magi." Preminger wanted Ogden Nash to write the lyrics and Leonard Bernstein to do the music. As Louella Parsons noted in her February 23, 1945, column in the *Los Angeles Examiner*, since the success of *Laura*, Preminger had become "the white haired boy at 20th, so nobody's saying a word." The project was shelved, though eventually the story was filmed by Henry King, without songs, as part of the omnibus *O. Henry's Full House*.

Preminger's next project was *Fallen Angel*, based on a novel by Marty Holland (a pseudonym for Mary Holland), which Fox had bought in 1944, before its first 1945 publication by Dutton. Preminger told a reporter that he liked the book because "its characters were all definite and real. This is a melodrama, and yet the suspense all builds out of those people's reactions."[1] Since the story contained elements that linked it vaguely to *Laura*, Zanuck may have seen in *Fallen Angel* an opportunity to repeat the anticipated success of that film (as yet unreleased at the time the book was purchased). Like *Laura*, the story pivots around the murder of a woman who is the object of obsession for several men. The murderer turns out to be a retired policeman, while his younger rival, a down-and-out former publicity agent named Eric Stanton, finds redemption through the love of a rich woman whom he had sought to seduce and fleece.

Preminger brought in Harry Kleiner, one of his Yale Drama School students, to write the script. Kleiner turned in his first draft on March 2, 1945. As was his custom, Zanuck filled the title page of his copy with penciled notes about casting. The notes indicate that Zanuck was considering borrowing Olivia de Havilland from Warners to play June Mills, the rich woman. This character could be considered the female lead by virtue of surviving to the end of the film, but it must have been obvious from the start of the project that the other main female character, that of Stella, the diner waitress who is murdered, was the showier role, which may explain Zanuck's worried note that "No star will play" June.[2] For Stella, Zanuck had already cast Linda Darnell. The twenty-one-year-old actress was not a top-rank star, despite her early exposure as Tyrone Power's costar in *The Mark of Zorro* and *Blood and Sand*; but her latest film, *Hangover Square*, which had just been released, proved her promise as a sexy siren.

In a conference on the script, Zanuck declared himself pleased with everything but the ending, which had Eric go to the District Attorney to report his suspicions of Judd, the murderous ex-cop. "Once we see the boy in the District Attorney's office, the story is over," Zanuck objected. "Stanton, himself, should solve the murder." In Zanuck's mind, *Fallen Angel* was taking shape as a follow-up to Preminger's previous success: on his script, Zanuck penciled, "Everything great up to last act—needs hypo like *Laura*." Eric's investigation of Judd and his return to the diner to confront the policeman would be incorporated in subsequent revisions.

The Production Code Administration and the Office of War Information both bombarded Fox with objections to Kleiner's script, in particular the scene in which Judd administers the third degree to the jukebox salesman Atkins, another of Stella's suitors. The objection was not to the beating itself (which could be tolerated since Judd's status as a policeman was established as only quasi-official), but to the presence of the sheriff in the next room. Script revisions would get the sheriff out of Stella's apartment when Judd beats Atkins. Joseph Breen also advised that June and Eric should not be shown in bed together in their San Francisco hotel room, because the British censor board would delete the scene, but the released film shows the couple lying side by side in bed. (Also notable in the final film is an openmouthed kiss between Eric and Stella.)

In early April, the studio announced that Alice Faye would play June. Before *Fallen Angel*, according to Louella Parsons, Faye had turned down sixteen scripts in succession, "holding out for a straight dramatic part."[3] A press release indicated that Preminger had courted the star to play the part, but according to Preminger, Faye's agent had asked him if he had anything appropriate for Faye, whereupon Preminger mentioned June in *Fallen Angel*, thinking she wouldn't be interested. To his surprise, she called the next day to accept it.[4] Hoping to meet the presumed expectations of Faye's audience, Zanuck planned to have her sing, as his penciled notes on the cover of Kleiner's March 31 final script show ("Song—justify Alice Faye—she plays organ—sings . . .").

Zanuck was concerned with making the story a better whodunit: "We must in direction put more suspicion on Clara [June's older sister, played in the film by Anne Revere], otherwise Judd is obviously guilty." He also continued to harp on the ending, which he thought weak, and on April 18 Kleiner injected more danger and action in the form of a fistfight at the top of a cliff between Judd and Eric. Meanwhile, in those two roles, Charles Bickford and Dana Andrews joined the cast. Andrews later said that he learned that Faye had asked for him: "She had seen *Laura*, and she liked me in this part . . . She said, 'I'll do this one if you can get Dana Andrews.'" Andrews first turned down the script, which he thought "in bad taste" and "unbelievable," but Preminger urged him to take it, and, threatened with suspension by the studio, Andrews reluctantly reported for work on *Fallen Angel*, which started production on May 1.[5] Unlike the largely set-bound *Laura*, the production of *Fallen Angel* involved considerable location shooting (some of it by a second unit), mostly in the Los Angeles area; footage was also shot in San Francisco. *Fallen Angel* was the first Preminger film to make extensive use of locations to enhance the texture of reality in the film.

Among the members of the *Laura* production team reunited for *Fallen Angel* were director of photography Joseph LaShelle, costume designer Bonnie Cashin, and assistant director Tom Dudley. Dorothy Adams, so memorable as the maid in *Laura*, reappeared in a small part as Stella's neighbor. In another apparent attempt to recapture the *Laura* magic, David Raksin was assigned as composer. His first contribution to the picture was the song "Slowly," which Faye was to sing on-screen. Raksin had written the song in 1939 as "a nightclub-style song" for his wife, a band singer, and he remembered it when he was asked to come up with a selection of tunes for Faye to choose from. "Alice was the one who was allowed to choose the song. So I went to see her, and she was a very gracious person, and I played her, in my inimitable style of bad playing, several tunes . . . I suddenly thought about this thing, and I played it for her, and she said, 'That's it! Wonderful, wonderful. I want to sing that.' And so she did, and very beautifully too."[6]

Faye called Preminger "very tough to work for. He didn't care what he said or how he hurt you. He got a lot out of me, though; I was proud of the performance I turned in."[7] Linda Darnell didn't get along with the director. Her sister Undeen said that the actress "was not one to dislike many people, but Preminger she couldn't tolerate. He was a good director, but a mean SOB. She hated him."[8] Darnell's aversion to Preminger was obvious during the shooting of *Fallen Angel* (Faye recalled that Darnell and Preminger "did not work well together, and made no bones about saying so")[9] and became sufficiently well known around the studio that during the production of *A Letter to Three Wives* three years later, Joseph L. Mankiewicz used a framed portrait of Preminger (its back to the camera) to elicit an appropriate reaction of distaste from Darnell when her character looks at a picture of the infamous Addie Ross, the unseen catalyst of that film's plot. (By then, Darnell had endured Preminger through *Centennial Summer* and all 125 days of *Forever Amber*. She would go on to do a fourth Preminger film, *The 13th Letter*.)

Asked about Preminger's reputation for ill temper, Dana Andrews said, "He gives some people a very bad time on the set. He doesn't have much patience with inefficiency. If an actor's got a job acting, he should be able to act. He shouldn't have to teach him how to act. He will go into these tirades and I'm sure that he has bawled out very competent actors but I have seen him—as I have seen many directors—go into tirades against incompetents."[10]

Principal production ended in late June. After the footage was assembled, Zanuck found the ending unsatisfactory, and so on July 20 and 21 a new ending was written, eliminating the action on the road and the cliff and playing the entire denouement in the diner, where Eric returns to confront Judd. It was this appropriately low-key ending, which Preminger probably shot in a day, that would appear in the final film.

Zanuck, who guided the development of all the scripts Twentieth Century-Fox produced, was legendary for also controlling his studio's films through editing. Screenwriter Walter Reisch recalled, "Once a picture had been shot, and the director had, according to his contract, submitted the first cut to Zanuck's office containing everything that had been shot, regardless of whether it was long enough or too long, Zanuck took over and edited the picture every day from after dinner till long after midnight. But he didn't edit it the way you would think pictures should be edited, with subtlety, with patience, a little frame from here and a little frame added there; he took out whole sequences."[11]

When *Fallen Angel* fell under his scissors, Zanuck excised Faye's rendition of "Slowly" and several dramatic scenes featuring her—a decision that turned her against him for good. She later said, "It nearly broke my heart . . . Zanuck . . . cut out most of my best stuff . . . Linda Darnell had one of the other leads and Zanuck, who was building her up at the time, wanted more of the focus on her." Comparison of the released film with the final script confirms that much material involving June was omitted, although it's unclear at which point she would have sung "Slowly" (the scene in church, the dance-club scene, and the beach scene had all been pencil marked in Zanuck's script as potential places for a song). A street scene in which Eric encounters several people—including Judd and his wife, as well as the Mills sisters, on their way out of a church service—was cut. Eric and June's first date originally included a visit to a bowling alley. Later, in another cut scene, Eric asks June to go with him to San Francisco; she refuses because of her concern for Clara. In the most extended of June's missing scenes, she returns home late to find Clara waiting for her. Asked where she's been, June replies in an angry outburst, "Why must I account to you? I'm twenty-four. I'm tired of doing the same things every day! Tired of this town! Tired of this house—tired of both of us." She goes sobbing into her room, slamming the door. The next morning, the two sisters are reconciled, but June pursues her tormented reflections, musing, "What good are all my books, and my music, if I can't enjoy the things other people do? If I'm always alone . . . I just mean nothing ever really happens." Zanuck, who liked movies to move, probably found June's reflections irritating. According to Preminger, "At Fox . . . all of us knew that Darryl Zanuck had no empathy for women in film. He liked women and was happily married but women's problems and feelings bored him totally."[12]

Though Faye's rendition of "Slowly" did not survive the final cut, the song is prominently featured at several points in the film. It's said to be Stella's favorite song and is repeatedly played on the jukebox in the diner. The film associates the song with Stella so firmly that it may seem hard to understand how the filmmakers thought they could justify its being sung by June, the Faye character. The probable explanation is that the song heard on the jukebox was to have been a different one, and that after cutting Faye's "Slowly" performance, Zanuck decided that rather than waste a good song, it would end up (in a version sung by Dick Haymes) on the jukebox. The question of whether to promote the song to the status of a theme, equivalent to the theme of *Laura*, became the subject of argument between Raksin and Preminger, as Raksin recalled:

> When we came to spot the picture, Preminger said, "Now of course, you're going to use the tune in the main title." I said, "Of course I'm not." He said, "You're not?! What kind of guy are you? Any composer would want to use his tune." I said, "But I don't want to use my tune if I'm going to ruin your picture. Look, here's a guy in a bus. We don't know anything about him. There should be some sense of the movement of this, going through the night, mysterious circumstances." So I wrote a bus-moving-in-the-night piece, and that's what we played.[13]

The final production cost was $1,075,000—slightly more than what *Laura* had cost. *Fallen Angel* was released in December 1945 to tepid reviews.

In interviews Preminger gave during the 1970s, *Fallen Angel* was one of several films from his Fox period that he claimed not to remember at all. The most he would say for it was that in contrast with projects like *Centennial Summer*, the reason for doing which he could not recall, "I know very well that *Laura* fascinated me, also *Fallen Angel*."[14] In the movement from *Laura* to *Fallen Angel*, Preminger repeats his own movement from the sophisticated, cosmopolitan world of the New York theater to the remote and isolated world of Hollywood. The New York depicted in *Laura* is still close to Europe (Waldo addresses guests at a party in French), and it's a world ruled—or so it seems at first—by reason, by the mind, by wit. It's also a world in which women have careers and rise to prominence in them; whereas in *Fallen Angel*, the most that not only Stella but even June aspires to is marriage.

Eric's relentless preoccupation with money is one of the most striking signs of the shift between the worlds of the two films. His poverty brings about his initial arrival in Walton and motivates most of his actions thereafter. When he tells June about his past life, his narrative is all about money (having sold his business, he lost half his earnings in a crooked dice game, then went through the other half in Las Vegas). Eric's economic bankruptcy becomes a metaphor for moral bankruptcy; as Judd says, "You're an expert, Mr. Stanton. You know the exact value of a man's word against facts."

Fallen Angel abounds in the kind of fluid camera movement that Preminger made a stylistic trademark in *Laura*. The section of the film devoted to Eric and June's furtive stay in San Francisco contains some notably expansive shots, but Preminger insists on this fluidity from the very first (post-credits) shot, in which the camera manages, apparently, to pan and track alongside a man walking down the aisle of a bus. This maneuvering in an apparently tight space (in reality, of course, a studio set) is Preminger's declaration of the freedom of his camera. Subsequently, the camera tracks behind Eric as he walks into Walton and approaches Pop's Diner. The visual emphasis on the character's back suggests exclusion and privateness, but at the same time, the viewer is drawn in to the film's world with Eric. Again and again Preminger uses camera movement to bring us into the worlds of his characters. In the first scene in the Mills house, the characteristically Premingerian switch in narrative interest from Eric to June is signaled by a tracking shot that follows Clara and June from the front hall through the parlor, then through the dining room, to the door of the kitchen. Once again, the camera follows the backs of people, suggesting that their existences are independent of our interest in them.

Throughout *Fallen Angel*, shots connect people and spaces in complex movement. In the séance scene, the camera cranes toward Professor Madley (John Carradine) onstage, then swings around to the audience, scans their faces, and bears down on Eric entering the theater. A lengthy traveling shot accompanies June and Eric as they walk outside a church and along a street, reach the corner, pause, and continue on into the street, Eric pausing (during his discourse about "the little things . . . [that] make up life") to pull June back by the arm just as two bicycle riders go by; finally, the couple reach June's house, where Eric invites her to dinner, the shot ending on Eric's slight smile of triumph after she accepts (a performance touch by Dana Andrews reminiscent of Mark McPherson's reaction when he hears from Laura that she has decided not to marry Shelby Carpenter).

Other camera movements merely insist on the inexorable domination of the camera, as when it pushes forward through several dancing couples at a nightclub to approach Eric and Stella. Sometimes scenes begin with a formal traveling movement toward or away from a character; for the most part these movements are on a plane parallel to the ground (like the track-in that isolates June at the breakfast table and the next, complementary shot of Stella behind the counter at Pop's). Other scenes begin with elaborate flourishes: a beautiful daytime exterior shot cranes down from a high angle on Eric as he walks around a corner, then reframes him in a low angle as he stops in front of and goes into a church. Sometimes the camera, on a crane, alternately drives forward into and pulls back from a scene. One of the most startling instances of this type of movement occurs in the dance-hall scene, when, in the pause between songs, the camera moves in to frame Eric and Stella in a close two-shot, separating them from their partners (June and Atkins, respectively); then, as the band starts the next number, the camera tracks out again, and the original couples resume dancing.

Throughout *Fallen Angel*, camera movement creates patterns of tension and release, linked to the characters' moods, their perceptions, and their knowledge or ignorance of their environment. The result is a fluid state of audience involvement in which we are led to identify with or detach ourselves from Eric's point of view and thus to constitute him as both participant and percipient. The sequence of June and Eric's wedding night combines long-take camera movement, heavy drinking (by Eric), and ominous scoring (by Raksin, again using the "Len-o-tone" tape effect from *Laura*) to portray Eric's psychic stress—a condition we share only incompletely, since the long take also accommodates, and pays respect to, both Clara's wistful and almost dazed compassion and June's patient, uninsistent expectation.

The narrative movement is sometimes fluid, sometimes uneven, halting, blocked (Zanuck's editing may be responsible). A short scene in which Eric starts to board a bus out of Walton, then (hooked on Stella) changes his mind, is followed by a scene that begins by showing us the end of an unsuccessful date: Atkins's car (always a fleeting apparition in the film, sometimes glimpsed coming or going and sometimes unnoticed) pulls up, Stella gets out, they say goodbye coldly, and he drives off. Both these scenes provide short glimpses of external results of processes that go on beyond and behind the scenes.

Preminger is more gripped by, and more persuasive with, Eric's attraction toward Stella than his redemption by June. The fake romanticism of Eric and June's night on the beach (with hot dogs) is undercut by back projection and by scoring it with "Slowly" (Stella's song now—though it was June's while the film was in production); and the conclusion of the scene—June's falling asleep!—seems clearly meant as parodic. The commitment toward romantic love required by the scene in Eric and June's San Francisco hotel room (which culminates with a sunrise in a window—an effect that Preminger will repeat in *Where the Sidewalk Ends*) is out of character for the brusque, imperious figure that we imagine, I believe, the narrator of *Fallen Angel* to be. The unceremonious way in which Preminger ends the story is a clue to the attitude of this narrator: Eric leaves the diner for the last time, finds June waiting for him in a car; they drive off, leaving the camera to hold on the studio mock-up of the space beside the diner, with its back-projected ocean. Preminger's succinctness here no doubt partly expresses his desire to be finished with these characters once and for all (as we've seen, Zanuck imposed this new, changed ending). Even in this desire, though, Preminger's attitude isn't merely the blank insouciance of a hack. It expresses the positive will to finish and takes a definite attitude—not one marked by a profound sympathy—toward the story being narrated.

It is surely indicative of his own life attitude that of the films Preminger made as an independent producer, only four center on the formation of a romantic couple: *The Moon Is Blue*, *Carmen Jones*, *The Man with the Golden Arm*, and *Tell Me That You Love Me, Junie Moon*. Perhaps the two most engaging couples in Preminger's independent films are formed by people who have wars to fight and whose preoccupations are not mainly with love and sex: Ari and Kitty in *Exodus*; Torrey and

Maggie in *In Harm's Way*. Finally, there is *The Human Factor*, in which a steady devotion replaces the transcendence of romantic love.

On the other hand, *Fallen Angel* is a key Preminger work for the way it addresses the problem of self-knowledge in terms of the difficulty of knowing any human being. As characters in a film, Eric, June, Stella, Judd, and Clara are known to us only through external signs of behavior and speech. Though Eric is, in a sense, our guide through the story, he is also more apart from us, more defined in terms of externals, than the other characters. One reason for this is his profession: as a publicity man, he gets by on a glib talk; his business is persuading others, manipulating external signs in order to obtain desired responses. Another reason for Eric's externality in the film is that his obsession with Stella alienates him not only from the other characters (from whom he must constantly hide the intensity of his commitment to the waitress) but from the viewer. A sign of this occurs in the scene of Eric's conversation with Stella in the doorway to her apartment: he looks insistently inside and she opens the door in order to facilitate both his view and ours, since the camera is positioned behind the back of his head and swivels as he scans the interior of the apartment. Later, when Eric takes it on the lam to San Francisco, his paranoia estranges him from June and from the viewer. It's only still later, in the hotel room, that Eric achieves a certain self-consciousness and comes to share, for the first time in the film, our capacity for viewing his life from the outside: his acquisition of this ability coincides with the end of his obsession with Stella.

Preminger is not impersonal, neutral, or indifferent, but in representing human events, he emphasizes the *outsideness* of both the participants and the narrator. Another word for outsideness is "embodiment," that is, taking on the characteristics of a body—among them, being in one place at one time. Preminger refuses to pretend to stand for the characters and look through their eyes: at most, his camera takes up a place behind the backs of the characters (for example, in the scene in Stella's doorway just mentioned), from which it may approximate their points of view. In *Fallen Angel*, the extension of many shots in time (through the duration of relatively long takes) and in space (through camera movement) characterizes the narrative agency of the film as an embodied being. The long take explicitly denies that the camera could, as it were, step outside itself (through a change of shot) and occupy more than one place within a scene, and camera movement lays stress on the physical, gestural nature of its possession of space and the continuity and uniqueness of a point of view that, in order to take in two different areas, must move through space. The rigorous and exciting use of the camera in *Fallen Angel* sets the parameters for Preminger's subsequent work.

8

A Bucket of Ashes

While Preminger was preparing *Fallen Angel*, he was also looking ahead to his next project, *Centennial Summer*, a musical version of Albert E. Idell's 1943 bestseller of the same title. Set in 1876 Philadelphia, the story concerns a middle-class family, the Rogerses, that is disrupted by the visit of Mrs. Rogers's sister, Zenia, who has been living (rather dissolutely by Philadelphia standards) in France. With Zenia comes her late husband's nephew, Philippe, who has been assigned to take charge of the French pavilion at the Centennial Exposition. In the rivalry of the two older Rogers sisters over Philippe, the outgoing Edith gains an advantage over the shy, romantic Julia by pretending to Philippe that Ben, an obstetrician who has long courted her, is Julia's beau, but Philippe eventually learns the truth. Since the Frenchman prefers Julia anyway, and since Edith will settle for Ben, a happy ending for all is easily secured.

In his first-draft script, dated January 22, 1944, Michael Kanin approached the story as a nonmusical romantic comedy. Zanuck exulted that through page 48 "it is *Life with Father* at its best" [*sic*], but found that after that the script became too complex and "it all amounts to nothing."[1] Kanin turned in a new outline in February and a temporary script in April. Zanuck then apparently put the project on hold. By the time of Kanin's revised temporary script (October 13), *Centennial Summer* had turned into a musical. This script contains a note: "The music is to be used in the same fashion that it is used in the stage play *Oklahoma*, and in our own film *State Fair*." *State Fair* was not yet in production, but the studio had high hopes for it, anticipating the post-*Oklahoma!* boom in midwestern musicals that MGM would be the first to profit from with its November release of *Meet Me in St. Louis*.

In January 1945, Jerome Kern signed on to *Centennial Summer*, agreeing to write the music for ten songs. The young leads were all non-singers: Jeanne Crain (Julia), Linda Darnell (Edith), Cornel Wilde (Philippe), and William Eythe (Ben). Preminger was definitely assigned to *Centennial Summer* by April 17, 1945, the date of a conference on the January 22 script. Years later, he told Peter Bogdanovich that he had worked on the script with Michael and Fay Kanin for a year before turning it in to Zanuck. Preminger's name doesn't turn up in connection with the project before the April 1945 conference, but there is no reason to doubt that he had been working on it before then. He told Bogdanovich, "It was a very unusual script . . . Zanuck . . . said that it would never make a motion picture. So he wrote a memorandum which straightened it out so that every character became a cliché, because he felt that only cliché characters could be in a musical comedy."[2]

The memo Preminger probably had in mind runs sixteen pages—long even for Zanuck. "We must first have a great boy and girl story. The other things should be treated merely as a subplot—just something that is going on behind the leading man and the leading lady. We must have someone to root for, and the obvious persons to root for are the young people. We have found out, in a couple of instances, that when you have aged people in the lead in your story you have a failure." Zanuck's insistence on emphasizing the romantic leads sabotaged Preminger's plan to make *Centennial Summer* into an unusual film—an ambition he had signaled by casting Dorothy Gish as Mrs. Rogers. What's left of Mrs. Rogers in the final film can't be called worthy of the distinguished actress (though the same must be admitted of her role in *The Cardinal* seventeen years later). Constance Bennett and Walter Brennan were also cast below their abilities, as Zenia and Mr. Rogers.

Dutifully reworking the script along Zanuck's guidelines, Kanin and Preminger finished a revised final script on August 8. By then, the Production Code Administration's few concerns about the film had been largely allayed. During the correspondence over *Centennial Summer*, Breen pounced on the detail of Philippe, overjoyed at learning that Ben's romance with Julia has been a ruse, kissing Ben on both cheeks. "It will be well for you to shoot this particular scene with the utmost care," Breen wrote on July 30, "in order that it will have about it no possible suggestion of the pervert." It was the kind of instruction whose ludicrousness must have provided fleeting compensation to filmmakers who had to contend with the PCA.

In late August, Kern supervised the recording of his songs. Shooting on *Centennial Summer* began in early September. Dorothy Gish found the stressful atmosphere on Preminger's set a far cry from her days with Griffith—"that feeling of panic all around me, that just terrified me"[3]— but she also found a tactful way of describing Preminger for a studio press release: "He is able to put into words the precise effect he is trying for in a scene. This avoids waste of time."[4] According to Cornel Wilde, "Dorothy was fun. She was perfect for the film. Even Otto would laugh."[5] Wilde disliked Preminger. "Otto liked to break actors down so that he would be in control," he said. "He would do cruel things, mostly to little people."[6] On the other hand, one of the little people, Barbara Whiting, the teenage actress playing the youngest Rogers daughter, found Preminger "nice but very strong."[7]

During production, a studio publicist asked Preminger to explain his preference for American over European subjects. Preminger replied, "For one answer, I might quote the American poet, Carl Sandburg. As he once wrote, 'The past is a bucket of ashes.' Many times, I have been asked to do again in America some of the things that turned out success-fully for me in Europe, but I have always said 'No,' because I have a hor-ror of going backward; I want to go forward. For me, Europe is the past and America is the future . . . As a new American, intensely interested in every facet of American life, I might just possibly have something new to offer to stories with American settings."[8] *Centennial Summer* bears out Preminger's "Europe: past/America: future" commonplace by juxtaposing the historical themes of the French pavilion with American innovation and ingenuity (as represented by Rogers). On the other hand, one won-ders if Preminger was aware of the grim irony in his use of the Carl Sandburg quote. If "the past is a bucket of ashes," *Centennial Summer* is the attempt to make these ashes flicker into the semblance of life.

The film wrapped in early November. After seeing the first cut, Zanuck felt that it was weak and needed extensive changes, and on No-vember 23 he sent Preminger an eight-page memo outlining six new scenes to emphasize the rivalry between Julia and Edith, the feigned romance between Ben and Julia, and the confused reactions of Ben (who now imagines, briefly, that he may be in love with Julia). These six scenes were duly scripted by Preminger and Harry Kleiner (replacing Kanin) over the next two weeks. As scripted, the added scenes follow Zanuck's memo scrupulously, to the point of reproducing much of his suggested dialogue, with only minor changes. This literalism is a sign of Preminger's waning enthusiasm for the project. Philip Dunne remarked, "Zanuck never intended his clichés to be taken seriously; he merely wanted the writers to explore a certain line, to try for a certain dramatic effect . . . [Zanuck's] conference notes . . . underlined the firm decisions which had been reached, but nothing was meant to be taken literally."[9] In writing the added scenes for *Centennial Summer*, Kleiner and Preminger take the path of least resistance, obeying Zanuck to the letter and doing little more.

In the November 23 memo, Zanuck summarizes his intentions in terms that imply something like a philosophy of film. The audience's sympathies must be firmly placed with one or two characters and not dispersed; a likable character, one we root for, must be "aggressive instead of passive" and should not be a "dope" or an "ass." Just as important, such characters should provide good showcases for the studio's contract stars. In his independent productions, Preminger would challenge this philosophy. Films such as *The Man with the Golden Arm, Bonjour Tristesse, Advise & Consent, Bunny Lake Is Missing*, and *Such Good Friends* all involve situations in which the audience's sympathies are not obviously manipulated; and all feature central characters who are weak, duped, ambiguous, or neutral.

The end result of Zanuck's tampering with *Centennial Summer* is no ringing justification of his avowed principles. The central pretense that Julia and Ben are in love remains what it was all along in this story, a contrived complication, and Julia's active participation in the illusion makes her a perverse and puzzling figure. Her support for the lie makes her, and the film, darker (and more Premingerian); and the surgery Zanuck ordered on *Centennial Summer* resulted in two of the grimmest scenes in the film, the confrontations between Julia and Edith in Julia's room.

No amount of surgery could have made a great film out of *Centennial Summer*. The plot and the characters remain trivial and contrived, and the film is rarely funny. Zanuck's insistence on minimizing the parents and the two younger children undercuts our sense of the family as a positive, vibrant centripetal force, so that the film (to a much greater degree than *Meet Me in St. Louis*) tends to be largely about individuals or couples, and only rarely about the group. The four young leads—Crain, Darnell, Wilde, and Eythe—are pretty rather than engaging: Crain is cold and subdued, and her scenes with Wilde are stiff and forced. The psychological center of the film is located in neither of the love relationships but in the bitter rivalry between Edith and Julia—a rivalry mirrored in the subplot between Zenia and Mrs. Rogers. Again, a worldly, sly coquette is pitted against a simple, aggrieved woman who must repress and falsify her reactions while the other is being splendid and flamboyant.

The film's abundance of night scenes adds to its fretful, rather cheerless mood. The interest of the film lies mainly in its mise-en-scène, especially its elaborate camera movements. The opening scene, in which a huge crowd witnesses the president's address at the opening of the Centennial Exposition, is marked by leisurely crane shots. Early in the film, intricate shots link the various members of the Rogers family, creating a fluid, orderly sense of bustling excitement. Alone in her room, Julia sings about "The Right Romance" that will someday come along—a scene staged in sensuous, curling movements of actress and camera. Later, a traveling shot passes along the front of the house, past the barn, through the yard, and to the back porch, to reach a maid churning butter, the family visible through the open door at right. Preminger tries to keep a continuous flow of movement during scenes: while singing "In Love in Vain," Julia crosses the porch to the parlor to turn out the lamp and close the windows, the camera tracking with her.

The two most interesting scenes of *Centennial Summer* are discrete showcases for guest performers, in which the principals figure only as spectators. One scene celebrates a precursor to the cinema. As a male performer sings "All Through the Day," painted color slides are projected behind him. The scene emphasizes the mechanics and the mystery of the spectacle: the golden slide projector wheeled into the hall, the lights dimming. The sudden eruption of this spectacle within the spectacle of the film seems to be an acknowledgment of the prevailing falsity of *Centennial Summer*, its project of fabricating an idyllic image of the past. The magic lantern is also, with the train and the clock, one of the inventions that point out from the film's imagined world of 1876 toward the world of the film's viewers seventy years later, for whom the past is produced as an object of nostalgia.

The second noteworthy scene takes place in a saloon, where Rogers and Philippe drown their sorrows together. Without preparation or explanation, a black man with a banjo enters the saloon, followed by five black children, four boys and a girl. Preminger draws our attention to the extraordinary nature of this intrusion by having the camera track forward slowly toward the new arrivals, reaching a close shot of the girl, the last to enter, as she shuts the door behind her. The banjo player proceeds to serenade her ("Cinderella Sue") while the boys dance and play harmonicas. Whereas the other musical numbers in the film tend to substitute for dialogue, transposing a dramatic situation to a new expressive plane, the "Cinderella Sue" number is self-contained, isolated. It answers no question that the narrative has posed, and poses no question for it to solve; it takes nothing from and gives nothing to the narrative. It is like a fantasy, a strangely oblique and contextless one. Its only function is to celebrate itself, as an assertion that could be made anywhere at any time, or (which amounts to the same thing) to celebrate the triumph, promise, and charm of Cinderella Sue as qualities deserving honor and display in any context, for their own sake. At the end of the performance, the performers wait for neither money nor applause but simply exit through the door by which they entered, closing the sequence.

The "Cinderella Sue" number is one of those moments in Preminger's films that acknowledge the artifice and fantasy nature of their narratives. It opens up the world of *Centennial Summer* and looks forward to that of *Carmen Jones*. In its sudden and inexplicable incursion into the narrative, it also resembles another of Preminger's bar scenes, the apparition of the Zombies in *Bunny Lake Is Missing*.

When *Centennial Summer* opened in July 1946, many of the reviews followed the lead of Bosley Crowther, who wrote in *The New York Times* that the film "has color but it lacks exuberance and warmth."[10] The color noted by Crowther was one of the factors that caused the production cost of the film to reach an exorbitant $2.275 million—the largest amount yet spent on a Preminger film. His next film, through no fault of his, would far exceed this amount.

9

The Limbo of Movies

It would be an understatement to say that *Forever Amber*, Preminger's film version of Kathleen Winsor's popular novel, has not endured as a classic. In 1957 Preminger called it "the worst picture I ever made."[1] Screenwriter Philip Dunne wrote, "The picture was finished, released, took its deserved lumps from the critics, and disappeared into the limbo of movies which never should have been made."[2] Yet *Forever Amber* is a characteristic Preminger film, even, within its limitations, a triumph.

On October 3, 1944, Fox's Colonel Jason Joy submitted to the PCA a synopsis of Winsor's soon-to-be-published saga of the English Restoration. Joseph Breen replied the next day that the story was "utterly and completely unacceptable under any one of a dozen provisions of the Production Code. As we read it, this story, from the standpoint of the Code, is hardly more than a saga of illicit sex and adultery into which enters the elements, on a wholesale scale, of bastardy, perversion, impotency, pregnancy, abortion, murder and marriage without even the slightest suggestion of compensating moral values." Breen's attempts at discouragement weren't heeded, and Fox went through with its purchase of *Forever Amber*. William Perlberg was assigned to produce the film, and Jerome Cady to write the first-draft script, which Philip Dunne was then given to revise. Dunne's first instinct was to make the film into a satire: "I thought that if we kidded the pants off everybody, including ourselves, the picture might get by. Zanuck refused, on the perfectly logical grounds that there was no point in tampering with success by making so radical a change in a book which had captivated the millions who like to lick their lips while reading."[3]

The book whose readership the Harvard-educated Dunne held in such contempt tells the story of Amber St. Clare, a foundling raised by a

Puritan couple in rural England in the mid-seventeenth century. Amber seizes her chance to escape her stifling circumstances by attaching herself to a dashing cavalier, Bruce Carlton, whom she accompanies to London. Bruce is sent off to sea, and Amber, left to fend for herself, lands in Newgate Prison. She manages to get free and, through a succession of lovers, raises her social rank, even becoming the mistress of King Charles II. Amber still regards Bruce, whose child she has borne, as the love of her life, and when Bruce returns to London only to succumb to the Great Plague, she risks her life to nurse him back to health. Nevertheless, Bruce marries an American and leaves for America, taking his and Amber's son with him.

Dunne labored on reshaping the material for several weeks and handed in what he called "a dreary, dutifully sanitized" script, which Zanuck submitted personally to Breen on October 9, 1945, with a cover letter assuring the PCA chief, "In this particular case I set myself up as a censor." Breen insisted on a stronger "voice for morality, and some further indication of punishment for both Bruce and Amber because of their sin," and Zanuck agreed to accommodate him. Although Breen may have left their meeting feeling that he had won major concessions from Zanuck, the producer's instructions to Dunne and Perlberg ("This will call for adroit writing, but I think it can be done without harming anything") show that the changes he thought he had obliged himself to make were mostly trivial. In any case, on the questions of "morality" that officially haunted Breen, Fox and the Production Code Administration were not in fundamental disagreement: the film would be the tragedy of a woman who tries to step out of her class and is justly punished.[4]

Dunne turned in a "final" script on October 27. It was submitted to Breen, who, after further discussion with Zanuck, Perlberg, and Dunne, wrote back that the script was acceptable, with the understanding that further changes would be made. Showing the lengths of his vigilance, Breen's letter includes this note on page 138 of the script: "Please make certain that the use of the word 'fire' be so recorded on your sound-track so as to make certain there will be no shouts or cries likely to upset persons, within ear-shot of the theatre, who might hear only the word." On December 13, in a letter to Francis S. Harmon, Breen celebrated what appeared to him to be the triumph of his efforts over *Amber*. "In so far as the Code is concerned, the basic story is not unlike that of fifty pictures

which have been produced here in Hollywood in the last several years."
As the letter shows, Breen had accepted Zanuck's interpretation of *Forever Amber* as a "tragedy"—i.e., a narrative in which an initial sin, after
being punished by serial indignities, culminates in a painful loss, these
proceedings accompanied throughout by a "voice for morality" and
dramatized against an exotic background.

Peggy Cummins, who was about to turn twenty, was a Dublin-born
discovery of Zanuck's whom he had spotted in a London stage production of *Junior Miss*. Cummins, who had been in a few minor British
films, would, it was announced, make her American film debut as Amber
under the direction of John M. Stahl, a longtime veteran director who
was riding high at Fox after the smash success of *Leave Her to Heaven*
(1945). Production started on March 11, 1946. With 103 days of shooting scheduled, the budget was estimated at over $3 million—Fox's
biggest to date.[5] Observers saw trouble brewing from the start. "I visited
the set on the third day," said Dunne, "and discovered cameraman Leon
Shamroy fortifying himself with a nip of brandy at eleven in the morning, always a sure sign that something was radically wrong with a production."[6] Zanuck continued to tinker with the script: on April 2 he held
a conference on suggested new scenes, which Dunne turned in on
April 6.

On April 30, a Tuesday, production was halted. It was announced
that Stahl would not continue as director, that Peggy Cummins would be
reassigned, and that production would not resume for at least three
months. This was the fourth halt in production: three others had been
attributed to Cummins's illnesses. Later accounts put the amount
charged against the production for the Stahl-Cummins footage at
$500,000 or as high as $1,000,000.[7] Zanuck told the press that filming
"has been suspended until late summer due to the quality of the film so
far shot not measuring up to the high standard originally planned."[8] The
fullest analysis of what happened with the Stahl-Cummins *Amber* came
from Frank S. Nugent in *The New York Times*. "Mr. Stahl is reported to
have complained on one occasion that she looked like a little girl dressed
up in her mother's clothes. Miss Cummins naturally resented this—no
hussy wants to be told she looks like a little girl, or vice versa—and she
and Mr. Stahl appear to have taken turns marching off the set in huffs.
After a month or so of this, Zanuck finally recognized that the picture

wasn't shaping up and suspended production."[9] This account was confirmed by Cornel Wilde, who played Bruce: "Peggy flashed her two expressions for thirty-nine days. At the end of thirty-nine days Zanuck
finally admitted she just couldn't do it."[10]

Zanuck informed Preminger and Charles Feldman (then the agent
for both Preminger and Stahl) that "Stahl was doing a terrible job" on
Amber and that Zanuck would replace him with Preminger. According to
Preminger, he tried in vain to refuse the assignment by reminding
Zanuck of the debacle of *Kidnapped* and warning him, "If I start it, you
will fire me."[11] Samuel Fuller remembered, however, that Preminger was
very excited to be connected with such a big picture, and he visited
Fuller's office, bringing a bag of "hot chicken," to celebrate.[12] William
Perlberg stayed on as nominal producer, "but he kept out of my way," as
Preminger later put it.[13]

Zanuck decided to replace Cummins with Linda Darnell. Preminger
thought Darnell wrong for the part and tried to promote his own choice,
Metro contract star Lana Turner, to no avail.[14] In compensation, Preminger asked for the services of Ring Lardner, Jr., to rewrite the script.
Zanuck agreed, but in a bid to retain control over the project, he also reassigned Dunne to work with Lardner: "a touchy situation," in Lardner's
words, "or, rather, it would have been if [Dunne] had been any less of an
exemplar of graciousness and professionalism. As it was, the three of us,
Otto, Phil, and I, established a strong bond based, in part, on a fervent
common desire to be working on almost any property other than the one
Zanuck had foisted on us."[15] According to Dunne, "though [Preminger]
had a reputation among writers as a monster, complete with horns and
cloven hooves, with me he was never anything but a considerate and
constructive collaborator."[16] Lardner approached the project with an eye
toward its potential for humor: "Nobody should take Amber too seriously," he told *The New York Times*, in apparent obliviousness to all
Joseph Breen's mighty efforts.[17]

The changes to *Forever Amber*'s script that were introduced after
Preminger took charge of the project are usefully summarized in an undated PCA document (probably from May 1947, when the PCA first
screened the film), signed by Stephen Jackson, listing substantial differences between the film as screened and the last script submitted to the
PCA, dated April 11, 1946. In their revisions, Preminger, Dunne, and

Lardner downplayed Almsbury's "voice for morality," strengthened the implications of sexual activity, and added, at the end of the film, dialogue making it clear that King Charles has made financial provisions for Amber and indicating that Amber would "continue with the kind of life she had been living." One can only speculate as to why the studio failed to send the October 10, 1946, shooting final script to the PCA—an omission that would come back to haunt the production.

On September 4 Preminger began rehearsing his principals. Much of the casting had been changed from the Stahl version, either because the original actors were no longer available or because Zanuck or Preminger had new ideas. Zanuck insisted, however, on having Cornel Wilde stay on as Bruce Carlton, a choice that probably displeased the director as much as it did the star; the two "were barely on speaking terms" since *Centennial Summer*. Wilde caused a stir on October 14 by refusing to appear in *Amber* unless he got a pay raise. The rate his agents negotiated for him—$200,000 a year for forty weeks—made him the third highest paid actor on the lot (after, one assumes, Tyrone Power and Betty Grable).[18]

Principal photography began on Thursday, October 24, in the kitchen of the cottage where Amber refuses her Puritan foster father's choice of a fiancé. A *New York Times* reporter watched Preminger make "six takes of the first shot with the cheerful serenity of a man who knows that nobody expects the picture to cost less than its tentative budget of $3,500,000."[19] On October 28, *Variety* reported that the film's costs were expected to reach $4.5 to 5 million.

One of the production's bright spots, for Preminger, was his first opportunity to work with Leon Shamroy, who became "a marvelous friend."[20] The two would work together again on *Daisy Kenyon*, *That Lady in Ermine*, *Porgy and Bess*, *The Cardinal*, and *Skidoo*. Shamroy said of *Forever Amber* that "the main photographic problem . . . was to deemphasize the color so that it would not detract from the characters or from the dramatic action."[21]

The film was completed on March 11, 1947, but Dunne and Lardner were reassigned to the film to write added scenes and retakes, including a revision of the final meeting of Bruce and Amber. Dunne and Lardner finished their revisions on April 8, and Preminger shot them over the next few weeks, wrapping the film in late April. At a final production cost of $6,375,000, *Forever Amber* was by far the most expensive film Fox had made to that time, surpassing by more than $3 million the cost of Edmund Goulding's *The Razor's Edge*, which had briefly held the cost record at the studio.[22]

The PCA viewed a complete cut of the film on May 21. The next day, Geoffrey Shurlock and Mr. Lynch of the PCA informed Fox that the film "was in definite violation of the provisions of the Code regarding the proper treatment of illicit sex." A confidential internal PCA memo dated May 27, setting forth the objections, clearly indicate the tone of Preminger's original cut of *Forever Amber*. "The finished picture is objectionable because it deals excessively in illicit sex and adultery. While it is true that these objections [*sic*] are treated deftly and without offensive details, by the same token they are made to appear attractive." The film concentrates on Amber's social and financial rise and indicates at the end that she still enjoys financial security, "and far from any moral regeneration or repentance for her misdeeds, she is, in fact, planning a continued life of virtual prostitution. Even the losing of her son has little of the agonizing tragic impact that might be expected on the part of a mother."

This memo became the basis for a list of changes that was drawn up on May 28 after Zanuck agreed to recut, redub, and reshoot to meet the PCA's objections. On June 2 the PCA reviewed a new cut of the picture and found that most of the proposed changes had been made. Notes from the studio dated June 9 conclude with the remark, "Our understanding is that the ending of the picture will be a matter for our decision," which suggests that Fox had persuaded the PCA to accept the ending of the film as shot, with the implication that Amber would return to her life of sin. On June 20, after viewing two reels of film including "the redubbed lines, re-edited sequences, and additional scenes shot," the PCA agreed that *Forever Amber* could be approved and granted a Seal.

The final battle of *Forever Amber* was still to come. On Wednesday, October 22, 1947, the same day that the film opened at the Roxy Theatre in New York (where it set a record opening-day gross for the theater of $25,308), the Legion of Decency announced that it had given the film a C, or "condemned," rating. Cardinal Francis J. Spellman, archbishop of New York, called it "a glorification of immorality and licentiousness" and warned his followers that they could not see it "with a safe conscience." The Legion left the door open to revising its rating if the film was changed, an opportunity Perlberg vehemently rejected even as studio executives convened to consider their options.[23]

Catholic clerics decried the film in Rochester, Providence, Indianapolis, Cincinnati, and Boston (where the commissioner of public safety banned Sunday showings of the film). Cardinal Dennis Dougherty ordered the one million Catholics of the Philadelphia Archdiocese to boycott the Fox Theatre, then home to *Amber*, for one year. State censorship boards in Maryland and Pennsylvania weighed in by demanding cuts in the film (notably in the scene of Amber's birth pains—already weakened to appease the PCA—and in the strangling of the homicidal nurse Mrs. Spong). The Legion's C rating left the Motion Picture Association of America (MPAA) out on a limb. It made the PCA's usefulness, already a subject of debate in the industry, increasingly doubtful. The administration's existence was premised on its ability to ward off external censorship and public boycotts of the kind that *Amber* was now facing. On the other hand, if *Amber* proved a hit despite the Church's disapproval, the film's success would prove that the Legion was not a serious threat and that one of the PCA's major functions—to prevent the negative consequences of a C rating—was unnecessary.

Since shooting the retakes for *Amber* in April, Preminger had shot and cut *Daisy Kenyon*. He was working with Ring Lardner, Jr., on adapting Christine Weston's novel *The Dark Wood* (in which a war widow struggling to accept her husband's death falls in love with a veteran whose wife has left him for another man) when he was called back into the fray for *Amber*. Fox president Spyros Skouras summoned Preminger to New York for a meeting on October 27 with Father Patrick Masterson, the Legion's new executive secretary. Preminger later gave a vivid description of Skouras pleading desperately with Masterson to remove the ban on *Amber*, kneeling in front of him, kissing his hand, and crying. Preminger said that he and Masterson, both embarrassed by Skouras's behavior, spent the rest of the day screening the film together in "a friendly mood," with Masterson detailing his objections after each reel,[24] but Masterson's notes on the meeting (which fail to mention Skouras's groveling) state that he, fearing a trap, refused Skouras's offer to review the film and make specific objections.[25]

A few days later, PCA officials Arthur DeBra and Stephen Jackson,

serving as liaisons between the studio and the Legion, came up with a
list of ten changes that could be made to *Amber* either by redubbing or
by eliminating footage. Their proposals had three main objectives: to
show that Amber leaves home not out of a desire for "finery and luxury,"
but in flight from her foster father and a proposed forced marriage; "to
eliminate the flavor of propositions on Amber's part to enter illicit relationships in order to achieve her ends . . . [; and] to remove offensive
material and strengthen the compensating moral value."

Preminger, doubtless under tacit or explicit pressure from his em-
ployer to placate the Legion, accepted most of the PCA's proposals. He
protested, however, a cut in the final sequence that would end the film
with Amber at the window of her apartment, after Bruce and her son
have gone to the coach. According to a PCA memo (probably written by
DeBra and Jackson) dated November 6, the day a temporary cut print of
Amber was sent to the Legion for review, "Mr. Preminger, director of the
picture, who has been exceedingly cooperative with respect to all of
these matters, has stated that as far as he is concerned, he is vehemently
opposed to this particular change. He takes the position that it is not
only contraindicated from the dramatic standpoint, but even with respect to the punishment of Amber, the present ending is the bitterest experience of all for her. He states that in the event that the studio
approves this change, he will disassociate himself from the entire matter
and on his own give a strong statement to the press criticizing the entire
situation." In the event, the change went through; so did several others
on which Preminger took no recorded stand, including eleven cuts and
new voice-overs at the beginning and end of the film to stress the proper
"moral" interpretation of the heroine's trajectory. On November 28 Fox
sent its exchange managers a set of instructions for cutting existing
prints of *Amber*. The voice-overs were contained in new inserts shipped
in early December, which were substituted for the beginning and end of
the film.

In the film as originally released, two further shots followed the exterior close-up, which now closes the film, of Amber closing the window of
her apartment. In the first, an interior medium shot, Amber turns from
the window, walks into the foreground (the camera pulling back), sits at
her dressing table, and calls for her maid, Nan (Jessica Tandy) who approaches. There was then a cut to a close two-shot of Amber and Nan,

reflected in the dressing-table mirror, as Amber instructs her maid, "Tell Sir Thomas Dudley I'll be happy to have supper with him tonight." Amber starts applying makeup to her face, Nan exits, and the camera moves into a close-up of Amber as she applies rouge to her cheeks: fade-out.

It is both understandable and revealing that Preminger fought, vainly, for this ending: understandable, since it's a much stronger ending than the one the film was left with; revealing, since it confirms Preminger's intentions for *Forever Amber* and shows that despite his reluctance to direct it and despite his later dismissals of the film, he took it seriously (though not so seriously that he didn't think better of his threat to make public his dissatisfaction with the new ending). That Preminger would repeat, substantially, the original ending of *Amber* in the ending of *Bonjour Tristesse* (with a crucial variation: in the later film, Cécile removes her makeup instead of putting makeup on) indicates the importance for him of the image of a woman reflected in a dressing-room mirror and of linking this image to the logic of continuing with a certain way of life (the implied signification of these endings—both of which also present the solitude of a woman before her own image as an affliction). It's unlikely that, had *Amber* retained its original ending, Preminger would have risked such blatant self-repetition ten years later. (Amber's attempted ruse of leaving Bruce's wife alone with King Charles anticipates Cécile's plot against Anne in *Bonjour Tristesse*; and both plots lead to disaster for their plotters, Amber's in its failure, Cécile's in its success.)

On December 4 Skouras announced that because of objections from the Legion and "other organizations representative of public opinion," *Amber* had been recut. Years later, Skouras claimed that the condemnation of *Amber* had cost the studio at least $2 million. Darryl Zanuck recalled that the Catholic pressure on exhibitors stemming from the C rating "meant that we lost practically one-third of the United States, and so, like Howard Hughes and his problem with *The Outlaw*, we finally cut the picture. The exhibitors wanted to support us as they wanted to play the picture, but when you gang up on a man and picket his lobby and threaten him with undermining the morals of youth, he finally gives in."[26] *Amber* brought in $8 million in domestic rentals—the number-4 slot for its year, but that was not enough to offset the film's high negative cost and other expenses.

In *Forever Amber*, Preminger and Shamroy film faces, windows, curtains, architecture—faces, mostly. We're not invited to be interested much in what these faces might conceal, in anything not visually explicit. It's a film with much darkness, thanks to Shamroy's magnificent lighting designs, but no dark side. Amber is the light that eliminates all shadows, that lights up lust on every man's face.

However compromised by censorship, *Amber* is Preminger's most extended study of the displacements of women—from country to city, from family to husband, from lover to lover—as social rituals revealing the underlying structures of society, rituals that are performed again and again in Preminger's films. His cinema is, moreover, filled with male heroes who are morally or intellectually weak, cold, misguided, inadequate, or willfully blind to some fundamental truth about themselves, their society, or the women who love them. Of all these men, none is as repellent as Bruce Carlton: weak in his desire, self-righteous ("there's a man over there who's dying: go to *him*"), grudging but also self-serving in his acceptance of Amber's insistent devotion. Bruce's one decent gesture occurs near the end of the film when he says to his son (who, on his mother's question, has impulsively stated his wish to accompany his father to Virginia) that he may go "if your mother says you can." Otherwise, Bruce is never admirable or likable at any moment. During his tenure as a Fox leading man, Cornel Wilde was the kind of limited actor whose defensiveness about his limitations is apparent in his performances. The personal antipathy between him and Preminger no doubt contributed to the effect, in *Amber*, of Wilde's retreating on-screen into a strained, choked remoteness that does nothing to make the character more sympathetic.

Among *Amber*'s many superb set pieces, we may point out first the theater sequence early in the film that begins with a fine Preminger crane shot that tracks back with Amber, Bruce, and Almsbury as they walk forward through a vestibule into the theater. Abandoning them, the camera continues backward through the crowded ground-level seating area (women passing among the spectators selling oranges) while also panning toward the stage, where an actor (Ian Keith) delivers the prologue to *Romeo and Juliet* as the curtain rises against a backdrop of

Verona. In a delightful instance of the film's documentation of the customs of seventeenth-century England, the appearance of the King (George Sanders) in his box not only causes the audience members to turn and bow but forces the onstage actors to interrupt their duel scene, doff their Italian caps, and bow also, before resuming their imaginary quarrel.

The scene of Amber giving birth is handled in an impressive single take, the camera tracking back as a door opens and a maid walks forward with a pot, the camera revealing, then passing, the bawd Mother Red Cap (Anne Revere), who stands with arms folded beside a column, then panning to a close shot of Amber in labor. Now the camera, reversing direction (as Raksin's score drowns out Amber's groans), finds the grotesque old midwife wiping her hands. The midwife bends down below the frame, and the camera moves past to approach Black Jack, who is separated from the foreground space by a standing screen. He stares distractedly out a window; the camera holds on him for a considerable time before we hear a baby crying, and Black Jack smiles in relief. In this shot, as throughout the film, Preminger insists on linking Amber to her surroundings, first to establish their sordidness and her isolation, then— in the emphasis on Black Jack and his obvious concern for Amber—to show the presence of a compensating human contact. At the center of the shot is Amber herself, her presence elided both by the camera and by the sound mixing, which, in accordance with the PCA's wishes, eliminated Amber's offscreen groans.

The duel scene, with its dark figures of people and trees looming against gray fog, and the plague sequence, a painterly chaos of smoke, carts, corpses, and lurid crosses in red paint, are highlights of the film's pictorialism. The camera's calm discovery of horror and its slow lateral movement as cargo is unloaded from Bruce's ship anticipate *Exodus*.

The scene in which the Great Fire of London reaches Radcliff Manor contains an astonishing moment. In a low-angle shot, Radcliff's servant carries the doomed Earl in his arms toward the camera and tosses him at it; Radcliff falls beneath camera range as flames rise in the foreground. In the same take, Amber and Nan, who have watched this event in shock, flee through a door in the background, whereupon the servant, his work done, turns and runs out the same door only about a second before the ceiling collapses and flaming rafters fall where he had been standing. Nothing has prepared us for the servant's action. The character has barely figured in the film, apart from a brief moment when Radcliff strikes him and another when Radcliff berates him (but these moments, and Richard Haydn's characterization of Radcliff in general, are enough to vindicate the killer). The staging of the scene is overpowering: the shock of the abruptness of the killing is heightened by the unleashing, at the very end of the shot, of a massive destructive power that gives the impression of having put the actors in physical danger.

The final sequences of the film, though shorn of the logical conclusion (Amber resuming her place in front of the mirror and preparing for her date with Sir Thomas) toward which Preminger originally guided them, remain a substantial achievement of Premingerian distanciation. This section of the film begins on a shot of Amber, hovered over by a hairdresser and a maid, reflected in a large mirror of approximately the dimensions of the film frame. The shot tracks back to a wide medium shot encompassing several courtiers who have come to pay Amber their respects and ask her for favors. A later scene shows her staring with dreamy anxiety into the same mirror: "I wonder if he [Bruce] thought I looked old. He knows I'm almost twenty-five." Preminger's original final capper of Amber again at the mirror would have retrospectively heightened the value of the mirror shots that remain.

As the King's mistress, Amber has reached the pinnacle of her social success. The artificiality of the world of the court and Amber's mastery of its conventions (she has even learned to speak French) are strongly marked in the formality of performance and the spaciousness of the sets, which Amber dominates. The world that Bruce rejects is on full display here. This rejection or denunciation of "the world"—what might be called Preminger's Beautiful Soul motif—is a key Premingerian gesture, performed, at various levels of the narrative, in all his major films. Many of his characters—including Laurent in *The 13th Letter*, Patty in *The Moon is Blue*, Billy Mitchell, Joan of Arc in *Saint Joan*, Anne in *Bonjour Tristesse*, Brig in *Advise & Consent*, and Stephen in *The Cardinal*—see themselves as too good for the world, or as summoned to correct it.

10

A Search for Lucidity

Elizabeth Janeway's novel *Daisy Kenyon*, a romantic quadrangle set mainly in New York during the years 1940 to 1942, was bought by Twentieth Century-Fox in July 1945, before its publication later that year. The story dealt with the then hot topic of divorce, and Janeway's worldly tolerance of adultery may have appealed to Preminger, who was assigned to the project. Margaret Buell Wilder and Ted Sills worked on a first-draft script that was scrapped; then David Hertz took over the assignment, which proved a lengthy one. A crucial decision made in the writing stage was to shift the time period to the present—one of the central characters, the neurotic Peter, becoming a veteran suffering from posttraumatic stress. Hertz turned in several "first drafts" between November 1945 and June 1946, at which time the project was apparently shelved for several months, no doubt because Preminger had been reassigned to *Forever Amber*. (Studio publicity reported that as of January 1946 the director-producer's plate also contained *The Dark Wood*, *Any Number Can Play*, and *Methinks the Lady*—which would become *Whirlpool*.)

In early March 1947, with the production of *Amber* near its scheduled close, Preminger turned again to *Daisy Kenyon*. (The further tinkering and special pleading that *Amber* would require meant that his attention was probably even more divided than usual during the production of *Daisy Kenyon*, but there is no external evidence to suggest that the film suffered from this.) On March 5, 1947, the studio sent Hertz's June 22, 1946, draft to the Production Code Administration. Breen's rejection came three days later. The basic story was not acceptable "because of its lack of regard for the sanctity of the institution of marriage . . . Further, the script contains an excessive and, in our judgment, unnecessary emphasis on drinking and liquor, which would have to be eliminated." On March 12 Preminger met with Breen to discuss what could be done to save *Daisy*, and Preminger agreed to some concessions—all of which concerned the adulterous affair between the title character, a fashion illustrator, and Dan O'Mara, a successful and married lawyer. First, the implication of "illicit sex" between them would be avoided; further, "the wrongness of the relationship" would be emphasized, and Daisy's attempts to break it off would be strengthened. Moreover, Peter Lapham, whom Daisy marries over the course of the story and who steps aside when Dan's wife, Lucille, sues Dan for divorce, "will not walk out on Daisy because he feels the breakup of their marriage is proper but rather to give Daisy an opportunity to solve her own problem; and the burden of the responsibility for the unhappy marriage of Dan and Lucille will rest on Dan and not as at present, largely on the wife. Also, we understand that hope will be held out for the ultimate reunion of Dan and Lucille." And, again, the characters would have to cut down on their drinking.

Zanuck, Preminger, and Hertz met on March 20 to discuss the script. The conference notes indicate that the participants' main concern was with meeting their obligations to the PCA. So Zanuck suggested that on page 10, "instead of mixing himself a highball, Dan should get a cup of coffee." Zanuck also proposed a sanctimonious speech for Daisy along the lines of: "I know this is going to sound crazy, but my marriage to Pete taught me something I never knew before. Marriage is an institution; it's the foundation of everything. Your roots are with your wife and children, Dan, and even though they may be unhealthy roots, they are yours, and that's where you belong."

Preminger and Hertz worked on a revised draft, avoiding the obvious moralism of Zanuck's proposal and bringing the ending closer to its final form by having Dan arrive at Daisy's Cape Cod cottage for a three-way showdown with her and Peter. Preminger, dissatisfied, asked Ring Lardner, Jr., to do some revisions. The final screenplay, dated May 7, omits Daisy's voice-over narration and an unwieldy flashback structure, narrating the story in a straight chronological fashion.

The PCA still found cause to reiterate its earlier complaints, and in response, the filmmakers went out of their way to reduce the characters' drinking. In several scenes of *Daisy Kenyon*, characters pour or are served alcoholic drinks but never drink them (a curious habit twice underscored in the dialogue); to gild the lily, Peter and Dan both drink milk (and Mary Angelus, Daisy's model, drinks cream). On the other hand, when it comes to the PCA's most substantial criticism, regarding the lack of "a good word for the institution of marriage," the film manages to satisfy the letter of the law. Coverly, Lucille's father, warns his daughter against divorce, but he is an unsympathetic character, and his desire to keep the O'Maras together is clearly self-serving (he wants to keep Dan as his law partner).

The sequel to the PCA's efforts to clean up *Daisy Kenyon* arrived when the Legion of Decency came down against the film, rating it Class B, with the note, "Light treatment of marriage; reflects the acceptability of divorce." Jason S. Joy, Twentieth Century-Fox's director of public relations, wrote to Stephen S. Jackson of the MPAA, "Apparently all of the preachment against divorce which we injected into the picture at the suggestion of the Production Code Administration was of no avail"—a reproach hinting at the ongoing tension between the studios and the PCA.

Joan Crawford was cast as Daisy; possibly she sought the role (Twentieth Century-Fox publicity indicated that the star had tried to buy the rights to the novel but was beaten to them by the studio). According to Bob Thomas, Crawford requested Dana Andrews and Henry Fonda (both of whom were under contract to Fox) as her costars. Fonda was switched from *Call Northside 777* to play Peter. The actor would later recall, "I didn't want to do it . . . It wasn't bad, so I couldn't fight too much about it." Preminger persuaded Dana Andrews to take the role of Dan, although as with *Fallen Angel*, Andrews was unenthusiastic about the film; he even tried to get out of the picture, but was warned by his attorney that if he dropped out, he would be liable for his two costars' salaries.[1]

In late May, Preminger and cinematographer Leon Shamroy went to New York to shoot backgrounds at La Guardia Field, the East River Drive, and a Greenwich Village movie theater. (The decision to shoot in New York was part of a trend: Twentieth Century-Fox had recently shot scenes there for *Miracle on 34th Street*, *The House on 92nd Street*, *Boomerang*, *Kiss of Death*, and *Gentleman's Agreement*.) Preminger and Shamroy returned to Hollywood, where studio shooting started on June 16. In July, for a scene set at the Stork Club, Preminger persuaded Walter Winchell and another columnist, Leonard Lyons, to do brief bits.

John Garfield, on the lot for *Gentleman's Agreement*, appeared as an extra (only the back of his head is visible, in the foreground of the shot in which Dana Andrews has a short exchange with Lyons).

The aspect of *Daisy Kenyon* that left the most lasting memory in the minds of those who worked on the film was the cold temperature of the sets, which Crawford stipulated had to be kept at 58 degrees. According to Ruth Warrick, Crawford "seemed to live in a crackle of tension one could almost feel like a physical thing around her." On the other hand, Fonda was impressed with Crawford's "consummate" acting. "With her you never saw the wheels turning. She was very true. She *was* the part, the character, not an actress merely playing the person."[2]

Preminger found Fonda, with whom he would work again several times, "completely professional," and got along well with Crawford, whom he called "a pro who knew how to get the effect she was after. She did not need much help from me."[3] Crawford later praised her director's work, saying of *Daisy Kenyon*, "If Otto Preminger hadn't directed it the picture would have been a mess." She remained fond of Preminger, saying toward the end of her life, "Otto is a dear man, sort of a Jewish Nazi, but I love him."[4]

Shooting was completed on August 12. On October 6, David Raksin's score was recorded. Raksin, who considered the score one of his lesser efforts, recalled a dispute he had with the director over a theme he used in the Cape Cod sequence:

> Preminger, when he heard it, said [sharply], "Where did you find that tune?" He was mad, he didn't like it. I was so horrified that he chose to say this in front of the guys in the dubbing room, where we're putting the film together, I was actually insulted, and I did the cruelest thing. I drew him aside, and I said, "Look, Mr. Preminger, if you want people to know that you don't know what's appropriate for this kind of a setting, you're doing it now." Terrible thing to do to a European guy, you know. He just sort of looked at me, and burst into laughter, as if to say, "Where did they find this idiot?" He accepted it. And of course, it worked fine.[5]

The final production cost was $1,850,000. *Daisy Kenyon* was released in December 1947. The mixed reviews and mediocre box-office performance must have confirmed the earlier misgivings of both Andrews and Fonda. The film would be one of several from its period that apparently left no impression at all on the mind of its director. During the 1970s, Preminger regularly told any interviewers who asked that he could not remember anything about it. Despite his reluctance to talk about it, *Daisy Kenyon* is among his best films.

In *Daisy Kenyon*, space, distance, place, and home are primary. The opening titles are superimposed over a detailed drawing of the front entrance to Daisy's apartment building—a space that will be contested during the film between Dan and Peter but which remains, for Daisy, the proof of her independence and freedom of choice. In the first sequence (after an amusing interchange with a taxi driver who offers statistics on New York's taxi crisis, bolstering the film's theme of competition), camera movement strongly marks Dan's entrance into the house and then into Daisy's apartment. The camera moves with him, benefiting from his power to cross thresholds while also bestowing on him its own power over visibility and perspective. The scene also asserts his mastery over filmic form (he has the ability to shut off Raksin's jaunty title theme, which turns out to have been playing on a phonograph).

The strong complicity between Dan and the camera at such moments (as, later, in the scene in which, in a single take followed by a moving camera, he enters the waiting room of his law office and passes through an intermediate room into his private office, greeting secretaries as he goes) makes *Daisy Kenyon* the culmination of what might be called Preminger's Dana Andrews series. The value of Dana Andrews in Preminger's films comes from his supercivilized nature, his smoothness and glibness, his imperturbability (which serves, of course, as a provocation to perturb). Dan O'Mara has perfected the ability to move smoothly through the world, to make himself liked, to claim unobtrusively the right to control situations—skills that also belong to such later figures as Slater in *The Moon Is Blue*, Raymond in *Bonjour Tristesse*, Leffingwell in *Advise & Consent*, and Stephen Fermoyle in *The Cardinal*.

It is in Preminger's films (more than in those of Fritz Lang or Jacques Tourneur) that Andrews's averageness becomes most meaningful. In *Laura*, his refusal to show emotion becomes an obstacle against which he visibly fights, and the audience feels each expression of his emotion as a triumph. In *Fallen Angel* he embodies the opportunism of the average American male, the moral corruption required to get ahead, along with the ambivalence that comes from a residual humanity that can't commit itself wholly to the worst in himself. In *Daisy Kenyon* he is a model of social and professional success. In *Where the Sidewalk Ends* he is, again, average, but his averageness is now ashamed of its origins, furiously seeking to stamp itself out; he must obliterate himself and assume the role of another (which he can easily do because his being is chameleon-like). Finally, in *In Harm's Way*, Andrews reappears as the total careerist, his individuality utterly submerged in the effort simultaneously to get ahead and to be invisible (he advocates an emasculated policy, waiting, doing the least possible).

Though in *Daisy Kenyon*, Dan drives the narrative much as Mark drives the narrative of *Laura*, Daisy, no less than Dan, is in complicity with the form of the film. Raksin's score is, after all, *her* chosen music: it is always associated with her, just as the theme of *Laura* is associated with Laura, as Raksin's "Slowly" is associated with Stella in *Fallen Angel*, and as the theme of *Angel Face* is associated with Diane. (In all four films, the theme emanates from a diegetic source linked to the female character: phonograph, jukebox, piano.) The problem in *Daisy Kenyon* is: Which man, Dan or Peter, should Daisy choose? (The problem is echoed, and parodied, on a minor level by Mary's plethora of suitors.) In the final sequence, the problem is posed concretely as the question of which of the two men will return alone to the train station. Daisy arrives at her answer after the salutary "shock treatment" of her car wreck: "You're both going back to New York."

Peter's overruling of her decision may be felt by some viewers as a brutal and unsatisfying end to a film that has advocated a woman's right to determine her own life. On the other hand, here, as throughout *Daisy Kenyon*, Preminger leaves the film open. I would even call its ending a model Premingerian ending, presenting a situation in a way that does not determine the film's meaning or give a final judgment on the characters, not requiring the viewer to see the situation as desirable or just, allowing the viewer to question the ethical and aesthetic validity of the situation. This is so despite Peter's position as the character in the film who, finally, knows where all the other characters are going (a role suggested by his temporary employment as compass adjuster).

Daisy Kenyon questions what kind of film it is and rejects categories and genres. "All right, have your tragedy, have your melodrama," Daisy tells Peter, criticizing his attempt to articulate the sense of acute loss and unreality he experienced after his wife's death and accusing him of "trying to sound like a case history." Daisy argues implicitly for a different mode of self-representation that is never characterized and that *Daisy Kenyon* attempts to imagine. The divorce trial sequence illustrates Preminger's position: the trial is ostensibly a mechanism for producing truth, but Daisy—with the support of the film—resists the pressure from Lucile's attorney to reveal intimate details about her life, questioning his right to demand them and asserting a basic human right to privacy. She resists representation, unwilling to portray herself for the public as a character in the story of Dan and Lucile.

The film is about a search for lucidity. Crucial to this search, for Preminger, is the camera's ability to pull back, to show more of the space around the characters. After Daisy's car accident, she opens the passenger-side door of the car, slowly gets out, and half leans on, half clings to the open door. As she does so, the camera (slightly elevated) cranes back, showing more and more of the snowy woods around her at the same time and, we imagine, at the same measure as she reorients herself in the space. The silence into which the film suddenly opens contrasts with the cacophony of Raksin's score during the previous driving scene (just as the increased distance of the camera contrasts with the progressively tighter intercut close-ups of the ringing phone and Daisy's face in the scene in the cottage). As the camera reaches its maximum distance and stops craning, Daisy starts, tentatively, to walk forward. Here, in contrast with the shots in which the camera tracks forward aggressively behind Dan, the camera movement is aligned with a spiritual process, suggesting a harmony between Daisy and her environment.

The crane back from the wrecked car is one of the grand Preminger gestures: the discovery of space as an expansion of the individual's powers of sense and action—that is, the gradual filling of space by consciousness. The camera movement suggests a reciprocal action: consciousness expands to fill space as the space also expands, creating more room for consciousness.

The crane shot takes to their extremes several tendencies apparent throughout *Daisy Kenyon*: to create space, to open the film and the characters to a wider world, to place pauses and gaps within the film as spaces for reflection, to find ways other than dramatic action to express the characters' dilemmas and decisions. These tendencies are clearly at odds with Zanuck's preferred style of filmmaking, and the logic and consistency of Preminger's pursuit of them within *Daisy Kenyon* are proof of his ability to do personal work at Twentieth Century-Fox.

Daisy Kenyon is possibly the first Hollywood film to allude to the internment of Japanese Americans during World War II. Dan says that his client, a Japanese American named Noguchi, was victimized by "some smart operator on the Coast" who stole Noguchi's home (on the basis of an obscure law "written by Cortez") while Noguchi was fighting in Italy. Despite the pussyfooting, the Noguchi story is a clear reference to the Japanese American internment, which affected almost exclusively people living on the West Coast, resulting in massive loss of property for the victims, the injustice of which was pointed up by the service many thousands of "Noguchis" performed for the United States in the war.

The Noguchi story directly anticipates the property case in *Hurry Sundown*, in which a racist judge tries to frustrate the attempts by a black man (just returned, like Noguchi, from World War II combat) to reclaim his property. (The June 22, 1946, draft of the *Daisy Kenyon* screenplay had a courtroom scene in which a racist judge denies the plaintiff's claim, but Breen would not allow such an attack on American justice. In the film, the defeat is merely mentioned.) Is this coincidence or is it another piece of evidence that despite Preminger's later effort in interviews to drive a wedge between the pre-independence and post-independence phases of his career, the two are continuous, and that Preminger took advantage of his freedom to pick up situations and themes he had been forced to abandon during his Fox period—as with the reprise of the censored original ending of *Forever Amber* at the end of *Bonjour Tristesse*?

11

Hollywood Crossroads

Since *A Royal Scandal*, Ernst Lubitsch had produced another picture (*Dragonwyck*, Joseph L. Mankiewicz's directorial debut) and directed a final masterpiece, underappreciated at the time: *Cluny Brown*. For his next project, he went back to a 1919 German operetta, Rudolf Schanzer and Ernst Welisch's *Die Frau im Hermelin*, which Fox had acquired for him in 1942.

Zanuck found the story of *That Lady in Ermine* "all too fancy" and insufficiently "honest," but he gave the project the go-ahead anyway, hoping that Lubitsch could, as he had done in *Heaven Can Wait*, "combine farce and a tear." For the stars, Lubitsch and Zanuck agreed on Betty Grable and Douglas Fairbanks, Jr. Lubitsch turned to his friend Samson Raphaelson to write the script. Overcoming his misgivings, Raphaelson took the assignment. "Lubitsch was a very sick man plodding along on formula," Raphaelson later said. "I couldn't fight a man who had had two heart attacks."[1] The Breen office found the first-draft script unacceptable in its comic treatment of adultery. The film deals, in fact, with two adulterous situations occurring three hundred years apart. In the framing story, set in 1861, Countess Angelina of Bergamo (Grable's character) sees her castle taken over by Hungarian hussars under the command of an irascible colonel (Fairbanks). The colonel falls in love with Angelina, arousing the jealousy of her cowardly husband, Mario. In a story told in a long flashback, Angelina's look-alike ancestor, Francesca (Grable again), saves the castle from an invading duke (Fairbanks) by entering his tent with him alone, while her husband, Alberto, watches sadly. Lubitsch mollified the Breen office by agreeing to make it "quite plain that the break-up of the marriage is brought about by Mario over the protests of Angelina, who wants to preserve the marriage, as is her duty" and by changing a dissolve (which Breen took as denoting a passage of some time) to a straight cut after Francesca enters the duke's tent and before she leaves it.

Shooting started on October 20, 1947, under the new title *This Is the Moment* (after a line in the lyrics of the film's superb romantic ballad by Leo Robin and Frederick Hollander). Lubitsch inspired the cast with his vitality and his enthusiasm for improvisation. Fairbanks found working with him "a joy."[2] Lubitsch was pleased with how the film was going, and Zanuck, apparently, liked the rushes. As the production went on, Lubitsch visibly lost energy. Forced by exhaustion to leave the set one day at 4:00 p.m., he told an assistant that he was considering having Preminger finish the scene for him.

On Sunday, November 30, Lubitsch died of a heart attack. On Wednesday, December 3, the studio announced that Preminger would finish *This Is the Moment*. Preminger's version is simply this: "When Lubitsch died, I was asked to complete *That Lady in Ermine* [as the film was eventually called]. I really didn't think that the script was interesting, nor was the picture. I finished it—that was it."[3] Lubitsch biographer Scott Eyman attributes Preminger's desire to take on the project to careerism, but it may be wondered whether Preminger could have seen it as furthering his career. At his own request, he would take no credit for directing *This Is the Moment* (although, of course, his role in the production was well publicized).[4] If a Lubitsch connection was a career boost, Preminger had already established it with *A Royal Scandal*, just as with *Centennial Summer* he had already proved he could direct a period musical in Technicolor. Finally, Preminger's later profession of apathy toward the picture must be given a certain weight, even allowing for the dampening effect the film's weak commercial performance may have had on his retrospection.

Preminger had nothing else that would be ready soon. His writer on *The Dark Wood*, Ring Lardner, Jr., had just been sacrificed to the anti-Communist terror that had taken over Hollywood. Lardner appeared as an unfriendly witness before HUAC on October 30 and was cited, with nine other Hollywood writers and directors, for contempt of Congress on November 24. On the same day, executives from all the major studios, including Spyros Skouras, began a meeting at the Waldorf-Astoria Hotel in New York, from which they emerged the next day with a resolution to fire the Hollywood Ten and, in the future, to deny employment to anyone known to be a Communist. Lardner recalled, "I was in the middle of a conference with Otto when his secretary came in to say that Mr. Lardner was to report to Mr. Zanuck's office. 'Only Mr. Lardner?' Otto asked, almost incredulous at the affront to his dignity as a producer-director. I reminded him that Zanuck might have something else on his mind besides our project. And I was right." Lardner was then told directly that he was fired.[5]

On Thursday, December 4, 1947, the day of Lubitsch's funeral, Sam Wood, Leo McCarey, George Marshall, David Butler, and Tay Garnett, all politically conservative directors, prepared for a meeting of the Screen Directors Guild that was scheduled for the following night. Also present at the meeting was an FBI informant whose name has been blocked out of the Bureau's report on the meeting and who, it may be presumed, was another member of the guild. They went through a list of members and checked off those who they thought were Communists. One was Preminger (whom David Butler had directed in *They Got Me Covered* five years before).

Preminger had been under suspicion before. The FBI's records concerning him show that he was linked to numerous individuals and associations that were deemed, at best, dubious, and at worst, blatantly communistic, including the European Film Fund (which Lubitsch had helped organize to help unemployed émigré artists), the executive committee of the Hollywood League Against Nazism, and the League of American Writers. Among the individuals with whom the FBI saw fit to log Preminger's contacts were Ernst Lubitsch (whom a source evidently well placed at Twentieth Century-Fox in 1944 judged "pink"), Joseph L. Mankiewicz (merely "liberal in his political thinking," said the same source), German émigré writer Lion Feuchtwanger, American writer Viola Brothers Shore (whom Preminger had hired to adapt Anna Seghers's *The Seventh Cross*), Harry Kline (former secretary of the Los Angeles County Communist Party), Fritz Lang (at whose house Preminger was a frequent visitor in 1943), Martha Dodd and her husband, Alfred K. Stern (both to be indicted for spying for the Soviets), and producer Boris Morros (a Soviet agent who, in 1947, turned counterspy for the FBI and later implicated the Sterns). The same source who mentioned Preminger's contacts with Lubitsch and Mankiewicz in 1944 described

Preminger as a "lone wolf" and said that "he had never heard Preminger express any political beliefs." Another informant thought that Preminger had "fellow traveler tendencies."[6]

Preminger was one of thirty-four honorary pallbearers at Lubitsch's funeral on December 4 at Forest Lawn. The next day, shooting resumed on *This Is the Moment*, with Preminger directing. Without exaggerating their symbolic significance, it should be noted that these events occurred at a historical moment in American cinema. The U.S. Supreme Court would hear the *United States v. Paramount Pictures* antitrust case in February 1948 and in May would hand down the decree that would end the ownership of movie theaters by producer-distributors. The competitive threat that television posed to film exhibition was starting to become clear. The Waldorf-Astoria resolution marked the beginning of the anti-Communist blacklist in Hollywood. These three forces—the divorcement decree, the rise of television, and the blacklist—defined the conditions for Preminger's emergence as one of the most successful independent director-producers, while marking the end of the period in which the Hollywood studio system functioned at its highest level of stability: a period in which Lubitsch flourished, and which he symbolized.

After taking over *This Is the Moment*, Preminger wasted little time in gaining the antipathy of his two stars. Grable thought his direction heavy-handed and was annoyed when he conferred with Fairbanks without including her in the discussions.[7] Fairbanks walked off the set when Preminger shouted at an electrician; the actor had to be coaxed back to the studio, where he found that Preminger had apologized. Walter Abel, who played Horvath, the colonel's much-put-upon second-in-command, recalled, "When Preminger came in he changed everything." Fearing that Preminger's conception would be at odds with Lubitsch's and render the film incoherent, Abel and Fairbanks approached their new director with "nothing but kindness and delicacy in our minds," in Abel's words, and tried to explain Lubitsch's intentions as they understood them. Preminger cut them short: "Mr. Lubitsch is dead. *I* am the director of this picture." From then on, Abel recalled, "There was no more fun in Hollywood, not with that man."[8] (Yet Preminger later paid Abel a compliment: "Not all actors are as nice as Walter Abel, otherwise it would be very easy to direct . . . Some actors need to be treated tougher, some easier—Mr. Abel, with silence.")[9]

Preminger's work on the film involved more than merely filling in the scenes left unfinished at Lubitsch's death. Preminger also reshot some of Lubitsch's footage ("because it was too subtle," quipped Fairbanks). Several scenes shot by Lubitsch were sacrificed in the final cut (although the decision to eliminate them was Zanuck's rather than Preminger's), including the original beginning and ending of the film and several production numbers.[10] According to Fairbanks, "Zanuck more or less took over and re-cut and re-edited things in a way which I knew Lubitsch would not have done. But he was adamant that as long as Lubitsch was no longer there he was going to do it the way he wanted. And what had been a very, very witty and very Lubitsch-y kind of picture was only fairly so."[11]

Shortly after finishing production on the film, now retitled *That Lady in Ermine*, Preminger landed in the gossip columns. Natalie Draper, who played the small part of King Charles's mistress for both Stahl and Preminger in *Forever Amber*, had been mentioned in Louella Parsons's columns as a "favorite dining and dancing partner" of Preminger's in May 1946, during the hiatus in that production. On January 12, 1948, Parsons reported in the *Los Angeles Examiner* that Preminger had written Marion in Romania asking for an immediate divorce. "If it is difficult for her to obtain her freedom in Europe," Parsons wrote, "Otto will get a divorce either here or in Nevada." Perhaps Preminger funneled this story to Parsons in order to prove to Draper, with whom he was still involved, that he intended to free himself from Marion.

The night before Parsons's story appeared, Draper was out on a date with Australian-born screenwriter Ivan Goff at Le Papillon, a Sunset Strip nightclub. According to Draper, who described the incident the following day to Parsons, Preminger, who was in the dining room, approached them, greeted Draper, and slapped Goff several times in the face. "Otto Preminger and I went together for a long time," Draper explained to the columnist. "He wants to marry me and has asked his estranged wife for a divorce. But I don't want any part of him. He's enraged with jealousy. He doesn't like anyone I go out with."[12] At the time, Preminger denied the entire incident ("I wish to make no statement that would involve a lady and particularly a lady that has been my friend"),[13] but in his autobiography, he (withholding the names of the other two parties) claimed that Goff had previously accused him of beating Draper and threatened to knock the director down. When, a few nights later, Preminger ran into Draper and Goff at the restaurant bar, Preminger confronted Goff—"So you want to knock me down? Well, here I am"—and slapped the writer across the face.[14]

That Lady in Ermine opened in August 1948. Most of the reviews managed to convey the respect appropriate to the final work of one of the cinema's acknowledged giants, while also regretting the film's failure to come up to his standard. Betty Grable's popularity assured the film a measure of attention, but many of her fans, when they saw the picture, must have wondered what she was doing in it. The film, which cost $2,485,000 to make, earned a disappointing $1.5 million in domestic rentals.

That Lady in Ermine is a bizarre film, combining fantasy, whimsy, and operetta in a manner that departs radically from Hollywood norms of the period. It belongs next to such mysterious postwar fantasies as *One Touch of Venus*, and it can also be seen as a belated and eccentric cousin to Lubitsch's Ruritanian romances of the 1920s and '30s.

As the second of the two minor films of which Lubitsch and Preminger will forever dispute authorship, *That Lady in Ermine* poses a different, and more interesting, critical problem than *A Royal Scandal*. The earlier film, whatever its weaknesses, is a coherent work, a legible design fulfilled with some skill; the authorship problem of the film, such as it is, consists mainly in determining whether the "skill" is essentially Premingerian or Lubitschian. I'm willing to leave this question open, although I expect to see few scholars avid to take it up.

That Lady in Ermine turns out, as Douglas Fairbanks, Jr., and Walter Abel had feared, a split film, internally contradictory, uneven in execution. The opening scene, in which Angelina and Mario return from their marriage ceremony as if in shock, is leaden and badly acted, casting a pall over the film. The next sequence, in which the portraits of Angelina's ancestors come to life and rally around Francesca, calling on her to save the castle, has much comic verve (culminating in Francesca's singing "Ooh, what I'll do to that wild Hungarian") that carries over to some extent into the following scene, in which the colonel surveys the captured castle and resigns himself to the inevitability of his soldiers' partying with the castle's large female domestic staff.

Grable's casting is already a Lubitsch touch (for an equivalent insertion of the quintessence of mid-Americanness in a European context, we need look no further than Grady Sutton in *A Royal Scandal*)—though one only a knife-edge away from mere commercial concession. Her performance is best when it is pure, unrestrained energy, but at too many moments she seems awkward and unsure of what effect she should be creating. Fairbanks, despite a grizzled appearance not improved by grotesque makeup, fares better, and he is really funny when, in a fantasy sequence, he finds that he has suddenly acquired the ability to belt out the song "This Is the Moment" (in someone else's rich baritone).

More clearly than *A Royal Scandal*, the film contains elements that link it to other Preminger films. The colonel's obsession with Francesca's portrait alludes to *Laura*, and the scene in which he and his officers stand staring at it, then turn to see Angelina, its living likeness, descend the stairs, is almost an explicit parody of the central scene of the earlier film. Later, another reminiscence of Preminger's masterpiece occurs when the colonel interrogates Angelina under a pretext of official business, just as Mark interrogates Laura. *That Lady in Ermine* also contains elements that point to Preminger's future work. No doubt the heavy comedy and overplayed burlesque of the flashback scenes do him no credit, but there is in them, perhaps, something of his 1968 acid poem, *Skidoo* (a film that many will charge does him no credit either). More surely, the mix of song, fantasy, and special effects (a knife flying backward; Francesca and the colonel flying upstairs and crashing through the ceiling) in *That Lady in Ermine* already suggests the explosive and libertine juxtaposition of incompatible elements that would characterize *Skidoo*.

12

Sick Children

A new film version of Oscar Wilde's *Lady Windermere's Fan* wasn't Darryl F. Zanuck's idea. According to Walter Reisch, who is credited as co-screenwriter (with Dorothy Parker) on the finished film, "That was precisely a non-Zanuck picture. Nothing could be further removed from his way of thinking than Oscar Wilde, or Lady Windermere, or Mrs. Erlynne. It was just too Victorian, too elegant, and too slow. Everyone spoke like everyone else, very stilted and mechanical dialogue—brilliant, the most wonderful dialogue on earth, but totally inhuman. Zanuck just didn't care for it, so Otto was left alone and it was dragged out."[1]

Preminger later (in 1970) called *The Fan* "a mistake I made on my own," adding, "whatever I did to that film was wrong. It is one of the few pictures I already disliked while making it."[2] Yet in 1953 he told Jacques Rivette (to whom he described the film as "an experiment, unfortunately failed"), "It's one of my children, and the ones who are sick are not the ones whom one loves the least."[3] This rather uncharacteristic comment (Preminger must have been in a sentimental mood that day) was (mis)cited by Jean-Luc Godard in a 1962 interview, explaining why of his own films to that date he liked most *Une Femme est une femme*.[4]

Preminger, it can be assumed, initiated the project and encouraged Zanuck in October 1947 to buy the film rights to Wilde's play from Warner Bros., which had produced Ernst Lubitsch's film of *Lady Windermere's Fan* in 1925. Preminger later told a reporter that he was drawn to the project "because of the vogue Wilde's plays have attained in postwar years."[5] Preminger had Reisch assigned to the project, and the writer turned in a first-draft script on January 20, 1948, a week after Preminger's contretemps with Ivan Goff. Reisch came up with the device of telling Wilde's story in flashback, through framing scenes, set after the end of World War II (Lord and Lady Windermere having perished in the Blitz), in which Mrs. Erlynne discovers the notorious fan at an auction and, to establish her claim to it, seeks out Lord Darlington, to whom she recounts the events surrounding the fan's memorable appearance in Darlington's house on the night of Lady Windermere's ball. (Similarly, Preminger and Graham Greene would add a reference to World War II to the epilogue of Shaw's *Saint Joan*.)

Preminger thought Reisch's script needed polishing and went to New York in early March to persuade Dorothy Parker (with whom Preminger had spent a period in 1939 working on a play script called *The Happiest Man*) to do a rewrite. Parker, in turn, brought along her partner, Ross Evans. Working quickly, the two turned in a revision on March 29. By early May, the title of the project had been shortened to *The Fan*, perhaps in an attempt to disguise the literary origins or the English setting of the work.

A temporary script dated May 7, bearing the names of Reisch, Parker, and Evans, "disturbed" Zanuck at several points. On May 11 he met with Preminger to discuss his concerns. Mrs. Erlynne's behavior baffled him. "She knows, when she starts the flirtation with him, that Lord Windermere is married to her daughter. I was amazed that she would want to run the risk of upsetting her own daughter's marriage and happiness." He also passed on an objection from Mrs. Zanuck, whom he had asked to read the script (a sign that he felt out of his depth in these waters): in accepting Mrs. Erlynne's word that there is nothing between her and Lord Windermere, Lady Windermere seems too gullible.

Gene Tierney, who had been set to play Lady Windermere, told Zanuck and Preminger that she was pregnant and withdrew from the cast. On May 17 Jeanne Crain sent Preminger a telegram:

Dear Mr. Preminger: You know how very much I hoped to be in your picture "Lady Windermere's Fan." I had abandoned this hope completely. However I heard reports last night about Gene. If these reports are true I wonder if there would be a possibility of your considering me taking her place. I need not tell you how very happy I would be for this opportunity. I am also wiring Mr. Zanuck and would deeply appreciate any consideration you might give me. With kindest thoughts I am, Sincerely, Jeanne Crain[6]

Crain's casting was announced on May 20. *The Fan* was her third Preminger film and would be her last.

Preminger went to England on May 21. There, he made location shots and signed up Hugh Dempster and Martita Hunt, who would come to Hollywood to do small parts. After his return, the script was changed slightly in accordance with Zanuck's wishes. On June 11 Zanuck sent a memo to Preminger. The tone of his opening paragraph seems dubious and resigned: "I am convinced that we will have a very brilliant film. Whether or not it will be popular or commercial is something that I am not prepared to know about." Zanuck urged delaying the revelation of the true relationship between Lady Windermere and Mrs. Erlynne and recommended, a little desperately, that the dialogue be pruned of verbosity. "While a great deal of our script is brilliantly written, to me at times it becomes terribly pretentious, talky and dull. In our effort to get in all of the Oscar Wilde epigrams we can easily frequently seem to destroy characterization. I cannot imagine everybody in the cast being so damn clever, subtle or witty. Now this does not mean that I recommend stripping all of Wilde from the dialogue, but I do believe that a great deal of it can be trimmed." Zanuck's insistence on this point would rob Wilde's play of many of its most brilliant quips, its most elegant turns of phrase, and its most exciting passages of sustained repartee— rob it, in short, of what makes it a great play, since on the level of its plot, *Lady Windermere's Fan* is an old-fashioned, sentimental melodrama in which an attempted seduction is averted thanks to a fallen woman's self-sacrifice on behalf of her daughter.

Even on these terms, Preminger, Reisch, Parker, and Evans fall considerably from the level of Wilde because of their mishandling of the mechanics of the plot. The action of Wilde's play occurs within a twenty-four-hour period comprising the afternoon before Lady Windermere's ball, the ball itself, and the next day. All the crucial events transpire in this period, producing an effect of concentration and crisis that does much to mitigate the talkiness Zanuck complains of. By pushing back the start of the action and showing events that Wilde's text merely alludes to or implies, Preminger and his screenwriters burden the plot with a series of bewildering and boring scenes, further slowed down by the presence of the modern-day frame scenes between Mrs. Erlynne and Lord Darlington.

The pressbook for the film noted Preminger's predilection for long takes, discussing it as a money-saving technical innovation rather than a stylistic signature: "In one continuous movement, the camera filmed all of the closeups, medium and distance shots needed for each individual sequence. The most difficult scene was one that called for the camera to move through three rooms of a house, filming scenes in each room, ending in a ballroom where the camera made a 360-degree arc. This scene lasts nearly five minutes on the screen, and took nearly a day to prepare, but it saved more than two days of the actual shooting time it would have taken under the old procedure. In all, Preminger was able to save twenty days in the production of the picture." No doubt Preminger's speed was impressive, but "twenty days" is surely an exaggeration. (After the close of production in mid-August, the *Los Angeles Times* reported that Preminger finished the film "in 32 days instead of the scheduled 42".) Moreover, no shot in the film lasts as much as "nearly five minutes" (although a take of such length might, of course, have been shot and printed and then shortened, or cut into, in editing). In any case, the article shows Hollywood acknowledging and publicizing Preminger's style at around the same time that Hitchcock's long takes in *Rope* and *Under Capricorn* were also much noted by film professionals.

Preminger may have needed the technical challenge of long takes to sustain his interest in the project. He may also have been under orders from Zanuck to reduce production costs to the absolute minimum. In the end, the picture came in at $1,420,000. "Nobody was hurt by the picture, and nobody was elated either," Walter Reisch concluded after it was all over.[7] The film opened in April 1949 in New York, where Bosley Crowther pronounced it "strangely uninspired."[8]

The Fan is a troubling film. Everything hinges on the relationship between Mrs. Erlynne and Lady Windermere—a relationship that, to move the audience, must involve love. Yet in their climactic scene together, Preminger directs Madeleine Carroll and Jeanne Crain as if they were Judith Anderson and Gene Tierney in the bedroom in *Laura*. Perhaps Preminger *wants* us to understand that Mrs. Erlynne really hates and resents her daughter and sacrifices her own "happiness" so that she can feel justified in her resentment, in her silent act of bidding farewell forever to the burden of motherhood. It's hard to know how else to explain the film's lack of warmth, the failure of the characters and their dilemmas to resonate. The script seems at odds with the film. It should be a different script to suit the meanings Preminger wants the film to have—a script that would let him make a dark, perverse film, like *Angel Face*. Preminger doesn't believe in the nobility of Mrs. Erlynne or in the beauty and importance of the Windermeres' marriage, but his script doesn't let him criticize these values openly.

Preminger's insistence on moving his camera through doorways (for example, in the scene in which Lord Darlington visits the house that Mrs. Erlynne has rented) suggests a conscious rejection of Lubitsch's famous trademark of lingering in front of closed doors. If Preminger didn't think of Lubitsch at all, that would have been an even surer way of killing him. Yet there is perhaps a recollection of *Heaven Can Wait* in the gentle mockery to which the film submits the aged roué Darlington, especially in Mrs. Erlynne's reply to his suggestion that they dine together sometime.

In adapting the play, Preminger and his collaborators have made it significantly less funny. The one purely comic figure who remains—the Duchess of Berwick (the splendidly eccentric Martita Hunt, in her first of three Preminger films)—has less to do in the film than in the play; Darlington is robbed of some of his best lines; and what remains of the cleverness with which Wilde was so lavish is distributed parsimoniously among the characters. The foreknowledge, planted early in the film, that the Windermeres will end their days being blown up by the first German bombs to fall on London casts a pall over the proceedings.

Though the performances of Carroll and Crain are better than adequate—Crain in particular pulls off her role with a spirit and panache not found in all her films—of all the principals, only George Sanders seems ideally cast. An actor not known for the ability to suggest deep reserves of emotion, Sanders brings the hint of a long-suppressed romanticism to the scene in which Darlington professes his love to Lady Windermere and asks her to run away with him.

The window on the Victorian past opened by Mrs. Erlynne's narration is tinted by no nostalgia. Mrs. Erlynne evokes the past without regret or idealization, but in a spirit of dry lucidity. Lady Windermere's much-anticipated ball not only falls short of Ambersonian dimensions but is so fraught with stress that it seems placed in the film less to commemorate the vanished glories of an age than to depict the age's anxieties. The ball sequence is an appropriately distressing centerpiece to a glum film.

The fakeness of the streets is a limiting factor. The film should be about London as a place that murmurs, knows things, suffers, and goes on—a living being, which the London of the film (despite the stray souvenir of Preminger's location expedition, such as the opening crane shot and a few back-projection plates) clearly is not. The studio abstraction weakens the film (which is not true of *Laura* and *Daisy Kenyon*, both of which give us a sufficient idea of urban place). In *The Fan*, stylization substitutes unsuccessfully for the concrete image of society, and Preminger fails to find the appropriate *style* for the film. Because Preminger's London doesn't exist, we are forced to seek the drama inside the character's souls—but these are spaces to which, in Preminger's mise-en-scène, we can never have access.

The high point of the film is the scene in Darlington's house. The sense of women trapped by male power, and specifically the male voice (as the men's conversation is heard over shots of Mrs. Erlynne and Lady Windermere hiding), is strong, and Preminger's tracking shot, accompanying them as they try vainly to escape, is a vivid expression of his sympathy.

The fan itself, one of a series of objects in Preminger's films that signify femininity, is a screen, a decoration, a source of coolness (as such superfluous, as the cynical auctioneer points out, in the London winter of the present-day frame scenes). It is a metaphor for film (it oscillates; it both reveals and conceals) and for the narrative (it opens and closes; it unfolds). Though men introduce it into the narrative circuit (in the first flashback scene Lord Windermere buys it as a present for his wife), the fan is also an object of exchange and an instrument of communication among women (instead of the letters that Mrs. Erlynne declines to write, she and Lady Windermere exchange fans), and it stands for women's self-determination and freedom of action. The fan also communicates between the past and the present, signifying a coming and going through time.

In its temporal telescoping, *The Fan* bridges *Laura* and *Bonjour Tristesse*, being about, on the one hand, the need to wear a mask to cover a dark secret and, on the other, memory and mirrors. In *The Fan*, the film frame becomes a window (or the window a frame) on a past that slips and interposes itself between two presents: in an unusual optical effect, a mirror in a tailor's shop becomes a frame within which the flashback is printed as an image that gradually increases in size, coming toward us like the Lumières' train, gradually engulfing the frame of the mirror and becoming one with the frame of the film. In *Bonjour Tristesse*, Preminger will find another visual metaphor for the past's invasion of the present: the glimmers of color that lap like waves over various parts of the CinemaScope frame—a figure that shows us that memory and cinema are like each other and that the past is not just a time, or a place, or an image, but a physical force. In *Tell Me That You Love Me, Junie Moon* and in *Such Good Friends*, a mirror will again be the site of a transition to the past.

13

From Self to Self

In Preminger's autobiography there is a single reference to a famous fellow Viennese: "According to Freud, the ability to forget is the sign of a healthy mind."[1] Later in his life, Preminger certainly seemed to have forgotten *Whirlpool*, though it is a fascinating work that reveals much about his conception of cinema.

Fox optioned Guy Endore's novel *Methinks the Lady . . .* in December 1945 and assigned it to Preminger. Endore worked with Harry Kleiner on two successive script drafts, the second dated April 2, 1946. These drafts remain close to Endore's novel. Joan, the wife of noted psychoanalyst Spence Gillian, is caught trying to shoplift a piece of jewelry from a department store. In addition to her kleptomania, Joan suffers from a raft of neuroses stemming from her relationship with her father. She is accused of the murder of one of her husband's female patients, but Spence demonstrates through deft psychoanalysis that the killer is actually Dave Harper, the insane store detective who caught Joan shoplifting and tried to blackmail her for sexual favors.

The project languished for more than two years. Then, in November 1948, Andrew Solt was assigned to work on a story outline and a script; and that same month, Gene Tierney and Richard Conte were announced for the leads. Meanwhile, Preminger had been keeping an eye open for other projects. He hoped to get Cary Grant and Rex Harrison to star in an adaptation of A. P. Herbert's novella *House by the River* (which Fritz Lang would eventually film with Louis Hayward and Lee Bowman). He told Zanuck he wanted to do *No Way Out*, Lesser Samuels's story about a racist criminal's vendetta against an African American physician, but the project went instead to Joseph L. Mankiewicz (who noted in a telegram to Zanuck: "I believe Otto, with his usual facility for stepping over the other customers, has already sent you a wire about it").[2]

Solt's December 11 outline for *Methinks the Lady . . .* , which gave the characters new names and changed the villain, encouraged Zanuck: "I believe for the first time we are beginning to get somewhere on this story." Zanuck told Preminger, "I like your idea of an 'outside story' and an 'inside story'—that is, I like the idea of it." What this idea was, exactly, is unclear, but it perhaps referred to either, or both, of two key dualities in the story: the surface charm of David Korvo (as the villain was rechristened) masking his hidden evil, and the surface normality of Bill and Ann Sutton (the new names for the psychiatrist and his disturbed wife) concealing unacknowledged tensions and weaknesses.

From Endore's clever and unusual novel only a few elements are retained. Of the many differences between the novel and the film, the most decisive concern the identity and motive of the killer. The film's David Korvo is an astrologer and hypnotist whose powers are so advanced that a few hours after having his gallbladder removed in order to give himself an alibi, he is able to hypnotize himself into feeling no pain as he leaves the hospital to commit murder. His victim is Mrs. Theresa Randolph, who, in addition to being Bill's patient, is Korvo's former lover. Korvo kills her in order to prevent her from revealing that he has swindled her out of large amounts of money.

Solt finished his script (now called *Whirlpool*) on March 21, 1949. Zanuck made some detailed comments in a March 30 memo, concluding, "I believe this story has the makings of a very unique and unusual picture. It can have much of the quality and strangeness of *Laura* . . . As now written it is contrived and artificial in many spots, but correcting this is mainly a matter of straightening out motivations and providing proper dramatization." In another reference to *Laura*, indicating that Zanuck and Preminger hoped (as with *Fallen Angel*) to recapture the earlier film's success, Zanuck notes that "we must make David an interesting and intriguing character, just as interesting as Clifton Webb was in *Laura*." To help ensure this result, Preminger went to New York in April to hire José Ferrer (then acting in a hit Broadway comedy, Robert McEnroe's *The Silver Whistle*) to play Korvo. Ferrer's casting was announced on April 13.

Preminger's New York trip came on the heels of another excursion taken on behalf of a different project. In late February, Preminger and Philip Dunne went together to Shanghai and Hong Kong for three weeks to do research for a "semi-documentary" film for Fox, tentatively titled *The Far East Story* or *Transit Hong Kong*. Shanghai was then one of the last outposts of Chiang Kai-shek and his Nationalists, who had lost most of the rest of the country to the Communists. Dunne and Preminger found it, as Dunne later wrote, "a dying city" in which "law and order . . . had almost completely broken down." After they returned from China in March, Dunne and Preminger worked on an adventure-story script, to be filmed partly on location and partly in Hong Kong studios, about the current Chinese conflict. Because, as Dunne recalled, "we included as one of the characters a corrupt Nationalist general," the studio canceled the project. Nothing came either of another project Preminger had going, something called *Modesta*, for the recent Fox import Valentina Cortese.[3]

Meanwhile, Preminger turned to Ben Hecht for a rewrite of *Whirlpool*. Known as a speedy writer, Hecht thrived at Twentieth Century-Fox. In his autobiography, he wrote that Zanuck was "quick and sharp and plotted at the top of his voice, like a man hollering for help." Hecht got on well with Preminger, whom he described as "witty and Boccaccian" and whom he included among the "sane and able" directors he had worked with.[4] A controversial figure because of his support for the Irgun, the Jewish Palestinian terrorist group whose activities Preminger would dramatize in *Exodus*, Hecht would be credited as "Lester Barstow" for the foreign release of the film. *Whirlpool* was not among the works that Hecht regarded with much pride. David Raksin recalled, years later, meeting Hecht and congratulating him on what he thought was "a very good job . . . He gave me an angry look, to dismiss me, and he stalked off, because he thought it was terrible."[5]

Hecht turned in his first draft on May 2. The next day, Zanuck, in a memo, pronounced Hecht's work "excellent," with the exception that "the last act lacks suspense or tension or excitement due to the fact that no one is in jeopardy." Zanuck then proposed the general outline of the ending sequences, set in Mrs. Randolph's house, as they were finally shot—including two perhaps unconscious links to *Laura*: Korvo's choice of a staircase as a hiding place and the playback of prerecorded speech on the sound track over a scene of death. Preminger went to New York to work with Hecht on the new ending. Hecht's revised script, dated May 16, elaborated on Zanuck's outline for the final scene. Another scene called for Ann, in her jail cell, to hear her own thought-voice and lines of dialogue from earlier in the film. This scene (which would have strongly suggested *Saint Joan*) was eventually omitted.

The script posed few problems to the Production Code Administration. Breen wanted one of Korvo's lines—"I've nothing against women betraying their husbands. It usually improves their manners"—rewritten. The new line was perhaps even more offensive, if offense was to be found: "Personally I have nothing against women betraying their husbands. Even our government is against monopoly." Production started on June 6 and closed without recorded difficulties on July 22; the final production cost was $1,295,000.

The completion of *Whirlpool* coincided with the close of a chapter in Preminger's personal life. On August 10 Marion Mill Preminger filed suit for divorce in Santa Monica Superior Court. She charged that Otto "left the house on January 17, 1946, and never came back." (Early 1946 probably marked the beginning of Preminger's affair with Natalie Draper.) The divorce was granted on August 25.[6] In her autobiography, Marion looked back on her Hollywood life, to which she now bid farewell: "I lived for ten years with my vanity hurt, until I lost it. All that time I was confused and disturbed and thwarted in my ambitions, until I lost them. All the time I was married to the greatest director in the world, what my own life lacked most was direction."[7] It's possible that Preminger modeled Theresa Randolph in *Whirlpool* on just such an uprooted and confused person as Marion, who also dabbled in hypnotism and psychoanalysis: "in Hollywood one takes lessons in everything," she wrote.[8]

Apparently the couple remained friends, for Louella Parsons reported seeing them dancing together at the Chanteclair nightclub a few nights later.[9] Subsequently, Parsons's column portrayed Preminger as a romantic figure, saying that he "beaus all the beauties in our town and makes their hearts beat faster" and calling him "the secret passion, as well as the café-society love, in the lives of many women who have cried salty tears over him."[10]

Preminger's films often begin *without* the viewer, forcing the viewer to catch up. *Whirlpool* begins just after the heroine has committed an act she has already forgotten when we see her at the start of the film. The film starts by taking us in, including us in her amnesia—as it will do later when, on hearing the clock strike, Ann mechanically performs a series of actions. By not showing Korvo planting in her mind the posthypnotic suggestion that these actions will fulfill, the film makes the sequence into a mystery. Preminger capitalizes on the interest of cinema in movement and the human figure; moreover, he capitalizes on the specific interest taken by Hollywood cinema in the figure of the female star. *Whirlpool* is a film about Gene Tierney, and Tierney delivers what is probably (alongside her performance in John M. Stahl's *Leave Her to Heaven*) her best performance.

Early in the film, the camera establishes an attitude toward Ann that could be described as relaxed but persistent in its continual medium-shot surveillance of her movements. This mode of observation suggests, by analogy, that we are watching Ann watch herself. The space around her, in the frame, figures the mental space of her own unconscious self-observation. The smoothness of the camera movements suggests this unconsciousness by emphasizing the mechanical quality of her actions, the regular, dancelike transitionality of all her movements.

Preminger's films constantly emphasize the splitting of the self into autonomous observer and automatic actor. The shot of Laura's return in *Laura* is one example of this splitting: the distance of the camera suggests that Laura enters her own home as a kind of object among its other objects. Another is the scene in *Where the Sidewalk Ends* in which Dixon is made to disguise himself as Paine's killer (i.e., as himself) in order to repeat, for the eyes of a witness, his own exit from the scene of the crime. Both these scenes fuse reality and dream, as does, in a more explicit manner, *Whirlpool*. The camera movement that accompanies Ann's descent into Theresa Randolph's living room is objective in its registration of visual images and subjective in its structure.

When Ann descends the stairs, she sees herself (is seen by the camera) from the point of view of a man watching her. This man could be Korvo, or Bill (to whom she says, "You made me play-act," and for whom she is "locked away in the characterization of a serene and devoted wife"), or her father. For Gene Tierney, it could be Preminger. Ann/Tierney displays herself and is conscious of doing so (as is Laura/Tierney presenting herself to the camera in the flashback montage of *Laura* and Morgan/Tierney modeling a dress in *Where the Sidewalk Ends*).

At the bottom of the stairs, Ann encounters Theresa's portrait, which both prescribes a place for her and denies her access to that place. The portrait of the murdered Theresa on the wall of her own living room recalls the portrait of Laura in her apartment: it occupies the heroine's attention in a shot composed in a manner reminiscent of the shots of Mark standing under Laura's portrait. (Gérard Legrand writes that when Ann discovers Theresa's corpse, "it's as if Laura returned home before Mark to find herself murdered in the guise of some boyfriend's 'ex,' but under her unforgettable portrait."[11] A later commentator, Odile Bächler, adds, "the cinephile has the impression that Laura returns here to take a step back from herself, in seeing her double . . . killed.")[12] Whereas Laura's portrait organizes the space of her living room, so that all the positions in that space radiate from it and refer to it, Theresa's portrait functions as a sign of death and closure, marking the space it dominates as off-limits.[13]

Whirlpool is Preminger's critique of the male need for perfection in the woman, just as the figure of the hypnotist Korvo, exploiting the weaknesses of women for his gain, is a critique not only of the director's role but of the activity of Hollywood cinema: promising escape ("I can release you from a torture chamber called Mrs. William Sutton"), designing traps for the unsatisfied desires of women. It is appropriate that on being introduced to Korvo at Tina Cosgrove's party, Baron Feruccio says, "You're in the movies, Mr. Korvo." Their hostess corrects him: "Mr. Korvo reads souls, guides human destinies with the aid of the stars, and makes fortunes for other people at a nominal fee." The double meaning of "stars" is no doubt significant: all the same words with which Mrs. Cosgrove describes Korvo could describe Preminger's function.

Korvo's hypnosis of Ann in a parlor at Mrs. Cosgrove's house allows Preminger to construct a triple metaphor of cinema. First, the therapeutic function of the hypnosis—to provide forgetting, escape, and rest—is also that of Hollywood cinema. Second, the hypnotist's control over his subject mirrors the director's over his actor (Korvo becoming an off-screen voice determining and commanding the visible—years later, Preminger would direct Liza Minnelli this way in *Tell Me That You Love*

Me, Junie Moon). Third, Korvo demonstrates the effectiveness of this control by ordering Ann to move around the room, producing movement for movement's sake (she is to perform three actions, crossing the room each time: drawing the window curtains, closing the door, and returning to her chair). This demonstration affirms the power of cinema to restore, or to reproduce, movement. Prior to Korvo's direction, Ann is, for the moment, motionless. In fulfilling his apparently meaningless instructions, Ann proves the magic of cinema, its superiority to photography and its closeness to life.

In this closeness lies the paradox that *Whirlpool* examines. For Ann acts, apparently, not under her own free will, but in obedience to Korvo. The image of life they produce together is not spontaneous and authentic, but staged and externally directed (in this, it echoes Mrs. Cosgrove's claim, "I don't have to attract society, I manufacture it"). Yet Bill later informs us, authoritatively, that a hypnotized subject will not act in a way contrary to her moral principles—a point that Ann affirms in this scene when she refuses to place her hand in Korvo's. Even in fulfilling the apparently innocuous agenda of his demonstration, Ann appears to balk. Midway between the window and the door, she walks into close-up and stops, a thoughtful, troubled expression on her face. Korvo prompts, "Close the door," and she proceeds. Ann's hesitation contradicts the effects of naturalness and flow created by the camera movement with which Preminger records the scene. Her hesitation marks a resistance to the surface flow of movement in which she is caught up, a consciousness of the alien nature of the characterization being imposed on her. *Whirlpool* expands from the conflict between self-will and external will, making this conflict an instance of the battle between a woman's self-definition and a definition imposed by men. In this, the film again follows *Laura*, in which the heroine declares at one point, "I never have been and I never will be bound by anything I don't do of my own free will," and, later, says, "For the first time in ages I know what I am doing." (In front of the window in Mrs. Cosgrove's parlor stands the same Asian statue seen in the first post-credits shot of *Laura*—another allusion to the battle of wills staged in that film.)

In the consciousness of self-will and in the knowledge of what one is doing, Preminger locates the possible region of autonomy of the heroines of *Laura*, *Forever Amber*, *Daisy Kenyon*, *The Fan*, and *Whirlpool*. Of these five statements of the theme, *Whirlpool* is the last and the most explicit. The ending of *Whirlpool* may seem ridiculous by external standards of verisimilitude, but within the terms of the film, Ann's ability to remember her previous visit to the Randolph house and, just as important, her refusal to help Korvo escape ("Bill, I'm lying. I can't lie to you anymore, no matter what happens") are necessary moments in a restitution to selfhood.

14

The Unseeing Witness

After *Whirlpool*, Preminger's next project was *Night Cry*, based on William L. Stuart's novel. Rights to the book had first been purchased in April 1948 by independent producer Frank P. Rosenberg, Jr.'s, Colony Pictures. Rosenberg was represented by Ingo Preminger, who, after following his brother to California in 1947 and getting a job with the Nat Goldstone Agency, had lately opened his own talent agency. Undoubtedly it was through Ingo that Otto learned of the story and recommended it to Zanuck, just as it was through Ingo's deal making that Rosenberg sold his rights in the book to Twentieth Century-Fox and got himself put on the Fox payroll as associate producer.

The studio assigned Ben Hecht to write the script. Working with his customary rapidity, Hecht turned in a rough first draft for *Night Cry* on November 26, 1949, followed by a final script, now titled *Where the Sidewalk Ends*, on December 7 and a revised final script on December 14. Zanuck held several conferences on the script, but his preproduction contributions to the film seem to have been more limited than on any of Preminger's previous films (at least since *Margin for Error*, which was produced while Zanuck was absent from the studio). In his notes on the December 7 script, Zanuck recommended several ways to mitigate the guilt of the main character, Mark Dixon, a tough and violent police detective who accidentally kills gambler Kenneth Paine, a suspect in the murder of out-of-town high roller Morrison, and then tries to cover up his responsibility for Paine's death. Zanuck's recommendations concerning Paine's killing were followed, and in the final film, an encounter in which Dixon slugs a night watchman while disposing of Paine's corpse occurs offscreen.

The December 7 script portrayed the gangster Scalise as a drug addict. At the Breen office's insistence, this angle was omitted in later revisions, although it did not escape Breen's notice that in Hecht's December 14 script, the character was described in stage directions as speaking in a "dreamy" voice. "This, of course, could be completely inoffensive," Breen commented, "and yet on the other hand, in view of the character of this man in the previous script, could be suggestive that he is under the influence of narcotics. As you know, the latter possibility could not be approved." Nevertheless, in the film as shot, Scalise repeatedly uses some kind of inhaler and is seen lying down in beds, and Dixon calls him Dream Boy.

The hint of another peculiarity possessed by Scalise—homosexuality—eluded the PCA, possibly because the agency was blinded by a more flagrant gay characterization in the script ("The character of Rafferty, in the model agency, is completely unacceptable. He is unmistakably a 'pansy' "; Hecht eliminated the character). Yet Scalise's penchant for surrounding himself with muscular young men (notably Neville Brand's Steve), his use of a sauna as a hangout, and his habit of receiving visitors while lounging in bed all carry strong gay connotations on-screen; and the exaggerated nonchalance actor Gary Merrill gives Scalise's comments about Morgan, Paine's wife ("There was a girl with him . . . I didn't quite get her name"), imply a contempt for women that also types him as homosexual.

Dana Andrews was cast as Dixon, Craig Stevens as Paine, and Gene Tierney as Morgan. Lee J. Cobb refused the role of Morgan's father, Jiggs, a cabdriver who becomes a suspect in Paine's killing. The part went to Tom Tully. Starting on December 27, 1949, Preminger shot for three weeks on twenty-two locations in New York, before finishing in Hollywood. Gary Merrill, who started his assignment on the film in New York, was uncomfortable with the role of Scalise. Visiting Preminger's hotel room to ask for advice, Merrill found Preminger sitting in his tub, shaving. "Otto, I've never played a gangster. I'm having trouble getting into the part." Preminger replied, "Don't tell me. Tell your psychiatrist."[1]

Where the Sidewalk Ends is one of the many films that Preminger, in later years, systematically forgot. He made a slight exception for Rui Nogueira, for whom, in 1970, he dug up memories of "Bert Freed [playing Dixon's partner, Klein], that actor with the round face who had to drive a car down Broadway and who didn't know how to drive. He was

such a bad driver that I had to help him hold the steering wheel." Preminger also recalled "Karl Malden, a beginner, to whom I had to explain
that there was an enormous difference between theater and film, and
that in film you shouldn't shout your lines."[2]

This was Preminger's version of an association that Malden, in his
autobiography, remembered as uninstructive. (Malden, by the way, had
appeared in several other films before *Where the Sidewalk Ends*.) His
first scene in the film was the one in which his character, police lieutenant Thomas, walks through Paine's killing as he imagines it. "The shot
called for the camera to be tracking me the whole time. And there was
Otto, stationed high above it all with the camera on the boom. I delivered all of two lines when he shouted, 'Cut! Karl, you are wrong!' He
started out full steam, shouting at me, I don't even remember what. Do
this and that, look here and there!" According to Malden, "After five or
six takes with Preminger berating me after each one, he had me so confused I didn't know whether I was in New York or Los Angeles, let alone
how to play the scene. I didn't know what hit me. All I wanted to do was
get out of there. Humiliation has never been the way to a great performance as far as I'm concerned, and it didn't work that time. Finally, after
another three or four takes, he hollered, 'Print!' and that was that. He
had done his job on me, initiated me into the Preminger school of filmmaking."[3]

After the close of production on March 10, Zanuck, whose involvement during the scripting had been, as we have seen, relatively restrained, viewed the assembled picture and found that it needed
extensive retakes. Hecht completed the required revisions on March 29.
Five scenes underwent extensive reshooting: Dixon's interrogation of
Scalise in the hotel room where Morrison (Harry von Zell) is killed; both
of the two scenes in Dixon's hotel room; the action sequence in which
Dixon tries to force Scalise and his men to kill him and then, when the
police arrive on the scene, foils their escape attempt (as first filmed, this
sequence took place in an off-season amusement park, with a final fight
between Scalise and Dixon on a Ferris wheel); and the final scene, in
which Dixon reveals to his superior, Foley (Robert Simon), that he killed
Paine.

The additions all play up a theme completely absent from the script
that was first shot: Dixon's father, it now emerges, was a gangster, and

Dixon's hatred of criminals—above all, Scalise, a protégé of Dixon's father—stems from his obsessive drive to prove himself different from his father. Thus Dixon acquires a new motive for covering up his killing of Paine: his dread of acknowledging his criminality, which he seems to believe is an inherited trait. In the script as first shot, Dixon's father had been a traffic cop who was killed during a jewelry heist. The new scenes thus turn Dixon's original motive with regard to his father into its opposite: instead of wanting to avenge his father, Dixon wants, symbolically, to kill him. The new scenes brought the story of *Where the Sidewalk Ends* closer to that of Sidney Kingsley's play *Detective Story*, to which Paramount had purchased the rights and which would shortly be filmed by William Wyler. (In January 1950 Paramount tried to dissuade Fox from filming *Where the Sidewalk Ends*, claiming—even before Dixon's father's profession was changed—that it was too similar to *Detective Story*.) One of Zanuck's motives in demanding the retakes may have been to capitalize on the similarity between the two films, knowing that *Where the Sidewalk Ends* would reach theaters before *Detective Story* and hoping to steal the competition's thunder.

The mostly sparse score included heavy use of Alfred Newman's "Street Scene," a staple in Twentieth Century-Fox thrillers. The film's final production cost was $1,475,000. The film was released in July; reviews ran to the favorable side, Philip T. Hartung in *Commonweal* noting that "it is seldom that a movie works up such anxiety in the audience, who can hardly wait to get the answers."[4]

"A cop is basically a criminal," Preminger remarked to writer Doran William Cannon during the story conferences for *Skidoo*. "Why do cops like to hit people? Because when they become cops, they satisfy an instinct for violence, only it becomes legalized violence."[5] Whether characterized as an attempt to avenge or to destroy his father, Dixon's violence (with his desire to escape responsibility for it) remains at the core of the film, and Dixon's ambivalence, characteristic of Preminger's conception of character and projected ideally through Dana Andrews's performance, supports the imposed new scenes.

In fluidity of camera movement, *Where the Sidewalk Ends* approaches the peak of *Fallen Angel* in Preminger's work to date. Space is elastic: the fight in the Turkish bath, after disrupting the partitions of the space, ends with an upward crane shot as Steve gets up from the floor. *Where the Sidewalk Ends* also shows a greater reliance on close-ups than is typical of Preminger, indicating his determination to strip this drama to its essentials and to emphasize Dixon's relationships with his savior (Morgan) and his gangster adversary (Scalise).

Where the Sidewalk Ends is one of Preminger's great films on obses-sion and anguish. The central moment of anguish in the film comes when Dixon is ordered by Thomas to put on Paine's coat and hat and thus to assume, for the witness Mrs. Tribaum, the identity of the mur-derer he really is. Preminger films this moment in a characteristic man-ner: the camera, in motion throughout the sequence, moves toward Dixon, not to isolate him or separate him from the group of policemen, but to underline his dual existence inside and outside the law, for others and for himself.

The numerous shots that crane and tilt down from the front door of Paine's apartment building toward the window of Mrs. Tribaum's base-ment apartment testify to a compulsion to repeat: again and again the camera's gaze is driven downward to the window, in search of the source of the complementary gaze, that of the woman, first to verify that she sees, or, more often (since for the most part she is asleep as she sits by her window), that she doesn't see. It's as if she held a key to the enigma of the film, an enigma that is elsewhere distributed across spaces and faces that offer no enlightenment. If indeed she holds this key, she is un-conscious of it. Only Lieutenant Thomas's questioning leads Mrs. Tri-baum to realize that the man she saw leave the building was not Paine. She remains, however, unable to recognize Dixon as the man, even when Dixon, at Thomas's insistence, again assumes the disguise of (a man dis-guising himself as) Paine.

The figure of the unseeing witness, who doesn't know what she sees, returns again in the film in the character of the cabdriver who, on his way out of police headquarters, passes Dixon, who is on his way in, with-out recognizing Dixon as the man he took to Grand Central Station on the night of Paine's death. Later in the film, Dixon enters another door-way to pass someone on the way out: Morgan, leaving Mrs. Tribaum's apartment after her father has been arrested. Such crisscrossings of characters illustrate, or are commented on by, a reproach made by Lieutenant Thomas: "A lot of fancy footwork you did last night, Dixon, you and Mr. Paine." When Dixon replies in self-defense that "it couldn't be helped," Thomas continues, "I don't understand how you didn't see him . . . You must have practically passed each other." Dixon himself comments later on his propensity, or fatality, for passing *through* places, when, on finding himself in Morgan's apartment without knowing how or why he came there, he wonders, "Where the devil am I? I keep coming and going."

If the dance of two characters passing each other is a significant motif, the repetitive camera movements toward Mrs. Tribaum's window suggest an impasse. At her window, there is a blockage, a stop in the continuity of the film, an insistence on a message that has not been transmitted. One meaning of this message is the knowledge of death. Paine is dead, but Mrs. Tribaum doesn't know it. This statement can be converted into a proposition that describes the general condition of the film's characters, who are dead without knowing it (as Paine bears his own death inside his head in the form of the silver plate left there from a war wound), who have yet to accede to the knowledge of their death. Dixon precedes them (just as he is the first to arrive at Paine's apartment and, for a while, the only person to know that Paine is dead). When he writes the letter to Foley ("To be opened in case of my death"), he knows he will die, and he writes from the perspective of one who is already dead ("I didn't have the guts to tell you this while I was alive . . ."). Dixon's foreknowledge of his own death finally liberates him to act against Scalise, but before he reaches that suicidal decision (which resembles Eddington's reconnaissance flight in *In Harm's Way*), he remains the anguished prisoner of the need to conceal his knowledge from the other corpses who, unlike him, have not yet been made aware of their death, among other dreamers who have not yet been wakened.

The failure to recognize, to see, which unites Mrs. Tribaum and the cabdriver, is shared by Thomas himself, who becomes fixed in his delusion that Jiggs Taylor killed Paine, and by Morgan, who unhesitantly transfers her faith to Dixon. In the whole film only two characters possess unerring insight: Dixon, who knows instinctively that Scalise killed Morrison, and Scalise, who realizes that Dixon killed Paine.

The secret that Mrs. Tribaum holds is a key to Preminger's cinema: sighted but blind, awake but asleep, she embodies the function and the quasi-hypnotic state of the film viewer (her habit of sleeping at the window, which she says she started after her husband died, is, no doubt, a commentary on female film spectatorship during and after World War II and on the urge to defeat loneliness by going to the cinema to sleep and dream). She represents the fallibility of the consciousness that mistakes itself for the creator of what it perceives. In seeing and not seeing, she is a figure exactly complementary to Dixon, who offers himself to view but at the same time hides himself. (The shot in the restaurant during which, having received word from Klein that Paine's body has been found, Dixon visibly shakes off his anxiety about the news as he prepares to rejoin Morgan, beautifully conveys this duality.) Furthermore, Mrs. Tribaum's vision, if she were able to take full possession of it (to repeat fully the moment of seeing Dixon descend the stairs in Paine's disguise), would be capable of dooming Dixon. That is, if she could truly see, her sight would be able to kill.

15

Private Arrangements

In 1950 Preminger negotiated a new contract with Twentieth Century-Fox. Starting on May 1, the contract called for him to direct four pictures within four years, at $110,000 per picture, for the studio, which had the right to use his services for one half of each year. This contract enabled Preminger to spend half of each year working in the theater, his first artistic love, and living in his favorite city, New York. The first film under the new contract was a remake of Henri-Georges Clouzot's *Le Corbeau*. Preminger was assigned to the project, initially called *The Raven*, on May 8, 1950. He told Jacques Rivette, "I admired Clouzot's film very much, and just for that reason, I changed its script considerably, keeping only the general theme and the nature of the main characters, in order to make a work totally independent from the original."[1]

Clouzot's 1943 film, based on a story by Louis Chavance and cowritten by Clouzot and Chavance, is set in a small French town that is thrown into turmoil by anonymous letters accusing various townspeople of misdeeds. The central characters are the town's new doctor, Germain; an attractive patient, Denise, who seduces him; an older doctor, Vorzet; and his young wife, Laura, who is attracted to Germain. At the end, Vorzet is revealed as the letter writer and is killed by the mother of a young man who was driven to suicide by one of Vorzet's letters.

On May 11, 1950, writer Howard Koch made detailed notes on the story, pointing out how the remake would differ from the original. Dr. Germain would now be a misogynist instead of, as in the Clouzot film, someone who appears to dislike children. The relationship of Germain and Denise would start as a purely sexual one, but "we will add some scenes in which we see that they are actually falling in love." Most interesting, and Premingerian, is the notation, "We will develop the subordinate characters as normal people with good and bad traits, not as consistently and entirely evil as they are portrayed in the French film." Among the other notes, one that seems to have been disregarded as the filmmakers proceeded was "Find opportunities for comedy relief." The filmmakers decided to set the film in Quebec, to which province a location scout was dispatched on May 17.[2]

In the early scripts, first called *The Last Letter* and then *The Scarlet Pen*, Zanuck balked at Koch's attempt to delve into the psychology of Laurent (Clouzot and Chavance's Vorzet) and his wife, Cora (formerly Laura), and he wanted to cut the scene in which their shared insanity is revealed: "The audience doesn't give a damn about *folie à deux*. They've come to see two crazy people committing murder." Koch objected: "Without that particular relationship, the picture makes no sense. It's an obligatory scene." Giving Koch a hard look, Zanuck replied, "In this studio I decide what's obligatory."[3]

Linda Darnell was cast early in preproduction as Denise, and Zanuck announced that Joseph Cotten and Maureen O'Hara would play Pearson (Germain) and Cora. Subsequently, Charles Boyer joined the cast as Laurent, and Cotten dropped out; Richard Todd was briefly sought to replace him, before Michael Rennie assumed the role. The substitution of Constance Smith for O'Hara in late August, just before the start of production, completed the casting of the main parts.[4]

Preminger and Koch tried to include in the film a reference to abortion (which had figured in Clouzot's original): the August 14 script has Laurent telling Pearson that a letter "implied that your relationship with Cora has had a rather embarrassing result—don't get excited now—and you took advantage of my absence to . . . get rid of the embarrassment with the aid of surgery." In a letter to the studio on August 21, Breen pounced on this detail and warned the filmmakers to expunge it. Breen also objected that the fade-out of a scene between Pearson and Denise, and the fade-in on Pearson waking up the next morning and stretching "with a relaxed air of well-being," seemed "indicative of a sex affair." Although the stretching was omitted from the next draft of the script, the finished film still fades out on Pearson and Denise embracing in her bedroom (in her bed, for that matter). The film also contains two unmistakable allusions to Laurent's impotence.

The film went into production in September. Much of it was shot on

location in and around St.-Denis-sur-Richelieu (near Montreal)—
though by no means "the entirety" of the film, the claim of an on-screen
title in the release prints to the contrary. Some scenes were shot in a
studio in nearby St. Hyacinthe, Quebec, and some in the Twentieth
Century-Fox studios in Hollywood. Still, the film marks a peak, in Preminger's films to its date, in the proportion of location to studio shooting,
and in this respect it points the way to *Anatomy of a Murder*.

According to Preminger's autobiography, it was during the Quebec location shooting that he made the acquaintance of Mary Gardner, a New
York model who visited Rennie several times. "Gradually her attention
switched from him to me."[5] Preminger and Gardner would marry in
Brooklyn on December 4, 1951.

After the company's return to Hollywood, Zanuck decided to do
some retakes and added scenes. These were filmed during November,
and at least some of the new material required Preminger and several
actors, including Rennie, to return to the Canada location at the end of
the month. Shortly after that, the picture was retitled *The 13th Letter*.
The final production cost was an economical $1,075,000.

A film of exhaustion and reflection, *The 13th Letter* is the grayest of
Preminger's films. The exterior shots are filled with characteristic camera movement, fluid and sometimes relentless, but the emotional tone is
depressed, slack. Joseph LaShelle's cinematography excels in the scenes
in the church: the glow of daylight through the windows, the clear light
and strong shadows on the altar are extremely effective in establishing
a somber, melancholy mood that is enhanced by the location sound
recording. Yet the dialectic of *Laura, Fallen Angel,* and *Where the Sidewalk Ends* is lacking in *The 13th Letter,* which presents, for our intellectual interest but not our emotional commitment, a closed world.

The tone of *The 13th Letter* is determined to a large extent by the
characterization of Pearson and the personality of Michael Rennie. Pearson has come to the town fleeing from intimacy, and he spends much of
the film continuing this flight. He is cold and withdrawn, only now and
then betraying any of the inner struggle to repress his emotions—by, for
example, his troubled looks as he tries to occupy his mind by working
on a clock while Denise talks to him. Bland and remote, Rennie cuts a
mediocre figure next to the sublime intellectual arrogance of Pierre Fres-
nay, who played the equivalent part in the Clouzot film. Joseph Cotten,

whom Zanuck had originally cast in the part, would have been more engaging, more obviously the sensitive, wounded man withdrawing from the world but pulled back into it by his essential humanity.

Preminger's lack of interest in the relationship between Denise and Pearson, once it has passed through its early stages of erotic tension and oral sadism (Denise twice bites him on the wrist), borders on the pathological. The scene in which Pearson tells her about his failed marriage is handled with startling conventionality in two over-the-shoulder close shots, Darnell glamorously lit in a conventional manner; only the fact that the scene is set on a moving ferry and filmed on location elevates it slightly. Preminger tosses off the film's ending, which establishes the happiness of the couple in a town now restored to normal, without even trying to make it convincing.

Only in its last fifteen or twenty minutes does *The 13th Letter* become fully engaging. Two late scenes, both confessions, exist at a higher level of realization and abstraction than the rest of the film. The first is the scene of Laurent and Pearson in Laurent's office, in which Laurent tells Pearson about his marriage. Boyer's performance and the quality of the writing elevate the scene, which begins with a single take of Laurent's reaction on being told that Cora told Denise that she was having an affair with Pearson. The camera pans with Laurent as he rises from his desk, passing beneath the portrait of Cora and behind Pearson, who is sitting in the foreground; then the camera tracks past the back of Pearson's head to dolly into a close shot of Laurent. The progressive concentration and abstraction of the shot turn it into the intense and sustained revelation of a character—for the first time—in a film that has been mainly occupied with shifting surfaces.

The second scene is that between Cora and Pearson in her hospital room. Preminger uses the bareness of the setting, with its largely blank walls, to great advantage, all the attention being concentrated on the actors' faces, and only two objects—the cross mounted on the wall over Cora's bed and the lamp blazing in the background (recalling the lamp during Laura's interrogation in *Laura*)—temporarily assuming prominence. (The scenic nudity anticipates the scene in *Exodus* in which Karen finds her father in the hospital.) The climax of the scene is Cora's remorse over the suicide of one of the recipients of the letters. It is after she expresses her sorrow over this unintended consequence of her actions that she begins to relax; by spontaneously touching Pearson's shoulder, she indicates that she is already free of her obsession with him and on the road to recovery. On the whole, *The 13th Letter* is one of Preminger's more indifferently acted films, but here Constance Smith's performance is natural, Rennie's is very simple, and the intimacy of the scene is touching.

A major theme of *The 13th Letter* is the rebuke of moralism. Denise reproaches Pearson for his "hateful coldness and superior airs, like someone standing in judgment." The dialogue (adapted from Clouzot's film) between Laurent and Pearson in the latter's office concerning the relativity of "good" and "evil" is obviously central to this theme and clearly anticipates Paul Biegler's speech in *Anatomy of a Murder* about people not being just good or bad, but many things. For Preminger, as for Laurent, no constant and immutable standard of morality exists. The metaphor of the swaying ceiling lamp (also borrowed from Clouzot), which Laurent uses to prove his point, is related to another symbol in the film, the clock that Pearson sets in motion. Preminger sets up a specifically cinematic analogy between time, the possibility and form of any movement, and the shifting basis for moral judgment. The metaphor will reappear in the child's swing at the end of *Bunny Lake Is Missing*: again, good and evil change places.

Finally, the importance of the folie à deux, the private arrangement, to Preminger's work as a whole cannot be overestimated. Laura and Waldo, Stella and Judd, Ann and Korvo, the Laurents, Ann and Steven Lake: each couple shares a private understanding that unites them against the world, but the bond cannot be maintained. In each case, it is the woman who breaks it, rejecting the man for the world and abandoning him to a solitary madness.

16

What the Jury Decides

The early 1950s saw Preminger in financial difficulty. In August 1950 Marion sued him for failing to pay $48,800 she claimed was due her under the terms of their 1949 property and maintenance settlement. At around the same time, the IRS put a lien on his Fox salary, claiming unpaid tax obligations from 1948 and 1949. In February 1951 the Treasury Department seized Preminger's Beverly Hills house and stationed guards on the property until he came to terms with the government. As of July 1951, he still owed the IRS $32,632.[1]

He does not seem to have let these troubles defeat his general optimism. His new Fox contract allowed him to shuttle back and forth between New York and Hollywood. "I think it's a wonderful life," he said. "I enjoy being in either place; it's childish to love New York and hate Hollywood, as some people claim to do, and the variety keeps me young and alive and stimulated."[2] In 1951 Preminger's setbacks were offset by a major success, the Broadway hit *The Moon Is Blue*, which will be the subject of a later chapter.

In February and March 1952 he worked as an actor (for the first time since 1944) in Billy Wilder's *Stalag 17*. His performance as German POW commandant Oberst von Scherbach became Preminger's most famous. Wilder recalled, "He had trouble remembering his lines and would get very embarrassed and say that he was rusty because he hadn't acted in so many years. He said he would send me a pound of caviar every time that he had a day when he blew his lines. Well, several pounds of caviar arrived for me in the course of shooting that film, but he gave a fine performance."[3]

Preminger's next film as director, *Angel Face*, was one of the films Howard Hughes rushed into production at RKO in 1952 to take advantage of Jean Simmons's talents before the expiration date on her contract. Chester Erskine's original script for the film was first submitted to the PCA in January 1952. Behind the placeholding title *The Murder* lay, perhaps, the writer's admission that coming up with a title was the least of his problems with the story, which may have been loosely based on a notorious 1947 case involving seventeen-year-old Beulah Louise Overell and her boyfriend, George Gollum, who were acquitted of blowing up Overell's parents aboard their yacht in Newport Harbor, California. (In his review of the film in the *Los Angeles Times*, Philip K. Scheuer noted that *Angel Face* "bears certain overall resemblances to a recent sensational case.")[4] In Erskine's script, a rich young woman conspires with a young man to murder her stepmother by rigging her car. The crime comes off as planned except that the girl's father, for whom she has what the studio script synopsist calls "an abnormal affection," is killed along with his wife, and the two killers quickly fall under suspicion and are arrested. A slick lawyer arranges for the couple to marry in jail and plays on the sympathies of the jury to get them acquitted. Conscience-stricken over the initial crime, the hero tries to kill the woman, who dies in an accidental fall downstairs, whereupon he goes to the police to turn himself in for killing her.

Irving Wallace worked on a rewrite on the film, which Hughes chose as a project for Simmons and RKO contract star Robert Mitchum. With Simmons's end date approaching, and probably suspecting that she would be inflexible in enforcing it, Hughes needed a director who could be trusted to finish her scenes on schedule. He turned to Darryl F. Zanuck for help. Zanuck recommended Preminger, who was then idle at Fox. (In August 1951 Preminger announced plans to film Harry Kurnitz's not-yet-published novel, *Reclining Figure*, a suspense thriller about art forgery, but nothing came of this.)

As Preminger told it, he reported to RKO and was given a script. "At four o'clock in the morning, I called Mr. Hughes, and I told him: 'Howard, I hate your story; please don't make me do this film.' He replied to me: 'My friend, I need you. You come tomorrow to my studio, and you come like Hitler: the studio will be yours, and you can hire whomever you want. And everything will be done the way you want it.' I couldn't say no because I was under contract, and also because he was my friend. If I hadn't made the film, Zanuck would have been angry. So

I hired two writers right away, and we wrote till eight o'clock in the morning. At nine o'clock, I shot the scenes, and each day we proceeded in the same way. I don't like this system, and I don't believe in it. It's a miracle that the film was a success."[5]

The writers Preminger hired were Oscar Millard (a client of Ingo's) and Frank Nugent. According to one source, Ben Hecht also worked on the script for Preminger.[6] Mona Freeman, cast as Mary, the discarded girlfriend of the Mitchum character, said before the film was released, "It was remarkable what was accomplished during the making of this film by director Otto Preminger, because he actually undertook to revise the script and made many notable improvements."[7] Publicity materials noted that the screenplay was done "under the close supervision of Producer-Director Otto Preminger. Millard handled the original adaptation [of Erskine's original story] with Nugent polishing the dialogue." No mention was made of Irving Wallace's contribution.[8]

A crucial change was made in the plot: the hero is no longer a conspirator in the murder, which the heroine now commits on her own. The ending caused some difficulties. Preminger, Millard, and Nugent proposed having Frank (Mitchum) commit suicide, leaving evidence inculpating Diane (Simmons) and ensuring that she would be punished. In a June 20 letter to RKO's William Feeder, Breen rejected the ending as violating the Production Code's provisions on suicide. In the ending as eventually shot, Diane kills herself and Frank in a car. Since this was still suicide, the Breen office hesitated, but Feeder noted on July 8, "We won our point on our contention that the scene does not glamorize or sentimentalize the suicide theme." Throughout the film's production Feeder continued to pass pages along to the Breen office as they were written. The last changes were submitted on July 14, late in production.

The best-known story about the making of *Angel Face* was recounted by Stewart Granger in his autobiography. Granger, then Jean Simmons's husband, recalled that "in spite of the bullying Otto Preminger who was directing it, Jean enjoyed the film. She adored Mitchum and used to tell me what a good actor he was, how funny and amusing and how easygoing, he just wouldn't let things get him down." According to Granger, "In one scene Bob was supposed to smack Jean, and she told the very gentle Mitchum to really let go. Otto insisted on take after take and poor Jean's cheek was getting redder and redder. As Otto insisted on yet another take, Mitchum turned to him and let him have one right across the face. 'Would you like another, Otto?' he said. Otto quickly agreed to print the last take."[9]

Mitchum would work with Preminger on two more films (*River of No Return* and *Rosebud*). The two men's public statements about each other were usually complimentary, even affectionate. Reflecting on his career late in his life, Mitchum called Preminger "one of the funniest men I know. And Otto gets so overwrought that he just becomes a pudding of inarticulation, frustration. I think that Otto is a very gifted producer. He has great taste. But I do not think that he is a very good director."[10]

The production reports for *Angel Face* (or *The Murder*, as it was still called until November) indicate no major difficulties. On the second day of shooting, the company wrapped early because Jean Simmons became "unable to continue." On June 21 Mitchum was ten minutes late. On June 23, thirty-two minutes were lost because of a back-projection machine malfunction on the set of Fred's café, Frank's hangout. Scheduled for twenty-eight days, the film finished in twenty-nine and only slightly exceeded its modest budget, coming in at a total cost of $1,039,000. Production closed in late July. The film was released in February 1953 to mixed reviews.

In an extraordinary sequence of *Angel Face*, Preminger gives us a model of how to see his characters. The sequence begins with a shot of Diane and her father, Charles Tremayne (Herbert Marshall), playing chess in his study. The shot is partly framed by the open balcony door, a frame that freezes the moment in time and makes of it an idyllic and emblematic scene. The chess game is intercut with shots of Frank alone in the room outside his bedroom. He looks out the window, then goes to the phone and calls Mary's workplace. Failing to reach her, he discontentedly removes his tie (the camera tracking forward to a close shot), darting glances, as he does so, offscreen right (in the direction of the window). (His look offscreen repeats the look by which he first sees Diane and is drawn into her world for the first time.) The staging of the scene implies that Frank has been waiting for Diane to emerge from the house and that, disappointed, he instead calls Mary, still wishing, no longer with much hope, for Diane to appear. (That instead of Mary he

reaches a third woman, one Janey, shows that women are interchange-
able for him at this point.)

Meanwhile, Tremayne concedes the chess game. "You could win any
time you wanted if you really tried," Diane tells him affectionately (and
reproachfully?), revealing that behind the play of the chess game lies another level of play, the fond father indulging his daughter by letting her
win—and behind this, the darker truth that if Tremayne loses, it's out of
boredom and lack of will, out of having given up trying at this game, as
he has given up trying at life. Diane refills his brandy glass ("just a little,"
he specifies—another idyllic detail, indicating the denied option of
overindulgence), then lets him know that she has laid out his bedside
table with his preferred objects: milk, cookies, cigarettes, matches. They
say good night on the balcony.

Diane wanders slowly into her room. Her face and manner suggest a
brooding discontent whose object we can only guess at. She goes to the
piano, on whose lid sits a framed photograph of her father (in his—
Herbert Marshall's—matinee-idol days), at which she pauses to look.
Then she sits at the piano and begins to play the film's theme as the
camera (which has followed her across the room) tracks forward into a
close-up. At first she looks downward; as she plays, she raises her eyes
slightly, then looks up and stares at a point just below the level of the
camera, so that light reflects from her pupils.

This shot dissolves slowly into a close-up of the face of a clock,
whose glass, too, reflects points of light (during the dissolve, the stars of
Diane's pupils seem to become part of a larger constellation with the
stars of the clock face). The camera tracks back to reveal that the clock
is sitting on a table outside Frank's bedroom; Diane, in a nightgown, enters hurriedly up the stairs and knocks at the bedroom door. Frank
emerges, and Diane proceeds to tell him that her stepmother has just
tried to kill her with gas.

What happens in this sequence? We can summarize it this way: Diane is placed between, and before, two men, one of whom is placed in
turn between two women, neither of whom is available to him. Choosing—or condemned to—solitude, Diane plays the piano, and as she does
so, the camera is concerned with the surface of her face, behind which
an imagination is at work, an imagination that at the moment we see it is
perhaps conceiving the false story that she will tell Frank. (Frank, when
he rejects her story, utters the crucial line: "I don't pretend to know what

goes on behind that pretty little face of yours, and I don't want to know.") The film identifies Diane as the source of narrative, of *the* narrative. The film, and Diane, will return to the settings and objects that this sequence mobilizes. When, late in the film, she wanders through the empty house, Diane returns to the chessboard (picking up the king, a symbol of her father and a reminder of the abdication for which she scolded him: "You could win any time you wanted"), then goes to the room outside Frank's bedroom. It is as if the first sequence were the source of the second one.

The dissolve from Diane's face to the clock face tells us that she, too, is present in the world of the film as an object—not any object, however, but a fatal one: death is at work behind the clock face, just as it is at work behind the human face ("like bees in a hive," as Cocteau tells us in *Orphée*). The film renders Diane inanimate: frozen in the very death that she contemplates. The points of light reflecting from her pupils—frozen on her face over the last seconds of the shot—are enough to depict her as an art object, an object of beauty. As she looks offscreen or, to be more precise, when she positions her eyes so that they reflect the light in the way Preminger and Harry Stradling want, she is looking at nothing. Out of the nothing she looks at will come the nothingness that spreads over the film as, two by two, the characters are evacuated from it (Charles and Catherine; then the servants, Ito and Chiyo, who leave the house to look for new employment; then Frank's friends, Bill and Mary, who pair off together; and finally Diane and Frank).

Diane's existence is characterized by a holding back, an inability or a reluctance to participate, a failure to commit herself fully to any particular line of action. As Jacques Lourcelles writes, "the key to her behavior, if there is one, is to be found not in her intentions but rather in an inexpressible wavering between her intentions and her acts, a wavering that the mise en scène is marvelously capable of suggesting at the very moment when she gives up justifying it."[11] The multi-planar existence of the character compounds the ironies in Preminger's treatment of the legal system, which, *Angel Face* makes clear, produces not truth, but a story. As Barrett, her lawyer (splendidly played by Leon Ames), says to Diane, "The truth is what the jury decides. Not you, not me, not Frank." In the courtroom, the District Attorney and Barrett offer competing narratives, neither of which is adequate to the truth as we understand it. (It is significant that neither Diane nor Frank, apparently, is called to testify.) Our own understanding of "the truth" is only partial. Because of the ellipses in the film's narrative, several facts remain unknown to us: whether Frank and Diane have had sex (as the District Attorney assumes), whether Frank knew that he was giving Diane information that she would use to kill her stepmother, whether Catherine would have gone into business with Frank (as both Barrett and the Tremayne family's lawyer, Vance, apparently believe), whether Diane engineered the gas leak in Catherine's room (as her unbelievable story to Frank, describing Catherine's attempt to kill her with gas, leads us to assume), why Catherine apparently takes no steps to protect herself even though she seems to believe that someone in the house has tried to kill her. It is not even out of the question that the killing of Charles along with Catherine was not, in some sense, an intentional result of Diane's manipulation (as Reynold Humphries postulates in his psychoanalytic reading of *Angel Face*).[12] The entire section of the film devoted to the trial and to Barrett's pretrial maneuvers is the construction of discourses that attempt to explain Frank and Diane's actions. In rejecting both Barrett's and the District Attorney's versions of the couple's story, we are brought to recognize that our own version is no more satisfying or complete.

The scene of Diane's attempted confession in Barrett's office is one of the greatest scenes in all Preminger's work, not only because of the hopeless truth made vivid by the contrast between Diane's stern, slow, dreamlike gravity and Barrett's indomitable cynicism, worldliness, and superficiality, but because, to form a triangle with the two principals, the scene introduces the key Preminger figure of the impassive witness, incarnated by the stenographer, Miss Preston. The mystery of this figure, who is reduced to the function of recording witness, permitted in no way to express any opinion or feeling about the drama that unfolds before her, will engage Preminger in several films, notably *Advise & Consent*, in the shots of functionaries during and after the Senate subcommittee hearing. (Capra has a marvelous version of this figure in *It's a Wonderful Life*: the servant who pushes Mr. Potter's wheelchair.) The impassive witness has a similar function to that of the interested but silent observer, incarnated in another scene in *Angel Face* by Bill when he and Mary listen to Frank's attempt to renew his relationship with Mary. (Cf. the two-shot of Maida and Parnell in *Anatomy of a Murder*, when Biegler asks Parnell to give up drinking and help him with the case; and the two-

shot of Munson and Brig Anderson in Munson's hotel suite in *Advise &*
Consent, in which Munson is a silent witness during the conversation
between Brig and the President.) Frank's words are directed to Mary
alone, who alone responds to them, but they also fall, so to speak, on the
blank and thoughtful face of Bill.

A major pleasure in certain Preminger films lies in the pure sensu-
ousness and the rhythmic quality, relatively divorced from narrative, of
their depiction of moving cars. This element becomes stronger as Preminger liberates himself from back projection, but even in the earlier films
he finds many opportunities to show cars in motion through real space:
the pulling up of cabs and other vehicles in front of buildings becomes a
refrain in *Laura* and *Daisy Kenyon*; *Fallen Angel* features numerous
scenes of moving cars; in *Whirlpool*, Ann drives from her house to
Theresa Randolph's house; in *Where the Sidewalk Ends*, Dixon and Klein
drive through New York at night in their patrol car.

In *Angel Face*, the car is both a potent symbol (the duality of Frank's
ambulance/Diane's sports car introduces a further level of complexity in
the film) and a signifier of Los Angeles culture, but at the start of the
film, at the same time as it becomes a meaningful sign, the car also
functions as a pure rhythmic element, an assertion of pure movement,
linked to the movement of the camera itself. The first section of the film
is structured by the departures and arrivals of cars: Frank and Bill's am-
bulance leaves its garage in the first shot to arrive at the Tremayne house
two shots later, and on its return trip it is followed by Diane's sports car.
The moving camera imposes on the movements of these vehicles a second, discreetly authoritative movement: in its forward motion toward the
points of the vehicles' departures and arrivals, the camera is urgent but
unhurried; its lateral pans after the vehicles as they drive away are calm.

Finally, the car is a death trap, a murder instrument. As Frank invol-
untarily drives it backward off the cliff, Diane's car appears as a purely
illogical and chaotic element: pure destruction taking over the film,
evacuating the narrative (which seems to end prematurely, before the actual end of the film). Preminger's impassive embrace of this destructive-
ness, with its threat of meaninglessness, marks the first clear emergence
in his work of a negativity that will become increasingly important in
Anatomy of a Murder, *In Harm's Way*, and *Bunny Lake Is Missing*.

17

The Accepted or Common Thing

Vienna-born F. Hugh Herbert's play *The Moon Is Blue* opens in the observation tower of the Empire State Building with the chance meeting of Patty O'Neill, an aspiring young actress, and Don Gresham, a successful architect. Patty agrees to accompany Don to his apartment but puts him on notice that she intends to remain a virgin. Over the course of the evening, these two characters, joined by a third, aging playboy David Slater, the father of Don's estranged girlfriend, discuss various aspects of sexual morality. Despite the interest that both men take in Patty (though they are also repelled by her embarrassing frankness), and her attraction to both, she gets through the night with her virginity intact. The next morning, Don and Patty return to the Empire State Building, where he proposes marriage.

In late 1950 Preminger teamed up with Richard Aldrich, Richard Myers, and Julius Fleischmann to stage Herbert's play. At the time, Preminger, Aldrich, and Myers were also embarked on another project, *Four Twelves Are 48*, a farce by Joseph Kesselring, who wrote *Arsenic and Old Lace*. The plot of *Four Twelves* suggests a kind of inversion of *The Moon Is Blue*: Kesselring's title refers to four Osage Indian women of successive generations, the first three of whom became unmarried mothers at age twelve. The production (which featured Anne Revere, Pat Crowley, Ernest Truex, Doro Merande, and Hiram Sherman) opened on January 17, 1951, to poor reviews and closed quickly.

By then, Preminger had already shifted focus to *The Moon Is Blue*. For the main parts, he engaged three accomplished actors: Barbara Bel Geddes, Barry Nelson (as Don), and Donald Cook (as David). Preminger was on his best behavior with the three stars. As Nelson recalled, "Maybe we caught him in a good mood because Otto never once raised his voice to any of us . . . He was very, very careful."[1] Though Preminger forced Cook, against his wishes, to use a fake southern accent, the actor praised his director's skill. "He didn't maneuver us just for the sake of movement, to break up a talky scene. He always found a good reason why we should move. And if he couldn't find it, he would have Herbert write something in."[2]

After the show opened in Boston on February 19, 1951, Herbert locked himself in a room for two days with coffee and Benzedrine to rewrite the third act.[3] The revised work opened in New York at Henry Miller's Theatre on March 8 and was an immediate success. Noting that the production "aroused almost continuous laughter in the audience," Ben Hecht called *The Moon Is Blue* "the perfect example of successful mental comedy. It is a play whose sole quality is wit . . . In its bright sentences are the whimsy and confusion of the civilization in which three characters exist."[4] Reviews tended to strike a note of skepticism won over. John Lardner wrote in *The New Yorker* that the play "seems to sparkle, and perhaps it does." Brooks Atkinson seemed to doubt that what he saw was actually a play ("It is more than likely that nothing happens after all") but admitted that the actors conveyed "a definite impression that something delightfully crack-brained is taking place in the most normal circumstances."[5] The play would run for 924 performances at its original theater before closing on May 30, 1953.

The Moon Is Blue marked the renewal of one of Preminger's most enduring professional relationships: Maximilian Schulz, whom Preminger had known since his Gymnasium days in Vienna and who later worked under Reinhardt and Preminger at the Josefstadt, functioned as Preminger's assistant on the production. While *The Moon Is Blue* was running, Schulz, taking the name of his favorite character in the play, changed his name to Max Slater. He would go on to serve as dialogue director on most of Preminger's films. According to Martin Schute, who worked on several Preminger films starting with *Bonjour Tristesse*, Slater "was there with the script, with Otto all the time. If something had to be done on the script, then Max would be off talking to the writer. Or if Otto wanted a particular kind of performance out of someone, he would get Max to rehearse it with that person before they came onto the set, which of course saved time. He would rehearse it the way Otto would have rehearsed it, because he knew him that well." Eva Monley, who worked with Slater on five Preminger films in the 1960s, recalled, "I think that O.P. could talk to him about doubts, about beliefs, and Max spoke well, thought well, and honestly. He always got a straight answer from Max . . . Probably a lot of things that none of us knew about, he always talked about with Max."[6]

In October 1951 Preminger announced that he and Herbert would produce a film of *The Moon Is Blue* independently in New York.[7] In April 1952 (following an unsuccessful attempt by Preminger to launch another comedy, Herman Wouk's *Modern Primitive*, about a painter and his model, which opened and closed in Hartford; Albert Bassermann appeared in it as a Dutch art critic), they contracted with United Artists to finance and distribute the film.[8] For the first time in his film career, Preminger secured creative autonomy, including what would become known (when such stipulations became more common) as final cut. *The Moon Is Blue* also marked the first time that Preminger shared in the profits of one of his films. He deferred his producer's and director's fees, and Herbert his fee for the movie rights to the play, in exchange for 75 percent of the film's profits.

If April 1952 was, thus, the month in which Preminger declared his independence from the major studios, it was also, strangely enough, the month that saw him laboring for the studios in the most anonymous job he ever undertook. Delmer Daves had wrapped *Treasure of the Golden Condor*, starring Cornel Wilde, at Fox and then left to England to set up his next film, *Never Let Me Go*. Zanuck ordered a last round of added scenes for *Condor* and assigned Preminger to direct them. "I don't want the script. Give me the *pages*," Preminger told the producer, Jules Buck.[9] Preminger later remembered a scene, set in a condor's nest, featuring Wilde, Constance Smith, and a snake. "I just let them shoot it . . . It was only one scene, it took an hour."[10]

Preminger cast David Niven as Slater in *The Moon Is Blue*, over the objections of United Artists, who considered the actor, then at a low point in his career, "washed up." To prepare Niven for the shooting, Preminger had him join Diana Lynn and Scott Brady in the California run of the play in the summer of 1952.[11] During rehearsals, Preminger got under Niven's skin once with the remark, "Mr. Niven, you are so charming off the stage. Why can't you be charming on it?" Otherwise the two men got along well.[12]

In November, William Holden joined the cast of the film as Don and became a partner in Preminger and Herbert's company, Holmby Productions, signing on (as had Niven) at less than his normal salary in exchange for a share of the profits (for Holden, 20 percent). The film's Patty would be Maggie McNamara, who had played the role in 1951 in Chicago (where her costars were Leon Ames and Murray Hamilton, both of whom also, like her, went on to appear in Preminger films).

Encouraged by the success of Herbert's play onstage in Germany, Preminger decided to shoot a German-language version of the film on the same sets and during the same production period as the English-language one. The writer to whom he entrusted the German script was Carl Zuckmayer, two of whose plays he had earlier been interested in: *The Captain of Köpenick* (which Preminger hoped to stage on Broadway in 1938) and *The Devil's General* (which Preminger considered filming in 1951).[13] As Preminger told a reporter, "The German market is very important in Europe, and a real German picture will do 90% more gross than one in English. *The Moon Is Blue* lends itself to this because it has a very small cast." Preminger estimated that shooting the second version would add only eight or ten days to the schedule and about 10 to 15 percent to the cost of production.[14] Johannes Heesters, Johanna Matz, and Hardy Krüger were cast in the leads.

The budget Preminger submitted to United Artists in late 1952 is a marvel of economy. The combined production cost for the two versions of the film would be about $350,000 (raised to $373,445 just before the start of shooting). This amount was exclusive of the deferred salaries of Preminger ($110,000), Herbert ($75,000), and Holden ($85,000) and the deferred payment of $200,000 for the rights to the play.[15]

After the film had become a success, Holden was reported in the *Motion Picture Daily* as admitting that he, Preminger, and Herbert had anticipated before making the film that the PCA would not approve it.[16] The first indication that *The Moon Is Blue* would run into trouble with the PCA came on July 13, 1951, when the Breen Office notified Herbert (who was already contemplating an independent film production of the play) that the play was in violation of the Code. Breen detected in the play "a light and gay treatment of the subject of illicit sex and seduction. While there is no actual seduction in the story, the general attitude towards illicit sex seems to violate that Code clause which states: 'Pictures shall not infer that low forms of sex relationship are the accepted or common thing.' Furthermore, the Code specifically provides that seduction or illicit sex should never be the subject for comedy or farce, or treated as material for laughter."

On December 26, 1952, Preminger sent a draft of the film script, dated December 11, to Breen. On January 2, 1953, Breen advised Preminger that the film could not be approved. Most of Breen's three-page letter consists of a list of lines of dialogue exhibiting "an unacceptably light attitude towards seduction, illicit sex, chastity and virginity." In chronicling the *Moon Is Blue* case in his memoirs about his work with the PCA, Jack Vizzard noted a few of these lines: "Men are usually so bored with virgins." "Godliness does not appeal to me." "Steaks—liquor—and sex. In that order." "I always feel uncomfortable on a high moral plane." As Vizzard wrote, "It was the flavor of talk such as this that created the question" about the script's acceptability—*not*, as legend has long had it (and as Preminger repeated in his autobiography), the utterance of the *words* "virgin," "seduce," and "pregnant."[17] (Nevertheless, in a *New York Times* piece published on July 12, 1953, Bosley Crowther reported that the film contained "some bits of language which, while they pass in contemporary talk, sound like minor explosions when they come from a film.")

Vizzard's analysis of the film pinpoints two more fundamental problems with the script. First, in having Don give as his reason for not seducing Slater's daughter, Cynthia, that she encroached on his male prerogative by coming to his apartment on her own initiative, "the story was saying that 'free love' was something outside the scope of morality altogether, was a matter of moral indifference." (This implication was only strengthened by Slater's indignation over Don's failing to make a pass at Cynthia.) Second, the film is so far from upholding the position of Patty, the film's champion of sexual abstinence, that it characterizes her (in Vizzard's words) as "eccentric" and firmly "puts her in her place" when Don criticizes her as a "professional virgin." For Vizzard, "this was the key to the entire controversy" and the reason why Breen, on the verge of retirement, chose "to make of this picture his last great orchestral flourish."[18]

On January 6 Preminger and Herbert told Vizzard and Geoffrey Shurlock that they disagreed with Breen and would shoot the film largely as written.[19] Off the record, the cultured and liberal Shurlock agreed with Preminger that *The Moon Is Blue* was not objectionable. Preminger "ultimately made Geoff his pet," Vizzard wrote, and the two had a long, amicable relationship.[20] United Artists head Arthur Krim and his partner, Robert S. Benjamin, accepted the risk that Breen would not be moved from his initial opinion on the script: in late January they deleted the clause from their contract with Holmby requiring the producers to deliver a film that would get the Production Code Seal.[21]

After ten days of rehearsing first the English-language cast, then the German, each for eight hours a day, Preminger started shooting on January 21. Unaware of the PCA's objections, journalists commented mainly on the bilingual production. The procedure was simple: first Preminger shot a scene in English, with the European actors watching; then he shot the same scene in German. Preminger later said that he liked only the English-language version of *The Moon Is Blue.* "It's an American play, typically American, and all the psychology, when it's translated into German, becomes very heavy."[22]

The brisk twenty-four-day production ended on February 18, and the film was ready for a Pasadena preview on April 8. Two days later, Breen phoned Preminger to say that he and his staff had screened the film and decided that it could not be approved for a Seal. The grounds were the same as those on which he had rejected the script: the "unacceptably light attitude toward seduction, illicit sex, chastity and virginity." In a rebuttal letter on April 13, Preminger affected a tone of outrage at Breen's "unwarranted and unjustifiable attack" on himself and Herbert, "not only as craftsmen who have served the industry for many years but as members of the community who have never been connected with anything shady, dishonorable, salacious or illicit." He argued that the film "is a harmless story" in which Patty and Don "represent the attitude of the picture," in favor of marriage, against Slater, whose libertinism they attack "in no uncertain terms." Preminger and United Artists, through lawyer Samuel I. Rosenman, appealed the PCA's decision to the MPAA board of directors and were denied, whereupon Preminger protested in public against "the standards of a group of competitors based on the hypocritical interpretation of an antiquated code."[23]

Exhibitors had been separated from distributor-producers by the 1948 "divorcement decree." Logically, it also freed exhibitors from the distributor-producers' association, the MPAA, and from the obligation of showing only films that had received the PCA's Seal, but this logic had not yet been subjected to a major test. *The Moon Is Blue* would be that test. United Artists decided that it would distribute the film without the Seal. The company devised a release strategy that would start with pre-release runs in major cities, hoping that the success of these engagements would encourage wary exhibitors to book the film.[24]

It was a move of great importance for American filmmaking. As Michael Conant has written, the Production Code was the instrument through which, "in essence, the five majors exercised censorship over the entire industry. The most important effect of this combination in limiting the supply of films was to restrict the production of pictures treating controversial issues. With a few notable exceptions, the code enforced conformity to a rigid, repetitious pattern of stories and plots that prevented new approaches to drama or new ideas in picture stories from reaching the screen."[25] By circumventing the Code, *The Moon Is Blue* showed that a range of possibilities existed outside this "rigid, repetitious pattern" of major-studio production—a range that independent producers were quick to claim as their own territory. By then, the eventual outcome—a marriage of convenience between the majors and the independents, in which the majors put up their persistent advantages in access to capital, distribution, and publicity against the independents' ability to develop projects rapidly and efficiently—was already foreseeable: in 1954, Preminger's own *Carmen Jones* would be the result of such a marriage.

The Moon Is Blue opened at the Woods Theatre in Chicago (which presented the film to adults only) on June 22 and at the United Artists Theatre in San Francisco three days later. On June 30, *Variety* made it official: "Any unity there might have been among the major industry elements against a film turned down by the Production Code Administration is now evidently broken."[26] The trade journal reported that three major chains had booked *The Moon Is Blue*.

Reviews tended to emphasize the rejection of the Seal and highlight the innocuous nature of the film. Manny Farber, in *The Nation*, found the film "flexible and interesting . . . [perhaps] because the director, Otto Preminger, can set up a modern apartment scene as shrill and phony as Broadway living actually is."[27] *Variety*'s year-end domestic-rentals charts put *The Moon Is Blue* at number 15 for the year 1953, with $3.5 million.

Exulting over the box-office success of the film, Preminger's publicity agent pointed out that "the picture has been shown without one cut and with advertising which in no way appealed or concentrated on the publicity which was forced upon it by the various censor groups."[28] (Graphic designer Saul Bass had come up with the design that was used in some, though not all, situations, showing two birds on a windowsill peeking under a blind—a modest beginning to what would become a prodigious collaboration between Preminger and Bass.) Behind the scenes, however, Preminger was fuming. In June he objected to United Artists' use of the line "Recommended for adults only" in advertising *The Moon Is Blue*, preferring the subtler "An adult story." UA executive Max E. Youngstein put his foot down, notifying sales director George Schaefer, "If I think one ticket sale will be lost, I must insist on using the words 'Recommended for adults only' everywhere."[29] Youngstein's intransigence annoyed Preminger, who complained to Schaefer that the advertising campaign both compromised him personally and endangered their battles with the censors.[30] But Youngstein insisted to Krim that "sex and the controversy about sex is selling the picture."[31] Preminger's contract with United Artists gave him the right to be consulted on advertising but left the studio final authority. This was a point that Preminger learned not to concede again.

The rulings in favor of *The Moon Is Blue* in state supreme courts in Maryland and Ohio and (in a suit against the Kansas film-censorship board) in the U.S. Supreme Court not only spelled the beginning of the end of the state censorship boards, but also, indirectly but crucially, weakened the Production Code. One of the key functions of the PCA was to help the studios craft their films in such a way that they would avoid local censorship. With local censors losing constitutional challenges, the PCA faced the imminent loss of a crucial justification for its own existence.

Times changed; Breen retired; Hollywood adapted. On June 27, 1961, the PCA granted Seals to both *The Moon Is Blue* and *The Man with the Golden Arm*, the film that brought Preminger into conflict with the agency again in 1955.

The Moon Is Blue remains a well-known title in film history, but it is not among the classic Hollywood films that are today much seen or discussed, and even among Preminger's admirers it has attracted little attention. The theme of most accounts of *The Moon Is Blue* is how innocuous the film seems from the commentator's later, more sophisticated vantage point. The film has suffered from its historical burden as a landmark case: the film itself, its qualities, its meanings, its style, have vanished behind the seemingly self-evident truth that it is actually not daring at all.

That *The Moon Is Blue* is in no way daring or provocative, by the standards of the United States in the early 1950s or by later standards, may be contested. Though no sexual act takes place within the narrative, the nearly exclusive concern of the dialogue with the possibility that sex could happen—or with the potential for a third party's being misled by appearances into assuming that two people have had or are going to have sex—makes *The Moon Is Blue* a highly unusual film for any period. Its singular atmosphere draws from romantic comedy and farce, but this is romantic comedy from which all sentimentality has been drained, and farce handled with a scrupulous and dry realism. It is an extremely pure work, its compression and rarefaction accentuated by the fact that it takes place, for the most part, within a single night, in a few periods of roughly "real time."

Preminger compounds the salaciousness of the play with the figure of Cynthia, who did not appear onstage. In the film, Cynthia watches from a fire escape through the window of Don's bedroom as Patty takes off her dress. Later, Cynthia, going out to meet Don, puts a coat over a short slip. When she joins him in the elevator, Don says, "Well, it didn't take you long to get dressed." As the elevator doors close, hiding the couple from the camera, Cynthia is heard saying slyly, "I've got news for you." (The closing of the elevator doors constitutes, perhaps, the film's one Lubitschian moment—one that is thrown away, happening on the margin of the story.)

The style of the film is elaborate in its plainness. More than any other Preminger film, *The Moon Is Blue* consists of people talking. Several passages are filmed as extended exchanges between two people, each in close shot: Patty sewing a button on Don's jacket while questioning him about whether he has a mistress; Don and Slater discussing the events of the previous night. Preminger follows the three characters assiduously and has his camera stay on them: when Patty hovers over

Slater on a couch, the camera frames their faces in a close two-shot from the side. When Don is on the floor and Patty bends over him, the camera is over her shoulder.

The concentration on faces is somewhat unusual for Preminger, suggesting a deliberate accommodation to a theatrical style of presentation, with an emphasis on dialogue. *The Moon Is Blue* is one of the Preminger films in which the relationship between film and theater can be considered most fruitfully. The theater is a world of speech, of language; but Preminger places this world within the world of silence and lets silence emerge through language. The mise-en-scène emphasizes the openness of the looks among the characters. Patty's calculated and affected air of being oblivious to the provocation created by her questions and revelations is as manifest on her face as the "look of wholesome rapture" that Slater takes as ample repayment for the $600 he gives her. Throughout the film, Don and Slater confront each other with frank, even affectionate looks, with an openness of gaze that is unusual between heterosexual men not only in American cinema but in American society. The emphasis on gazes shared and met is a device by which Preminger underlines the importance of the dialogue *as* dialogue—that is, as interpersonal verbal communication—and that gives it a material existence.

The relative closeness of the camera to the characters during much of the film (which takes place almost entirely in interiors) enables Preminger to make a dramatic point in the infrequent moments when the camera withdraws. When, brooding aloud to Don over the possibility of their becoming romantically involved, Patty remarks, "You picked me up, and no matter what happens, you'll always wonder . . . about all the other men who might have picked me up before you did, in just the same way," the camera pulls back to a wide shot that shows her wandering around the apartment, touching things and looking at the pictures on the walls. The medium-long-shot distance underlines Patty's troubled feelings and the gravity of the sentiment she has expressed. Near the end of the film, after Slater leaves Patty alone in Don's apartment, Preminger cuts to the widest possible shot of the living room, Patty sitting in an armchair in the background at screen right (perhaps it would be better to say upstage left, since the shot is so pointedly theatrical, exhibiting the set as a proscenium stage), contemplating whether to knock at Don's closed bedroom door. The wide view insists on a spatial unity that is also a temporal perspective, looking back on the whole momentous night that is now approaching its end. It is a summing-up, indicating that the drama has been moving all the time toward this decision; a gathering together of the scenes of the film into a meaningful coherence. Yet this coherence is alienating: it excludes the audience, which now sees Patty at a great distance, as someone present within the space of a set rather than inhabiting a world.

The modernity of the decor, accentuated in such shots, plays a role in this alienation of the viewer. The design of the sets in *The Moon Is Blue* is an implicit commentary on the society in which the film takes place, with its unreality, its regular geometry, and its lack of reference points (that Manhattan is shrouded in fog at the beginning of the film, so that Patty doesn't know in which direction to look for Brooklyn, is not accidental). Don's apartment is starkly and resolutely modern. Even in closer shots, Preminger makes a point of positioning and framing the actors so that, for example, a framed modern painting on the wall is visible in the background, between two faces, in the exact center of the shot. Don's decorative taste is important to the film: it signifies above all the quality of being contemporary, and it emphasizes the science-fiction aspect of the film's excursion into experimental morality. The decor of Don's apartment also defines the world of the film as an artificial world—and one, therefore, with strong affinities to the world of theater.

The Moon Is Blue is a key transitional work in Preminger's career. Marginally but amusingly, it looks back to *Where the Sidewalk Ends*, from which it brings back Tom Tully as a father who, outraged by an attempt on his daughter's honor, shows up at the malefactor's apartment ready to do him harm. (Since Mr. O'Neill is also a policeman, the Tully character here is a fusion of Jiggs Taylor with Mark Dixon. After knocking out Don, O'Neill kneels beside him and takes his pulse just as Dixon does with Paine in *Where the Sidewalk Ends*. O'Neill is luckier than Dixon, or perhaps more skilled, as he suggests by saying, "Twenty-three years on the force taught me just how hard to hit a man.") Don's line to Patty, "A girl's supposed to be intuitive about those things" (i.e., about whether a man intends to seduce her) is rephrased in *Anatomy of a Murder* in Biegler's question to Laura: "Doesn't a woman sort of instinctively know when a fellow's on the make?" Later, Slater alludes to "the unwritten law" that allows fathers to use violence to defend their daughters' virtue, the same law that Manion thinks also protects violent husbands. These repetitions show that *Anatomy of a Murder* can be seen as a sequel to *The Moon Is Blue*, continuing the earlier film's investigation of sexual morality.

In declaring his independence with *The Moon Is Blue*, Preminger also declares something of his philosophy. No doubt all "men of the world" could agree that it is normal for men to seduce women, or that Patty is justly reproached for being a "professional virgin." In making a film in which these implications are allowed to stand, Preminger criticizes the hypocrisy that weakened his *Forever Amber*. *The Moon Is Blue* implies a world in which people are free to make love to each other, exploit each other, and hurt each other, the world of gray and vague and experimental morality that Preminger would explore for the rest of his career.

18

All Things Are in Process, and Nothing Stays Still

River of No Return started out as an idea of writer Louis Lantz, who proposed an Old West variation on Vittorio De Sica's *Ladri di biciclette* (*The Bicycle Thief*), with the hero now a farmer who loses his horse (and his gun). As in De Sica's film, the stakes are raised by the hero's responsibility for the care of his young son. Lantz wrote a twenty-one-page treatment and worked on the screenplay under Stanley Rubin, a new producer at Fox, throughout the second half of 1952. In 1953 Rubin brought in Frank Fenton to improve on Lantz's work. Fenton turned in two drafts in March before completing a final screenplay on April 17, 1953.

Set in the American Northwest during the Gold Rush, the story concerns widower Matt Calder, who, having just completed a prison sentence for shooting a man, rejoins his young son, Mark, intending to replant his farm. Matt comes to the aid of a gambler, Harry Weston, and Weston's saloon-singer girlfriend, Kay, who are making their perilous way by raft to Council City to register a gold claim. Weston steals Matt's gun and horse and continues the journey alone. Chased off the farm by Indians, Matt, Kay, and Mark pursue Weston by raft, and after enduring many hardships, they reach Council City. Weston is about to kill Matt when Mark shoots the gambler, saving his father. Matt and Kay, now a couple, return with Mark to the farm.

This script was sent to the Breen office, which commented on April 27 that it appeared largely unobjectionable. The major sticking point was the killing of Weston by Mark. Breen wrote, "It has been the invariable policy of the Production Code Administration not to approve scenes in which children are shown taking the life of another. Accordingly, before your finished picture could be approved, it will be necessary that some other sympathetic character in your story do the shooting." On this crucial point, the filmmakers successfully resisted Breen.

A Zanuck memo on April 22 indicates that he had conceived of the film as a Marilyn Monroe vehicle in Twentieth Century-Fox's new CinemaScope process, with a heavy emphasis on spectacle and sex. "These episodes of the raft going down the river have got to stand an audience on its ear. It has got to be the Cinerama [sic] equivalent of the roller coaster." *River of No Return* was announced in early May 1953, with Monroe starring and Preminger directing. Stanley Rubin was happy with the former choice, but not the latter. "I thought of *River of No Return* as a piece of Americana, and I thought it needed a director who had worked in that area, which Preminger had not done . . . I was thinking of somebody like Raoul Walsh." Zanuck needed a project for Preminger, to whom the studio had to pay $2,500 a week whether he was working on a film or not. So Preminger was forced on Rubin, who got off on the wrong foot with his director by letting him know, over lunch in the studio commissary, that Preminger had not been his first choice. "I was a young producer then," Rubin said later. "I didn't realize it when I said that, but this was not the way to start a relationship with your director."[1]

After the autonomy he had enjoyed on *The Moon Is Blue* and "the almost-freedom" Hughes gave him on *Angel Face*, "I found myself more reluctant than I had expected to be back at Fox," Preminger recalled.[2] Since by the time Preminger was assigned to *River*, the writing was nearly completed, he had less opportunity to guide the development of the script than on any of the films he had done for Fox as producer-director.[3]

Rubin related a distressing incident involving himself, Preminger, and Zanuck. Rubin and Preminger had agreed to try to resist a change that Zanuck wanted to make in the script. They went together into a meeting where "Zanuck was explaining this change that he wanted, and I spoke up against it, and I waited for Otto to join me. And he never did. That was annoying. I lost that battle, and we made the change he wanted." This account parallels Dana Andrews's account of the meeting among Preminger, Zanuck, and Rouben Mamoulian about the characterization of Mark McPherson in *Laura*. In both cases, Preminger either deliberately deceived his colleague or (the more benign interpretation), at the last moment, simply thought it wiser not to disagree with Zanuck.

Whatever Preminger's motives, the result was the same: a decrease in the influence of his collaborator (first Mamoulian, then Rubin) over the film, and an increase in his own influence.

Shooting started at Devona Flats, Alberta, on July 28. By agreement with Preminger, Rubin did not accompany the unit to the location. *River of No Return* was Preminger's first film in CinemaScope. Rubin recalled that Preminger and cameraman Joseph LaShelle "just adjusted to the size of the screen, and I think it did not make as enormous a difference in setting up a shot as we had talked about before we went into production."[4] In an interview he gave to Jacques Rivette in Paris shortly after finishing production on *River*, Preminger said that CinemaScope created "a subtle change" in his mise-en-scène. "He appreciates it for the possibility of having a greater number of actors play at the same time," Rivette reported, "of combining more effectively, with the movements of the camera, those of the characters *in relation* to it."[5] Years later, with a long series of anamorphic wide-screen films behind him, Preminger claimed that the wide-screen process "really didn't make that much difference . . . What counts isn't the frame, it's what you put in it."[6]

Part of what he had to put in the frame of *River of No Return* was Marilyn Monroe, and neither of them was happy about it. According to Stanley Rubin, "It's very possible that if we hadn't cast Monroe before we hired Preminger, he would have fought against Monroe. Her style of acting, which was rather self-conscious, probably annoyed him . . . Then with the addition of Natasha Lytess, and the imbroglio that happened because of it, they were on the wrong foot from the word go."[7] Preminger, who first met Monroe's infamous acting coach in the dining car of the train taking the company from Los Angeles to Canada, soon came to despise Lytess. Paul Helmick, assistant director of *River*, later retained "a mental picture of her slinking around the set, standing in the shadows as she watched a scene being rehearsed or shot" so that she could privately advise Monroe on how to play it and whether to ask for a retake.[8] Monroe's costar, Robert Mitchum, later recalled, "Marilyn thought there was some magic in Natasha. She felt she needed someone other than a director, preferably a woman, to tell her when she did something right."[9] The clash was inevitable. Directors less autocratic than Preminger might well be expected to show irritation over having to direct an actor who is receiving, and heeding, competing instructions. According to Preminger, Lytess urged Monroe to drop her characteristic "soft, slurred voice" and "enunciate every syllable distinctly. Marilyn didn't question Natasha's judgment. She rehearsed her lines with such grave ar-tic-yew-lay-shun that her violent lip movements made it impossible to photograph her . . . I pleaded with her to relax and speak naturally but she paid no attention."[10]

As Preminger told it, Lytess's ill influence on the production culminated when she privately warned young Tommy Rettig that without a coach, he was in danger of losing his talent. At work the next day, Rettig, usually letter-perfect, had trouble remembering his lines and broke down in tears. When Preminger learned from Rettig's mother what Lytess had said to the boy, Preminger banished Lytess from the set. In this decision, he had the support of Rubin. On August 8 Monroe fought back through her agent, Charles Feldman, who spoke to Zanuck about the situation. Zanuck wired Preminger and ordered him to permit Lytess back on the set.[11] This incident, it can be assumed, hardened the mutual dislike between Preminger and Monroe. For a few days after the blowup over Lytess, Helmick recalled, "the tension on the set between the two of them made things unpleasant," and Preminger usually conveyed his directions to Monroe through either Helmick or Mitchum.[12]

On August 19, during the shooting of a raft scene, Monroe suffered a leg injury—fabricated it deliberately, according to her friend Shelley Winters, who was then working on a nearby location in Raoul Walsh's *Saskatchewan*—that was widely reported and stopped production for several days. In Stanley Rubin's opinion, "it was a legitimate accident, it was not a faked accident. She may have exaggerated it, as Marilyn could do. The publicist ran with it too and made it more than it was."[13] When she reported back to work to finish the aborted raft shot, she was on crutches, a walking cast on her ankle. Preminger, realizing (in Winters's view) that both the crew's sympathies and those of the studio were entirely with Monroe, proceeded to direct the actress "with a great display of European manners."[14]

Paul Helmick noted an improvement in the relationship between Preminger and Monroe for the rest of the production, though Monroe continued to have trouble with dialogue. "Some of it had to be done in short takes because she couldn't remember her lines," said Preminger later. "I didn't want to spend my entire life in Canada."[15] Forced to accommodate Monroe, Preminger had already learned from *Angel Face* to stay out of Mitchum's way. Stanley Rubin recalled, "He treated Mitchum differently from the way he treated Monroe. He didn't try to dominate Mitchum, which I thought was a very good decision on his part."[16]

Rubin's position on the production is indicated by another anecdote the producer recounted. "I had a quarrel with Otto about something in the script that I didn't think he had achieved. I can't remember what it was. He was annoyed about that. I was very upset in one phone call to him, when I had run the dailies, and I thought a scene had not done the script justice. He thought the scene was OK. He disagreed with me openly about it. That's where his veteran status, and my novice status, gave him the edge."[17] Preminger did not retake the scene.

The unit returned to Hollywood in early September to finish the film in the studio. Here, Preminger, Mitchum, Monroe, Rettig, and the crew labored for days on the many back-projection shots required for the long raft sequences. Monroe "hated getting into that tank on the raft and getting soaked for hour after hour," said Rubin, "and there was a point when she just didn't want to come out of her dressing room and get on the raft again. They called me to the set, and I went up there and talked to her, and she got back on the raft."[18]

After finishing shooting *River* in September, Preminger edited the film with Louis Loeffler in Hollywood. Somehow, Preminger found time to stage the American premiere of Gottfried von Einem's opera *The Trial*, based on Kafka's novel, at the New York City Opera, in October. According to a reviewer, "Each scene was hemmed in by high, grey walls broken only by gaping black windows. The action took place on a succession of movable scaffoldings, arranged to suggest a shabby room, an artist's studio, an office."[19] From *River of No Return* to *The Trial* is a considerable leap, even by the perpetually self-negating standard Preminger was rapidly defining. *The Trial* is both a logical and revealing choice of subject for Preminger: logical because the trial is a recurrent, even obsessive motif in his films, as commentators have often noticed (usually referring the theme to Preminger's own legal training—though, since Otto never actually practiced law, as a biographical motif it might be more plausibly and more interestingly linked to his relationship with his father, who was a trial lawyer), and revealing because Kafka's story, by making clear that the Law is both absurd and terroristic, points to a sub-versive, parodistic, critical strain in the treatment of legal proceedings and justice in Preminger's films.

Near the end of October, Preminger brought a rough cut of *River of No Return* to Paris to show Zanuck. On October 29 Zanuck expressed his dissatisfaction in a memo: "Not only do we need additional footage, but our picture is inarticulate. We have got to stop guessing about these relationships. Once and for all, we want to lay it on the line so there can be no doubt or confusion as to what our people mean and how they feel." He demanded three new scenes: a scene in Kay's tent-saloon dressing room with Weston (Rory Calhoun); a moment in which Kay ac-cuses Matt of shooting a man in the back and is overheard by Mark; and a "sex scene" in which Matt grabs Kay and pins her to the raft. (A trailer for *River of No Return* preserves a brief shot from Preminger's original scene, which was excised to make room for the new one: standing on the raft, Matt and Kay are framed against the shimmering water; Matt em-braces and kisses her passionately; Kay responds; there is no suggestion of his forcing himself on her.)

Jean Negulesco (with whom Monroe had worked on *How to Marry a Millionaire*) may have been assigned to shoot the new scenes (written by Frank Fenton) in November.[20] On December 2, Negulesco, but not Preminger, was on the list of recipients of a memo in which Zanuck con-tinued to rework *River*, demanding that what he was now calling "the attempted rape" be shot again, with increased violence, and devising a new scene of Matt giving Kay a massage. These scenes were written and shot to Zanuck's specifications. Though Negulesco's contribution to the film was not publicized, he later revealed it in interviews. When cinephiles turned to Preminger for verification, he said, "If there were retakes, they were not of any importance. Maybe I was out of town."[21] The added scenes don't ruin the film, though they make the progression of Matt's and Kay's feelings toward each other a bit confusing. The cave scene, in which Matt massages Kay (who is naked under a blanket), is an undoubted erotic high point, but the plot has to stop dead for it to occur, and one feels confident that Preminger's original film must have been more fluid.

Released at the end of April 1954, *River of No Return* reached number 19 in *Variety*'s year-end box-office report. According to Twentieth Century-Fox's internal accounting, the film's rentals for the year were $3,903,000 domestic along with $3,445,000 foreign, for a total of $7,348,000—allowing the studio to reap the handsome profit of $2,089,000 after print costs, advertising, and overhead. (The final negative cost of the picture was $2,197,000.) Keyed to Zanuck's intentions for the film, the reviews treated *River of No Return* as escapist drivel and noted its successful exploitation of Monroe's physique.

River of No Return is memorable above all for its mixture of a great sense of serenity and freedom, stemming as much from the use of Cinema-Scope as from the Canadian landscape, with a brooding sadness that emanates from the loping title song (recorded with eerie echo-chamber effects); from another song, the desolate minor-key "One Silver Dollar"; and from Marilyn Monroe's rendition of them.

Preminger's use of CinemaScope in *River of No Return* has attracted much attention from commentators, for whom André Bazin, in 1955, paved the way by calling *River* the one CinemaScope film he had seen "in which the format really added something important to the mise en scène."[22] Two scenes, one of them often discussed, the other not, illustrate what Bazin may have had in mind. The less-discussed scene comes early in the film: Matt, searching for Mark, circles around the stage of the tent saloon where Kay sings "One Silver Dollar." Given the limitations on the size of the space, the duration of the shot is a function of the width of the screen. If the scene had been filmed in standard ratio, to keep Kay in the frame as Matt circles the stage, and to preserve the scale of the CinemaScope scene (i.e., with Kay, the central figure, at the same proportionate height in the frame), Preminger would have had three options. One, he could have had the set built smaller, in which case it would have taken Matt less time to circle the stage. Two, the camera could have circled the stage with Matt (or opposite him), in which case the meaning of the shot would have changed completely: it would now have become a statement on Kay's total availability, emphasizing her status as a visual object for Matt in a way that the scene as Preminger filmed it (in which Matt apparently takes little interest in Kay) does not. Three, the scene could have been done in several cuts, in which case the composition would have changed drastically over the course of the scene, and again, the film's effort to frame the two figures together would have laid a greater stress on their relationship than is evident in the scene as it was filmed.

What does CinemaScope bring to this scene? First, as we have seen, duration—as a function of the size of the set, the unhurried pace of Matt's movement, and the proportions of the frame. Second, the creation of a continuous visual framework to link these elements, and duration itself, to Kay's song, the lyric of which concerns gambling, chance vicissitudes, and the transference of an object from one possessor to the next. The song is thus a commentary on the set (bounded by a craps table on one end and a roulette wheel on the other), on the town (which exists to support gold prospecting), and on the larger issues—as yet undisclosed—in the narrative (Weston's cheating Colby of his gold claim and his stealing Matt's gun and his horse; Mark's passage through the hands of successive custodians; Kay's passage from Weston to Matt). Third, and perhaps most obviously and most importantly, the linking of Matt and Kay in space in such a way that the chance, contingent quality of their presence together is underlined while, simultaneously, the necessity of their association—its fated or fateful quality—also becomes clear. The two figures are linked by standing out in different ways. Kay is the central object of the scene, and Matt spans the entire space of the saloon in his movement: not only is he the only figure to do so, he is also the only person around the stage whose attention is not constantly fixed on Kay. The dialectic of necessity and loose contingency is visually expressed in a very dynamic way when Matt reaches the farthest point on the ellipse his movement traces around the set: the camera cranes back slightly and reframes Matt and Kay so that they are at opposite corners of the frame.

In a celebrated shot later in the film, after Matt has saved her and Weston from being carried downstream on their raft, Kay inadvertently lets go of her suitcase, which floats away as Weston brings her ashore in his arms. The shot of the suitcase floating down the river—its "symbolism . . . so completely absorbed into the action that it may easily pass unnoticed,"[23] in V. F. Perkins's words—has become central in the highly influential critical construction of Preminger as an author who, as Perkins writes, "presents the evidence but . . . leaves the spectator free to draw his own conclusions."[24]

In fact, as David Bordwell has pointed out, Preminger's direction of the scene is not as unemphatic as Perkins suggests: the loss of the suitcase is highlighted by dialogue (Kay cries out, "My things!" and Weston says, "Let it go"), by camera movement (a slight reframing pan in the direction of the current as the suitcase floats offscreen), and by a musical sting in the score.[25] For my purposes, the key moment in the shot comes later, when Weston and Kay reach the riverbank and are met by Matt. As Weston, carrying Kay, walks forward through the water, the camera tracks back and pans slightly to the right, so that the suitcase, still floating downriver, becomes visible again at the right of the screen, and when Matt walks into the shot, a symmetrical composition is briefly formed with Weston and Kay in the center, Matt at left, and the suitcase at right, until, for the second time in the shot, the suitcase floats offscreen. At this moment, it becomes clear that the entire shot has been conceived for and made possible by CinemaScope. The shape of the screen corresponds with the horizontal movement of the river, a correspondence emphasized by the camera angle, which is perpendicular to the flow of the river. The only way for Preminger to maintain our sense of the river as a horizontal, lateral force, and of the current as flowing parallel to the camera plane, while also highlighting the suitcase by panning to include it *and* remaining close enough to the actors to frame them in medium shot (above the knees)—all in a single, unbroken shot—is with CinemaScope. With a standard-format frame, he could have shown the suitcase again without a cut only by panning drastically to the right—which, to be sure, Preminger does, but only at the very last moment, as Matt and Weston walk to the house and we see, for the last time, the suitcase drifting away down the river.

In both these shots, then, Preminger uses CinemaScope to extend the duration in which the people and objects in a scene can be kept in a dynamic and coherent relationship. Preminger also uses the wide screen to emphasize the distance between people in the composition as a meaningful element, as in the moment in the saloon shot when Matt and Kay are at their greatest distance from each other, or near the end of the river shot, when Matt leads Weston toward the house and Kay's suitcase is a visual point in the middle of the space between them. Moreover, Preminger uses CinemaScope to emphasize, in the second shot, the horizontality of the river and, in the first shot, Kay's solitude onstage.

Based on a story that Preminger did not select or develop, made from a script that had been largely written by the time he was assigned to the film, starring an actress he disliked, and, finally, partly reshot by another director, *River of No Return* can't be considered a Preminger work in the same right as his independent productions or most of his previous films for Fox. Yet *River of No Return* proves that his ability to control a film through direction depends neither on his prior control over the script nor on his functioning also as producer. The same can also be said of *The Court-Martial of Billy Mitchell* and *Porgy and Bess*, the only later films that Preminger directed without also producing. These three films constitute an unofficial trilogy.

19

Taboo

Billy Rose's production of *Carmen Jones*, an all-black-cast restaging of *Carmen* with the locale moved to the contemporary American South, enjoyed a long and successful run after its Broadway opening in 1943. In 1953 Preminger secured the screen rights. Since *The Moon Is Blue*, he had been looking for the right project for his next independent picture. Before leaving for Canada in July to shoot *River of No Return*, he tried unsuccessfully to get the rights to John Van Druten's play *Bell, Book and Candle*. Another interested party, producer Irene Mayer Selznick, noted in a memo to lawyer Lee Moselle: "Now I must tell you that [there is] a tremendous resistance—this is confidential—among actors to Preminger, certainly top actors. I don't know about stage, but certainly about screen."[1] Her remark is evidence of a tension between Preminger and the Hollywood establishment, a tension that the success of *The Moon Is Blue* in defiance of the MPAA can only have exacerbated.

Dissatisfied with Oscar Hammerstein II's text, Preminger told Harry Kleiner, whom he hired to write the script for *Carmen Jones*, to return to the original source, Prosper Mérimée's novella about the doomed love between Carmen, a fortune-telling Gypsy, and Don José, a Spanish soldier who gives up his profession for her and finally murders her out of jealous possessiveness. "I had decided to make a dramatic film with music rather than a conventional film musical," Preminger said. During the editing of *River of No Return*, Zanuck, hearing of Preminger's inability to find a production deal for *Carmen Jones* (United Artists had turned it down, calling it "too rich for our blood"), asked to read the script. Two days later, Zanuck offered to back the film. The agreement between Carlyle Productions (Preminger's company) and Twentieth Century-Fox called for the studio to advance Carlyle $700,000 (later raised to

$775,000) on account of the negative cost of the film; Carlyle would be liable for all negative cost over that amount. The studio would recoup its advance from the distribution of the film, after which Carlyle would begin to realize its 50 percent share of the profits. (In 1960 Preminger sold his rights in *Carmen Jones* to the studio.) Zanuck had script approval, and Preminger was obliged to comply with suggestions for changes "from the viewpoint of approval by M.P.A.[A.] and censorship organizations." Zanuck also had "personal approval" of the final editing, and Preminger agreed to comply with Zanuck's editing "suggestions," though he won the concession (which no doubt was especially meaningful in view of his recent experience on *River of No Return*) that he would not be required to do any retakes or added scenes.[2]

Kleiner's April 19 first-draft script was submitted to the PCA, which was concerned about "an overemphasis on lustfulness" and the lack of a "voice for morality." The scene of Carmen and Joe (Hammerstein's Don José, a G.I. stationed at the army base that also houses the parachute factory where Carmen works) in their Chicago apartment was too "sex suggestive" for Breen, who urged that Joe not be shown shirtless, as envisioned by the script; requested that "the bed . . . be minimized as much as possible"; and objected to such details as Joe playing with Carmen's legs. In the event, Preminger's version of the scene made it into the finished film. A sticking point was the phrase "fight like hell" in the number "Stan' Up an' Fight," sung by Husky Miller, a prizefighter who eventually becomes Carmen's lover. Breen refused to approve the word "hell." Though Oscar Hammerstein agreed to make some other changes in the lyrics to appease Breen, he and Preminger drew the line here. Twentieth Century-Fox appealed Breen's ruling to the MPAA board of directors and won.

Throughout April and May, Preminger set up *Carmen Jones*. Harry Belafonte was cast as Joe, and Pearl Bailey as Frankie, an acquaintance of Carmen's who persuades her to join Husky Miller's entourage on a trip to Chicago. Preminger auditioned newcomer Diahann Carroll for Carmen but instead cast her in the small role of Myrt, Frankie's friend.

Thirty-one-year-old Dorothy Dandridge had appeared in a number of films in supporting roles, had played the lead in the little-noticed MGM low-budgeter *Bright Road* (1953), and was enjoying some success as a nightclub singer. Earl Mills, her personal manager, persuaded Ingo

Preminger, whose offices were in the same building as Mills's, to help Dandridge get an interview with Otto. At their first meeting, for which she dressed in a sedate blue dress, Preminger insisted that she was "too sweet, too regal" for Carmen and told her to come back when she had learned the part of Cindy Lou (Hammerstein's counterpart to the Micaela of Bizet's opera).[3] More determined than ever, Dandridge returned for her next interview armed with a black wig, a low-cut blouse, a slit skirt, high heels, and pointers from her mother on "how some of those girls who are factory workers behave."[4] Preminger took one look and said, "My God. You are really Carmen."[5]

On May 11 Preminger directed Dandridge in a screen test of the scene of Carmen and Joe in their Chicago hotel room. Playing Joe was James Edwards, one of the most distinguished African American actors then of leading-man age in Hollywood. Mills said, "Every bit of support that could possibly be given an actress was given by Preminger. He treated the test as if it were an important scene in an important movie."[6] Preminger was elated over the test, and Dandridge signed her contract for *Carmen Jones* on the same day.

Soon she had doubts. Winning the part—the first leading role for an African American woman in a major Hollywood film in several years—had made her a target for envy. She doubted her ability to carry the film. Moreover, she was concerned about the image of African Americans that Carmen represented. Learning of Dandridge's misgivings, Preminger visited her Sunset Strip apartment one evening. She cooked him a steak, they drank champagne, and he told her to forget her fears. "We can make the best picture of the year," he said. He fascinated her with tales of his past. He also disclosed that although he and his wife lived in the same house and entertained together, "they were not exactly husband and wife." As the evening went on, Dandridge felt more and more comfortable with him. He told her that it was a "Hollywood custom" for a director and a star to have an affair for the duration of a picture and that such intimacy could help the picture: "If star and director know each other heart and soul—and the rest—the spark of it all might well leap into the beauty of the film." To Dandridge, he was both a father figure and "physical, all-male—no problem there." That night, the two began an affair that would last long after *Carmen Jones*.[7]

During the days, they rehearsed. The three-week rehearsal period included extensive sessions in which Dandridge worked with mezzo-soprano Marilyn Horne, then beginning her career. (Preminger decided early on that the libretto would be sung by trained operatic singers and that Belafonte's and Dandridge's voices would be dubbed.)[8] The music was recorded on June 18. Choreographer Herbert Ross blocked all the dances and staged the roadhouse sequence, including the quintet "Whizzin' Away Along de Track." "After it all was rehearsed," Ross recalled, "Otto went through everything with a cameraman. Everything was pre-rehearsed, pre-recorded, and then shot on a tight schedule."[9]

Shooting began on June 30 at the RKO studios, which Preminger perhaps chose in preference to those of his financial partner in order to lower his overhead. The director of photography was Sam Leavitt, who proved his ability to get good results fast and would go on to do five more films for Preminger. Usually keeping to herself when not working in a scene, partly because she felt others in the company mistrusted her and suspected her relationship with Preminger, Dandridge matched her director in meticulousness and discipline.

According to Herbert Ross, Preminger "bullied everyone with the exception of Pearl Bailey."[10] As Joe Adams (Husky) and Diahann Carroll both remembered, Dandridge walked off the set once when Preminger screamed at her. On returning to the set, Dandridge played the scene perfectly. "Which is exactly what he wanted her to do," Adams said. "He made her angry deliberately. She was doing more than she knew that she could do. And he brought it out of her. And then, of course, she was very happy. He had a way of doing that." "He often screamed at her to force her to rise above her inexperience," Carroll said. Nevertheless, Geri Branton, Dandridge's close friend and confidante, recalled that after the incident, "She gave him hell for two weeks. She didn't yell back on the set, but I'm telling you she gave him hell."[11]

Brock Peters (then billed as "Broc," and cast as Sergeant Brown, Joe's persecutor) remembered an on-set incident between him and Preminger that almost turned violent. "He chewed me out in front of a lot of people, crew and cast and extras. He said something about 'this New York actor . . .' Some disparaging things. And, of course, I was on the spot. It was my first picture. I was wanting desperately for it to work. I lost my temper, and I went for him. And Pearl Bailey and somebody else grabbed me."[12] When the difficulties of Olga James (Cindy Lou) during an exterior scene endangered the schedule, Preminger "really unleashed on her for quite a while,"[13] Peters recalled, bringing her to tears. But James got it right after that. After six takes of the "Stan' Up an' Fight" scene, Preminger, dissatisfied with Joe Adams's work, yelled through a megaphone, "Mr. Adams. What exactly is it you call yourself doing? I've got a milkman that's a better actor than you." Controlling his anger, Adams went through the scene again, this time satisfying the director, who pronounced the take "fantastic." The actor later praised Preminger: "He was just as great to rave about you when you got it right."[14]

Carroll, making her film debut, felt that Preminger liked her enthusiasm and made her his "mascot."[15] On the set, "He allowed me to stand behind him at first, and then eventually he'd say to me, 'Come closer, come closer.' And I watched the way he observed the scene and what it was that disturbed him and how he went about correcting it and getting what he wanted from his actors. Very often I thought, 'God, is this a cruel man.'" For Carroll, who was raised in New York, "working with someone like Otto who liked young people" was part of the fun of her first sojourn in Los Angeles. "I don't know if it had anything to do with the fact that I was female, but I do know that we developed a friendship from there."[16]

The actors were under no illusions that the opportunity of *Carmen Jones* meant a breakthrough. Diahann Carroll recalled, "It became clear as the weeks went by that none of us was likely to have much of a future here . . . The unspoken assumption seemed to be that we were outsiders, in town for only a short while to do our 'black' feature film (there was a 'black' film every few years), and when it was over we would go back to wherever we came from and no one would ever see us again."[17] Brock Peters concurred with this assessment. "At that point in the history of African American talent, there hadn't been very many opportunities for us, we weren't being sought out . . . The span of time between those films was fairly significant in our young lives, and to find ourselves in a film like *Carmen Jones* didn't necessarily say to us, oh, now you're going to have glorious careers . . . We were hired, and came out, and did the work, and did our best, so that hopefully someone would think to cast us in something else, each of us thinking that, given the climate and the opportunities that were available, it was highly unlikely!"[18]

The twenty-four-day shooting period ended on July 27. Preminger managed to bring in the production at the modest negative cost of $800,000.

Preminger screened *Carmen Jones* for Twentieth Century-Fox executives in New York on September 24. Before the film was released, he turned to a project for television, a live telecast of *Tonight at 8:30*, a trilogy of one-act plays by Noël Coward, which Preminger had undertaken to direct for NBC's *Producers' Showcase* series in an adaptation by F. Hugh Herbert. Ginger Rogers essayed the lead female role in each of the plays. In October, Preminger rehearsed the cast of *Tonight at 8:30* for a week at NBC studios in New York. Rogers recalled that Preminger "was very gracious toward me, but he was a very picky man and nearly drove Gig Young [her costar in the third episode, "Shadow Play"] crazy. Otto was constantly on his case—pick, pick, pick—unnecessarily. I was embarrassed by Otto's constant fault-finding and Gig was nearly in tears. How he stood Otto's behavior I will never know."[19]

Broadcast on October 18, *Tonight at 8:30* did not come off. Preminger, in a tuxedo, introduces the show, speaking slowly. In the first episode, "Red Peppers," about a married couple whose music-hall song-and-dance act is on its last legs, Preminger paces the dialogue very fast and uses more close-ups than he would use in a film. Clearly, the evening has been conceived as a piece of televised theater, with the camera serving as a recording device, at the same time self-effacing (because blunt and unaesthetic) and obtrusive (for the same two reasons), to catch the actors' performances. In "Still Life," Rogers and Trevor Howard (who had played the same part in David Lean's adaptation of the play, *Brief Encounter*) look mismatched: she is distant, artificial, and under-rehearsed; next to her, he comes off as too practiced and smooth. Their scene of high emotion feels rhetorical, declaimed. "Shadow Play," in which a marriage in an advanced stage of breakdown is magically saved through a long excursion into nostalgic fantasy and song, is the most elaborate and bizarre of the three episodes and the one that suffers most from the hazards of live TV. At one point, a boom mike dips down in front of Gig Young's face; there's a hasty cut to an empty chair, from which the camera then pans back to Young. The musical numbers pose problems for both Rogers and Young: if it's a duet, the song will be either in his key or in hers, leaving the other stranded. During one song, Young fails to keep up with the orchestra. The performers have no choice but to keep going, and their doggedness in the face of insurmountable adversity only heightens the surrealist charge of the play. For those in search of cinema, none is to be found here. *Tonight at 8:30* suggests instead that there was a basic gap between Preminger's conception of theater and his conception of cinema, a gap that he made no effort to bridge and which may even have been the precondition for his success in both forms.

Meanwhile, *Carmen Jones* and Dandridge were the beneficiaries of extensive prerelease publicity in both national general-interest magazines and the African American press. Dandridge made the cover of the November 1, 1954, issue of *Life*, which hit the stands three days before the film's premiere at the Rivoli Theater in New York. The film opened to positive—often exultant—reviews and became a box-office success. By the end of 1955, *Variety* reported, it had racked up $2.5 million in domestic rentals, not enough to make it a blockbuster, but enough, when non-U.S. rentals were added, to show a more than respectable profit.

Carmen Jones is one of Preminger's best-remembered films—though not for reasons that have much to do with his direction. As an all-black Hollywood film released in the year of *Brown v. Board of Education*, the film has inevitably become a central and contested document in the historiography of the representation of African Americans in popular culture. Since the 1990s, *Carmen Jones* has acquired further renown thanks to heightened interest in the life and career of Dorothy Dandridge.

Carmen Jones is an ideal Preminger project in one respect: the opera is itself an analogue to his own cultural situation as a European artist, heir to nineteenth-century European culture, transplanted to twentieth-century America. From Mérimée's story, by way of the opera by Bizet, Meilhac, and Halévy, *Carmen Jones* inherits a number of themes central to nineteenth-century European literature and art: exoticism, occultism, the (self-) critique of patriarchy as performed by white male artists privileged to cross class and ethnic boundaries, the dangerous and attractive figure of the prostitute (although Carmen is not a prostitute, prostitution remains a subtext of the film, and is hinted at unmistakably when Frankie bristles at Rum's invitation to join him on the trip to Chicago).[20] That the theme of prostitution is central to Preminger is evident from David Raksin's recollection that Preminger saw Laura Hunt as "a whore." Like Laura, Amber, Mrs. Erlynne in *The Fan*, Bess in *Porgy and Bess*, Laura Manion in *Anatomy of a Murder*, Mona in *The Cardinal*, and Ann in *Bunny Lake Is Missing*, Carmen puts herself outside the norms governing women's sexual conduct and thus loses the protections afforded women by patriarchy and becomes vulnerable to patriarchal violence. All these characters, while not prostitutes, are sexually experienced, and a central concern of these films is to show how women are victimized by patriarchal discourses that castigate them for extramarital or polygamous sex, in effect putting them into the category of prostitutes.

Carmen Jones is the most straightforward example in Preminger's work of his rejection of the cliché of the "femme fatale." Already, *Fallen Angel* and *Angel Face* criticized the misogyny of this cliché. The whole point of Preminger's visual strategies in *Carmen Jones* is to resist the fatalism suggested by Joe's entrapment as he hides from the military police and by Carmen's apparent belief in an inescapable destiny. The film makes it clear that although she seduces Joe, she can't be blamed for his downfall. Her abandoning Joe to become Husky's mistress is a dual rebellion: on the one hand against Joe's attempts to "own" her ("There's only one that does," she tells him, "that's me, myself") and on the other against fate, imaged in Frankie's nine of spades.

By updating the story, placing it in the United States, and making all its characters African American, Hammerstein's adaptation suggests that the themes of *Carmen* are universal, while also eliminating the transethnic quality of the central love relationship and transposing it, as Susan McClary perceives, "in such a way that the whole cast now stands as exotic for the gaze of a mostly white, affluent audience."[21] As James Baldwin comments, the absence of white people from the world of *Carmen Jones* "seals the action off, as it were, in a vacuum in which the spectacle of color is divested of its danger. The color itself then becomes a kind of vacuum which each spectator will fill with his own fantasies." For Baldwin, Preminger's film makes it impossible to forget "that this is an opera having nothing to do with the present day, hence, nothing, *really*, to do with Negroes," while the use of black actors mainly makes possible "a sterile and distressing eroticism," more potent than that of a Lana Turner film only because "Negroes are associated in the public mind with sex."[22]

Preminger defended *Carmen Jones* by acknowledging its central artificiality and arguing that this quality enabled the film to be socially progressive. "This was really a fantasy, as was *Porgy and Bess*. The all-black
world shown in these films doesn't exist, at least not in the United
States. We used the musical-fantasy quality to convey something of the
needs and aspirations of colored people."[23] Some weight can be given to
Preminger's assertion. The narratives of both *Carmen Jones* and *Porgy
and Bess* represent the African American exodus from the rural South to
the urban North (Chicago in *Carmen Jones*, New York in *Porgy and
Bess*)—while, to be sure, occulting the major historical causes of this migration. In *Carmen Jones*, the underdeveloped infrastructure and the
poverty of the South become apparent (during Joe and Carmen's aborted
trip to Masonville), establishing a background against which Carmen's
longing to see Chicago, and the desire expressed by Frankie and Myrt
for luxury items obtainable there, such as jewels and mink coats, become understandable. The star power of Husky Miller, who is hailed as
a hero wherever he goes, reflects the truth that during much of the
twentieth century, sports was one of the few professions by which black
people could achieve wealth and fame, and thus Husky embodies the
historical potential for the black sports star to serve as a role model and
as an example of a self-reliant or insurgent, aggressive racial identity, of
which Husky's anthem, "Stan' Up an' Fight," could be heard as a veiled
assertion. (I hasten to add that I have no evidence that it was heard this
way, either in 1943 or in 1954. In 1943, the song was likely to have been
heard in reference to the war effort.)

White racism becomes, by the very conception of the project, the
major structuring absence of *Carmen Jones*. Yet if the absence of white
people from the parachute factory, or from the auditorium where the
boxing match takes place, clearly places the film in the realm of fantasy,
the segregated spaces that were a reality for most black people in the
United States find a recognizable image in the all-black Chicago streets
we see in the film.

The use of Bizet's score (sung, largely, by white singers) necessarily
closes the film off from one of the most powerful forms of African American culture: African American music. Only in Max Roach's drum solo
(and in the Pearl Bailey number that follows it, "Beat Out That Rhythm
on a Drum") does that music enter the film, bringing with it some sense

of density and urgency. Throughout the rest of *Carmen Jones*, the absence of jazz, blues, gospel, or contemporary popular music styles accentuates the artificiality of the film. Bizet's music becomes an element of stylization, a metaphor, a foreign idiom. The problem of dealing with another's speech, of acknowledging it as other, can be considered the central problem posed by *Carmen Jones*.

Though *Carmen Jones* encompasses the tragic visions of its protagonists within a total vision that is sympathetic but basically ironic, the text demands, and the conventions of the opera form make possible, a greater exteriorization of interior states than Preminger's films usually provide. Joe's "Dis Flower" is a private monologue, sung during his labor sentence for going AWOL, while he is isolated spatially from the other workers. Cindy Lou's "My Joe" is heard in voice-over accompanying a traveling close shot of Cindy Lou walking on a Chicago street. Carmen's "Card Song," though sung in the presence of other characters, is essentially monologic. Preminger's contribution to these songs is to ground them in an external reality, so that the inner world of the characters appears not to violate the outer world but to communicate with it. The elegance and bleakness of *Carmen Jones* make clear Preminger's skepticism toward the stylized exuberance that the play irresistibly demands.

As an exercise of camera fluency and skill at staging lengthy scenes, *Carmen Jones* is not far from Preminger's peak (he will not surpass it until *Exodus*). What stands out first in *Carmen Jones* is his success at opening up the opera. From the first shot of a bus arriving at the parachute factory, he announces the intention of bringing the opera into contact with a real, external world, of not only letting into the film the weight of this world and the recalcitrance of its objects, but dwelling on that weight and this recalcitrance. Preminger's staging of Carmen's "Dat's Love" (to the tune of Bizet's "Habanera") in a factory cafeteria epitomizes the deglamorization to which he subjects the material. More than just the setting, it's the way the setting is used that strikes such a note of incongruous and irredeemable banality, a hard American ugliness that will endure past the passions and rivalries of the characters (even though the war will end, as the dialogue later reminds us, and the factory will be either shut down or turned to other purposes).

The film documents the transformation of space by personal imperatives and expressiveness. The camera registers the squareness of the cafeteria space, its rows of people at long tables laid out in parallel, the counter at a right angle to the tables. The squareness is never contradicted by the camera, whose orientation is always parallel to the counter (either behind the counter or at the opposite side of the set, at the ends of the tables). Yet Carmen's weaving movements between the tables and along the counter demonstrate an effortless domination of the space, and the entire sequence is staged as a showcase in which she is the moving center of attention for the other characters, whose places are more or less fixed.

Throughout the film, Preminger extends space and duration in order to create the sense that the story is generating itself within a dynamic field of possibilities. *Carmen Jones* approaches Preminger's ideal of a film without cuts, in which each moment appears to call forth the next in an unbroken flow. The film begins and ends in motion: in the first shot, a bus approaches the camera; in the last, Joe, after killing Carmen, walks away from the camera down a hall to meet his fate. The entire film can be seen as an attempt to explain the progression from the first shot, with its fluid expansiveness, to the last, in which our view of Joe is bounded by the narrow frame-within-a-frame of the doorway to the storage room, within which the camera remains (with Carmen's dead body offscreen).

Carmen Jones was Preminger's second film in CinemaScope, and as in *River of No Return*, his response to the increased width of the screen is to expand the characters' fields of action and motion, emphasizing the vastness of both their physical environment and their sphere of moral decision. The dislike of confinement expressed by Dorothy Dandridge's Carmen cries out for the wide screen, and Preminger obliges her with a generous and elastic mise-en-scène, staging scenes as unfurling ribbons of movement, gesture, and reaction. As in the earlier black-and-white films, the long takes and camera movements are also a source of tension, and it is clear throughout *Carmen Jones* that Preminger likes the pressure the long take puts on actors, as when he saves a difficult fight (between Harry Belafonte and Brock Peters) for the end of an already lengthy and complicated dialogue take.

For Dorothy Dandridge, the success of *Carmen Jones* marked a plateau that she would never be able to recapture. She became the first African American to be nominated for the Academy Award for Best Actress, but as Preminger had predicted, she did not win. ("The time is not ripe," he told her; on March 30, the award, presented by William Holden, went to Grace Kelly for *The Country Girl*.) Zanuck signed Dandridge to a contract, which she negotiated under Preminger's behind-the-scenes tutelage. ("You must ask Zanuck for more than he wants to pay," he told her. "He will have no appreciation of you otherwise.")[24]

Perhaps, as Dandridge's biographer Donald Bogle (who worked for Preminger as a story editor in the late 1960s) thought, Preminger misread the American culture of the period and "refused to believe that Dorothy might be limited by the movie industry because of her race."[25] Why, then, did Preminger not take a more active role in furthering Dandridge's film work? He still owed Fox a fourth picture under his April 15, 1950, contract (*The 13th Letter*, the RKO loan-out *Angel Face*, and *River of No Return*, but not *Carmen Jones*, were regarded as falling under the contract). There might have been a role for Dandridge in Preminger's projected film on Gandhi, in preparation for which he spent three weeks in India in November and early December 1954, meeting Prime Minister Nehru and others. When he sought to buy the film rights to *Porgy and Bess* in or around 1955, he probably had Dandridge in mind for Bess. During his leave from Fox that year, Preminger turned his attention to *The Court-Martial of Billy Mitchell*, in which there could have been no question of casting Dandridge, and *The Man with the Golden Arm*, in which it is interesting to consider what (in a color-blind filmmaking universe) the actress might have made of one of the two main female roles.

For some time after *Carmen Jones*, Preminger continued his affair with Dandridge. Vivian Dandridge confirmed, "Otto was crazy about my sister."[26] He took charge of Dorothy's career, her business, and her persona, telling her how to dress, giving her suggestions on her nightclub act (including lighting), and proposing real-estate investments for her. He followed her around the country, sometimes annoying her by showing up without notice at nightclub openings. "He couldn't get me out of his system," Dandridge wrote, "nor could he make any proposals of substance to me—neither a new film nor marriage."[27] Preminger paid the down payment on her new showplace house in the Hollywood hills and kept her checking account replenished. The couple gave small dinner parties for friends. They were discreet enough—or Preminger had sufficient clout—for their affair not to cause a scandal.

Surrounded by social prejudices and career pressures, the two of them were, she realized, playing "a game—I to get him, he to lose me." She understood that "Otto was another confrontation with a white man who would not follow through."[28] Geri Branton recalled that Dandridge would sometimes show her resentment openly. "Sometimes she was so *insulting* to him. She used to say, 'Stop chewing your food. Your teeth clack. You got an ugly old bald head.' It kind of hurt him. But you know you don't say that to a *Prussian*."[29]

Dandridge remembered: "Behind what we saw and knew and felt of each other, behind the confrontation of our polar interests, sex, color, status, legality, all the other tangibles and intangibles of human relationships, behind all that, we had a good relationship. I kept it harmonious. There was tenderness, affection. He was a wondrous gift-giver. I did not love him, but if he had proposed marriage, love would automatically follow."[30] Even Earl Mills, who resented Preminger's influence on Dandridge, acknowledged that he "gave as well as took which wasn't true of her other lovers."[31]

None of the published Dandridge biographies make it clear when her affair with Preminger ended. During the entire period of their intimacy, he was still married to Mary Gardner, and Dandridge also dated others. In a gesture worthy of Orson Welles's Gregory Arkadin, Preminger, calling from California, once reached Dandridge at Idlewild Airport in New York to summon her home from an assignation with a rival. She obeyed. Preminger met her at the Burbank airport under rain, wordlessly draped a raincoat around her, and took her home in a limousine, holding her in his arms "as if I were a perverse child who had done some ridiculous thing."[32]

Later, she embarked on a longer-lasting relationship with Jack Denison, a Las Vegas maître d' rumored to have mob connections. Preminger, who met Denison, later noted, "He had long white hands and fingers. He had *white* hair, and *white, white* skin." In Bogle's view, "Preminger committed a terrible injustice against her with his comment that she was attracted only to white men. That was Otto, the spurned lover, trying to strike back, particularly at her relationship with the very white-looking Jack Denison."[33]

Earl Mills claimed that Dandridge became pregnant with Preminger's child and that when Preminger refused to marry her, Mills arranged for a prominent Beverly Hills physician to perform an abortion. According to Mills, the event caused her to end her relationship with Preminger, against whom she subsequently felt bitter. Geri Branton insisted, however, that Mills's story was untrue, and Dandridge's own autobiography makes no reference to an abortion.[34]

About all that can be said about the end of Preminger's affair with Dandridge is that it occurred before July 1958, when Preminger took over as director of *Porgy and Bess*, in which Dandridge had been cast: "When Otto entered as a director, our relationship was a professional one . . . The old romance was now as cold as iced cucumbers."[35] Since Preminger was still close enough to Dandridge for her to have heeded his advice (when Samuel Goldwyn was preparing the production with Rouben Mamoulian as director) to take the part of Bess, the two may have still been intimate as late as December 1957, when her casting in the film was announced. That the affair lasted several years seems definite.[36] The best surmise is that the affair ended, probably at Dandridge's initiative, in 1957 or possibly 1956.

20
A Conservative Liberal

William "Billy" Mitchell achieved distinction in the U.S. Army's Air Services during World War I, rising to the rank of brigadier general. In 1921, his advocacy of the military use of aviation and an independent air force got a widely publicized boost when, in a test, Mitchell used bombers to sink the captured German battleship *Ostfriesland.* In September 1925, the crash of the navy dirigible *Shenandoah* prompted Mitchell to make a statement to the press in which he blamed the accident on "the incompetency, criminal negligence, and almost treasonable administration of the national defense by the War and Navy Departments." Mitchell was relieved of duty and ordered to explain his remarks before a court-martial in Washington. The trial, which attracted much publicity, ended with Mitchell being suspended from duty for five years without pay. Mitchell, who died in 1936, was posthumously vindicated when his warnings about the threat of Japan proved accurate. In 1946 Congress awarded him a Medal of Honor; the following year, the air force was designated an independent branch of the U.S. Armed Forces.

Warner Bros. considered making a film on Mitchell in 1941 but scrapped these plans after Pearl Harbor. Years later, Milton Sperling, a quasi-independent producer with close ties to Warner Bros., revived the project and secured the cooperation of Billy Mitchell's family. Leon Uris did a story outline, but the revised final script, dated June 9, 1955, is under Milton Sperling's name, as is the shooting final dated June 23. (The final script is credited to Sperling and Emmet Lavery.) Gary Cooper was cast as Mitchell.

Why, at this stage in his career, having directed and produced two successful independent productions and about to embark on the third, did Preminger choose to hire himself out again as a studio employee and submit to the control of a producer? The obvious answer may well be the right one. He got $110,000 for up to eighteen and a half weeks of work on *The Court-Martial of Billy Mitchell*, plus 10 percent of net profits. (Otto and Ingo had sought to get Otto's name above the title, but Sperling refused.) Preminger's contract, dated June 7, 1955, gives April 26 as the start date for his services on *Billy Mitchell*. The film was budgeted at slightly under $1.5 million (plus overhead of about $600,000).

Preminger's own productions were stalled at the time. After his trip to India in 1954, he set up a deal for his Gandhi film with Harry Cohn at Columbia. It would have been, as Preminger told François Truffaut at the time, less about Gandhi than about his doctrine. "He himself will play a symbolic role. We'll show the effects of his principles on the life of another man."[1] After the project (for which Alec Coppel worked on a script) was aborted, its tentative title, *The Wheel* (referring to the Hindu prayer wheel), became the name of one of Preminger's ad hoc production companies.

On June 8 Preminger traveled to New York, where he cast the small parts for the scenes of *Billy Mitchell* to be shot in Washington. He then proceeded to Washington, where on June 18 he started shooting at Union Station. On June 20 the unit moved to the Army-Navy Club for three long nights of shooting. The results displeased Jack Warner, who sent a telegram to Sperling (who had accompanied the unit to Washington) on June 25: "Everything good but was disappointed in minute amount film. Could not believe only had 100 feet film one night . . . Know hours of shooting in Army-Navy Club restricted therefore appears should have been done here and not worry about authenticity which am sure not going make picture any better or worse." Whatever Sperling's own feelings about the matter, he had already committed to shoot in Washington for nine days, and Preminger completed the location schedule. Much of the shoot consisted of exterior shots, but in addition to the interior at the Army-Navy Club, Preminger had managed to secure the interior of a committee room at a Senate office building for a day's work.[2]

Don Kranze, working as second assistant director on the Washington shoot, recalled, "Gary Cooper at that time was not too hot on his lines. I don't know why. He was having trouble . . . He was not dead perfect on his lines, that's all I'll say. I was used to stars coming in, and bingo. He was not, he was fluffing."[3] Kranze may have misunderstood Cooper, of whom Preminger had a higher appreciation: "Everything that he did, he did deliberately. He knew what he was doing. That slow talk, that looking down, that was all deliberate. But he had this personality, also, you know, that at least exuded realism and reality. But he was also a very good actor."[4]

Unlike some who worked for Preminger, Kranze admired his boss, even when Preminger's temper was directed at him. "If you didn't hem and haw, and if you said, 'I did it. I screwed up,' that was the end of it. No reproachment, no nothing, just 'Okay, let's move on.' But if you hemmed and hawed—and here's where you hear these terrible stories— he'd open up on you. I screwed up one time. We're in Washington, D.C. And I'm out in left field, and they told me to hold the people back from this building, don't let 'em go out. Well, I didn't pay attention, and some people walked out in their modern-day dress. That ruins a big shot. A lot of effort setting up the shot, a lot of time . . . So he said, 'Mr. Kranze, what happened?' I said, 'I screwed up. It won't happen again.' That's the end of it."[5]

On Sunday, June 26, Preminger finished in Washington and returned with Sperling to Los Angeles. Shooting resumed in the studio on June 28. A second unit headed by Russ Saunders, shooting continuously throughout the schedule, took exterior shots at the Fletcher Airport in Rosemead, California, and other locations, process shots for flying scenes, and shots of the miniature that was used for the *Ostfriesland*.

Preminger brought in Ben Hecht at the last minute to work on the screenplay. One of Hecht's conditions for doing the uncredited work was that Preminger should get him some Demerol, which the writer was in the habit of taking to help him sleep.[6] Production reports of the studio scenes indicate that the script was being rewritten during productions, with, among other changes, several added scenes involving Zachary Lansdowne (a protégé of Mitchell's and the commanding officer of the doomed *Shenandoah*) and his wife (played by Jack Lord and Elizabeth Montgomery).

Sperling, though Preminger found him "a very nice and intelligent man," proved a less than ideal collaborator. "He had a tremendous inferiority complex," recalled Preminger. "Whenever he suggested something, and we liked it and incorporated it in the script, he came back the next day and changed it again. This went on until neither Ben Hecht nor I had the patience to go through with it." Preminger still managed to put his stamp on the film. "I didn't have troubles with [Sperling]—he had troubles with me," Preminger said.[7] Sperling's script had envisioned starting the narrative with Billy's arrest, recapitulating most of the story in a long flashback culminating with Billy's statement to the press, and then returning to the present for the court-martial. This idea was scrapped, and in the final film, narrative events proceed chronologically in the present tense.

Gregory Walcott, cast in the small part of a reporter, considered Preminger a "fastidious" director, recalling that after watching a rehearsal of a scene in which reporters question Mitchell, Preminger redistributed the reporters' dialogue among the actors before shooting the scene.[8] The production reports show that it was not uncommon for scenes involving dolly-boom work to require eleven, twelve, or as many as fourteen takes. On July 18, the first day on the courtroom set where Preminger would work for two weeks, one setup (in which Mitchell's lawyer, Reid, challenges Guthrie, the head of the court-martial, for personal prejudice) took nearly four hours to light and rehearse, then eight takes to shoot. At the end of production on August 13, the film was seven days behind schedule.

Released in December 1955 to lukewarm reviews and fairly good box office (*Variety* reported domestic rentals of $3,000,000), *The Court-Martial of Billy Mitchell* is an impressive film. Of all Preminger's films, it is (with *Saint Joan*) the one that is most purely about the public, professional world, and in which the characters are least engaged or influenced by private motives. The best sequences are undoubtedly those of the trial. The mise-en-scène highlights the starkness of the setting, the rigidity of the conduct of the judges. Preminger uses the depth of the cavernous space behind Mitchell, where the faceless audience members are seated, to suggest a vast and inhospitable arena. The scraping of the judges' chairs on the stone floor as they troop en masse in or out of their places adds to the dismal and harsh atmosphere.

With uncanny exactness, the trial scenes anticipate *Anatomy of a*

Murder in a number of details. The dramatic structure is similar in both films, hinging on a key line of evidence that the defense is eager to bring into the trial, the prosecution equally eager to keep out, which the court rules inadmissible until a climactic mid-trial turning point. In *Billy Mitchell*, this line is the "justification" for Mitchell's denunciation of his superiors; in *Anatomy*, it is the rape of the defendant's wife, Laura, by the murder victim. Both films emphasize the word "justification" in relation to the defendant's action: in *Anatomy*, it is distinguished from "excuse" (defense attorney Biegler tells his client that the killing is unjustifiable, but possibly excusable). In both films, a bereaved woman appears as a crucial defense witness; her bereavement endows her with a special status in the courtroom and gives her words the unimpeachable stamp of truth (Margaret Lansdowne in *Billy Mitchell*, Mary Pilant, the victim's daughter, in *Anatomy*). Both trials include lengthy prosecutorial cross-examinations whose dramatic power is heightened by the fact that the defense witness is incapacitated: Mitchell by malaria, Laura by her desperate need to conceal her promiscuity.

Finally, both *Billy Mitchell* and *Anatomy* propose the same conjunction of a dramatic motif with a casting strategy. In both trials, the prosecution is bolstered by a visiting attorney of legendary powers who takes over the case from his colleague. Both these fearsome antagonists are played by young actors from the New York stage who are not yet established in films—Rod Steiger in *Billy Mitchell*, George C. Scott in *Anatomy*. Since the protagonists are played by long-established Hollywood stars (Cooper, James Stewart), the two trials take on a subtextual charge of meaning: the old versus the new, tradition versus innovation, which is conveyed, in each case, not only through the audience's extrafilmic awareness of the relative stature of the two actors but also through their sharply contrasting styles of performance. Appearing in *Billy Mitchell* for the first time eleven minutes before the end of the film, Steiger brings an intensity and a willfully grating tenacity that are markedly at odds with the performance styles of all the other actors: if they are smooth, he is rough. The open irony of Gullion's exaggerated respect for Mitchell's accomplishments can be read in terms of the attitude an actor like Steiger might be imagined to have toward an exemplar of old Hollywood royalty like Cooper. Conversely, the visible discomfort of Mitchell before Gullion's onslaught (like the discomfort of James

Stewart's Biegler before Scott's Assistant State Attorney Claude Dancer) might be interpreted as the discomfort of the *actor* before a probable future star who is having a field day in a showy supporting role.

In each film, furthermore, the casting of the younger actor carries a similar complicating irony, since, contrary to expectations that might be founded on his own persona apart from the film, his character embodies the reactionary position in the film's ideological struggle, whereas the older actor defends the progressive, enlightened position. Asserting, like the prosecutors in *Saint Joan*, the necessity of unquestioning obedience to authority, Gullion criticizes and mocks Mitchell for independent thinking and for trying to move the army forward. In *Anatomy*, Dancer, in order to cast doubt on Laura's testimony, tries to associate the jurors with his own misogyny and to cast Laura in the stereotypical role of "huntress."

This reversal indicates how *The Court-Martial of Billy Mitchell* can be read as an allegory of Preminger's own relation to tradition. It is crucial to the inner structure of the film that an established star play the beleaguered but ultimately vindicated rebel, while a younger actor becomes the key spokesman for an oppressive tradition. Preminger's own relation to power is ambivalent, and his films acknowledge this ambivalence. In *Saint Joan*, the casting of the untrained Jean Seberg, opposite the likes of John Gielgud, Anton Walbrook, and Felix Aylmer, doesn't exactly compromise Joan's moral, social, and political force, but it complicates our attitude to it. With *The Moon Is Blue*, Preminger cast himself as a rebel against certain traditions of Hollywood. *Billy Mitchell* can be seen as a self-portrait that shows how Preminger wanted his own rebellion to be perceived: not as a self-promoting and nihilistic gesture, but as a bid to rehabilitate and modernize American filmmaking and to enable it to thrive in the changed environment created by television and the divorcement decree. Preminger, who could thus claim that he was, despite a political liberalism that he would make increasingly public, a conservative, might well identify not only with Mitchell—who, like him, had achieved success and high responsibility within a large bureaucratic structure—but also with Gary Cooper, who was politically conservative (he appeared as a friendly witness before HUAC in 1947).

The Court-Martial of Billy Mitchell shows that "conservative" and "liberal" are relative terms, that retrograde and progressive tendencies both function within an institution, but that individual initiative and courage are needed to tip the balance and change the institution for the better. In this demonstration, *Billy Mitchell* is already close to Preminger's major institutional studies, *Advise & Consent*, *The Cardinal*, and *In Harm's Way*.

21

Hooked

___

Nelson Algren's 1949 novel *The Man with the Golden Arm* took a long, shadowy road to the screen. John Garfield was interested in playing the drug-addicted hero, Frankie Machine; and his company, Roberts Productions, bought the movie rights in 1949 or early 1950. Garfield's death in 1952 halted the project, but its chances of making it to the screen had always been in doubt because of the Production Code's strictures against drugs: "The illegal drug traffic, and drug addiction, must never be presented."[1]

The Man with the Golden Arm came to Preminger's attention by way of Ingo, who represented Lewis Meltzer, who had done a draft of the screenplay for Roberts. (In 1938 Otto had directed Meltzer's play *Yankee Fable*, which closed out of town.) Ingo sent the script and the book to his brother. At first Otto was unenthusiastic, but then he saw the possibility of using the film as a vehicle for breaking the Code restriction on drugs.[2] Preminger, probably negotiating through Ingo, acquired the rights to *The Man with the Golden Arm* either directly from Bob Roberts, Garfield's blacklisted former partner, who was now living in Europe, or from someone else to whom Roberts had sold the rights.

In late 1954 Preminger approached United Artists with the project. On terms similar to those that had governed the deal on *The Moon Is Blue*, the company agreed to fund *The Man with the Golden Arm* at a production cost of $500,000, exclusive of stars' salaries, story costs ($140,000), and Preminger's fees as producer and director ($110,000, deferred). Preminger would also receive the first $250,000 of net profits and 75 percent of net profits thereafter.[3] Back in the MPAA fold after *The Moon Is Blue* had finished its run, UA knew that it would have to defy the MPAA again over *Golden Arm* and was confident of success, even if it meant once again withdrawing from the association.

Seeking "a hard-hitting writer to do a rewrite" of the script, Preminger had Nelson Algren brought out from Gary, Indiana, to Hollywood.
For Preminger, this journey and Algren's association with the film perhaps came to little more than a brief and inexpensive waste of time, but
for the writer it was a catastrophe that, according to his biographer,
"marked a turning point in Algren's life."[4] For Algren, Preminger would
become an obsession, a symbol of the crass arrogance of power, an enemy with whom he would grapple again and again in his writing and his
reminiscences.

On arriving in Los Angeles at the end of January 1955, Algren was installed at the Beverly Carlton Hotel and urged to "be nice to Otto."
Showing up in a red Cadillac to pick up Algren for their first conference,
Preminger immediately made himself an object of contempt to the
writer by demonstrating a fascination with his automatic power windows. In Preminger's office, Algren watched as Preminger continued his
"producer" antics, having himself made up in his chair for a photo shoot,
taking phone calls (hanging up on one disappointed caller, Preminger explained to Algren, "Everybody wants to be Mahatma Gandhi"), pushing
buttons on his desk to summon assistants.[5] Perhaps to break the ice,
Preminger asked Algren about the characters of *Golden Arm*—petty
criminals, gamblers, prostitutes, and alcoholics mired in a squalid section of Chicago: "How do you know such people?" The classist implication of the question, or maybe the way Preminger asked it, rankled
Algren. When the writer left the producer's office, not only was he convinced that Preminger was incapable of making a sincere film of the
book, but "I saw no chance of having a relationship with this guy at all."[6]

Their next meeting was at Preminger's Malibu house. In the meantime, Algren had gone to a movie theater and noticed a line on the poster
for a jungle movie: "White Goddess say not go that part of forest." In the
twelve-page treatment Algren handed Preminger ("So little pages?" was
the latter's comment), he gave the line to Frankie Machine. The meeting
must have ended not long after Preminger read it. According to Algren,
"He just picked up the phone and told the agent, 'Mr. Algren and I have
agreed that he doesn't care to do the sort of script I want, so . . .' His last
gesture to me was very insulting. He said something like, 'Thank you for
letting me meet a very interesting person.' "[7]

Algren refused to accept any money from Preminger and on February 10 wrote him a sarcastic and insulting letter turning down, one by one, each item Preminger had offered: $203.78 for train fare; a $35 per diem "for listening to the expression of certain thoughts, after a manner of speaking, by yourself . . . all of them . . . the property of other persons"; and $750 for his work on the script ("since my work served only to confuse you further, no moneys are rightfully due"). Still smarting from Preminger's epithet, the writer concluded, "Although I did not find you an interesting person, I did discover in you an uncanny one. Upon the basis of mutual amusement, therefore, I am the debtor. And since you are decidedly more uncanny than I am interesting, I must, at a rough estimate, owe you close to forty dollars. I will send you this sum confident of your satisfaction in alms from any quarter however modest."[8]

After this, and after the lawsuit Algren later filed against Preminger, Preminger's version of his encounter with Algren may fairly be called forgiving. "He was an amusing, intelligent man but he couldn't write dialogue or visualize scenes," his autobiography states. Perhaps the most substantial charge Algren ever leveled against Preminger was contained in Algren's review of that autobiography. Quoting Preminger's account of the process of adapting a literary work for a film—"When I prepare a story for filming, it is being filtered through my brain, my emotions, my talent such as I have"[9]—Algren counters, "The trouble with this is that the life of the common man has never filtered into Otto's brain and emotions; or into his talent such as he has. The book dealt with life at the bottom. Otto has never, not for so much as a single day, had any experience except that of life at the top."[10]

Preminger looked around for another "hard-hitting writer" to do the script. When Walter Newman (having been sounded out by Ingo about his interest and availability) first met Preminger, the director told him that he saw *Golden Arm* "as a murder mystery."[11] Preminger's remark suggests that he already had in mind some version of a crucial plot twist introduced by the film. In both the novel and the film, Frankie's wife, Zosh, was injured in a car driven by Frankie and is now wheelchair-bound. In the film, it's Zosh, not Frankie, who kills the drug pusher Louie—to prevent him from exposing her secret: that she has been feigning paraplegia in order to exploit Frankie's guilt and keep him from leaving her.

At the first meeting, Newman was adamant that the book was too good to be tampered with, and the two argued loudly for two hours. Finally Preminger told Newman, "Let's talk about it tomorrow. You're going to work with me and we'll iron it out." Newman was hired in February; in March, it was reported in the press that he and Preminger were at work on *Golden Arm*. A Preminger spokesman—clearly being disingenuous—said that his boss "intends to come up with an adaptation to which the Production Code people will not object."[12]

Over a series of daylong sessions, the director and the writer worked out a dramatic line for the film. The crucial change from the novel was to make Frankie Machine (who, in Algren's book, ends up hanging himself while on the run from the police) a protagonist who struggles to change his life and wins. "This provided the necessary conflict and I think made it workable as a film," said Newman. According to Newman, "I worked very hard to use as much of the book as I could, as many of the people, as much of the dialogue, as many of the incidents as I could—except that I turned them upside down."[13]

In the novel, Frankie is first exposed to morphine in an army field hospital in France while recuperating from a battle wound. Preminger decided to eliminate the war wound and the medication as excuses for Frankie's drug use in order to widen the application of the story and to emphasize the psychological, rather than physical, aspects of addiction. "If people take it for 'kicks,' as they call it, and they think, as he says in the picture, 'I thought I could take it or leave it, and suddenly I noticed I couldn't leave it any more,' there is the danger: that we all feel we are exceptions in these matters, we can just try it, and then let it go. This is the danger with alcohol, with narcotics, with all kinds of things—that we feel we are stronger than other people . . . I also tried to show in the picture, that the psychological cause is really what keeps the man on narcotics . . . Statistics show that people fall back into the habit in alarmingly high numbers, because of mental unhappiness. Maybe it starts with the pace of the life we live, with mature people taking sleeping pills and benzedrine. Then they go to more harmful poison."[14] As these comments make clear, Preminger sought to make Frankie Machine a character whom middle-class audiences could identify with. In doing so, the film eliminates an important dimension of the novel, the radical critique of American society that Algren announces in the first chapter of the book, which describes Frankie and his fellow jail-cell oc-

cupants as sharing "the great, secret and special American guilt of own-
ing nothing, nothing at all, in the one land where ownership and virtue
are one."[15] By elevating Frankie in class (and by removing Algren's important insistence that the police manhunt for Frankie is driven by ward
politics), Preminger makes Frankie a hero responsible for his fate instead of a victim of specific social and political forces. Preminger's
Frankie *is* victimized, to be sure, but by perverse and vicious individuals—Zosh and Louie—rather than by a social system. Nevertheless, one
could argue, with Preminger, that these changes to the story make its social criticism stronger by implying that anyone, not just the poor and
wounded, can become an addict—challenging U.S. drug czar Harry J.
Anslinger's attempts to portray drug use as largely confined to a criminal
underclass.[16]

Newman enjoyed working with Preminger: "I had to learn Otto and
he had to learn me . . . I found him to be *endlessly* patient, always cour-
teous, much more so than I was. We argued a lot, we used to have desk-
banging discussions, but it was just part of the business, there was never
anything personal in it. It was a pleasure to work with him, always exciting." After about a month of desk banging and research, during which
Preminger and Newman spoke with LAPD narcotics authorities and
other experts, Newman was ready to go off on his own and write. Three
or four weeks later he gave Preminger the first fifty pages. After reading
them, Preminger called Newman and said, "I'm delighted," which Newman thought was "extraordinary behavior for a director or a producer.
Almost all of them, at this point, would have begun the conversation
by saying, without even a hello, 'On page eleven there's a misplaced
comma—on page fourteen I don't understand the motivation'—and so
on and so on. This is Standard Operating Procedure and it's meant to
put the screenplay writer in his place—in other words, to put him
down."[17]

Preminger sent Newman's first fifty pages to Marlon Brando's and
Frank Sinatra's agents (and also, possibly, Montgomery Clift's). Sinatra's
agent called him back two days later saying that his client was ready to
sign a contract and didn't need to wait for the rest of the script. On
May 2 Preminger announced to the press that Sinatra had committed to
do the film. Sinatra's deal got him $100,000 plus 12.5 percent of the
profits.[18]

After Newman finished the script, Preminger brought in Ben Hecht to do some rewriting. (Hecht's contribution to the film, like his last-minute work on *The Court-Martial of Billy Mitchell*, went uncredited.) On June 27 Preminger sent the script to Geoffrey Shurlock, who had replaced Joseph Breen as the PCA's director in October 1954, with a request that the administrator read it personally. "As I told you on the phone I consider the theme and the way it is handled in this script very important. I sincerely believe that this picture done with integrity can be a public service."[19] On July 6 Shurlock told Preminger that the PCA could not pass *The Man with the Golden Arm* because of the Code provision on drugs. Off the MPAA record, Shurlock hoped to make *The Man with the Golden Arm* the occasion for an overhaul of the Code, as he told Preminger and several United Artists executives.[20]

Preminger assembled the cast, recruiting Arnold Stang, Robert Strauss (from *Stalag 17* and, long before that, the ill-fated *Yankee Fable*), and Doro Merande (who had been in Preminger's Broadway flops *Beverly Hills*, *The More the Merrier*, and *Four Twelves Are 48*, and whom he would use again in small parts in *The Cardinal*, *Hurry Sundown*, and *Skidoo*) to play colorful denizens of Frankie's neighborhood. He was pleased enough with Darren McGavin's work in a small part in *Billy Mitchell* to promote him to the role of Louie in *Golden Arm*. For Zosh, Preminger considered Barbara Bel Geddes and Joanne Woodward, only to settle on Eleanor Parker. For the role of Molly, the sympathetic neighbor who helps Frankie beat his addiction, Preminger wanted Kim Novak badly enough to meet Columbia's loan-out price of $100,000, a large sum for a star not yet risen. Preminger would have liked (he later said) to shoot on location in Chicago, but to keep costs down he settled for the RKO back lot. Reflecting the exhibition practices of the time, Preminger's contract with United Artists stipulated that the film should be in a "wide-screen" (i.e., anamorphic) process or in the 1.85:1 aspect ratio; Preminger chose the latter.

Sinatra and Preminger got on well together, the star surprising himself by discovering a taste for rehearsal. "He wasn't a professional actor," as Preminger noted, "but he was very good, and reliable, and I loved him." Sinatra teased Preminger by calling him Herr Doktor or Ludwig, perhaps in reference to the director's early Twentieth Century-Fox days, when his credit included his middle name. In return, Preminger dubbed

Sinatra Anatol, after Arthur Schnitzler's famous creation, an easygoing philanderer in late-nineteenth-century Vienna. Preminger enjoyed his banter with Sinatra enough to incorporate the two nicknames into a line in *Anatomy of a Murder*. When the accused Lieutenant Manion tells his attorneys that the army psychiatrist who pronounced him temporarily insane was named Smith, one of the lawyers, Parnell, expresses the hope that, the better to impress the jury, the doctor's full name was "Anatole Ludwig Smith."

Sinatra made an extra effort to accommodate the frightened, inexperienced Novak, the two stars often working alone with Preminger on a closed set. Once Sam Leavitt's camera started rolling, however (shooting started in late September), Novak lost her self-confidence. Preminger had learned that Novak's performances at Columbia had required extensive dubbing because of her problems with dialogue. Refusing to dub, Preminger managed to break her of her bad habits, although sometimes it took as many as twenty takes to get her "to forget to be afraid."[21] "Sinatra went through all the takes, just like a pro," Preminger recalled.[22] "He never complained and never made her feel that he was losing patience through any of it, even when we had to do some scenes again and again." It helped that Novak was able to identify with her character, of whom she later said, "She was compassionate and acted the way I would have done had I been faced with such a problem in real life. I could understand all her feelings."[23]

Preminger was tough with Stang and so much so with McGavin that even Preminger admitted, "I treated him pretty rough." One day, Preminger, directing from his usual perch on the boom, yelled at McGavin, who replied, "Don't you shout at me." According to an onlooker, "Preminger, the actor, let the silence hang, then said very quietly, 'Very well, Mr. McGavin. You're a bad actor on stage, you're a bad actor in front of the camera. Can you hear me, Mr. McGavin? Shall we proceed?' " McGavin "almost chased him up the boom." Sometimes Sinatra helped break the tension by teasing Preminger with imitations of his accent. "It was his way of fighting for us," said McGavin.[24]

Walter Newman visited the set to witness the scene in Louie's apartment in which Frankie knocks out the pusher, searches frantically for drugs, and runs out the door. After the one-take scene was finished, a technician pointed out, "When Frank ran out of the room, he missed one of the lights he was supposed to pass under—we'll have to do it again." Sinatra said, "Uh-uh. That was *it*. I couldn't possibly do it again." Preminger concurred with his star: "Never mind the light."[25] For the key sequence of Frankie going cold turkey in Molly's apartment, Sinatra asked Preminger to skip the rehearsals and start shooting, confident that he knew how to play the scene. Preminger acceded to his request, and Sinatra proceeded to nail the scene well ahead of Preminger's schedule.[26] Still photographer Bob Willoughby recalled, "When Otto yelled 'Cut!' and said something about doing another take, Frank looked up at Al Myers, the camera operator, and asked him if he'd got it. Al quietly nodded, and Frank walked back to his dressing room. There would be no retakes on this scene."[27]

While the film was still in production in mid-October, Harry J. Anslinger, commissioner of the U.S. Bureau of Narcotics, condemned the film for showing that the hero had freed himself from addiction—an outcome that, in his view, was unrealistic. This position was consistent with Anslinger's career-long policy of stigmatizing addicts as beyond-the-pale deviants. (Anslinger advocated compulsory imprisonment for users instead of medical treatment. He also thought that drug trafficking in the United States was a Communist plot.)[28] Preminger had already baited the commissioner by observing at a press conference in late September that the PCA would not oppose the film but for the narcotics clause in the Code, whose reinstatement (the clause was softened in 1946, but the amendment was rescinded five years later), as Preminger noted, Anslinger had pushed for. Pointing out that the Bureau of Narcotics was part of the Treasury Department, Preminger wondered, "Suppose the Treasury asks movies to stop saying anything about taxes? It's the closest thing to government censorship, which they should either have or not have."[29] Preminger pounced on Anslinger's attack, sending Secretary of the Treasury George M. Humphrey a telegram that was published in *The Hollywood Reporter* on October 25, in which he criticized Anslinger for seeking to control the content of films. Over the following weeks, as the controversy over *Golden Arm* ensured him access to the press, Preminger kept up his onslaught against Anslinger, noting the commissioner's "singularly unsuccessful" record of stemming drug traffic and, during a televised panel discussion, calling him "the most unsuccessful public official in America."[30] Preminger also attacked Anslinger in the trailer for the film.

Shooting ended at the end of October, and a rough cut was ready in time for UA executives to see it over the November 5–6 weekend. UA president Arthur Krim claimed to be confident that the PCA, recognizing the film's "immense potential for public service," would approve it, and Preminger echoed this opinion in a press conference in New York on November 14, but he also disclosed that the Fox West Coast circuit (which had turned down *The Moon Is Blue* because of the lack of the Seal) had committed to showing *Golden Arm* whether or not it got a Seal.[31]

After the PCA screened the film on December 2, Shurlock wrote Preminger, "The picture is basically in violation of the clause of the Production Code which states 'The illegal drug traffic, and drug addiction, must never be presented.' For this reason, it will not be possible for us to issue you the Association's Certificate of Approval." UA appealed and, in a meeting of the MPAA board of directors on December 6, was denied, despite president Eric Johnson's recommendation to the board that *Golden Arm* receive a special exemption from the Code rule on drugs. The next day, UA announced that it was withdrawing from the MPAA and would distribute the film without the Seal. *Variety* editorialized that the MPAA was bound to liberalize the Code statute on drugs but didn't want to give the appearance of doing it under pressure from a producer who "made it so perfectly plain that he more or less didn't care what they did . . . While they are generally agreed for [sic] the need for a change, film company toppers have a deep-seated resentment against Preminger's tactics. 'If we're going to change the Code every time someone deliberately puts us on a spot, pretty soon there wouldn't be a Code,' said one."[32]

Preminger declared himself unsurprised that the MPAA upheld the PCA ruling. "What can you expect when the jury consists of your competitors?" he asked. "It might have been quite different had they appointed a group of top directors to do the reviewing of my picture. They might have appreciated its value."[33] At a December 27 press conference in Hollywood, Preminger went further, charging that despite the MPAA's claims that the Production Code protected filmmakers from censorship, the Code really functioned as a means for the major studios to restrict film content. Preminger cast himself as a champion in the fight against censorship ("If you don't defend your right to exist without censorship, that right deteriorates").[34]

Meanwhile, UA found little difficulty in lining up bookings for
Golden Arm. Some exhibitors who may have been reluctant to book the
Seal-deprived film took heart from the Legion of Decency's decision to
give the film a B rating instead of the expected C, a move that was
widely taken as a snub to the Code.

According to *Variety,* after considerable back-and-forth argument
with the New York State censors, Preminger agreed, shortly before the
film's New York release, to cut thirty-seven seconds of footage showing
Louie preparing Frankie's fix in a spoon. The *Variety* article also stated
that to avoid having to fight this particular battle over and over across the
country, Preminger made the same deletion in all prints.[35] This statement appears inaccurate. On January 12, 1956, the Maryland State
Board of Censors demanded a cut from the moment when Frankie rolls
up his sleeve to the point just before he reclines on Louie's couch. In
testifying at an appeal hearing, United Artists sales supervisor George J.
Schaefer claimed that the film had been passed by censors without cuts
in every state except Maryland.

The film opened on December 15 in New York and went into general
release in early 1956. Reviews ranged from high praise to moralistic condemnation. Preminger's campaign for *Golden Arm* set him against much
of the Hollywood establishment in an even more stark way than had the
fracas over *The Moon Is Blue.* Louella Parsons, long a Preminger sup-
porter, turned against him in her December 30 column, in which she declared, "On all sides there is a feeling that Otto Preminger overstepped
the bounds of decency in making a picture that could very well bring
down Federal censorship."[36]

In the controversy caused by the film's treatment of drugs and the
MPAA's denying it a Seal, two other unusual aspects of the film did not go
unnoticed. Composer Elmer Bernstein, whom Ingo had recommended to
Otto (and who was then on a kind of "graylist" in Hollywood because of
his presumed political associations), came up with a score that featured
both a jazz ensemble, Shorty Rogers and His Giants (who also appeared in
the memorable scene of Frankie's disastrous tryout as a band drummer),
and a symphony orchestra. *The Hollywood Reporter* exulted that with his
score, Bernstein proved that jazz could function in a film "as a sustaining
and continuous story-telling element in underscoring the mood elements
of an entire picture."[37]

Having learned his lesson after his dispute with United Artists over the publicity campaign for *The Moon Is Blue*, Preminger had insisted on the right to approve the content and design of advertising and publicity for *The Man with the Golden Arm*.[38] Though he had previously done the campaign for *The Moon Is Blue* and the titles for *Carmen Jones*, Saul Bass considered *The Man with the Golden Arm* his first significant collaboration with Preminger. Late in his life, Bass remembered Preminger as "a bundle of contradictions . . . the best client I ever had and the most difficult one," and a man in whom "intuitive processes [were] at work . . . that enabled him to identify when it was really working and when it was not." Bass broke new ground with his campaign for *The Man with the Golden Arm*. "The thing that was singular about what happened with *Man with the Golden Arm* and a number of other things we did was the notion of making a commitment to one central idea. A notion that it was possible in a totally reductive way to say, 'This is what the film is about,' and develop an evocative, visual configuration and image that would express that notion and express it in a sufficiently seductive and perhaps metaphorical, or a provocative way, that would cause a large enough number of people to say, 'Hey, I'm interested in that film and I want to see it.' That notion was an absolutely frightening one . . . for all the distributors, but that was the notion that Otto and I committed ourselves to."[39]

For *The Man with the Golden Arm* campaign, Bass devised the image of a crooked arm. Preminger liked the image so much he had Bass incorporate it into the titles of the film as an animated sequence. This would be the first of Bass's renowned title sequences in films for Preminger, Alfred Hitchcock, and others. It opens with white bars, which could be interpreted as drumsticks (a visual correlative to Shelly Manne's cymbal pattern, the first sound heard in the film), sliding down from the top of the screen against a black background. At the end of the sequence, the sticks change into an arm, which twists itself into the form of the ad campaign image, at the same time as Preminger's producer-director credit appears on-screen. Future Bass titles would again link Preminger's name to arms and hands: the severed arm in *Anatomy of a Murder*, the hand lifting the dome off the Capitol in *Advise & Consent*, the forearm and pointing finger in *In Harm's Way*, the hand ripping the screen in *Bunny Lake Is Missing*.

Preminger's commitment to Bass's graphic overrode the doubts of marketers and exhibitors. Bass overheard Preminger talking on the phone with a Texas exhibitor who wanted to replace Bass's simple design with a more conventional campaign. Preminger replied, "If you change one hair in any of these ads, I will pull the picture." For Bass, this incident confirmed his opinion of Preminger. "That strength and that belief and commitment, I would have jumped off the roof for Otto . . . Those qualities that made him difficult also made him a man that you could count on. Let's put it this way, he is a man I would be willing to go to combat with."

Bass's ads bore the phrase "A Film by Otto Preminger." Some in Hollywood took exception to the slogan, which, claimed screenwriter Dan Taradash, president of the screenwriters branch of the Writers Guild of America, "could only be justified if [the] film had been written, produced, and directed by one man."[40] A well-known Hollywood witticism went like this: a car is driving through Bel Air; someone says, "There's Otto Preminger's house. Excuse me, I mean, a house by Otto Preminger." In 1956, Nelson Algren, filing suit against Preminger and other defendants, sought an injunction to stop Preminger from claiming authorship of the film. (The suit was eventually dropped because Algren lacked funds to pay his attorney.)[41]

Sinatra was nominated for the Best Actor Academy Award but lost to Ernest Borgnine (*Marty*). *The Man with the Golden Arm* had a highly successful run, ending up at number 13 on *Variety*'s list of the top-grossing films of 1956 ($4,350,000 in U.S. and Canadian rentals). Some highlights of the later career of *The Man with the Golden Arm* should be noted. In December 1956 the Production Code statute on drugs was amended, as was widely predicted during the *Golden Arm* fracas; the new rules opened a few loopholes (perhaps less in direct response to Preminger's film than to accommodate such major-studio projects as Fox's *A Hatful of Rain*, released in 1957). In December 1966, in leasing *The Man with the Golden Arm* for TV broadcast, ABC agreed to show the film without deletions and to let Preminger choose, as he put it, the "least harmful places" for commercial interruptions. This agreement, possibly unprecedented in U.S. TV, compensated Preminger for his failed lawsuit the previous year to prevent the mangling of *Anatomy of a Murder* on TV.[42]

The fluidity of *The Man with the Golden Arm* (evident from its impressive opening crane shot, which crosses the street to frame Frankie alighting from a bus, then follows him two blocks to the window of Antek's bar) reflects the domination over the profilmic that studio shooting affords. It is a domination that Preminger had already begun to renounce, and with which he would dispense altogether, or as much as possible, in *Anatomy of a Murder* and the films following it. Like *The Moon Is Blue*, *Saint Joan*, and, especially, *Porgy and Bess*, *The Man with the Golden Arm* is in this sense an exception to the main movement of Preminger's work after his departure from Fox and before *Skidoo*: an abstract, hermetic film rather than one that involves itself with a reality that exists outside, and for other purposes than, the filmic project. The sets render Algren's skid row as an isolated and self-contained world, accentuating both its hopelessness and its lack of historicity. This world has no past and no future; it is ready for the bulldozers. The stylization of some of the performances—Robert Strauss's and Arnold Stang's, notably—suits this desperate and artificial quality perfectly.

Also at work throughout the film is a highly coded "realism," manifested, for example, in the studied intrusions of characters in the backgrounds or on the sides of compositions to whose foreground actions they are ostensibly irrelevant. As Frankie, in the foreground of the shot, uses the common phone of his apartment building to call the man to whom he has been referred for a job interview, John, Molly's boyfriend, leans against the wall in the background, waiting for her to emerge from the apartment. John's eyes drift around the scene in a bored manner, occasionally lighting coldly on Frankie's back; Frankie, after registering John's presence at the beginning of the shot as he descends the stairs to the hall, pays no attention to him. John's obtrusive presence in the shot, as if he just happened to be there, is an element of realism, distracting from rather than supporting the ostensible concerns of the plot. The quality of distraction is deceptive, however, since in fact John's presence sets up the important revelation of Frankie's past relationship with Molly. Later, John and Molly, sitting in a booth in Antek's bar, are visible in the background of a shot in which Frankie, Sparrow, and Schwiefka talk in the foreground. The placement of the background figures appears to call out to be read as an irrelevant distraction and thus as an element of realistic detail, but it is clear that Preminger also wants us to be aware of Molly's looking across the room at Frankie, and of the fact that she and John, though physically close together, have nothing to say to each other.

One of the most striking examples of this kind of recuperated distraction that reads as an element of realism is the use of the figure of the anonymous junkie cellmate (played by Jered Barclay) in the scene of Frankie in jail. The character calls attention to himself by yawning and wiping his nose, as well as by his rather startling physiognomy, and he is placed in the composition not only as a distracting element, but as one that Frankie must actively avoid noticing (after first inattentively sitting next to the man, Frankie looks at him and immediately moves away) in order not to be reminded of his own barely suppressed craving for a fix. The distracting element is thus one that Frankie seeks to suppress but cannot. The composition that holds Frankie together with the junkie is a metaphor for Frankie's consciousness. This mental aspect of the image is so strong that the realism of the shot is hardly more than a vestigial element.

Throughout the film, the drama is interiorized, psychological, played out seemingly among the mental images of beings and things (the second shot in the film, a close-up from inside Antek's of Frankie peering in through the window, already alerts us to the privileged emphasis that Frankie's subjective experience will receive throughout). Drawn to ever smaller spaces, the film seals itself off (as Schwiefka's marathon poker game seals itself from the sunlight), locks itself in (as Frankie has himself locked in Molly's bedroom when he tries to kick his habit). Camera movement in *The Man with the Golden Arm* tends to define subjective mental states rather than explore the contours and surfaces of an outer world, and it creates a suffocating atmosphere, relentless in its emphasis on the registration of consciousness, as in the repeated track-ins on huge close-ups of Frankie's eyes, first as Louie injects him, then as he lies back, then again (in a later scene) when the lighted match Molly holds near his face provokes the giveaway blinking that reveals he's back on the stuff.

The Man with the Golden Arm is largely a film of faces: scenes are staged as abstracted, displaced encounters among people who face toward the camera from various planes in the same shot. Frankie and Louie are often shown in this way, one confidently turning his back to the other so that both are seen looking forward, the man closer to the camera asserting the greater power ("I'll be around," Louie tells Frankie). In the superbly acted long-take seduction scene, the two men both face front and occupy the same plane (sitting side by side at Antek's bar), so that the underlying contest between them appears even, and a surface of mutual liking and respect is foregrounded.

It is a frontal, vertical film, done in repetitive, driving, elastic movements. The camera tracks back across the floor of the apartment from Zosh before she gets up out of her wheelchair, showing us, for the first time in the film, that she can walk. When Louie enters the apartment and finds her standing up (becoming the first character in the film to share our knowledge of Zosh's hidden ability), the camera reverses its previous movement by tracking toward her. Repeated shots follow characters up the stairway to Schwiefka's card game.

Like *Fallen Angel*, *The Man with the Golden Arm* (Preminger's, not Algren's) is a story of redemption. In both films, the hero's triumph over his demons is signaled by morning sunlight streaming through the window of a transient dwelling. That transience itself—a particularly American rootlessness, linked to the refusal to accept, and the inability to reject, one's surroundings—is a theme of both films is indicated by their beginnings, which find the protagonist deposited from a bus in his new environment.

22

Too Much Reason

Preminger's fascination with Shaw's *Saint Joan* dated to his Vienna years. "I think it's the greatest masterpiece ever written for the theater, and that's why I was always interested in making this filmed version of it."[1]

On May 3, 1956 (in the middle of the Cannes Film Festival, where Preminger was on the jury—they gave the Palme d'Or to the Jacques Cousteau documentary *Le Monde du silence,* directed by Louis Malle), after two years of on-and-off negotiations, Preminger concluded a deal with George Bernard Shaw's estate for the film rights to *Saint Joan.* The contract was unusual in quantifying the fidelity of the adaptation: Preminger would have the right to change up to 25 percent of the original. Already, in March, Preminger had signed with United Artists to produce *Saint Joan* in England under the Eady Plan, which provided a government subsidy for films that employed a quota of British personnel. (The fact that the decision to shoot *Saint Joan* in England was made long before Preminger discovered Jean Seberg shows that, though the Iowan's presence among the otherwise almost entirely British cast heightens the sense of Joan's isolation, the desire to achieve this effect did not dictate the production circumstances.) The terms were similar to those of *The Man with the Golden Arm*: the production cost was not to exceed $750,000, unless Preminger hired stars.[2]

Preminger hired Graham Greene to write the script for the film, no doubt to ensure that the film would have something to say about Catholicism. Preminger found the writer "a delightful companion" and discovered that "sex is on his mind all the time."[3] On July 19, in New York, Preminger announced that to cast the title role of *Saint Joan,* he would launch a talent search throughout the United States, Canada, and Western Europe. "I wanted audiences to identify this actress only with

Joan, not to identify Joan with an actress they already knew."[4] Entry application forms were distributed in 9,000 theaters in North America and 2,000 in Europe. "I have no specific image or character in mind," Preminger said. "I only know there are certain qualities necessary to play this part, which I hope to recognize when I meet the girl."[5] Eventually, 18,000 applications were received, and Preminger personally auditioned 3,000 girls.

"Apart from the possibility of finding a girl," Preminger explained to Myer Beck of United Artists' publicity department in a letter that, incidentally, provides some insight into Preminger's capacities as a businessman,

> the fact that my trip will take me to almost all key cities in America, Canada and England will help to pre-sell the picture. In order to achieve this I want you and Thomas, in association with the United Artists field men, to be absolutely sure not to overlook any possibility for me to appear on TV, radio, speak to colleges and literary societies wherever I go. All this can be achieved without feeding hundreds of people with lunch and pouring drinks into hangers-on at our expense. It has become too much of a custom in film publicity to pick up checks without giving any thought to it, but these $4., $5., and $12. bills add up to big sums without creating anything but hangovers.[6]

The auditions started on September 4 in New York, where Preminger spent an exhausting day seeing more than 250 candidates in the Trianon Room of the Hotel Ambassador. While in New York, he met Richard Widmark and cast him as the Dauphin.[7] Widmark later recalled, "I said to Preminger, 'What the hell do you want me in it for?' He said, 'I think it would be very interesting.' It was interesting all right. It practically did in my career."[8]

Preminger moved on to Boston, Montreal, Toronto, Detroit, and Cleveland before arriving in Chicago, where he found his Joan. Born in Marshalltown, Iowa, in 1938, Jean Seberg had graduated from Marshalltown High School in June 1956. Encouraged by her drama teacher and a local businessman, she sent in an application to the *Saint Joan* contest. She received a form letter instructing her to learn two speeches from

Shaw's play and to appear at the Sherman Hotel in Chicago on September 15 for her audition. When Preminger saw Seberg, "something clicked," he said. "She was a vital young woman and she had great personality. And she was very anxious to play the part." At the end of the day, Preminger met Seberg's parents and told them to bring the girl to New York in a month for the last round of auditions.

The auditions continued: St. Louis, Denver, Seattle, San Francisco, Los Angeles, Dallas, Atlanta. On September 28, Preminger was in Washington, D.C., his last U.S. stop on the audition tour before crossing the Atlantic to see the European hopefuls.

Three possible Joans faced one another in the final auditions at the Fox Movietone studios in New York in mid-October: Kelli Blaine, Doreen Denning, and Jean Seberg. Directing each in a screen test, Preminger lavished the most time, attention, and criticism on Seberg. The actress bore up under his demands and showed considerable nerve. "At the beginning Mr. Preminger did everything he could to upset me," Seberg told Art Buchwald. "He called me a ham and a phony and I was so upset I didn't know what to do. But then I realized he was just trying to see if I could take it."[9] When Preminger, who made her repeat her audition monologues several times, asked her if she was tired, she replied, "Mr. Preminger, I'm willing to go on and on with this until *you* drop dead."[10] Seberg recalled, "He went at me and I fought him back. I still had a lot of Midwestern strength. I really sometimes think that's why he took me; unconsciously, he saw a spirit to break."[11] After more of the ordeal, she finally broke down sobbing, whereupon Preminger lifted her up, comforted her, and assured her that she had done well. According to Bob Willoughby, whom Preminger had hired as still photographer for the sessions, "There was no question that Jean was the winner. The others were more polished, but Jean had the sincerity Otto was after."[12] That night, Preminger told Seberg that she would play Joan and swore her to secrecy until he announced his decision on *The Ed Sullivan Show* on October 21.

Preminger signed Seberg to a seven-year contract. Although it was rumored during the time of their association together, and has frequently been suggested or imagined since, that the two had an affair (Louella Parsons even reported that Hollywood was betting that the two would marry),[13] Preminger denied it, and Seberg's biographer, David Richards, believes that Seberg herself found such rumors puzzling.[14]

On October 21, Seberg was presented to the press. *The New York Times* called her "a personification of the Cinderella story."[15] During the following months, her break would continue to capture the imagination of magazine editors, and she was featured in a number of profile articles and cover photos. Though United Artists had grumbled at the cost of Preminger's talent hunt (initially budgeted at $50,000, the trip ended up costing twice that), UA vice president Max E. Youngstein noted to his colleagues that Preminger's talent search had paid off in free publicity and given them "a theme for selling the picture which might bring in young people to a George Bernard Shaw play, and that is to keep hammering home the Cinderella theme of Jean Seberg."[16]

Preminger went to London to set up the production. Anton Walbrook was cast as Cauchon, Felix Aylmer as the Inquisitor, and Barry Jones as Courcelles. Richard Burton, announced as the Earl of Warwick,[17] was replaced by Sir John Gielgud, who thought Greene's screenplay "very clever."[18] Meanwhile, Richard Todd was added to the cast as Dunois, Harry Andrews as Stogumber, and Kenneth Haigh (replacing Paul Scofield) as Brother Martin. For the production team, Preminger recruited—probably by design—several veterans of Olivier's *Hamlet*, including production designer Roger Furse, assistant director Peter Bolton, makeup artist Tony Sforzini, and editor Helga Cranston, who believed that she owed her hiring partly to another connection: "When he asked me where I was born in Germany, and I said Darmstadt, he said, 'Ah, I performed there, in my first stage appearance, in *Cabala and Love*, by Schiller.' And I quoted a line from that. Of course he roared with laughter. That broke a lot of ice. He also was fascinated with the fact that I worked with Olivier."[19] Another *Hamlet* veteran, cinematographer Desmond Dickinson, left over a disagreement with Preminger over how the film should look; in his place, Preminger hired another distinguished cameraman, Georges Périnal. Preminger had decided early on to shoot the film in black and white. "I want to put the emphasis on people, on characterizations, on emotions, and on the words by Bernard Shaw . . . Color, or too much spectacle added to it, would distract rather than help to give this play to the public."[20]

Preminger installed Seberg at the Dorchester Hotel, where he also had a suite, and took charge of her entire schedule, which included French lessons, elocution lessons, riding lessons, and instructions in handling a broadsword and encountering the press. Seberg, who at first imagined Preminger as a "father" and "savior,"[21] came to see him differently. "He decided she had to be fearful and depressed and he saw to it that she was, finally," said Cranston. "He virtually imprisoned her in the hotel. She was not allowed to go out at all. He sent her food and everything she needed . . . Because she was so inexperienced, he really made her miserable in order for her to perform miserably, you know. It was as simple and as cruel as that."[22] Bob Willoughby, who accompanied Preminger and Seberg to London to serve as still photographer for the production, noted, "Otto wanted nothing less than total control."[23]

On December 17 Preminger and the cast assembled for the first of a series of rehearsals at Shepperton Studios. If Seberg had not yet been sufficiently overwhelmed by Preminger's provisions for her, the presence of some of England's best actors playing supporting parts in a film of which she was the star must have given her an acute appreciation of the burden she had to carry.

Shooting started at Shepperton on January 9 with Joan's arrival at the Dauphin's court. Preminger's direction of Seberg was rigorous. Describing his work with the young actress, which journalist Stephen Watts suggested might have something in common with the technique of a famous literary hypnotist, Preminger explained, "I try to teach her to think. Surely that is the opposite of Svengali. His trick was to insure that his victim didn't think. I can't get out of Miss Seberg what isn't there." One day, indeed, he yelled at her, "You're not thinking the part!" According to Bob Willoughby, "I really think Jean worked her heart out to please Otto. She was very frightened and insecure, but she was determined to do a good job. Otto was a tyrant on the set, though. Nothing had an effect on him. He kept her on a constant emotional pitch, which isn't a professional way of acting. Often at the end of the day's shooting, she would be sobbing hysterically."[24]

According to Otto Plaschkes, second assistant director on the film, "You could see that she was trying very hard, but no matter what she did, she was never good enough for Preminger . . . Every word she had to say, he wanted to alter the emphasis."[25] Gielgud recalled, "Having chosen her but then decided it was a mistake, Preminger was utterly horrible to her on the set and I desperately wanted to help in any way I could. There wasn't an unkind bone in her body, but she was desperately insecure about everything and when one day I gave her a cup and saucer that had belonged to my great-aunt Ellen Terry, she simply broke down

in tears. She didn't know anything about phrasing or pacing or climax—
all the things the part needed—but she was desperately eager to learn,
and we became great friends."[26] Richard Widmark said that Preminger's
treatment of Seberg made *Saint Joan* the worst experience of his career.[27] "The way he treated Jean Seberg was indescribable. He criticized
her constantly. He yelled at her, he insulted her, without ever letting
up . . . We all asked him to leave her alone. Nothing did any good.
Maybe it was a test of toughness. But, to me, it was sadism."[28]

Off the set, Preminger could be kinder. He gave Seberg presents and
treated her with affection, running his hand through her hair and calling
her "baby." Helga Cranston thought that his affection for Seberg "was
like the affection of a father. He would call her 'Jeanie.' "[29] Once, Seberg
managed to play a practical joke on her tormentor. During a dinner party
at the Brompton Grill in London (on the occasion of a visit by Harry Belafonte), Seberg, Willoughby, and another friend arranged with the
restaurant staff to give Preminger red-carpet treatment but to refer to
him always as "Mr. Hitchcock." According to Willoughby, "The first few
times, he let it pass. But by the end of the evening he was pounding the
table with his fist and screaming, 'That is not my name! I am Otto Preminger!' "[30]

Helga Cranston thought that the two directors had something in
common. She observed years later that

> Hitchcock . . . worked out the story and the shooting so well, he
> gets rather bored during the actual time when the film is in pro-
> duction, because he saw it all out and he is no longer interested.
> There was something like that in Preminger, but different. When
> Preminger was shooting I felt he was a sort of quick sketch artist.
> He did not ponder about what was happening in front of the cam-
> era. Most of the time he put in all the ingredients: he had the
> best actors possible, he had the best art direction. All these ingre-
> dients guaranteed him a quality of film, rather than a sort of cre-
> ative inspiration during the direction.[31]

Cranston's assessment echoes Ingo Preminger's view of Max Reinhardt:
"His way of looking at art, was, you hire the best, and that has to pay
off."[32]

Preminger got along well with Georges Périnal, whom he had been

warned against for slowness. Comparing Périnal with Sam Leavitt, Preminger remarked, "While Périnal also does exactly what the director
wants, he understands why the director wants it . . . He was the most
efficient and conscientious cameraman I can imagine." Said Otto
Plaschkes, "Périnal seemed slightly removed from the hustle and bustle
of filmmaking. Preminger bowed to him totally, never interfered with
what Périnal was doing. There was a quiet authority to Périnal. Not a
very good communicator. One never quite knew how much time he
wanted before the set was ready, you had to guess. But he was good."[33]

A *Newsweek* reporter described the director as incensed by the time
and money wasted on tea breaks during production—a detail that suggests that Preminger's first experience with an English crew (apart from
his location trip for *The Fan*) required some painful adjustment on both
sides.[34] "The crew were slightly in awe of him," Plaschkes noted, "and
slightly terrified of him. I suppose we all said to each other, 'We'd better
be careful. This could happen to us too.' The mood was slightly subdued. It wasn't at all unhappy, but there was no sense of camaraderie.
Some directors can inspire a unit to become better than themselves.
That wasn't true of Preminger."[35]

During the trial scenes, Preminger kept demanding "more passion,
more passion, more passion" from Seberg, said Plaschkes. "And one
could almost hear Jean Seberg saying to herself, 'I'm giving it as much
passion as I can. I can't give any more without being phony.' My impression is that her performance never improved. Maybe a word here, a word
there, under Preminger's guidance, or shouting rather. I think at that
point she knew her limitations."[36] After the end of shooting, Seberg told
Gilbert Millstein, a *New York Times* writer, "Three weeks before the end
of the picture, the night before we made the perpetual-imprisonment
scene, Otto had a long talk with me. He said I had to stop worrying
about all exterior things, the impression I was making on people and, oh,
a lot more."[37] Helga Cranston said, "During the trials there was one
scene when she has a pretty long speech. She had 29 takes. She
was completely at the end of her tether. She hated him. She said to
me, 'I wish he would fall in love with me; I would give him such
hell.' "[38] Meanwhile, Preminger was on his best behavior with some of
the more distinguished actors. "He never said boo to John Gielgud or
Anton Walbrook," said Plaschkes. "These were two tough professionals,

he wouldn't dare touch their performance."[39] Gielgud occasionally dried up on his lines, "which didn't seem to faze him or Preminger," said Plaschkes.[40]

Disaster struck in the last week of filming. In the first take of Joan's burning, a misfire by the gas cylinders hidden under the pyre produced a sudden burst of flame that engulfed the actress. One of the executioners leaped up and freed Seberg, while studio firemen extinguished the blaze. Seberg recuperated in her dressing room and offered to continue working, but Preminger canceled the rest of the day's shooting. For the rest of her life, she would bear scars on her belly from the fire.[41] Preminger allowed himself to be quoted in *Newsweek* as saying, "We got it all on film. The camera took 400 extra feet, and the crowd reaction was fantastic. I'll probably use some of it."[42] He did. When work resumed on the burning scene, precautions were added that made it impossible for Preminger to shoot Seberg on the burning pyre in long shot as he had wanted.

Early the next morning, Preminger and Seberg were on their way to the studio in Preminger's car. The conditions were icy, and the car skidded off the road. Already shaken from the fire, Seberg became hysterical. Rumor around the set had it that it was at this point that Preminger promised her the role of Cécile in *Bonjour Tristesse*.[43]

When Helga Cranston first met Preminger, he told her that it was " 'very easy to cut my films, all that you have to do is take off the clapperboards.' But it wasn't so easy in all cases," Cranston remembered. "Sometimes it worked, but we also had problems, because he didn't shoot any closeups, and he didn't make sure that you could shorten a scene or that you could speed up a scene."[44] Preminger hired Mischa Spoliansky, whom he had known in Vienna, to compose the score for *Saint Joan*. "He was quite difficult with Mischa," Otto Plaschkes recalled. "He didn't quite like the shape of the music, so he wanted to alter certain things. He actually had a very good ear, Preminger."[45] Once, when Cranston shortened a Spoliansky organ piece to get it to fit the scene, Preminger flew into a tirade that reduced her to tears. That evening, he called her and took her out to an excellent dinner. "He was terribly generous with money," Cranston said. On another occasion, she asked to stop on the way to the cutting room to buy a blouse in a department store. "What do you mean? When you work with me you don't go to a department store. Tomorrow you go to Dior and buy a blouse . . .

But he started to scream at me again in the cutting room, and I felt I should have taken that blouse and thrown it in his face. He was very sentimental with his screaming."[46]

The film premiered in Paris on Sunday, May 12, 1957 (as he would do on a number of his later films, Preminger had announced the date of the premiere before the start of production), before its U.S. release. The glee with which U.S. reviewers vented their spleen on the film, Preminger, and Seberg is explainable as a delayed outburst of resentment against the massive publicity that had surrounded the talent search and the casting of Seberg. The *Time* reviewer, in a piece that alluded to the film's "panting publicity," got off the most memorable lines in a snide attempt to convey the extent to which the actress was miscast. "Shaw's Joan is a chunk of hard bread, dipped in the red wine of battle and devoured by the ravenous angels. Actress Seberg, by physique and disposition, is the sort of honey bun that drugstore desperadoes like to nibble with their milkshakes."[47] The *Saint Joan* talent search, the discovery of Seberg, and the fizzle of Seberg's debut would remain crucial in defining the public persona of Preminger and the journalistic discourse on it.

Preminger later reconsidered *Saint Joan*. "It was one of my least popular films. But even now, I don't care, and even though it lost a lot of money, I would do it again. I loved it. Yes, I love this film."[48] He admitted that he had miscalculated in directing Jean Seberg. "I didn't help her to understand and act the part, indeed I deliberately prevented her, because I was determined she should be completely unspoilt. I think the instinct—to cast a very young, inexperienced girl—was right, but now I would work with her for perhaps two years until she understood the part right through."[49] Trying to explain the failure of the film to excite a large audience, he speculated, "Something is missing—something that could make people cry. Perhaps Joan is too convinced herself. You just don't believe that she is a saint—that everything is vision and instinct and passion. There is too much reason in it for pictures."[50]

Saint Joan holds in balance the faith, charisma, and innocence of Joan—her absolute belief in herself and her voices—together with the realism of those around her. Preminger is on both sides, and the richness of the text in permitting both points of view—Joan's and that of the world—to expound themselves makes *Saint Joan* an ideal Preminger project. The efforts of the churchmen on Joan's behalf—so evident in the first scene in the cell—resemble Preminger's efforts on behalf of the other side in, for example, *Exodus*, still more *The Cardinal*: to give the other side the greatest benefit of the doubt, to avoid convicting the other side on mere technicalities, to avoid too easy a victory. (On the other hand, there is no doubt in whose side the scales are tipped, and the underlying directive of the churchmen's effort remains Warwick's cynical "Do your best for her, if you are quite sure that it will be of no avail.")

Seberg's performance, though deficient in nuance, is by no means the naked disaster it has been taken for. She and Preminger emphasize Joan's vulnerability and sadness, her uncomprehending sense of having been betrayed by the people and institutions she has fought for. In the scene after the coronation, her distress and her solitude are strongly emphasized. Leaving the throne room, she walks toward the camera, stopping as she hears the King say, "Of course, she had her uses." Then she starts crying and walks past the camera.

Preminger isolates Joan as much by her reactions and her looks as by staging and composition. Joan's troubled look up to the sky after the death of "Foul-Mouthed Frank," the soldier who tries to have his way with her, is strongly marked. Certain effects in the film depend on an ambiguity Preminger must have consciously sought, the impossibility of distinguishing between the discomfort of the actress and the discomfort of the character. Joan's nervousness at court is expressed by Seberg's shifting her body from side to side, as though she were uncertain where or how to stand. The exhaustion evident at the beginning of Joan's appearance at her trial was quite probably the direct result of Preminger's method of directing Seberg. The pressure on Seberg/Joan is expressed through her aggrieved, tormented delivery of the line, "What other judgment can I judge by if not my own?"—directed toward and past the camera, which she approaches with an exasperated, pleading defiance. Seberg is also effective in her more positive moments, such as Joan's beatific acceptance of death ("You are not fit that I live among you") and her final address to God.

Preminger insists on bringing out the erotic undercurrent of Joan's story. When Joan talks of wanting to baby Dunois, he takes it in a sexual sense and makes a pass at her: aware that an unwanted element has entered their relationship, she becomes uneasy. Yet Preminger and Seberg are fully conscious that Joan's effect on the soldiers and courtiers is a kind of seduction. In the epilogue, the intimacy with which she addresses the English soldier as "you, my one faithful" has more than a slight sexual hint, in which is activated the implicit eroticism of Joan's apparition in the bedroom of the dreaming Charles.

Saint Joan provides a template for Preminger's major works to come, studies of the workings of the law (*Anatomy of a Murder*), of nationalism (*Exodus*), of politicians (*Advise & Consent*), priests (*The Cardinal*), and military men (*In Harm's Way*). In *Saint Joan*, we find what may be called the Preminger Moment: a scene in which people discuss the code and logic of their profession in another language than the one they use in their public performance of their profession. The behind-the-scenes conferences among Warwick, Stogumber, Bishop Cauchon, and the Inquisitor are scenes of this type. Another example occurs earlier in the film, when, assuring La Trémouille that Joan's ability to see through Gilles de Rais's imposture and pick out the real Dauphin is indeed a "miracle"—though one based merely on observation combined with general cultural knowledge—the Archbishop of Rheims offers a pragmaticist definition of a miracle as "an event which creates faith." The Archbishop explains, "You are not so accustomed to miracles as I am. You see, it is part of my profession." The context in which we are to interpret "the miracle of the leaking pipe" in *The Cardinal* is already defined here as a nexus (a "coincidence," to use a word that is uttered, and questioned, in *Saint Joan*) of historical necessity and divine will. The camera movement in *Saint Joan* suggests that the trial is essentially a kind of ceremony rather than an attempt to persuade or to decide a truth.

Pageantry is part of the film, but Preminger doesn't make a big deal of it: he lets the sets fill the screen, making the world seem small and confined. Yet Périnal's sumptuous lighting creates a density and complexity of texture that could even be called extravagant. The constantly moving camera is methodical, inquisitive. Preminger uses camera movement as part of a rhythmic form that underlines the characters' emotions. An exchange between Joan and the Dauphin is given great force: Joan, leaning down toward the Dauphin (in foreground) as the camera tracks forward into a tight two-shot, asks him, "Are you afraid?" He turns toward her and nods before replying, "Yes, I am afraid." Later, the Dauphin, pacing slowly into close-up as he worries over Joan's exhortation to him to have himself crowned, exclaims, "Oh, if I only dared!" Over the close-up of him, the sound of laughter from the courtiers is heard. He looks offscreen right, then walks in that direction, the camera panning and tracking behind him to reframe a hanging tapestry, hubbub from the court audible. Then he walks back into close-up and repeats, "If I only dared." The shot draws out the Dauphin's state of being over a succession of compositional moments while making clear, through the sound track and the Dauphin's movement, that the source of his unease is society.

Saint Joan is one of Preminger's most underrated films, and one of his most personal. It may not be going too far to see in Joan an image of Preminger himself. Her seemingly paradoxical self-defense, "I am not proud; I never speak unless I know I am right," might have been written for Preminger. A stage direction in Shaw's play describes Joan as "naively incapable of seeing the effect she is producing."[51] Surely there is something of Preminger in that, too, although those who knew him would probably object that there was nothing naive about the incapacity in his case. Joan's inability to understand why she is not better liked strikes a note familiar from Preminger's mock-rueful comments to interviewers. *Saint Joan* is, seen from one angle, the self-justification in dramatic form of one who is too good for the world—that is, too convinced of her own rightness to bother with anyone else's feelings. Joan's progress among soldiers, politicians, and churchmen enables Preminger to depict a conflict between a world that demands "reasons" and a protagonist who obeys only intuition. Joan tells Dunois, "I have to find reasons for you, because you do not believe in my voices. But the voices come first, and I find the reasons after, whatever you may choose to believe." Joan's insistence that "it is God's business we must do, not our own" hints at a way to interpret the oft-alleged "impersonality" of Preminger the artist.

23

An Invisible Wall

Françoise Sagan's bestseller *Bonjour Tristesse*, published in 1954, involves the attempt by the first-person narrator, seventeen-year-old Cécile, to separate her widowed father, Raymond, from his new fiancée, Anne, whose presence at Raymond's vacation home on the Côte d'Azur disturbs Cécile's carefree summer. Cécile plots to reunite her father with his discarded mistress, Elsa. The plan succeeds only too well, as Anne catches Raymond together with Elsa, flees the house in a panic, and perishes in a car crash. Raymond and Cécile resume their hedonistic existence, but Cécile is now consumed with a sadness that she keeps secret from her father.

In April 1955 Preminger completed negotiations with Famous Artists, Sagan's representatives in New York, for the rights to *Bonjour Tristesse*. Preminger paid $150,000 for the rights. As in Nelson Algren's case, little or none of the windfall found its way to the author's pocket; Sagan had already sold the film rights to French producer Ray Ventura. On February 21, 1956, Preminger arrived in New York to confer with S. N. Behrman on the script for *Bonjour Tristesse*, and the two traveled by sea to Europe to work together on it.[1] That was perhaps the same spring trip on which Preminger went to Madrid to try to interest Cary Grant (then shooting *The Pride and the Passion*) in playing Raymond.

Dissatisfied with Behrman's work, Preminger hired Arthur Laurents to revise the script. Laurents later recalled Preminger introducing him to Jean Seberg in Paris. This may have been in May 1957, when Preminger and Seberg attended the world premiere of *Saint Joan*, or it may have been as early as December 1956, when Preminger first took his new star to Paris. Laurents remembered Seberg as "a shrewd cookie; I don't care what they say about her." According to Laurents, Preminger left him completely alone while he wrote the script, which he finished on June 28. The writer said, "It's a very slight, ironic story, and that's the way I tried to write it. But Otto, whom I liked, was a heavy-handed Austrian, and he tried to make it so melodramatic."[2] Despite Laurents's reservations, the film reveals that he and Preminger were at pains to tone down the more melodramatic aspects of Sagan's work. For example, the conversation between Raymond and Cécile about the differences between their way of life and Anne's is treated very seriously by the two in the book, but in the film they make it a subject for conscious humor and irony, so that the scene becomes a charming demonstration of the easygoing mutual understanding between father and daughter.

Bonjour Tristesse marked the beginning of two enduring professional associations for Preminger. One was with production executive Martin Schute, whom Columbia, the studio that undertook to finance and distribute the film, assigned to the production to look after its interests. Schute got along well enough with Preminger to play the same role on Preminger's next project, *The Other Side of the Coin*, then left Columbia to serve as general manager on *Exodus*. Schute would go on to work as associate producer on *The Cardinal* and *Bunny Lake Is Missing*.

Bonjour Tristesse was the first film on which Hope Bryce, who would become the last of Preminger's three wives, worked for him as costume coordinator. He had met Bryce, a model and fashion designer, a few years earlier, through Mary Gardner. Bryce's association with Givenchy, who was to design the women's clothes for *Bonjour Tristesse*, made her a logical choice for the role of costume coordinator on the film. Bryce later recalled, "I thought a little vacation in France would be pretty nice. So I went, and then I got plunged into all kinds of [questions of] how you translate fashion to film or even design to film . . . And, we just fell in love. He was my best friend, and always was from that point on."[3] She would continue as costume coordinator on all of Preminger's later films except *Porgy and Bess* and *Rosebud*.

Shooting started in Paris in July, with eight days of work in Les Halles, at the Place de la Concorde, at the Latin Quarter jazz club La Huchette, where Juliette Gréco's memorable performance of the title song was filmed, and at Maxim's, where, at a dinner party, Martin Schute saw Preminger dress down Columbia production manager Jack Fier, an old-timer with a reputation nearly as intimidating as Preminger's, over Fier's attempt to saddle the production with two Mitchell cameras whose noise made it impossible to record usable direct sound. "Otto just laid into Jack Fier, I mean, mercilessly. 'How dare you do this and this to me? Are you trying to ruin my picture?' It was very much 'my picture,' you have to remember. Columbia's only involvement was providing some money. He didn't think they had a word to say about anything else. They weren't allowed to change the cut of his picture, which was unusual . . . I remember the next day Jack Fier calling me up and saying, 'Martin, you just do whatever you can to keep the picture on track.' "[4]

The use of a sufficient proportion of British nationals among the cast and crew enabled Preminger to win for *Bonjour Tristesse* designation as a British production, with the attendant financial advantages. Because he was shooting in France, however, he was required to accept a French crew. According to Serge Friedman, the French assistant director imposed by the French union, Preminger's relationship with the French crew was bad throughout the production. On the second day, an incident with the French sound engineer (who would work only one day) resulted in a brief strike. Friedman won Preminger's respect by his meticulous and arduous preparation for the scene at Maxim's, which took a whole night and the following morning to film.

Though they had worked well together on *The Moon Is Blue*, Preminger and David Niven (cast as Raymond) got off to a bad start on *Bonjour Tristesse*. Niven, believing he wasn't needed for the day, went off to Deauville to attend a party, only to be summoned back for an unscheduled car scene. When Niven arrived at the location (having been whisked back at great expense by hired plane and helicopter), he was met by an enraged Preminger, yelling, "Don't walk—run!" The two had what Friedman remembered as a "terrible row" lasting an hour. According to Schute, "Ten or fifteen members of the French press were there while it was all happening. Having had this shouting match, [Preminger] came back where I was standing, and he said 'Well, Martin, that will probably make the headlines in the paper.' " Two days later, Niven and Preminger were on good terms again. "Niven's professionalism was perfect," marveled Friedman. "Each take was impeccable."[5]

At the end of the first week on the French Riviera (where, for Raymond's summer house, Preminger rented the magnificent seaside villa of publisher Pierre Lazareff, in Le Lavandou, near Cavalière), Preminger summoned Friedman to his hotel room, offered him a glass of champagne, and said, "I'm going to be a pain in the ass, but don't ask me to change. I am what I am. That's the way I work, that's my nature." For the rest of the shoot, Friedman observed, Preminger, without asking directly for advice, "ensured his collaboration, very often in a devious way by sarcasm and ironical questions . . . He would take into account the opinion of people who had proved their qualities."[6]

By now, the bloom had worn off Preminger's relationship with Jean Seberg. Already, by April 1957, he had told her, "I don't like the way you talk, walk, or dress."[7] According to Serge Friedman, Preminger made no secret of his dissatisfaction with her performance throughout the production of *Bonjour Tristesse*. Calling her "wooden," he often put her through repeated takes of a scene, only to give up after four or five, realizing he would get nothing more from her. Taking the path of least resistance, Seberg simply followed his instructions to the letter.[8] One day on the set when Preminger gave her a line reading, she responded by delivering the line not only with his exact intonation but with an imitation of his accent. "The crew guffawed. Preminger, taken aback, walked away, muttering that film was too expensive to waste."[9]

Mylène Demongeot (whose performance as Elsa is one of the glories of the film) recalled, "Preminger, always apoplectic and crimson, shouts and erupts non-stop. All day. Everyone is terrorized, and Jean Seberg more than anyone. He is absolutely hellish with her. Nothing works, ever. Nothing is ever just all right." Willi Frischauer, a visitor to the set, observed that "almost every one of [Seberg's] scenes involved a test of nerves." Once, Preminger, against Seberg's protests, scheduled a scene between her and Geoffrey Horne (cast as Philippe, Cécile's boyfriend)— in which Seberg had to remain in the water—for a day on which Seberg was having her period, as she had warned the production in advance. Seberg fainted several times while languishing in the mistral-chilled sea.[10]

Both Niven and Deborah Kerr (who played Anne) tried to help Seberg when they could, though Kerr thought the younger actress capable of dealing with Preminger on her own. "I think any other woman would have collapsed in tears or just walked out. But she calmly took all the berating and achieved a very interesting and true Sagan-type heroine." Bob Willoughby noted that in the short time since *Saint Joan*, Seberg had become more independent and more confident of her own sexual magnetism. During the shooting of *Bonjour Tristesse*, she embarked on a romance with twenty-three-year-old lawyer François Moreuil. Nevertheless, according to Seberg's friend Aki Lehmann, "Jean was very unhappy during much of that filming. She admired Otto as a father figure, and at the same time she hated his guts." "He just isn't human," Seberg confided to a friend from Marshalltown. "Sometimes I wish he would just die!"[11]

Demongeot recalled the nightly ordeal of watching the rushes, which Helga Cranston would bring down to Nice each week after working on them in England. "Preminger is the only director I've known to leave the projection room absolutely mad with rage, insulting everyone. Everything is lousy. Everything is abysmal. The actors. The photography—poor [Georges] Périnal, who tears out his hair trying to get shots of the Mediterranean, which changes color all the time, to match. The sets. The framing. The costumes . . . Nothing finds grace in his eyes. It's pretty depressing for everyone."[12] David Niven kept his temper, but Demongeot, out of the corner of her eye, noticed occasionally that he looked as if he wanted to strangle Preminger.

Demongeot was unafraid of her director, as she demonstrated when, the first time he yelled at her, she calmly warned him that if he kept going like that, he would have a heart attack. "That stopped his breath. Literally. Afterward, he left me alone"—except during a scene in which Elsa watches a conversation between Cécile and Philippe. Demongeot was unwise enough to start to say she had an idea—"Mr. Preminger, I think—"; Preminger cut her off, shouting, "Demongeot! Don't think! Act!" Despite everything, Demongeot liked Preminger. "He was a very intelligent man, a fascinating storyteller with his thick Viennese accent, and he could even be charming, and very funny, outside of work!"[13] According to Martin Schute, Demongeot even found Preminger funny on the set: his irritated attempts to control her performance sometimes caused her "to collapse into laughter, and he really didn't know what to do with that."[14]

Friedman's comments on Preminger's way of working are instructive. According to Friedman, Preminger followed the script to the letter. Rather than coming to the set with a visual schema worked out in his mind, ready to impose it on the cast, he invented both the blocking and the camera moves while rehearsing the actors. "Sometimes he had to do a lot of thinking before he could find the right place for the camera," recalled Friedman. To facilitate the work, the floor of the set was treated with gelatin to allow the camera to move as freely as possible. Preminger generally did only a few takes of a shot and was not above modifying his plan when a particular effect proved impossible. "When something really imperfect occurred, especially concerning Jean Seberg, he would decide to cut to another actor."[15]

After finishing in France, Preminger went to London with a reduced cast and crew to film, at Shepperton, the final apartment scene and some back-projection shots. The last shot in the film, in which tears form in Cécile's eyes as she removes her makeup with cold cream in front of her bedroom mirror, took an entire day. Demongeot recalled, "He wanted the face to remain a child's face, with no expression at all. And when the tears don't come just like that, your face is trembling, your eyes are blinking, your nose is wrinkling . . . I think he would have been better off doing it as a special effect!"[16]

During its last days, the production suffered a calamity. Preminger's design called for the present-time sequences to be in black and white and the flashbacks in color. Périnal neglected to instruct the lab to process the color negative of the Shepperton footage with the filters required for it to print properly in black and white. Martin Schute recalled: "Two days of shooting came back with color rushes, which couldn't be made black and white. Two days of shooting all of which had to be done again, with Seberg and Niven. Périnal was getting [to be] quite an old man, then, though he was an amazing cinematographer. Otto couldn't do anything. You don't tell people of his caliber, or give them a going-over, if they make a mistake. But that was one of the big ones."[17]

Preminger remained in London in October and November to cut the film with Helga Cranston. "The work was very quick," said Cranston. "The moment the sequence was finished, I cut it . . . I think I had a rough cut about two or three days after the shooting. So it was very fast and all the corrections were done in no time."[18] The dance sequence became the matter of a brief dispute between the director and the editor. "It was very rhythmic, and I cut it quite fast. He screamed at me: 'Put it back!' In the end, I had my way. He realized."[19]

Some additional shots were done at Pinewood, as was the looping that was required because of the difficulties in recording good sound in outdoor scenes on the French Riviera. "Niven was a fantastic technician," marveled Helga Cranston years later. "I have never seen anybody do a post-synch on a whole speech with everything in place. Total concentration and ability to repeat himself."[20] Demongeot's ability to loop her dialogue in a language unfamiliar to her evoked expressions of satisfaction from Preminger, which gratified the actress.[21]

According to Cranston, Preminger "badgered and criticized" Georges Auric, who wrote a superb score for the film. The composer's parting words to the director: *"Vous êtes insupportable!"*[22]

The finished work was approved for a PCA Seal on December 3. Later that month, Preminger was hit by two lawsuits. Mary Gardner Preminger filed suit for divorce on December 5. She claimed that they had been separated since April 20 and that lately Preminger had been causing valuable art objects and financial records to be removed from their Malibu home, allegedly in a bid to lower the value of the community property.[23] On December 27, Twentieth Century-Fox sued Preminger to recover $60,000 that it had paid him for the fourth of the four films he was supposed to have made for the studio under his 1950 contract (since renegotiated), claiming that Preminger had violated the contract by missing the deadline for starting work on the fourth film. The studio dropped the suit on February 18, 1958, after Preminger paid them a third of the sum and agreed to pay the rest in two later installments. Meanwhile, Preminger had another new play close out of town in early 1958: Bentz Plagemann's *This Is Goggle*, a comedy starring James Daly and Kim Hunter. Also in the cast were Doro Merande and a nine-year-old Bernadette Peters, in her professional debut.

Bonjour Tristesse premiered in New York on January 15, 1958. The mostly negative reviews in the United States gave further evidence of the press's tendency to respond to the public perception surrounding a Preminger film, notably a supposed intended scandalousness, rather than to the film. Philip T. Hartung thought that *Bonjour Tristesse* had a "large number of scenes that are meant to be shocking but really aren't." Cultural changes have, perhaps, made it hard for us now to understand this criticism, or why Arthur Knight found the film "repellent, even slightly obscene—in the way that window-peeping is obscene," or why the most positive phrase *Time* could come up with for it was "somehow repulsively alluring."[24]

In August, Preminger sold his contract with Seberg to Columbia, reserving the right to use her in one movie a year. He would never exercise this option. "He used me like a Kleenex and threw me away," Seberg lamented.[25] In the summer of 1959 Seberg ran into Preminger and Hope Bryce at a party for Françoise Arnoul. Seberg chatted amiably with Preminger for some time, an achievement that caused her to boast to her acting teacher, "I think I'm beginning to overcome my DTs about him."[26]

Jean Seberg committed suicide in September 1979. Preminger, who had just finished production on his last film, *The Human Factor*, was asked by a journalist for his reaction. "I was in a restaurant in my London hotel when I heard the news. I am told my face went white. While I had not seen her for fourteen years—I was never close to her—I was shocked. She was such a symbol of living, she wanted to do so many things, that it is hard to accept the idea that she committed suicide."[27]

Throughout *Bonjour Tristesse*, doorways, windows, and partitions—metaphors for the film screen—give access to successive planes of the world, just as the assumption of narrative form by Cécile's consciousness gives access to successive planes of memory and time. The flashback's gradual breaking through the present takes the form of successive openings of color images in various zones of the frame. This optical device implies that Cécile's recollections of the past—the "invisible wall made of memories I can't lose" that bar her from the present—form a constantly available layer of potential consciousness underlying the present.

The sense of an invisible wall blocking Cécile from the world is both contradicted and reaffirmed in the shots near the beginning of the film in which Cécile dances, first with Jacques, her new admirer, and then with Raymond. In these shots, which are accompanied by Cécile's voice-over, she stares past her partners' backs directly at the camera lens. Both her voice-over and her look imply a direct connection with the viewer, as if we were being granted access to her consciousness. On the other hand, the expressionlessness of her face makes her direct gaze appear more a challenge than an intimacy. The gaze appears to see nothing outside her, nothing in the world beyond the camera. With her unchanging expression, she seems not to be hearing her own voice, whose changes in pace and pitch reflect the transition of her feelings from monotony to wistfulness to pleasure as she imagines herself again in her position at the beginning of the previous summer. The split between the image and the voice—between Cécile as a visible person and Cécile as the narrator—doubles the split between Cécile and the outside world. Her face, with its perfect smoothness (a perfection to which the final images of the film again call our attention, as Cécile smears her face compulsively with cream), is itself a wall—the "tragic mask" of which G. Cabrera Infante writes in his beautiful review of *Bonjour Tristesse*.[28] (Frank said to Diane in *Angel Face*, "I don't pretend to know what goes on behind that pretty little face of yours, and I don't want to.")

This opacity of the transparent is not Cécile's exclusive property; it characterizes the whole opening section of *Bonjour Tristesse*. In the first shot after the credits, the city of Paris lies spread out before us, visible yet hidden, under a dismal sky. The following shots are utterly matter-of-fact and plain: not just readable, they are visibly constructed for readability (for example, the back projections behind Cécile and her artist friend, Hubert, as she drives her convertible). The atmosphere is slack, desultory; meaning appears exhausted or suspended in material evidence. "Cécile!" Hubert exclaims accusingly, chasing her out of the gallery into the street. "Aren't you interested in anything?" "Yes, in going someplace else." (Compare her later remark, when Hubert asks her why she's leaving the club: "I don't really know. You go to a place, you leave a place.") Cécile's indifference, her refusal to acknowledge any motive for action or change other than the principles of movement and succession themselves, seem to correspond to the indifference of the camera, which records her activities with a bland and cold neutrality, neither hostile nor sympathetic. The windshield of her car, like her face, is a wall or a screen, reminding us that the cinema screen itself divides us from the figures to which, at the same time, it gives us access.

In the opening sequence of *Bonjour Tristesse*, the camera is attracted to movement. If this rule reaches its extreme expression, in Preminger's work, in *Rosebud*, which for long passages seems to be nothing but movement, all his films exhibit this attraction to some degree, and many of them make it their subject. In *Bonjour Tristesse*, movement is linked constantly to the flow of time and to the awareness of the fleetingness of things and the imminence of their end. One function of cinema, for Preminger, is to show the movement of people and things away from us, to make visible in movement the impossibility of ever possessing them. Again and again in *Bonjour Tristesse*, scenes end on people walking away from the camera, on an increase of distance: Anne walking down to the sea, followed by Raymond, who is followed in turn by Cécile; Anne walking back to the casino after Raymond drives away with Anne; Cécile disappearing after crossing the nightclub dance floor, away from the camera. Through metonymy, a person can become just a period of time that has passed ("How long did any of them last?" Cécile says of her father's lovers). The film criticizes its own attraction to movement as a fatal displacement that merely conceals a fundamental placelessness ("You know where I live? Limbo, with my father"). Movement, too, is a disguise, a false surface, a lie.

Laurents's exceptionally well-balanced script enables Preminger to make a film on subtleties of behavior (though the writer himself, oddly, thought the director's approach "melodramatic"). Anne's regal self-possession, in Deborah Kerr's marvelous performance (the first of three indelible performances of women of early middle age in Preminger's films; the second will be Eva Marie Saint's Kitty in *Exodus*, and the third Patricia Neal's Maggie in *In Harm's Way*), becomes a marvelous instrument that can divide Cécile from Raymond by making her seem younger and him older. Anne sometimes seems rhetorical and affected in a way that Cécile, Raymond, and Elsa never are, as when, relaxing on the couch after returning home from the dance, Anne exclaims, "What a lovely, lovely, *lovely* evening!" What might be seen as inauthenticity is really the sign of the special relationship Anne enjoys with language and expression, a relationship that sets her apart from the other characters in the film and implies an awareness of the various distances that a person can take up with respect to her utterances. "*Really* welcome." "And *really* thank you": this exchange between Cécile and Anne at Anne's arrival shows the consciousness of the deceptive possibilities of language that seems to accompany Anne. When she says in the parked car, "Raymond, I cannot be casual," the line insists on the importance of language for her, and it justifies her earlier rebuke to Cécile, which seemed prudish and inappropriate ("I don't like vulgarities, Cécile, even when they're funny").

Anne's awareness of language enables her to usurp the role of narrator from Cécile. Their relationship is a battle for possession of the narrative—that is, of the terms in which the film describes its characters and events. The scene between Raymond and Anne in Raymond's parked car outside the casino is the first scene in the film that takes place apparently without Cécile's being present (though her emergence from behind a bush at the end of the scene retrospectively claims the scene for her point of view). In this scene, Anne's stiffness appears normal, and it summons a corresponding gravity in Raymond's behavior. It's as if it were only when Anne is together with Cécile that Anne seems unnatural.

The film makes it clear that Anne projects her fears about Raymond as a partner onto Cécile—that is, Anne unconsciously displaces her own worries about marrying Raymond onto her worries about Cécile's acceptance of their marriage. In the exchange of crosscut close shots between Anne and Cécile on the terrace, after the engagement is announced to Cécile, the shot of Anne is slightly closer; it's *her* psyche, not Cécile's, that creates this scene and casts the roles. The relay of figures that begins here continues in the ensuing scene, when Cécile turns to Philippe, asking him to give her what her father has given Anne, to such spectacular effect: "She looks softer, she moves easier. In the morning, she seems . . . as though she had the most wonderful secret in the world. I wish I walked the way she walks now. I wish I had the look she has." Later, when Cécile takes out her resentment of Anne on the surrogate of a doll, the sense established by the earlier crosscutting—that Anne and Cécile are each other's mirror images—is reaffirmed directly when Cécile, looking at herself in a mirror, suddenly turns her hatred of Anne against herself: "You're spoiled and willful and arrogant and lazy—a mean little monster!" This shot, in which the camera dollies in on Cécile's reflection in the mirror, dissolves to the nightclub washroom in the present time of the narrative, as Cécile looks at herself in another mirror and says (in voice-over), "Anne had made me look at myself for the first time in my life. And that turned me against her. Dead against her." The terrible final exchange between Anne and Cécile again confirms the equivalence between the two women: "Forgive me!" "No, *you* forgive *me*!"

The hidden turning point in their relationship is the scene in which Anne tries to call a truce with Cécile. Returning from Philippe's house, where (the coded dissolve lets us know) they have just had sex for the

first time, Cécile finds Anne alone on the terrace, writing. An awareness of perspective dominates the scene from the start: the terrace re-
cedes across the screen behind Anne (who is in the left foreground) in
the slightly high-angled shot; the railing at the edge of the terrace in the
background marks a visual barrier, beyond which the sea stretches to the
horizon. It is, moreover, a change in perspective that Anne presents to
Cécile as her peace offering, as she apologizes to Cécile for failing to
keep in mind that Cécile is still only a child and sees things from a
child's point of view.

After a succession of scenes in which we have been made to share
Cécile's attitude toward her prospective stepmother, we now realize that
Anne speaks for the film in her criticism of the superficiality of Raymond's friends, the Lombards (whom we have not yet met). To Cécile's
attempted defense—"At least they're having a good time now"—Anne's
rejoinder seems definitive: "Are they? Then why do they drink so much
and so often? Why are they never alone with each other? In the end
their only memories will be of hangovers." Anne's view of the future (her
prediction of details of the imminent night out with the Lombards will
prove accurate) dictates a reading of the temporal metaphor in the visual
design of the scene. At the end of the scene, Cécile walks away into the
background of the shot, and Anne walks forward, leans on a railing, and
looks out, prompting the camera to pan over the woods and the sea in
the direction of her look: having come to share her attitude toward Raymond's frivolous social life, we are now made to share, approximately,
her visual point of view. This is a necessary step in the progress of the
film toward tragedy, since Anne's witnessing of Raymond's infidelity will
precipitate her suicide.

The equivalence between Anne and Cécile is the main force behind
Preminger's staging of the scene in which Cécile follows Anne down
through the woods to the place of Raymond and Elsa's assignation. (This
scene was invented for the film; in Sagan's novel, Cécile returns from a
swim to find Anne—who has, we gather, just seen the lovers together—
running from the woods to the car.) This staging is deliberately highly
theatrical, Preminger contriving to keep Cécile and Anne in the same
frame almost constantly, so that Anne's failure to see Cécile assumes
practically the quality of a theatrical convention. The discovery of Raymond and Elsa (whom Preminger keeps offscreen; we hear their voices

over shots of Anne and Cécile) causes the mise-en-scène to break down, splitting up Anne and Cécile into separate shots, suggesting that the lovers' conversation acts on both women with a similar impact.

The last movement of the film finds Cécile renouncing a power she has enjoyed throughout: a power equivalent to that of the director. Not only has her consciousness, seemingly, willed the flashback portion of the film into being, but Cécile takes on a director's functions, casting Philippe and Elsa in their roles, giving them their actions, and staging scenes. In the scene of Anne's discovery of Raymond's infidelity, however, Cécile becomes the audience, rather than the director, of the spectacle she has set in motion, a spectacle that becomes an appalling rebuke of the director's power.

In the moral force of this rebuke and the irresistible narrative logic that leads up to it, *Bonjour Tristesse* is the most stringent of Preminger's films, though it's also one of the most pleasurable—not least because of the grandeur of the locations and Périnal's admirable CinemaScope photography, but not only because of them. Like *The Moon Is Blue*, *Bonjour Tristesse* catalogs and criticizes pleasure, and in both films, David Niven offers what is undoubtedly the most engaging account in Preminger's work of the male seducer or Don Juan (a figure Preminger usually views with contempt and mockery, as with Shelby Carpenter in *Laura* and Korvo in *Whirlpool*). But *Bonjour Tristesse* subjects Raymond to a critique that becomes all the more devastating the more likable he appears. The brief moment of Raymond's uncertain isolation in front of a bistro after he has made Cécile reassure him that the two of them "have great fun," is enough to reveal the obsessiveness of his need to be together with his daughter and to suggest the depth of the chasm that Anne's death has left in their relationship. As a critical examination of worldliness, *Bonjour Tristesse*, one of Preminger's greatest films, marks the culmination of a movement in his work that starts with *Laura* and proceeds from *Forever Amber* through *Saint Joan*, to be resumed in *Advise & Consent*, *The Cardinal*, and *Such Good Friends*.

24

Plenty of Nothing

The rights holders had long held out against offers from Hollywood to film George Gershwin, DuBose Heyward, and Ira Gershwin's opera, *Porgy and Bess*, which was first staged in 1935. Preminger himself made an offer, but Samuel Goldwyn finally secured the rights. The producer commissioned N. Richard Nash to write the script and picked as director Rouben Mamoulian, who had directed the original Broadway productions of both *Porgy* (the 1927 play by DuBose Heyward and Dorothy Heyward) and *Porgy and Bess*.

To get his cast, Goldwyn had to triumph over the perception in the African American community that *Porgy and Bess* represented a retrograde step for the image of blacks in the United States. The opera had long been criticized for misrepresenting African American society, speech, and music and for bolstering negative stereotypes, not just because it featured gamblers, a drug pusher, a murderer, and a drug-addicted, faithless woman among its all-black cast of characters, but also because of its portrayal of its hero, Porgy, as a gentle, passive cripple, satisfied with the "plenty of nothing" (or "nuttin' ") that is his lot. Harry Belafonte, mentioned as a possible Porgy, publicly declined to play a part in which he would have to appear on his knees. Sidney Poitier, who later said, "I had a considerable aversion to *Porgy and Bess* because of its inherent racial attitudes,"[1] tried to turn down the part, but pressure was put on him from several sides, and he finally signed on to *Porgy and Bess* in the belief that if he refused to do it, he would be prevented from doing *The Defiant Ones* for Stanley Kramer.

For Bess, Goldwyn wanted Dorothy Dandridge; it's hard to think of another performer then established in films whom he would have considered. Belafonte urged Dandridge to refuse the role, but Preminger told her, "Do it. It'll make you as big a star as you were when you did *Carmen*." Dandridge accepted the part. Sammy Davis, Jr., campaigned for and won the role of the flashy drug pusher Sportin' Life (in which Goldwyn had envisioned Cab Calloway). Three veterans of *Carmen Jones*, Pearl Bailey, Diahann Carroll, and Brock Peters, filled the other principal roles: Maria, the local "cook shop" proprietor; Clara, a fisherman's wife; and Crown, Bess's brutal lover.

Mamoulian told production designer Oliver Smith, who was building Catfish Row (the name of the all-black neighborhood where most of the opera's characters live) on Goldwyn's mammoth Stage 8, "While stylized, the set should still carry the illusion of reality and the flavor of authenticity—it should convincingly belong to the Charleston of 1912."[2] Brock Peters recalled, however, that the set "didn't look like Charleston or anything, it had a very European, sort of Old World, fairytale [quality]."[3] The set would never be seen in the film. Early in the morning of July 2, 1958, hours before the first scheduled dress rehearsal on the newly finished set, a fire (later blamed on faulty wiring) broke out on the soundstage. The soundstage itself, Smith's elaborate set, and Irene Sharaff's costumes were all destroyed—a loss that was later estimated at more than $2,000,000. Undaunted, Goldwyn announced that the set would be rebuilt and the costumes redone and that production would start after a six-week delay.

Mamoulian used the delay to try to impose his vision for *Porgy and Bess*. He also hired a press agent, Russell Birdwell, to funnel statements to the press about the film. This move may have been, for Goldwyn, the last straw: repeatedly at odds with the director during the eight months of their collaboration on the film, Goldwyn fired Mamoulian on July 27, stating, "Rather than go on with basic differences of opinion between us, I have relieved him."[4] Ivan Dixon, who played a small part in the film, thought that Goldwyn, "a shrewd man," had tricked Mamoulian into serving as casting director for the film and preparing the production.[5] Indeed, Mamoulian would later argue that preparation work on *Porgy and Bess* entitled him to codirectorial credit, but the Screen Directors Guild rejected his bid.

Mamoulian's replacement, announced at the same time as his firing, was Otto Preminger. Doubtless the presence on Preminger's résumé of *Carmen Jones*, the last all-black film from a major studio and a financial success, was decisive in Goldwyn's decision. Preminger had recently returned from a trip to Asia to explore the possibility of setting up a production of *The Other Side of the Coin*, an adaptation of Pierre Boulle's novel (published in French as *Les Voies du salut*) about a French rubber planter and his American wife contending with Communist guerrillas in Malaya. Preminger would work on this script, on and off, with A. E. Hotchner and then with Dalton Trumbo, before abandoning it.

In New York at the time of the announcement of his hiring for *Porgy and Bess*, Preminger arrived in Hollywood on July 30 to meet with Goldwyn. On August 6 Russell Birdwell staged a press conference at which Leigh Whipper, cast in the film as the Crab Man (the role he had created for Mamoulian in 1927), announced that he was withdrawing from the cast and claimed to "have first-hand information concerning the new director which brands him, to me, as a man who has no respect for my people." Goldwyn's publicists immediately set about repairing the damage from Whipper's bombshell. Pearl Bailey, Sammy Davis, Jr., Brock Peters, and actor Joel Fluellen leaped to Preminger's defense, all insisting that they had never known him to be anti-Negro.[6] Conspicuous in her absence from the chorus of Preminger's supporters was Dandridge, who had been told by her publicity advisers (she later said) to stay out of the controversy. "Later I heard that Otto was disappointed because I didn't go to the fore and explain that he was not prejudiced."[7] Her final, ambiguous word on the subject, published in her autobiography: "If Otto was prejudiced, he didn't know it."[8]

If he had produced *Porgy and Bess* himself, Preminger later remarked, the film would have been very different from the one that he made for Goldwyn. "It could have been better if it had been, like *Carmen Jones*, a film with music instead of a musical film."[9] N. Richard Nash claimed, however, that "Preminger just changed the whole thing"[10]—though the writer stayed involved with the film and contributed some rewrites. Although Nash's script had retained Heyward and Gershwin's caricatured demotic forms—"dat," "de," "wid," "nuttin'," "I knows," "I hates," and so on—the film that was made shows a consistent tendency to replace these forms with their standard English equivalents. So, for example, Bess says to Crown, "You don't look almost dead," instead of "You ain't looks most dead" (as in Nash's June 12 script). The actors apparently insisted on these changes. Brock Peters said, "There was the pressure of whether we were doing something that was contributing negatively to Black culture and one's view of what that was, and we didn't want to be guilty of that. And so in essence the sense we had was that we could clean it up somewhat in terms of language . . . We talked about it [those who had dialogue] . . . We just wouldn't do the dialect, the quote-unquote Southern Black dialect. We would go at it straight."[11] The song keys were also altered to enable the singers to achieve a more natural, less operatic sound. Peters, Davis, and Bailey sang their songs themselves; as on *Carmen Jones*, many cast members were doubled by other voices, with Robert McFerrin singing Porgy, Adele Addison singing Bess, and Loulie Jean Norman singing Clara (who opens the opera with the famous "Summertime").

Preminger persuaded Goldwyn to let him film the picnic on location and had some influence on the redesigning of the sets, which he thought too stagelike: "I wanted them changed and Goldwyn agreed," he later wrote.[12] Brock Peters confirmed that the new set was "very different" from the old.[13] Still dissatisfied, Preminger and cameraman Leon Shamroy met each night during production to repaint the set, against Goldwyn's wishes.[14]

From Sidney Poitier's point of view, Preminger's tenure on the film began with promise. "At our first meeting I looked for telltale signs to confirm the presence of furies lying dormant somewhere in the strong, muscular, baldheaded director. Unless I missed something, no sign appeared, he was as charming as a minister, and checked out normal—he was sweet, kind, loved to tell stories, laughed a lot, and was fun to be around. During rehearsal time he never once raised his voice, and was very patient and considerate with each actor, even those who were slow in getting to what he was attempting to convey."[15]

After a week of rehearsals, production began on Monday, September 22, 1958, on Venice Island in the San Joaquin River near Stockton, California, where the art department had re-created the Charleston Wharf and pier for the opening scene and the scene of the departure for the picnic. The company next moved across the river to Tule Island, which represented Kittiwah Island. Here, they shot the picnic, the fish fry, and Sportin' Life's "It Ain't Necessarily So" number. Sammy Davis, Jr., boasted, "It took only a couple of takes to finish 'It Ain't Necessarily So,' which was a record for the film."[16] By now, Dandridge had come to feel that the company was "manufacturing a cut-up bastard of a film which would never be all one thing or another."[17] This opinion does not necessarily contradict Brock Peters's assessment that in directing *Porgy and Bess*, Preminger "tried to make it as natural as he could."[18]

After ten days of location work, the company moved to the studio. Spared Preminger's anger on *Carmen Jones*, Dandridge now found it falling full on her. Poitier, who had not been needed for the location scenes, was startled on his first day of work to find that the kind, patient Preminger of the rehearsals had vanished. "Otto Preminger jumped on Dorothy Dandridge in a shocking and totally unexpected way. She had done something that wasn't quite the way he wanted it. 'What's the matter with you, Dorothy?' he exploded at her. 'You're supposed to be an actress. Now what kind of an actress are you that you can't do such a simple thing?'" She tried again, and Preminger interrupted the take to berate her further: "That's stupid, what you're doing—you don't have any intelligence at all. What kind of a dumb way for a girl to behave! You don't even know who Bess is." Dandridge "fell apart," in Poitier's words.[19] Other cast members were appalled by Preminger's treatment of Dandridge, which, said Nichelle Nichols, "daily . . . had her dissolving into tears." Once, while Dandridge enjoyed a two-day break in the schedule, members of the cast met with Preminger to protest his treatment of her. According to Nichols, "We told him to treat Dorothy Dandridge differently. She was our queen. It demeaned *us* to see this man attempt to destroy her every day. Everyone knew they had had a relationship. After the meeting, he was more respectful of us. He was a little more respectful of Dorothy."[20]

During the filming of Porgy's "Bess, You Is My Woman Now," Preminger twice interrupted takes to criticize Poitier loudly in front of the cast and crew. "You call yourself an actor? What kind of an actor are you, Mr. Poitier? . . . You don't even know how to play a warm scene—a warm scene with the woman you love." During Preminger's second tirade, Poitier silently unstrapped the shin shoes from his lower legs, stood up, and walked off the set. Preminger cajoled the star back, and, Poiter wrote, "Never once throughout the film, and I worked my tail off for him, never once did he raise his voice to me again—ever. Of course, he raised it to a lot of other people, that's the way he was."[21]

With the two other major stars on the production, Preminger was cir-

cumspect. Pearl Bailey found Preminger as much of a "pussy cat" as he
had been with her on *Carmen Jones*.[22] Sammy Davis, Jr., said of the director, "Maybe he can be a tyrant, but I never once saw that side of him.
Sure, he was a perfectionist, and he would never tolerate anything but
the best performance. He used to say, 'You are paid a very great deal of
money to act. Now please get on with it.' " Davis and Preminger developed a bantering rapport. "I found I was the only one who could talk
back to him," Davis recalled, "and he let me get away with murder." Attracted to Davis's high living style, Preminger hung out with the enter-
tainer. "Almost every day we lunched together, and we'd hit the
nightclubs most nights. All he ever wanted to talk about was broads. He
never tired of the subject. As I could always muster up half a dozen
good-looking ladies with a couple of phone calls, I soon found I couldn't
get rid of Otto even if I'd wanted to . . . Most nights we would go out
with a bunch of broads until the early hours." During filming, Davis said,
"Otto left me almost completely alone. If I wanted to do something my
way, I checked with him. But he never gave me the thumbs-down on an
idea."[23] In his limited screen time, Davis gives the most ebullient performance in the film, showing up the restraint of Poitier and Dandridge
as timid and embarrassed.

Davis remembered that Goldwyn "got very upset by certain aspects
of *Porgy*. He had a vision of the film which he didn't think Otto Preminger was holding to."[24] As for Preminger, he thought that Goldwyn
"didn't contribute one useful thought or word of advice throughout the
entire production."[25] Relying on his contract, Preminger barred Goldwyn
from the set. Counting on Preminger's dislike of the producer, Paul
Helmick, the assistant director, sometimes amused himself by casually
mentioning to Preminger, while the two relaxed over brandies together
in the director's office at the end of the workday, that it was rumored
that Goldwyn had sneaked onto the set that day. "The mere mention of
such a bold violation would have Otto ordering his secretary to get his
lawyer on the phone, no matter where he was or what he was doing."[26]
Art director Serge Krizman sometimes served as a go-between between
producer and director. "I would have to tell Otto, 'Mr. Goldwyn wanted
the scene played differently.' He would say, 'He's not directing this picture, *I* am!' "[27]

Preminger said, "I remember coming out of my office one day and finding some chairs underneath the window of my room: some of the staff had been standing on them for the sheer pleasure of tuning in to our conversations. I think they had good value."[28] "You couldn't miss that," recalled Brock Peters with amusement. "Sometimes when they argued, you could hear them if you were outside on the lot in front of the soundstage."[29]

Evidence that Preminger's work on *Porgy and Bess* was subject to considerable second-guessing and input from Goldwyn and others is provided by a letter from Nash to Goldwyn dated December 4. The letter accompanies Nash's revisions for the scene with two vendors, the Strawberry Woman and the Crab Man, "indicating the business which Ira Gershwin described to us today." Nash also writes, "I agree with you that it is necessary to re-shoot early sections of the picture which give the important characters special entrances." Nash proceeds to suggest ways of handling the first entrances of the Honey Man, Porgy, and Crown and Bess, footage of which he had screened with Goldwyn and Gershwin. Evidently taking up a comment of Goldwyn's, Nash goes as far as to propose a new mise-en-scène for the entrance of the last-named couple: "In the present version of the picture, Crown is first seen standing as if waiting in the wings for an entrance. I agree that it is most important to watch Crown enter at a greater distance and HOLD on him and Bess for a longer time and make their entrance considerably more important. Also, I think it most advisable to drop Sporting Life out of this shot, since his presence in the shot diffuses the entrance of the two erstwhile lovers."[30]

Production lasted ten weeks and ended on December 11. Faced with Preminger's long takes, there was little Goldwyn could do to put his stamp on the film in postproduction, although the pressbook for the film suggests that he ordered some rerecording: "Mr. Goldwyn had made it a special point that every word of the lyrics and of the dialogue should be absolutely understandable."

In view of the later fate of the film, it is worth pointing out that Ira Gershwin allowed his name to be used in the pressbook as the source of rapturous praise: "It is everything we hoped for. For *Porgy and Bess* to have reached the screen under Mr. Goldwyn's guidance, with his devotion to fine pictures, is a matter of great importance and satisfaction to all of us." Also quoted in the pressbook is Dorothy Heyward, widow of

DuBose: "The film exceeds our highest expectations. I have never heard the music performed so magnificently. Mr. Goldwyn has done a superlative job." (Heyward did complain, not for the pressbook, that the ending was supposed to be pathetic rather than uplifting.)[31]

Before the film was released, Preminger defended it on Chicago journalist Irv Kupcinet's weekly TV talk show, At Random, in a debate with Lorraine Hansberry, author of A Raisin in the Sun. Hansberry accused Preminger, in both Porgy and Carmen Jones, of trading in stereotypes and staying within Hollywood's "exotic tradition" of portraying black characters. Hansberry said, "We, over a period of time, have apparently decided that within American life we have one great repository where we're going to focus and imagine sensuality and exaggerated sexuality, all very removed and earthy things—and this great image is the American Negro." Preminger contended that the playwright was "a minority of one" in her objections (a claim that callers to the TV station were quick to refute) and defended both Porgy and Carmen Jones on the grounds that they were depictions of "a world that really doesn't exist"—an argument that Hansberry, understandably, took as conceding her point.[32]

The film opened in New York on June 24, 1959. Reviews were lukewarm (Time taxed the film with "cinematic monotony" and claimed, "Preminger has directed it as though it were a Bayreuth production of Götterdämmerung"),[33] and the film did weak business. According to A. Scott Berg, Goldwyn's biographer, the film, whose final cost was estimated at $7 million, "earned half its cost."[34]

Asked what he had learned from Goldwyn, Preminger quipped, "One of the main things I learned from him is never to mention the other fellow's name."[35] Preminger complained to Hedda Hopper about Goldwyn's publicity for Porgy and Bess. "You'd think the picture directed itself," he said. "No mention of me has been made."[36] Goldwyn's final insult was to deny Preminger a share of the profits (which, according to Preminger, the producer promised, but without specifying the percentage), although such a share would have been only a formality, since it's probable that even as of this writing, the film is still in the red. Despite everything, when the experience was a couple of years behind him, Preminger declared himself "very happy" with Porgy and Bess.[37]

Porgy and Bess is unavailable for public exhibition. In his deal with the Gershwins, Goldwyn had not bought the film rights outright but only leased them for a fifteen-year period beginning with the signing of the contract in 1957. After the end of this period, exhibition of the film required permission from the authors or their estates. Michael Strunsky, the nephew of Leonore Gershwin and the executor of the Gershwin estate, said in 1993, "That film was unfortunate, but typical of attitudes of the time. My aunt didn't want it distributed. She and my uncle [Ira] felt it was a Hollywoodization of the piece. We [the estate] now acquire any prints we find and destroy them. We are often approached for permission to show the film, which we consistently deny . . . The [set] looked like the Place de la Concorde—large, opulent, paved with cobblestones. It gave no flavor of Charleston at the time at all."[38] The hatred of art and contempt for history revealed in these ignorant remarks speak for themselves. Strunsky's remarks also suggest the deeper reason why he tried to destroy all traces of Preminger's film. For Strunsky, who no doubt had as part of his agenda the rehabilitation of *Porgy and Bess* as a progressive rather than reactionary phase in the representation of African Americans, a supposedly realistic representation of period and setting would affirm the social value of Gershwin's work.

"I thought it was a beautiful film with a beautiful Gershwin score," Preminger said years later.[39] Beauty is indeed the main feature of *Porgy and Bess*. The impulse toward beauty is evident from the opening scene on the wharf, with the camera slowly drifting toward the water as Clara sings "Summertime" to a baby in her arms. The sequence builds as the gradual unfolding of space: the rails of the plank along which Clara walks are used as an architectural element reflecting the width of the screen. By the third shot, in which a boat arrives at screen right and boys climb onto and jump off the railing of the pier in the background, the orchestration of movement and details has begun to suggest a whole world in the process of revealing itself.

The artificial and closed world of Catfish Row unfolds further as night falls (the passage between day and night, marked by the changes in light on the set and on the actors' faces, is a major atmospheric and temporalizing element throughout *Porgy and Bess*). The sweep and the beauty of the compositions are overpowering. The staircase and the railing of the housefront that serves as a gathering point for numerous characters, including a group of craps-shooting men, function as architectural elements organizing the composition and directing the viewer's eye in staggered or flowing movements across the width of the screen. Porgy establishes himself as the central figure merely by moving to the camera side of the railing to sing about his loneliness: his head is positioned at the point in the composition where the railing comes to an end, so that the railing's force and meaning seem to be imparted to him. In contrast, Sportin' Life is the most restless figure, spanning the frame horizontally and vertically as he emerges from a garret window, walks across the gutter of a roof, and slides down a rain pipe to the courtyard.

The arrival of Crown and Bess prompts a reversal in the dominant camera position on the housefront, so that the movement of the railing across the screen is now reversed, and Porgy occupies a relatively inconspicuous position at the left of the frame. This very long take ends with Porgy departing into the background across the wide, empty courtyard as a boy emerges with a lamp beneath the arch at left to open the door to Porgy's shack. The eruption of a fight between Crown and Robbins occasions one of the film's most striking shots: against a panorama of window shutters opening and people looking out, the two men rise in silhouette in the foreground from beneath the frame, grappling with each other. After Crown kills Robbins on the stairs, the camera pulls back and pivots right to reveal Bess at the right of the screen—the camera movement and her placement immediately establishing that the effect of the murder on the narrative will center on Bess. The hasty dispersal of the crowd into their homes leaves only Serena (grieving over her husband's corpse), Crown, and Bess in the vast space: the lengthy sequence has vividly expressed the key duality in the film, community versus isolation. The inescapable stylization of the film, the massiveness of the set, and the theatricality of the duration—time and space constituting together a huge block, rather than the smooth flow characteristic of other Preminger films (the fades to black at the ends of some sequences emphasize this blocklike quality)—all serve this meaning.

Bess tries to escape Catfish Row through the archway (which has been established as the link between this place and the outside world) but returns when she hears the police approaching. This shot (with its wonderful depth of field of the unattainable space beyond the arch) conveys that the courtyard, though an idyll, is also a prison. The beginning of intimacy between Porgy and Bess, as Bess hides from the police in Porgy's shack, is conveyed through a fairly distant medium shot that is compassionate in a way hard to define. Much of the meaning of the scene comes from the placement of the lamp on a table in the foreground, both a light source and a symbol of shelter and hope, in contrast with the shuttered window in the background, through which the policemen's voices and flashlights are perceived.

Preminger delays cutting, producing a heightened theatrical effect. When Crown, hearing thunder, tells the crowd of shelter seekers in Serena's house that God is laughing at them, an offscreen woman is heard singing "Oh de Lawd Shake de Heavens." Faces in the foreground turn to look past the camera: there is a noticeable delay before Preminger cuts to the reverse angle, revealing the singer on the stairs. A few minutes later in the same scene, the pause after Crown's song "A Red Headed Woman" is filled by Clara's offscreen wail, which causes Crown and others in the frame to look offscreen, before the cut to the space including Clara.

Throughout the film, Preminger's use of masses of people and architectural forms is very effective. One example is the scene in which Bess, walking forward from the back of the set and singing "Oh, the Train Is at the Station," leads Robbins's mourners up the stairs and offscreen. The arch of the huge fireplace in Maria's "cookshop" is repeatedly used as a compositional element (and the arch, whenever it is seen, is typically seen in full, flowing across the frame in the background). The largely static mise-en-scène of Serena's "My Man's Gone Now" is effective: the music conveys the emotion and is extremely powerful.

The duet in "Bess, You Is My Woman Now" is a model of abstraction and simplicity: Bess and Porgy are clasped together in mid-frame; through a small window at left, behind Bess, we see, out of focus, a largely empty field in which a few people are visible; at right, a door is closed. All our attention is focused on the center of the composition, and the two rectangles offer abstraction. Earlier in the same sequence, the staging of the action of Porgy's hurling Sportin' Life across the room emphasizes the relationship between the two rectangles, as Sportin' Life is thrown from the window (through which he entered the room to talk to Bess) across the space to the open doorway at right. The peak of the film's use of doors and windows as frames within frames or as abstract rectangular forms comes when Maria opens her window to see, across the courtyard, Porgy and Crown fighting in the window of Porgy's shack.

"Bess, You Is My Woman Now" is followed immediately by Maria's ebullient "Picnic Day," which culminates in a succession of left-to-right crowd movements toward the boat. The color is gorgeous: the reds of band uniforms, the pink of Bess's dress, the yellow and white of the other costumes, a U.S. flag at the stern. In the picnic sequence, Sportin' Life's "It Ain't Necessarily So" is an exercise in verticals and movements perpendicular to the camera plane. At one point, Sportin' Life approaches the camera relentlessly; then a cut to a new shot has the camera tracking forward. These movements prepare the viewer for Crown's emergence through the woods to seize Bess.

A lurid yellow-orange light splashes over the scene of the delirious Bess in bed. In the courtyard, the cobblestones now gleam a bright yellow. Poitier scores with the simplicity of his delivery ("God give crippled to understand lots of things he didn't give strong men"); his resignation over Bess's inevitable defection to Crown, contradicted by his arm stretched toward her across the small table against the wall, is quite moving. On the other hand, Dandridge is not enough of a presence in the film to make *Porgy and Bess* fully tragic—and this is doubtless Preminger's fault (he doesn't give Bess a reaction to Crown's death, for example).

Porgy and Bess is an overwhelming film, if a marginal one. Though there is undeniably something oppressive about it, it is expansive, too: it opens in multiple directions. Commentators viewing it within an auteurist framework have generally coupled it with *Carmen Jones*. But *Porgy and Bess* might better be viewed as a counterpart to *The Man with the Golden Arm*. Both films cut themselves off from the world to isolate themselves inside studio-built urban areas. Both films even feature dandy drug pushers, and the role played by the police in both films is rather similar. The artificiality and hermeticism of the two films make them exceptions in Preminger's film career, while irresistibly pointing back toward his origins in theater.

25

Man's Disorganized Soul

"Robert Traver" was the pen name of John D. Voelker, for seven terms the prosecutor of Marquette County in the Upper Peninsula of Michigan. Voelker based *Anatomy of a Murder* on a 1952 trial in which he (having lost his bid for an eighth term in 1950) defended Coleman A. Peterson, a U.S. Army lieutenant accused of killing a bar owner, Mike Chenoweth, who had, it was alleged, raped Peterson's wife. The jury found Peterson not guilty by reason of insanity. Voelker's lengthy novel is narrated in the first person by the defense lawyer, Paul Biegler, who has recently been voted out of the prosecutor's office in "Iron Cliffs County," Michigan. Biegler's client is renamed Frederick Manion; his wife is called Laura; the slain bar owner is named Barney Quill.[1]

Published in 1957 (by which time Voelker had been appointed to the Michigan Supreme Court), the book stayed on *The New York Times* bestseller list for sixty-six weeks. Preminger, one of the book's most assiduous readers, was first only "intellectually interested" in the story. Then, after repeated readings, he found himself "really captivated."[2] He bought the rights to the book in April 1958 and retained Voelker as technical adviser.

Looking for a writer, Preminger consulted Billy Wilder, who recommended Wendell Mayes, with whom he had worked on *The Spirit of St. Louis*.[3] Preminger and Mayes worked well together and developed a standard procedure that would stead them through their subsequent collaborations on *Advise & Consent* and *In Harm's Way*. According to Mayes, "When I work with Otto, we discuss over a period of time, say, the first fourth of a screenplay, where we want to go with it; and then I will go off and sit down, and I will write the first fourth. Then I come in and Otto reads it and we discuss it again and we get the construction and the arrangement of scenes to please both of us. Then we move on to the next fourth of the story. I've never gone through a whole screenplay with Otto and then gone off to write, because Otto doesn't like to plan that far ahead—and actually, I don't either because sometimes good things come without planning step-by-step straight through a screen-play."[4]

In adapting *Anatomy of a Murder*, Preminger and Mayes followed Voelker's plot closely and included technical and legal detail in such vast quantities as to ensure for the film an unusually long running time (161 minutes). Perhaps the most significant change to the story involved Mary Pilant, a local woman believed to have been the dead Quill's mistress. In the novel, Mary tells Biegler that her relationship with Quill was platonic ("I regarded him almost as a father")[5] and that they were drawn together mainly by her attachment to the daughter he had had by his estranged wife. Preminger and Mayes make Mary the illegitimate daughter of Quill, a change that draws *Anatomy* further into Preminger's thematic orbit, making Mary another of Preminger's daughter figures and linking her to such characters as Amber St. Clare and the unwed mother in *Bunny Lake Is Missing* (to which Preminger had recently bought the rights), forced by social prejudice about sexuality to live a partly concealed existence of uncertain status. The revelation that Mary is Quill's daughter also furnishes a courtroom coup de théâtre.

Preminger and Mayes added emphases that deepened the novel. They expanded on the relationship between Laura and Biegler by having Laura repeatedly make advances to Biegler and by showing, ambiguously, Biegler mastering his desire for her by ignoring or rejecting her advances. The script's omissions are also significant. In the novel, Biegler uses his courtroom summation to issue a moralistic condemnation of Dancer as well as of the prosecution's expert psychiatric witness, who denies that Manion was insane when he shot Quill. The screenplay omits the attorney's summations and minimizes the moral issues raised by the trial in order to concentrate on pragmatic issues of truth, evidence, plausibility, and dramatic presentation.

On December 8, 1958, Preminger met with Production Code Administration head Geoffrey Shurlock over the script. Shurlock was most concerned with two scenes in which clinical details concerning the rape are discussed. In a letter to Preminger summarizing their meeting, he wrote, "The references to 'sperm,' 'sexual climax,' 'penetration,' etc., seem to us to be hardly suitable in a picture to be released indiscriminately for mixed audiences. It also seems to us that there is an overemphasis on the words 'rape' and 'panties' to the point where this element possibly becomes offensive." Preminger complied by eliminating a few lines and changing a few others (substituting the less precise though still unambiguous "evidence" for "sperm," and, when Biegler asks whether Laura is pregnant, by changing—felicitously—Manion's reply from "Not unless Quill knocked her up" to "Not unless Quill started something"). On the other hand, Preminger kept the word "bitch," which Shurlock objected to, as well as a line Shurlock questioned: "I know that he tore my panties off—and did what he wanted."

When the MPAA insisted on removing the word "penetration," cited in the film as part of the legal definition of rape in Michigan, Mayes and Preminger agreed to change it to "violation." On April 29, however, while the film was in production, Preminger wrote Shurlock that Voelker had objected to this change. "He points out that in the statute of Michigan, and other states, only the word 'penetration' is used. He does not understand why 'violation' should be less censorable than 'penetration.'" Shurlock held firm in his response the next day. Preminger retained the less graphic word.

The traces—and the stakes—of such lexical battles are evident in the film. The screenplay of *Anatomy of a Murder* shows extraordinary concern with words, with where they come from, what other words they might be covering for, what effect they might have on people's perceptions of the objects they intend. Laura tells Biegler that Quill said to her, "I'm going to rape you," and Biegler asks, "Were those his exact words?" Biegler picks up on Sergeant Durgo's statement that Manion had told him that his wife had had trouble with Barney Quill, recognizing (as Durgo confirms) that the prosecutor asked him to use that word instead of the word "rape." Biegler presses bartender Alphonse Paquette over the distinction between "tight" and "high" as characterizations of people affected by alcohol. Biegler objects to a reference to Laura's nighttime "prowls" by Assistant Attorney General Dancer, who turns his apology— "I didn't mean to imply that you were a huntress"—into a veiled attack by deliberately pausing before the word "huntress" (suggesting that he is substituting it for the more offensive possibility he has had in mind all along). Judge Weaver polls the attorneys on possible words to substitute for the term "panties," which he believes carries "a certain light connotation." Paquette's seemingly damning description of Manion bringing death to Quill "like he was the mailman delivering the mail" is taken up by Biegler in examining the psychiatrist Smith to show that such a characterization could fit someone acting under "irresistible impulse"—just as Biegler's "high school debate" line is turned against him by Dancer.

Preminger's insistence on filming the trial with as many details about the rape as possible intact, and many more such details than had ever been aired in an American film, made *Anatomy of a Murder* as great a triumph over Hollywood censorship as *The Moon Is Blue* and *The Man with the Golden Arm* had been, and perhaps a more persuasive triumph, since, unlike those films, *Anatomy* would be released with the Production Code Seal and would thus demonstrate the flexibility, rather than the restrictiveness, of the Code. *Anatomy of a Murder* would be Preminger's major example of the kind of adult entertainment he often told interviewers he had been fighting to make possible since *The Moon Is Blue*. "I hate people who say, 'Do this for the industry,' or that 'this will hurt the industry.' The truth is: there is no more industry. Going to the movies has become a selective process for most Americans. If they can get their entertainment on television free, they will not go to the movies unless the films are top-flight. Making movies today is no longer an 'industry' operation but rather a team operation. The day when theater exhibitors did not want too high a standard in film content because people would then grow dissatisfied with the mediocre product—that day is disappearing."[6] Preminger's distaste—which he often expressed in interviews and press conferences—for the word "industry" is revealing. With *The Court-Martial of Billy Mitchell*, he had begun to define himself as a filmmaker of institutional anatomies—a definition that the films from *Anatomy of a Murder* through *In Harm's Way* would solidify. His rejection of the term "industry" was as much a statement of his own independence from—his position of outsider with respect to—the *institution* of filmmaking as his preference for New York over Los Angeles. His examination of the institution is never merely a neutral document but always (as with Frederick Wiseman's great films of the 1960s and 1970s) a critique founded on the position of the outsider.

Early in his planning of *Anatomy of a Murder*, Preminger decided to shoot the film on location in the Upper Peninsula. Voelker's house would serve as Biegler's residence in the film.

For the all-important role of Biegler—which can be seen as Preminger's tribute to his father (who had died in 1952), who also left the position of state prosecutor to defend clients—Preminger cast James Stewart. Along with his authority, humor, and intelligence, the star brought to the part his identification (stemming from his performance in *Mr. Smith Goes to Washington*) with the rural-American values of honesty, folk wisdom, and unpretentiousness—values that the film celebrates ironically by pointing up Biegler's exploitation of his "humble country lawyer" image for the jury.

Lana Turner was cast as Laura, Ben Gazzara as Manion, George C. Scott as Dancer, and Murray Hamilton as Paquette. Preminger offered the role of the judge to Spencer Tracy and Burl Ives, both of whom turned it down. Nat Rudich, then at the beginning of his long tenure as Preminger's assistant, suggested casting a real judge, an idea that led Preminger to offer the part to Joseph N. Welch, the U.S. Army counsel who, during televised Senate subcommittee hearings, helped end the career of Senator Joseph McCarthy with the famous rebuke, "Have you no sense of decency, sir? At long last, have you no sense of decency?" Welch was eager to do the film and signed his contract in January. Welch's casting became one of the most widely publicized aspects of the movie; another was Preminger's hiring of Duke Ellington to write the score, his first for a feature-length film.

In late February or early March, Lee Remick learned from her agent that Preminger had fired Lana Turner and now wanted Remick for the part of Laura. Announcing Remick's hiring in Hollywood on March 4, Preminger said that Turner had quit over a costume that she thought "wasn't glamorous enough. I told her I was trying to achieve a certain kind of realism, that I was not interested in old-fashioned glamour."[7] In her autobiography, Turner wrote, "Preparations moved along nicely until costuming time, when Hope Bryce, Preminger's assistant, wanted to dress me in a simple little suit right off the racks. I have never favored ready-to-wear clothing onscreen. So I suggested that my dressmaker run up the kind of suit she had in mind." According to Turner, Preminger called her on the phone at home that evening and shouted at her abusively, whereupon Turner hung up and called her agent, Paul Kohner, to tell him to get her out of the film.[8] With Turner, *Anatomy of a Murder* would have been a very different film from the one that was made. Preminger said, "With Miss Turner, I would have played the part differently— it would have been a study of the lieutenant's fascination with an older woman, and she would have been excellent in it."[9] In his next film, *Exodus*, Preminger would have another chance to explore this theme.

Shortly before the start of production, a chapter in Preminger's personal life closed with humiliating publicity: Mary Gardner Preminger was granted a divorce with a substantial financial settlement totaling some $250,000. She had first sought the divorce in December 1957, charging cruelty. In May 1958 she added to her petition the charge that Preminger had been intimate with at least three women: Hope Bryce and two London models, Laura Simpson and Pat Williams. (Pat Williams sold the details of her one-night stand with Preminger, which apparently took place in London in October 1956, to scandal magazines, and gave a deposition admitting the affair to Mary Gardner Preminger's attorneys.) Preminger called the three "innocent victims" and countercharged that Mary had been intimate with Michael Rennie over a three-year period while she was married to Preminger.[10] Rennie formally denied this claim and explained to Louella Parsons, "He's just clutching at straws. I was a friend of both Otto's and Mary's, and when Mary was alone and needed her friends, I did go to see her and took her out. I was concerned about her because her because she has gone through so much."[11] (Mary had undergone abdominal surgery in Los Angeles in early 1957, while Preminger was in England for *Saint Joan*.) The financial settlement brought the acrimonies and the public revelations to an end, and Mary was granted a divorce on the mere grounds of mental cruelty, which she established by testifying that her husband became "so violent" that "he beat his head on the floor and threw himself around the room."[12] The divorce would not become final until March 1960.

With the trial behind him, Preminger could embark on *Anatomy of a Murder* in an unencumbered spirit. "The special train carrying cast, crew, and equipment arrived at six-thirty on a March day, but half the population was at the station to greet us," recalled Preminger.[13] Hope Bryce remembered arriving in Ishpeming, Michigan, with the Hollywood contingent on the train from Chicago. "The snow was packed above the train. We looked out and it was like a cleaver had come along and cut

Joan Bennett and Preminger in *Margin for Error* (Twentieth Century-Fox)

Frank Latimore and Jeanne Crain in *In the Meantime, Darling* (Twentieth Century-Fox)

Otto Preminger and Gene Tierney on the set of *Laura*
(Twentieth Century-Fox; courtesy of the Everett Collection)

Dana Andrews, Clifton Webb, and Gene Tierney in *Laura* (Twentieth Century-Fox)

Gene Tierney and Judith Anderson in *Laura* (Twentieth Century-Fox)

Charles Coburn, Anne Baxter, William Eythe, and Mischa Auer in *A Royal Scandal*
(Twentieth Century-Fox)

Dana Andrews and Linda Darnell in *Fallen Angel* (Twentieth Century-Fox)

Cornel Wilde, Jeanne Crain, Linda Darnell, and William Eythe in *Centennial Summer*
(Twentieth Century-Fox)

Pati Behrs, Jeanne Crain, and Jessica Tandy in *Forever Amber* (Twentieth Century-Fox)

Daisy Kenyon: Joan Crawford, the wrecked car, and the expanding landscape
(Twentieth Century-Fox; courtesy of the Everett Collection)

Joan Crawford, Dana Andrews, and Henry Fonda in *Daisy Kenyon* (Twentieth Century-Fox)

Reginald Gardiner and Betty Grable in *That Lady in Ermine* (Twentieth Century-Fox)

Richard Greene and Jeanne Crain in *The Fan* (Twentieth Century-Fox)

Gene Tierney and José Ferrer in *Whirlpool* (Twentieth Century-Fox)

Gene Tierney, Dana Andrews, Bert Freed, and Karl Malden in the ending of *Where the Sidewalk Ends* as originally filmed (Twentieth Century-Fox)

Charles Boyer and Michael Rennie in *The 13th Letter* (Twentieth Century-Fox)

Jean Simmons and Leon Ames in *Angel Face* (Turner Entertainment/RKO-Radio Pictures)

Maggie McNamara in *The Moon Is Blue*
(United Artists/Otto Preminger Films; courtesy of the Everett Collection)

Robert Mitchum, Marilyn Monroe, and Tommy Rettig in *River of No Return*
(Twentieth Century-Fox)

"Stan' Up and Fight": Joe Adams and Dorothy Dandridge (on balcony) in *Carmen Jones*. Diahann Carroll (in profile) and Pearl Bailey are at Adams's left. (Twentieth Century-Fox)

Preminger directing Frank Sinatra in *The Man with the Golden Arm*
(United Artists/Otto Preminger Films; courtesy of the Everett Collection)

Rod Steiger, Gary Cooper, Ralph Bellamy, and Charles Bickford (back to camera, right)
in *The Court-Martial of Billy Mitchell* (Warner Bros./United States Pictures)

Preminger and Jean Seberg in 1957
(Courtesy of the Everett Collection)

Jean Seberg and Kenneth Haigh in *Saint Joan* (United Artists/Wheel Productions)

Jean Seberg, Mylène Demongeot, and David Niven in *Bonjour Tristesse*
(Sony Pictures/Columbia Pictures)

Porgy and Bess. At left: Sidney Poitier, Sammy Davis, Jr., Dorothy Dandridge, Brock Peters; center: Leslie Scott (wearing hat), Ruth Attaway (behind Scott), Joel Fluellen (to Scott's left), Ean Jackson (to Fluellen's left); on stairs, holding baby: Diahann Carroll

Lee Remick and James Stewart in *Anatomy of a Murder* (Sony Pictures/Columbia Pictures)

Kathryn Grant and James Stewart in *Anatomy of a Murder* (Sony Pictures/Columbia Pictures)

Jill Haworth and Eva Marie Saint in *Exodus* (© 1961 United Artists/MGM)

Unidentified actor (as stenographer), Burgess Meredith,
and Henry Fonda in *Advise & Consent* (Columbia Pictures/Otto Preminger Films)

Tom Tryon and Romy Schneider in *The Cardinal* (Columbia Pictures/Otto Preminger Films)

John Wayne and Patricia Neal in *In Harm's Way* (Paramount Pictures)

Laurence Olivier and Carol Lynley in *Bunny Lake Is Missing*
(Sony Pictures/Columbia Pictures/Otto Preminger Films)

Hurry Sundown: Beah Richards, Jane Fonda, John Mark, and Preminger
(Paramount Pictures; courtesy of the Everett Collection)

Luna, Preminger, and Groucho Marx during a break in the shooting of *Skidoo*
(Paramount Pictures; courtesy of the Everett Collection)

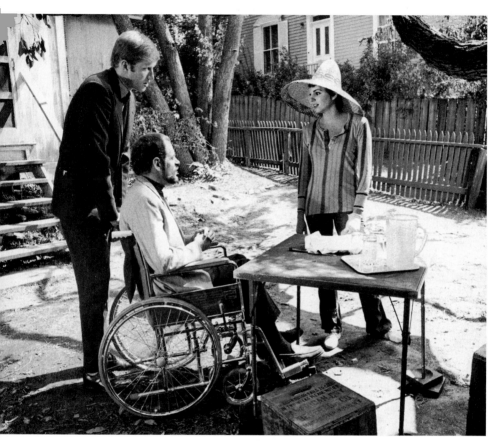

Ken Howard, Robert Moore, and Liza Minnelli in *Tell Me That You Love Me, Junie Moon*
(Paramount Pictures)

Ken Howard, Bette Howard, Nina Foch, and Dyan Cannon in *Such Good Friends*
(Paramount Pictures)

Preminger and Peter O'Toole during the production of *Rosebud*
(United Artists/MGM; courtesy of the Everett Collection)

Joop Doderer, Iman, and Nicol Williamson in *The Human Factor* (United Artists/MGM)

just the tracks' width. It was 32 below zero, and it stayed 32 below zero for almost the whole time."[14] Shooting started on March 23 at the Marquette County Courthouse; on that date a Saul Bass–designed ad, printed in papers in New York and Los Angeles, announced both the commencement of work and the July premiere of the film. At least part of the reason for the accelerated schedule was that Preminger wanted to have the film in release before interest in the book waned. "I didn't rush, but worked very concentratedly," Preminger said.[15]

Preminger thought that "the use of authentic locales helped the actors in some ways. We suddenly had the feeling that the actors themselves were really more lawyers when they appeared in the courtroom, or in those real places, than just actors: and they started to ask legal questions."[16] Expanding on these comments, he told Peter Bogdanovich:

> I feel realistic films gain by being shot on location in two ways. It's not only verisimilitude. Certainly you can copy almost any location. I could have gone there, photographed the courtroom, and had a replica built here in Hollywood. But if you shoot on location, you can't shoot in every way you want; you can't move walls, you have ceilings, you can't light exactly the way you want to. That makes you direct in a more realistic way. You have to be inventive. It's a challenge.
>
> The second thing is that I feel professional extras are usually disgruntled people who don't care much anymore. Either they wanted to be actors and didn't make it, or it's a kind of profession—they go from one picture to another and put on the same makeup and the same laughs and the same moves. But there is a reality if you have the real people—if you go to the Upper Peninsula of Michigan and get real people to sit in that courtroom, and the jurors are real people. Somehow it influences everybody; it influences the other actors. It gives them a reality and a feeling which they wouldn't get otherwise.[17]

In another interview, Preminger admitted, "The actual work on *Anatomy of a Murder* was more difficult, because I couldn't get natural movements either for the characters or for the camera. That's also what caused the dialogue to take on more importance . . . As far as the camera is concerned, a film like that demands more invention."[18] In an account of the production published in *The New York Times*, James W. Merrick observed that "Preminger's passion for realism is reportedly not meeting with the unqualified approval of cameraman Sam Leavitt . . . whose ingenuity has been taxed to the limit maneuvering his equipment and setting his lights in an area normally devoted on a Hollywood soundstage to the producer's canvas-backed chair."[19]

Ellington's collaborator, Billy Strayhorn, joined the unit shortly after the start of filming and worked on the score during production; Ellington would not arrive until April 29. Contrary to normal Hollywood practice, Preminger liked to have the composer on the set and would do so whenever possible for the rest of his career. "By watching the progress of the shooting, seeing the dailies with me, discussing the music daily, he becomes part of the film."[20] Ellington also appeared in one scene as roadhouse pianist Pie-Eye, who lets amateur jazz pianist Biegler share the piano bench and the comping chores with him during a hot up-tempo number by his quintet. Strayhorn contributed the piano solo played by Biegler while he waits for the jury to return with their verdict. "He asked me to play something I liked," said Stewart, who had studied piano and played with a jazz band as an undergraduate at Princeton. "What I think he did, you see, was write something for me that I would have played myself. It was very interesting the way he did it."[21]

Stewart had prepared for his part by studying the script while on vacation in India. "That picture demanded a lot of work and thought," he later said, and the opportunity for relaxed concentration afforded by his vacation left him "better prepared, physically and mentally, than I'd ever been." In Michigan, Ben Gazzara was impressed by the intensity of Stewart's work. "He closeted himself, because he had a great deal of dialogue. I never even saw him taking lunch, actually. I think he did that alone, totally concentrated on this character, totally immersed in it." Gazzara found Stewart's acting an inspiration: "I watched in awe. I said, 'Holy shit, look at this, look at this. Actors Studio, schmactor's studio. This guy can act.' How natural, how simple, what a sense of humor, tongue in cheek, how he could pause and hold it forever, hold your attention. He had all the moves. I was really awestruck. It taught me a great deal . . . You never had a sense from Jimmy Stewart that he wanted to crowd you out, that he wanted his moments framed, that he wanted you to change your rhythm to help him along, which a lot of greedy actors do. He let you be yourself and work and think."[22]

Preminger allowed the actors freedom to build their characterizations. To prepare her part, Remick asked Voelker and several Ishpeming residents about their impressions of the real-life model for her character. "Everybody had a different viewpoint about this lady and about the story itself. Some of them said she was so sweet and so good and she loved her husband so much, she never would have done such an awful thing, and then others in the same town would say, oh, she was a dreadful woman, dreadful, wild hellion, crazy lady, flirted with everybody, would have done anything. So then one makes up one's own mind, and I think she was probably a bit of both." Preminger, Remick recalled, "left a great deal, I think, to each of us. There were times when there were specific things that he wanted, specific lines or at a particular moment in the scene, and he was very definite about what he wanted then, but for the most part it seemed he left most of us to our own devices. If he didn't like it, he would certainly say so. But there wasn't elaborate discussion about it . . . He doesn't say here, come look at this house, come look at this trailer camp where you live, come look at the courtroom where the trial took place. You just show up there, ready to shoot, and you shoot . . . We didn't sit around and talk about the piece or the characters very much. Whatever discussion took place happened on the set, just before one shot a scene, or in between takes."[23]

Ben Gazzara said that Preminger gave him "no direction at all. With that, I think, he made a wise choice. If an actor is bringing it to you, why interfere with him? I don't think he liked to intellectualize over a performance . . . Otto didn't use rehearsal time between the actors. He used most of the time with the crew and the cameraman. The actor was supposed to take care of that himself." Though Gazzara found Preminger "rather a stand-off-ish fellow [who] seemed to be apprehensive about exuding too much enthusiasm in work or in friendship," he acknowledged that "if he liked you, he could be very, very charming. And thank God he liked me, and he liked most of the people on *Anatomy of a Murder* . . . It may have been because he was surrounded by people like Joseph Welch, and John Voelker, who wrote the book, and Jimmy, that he was rather mellow during the shooting of that picture."[24]

One exception Gazzara observed was Preminger's treatment of an actor who had come out from Hollywood to play the small part of one of the trial witnesses. The actor "was obviously not giving Otto what he wanted. After about the fourth take, Otto became insulting, accusing the actor of not doing his homework."[25] Gazzara concluded, "I think that Otto just didn't know how to work with actors, really, didn't know what to tell them to make them better, so he would become frustrated and become abusive."[26] George C. Scott, who liked Preminger, though one observer noticed that the two "often had disagreements,"[27] concluded similarly, "Otto is really too emotional to be a terrific director."[28]

Hope Preminger recalled that one member of the cast whom Preminger had little use for was Kathryn Grant (cast as Mary Pilant). At one point during the production the actress went to his office to insist on wearing her hair in spit curls. "After all, it's my personality," she said. "What personality?" Preminger replied.[29] Yet he treated the actress with forbearance when she was having trouble remembering her dialogue during the late-night bar scene in which Biegler asks her to testify for the defense. "His face was extremely taut," according to an observer, but instead of tearing into Grant, Preminger called a break in shooting and sent her off the set with an assistant to brush up on her lines.[30]

In directing Joseph Welch, Preminger avoided putting too many demands on him. "I was very careful . . . never to make him move and talk at the same time," recalled Preminger.[31] Welch said that Preminger told him, " 'Just be yourself, as you are in your day-to-day life, and forget there's even a camera there!' That carried me through splendidly."[32]

Eve Arden (playing Biegler's secretary, Maida), whose husband, Brooks West, accompanied her to Michigan as a late addition to the cast in the part of Mitch Lodwick, the district attorney, remembered the shoot as an enjoyable and sociable one. "The picture went smoothly, with only occasional flashes of the well-publicized Preminger temper."[33] Nor did Orson Bean, cast as the army psychiatrist who testifies for the defense, have any problems with Preminger: "On our show it was all going swimmingly. He would order a take. He would say, 'Action.' The take would finish and he would say, 'Cut. Print. Perfect. Next.' Just like that. And everybody was happy."[34] Remick agreed that few scenes required a large number of takes. "If he saw a take going bad, he'd cut it, and then we'd start again, and he'd get it fairly quickly. He doesn't go into it fifteen, twenty takes. He's very economical, in terms of getting what he wants fairly quickly and succinctly. You know quite definitely what he wants without lengthy, lengthy chats." Remick believed that Preminger left little to chance and relied little on improvisation or sudden inspiration. "I think he sees the entire film before he shoots a foot. I really do. I think he knows every shot, every angle, every bit, every piece of business. Occasionally he's surprised by something an actor does, and he either likes it or he doesn't, and it's either in or it's out, but I do think that there's relatively little that comes to him as a great spur-of-the-moment flash of something new on the set. It's all prearranged in his head."[35]

Shooting ended on May 16. Ellington and his orchestra recorded the score in early June. On June 17 the cut film was previewed in San Francisco. Said Preminger, "It was an obvious success with the public there. I did not change or cut anything, and it went right into release."[36] *Anatomy* received positive reviews and became one of the most popular pictures of 1959. *Variety*'s year-end box-office wrap-up put it at number 7 for the year, with $5.25 million in domestic rentals.

Anatomy of a Murder asks: How do we know anything about other people? The tension between a person's public and private roles is a constant preoccupation of Preminger's work, and the Preminger films that feature sequences in courtrooms highlight this tension in a particularly stark way, making the court the space where the private must account for itself. Of all Preminger's films, *Anatomy* dwells the longest within this space and elaborates most fully the questions of how to articulate the private in a public forum and whether the private life will be able to find an image for itself that can stand up in this forum.

The subtlety of Preminger's handling of the courtroom sequences is remarkable. He sustains interest through details of characterization and behavior; through contrasting one kind of performance with another (as in Biegler's two cross-examinations of the sullen and defensive Paquette); through variations of rhythm in speech and movement; and through the compositional choices, out of the limited range available, by which he highlights the meanings of the various exchanges. During Biegler's questioning of Manion, Preminger repeatedly frames him so that we see, in the background behind him, the faces of the jury fixedly staring offscreen at the defendant: these shots underline Biegler's role in staging Manion's self-presentation to the jury. On the other hand, during Laura's testimony, Preminger shows the jury only briefly (during the demonstration with her dog and at the beginning of the cross-examination). The role of the audience for whom the testimony is presented is now occupied by the courtroom spectators (already established, through their laughter at the word "panties" and the commotion raised by Laura's letting down her hair, as a public of consumers and spectacle seekers for whom Laura is the central object) and, in particular, by Mary Pilant, who arrives early in Laura's examination and sits among the spectators (observed by Biegler, as we are made aware by his grateful look offscreen at her).

Biegler's search for the truth structures the narrative, and Biegler's own interest in the case progressively complicates the search. In the first scene in the Sheriff's office with Manion, Biegler sits with his back to the window while Manion sits on a desk against a wall decorated with WANTED posters. The two men are opposed in shot/reverse shot, a device that emphasizes the early hostility between them: Manion wants to diminish Biegler by pretending he doesn't need him, while Biegler seeks to puncture Manion's illusion of invincibility. (Gazzara's acting contrasts with Stewart's. With his flamboyantly concessive hand gestures and his cigarette holder, Manion flaunts his unconcern and uninvolvement. The new, postwar male he represents is cool, uncaring, unimpressed by authority.) In their second scene together, Biegler assumes Manion's previous position, with his back to the WANTED posters, a taking over of territory, depriving Manion of space and options. Again, the scene is done in shot/reverse shot, but this time Manion is left, first, to float (in close-up) against the gray wall. This abstraction of the person is shown as the direct result of Biegler's taking over of space. Biegler recalls Manion to reality, informing him that of the four possible defenses against a murder charge, only one is available to him. As he ponders Biegler's riddle, Manion goes back to the window. Then, returning toward Biegler, he passes a driver's-test poster and a vision-test chart. The two posters reaffirm the "test" aspect of the scene, which Biegler has set up by telling Manion, "Let's see how bright you can be," and Manion confirms again by asking, "Am I getting warm?"

In the third scene with Manion, Biegler stands in the background in front of the cell door as Manion paces in the foreground, recounting his memory lapse during the shooting of Quill. The composition poses Biegler as the audience for Manion's performance: Biegler is also its evaluator, his position of power emphasized by the low angle. The unspoken question is whether Manion's claim that he was insane while shooting Quill can convince a jury, and Biegler's decision to take Manion's case gives the answer. At that point, the two men sit down side by side on a bench, and the camera pans to reframe them together. This moment is crucial. From here on, Biegler can no longer claim (before the film audience) to be a disinterested seeker after truth; he is (literally, in this shot) on his client's side.

As Preminger told interviewers, *Anatomy* demonstrates "that there is no absolute truth, and that it is better to free a criminal than to condemn him if there is the least doubt about his guilt."[37] The narrative construction withholds direct depiction of what happened among the Manions and Barney Quill on the night of Quill's death—and does so in a manner that doesn't seem like withholding. The non-depiction of the events in question presents itself not as some hole or lapse in the narrative, but as the inevitable consequence of the screenplay's choice to limit the narrative information to what Biegler knows. The absence of any absolute truth is thus equivalent, in the film, to the absence of a viewpoint outside Biegler's that would be able to compensate for the gaps in his knowledge.

The absence of absolute truth also finds expression in the mechanism of the trial itself, in which the diversity of testimonies, each given under the heading of "the truth, the whole truth, and nothing but the truth," shows that there are always holes in people's knowledge and that the best one can hope for, in trying to reconstruct a series of events, is an approximation. The body of truth can no more be knit together than the pieces of Saul Bass's anatomized body in the credits sequence, but at least the parts can reassume more or less the same configuration they had in life.

If Preminger's is, as it has been called, a "detached" cinema, Bass provides a perfect image of detachment by separating body parts. Detachment means not merely the physical or mental removal of the observer, declining to participate in the perceived world (as, at the beginning of *Anatomy*, Biegler is removed, physically apart from the community and disconnected from its news and concerns; he tells his friend

Parnell of his reluctance to take Manion's case; later, he declines Laura's invitation to enter her trailer), but also the act of separating what was formerly joined. Bass's titles for *Anatomy* also indicate that the film is mainly concerned with the community, represented as a "body." What the film will anatomize is not, in fact, the murder, but the murder trial. As Parnell's encomium on juries indicates, the film is concerned with the formation of a collective identity ("It's one of the miracles of man's disorganized soul that they can do it, in most instances do it right well"). This process is not directly represented in the film; it doesn't need to be, since the analogue to the process is under way in the film audience, which is also asked to judge Manion and "become of one mind." When Maida says she doesn't know what she would do if she were on the jury, she gives voice to the uncertainty of the film audience, for which she functions (here and at other points) as a representative within the film.

Another body central to the film is Laura Manion's. It would be too easy to stop at pointing out that the film is concerned with displaying this body, with exploiting it as an object of visual pleasure. At two striking moments the film performs in concert with Laura's body; the body of the film and Laura's body coincide. Throughout the scene of Biegler interviewing Laura in his office, she sits on the sofa. The shots of her contrive to keep her upper body and arms within the frame at all times, with an effort that becomes conspicuous when she leans forward to flick the ashes of her cigarette into an ashtray, and the camera, shooting her from a high angle in a general approximation of Biegler's point of view, tilts down to keep her arm in frame as she leans forward—it could be a moment from a musical. Thus celebrated by the camera, her gesture becomes extravagant. Near the end of the scene, their interview over, Laura puts on her sunglasses at the same time as she unbends her right leg and moves it from the sofa to the floor, the camera tracking back to keep the leg in frame.

The later comment on this scene comes during the testimony of Alphonse Paquette, who describes, with relish, Laura's behavior while playing pinball in Quill's bar. On cross-examination, Biegler deflates Paquette's and Dancer's attempt to implicate the jury (and the film audience) in their own misogyny by getting Paquette to admit that only he and Quill were paying attention to Laura. Yet the film, through its visual strategies no less than through its dialogue, has persistently asked whether Laura deliberately attracts men's attention, and has suggested that the answer to this is central, somehow, to her husband's case. The camera movements and framing in the scene of Laura on Biegler's sofa complicate the question by establishing a fit between Laura's presentation of herself and the film's interest in looking at her.

Another crucial moment in the film's relationship with Laura occurs at the end of her second interview with Biegler, in his car underneath the jail-cell window. Replying, after some delay, to his question about whether her husband has any reason to be jealous ("No, not once, not ever"), she turns to face Biegler and the camera, wearing the sunglasses she has just put on again. The fade-out that ends the shot here complements and mirrors her gesture of putting on the sunglasses, while also participating in her darkening of her own vision (just as in the earlier office scene, the camera's tracking back complements her putting on the sunglasses). The shot fades, not merely in the presence of Laura's putting on her sunglasses, but in consequence of it. Whereas a dissolve would have implied a continuity between scenes and between consciousnesses, the fade to black at this point registers a break in continuity, a disruption caused by, or analogous to, the masking of Laura's eyes and the darkening of her vision.

Anatomy of a Murder, then, *is* the woman; or, as in *Laura*, Preminger seeks to hold in balance two points of view that represent two poles organizing the world of the film—that of the subject drawn to the woman, and that of the woman herself. (In instructing Laura how to dress, Biegler repeats Waldo Lydecker's relationship with Laura Hunt; the Manions' matching cigarette lighters are another link to *Laura*, recalling that film's duplicate clocks.) The film shares a secret understanding with Laura Manion, a complicity that, rather than transcending the doubt or hatred or horror or longing with which the men in the film regard her, remains held in a complex pattern with the men's attitudes.

In the nighttime scene of Biegler bringing Laura back to her trailer after her visit to the roadhouse, the film overtly sympathizes with Laura, closing the scene on a shot of her anxious and tormented face as she is left alone in the doorway of the trailer. This gesture unequivocally signifies Preminger's refusal to permit any simple characterization of her as an "army slut" (Quill's epithet, as remembered by Laura). The shot enables us to view her as a tragic figure (a view we've been prepared for earlier in the scene by Remick's reading of the line "I'm lonely, Paul, aw-ful lonely" as a plea for sympathy rather than a come-on): above all, someone who is lost, misplaced (significantly, she lost her eyeglasses during the rape). This shot, like the shot with the sunglasses, concludes the scene with a face to black, signifying a break in the film, Biegler's temporary taming of Laura's sexuality, which allows the film to move into its next phase, the trial, with the ensuing fade-in on Judge Weaver enter-ing the courtroom.

This entrance is itself highly revealing. Preminger knows well that *Anatomy of a Murder* exists within a social-temporal space, that of a media-conscious America, where Joseph Welch is a recognized public figure and not a professional actor. Judge Weaver, taking over the court-room, must introduce himself, conscious of being an unknown quantity and an object of speculation, just as Welch must introduce himself (at the same time and through the same words and movements) to the film audience. This equivalence between actor and character activates the social dimension of the film, reminding us that the film comes out of and flows back into the real world.

The casting of Welch is one of Preminger's grandest gestures, and *Anatomy of a Murder* is an ideal proof of Preminger's assertion that the function of the producer is inseparable from that of the director. Prem-inger the producer provides the location, which Preminger the director films in a way that ignores its scenic beauty: we see nothing of the Up-per Peninsula that would likely qualify as a tourist attraction. We never see Biegler fishing (an activity that would certainly have afforded some scenic opportunities); we see only his return home at night. What we see of the area is what the characters see of it as they take part in the murder case. The landscape enters into the film mainly in driving scenes, as a purely incidental element. Landscape never exists for its own sake in Preminger's work, and he never celebrates it for its own sake—not even in *Exodus* (which opens with a panoramic shot of Cyprus, narrated by a tour guide for the benefit of a tourist). More than this, he never uses landscape merely to authenticate the reality of a loca-tion or a background, in other words, merely as a sign of realness—not even in *Rosebud* (in which the dispersion of the narrative across loca-tions in England, France, Germany, Corsica, and Israel threatens a cer-tain ostentatiousness). Landscape is always merely *place*: every event must take place somewhere. Preminger has no other interest in, no other use for landscape than to specify and characterize place.

To be sure, few shots in *Anatomy of a Murder* fail to announce that the film was made on location. Preminger makes sure that if there is a window on the set, we see what is outside the window (even in such a minor scene as that of Maida gathering intelligence at the beauty salon), or at least we see the natural light from outside filtering through a curtain. This isn't just a matter of what a film producer might call "putting the money on the screen": the presence of windows becomes a thematic and visual motif whose significance is suggested in an early dialogue exchange. When Parnell reproaches Biegler for drinking alone, Biegler observes, "You're living in a glass house," to which Parnell replies, "My windows have been busted a long time ago."

In the scene of Manion's interview with Biegler in the jail, a window serves as an opening, an area for reflection, a sample and a sign of the freedom that is at stake for Manion. (As Biegler tells Mary, "Manion loves his freedom. He'd like to have a little more of it.") While looking out this window, his back to the camera, Manion realizes that when he shot Quill, he "must have been mad"—amended, on Biegler's deliberate misunderstanding of the term, to "crazy." Manion turns toward the window, concealing his face from the camera, in order to think: when he turns back to the camera, he now has his excuse, his defense, his version of history. A moment like this occurs in *Advise & Consent*, when the President of the United States, during a private conference with his nominee for Secretary of State, turns to look out the window before asking, "Does anybody know you lied?"—meaning, Is there anyone to contradict your version of history? Again, the window at the back of the set offers an escape, a way out, a space of possibility, where stories and thoughts are gathered.

In *Anatomy of a Murder*, the breadth of this space of possibility finds expression in the much-admired score, which Tom Piazza has called "the closest thing we have to a vernacular American symphony." Another commentator, Krin Gabbard, complains that "the music sounds randomly tacked on," a state of affairs he attributes to Ellington and Strayhorn's having, contrary to usual film-scoring practice, written "a good deal of music without knowing exactly how it would turn up in the film."[38] But this apparent randomness actually enhances the texture of

the film. Ellington's music, in floating above the film and only rarely pinning itself to the images (e.g., the accentuating phrases when Biegler
finds the gun racks concealed behind Paquette's bar), expresses a freedom and a spaciousness that make clear the extended context of the
drama in three dimensions: temporal, geographical, and moral.

Anatomy of a Murder defines the freedom of its characters in terms
of their ability to move by car, and the traveling of distances, great,
medium, and small, is a major concern of the film. The first shot, after
the credits, is a nighttime exterior long shot of Biegler driving home from
fishing (he, too, "loves his freedom"). Other scenes show Biegler driving
(toward the county jail, where he finds Laura standing in front of a
parked car; toward the Thunder Bay Inn; away from the roadhouse, with
Laura, and toward the trailer camp; finally, toward the trailer camp
again, with Parnell). Parnell's disastrous drive back from Canada forms a
memorable interlude. Laura provides the key to her character early in
the film when she tells Biegler, "I grew up on the move . . . Manny likes
to go; we're always going, whenever we get the chance; we've been all
over." Anticipating the ending of the film, the line defines her freedom in
terms of her freedom of movement. She is from "no place in particular";
her father was a migrant construction worker. The durability of her relationship with Manion seems based on a shared love of movement. The
film repeatedly links Laura to parked cars (the car in front of the jail,
where Biegler first meets her; Biegler's car, where she sits and talks with
him; the trailer) that symbolize the predicament of someone who loves
"to move" but, for the moment, can't.

Moments in *Anatomy of a Murder* reveal Preminger at his most generous (confirming the testimony of those who recalled *Anatomy* as a
happy shoot by Preminger's standards). I think particularly of the beauty
and elegance of the shot in which Parnell, asked by Biegler if he can stay
sober and work with him on the case, considers his own capabilities and
the excitement, denied him during the law career he believed finished,
of working on a big murder case. During the fairly lengthy take, Maida is
sharply in focus at her desk behind Parnell, who is at right. Parnell is
given prominence by being slightly closer to the camera and also at the
right of the frame (which our eyes "read" last and want to rest on), but
the space of the frame is divided laterally between the two people—an
aspect of the scene that gives weight to Maida's interjections, her sym-

pathy for Parnell, and her admiration for Biegler (who, in offering Parnell a job, is unobtrusively trying to help the aging alcoholic regain his self-respect). In such a scene, we find a relaxation of the characteristic Preminger tension. The shot contains different perspectives—those of Maida, Parnell, and the offscreen Biegler—without making this difference a source of stress. Rather, the perspectives complement each other: there is a collusion between the look of Maida and the offscreen (implicit) look of Biegler, the former making the latter explicit.

At crucial moments in the film Preminger's camera hovers in space, draws back slightly to reframe people pressing forward: Manion as he seeks verification from Biegler that his guess at an "excuse" is correct; Biegler as he "begs the court" to let him introduce testimony about the rape. The hovering quality of the camera at these points is very expressive. Manion and Biegler extend themselves in space as they extend themselves in their words. Overstepping what they know, they enter into an area where they require the justification of another person, and the camera, by moving back slightly, gives the impression that it, too, is poised tensely at a place where it can't long remain, where some further action is needed to allow it to return to repose.

Preminger achieves a powerful effect by joining different shots on a continuous action, as when Biegler, distressed when Laura asks him if he doesn't like the way she dresses, quickly gets up and tries to return to the topic at hand; and when, during his cross-examination of Laura, Dancer ironically apologizes, "I didn't mean to imply that you were a— huntress," and then pursues his interrogation. In the latter moment, a cut appears to suppress what would have been a natural pause as Dancer shifts between the two modes of speech he alternates throughout the cross-examination: one soft, familiar, and intimate, the other driving, insistent, and public. Contradicting Preminger's inveighing against cuts ("It is my conviction that every cut interrupts the flow of story-telling"),[39] these moments use editing to intervene in the presentation of behavior; and *Anatomy of a Murder*, with its many scenes of interrogations filmed either in shot/reverse shot or in single takes with cutaways to listeners, in general constitutes an obvious counterexample (not the only one) to the opinion that unbroken long takes invariably characterize Preminger's style.

Sam Leavitt's lighting, often relatively flat for an American commercial film of the period, registers faces as absorbed within a space whose tonal boundaries are indistinct and where zones of light and shadow are not sharply differentiated. It's a kind of lighting that, within the range of options used in the period, connotes realism, and it is decisive in presenting the world of the film *as* a world—just as, even in the scenes in the courtroom (a self-contained world whose exact duplication in the studio was easily within Preminger's resources), the resonance of the voices in the live space reminds us that we are "in the world." *Anatomy of a Murder* locates itself triumphantly as a concentrated, limited effort within a real space and time that it lets us perceive clearly as continuing in multiple directions. This effort itself resembles a film production—a metaphor that will be active again and again in Preminger's films of the 1960s, a series of masterpieces that *Anatomy* inaugurates.

26

Make Them All Brilliant and I Will Direct Unevenly

Known as a political progressive, Ingo Preminger, who had by now established himself as an important talent agent, numbered among his clients several blacklisted writers, including Dalton Trumbo, one of the Hollywood Ten—the ten writers and directors who, in 1947, after being summoned as "unfriendly witnesses" before the House Un-American Activities Committee (HUAC), refused to testify, were cited for contempt of Congress and were convicted and sentenced to prison. Ingo also helped structure the deal by which, in 1955, MGM commissioned Leon Uris to write *Exodus*, a novel about the birth of the modern-day nation of Israel. MGM, then under Dore Schary's management, underwrote Uris's research in Israel and acquired the movie rights. After three years of work, Uris delivered the book in 1958. The pages of the massive manuscript, piled in boxes in Ingo's house, caught Otto's attention during a visit to his brother. "I started reading it after dinner and couldn't put it down. I sat up most of the night and when I finished I knew I wanted to make that film."[1]

An epic-length page-turner written in a brisk, journalistic style, Uris's *Exodus* starts in late 1946. In deference to the Arabs, the policy of the British mandatory government in Palestine strictly limits Jewish immigration, and the British have set up detention camps in Cyprus for European Jewish refugees caught en route to Palestine. Ari Ben Canaan, a leader of the Jewish underground military organization Haganah, plots the successful escape of three hundred detained children aboard a decrepit freighter, renamed the *Exodus*. Also on board is Katherine "Kitty" Fremont, an American widow who has volunteered as a nurse at the camps. Once in Palestine, Ari and Kitty fall in love against a background of three conflicts—between the Jews and the British; between the moderate Haganah and the extremist Irgun Zvai Leumi (or Etzel; called "the Maccabees" by Uris); and between the Jews and the Arabs. The third conflict intensifies after the United Nations' November 29, 1947, vote to partition Palestine into a Jewish state and an Arab state. The book ends with the surviving main characters fighting the Arab-Israel War in late 1948.

Uris interrupts the main narrative at several points to give lengthy background information on several characters whose experiences and genealogies allow him to encapsulate the entire history of the Jews: Karen Clement, a German Jew who spent the war sheltered by a Danish family; Dov Landau, a Warsaw Jew who became a *Sonderkommando* at Auschwitz, helping to dispose of bodies from the gas chambers; and Ari's father, Barak, and his uncle, Akiva, fugitives from the pogroms of late-nineteenth-century Russia who became, respectively, an official of the Jewish Agency in Palestine and a leader of the Irgun. Among the liberties Uris takes with the historical record, those concerning the freighter are especially worth noting. The historical ship *Exodus 1947* was crammed with 4,500 displaced persons of all ages, not just children, and they boarded not at Cyprus but at Sète, France. Her voyage was tragic: the British rammed and boarded her within Palestinian territorial waters and escorted her back to Europe, finally forcing the passengers to disembark at Hamburg, an incident that helped turn international opinion against Britain and in favor of Jewish statehood. (Preminger's film approaches the historical record more closely than the book in that the passengers— who now number 611—are of all ages.)

Apart from its popular appeal—the book became an instant best-seller on its publication in September 1958 and has remained in print ever since—*Exodus* enthralled Preminger for personal reasons. As early as 1950, Preminger had briefly planned to make an independent film called *A Candle for Ruth* in Israel, with first John Garfield, then Kirk Douglas under consideration for the lead role of an American who becomes involved in Israel's struggle for independence.[2] "He was not a religious Jew per se, but he was a political Jew," Hope Preminger said of her husband.[3]

Preminger learned that with Schary having left the studio in 1956, MGM was no longer eager to produce *Exodus*, a film that was bound to irritate the British and would probably be banned in the Arab world.

Preminger went to Joseph Vogel, president of Loew's, Inc., MGM's parent company, to negotiate for a transfer of MGM's contract with Uris. He got the rights to *Exodus* for $75,000, a price that also included partial payment for Uris's services as screenwriter.[4] Preminger approached United Artists to set up a deal for *Exodus*. On May 12, 1958, UA vice president Max E. Youngstein, then a third of the way through reading Uris's manuscript, wrote Arthur Krim: "This is, by far, the best thing on an Israeli picture that has come across our desks . . . I don't want to lose this one if we can find a way of putting it together."[5] Shortly afterward, United Artists and Preminger (represented by Ingo) made a deal for *Exodus*. The picture would cost $1,750,000, exclusive of stars. (This amount was later raised, with UA's agreement, to $3,006,000.) Preminger would receive $160,000 for his services, the first $250,000 of profits, and 75 percent of profits thereafter.[6]

Uris's first-draft screenplay dissatisfied Preminger, who later said of the writer, "I don't think he can write dialogue . . . In telling a story he becomes too much of a partisan."[7] After some period of effort, Preminger fired Uris (earning the writer's undying ill will; after the film was released, Uris publicly repudiated it) and started again with Albert Maltz, a member of the Hollywood Ten who was now working in Mexico. Maltz did a lot of research for the film and visited Israel at least once before the end of May 1959, at which time he was planning another trip in July. In addition to drawing on Zionist literature on Jewish settlement in and territorial claims to Palestine, Maltz made use both of pro-Israeli and pro-Arab sources on the 1947–48 conflict and conducted interviews with Israeli citizens (both Jewish and Arab).[8]

In July 1959 Preminger went to Israel to forge the alliances he would need to film *Exodus* entirely on location. Meyer Weisgal, whom Preminger had known more than thirty years before in Vienna as Max Reinhardt's friend and backer, was now head of the Weizmann Institute of Science in Rehovot. Through Weisgal, Preminger met Prime Minister David Ben-Gurion, Minister of Finance Levi Eshkol, and Pinhas Sapir, the minister of commerce and industry. The latter body, which administered Israel's small film business, did all it could to accommodate the biggest production to shoot in the country to date.[9] The Israeli government was eager to cooperate with *Exodus*, both because of the money the production would spend in the country and because of the goodwill and stimulus to tourism the film would generate (as had Uris's book). In gratitude to Weisgal, Preminger donated all revenues from Israeli exhibition of *Exodus* to the Weizmann Institute.[10] Preminger would remain in love with Israel for the rest of his life, though he could see some of the country's shortcomings. At a press conference during production of *Exodus*, Preminger said he was shocked to learn that censorship existed in Israel. He warned that it was the first step toward totalitarianism and hoped that as the nation developed, it would abandon it.[11]

In October and early November, Maltz sent Preminger, in installments, a complete detailed treatment for *Exodus*, totaling 246 pages. Among other criticisms, Preminger objected to the "low-level bickering" Maltz had written for the early stages of Ari and Kitty's relationship: "It is not on a mature level. They should be searching each other out."[12]

Meanwhile, Preminger set up his cast, headed by Paul Newman and Eva Marie Saint as Ari and Kitty. Newman later said that he tried to get out of the film, which he thought "too cold and expository."[13] Saint remembered talking with Preminger at her house in Brentwood: "He came over, and we talked about the script, and I had some ideas. It was a lengthy meeting. When we started filming, we didn't use my ideas, but that was all right."[14] Peter Lawford took the part of the anti-Semitic Major Caldwell (arming himself with this advice from David Niven: "There is only one way to handle Preminger. If you get into an argument with him, walk up to him, put your face right up against his—nose to nose—and scream, '*Fuck you, Otto!*' And you'll win. But remember, it's got to be nose to nose").[15] David Opatoshu, a star of the Yiddish theater in New York who had gone on to distinguish himself on Broadway and, to a lesser extent, in films, badly wanted to play Akiva and courted Preminger for the role. It proved one of the movie's most felicitous strokes of casting.[16] Adding to the necessary all-star status of the cast were Ralph Richardson as General Sutherland; Sal Mineo as Dov; Lee J. Cobb as Barak; John Derek as Ari's Arab friend Taha; and Hugh Griffith as a Cypriot who helps the Haganah. Preminger signed his old friend Gregory Ratoff to play a small but flamboyant cameo as one of the passengers of the *Exodus*. One of the last roles to be cast was one of the key ones—Karen. Preminger auditioned hundreds of candidates of various nationalities before choosing fourteen-year-old Jill Haworth, a product of London's Corona Stage School, and signing her to a seven-year contract.

On November 15 Preminger returned to Israel to scout locations. Among those accompanying him was Eva Monley, who started on the film as location manager and was soon promoted to production manager. Monley, then thirty-six, had worked on many Hollywood productions shooting overseas. She would prove to be one of the most durable and loyal members of Preminger's production team. "I did five pictures with him over ten years. That's unbelievable. I'll tell you why. Purely because I was a woman and not a male. Because he would clench his fists and holler at me and his eyes would pop out and then he'd suddenly realize he was talking to a girl, and not a very old one either. And he just backed off."[17] It was Monley who chose the all-important freighter that would not only play the role of the *Exodus* but would also carry personnel and equipment from Naples to Haifa and from Israel to Cyprus.

A start date in March 1960 was set. Throughout November and December, Maltz worked on a first-draft script: Preminger's assertion in his autobiography that Maltz "never got around to writing a line" is untrue.[18] The material Preminger received from Maltz by early December convinced him, however, that he needed to find another writer. On December 10 he called Dalton Trumbo. Throughout most of 1959 Trumbo had been tied up on Kirk Douglas's production of *Spartacus*. With his obligations to *Spartacus* discharged, he was free to devote himself to Preminger. Ingo Preminger recalled, "Maltz wrote a terrible script. I think it was 400 pages. It was ridiculous. Maltz was too serious. He was a good writer, but very serious. Maltz and Trumbo were like opposite poles. Trumbo was very lively, a pleasure to be with. I really loved Trumbo."[19]

Preminger arrived in Los Angeles on December 16. For the next forty-four days, seven days a week, he and Trumbo worked on the script. At seven each morning, Preminger, who had taken up residence at the Beverly Hills Hotel, arrived at Trumbo's house in Highland Park. While Preminger went over Trumbo's last set of pages, Trumbo worked on new ones. Then Preminger gave him back the first set of pages with suggestions, which Trumbo would follow while Preminger read the new material. Thus they kept going till the early evening, at which point, Preminger later recalled, Trumbo would "mix himself a martini and after a few sips he was too relaxed to continue working." (Preminger, meanwhile, was on "a straight steak diet," Trumbo remembered: "16 oz. of beef for lunch, very rare, each day . . . The butcher, I'm sure, thought I was keeping a pet lion in the house—and so I was." Trumbo liked Preminger. "He's a charming man, and unlike most directors, full of protein instead of shit.")[20]

Trumbo found their collaboration a valuable experience. "I'm verbose and sentimental," he told reporter Irwin Ross. "He has a sharpshooter's eye for verbosity and he knows how to assassinate sentimentality. He's also most helpful in construction. I had more pleasure working with Otto than with anyone in my life. More fun, more amusement, more tact, and, of course, more hard work." Once, Preminger objected that Trumbo had written a scene that fell short of the writer's standard. Trumbo defended himself: "If each scene in this film is of uniform brilliance, we will have a lot of monotony." Preminger thought about this for a moment and then replied, "Make them all brilliant and I will direct unevenly."[21]

As work continued, Preminger joked to Trumbo that if *Exodus* turned out a failure, he would make sure Trumbo got the blame. Both men knew that this was no idle threat. The possibility of ending the blacklist and openly acknowledging what everyone in the industry knew—that producers were buying and filming scripts written by people who were denied credit because of their presumed political affiliations—was more real now than at any time during the twelve years of the blacklist. In January 1959 the Academy of Motion Picture Arts and Sciences quietly rescinded its bylaw denying Oscar nominations to artists who refused to cooperate with HUAC. During the same year, Trumbo's identity as the author of the screenplay of *Spartacus* was disclosed in trade magazines and gossip columns.

On January 19, 1960, Preminger told A. H. Weiler of *The New York Times* that he had hired Trumbo for *Exodus* and would give him screen credit. The story broke on the front page the next day. Preminger underplayed the revelation. If he had chosen this moment to disclose his intention to give Trumbo credit, it was, he said, "simply because your newspaper asked me." His decision to hire Trumbo was "simply realistic and practical and not political . . . I feel that it is my duty to get the best screenplays I can . . . I am not an authority on the Hollywood blacklist. But assuming that such a thing exists"—here he alludes drily to the tacit nature of a blacklist that the studios had never acknowledged—"I will not participate in it. In my opinion, it is illegal and immoral."[22] Preminger was the first Hollywood producer to announce that he had hired a writer known to be blacklisted, and he deserves unqualified credit for breaking the blacklist. It takes nothing away from this distinction to note that it may have seemed likely in January 1960 that Kirk Douglas would prevail over the more cautious executives at Universal over the question of Trumbo's credit on *Spartacus*. In the event, *Spartacus*—released in October, two months before *Exodus*—became the first film to bear the name of a victim of the anti-Communist blacklist on its titles as screenwriter.

Was Preminger's announcement driven by desire for publicity—and was his timing of it motivated by the desire to forestall Douglas? Trumbo denied this firmly. "It has never entered my mind, nor I think his," he wrote in 1970, "that he gave me credit because of the publicity that was bound to attend such a move. He gave it because he strongly opposed the hypocrisy of the blacklist as a matter of principle."[23] Preminger had, in fact, long opposed the blacklist. According to Abraham Polonsky, "throughout the entire blacklist period Preminger kept someone employed who was officially on the blacklist."[24] By the time of *Exodus*, Preminger was ready to take his stand against the blacklist to the public. He was already considering such a move when he hired Albert Maltz, who wrote discreetly to Trumbo on November 11, while Maltz was still engaged on *Exodus*, "The producer of the current film I am working on is very eager to have my name on it."[25]

It has been said that in the climate of 1960, Preminger and UA risked little by flouting a blacklist that was all but finished. The outcry over alleged Communist infiltration of American politics and culture had died down since the heyday of McCarthy and HUAC. The most vivid proof of the failure of the blacklist was not Trumbo's credits on *Exodus* and *Spartacus*, but the tepidity of the protest the credits aroused. Right-wing campaigns induced a spurt of denunciatory letters, and the American Legion picketed the two films on their release (some legionnaires who marched against *Exodus* may have felt uneasy on seeing themselves joined by members of the American Nazi Party), but faced with the success of both films and the general indifference about who wrote them, the right could only slink away. Nevertheless—and apart from the obvious point that though the blacklist may have been effectively over, *somebody*, after all, had to be the first to make the fact public—Preminger's act took courage, even though he was the last person who would have said so. In attacking the blacklist, he implicitly criticized the film producers who had consented to, tolerated, and profited from it. The 1947 "Waldorf Statement," in which the major studios pledged to fire the Hollywood Ten and not to hire any known or suspected Communists, "wasn't agreed upon out of any desire to fight Communism," Preminger told a reporter. "It came to be because of fear."[26] To the current crop of studio executives—some of whom had been among the signers at the Waldorf—Preminger's defiance of the blacklist was yet further arrogance from a man who had already shown more than once that he neither feared their power nor needed their patronage.

Trumbo's notes to Preminger on the script, undated, but probably from February 1, 1960, indicate that Trumbo perceived—and solved—a structural problem in Uris's novel: the fragmentation of the historical story into three parts, one about the *Exodus*, one about the Haganah's rivalry with the Irgun, and one about the conflict between Jews and Arabs. Trumbo's solution was to emphasize, throughout the film, the UN vote on partition as the main factor in all the characters' determinations. This could be done without "any sweeping changes, nor the slightest change of action as presently written," simply by having the characters make references to the upcoming partition vote whenever appropriate.[27]

Trumbo also sought to change the character of Kitty: "She must *not* be a neurotic woman. Let us therefore eliminate all reference to her lost infant. That cuts off one area of neuroticism." Preminger rejected Trumbo's proposal on this point: a revealing decision. The loss of Kitty's child lies behind Kitty's need for Karen, and it was doubtless Preminger's insight (and it is communicated in the film through Eva Marie Saint's splendid performance) that there should be something obsessive, excessive about this need (which links Kitty to the heroine of *Bunny Lake Is Missing*, a narrative whose problems Trumbo would later tackle for Preminger but fail to solve).[28]

On February 11 Trumbo finished a "final script" for *Exodus*. The notes he sent to Preminger (undated, but probably accompanying this script) reveal much about the two men's priorities and biases in dealing with the historical record.

By their willingness to compromise and to accept partition, the Jews persuaded the world of their reasonableness as opposed to

the unreasonableness of Arab claims. This is regardless of the fact
that actually the Jews, too, wanted the whole land for themselves.
I choose to dramatize their perhaps reluctant acceptance of partition as a *desire* for it. It is better dramatically, and better for Israel
that it be that way, rather than to dramatize their desire for *all* of
it (which would place them on the level of the Arabs in the audience's mind).

We have, by increasing the Arab menace (as we had) over the
first script, run the risk of being just a little unjust historically. We
have covered the essence and the excuse for this injustice in
Akiva's speech on injustice and justice for the Jews and Arabs.
But I think it essential for our dramatic balance, for historical ac-
curacy, and for audience believability, to hit it once again.[29]

Accordingly, Trumbo now had Ari say of the Arabs of Abu Yesha, "This is
their home as well as ours."

The film is far less anti-Arab than the book (as it is less anti-British),
expunging Uris's hard-line propaganda and making Taha a wholly sympathetic figure and a martyr to Arab-Jewish friendship (in the book he becomes alienated from Ari by his love for Ari's sister, Jordana—an element
the film ignores—and he lets the Grand Mufti's soldiers pass through
Abu Yesha without warning Ari; he is killed defending the village against
the Palmach). Preminger and Trumbo also remove most of Uri's constant
references to biblical lore and—crucially—every overt reference to the
claim, very strongly presented in the book, that the Jews have a *divine*
right to Palestine (when Ari invokes the Bible in the film, it is as history
rather than as prophecy).

In the context of a fictional film whose overarching commitment is to
the Zionist cause, Preminger puts the Arab case in the most favorable
light possible by having the most extreme Zionist in the film, Akiva, admit that "one can argue the legitimacy of Arab claims on Palestine as
well as one can argue the legitimacy of Jewish claims." Earlier in the
film, Sutherland tells Kitty that Britain made promises to both the Jews
and the Arabs. It is crucial to Preminger's strategy that the case for the
Arabs be made not by an Arab, but by a liberal Englishman and a radical
Jew. Like so much in *Exodus*, this choice can be seen in two lights. If
Exodus can be praised for its fairness, it can also be criticized for sup-

pressing the voices of Arabs in order to project Zionist myth. Putting a pro-Israel spin on the Arab flight from Palestine, the film lets us hear Barak implore the Arabs to stay in their homes (echoing the stated policy of the Jewish leaders of the period) but shows us nothing of the Jewish expulsion of the Arabs. Ari's campaign to capture Abu Yesha is justified by the Arabs' use of the village as a base for their attacks on the Jews—and when he reaches the village, the Arabs have already abandoned it. The absence of scenes portraying such events from an Arab point of view seriously limits the film's ability to provide an objective account of the conflict.

The February 11 script also contained a reference to another historical subject close to Preminger's heart. Arguing with Ari about the Irgun's tactics, Barak says, "May I remind you that one of the greatest men who ever lived once said there is no end—however great—which justifies the use of violence? That man was Mahatma Gandhi!" Preminger and Trumbo later removed these lines from the script, possibly just in the interest of shortening an already extremely long film, or possibly to avoid overcomplicating the audience's response to the Jews' actions.

Geoffrey Shurlock reported to Preminger on his review of the *Exodus* script on February 16. Replying from London on March 4, Preminger urbanely agreed to cut the word "bastards" (the American captain of the *Exodus*, Hank, was to have exclaimed, "The dirty bastards are just going to make another concentration camp out of this ship!") but refused to remove the allusion to the Nazis' homosexual abuse of Dov at Auschwitz. "This is a reference to a very well known historical fact and, particularly in these days when synagogues and churches all over the world are again being smeared with swastikas, I believe that any soft pedalling of historic Nazi crimes would be criminal in itself . . . This is one point on which I cannot give in under any circumstances."

With a shootable script for *Exodus* finally in hand, Preminger laid out an ambitious fourteen-week shooting schedule with general manager Martin Schute, Monley, and first assistant director Gerry O'Hara. The unit gathered in Haifa in March. The crew was mostly British, with an Italian team of electricians; Israeli production assistants, translators, and technical advisers; and Arab workers. With the mix of nationalities and religious customs, the question of which day of the week to take off became thorny. Preminger impressed the Israeli contingent at a production meeting by ruling that the unit would observe the local custom and take the Shabbat off. (In the heat of shooting, nothing was sacred but the film. Otto Plaschkes, second assistant director, recalled, "We were shooting . . . on a Friday evening, with kids from school, accompanied by their teacher; it was getting down to sundown, and the teacher became very agitated, obviously wanted the kids to go and disappear by sundown, because of the Shabbat. And Preminger turned to the teacher and said, 'I will tell you when the Shabbat begins!' ")[30]

Two days before the start of shooting, on Friday afternoon, March 25, Preminger and Hope Bryce (serving for the third time as costume coordinator on a Preminger film) were married in Haifa. No civil marriage exists in Israel, and the couple had assumed they would have to fly to Cyprus to be married, but Abba Khoushy, the mayor of Haifa, insisted that the wedding take place in his city. On finding that Hope was not Jewish, the panel of rabbis who questioned the couple initially refused to perform the service, but they fell in line after the mayor threatened to take away their garbage trucks. For the sake of the ceremony, Meyer Weisgal testified that Hope was Jewish. (Years later, the publication of Weisgal's memoirs, which contained an account of the event, raised questions about the validity of the Premingers' marriage. To remove any doubts, the couple got married again by a New York justice in 1971, with their eleven-year-old twins present.)[31]

Paul Newman's working relationship with his director got off to a bad start. Soon after arriving in Haifa, Newman gave Preminger several pages of notes on ideas for rewrites. Probably Newman wanted to make Ari a more ambivalent figure. On departing from Israel ten weeks later, he told a reporter, "I had first criticized the 'superman' quality attributed to Ari Ben Canaan in the book and the film script." Preminger read Newman's suggestions but refused to consider them. "If you were directing the picture, you could do it your way. But I'm directing the picture and we'll do it my way." Newman conceded the point to Preminger, and for the rest of the shoot the two remained on professional terms. Newman later summed up the production as "chilly" and said, "We had some problems, Otto and I. He's a delightful man and a politically aware person. I love to sit and eat caviar with him, but in making a picture there's none of the give and take."[32]

This seems a mild assessment. Trying to find a way into a character he found opaque, Newman asked the Israeli technical adviser Ilan Har-tuv to help him meet a number of the real-life characters, such as Moshe Dayan, Yigal Allon, and Yigael Yadin, on whom Uris had modeled Ari. "He wanted to meet with each for hours and study their way of thinking, their gesticulations, etc. . . . Then Otto heard about it and told Newman, 'Stop the nonsense. I'm the director and I'll tell you what to do.'" (Hartuv also arranged meetings with Arabs for John Derek, which Preminger stopped, too.) Larry Frisch, a second assistant director on *Exodus*, recalled that when Newman offered some suggestions on Ari's final speech, Preminger cut him short with: "If you want to compare which of us is more intelligent, I'll save you the trouble."[33]

No doubt Preminger saw Newman's memo as a power play that had to be dealt with firmly. Also, it was one of his principles never to make major changes to a script to accommodate an actor. Maybe he was also giving Newman an object lesson in how he wanted him to play Ari: direct, hard, arbitrary. Early in the film, a collaborator expresses doubt about the feasibility of Ari's plan for getting the refugees out of the camp. The terms and the manner in which Ari replies make it clear that as far as he is concerned, the discussion is closed: "Look, I want to hear every criticism, every objection, but only once." When he said this line, was Newman thinking of Preminger?

Not that Preminger was likely to encourage criticisms and objections from his staff. Paul Kohn, reporting on the production for the *Jerusalem Post*, heard the director-producer lecture the cast and crew at the Zion Hotel headquarters: "I want discipline. You must do what I tell you to do, because I know what I am doing. If I make mistakes, let's do it anyway, and get it done with."[34] Eva Monley confirmed that there was no debating with Preminger. "He insisted on being right. And it was very hard to argue with him. Even if you knew you were right, it was hard to argue with him. Because he was convinced that his thinking was the best."[35]

Shooting began in Paris Square in Haifa on Sunday, March 27. On that day, a Saul Bass–designed ad announcing the start of production appeared in newspapers in the cities—New York, Chicago, and Los Angeles—where *Exodus* was scheduled to open. It was the first of four ads intended to promote advance sales of tickets for the film's opening engagement in December. The other three ads were timed to coincide with the production's migrations to Jerusalem (scheduled for May 20) and to Cyprus (June 5) and the close of production (July 3). (The *Exodus* advance sale, the largest for any film to that time, eventually exceeded $1,000,000.)

Jean Wagner, a correspondent for the devoutly pro-Preminger *Présence du cinéma*, spent several days observing the shoot in Galilee. On first arriving at a tiny village that Preminger had transformed into a set, he heard the director's shouts emanating "with metronomic regularity and variable pertinence" from inside the little house where he was filming Kitty's visit to the Ben Canaans. Wagner later joined the crew at the site of Ari and Kitty's hilltop scene and found Preminger upset because the three trees before which the actors were to cross had been planted too close to the edge of the hill. "Otto bellowing in English with German usages and a word of Hebrew from time to time, before the most beautiful landscape in the world under a blazing sun, is a spectacle that must be seen and that should be on film." Wagner found Preminger equally hard on the cast as on the crew: "On the set, he crushes them, abuses them, and poor Paul Newman must have often needed to call on all his patience to keep from exploding. He spends his time, next, winning them over again, which is easy for him, since his charm is as great as his culture. On the whole, in spite of everything, it's difficult to say that Preminger is loved."[36]

Occasionally Wagner heard someone mutter against the tyrant behind his back. On or off the set, such moments had to be carefully chosen because it seemed Preminger (first to rise and last to sleep) could show up anywhere at any moment. "He knew what was happening behind him," said Ilan Eldad, who worked on *Exodus* as both second assistant director and unit production manager. "He knew if an actor and an actress kissed, or if there were a romance—little, human things. He would say, 'Don't count on it, that I don't see what's happening there.'" The rigors of the shoot took their toll on everyone. According to Martin Schute, "Some of the crew were of the feeling that they had agreed to do a six-day week, but they hadn't really agreed to do 14 hours a day doing it . . . So there was a certain amount of ill feeling at times. But by and large it all sorted itself out, because they all had enormous respect for the way Preminger worked. He didn't sort of sit around and scratch his head. He was at it the whole time. He was a director who knew exactly what he wanted." Paul Kohn remarked on "the high regard everyone has for Preminger and . . . the warm regard for him of those who know him well . . . At lunch on the set, he takes his turn in a long queue together with drivers, technicians and extras. He will also personally go over to an extra, and congratulate him on work well done. He is extremely generous, unpredictable and accessible to all." Wagner was astonished by the director's mastery, his awareness of what each of the numerous assistants was supposed to be doing, the "maniacal meticulousness" with which he controlled every phase of the production. "The knowledge he had of this immense machine, in its least details, was stupefying."[37]

Preminger left Newman alone and was tactful with Eva Marie Saint, who recalled, "Preminger really didn't talk too much about the feelings or how a character should be designed. That was usually left up to the actor. Preminger guided us. If anything were wrong, he would know. He was very positive. I enjoyed working with him. I think he's a fine director. Like Hitchcock, he certainly had in mind what he wanted to shoot. And he had to, it was such a huge undertaking." Preminger gave some of the other actors a rough time. Many of Saint's scenes were with Jill Haworth, a far less experienced actress. Saint recalled, "He had to work with Jill Haworth, because she was so young." Under his demands, Haworth developed a simple, stubborn calmness that translated to the screen. "When he screamed, I wouldn't know what was the matter, so I'd just ask him instead of quaking like the others," she told an interviewer. According to Otto Plaschkes, who had also worked on *Saint Joan*, "Preminger didn't shout at Jill as much as he shouted at Jean Seberg. But he certainly pushed her, hard."[38]

For the intense scene in which Dov, seeking to join the Irgun, is interrogated by Akiva and made to confess that at Auschwitz the Nazis "used" him "like you use a woman," Preminger drove Sal Mineo and David Opatoshu through a grueling cycle of takes that lasted through an entire night and on into early the next morning, by which time, Otto Plaschkes recalled, Mineo had become "jelly." Yet Mineo came away from *Exodus* with affection for Preminger (and an Oscar nomination, owing, no doubt, to his performance in this one scene). "Otto Preminger made it more than just a movie," the actor told writer Boze Hadleigh. "Preminger had a lot of guts. He was real anti-censor, 'cause he was so pro-liberty . . . You know, Otto sounds like a Nazi, and he's a tough buzzard, but he's got a great heart. Nice man."[39]

The *Exodus* machine kept rolling. To attract the masses of extras he wanted for the scene in which the United Nations vote on the partition of Palestine is announced, Preminger organized a lottery. The six grand prizes were trips to New York for the premiere of *Exodus* in December. Each ticket cost one Israeli pound, about 45 cents; to be eligible to win, the purchaser had to show up at the Russian Compound in Jerusalem on May 23 and act as an extra in the partition announcement scene. The drawing would be held after the scene was finished. The day the scene was shot, Ben-Gurion revealed that Adolf Eichmann had been captured and brought to Israel. By 5:00 p.m. the news was the talk of the country. The thousands of raffle contestants who had filled the Russian Compound by 8:00 to appear as extras in *Exodus* were in an appropriately jubilant mood. The three-hour wait before the crew was ready to film the partition announcement put a damper on this euphoria, which was dulled further by the numerous takes required by Lee J. Cobb, who, as Barak Ben Canaan, had to make the announcement from a balcony above the crowd. "To get the actors in the square in sync with what Lee was saying was quite difficult," recalled Otto Plaschkes. "It was done on loudspeakers, and they weren't responding in the way that Preminger wanted, so it was take after take. Mostly I think it was the crowd's fault, but sometimes it was Lee's fault." According to Israeli second assistant director Yoel Zilberg, Cobb "wasn't ready with the lines." After about fifteen takes, Preminger blew up at Cobb, who insisted: "I can't work like this! I need time to concentrate." Preminger replied: "Time! Twenty thousand people are waiting, and you need time?"[40]

The incident brought to a head the strained relations between Preminger and the temperamental actor. Weeks earlier, an observer on the set had reported for the *Jerusalem Post* that Cobb "is acknowledged as the only actor in the company who is unafraid of the producer, and he interprets his role without direction. He even takes the liberty of breaking tense moments with a joke." If Cobb ventured humor on this occasion, it went over badly. According to Meyer Weisgal, whom Preminger had recruited to impersonate Ben-Gurion for the scene, Cobb "revolted in the midst of general pandemonium, rushed to the balcony and delivered himself of a speech which was not part of the script but highly dramatic nonetheless." Preminger yelled back at Cobb, "You're an idiot!" Cobb threatened to walk off the picture, and Martin Schute, as general manager, had to step in to remind the actor of his contractual obligations before shooting could continue. Paul Newman also helped by taking Cobb aside and talking with him privately. The scene was finished (though Preminger had to relent and do it in short takes, instead of the unbroken shot he had wanted), the winning lottery tickets drawn, the crowd sent home, and fortunately for both men, the scene was the last Cobb ever played for Otto Preminger.[41]

On June 5 the company moved to Cyprus, where the last few weeks of shooting went on without incident. The scenes at General Sutherland's house were filmed at the commissioner's house in Nicosia, the scenes of the blockaded *Exodus* at the harbor of Famagusta. Dalton Trumbo visited the set, now that he could do so without risking a run-in with Lee J. Cobb (pegged as a Communist, the actor testified before HUAC in 1953, naming names). To make it clear to everyone that Trumbo was there only as an observer, Preminger scolded Peter Lawford when he heard the actor ask the writer a question about the script. They also argued about characterization. Otto Plaschkes recalled, "The bully in Preminger came out with Lawford. He bullied Peter. And Peter gave back a bit. He argued with Preminger. You can argue up to a point with Preminger, but at the end of the day, whatever Preminger wanted, you had to produce. And Peter did, or tried to. Preminger wanted Lawford to play it more broadly, and Peter held back."[42] Preminger wrapped *Exodus* on schedule on July 3.

Postproduction took a little over three months—a few days less than the fourteen weeks of shooting. Louis Loeffler, Preminger's regular cutter, wanted to shorten Paul Newman's funeral oration at the end of the film, but the director's minimal coverage—a four-minute take of Ari addressing the mourners and an insert of the shrouded bodies of Taha and Karen—left Loeffler no other option but to let it run its full length. The film ended up at 212 minutes. "United Artists bugged him and bugged him to cut it," Hope Preminger recalled, but Otto was adamant.[43] At around the same time the final cut was complete, in October, Hope delivered twins, a boy and girl. They were named Mark (after Preminger's father) and Victoria.

Before the opening of *Exodus*, Preminger kept busy staging *Critic's Choice*, a new comedy by Ira Levin. Henry Fonda took the lead role of a famous drama critic whose personal life is thrown into an uproar when his wife finds a vocation for playwriting. Gena Rowlands was cast as the wife, and Lou Antonio as a director. Eddie Hodges, cast as the couple's son, recalled, "Preminger was so hard on Gena and Lou, screaming at them from the back of the theater and stomping down the aisles flailing his arms." Rowlands and Antonio left, to be replaced by Georgann Johnson and Murray Hamilton. According to Hodges, "Preminger had a different relationship with each member of the cast and seemed to know just which buttons to push to get what he wanted. I think he liked having the power to make people do as he wished—on or off the stage." Hodges noticed that the director and his star had a special relationship: "Preminger did not make the kind of comments or critique to Fonda openly like he did to others. I just assumed they had things worked out already and there was no need for such comments. If Preminger had any direction for Fonda, he would offer it in a sort of matter-of-fact way, and Fonda would respond accordingly . . . Fonda and Preminger were very serious when they were together—I saw very few light moments. They were both very intense in their own individual ways."[44]

Critic's Choice opened on December 14 to tolerant reviews (it would become a hit, lasting 189 performances). The next day, *Exodus* opened in New York. *Variety* set the tone for the reviews, calling the film "frequently soul-stirring" and praising many of the actors, but expressing the wish that Preminger and Trumbo "had been blessed with more dramatic incisiveness."[45] Speaking most memorably for those who thought *Exodus* too long, comedian Mort Sahl got up during a preview, turned toward Preminger, and implored, "Otto, let my people go." Despite the mixed critical response, *Exodus* earned more than $8 million in domestic rentals, making it a profitable venture for United Artists. (The final negative cost of the film would be assessed at $3,700,000.)[46] In 1962 Preminger sold his interest in the film to the company (85 percent of the profits, according to an amended agreement) for $1 million—a deal that, Preminger would later claim, saved UA.

Exodus is a film of speeches. Characters explain to each other the interests, policies, and goals of the groups they represent, sometimes to persuade (as when Ari urges cooperation between the Haganah and the Irgun and between the Jews and the Arabs), sometimes to enlighten (as when Sutherland recounts, for Kitty's benefit, Britain's "troublesome commitments" to both the Arabs and the Jews), and sometimes merely to state positions (as in Ari's visit to Akiva). The film ends with Ari's funeral oration over the bodies of Taha and Karen. Preminger makes *Exodus* an epic of the voice. Action—the blowing up of the King David Hotel, the attack on Acre Fortress, the fighting between the Jews and the Arabs—takes over only when speech is denied or repressed.

No other film has so many scenes in which voices cover people, speak over their bodies and faces. *Exodus* (like *Laura*) begins with a voice-off in conjunction with a camera movement, and thus begins by posing the question: Who is speaking? As Kitty's driver/tour guide breezily lists the foreign powers that have conquered Cyprus, the camera pans over a landscape until it reaches the speaker and his addressee, side by side. This movement of the camera in search of the source of the voice is emblematic of *Exodus*. The shot unites several consciousnesses, several voices: first the guide's (and behind him, a standard-ideological history that speaks through him, narrating the history of Cyprus as an always alienable property, a land that has been "conquered many times"); but also Kitty's, since it is she who looks (the guide, when we see him, is looking not at the landscape, but at her—showing that though the uttered words were his, the image did not belong to him); and that of a third person who is not a person but an agency: the cinema, Otto Preminger's.

Again and again in Preminger's cinema, the question is raised: Who is speaking? Whose voice is making itself heard (sometimes through other, intervening, mediating voices)? This is the question Biegler asks of Sergeant Durgo in *Anatomy of a Murder*, when the latter testifies that he was told of "some trouble" Laura had with Barney Quill. In *Saint Joan* the question is posed in another form: Where do the voices come from? In *The 13th Letter*, behind the different question, Who writes?, lies the same one, Who speaks?, since the written letters are the transcriptions of a spoken message. In *Bonjour Tristesse* it is obvious from the beginning that the Cécile who speaks is not the same as the Céciles we see (both in the present time of the film and in the flashbacks). And in *Exodus*, Akiva reproaches Ari, when the latter objects to the tactics of the Irgun, for delivering the standard Haganah line.

In *Exodus*, Preminger often cuts between a shot of the "live" source of a voice and a shot in which the amplified voice is heard over the image of the listeners. This happens when Caldwell and Sutherland, at the observation tower in the harbor, address the blockaded *Olympia/Exodus* over a loudspeaker; when Ari replies to them; and when Reuben reads news bulletins to the passengers. Such intercutting becomes a key stylistic figure in the film (although, because it is always done in a smoothly naturalistic way, it is all but invisible). The insistence on the difference between the live and the amplified voice has several effects: it emphasizes the characters' physical dispersion; it asserts the continuity of social fact and individual situation; and it creates a textural contrast between two different treatments of the voice (one close, clean, and full; the other flattened and remote), heightening the sensual experience of the viewer and the feeling, so potent in Preminger's films, of assisting at the revelation of a real world. (*Exodus*, by the way, is in stereo. The simple elegance of the six-track sound design, reflecting the sweep of the Panavision wide screen, is far removed from the surround-sound fanaticism of our current Dolby era. A contemporary reviewer found the sound mix disconcerting, however: "The sound track, for which Preminger tried some interesting effects with off-stage noises, often proves distracting and drowns out the dialogue.")[47]

When the massive crowd in the Jerusalem square hears Barak announce the partition of Palestine, the high-angle long shot represents the crowd as a visual unity, while Barak's amplified voice determines the crowd as a community of hearers. Amplification puts the on-screen characters and the film's viewers in the same relationship to the voice: both they and we are addressed by a message conveyed by an electronic signal. (Loudspeakers are prominent in many scenes in the film: the first thing Ari demands for his ship is a loudspeaker; the inhabitants of Gan Dafna set up a speaker to blare music in an attempt to fool the Arabs into thinking that the settlement is heavily manned; the radio in Akiva's death car is tuned to a news and music broadcast.) This message summons the listener to make an existential choice. The Jewish people are called on to reaffirm their choice to become a nation, and the viewer of the film is, implicitly, asked to support this decision. For Karen, assuming her Jewishness is a conscious choice: Kitty finds her an acceptable object for her displaced maternal love because Karen "thinks and acts just like an American," and the moral importance of Karen's journey through the film comes from the fact that she can pass for Aryan (and did so in Denmark). In calling on the passengers of the *Exodus* to observe silence for twenty minutes before voting on whether to go on a hunger strike, Ari affirms the function of the amplified voice as a call to decision. He also implicitly acknowledges the coercive power of broadcast speech. By shutting it off, Ari permits those who have hitherto only listened (and been spoken for) to consult their own consciences: the silence of the broadcast voice is to swell with the self-presence of the internal voice.

The theme of conscience and choice receives its fullest development in *Exodus* through the portrayal of Kitty. The sunglasses Kitty wears at the beginning of the film mark her as a stranger and an enigma (like Cécile's sunglasses in *Bonjour Tristesse* and Laura Manion's in *Anatomy of a Murder*); they shut her off from a landscape that the film presents to her (via the travelogue-like pan of the opening shot) and which it also relates to her (by including her in the shot at the end of the pan, and earlier by including the taxi, which is her trace in the landscape). Her taking off her sunglasses shows that her journey through the film will be one from separation to participation, from concealment to disclosure, from darkness to light (Karen is twice called "child of light," an epithet that hints at the therapeutic role she plays for Kitty). Later in the film, when Dr. Odenheim warns her that Karen "will drain [her] of love," Kitty stares fixedly offscreen and says with certainty, "That's exactly what I need." Her stare into the void suggests the pathological nature of her attachment to Karen.

Eva Marie Saint's performance, one of the subtlest by an actress in any film, conveys with admirable sensitivity the guardedness, hesitations, private judgments, and veiled condescension with which Kitty defends herself from becoming involved too closely with Ari or from becoming hurt by Karen's acknowledgment of her own Jewishness. (At their beachside table, when Karen asks for more time to consider her invitation to go to America, Kitty's passive-aggressive reaction is marvelously played.) Saint also gives a recognizable portrait of a politically liberal and financially comfortable but emotionally destitute American woman. The script, unfortunately, lets Kitty down in the last part of the film: the scene in which she saves Ari's life with a shot of adrenaline is an unsatisfactory substitute for the needed, but absent, turning point in which she surrenders to her rage and then to her love.

Thanks to Saint's performance, Kitty remains, however, an engaging heroine, and Paul Newman's restraint makes Ari an interesting hero. Their scenes together, especially the hilltop scene and their chance meeting in the terrace restaurant of the King David Hotel, are among the highlights of the film—and to say this of the love-interest scenes in a supposed action epic is already to indicate how extraordinary an action epic it is. Preminger cares about this couple as individuals; he's interested in their moral blossoming; and he makes us see the film's larger, transpersonal issues in relation to Kitty's development, and to a lesser extent Ari's. In two parallel scenes aboard the *Exodus*, first Kitty and then Ari are posed as on-camera witnesses. Kitty watches through a cabin window as two mothers, holding their young children, defy Ari's order that all children under thirteen be returned to Caraolos; then Ari, walking on deck at night, stops to listen as Dov denounces all Britons, Russians, and Poles, and Karen counters with her story of the Christian Danes. Each foreground situation is calculated to touch its observer: Kitty's miscarriage and childlessness have led her to value the life of a child over everything else; and we have heard Ari voice his conviction that Jews are alone in the world and can't count on the help of Gentiles. By moving Kitty and Ari into the backgrounds of the shots and refusing to cut to close-ups of their reactions, Preminger undercuts the schematic quality of these situations. He stages them as accidents in space. The confrontational, didactic aspect of each scene doesn't feel imposed by the script or director; it arises from how the incident compels the witness to stop and pay attention. Above all, Preminger leaves open the question whether Kitty and Ari learn their lessons from these encounters. This is because Preminger has no faith in "learning lessons" in the abstract and is interested in such learning only to the extent that it bears fruit through a character's later actions and speech.

Even in dealing with a subject as emotionally charged as that of *Exodus*, Preminger is above all a pragmatist, and he always sees the characters' moral choices in terms of their practical consequences. The terrorist actions of the Irgun are condemned not on ethical grounds, but because, as Ari says, "these bombings hurt us with the UN" (a line echoed by Barak's complaint that Akiva "presents us to the world as a bunch of murderers"). The reason Paul Newman's performance as Ari is so successful—despite Newman's own misgivings—is that it is precisely

in the spirit of the film: unsentimental, economical, and in love with the
practical. Preminger, like Ari, keeps things moving. When the Haganah
and the Irgun take over a Turkish bathhouse as the first stage of the attack on Acre prison, the raiders' entrance and the bathers' lining up
against the wall with their arms raised appear less as a cause and its effect than as two parts of a single mass movement. At Gan Dafna, Kitty
has no time to react to Karen's decision not to go to America: a loudspeaker summons Kitty to the infirmary just after Karen declares her
choice. So little time is given to reflection in this film that when somebody does pause to react to something, the moment has great weight:
Dov finding the body of Karen; Ari discovering the body of Taha—in a
shot that holds on his sinking reaction before revealing, by continuing to
track and pan with him, the object of his sorrow.

Preminger's camera discloses the unfolding of events in an unbroken
whole, putting us in the position of witnesses. In the second shot of the
film, the camera slowly tracks parallel to a column of people who shuffle
listlessly from right to left across the screen: these are the passengers of
the *Star of David*, whom the British are relocating to the Caraolos detention camp. The distance of the camera, its slight drift relative to the pace
and direction of the line, imply a certain detachment: we are witnesses
to this movement; we are not supposed to participate in it emotionally.
We're in the intellectual position of Kitty (her physical position is nearby
in a blocked taxi), uncomprehending and apart. Like the camera movements in Preminger's earlier films, this type of camera movement creates
a sense of temporal unity and flow, but whereas the temporal unity of a
shot in, say, *Laura* or *Fallen Angel* highlights a psychological development, the unity created by the camera in *Exodus* highlights processes
that are both physical and historical. The relocation scene suggests a
pointless, dehumanized, and externally directed movement characteristic both of this specific group of people and of the mass of European
Jewry immediately after the war.

The scene also crystallizes the distinctive narrative mode of *Exodus*: a
relay of interest among several main characters. In the shot of the
refugees, the camera's drift is loosely anchored to Karen, who thus becomes the center of our attention and speculation. Later in the sequence, Preminger underlines our identification with Kitty by having her
watch the proceedings from her taxi and ask the guide to explain what is

going on. Then our attention (alerted by an offscreen commotion) shifts to Dov, who jumps off a truck and tries to flee. After soldiers subdue Dov, we rejoin Kitty on her visit to General Sutherland. Throughout most of the rest of the film, the narrative keeps shifting from one character to another, and thus from one problem, goal, or theme to another and also, to some extent, from one landscape or visual quality to another: Ari is typically associated with open spaces and Dov with constricted spaces.

This narrative splintering (which has its source in Uris's novel) strengthens the thematic emphasis on the quest for unity. In the Cyprus section of the film, a sense of opposition is conveyed simply through alternating between scenes involving Ari and the *Exodus* and scenes involving Sutherland. After the *Exodus* lands in Palestine, the narrative breaks apart more intricately, and we follow, in turn, Dov, Ari, and Kitty as they move among Haifa, Jerusalem, Acre, and Gan Dafna. This richness of background can be felt as merely one of the surface pleasures of the film or as an element contributing to its hard-to-analyze wholeness. By playing one character against another, the film also asserts their connectedness. In their movements through the plot, the characters form a human chain. Karen urges Kitty to plead for the Jews of the *Exodus* to General Sutherland. Inspired by (and probably in love with) Kitty, Sutherland returns to England to plead, successfully (though at the cost of his career), that the *Exodus* be allowed to sail. Thus Dov reaches Palestine, where he joins the Irgun and blows up the King David Hotel. In the film (not the novel), the bombing occurs just after the suppressed heartbreak of Karen's meeting with her father, who has been reduced to a shell by the concentration camps and fails to respond to her. The explosion triggers Karen's emotion—the film's most powerful melodramatic stroke, lighting up all the film's main themes at once.

In an interview, Preminger discussed the balancing of characters in *Exodus* in terms of ideology. "It's an American picture, after all, that tries to tell the story, giving both sides a chance to plead their side. This leads to a danger which you are very well aware of, that is, in doing something like this and in presenting both sides of the question, events are apt to look contrived . . . a good person here, who is balanced by a bad one over there, and the other way round."[48] Trumbo and Preminger overcome this danger through two pivotal characterizations: Sutherland and Akiva, two mixed, divided figures who speak for the film in ways denied to the others. When Sutherland—a British soldier who is reduced against his will to running a detention camp and whose compassion for his charges leads others to believe that he is secretly Jewish himself—tells Kitty, "Nations are very much like people," he expresses an insight fundamental to the film, one that grounds the film's strategy of having individuals stand for groups in the microcosmic narrative. And it is Akiva—the terrorist who is mild and reasonable in manner, who acts in violence but values more than everything the family he has lost—who brings into the film the Premingerian dialectic of truth. He demands the truth from Dov, but he shrugs off Dov's question, "Why shouldn't I tell the truth?" with "That's always hard to answer"—a great line that resonates with Shaw's "I cannot tell you the whole truth: God does not allow the whole truth to be told" from *Saint Joan*.

The end of the film, the double funeral of Taha and Karen, is not in the book. Preminger's Israeli technical adviser, Ilan Hartuv, and others urged him not to shoot the scene. Hartuv recalled, "We told Otto that burying a man and a woman not his wife side by side was totally against the customs of both the Jewish and Moslem religions. So is burying people from different religions. Other people tried to intervene, but Otto was adamant."[49] Preminger's insistence on burying Taha and Karen together shows that he feels a greater responsibility to the future than to the past. At the end of *Exodus*, he looks toward a future reconciliation whose prefiguration in the symbol of the double burial overrides the demands of tradition. In his funeral speech, Ari, too (backing down from his tough "people are different" stand in the hilltop scene), sees this reconciliation coming: "It's right that these two people should lie side by side in this grave because they will share it in peace. But the dead always share the earth in peace, and that's not enough. It's time for the living to have a turn . . . I swear on the bodies of these two people that the day will come when Arab and Jew will share in a peaceful life this land that they have always shared in death."

The force and beauty of the film come from Preminger's embrace of contradiction. The consensus toward which *Exodus* builds is never achieved. Tensions remain unresolved: at the burial of Karen and Taha, Dov, instead of throwing earth on the grave, thrusts the shovel into the earth—an act of protest that in its ambiguity (Is he outraged at Karen's having to share her grave with an Arab? Does he simply refuse the fact of her death?) is a fitting gesture with which to end such an open film.

With *Exodus*, Preminger opened a new phase of his career—one that would encompass what is both the most important part of his work and the most neglected. For a certain kind of film lover, the imperishable mystique of *Laura* and the other Fox noirs will always define Preminger: *Anatomy of a Murder* has the widest appeal, and some connoisseurs prefer such relatively intimate works as *Angel Face*, *Bonjour Tristesse*, *Bunny Lake Is Missing*, and even *Such Good Friends* or *The Human Factor*. Nevertheless, the four large-scale works on questions of national and institutional destiny—*Exodus*, *Advise & Consent*, *The Cardinal*, and *In Harm's Way*—constitute Preminger's most radical and original achievement and the core of his self-definition as a filmmaker.

27

Gratuitous Acts

Preminger bought the rights to Allen Drury's *Advise and Consent* for $200,000 on November 9, 1959, a few days before leaving on a trip to London and Israel to set up the production of *Exodus*.[1] Preminger made a deal with United Artists for the film version of Drury's novel (he would eventually move the production to Columbia) and hired Wendell Mayes to write the script. Preminger and Mayes's adaptation of *Advise and Consent* follows the novel in providing an insider's view of the Senate's decision-making on whether to confirm Robert A. Leffingwell, the President's nominee for Secretary of State. Leffingwell is controversial because he once antagonized a powerful southern senator, Seab Cooley, and because he has given public speeches suggesting that he would seek a closer entente with the Soviet Union. (In the novel, the Soviet Union is named; in the film, the United States's foe is referred to collectively as "the Communists"—a bit of reticence in keeping with another in which the film follows the novel: the party affiliations of the characters are not specified. Anyone with a passing familiarity with U.S. politics will assume that the President and the Senate majority are Democrats.) At confirmation hearings held by a Senate subcommittee, Cooley presents a witness, Herbert Gelman, who claims that he and Leffingwell once belonged to a Communist cell. Leffingwell denies the charge and exposes Gelman as mentally ill. In fact, the charge is true, as Cooley ascertains by tracking down a third member of the cell, Hardiman Fletcher, a government administrator. Under pressure from Cooley, Fletcher reveals the truth to Senator Brigham "Brig" Anderson, the chairman of the subcommittee. Brig threatens to reopen the hearings and expose Leffingwell, but the President refuses to withdraw the nomination. One of Leffingwell's principal supporters, Senator Fred Van Ackerman, blackmails Brig over a homosexual episode from his past. Unwilling to compromise his integrity by recommending Leffingwell for confirmation, and unable to bear the revelation of his secret, Brig commits suicide. The appalled Senate rejects Leffingwell's nomination, and the death of the ailing President elevates Harley Hudson, the Vice President, to the executive office.

"While the author of *Advise and Consent* is a conservative Republican," Preminger said, "I eliminated everything in this book I considered reactionary. I do not belong to any party, but I believe in progress."[2] The major changes Preminger and Mayes made in adapting Drury's very long book tend to reduce the novel's moralism and anti-Communism. Mayes recalled, "The author of the novel, Allen Drury, hated the picture. He's very conservative—as a matter of fact, he's an archconservative—and Otto and I are liberals, so we didn't do justice to his conservative point of view."[3] Leffingwell is a more sympathetic figure in the film than in the novel, in which he comes off as glib, proud, conceited, and defensive. Preminger and Mayes added several scenes that reveal Leffingwell as humane and principled, including one in which Leffingwell confesses to the President that he lied at the hearings. The script gives greater weight than the novel to the suggestion that, since admitting the truth would destroy his career, Leffingwell was forced to lie about his flirtation with Communism. (In the novel, the truth comes out, but Leffingwell's career, it is implied, will survive.) Also, whereas Drury portrays Leffingwell and Van Ackerman as allies, Preminger and Mayes dissociate Leffingwell from Van Ackerman. The different attitudes toward Leffingwell in the book and the film are reflected in the respective Senate votes: Drury's Senate votes 74–24 against Leffingwell; in the film, the Senate is deadlocked, and only the Vice President's refusal to cast a tie-breaking vote ensures Leffingwell's defeat.

In the novel, the attempt to blackmail Brigham Anderson is a conspiracy uniting the three branches of government, since the compromising photo that serves as the basis for the blackmail passes through the hands of a Supreme Court justice, Senate Majority Leader Bob Munson, and the President. The film eliminates the character of the Supreme Court justice and exculpates Munson and the President, pinning the responsibility for the blackmail solely on Van Ackerman. This choice simplifies the story, ensures a less complicated response to Munson and the President, and, by scapegoating Van Ackerman, shows the morality of the leaders of American government in a more favorable light. Preminger could be charged here with weakening Drury's critique of politics. (Raymond Durgnat claims that the film "contrive[s] to see all sides of the question, so disturbing everybody a little and nobody much; a mountain-size framework produces a mouse-size thought.")[4] On the other hand, as with *Exodus*, Preminger views the characters of *Advise & Consent* (in the Saul Bass–designed logo and titles, an ampersand replaced the "and" of the book's title) with greater fairness than their first creator, eliminating the most inflammatory evidence against them, giving them a chance to present their own justifications for their actions, and thus furnishing the audience with a more intellectually complex experience. Even Van Ackerman's portrait is softened from the novel: Drury repeatedly assesses Van Ackerman as psychopathic, but in George Grizzard's performance in the film, the character comes off as arrogant and rude but still capable of seeing himself as others see him.

Another major change from the novel is the reduction in stature and narrative importance of Senator Orrin Knox. In denouncing Leffingwell as an "appeaser," Knox apparently speaks for Drury, and the rhetoric he employs is of the Cold War–era right: "Only firmness will save us now. Only a steadfast adherence to principles we know to be sound, and an absolute and unyielding willingness to die for them if need be, will rescue America from the plight which confronts her."[5] Reducing Knox to a minor character of no weight, Preminger and Mayes eliminate Drury's apocalyptic overtones and deepen the ambiguity of the story: there is now no personification of a fixed moral stance and no spokesman for the author's position. Or, if there is one, it is now Munson, the pragmatist, and not the idealist Knox.

Preminger and Mayes expanded on the homosexual theme of the novel, adding a sequence in which Brig goes to New York in search of his former lover, Ray, and visits a gay nightclub. This sequence allowed Preminger to clarify, and also to make more complex, the reasons for Brig's suicide. Preminger explained, "I feel that what really drives him to suicide is not the blackmail alone, but the sudden realization on his part when he gets into contact again with this homosexual world, that he has inside, in spite of his struggle, in spite of his marriage and his child, not quite overcome the temptation and the inclination to belong to this

world. In other words, he is at once repelled and attracted. He is not adjusted enough, like many people are, and in my opinion should be, to accept their homosexual feelings . . . This is the reason for his suicide
more than the blackmail."[6]

Don Murray took the key role of Brig after being warned by Preminger "that some of the greatest artists in our industry have turned this
part down, because they don't want to play a part that has this intima-
tion of homosexuality."[7] Charles Laughton took the part of Cooley (and
developed a close friendship with Preminger), and Burgess Meredith
was cast as Gelman at the suggestion of Laughton, a longtime friend.
Meredith, whose brief appearance is one of the highlights of *Advise &
Consent*, would become a mainstay of Preminger's films, appearing in
The Cardinal, *In Harm's Way*, *Hurry Sundown*, *Skidoo*, and *Such Good
Friends*.

Critic Walter Kerr found Henry Fonda in *Critic's Choice* (in which he
had lately acted under Preminger's direction) "so full of integrity he
should be Secretary of State."[8] The phrase proved prophetic when Preminger cast Fonda as Leffingwell. Walter Pidgeon was cast as Munson.
Preminger gave comeback roles to four actors who had long been out of
films. Lew Ayres (Vice President Harley Hudson), whose stand as a conscientious objector during World War II had hurt his Hollywood career,
had not made a film since 1953; Gene Tierney (society hostess Dolly,
Munson's mistress), institutionalized after a mental breakdown, had last
appeared on the screen in 1955; Will Geer (the Senate Minority
Leader), blacklisted, had last made a Hollywood feature in 1951 (earlier,
he had acted for Preminger in the Broadway flop *The More the Merrier*);
and Franchot Tone (the President) had largely abandoned films since
that same year (when he was part of a scandalous love triangle also involving two other actors, Barbara Payton and Tom Neal).

Peter Lawford thought that Preminger cast him in the minor role of
Lafe Smith, a womanizing senator, in the hope of using Lawford's family
connections to ease the way for *Advise & Consent* in Washington. In the
end, Lawford failed to get permission to shoot in the Senate chamber,
but he did secure his brother-in-law's consent—though it was later re-
tracted—to shoot in the Oval Office of the White House.

Wendell Mayes's script, dated July 5, 1961, was submitted to the
Production Code Administration. On July 28 Geoffrey Shurlock met

with Preminger. "I explained that as matters now stood, any formal letter would have to be a rejection of the script, in view of the inference of homosexuality. Therefore, pending some possible new directive concerning the treatment of this subject matter, I explained to Mr. Preminger I wanted merely to talk about details."

The points Shurlock discussed were the characterization of Ray's roommate and pimp, Manuel ("there will be no suggestion of the 'swish' in his case"); the gay-bar scene (no swishes allowed here either; "also, none of the men would be painted as described, or portrayed in any unduly shocking manner"); the shot of the photograph of Brig and Ray ("there will be nothing questionable"); and the text of Brig's letter to Ray ending their relationship (which should be "rewritten so as to avoid the present semi-condonation of homosexuality. Mr. Preminger states it will be a very moral statement"). The only point not having to do with homosexuality was Dolly's use of the word "bitch," an epithet that, Shurlock said, the PCA had rigorously kept off the screen. Preminger insisted on retaining the word, observing that as the speaker was using it, in a humorous manner, to describe herself, it couldn't give offense. As for Brig's letter, the text that appears in the film is neither a condemnation nor a condonation (it's not even a "semi-condonation"). It makes no judgment about homosexuality and does not even pass judgment on the rightness or wrongness of Brig and Ray's relationship, making it clear that Brig not only still has warm feelings for Ray ("you are generous and kind") but perhaps still loves him ("it won't be easy . . .").

Shurlock's hint at "some possible new directive" would be confirmed in October, when the MPAA announced that "in keeping with the culture, the mores and the values of our time, homosexuality and other sexual aberrations may now be treated with care, discretion and restraint."[9] By then, Preminger had begun shooting *Advise & Consent*, probably with the assurance that a Code change was imminent. (Another major film dealing with homosexuality, William Wyler's *The Children's Hour*, based on Lillian Hellman's play, had already been completed and would be released later in the year.)

Shooting started in Washington on September 5. Jerry Fielding, hired to compose the score, accompanied the unit to Washington. Production headquarters and lodging were at the Sheraton Park Hotel, "much more baroque, much more demented, much more fabulous than the hotel of

Marienbad," according to Jean Domarchi.[10] Democratic national chairman John Bailey let the production use his suite at the hotel for the sequences in Munson's hotel room. On September 25 the hotel ballroom
served as the set for the scene of the White House correspondents' dinner. The elaborate scene of Dolly's party was shot at an actual party
thrown for the film on Tuesday, September 19, at Tregaron, a huge man-
sion once owned by Joseph E. Davies, an ambassador to the Soviet
Union.

Don Murray thought Gene Tierney "very nervous and apprehensive . . . She needed constant reassurance by Otto, and as I remember
he gave it to her. I think he was very good to Gene Tierney."[11] According
to George Grizzard, "She was frightened by him. She would say, 'Do you
think he's going to yell at me today?' She was just frightened to death. I
don't know why, because I never saw him ever be anything but gentlemanly with her."[12]

Murray got along well with Preminger. "I found with people like Preminger, these very dictatorial shouters with the reputation of being real
despots, that what you had to do was never show them any weakness,
you had to be very definite about everything with them. You had to say,
'Otto, this is what I think.' I did that, and I never had any trouble with
him." Once, however, Murray made the mistake of hesitating in asking
for a retake. "Instead of saying, 'Otto, I'd like to do that scene again because I was out of camera range,' which is how I should have said it, I
approached it tentatively and said, 'Otto, maybe it's none of my business—', and he said, 'You're right, it's none of your business. Just act.' I
thought, 'Dammit, I messed up! I showed a weakness. The shark
smelled blood and attacked.' I never did that again."[13]

Grizzard liked Preminger but saw him (as did many others) as someone with two personalities:

Off the set he was charming and generous and kind. And something happened when he got on the set. I don't understand, there
were like two men there somewhere. I don't know whether it was
because he was producing and it had something to do with
money, or whether it had to do with keeping everybody's blood
boiling and energy up, or what it was. On the set he was an absolute monster. He made Franchot Tone cry, he would go home

crying at night. He said to the director of photography [Sam Lea-vitt], "If it weren't for me, you would be shooting B pictures." I mean, this was the man who was photographing his film. He yelled at everybody. He yelled at me one time. He yelled at Paul Ford. "Mr. Ford, why aren't you funny? I hired you to be funny." Well, you can't say that to a *comedian*. It's just crippling. And Paul was such a sweet guy.

The other [Preminger] was very kind. And one time on the set there was an actor who showed up drunk. He had been waiting around for, I don't know, a couple of weeks to do his scene, it was a tiny scene, and when it came time, he was just drunk. And Otto was so gentle with him, and so kind and so understanding. He just said very quietly, "Well, he has an illness." He was very gentle with him, the kindness was just astounding to see. That's what I saw off the set, too.[14]

The one piece of direction Grizzard remembered receiving from Prem-inger was given during the shooting of a scene in the Senate chamber. "I took this young hotshot senator as a firebrand, and Otto said, 'You're making too much noise!' He did teach me, if I didn't yell so much, he'd have to come in closer to find out what I was saying. That was good advice."[15]

Second assistant director Don Kranze recalled, "Lew Ayres hadn't worked in quite some time, and now he gets this spot in a [big picture]. And he got sick." Preminger considered recasting him, but Ayres, who badly wanted the part, persuaded Preminger to keep him. "I could feel the terror," Kranze said, "the need. And then Ayres was fine when it came to shooting."[16]

Eddie Hodges, cast in the small part of Leffingwell's son, recalled that Preminger was "somewhat calmer during shooting of my scenes than he was during rehearsals for *Critic's Choice*. He was also compli-mentary to me, which was a surprise. I wondered if he had thought I was not a serious actor before then. He could be very warm when he wanted to be . . . I was not one for many takes on any scene. I liked to put every-thing I had in the first take—Preminger seemed to like that."[17]

Shooting inside the Senate had to wait until the Senate adjourned—which it finally did, later than anticipated, in the early morning of September 27. Thereafter, Preminger took over the Russell Senate Office Building, starting with a superb exterior shot of Cooley dismounting a streetcar. The subcommittee hearings were filmed in the Senate Caucus Room, site of the 1954 Army-McCarthy hearings where, on live TV, Joseph N. Welch helped bring Senator Joseph McCarthy's career to an end. One day in the Caucus Room, Burgess Meredith marveled, "In the midst of directing, I suddenly looked for [Preminger], and he was over signing checks! There's nothing that he himself doesn't personally supervise."[18]

Jean Domarchi, invited to observe the production for *Cahiers du cinéma*, noted that shooting in the Caucus Room proceeded with none of the legendary Premingerian outbursts of anger. In the Senate locations, Domarchi observed, Preminger often used two cameras to gain time. Rarely were more than two or three takes needed. Preminger let Domarchi view the rushes in order to demonstrate his point that the editing of his films posed no particular difficulty. "The finished film corresponds with the film conceived in the *découpage*" (*découpage*, a French term with no exact equivalent in English, means the choice of shots and their arrangement); and the *découpage*, in turn, was not conceived "a priori," but created "on the fly, in function of the limitations and the possibilities of the decor." Domarchi found that "Preminger, whom one might describe as an egotistical and imperious tyrant, hides behind a cold and intimidating aspect a great kindness which gradually reveals itself. Like Hitchcock, he has considerable modesty, a horror of displaying his deep preoccupations in public."[19]

Preminger offered the Reverend Martin Luther King, Jr., the part of a Georgia senator—a move that won the film some publicity and was widely criticized by white southern politicians. King settled the controversy by declining the offer, saying, "I feel that the brief role could not be of any significant value in advancing civil rights and, therefore, have not accepted the proposal."[20] Preminger continued to make it clear to journalists that his film was in no sense anti-American. "We had a taste of Communism before this country ever became aware of it," he told Hedda Hopper. "I am against it." Presumably he was referring to the period after the First World War when Austria was under the domination of the Social Democrats.[21]

For the benefit of a visiting journalist, Preminger fired three crew members (including key grip Morrie Rosen, a Preminger veteran), only to hire them back after the journalist was gone. (One of the three refused to come back.) Firing people on the set was a Preminger trademark, though those who understood and could deal with his personality knew that such decisions were not always to be taken as final. "If you believed him the first time he said things . . . he was sometimes sorry about it," said Yoram Ben-Ami, a production manager on *Rosebud*.[22] Preminger fought several battles with unions on the production. One concerned second assistant director Don Kranze. Intending to bring Kranze back with him to Hollywood to finish the picture, Preminger was told that as a member of the Screen Directors Guild on the East Coast only, Kranze was ineligible to work in California. Preminger called the president of the West Coast guild and persuaded him to make Kranze a member. On the other hand, Preminger had no success trying to get camera operator Saul Midwall, who had worked on *Advise* in Washington, into the Los Angeles photographers' union so that Midwall could finish the film in the studio. When *Advise & Consent* premiered in Beverly Hills in June, Preminger held a press conference to complain about the rejection of Midwall and about featherbedding by the East Coast unions, which, he said, had raised the cost of production by $150,000 to $200,000.[23]

In Hollywood, Kranze witnessed a flare-up of Preminger's well-known wrath, directed against actor Larry Tucker, playing Manuel, Ray's roommate and pimp. Tucker was having trouble with a complicated scene combining movement and dialogue, and between repeated takes, Preminger loudly criticized the actor. "It was embarrassing to watch, embarrassing for the actor, embarrassing for everybody . . . It went on and on and on, and since it was a small person—I never saw him take off on a big person."[24]

Production closed on November 16. True to his word to Domarchi, Preminger raced through the editing in time for the PCA to approve *Advise & Consent* on December 12. He and Columbia wanted to release the film in time to qualify for the 1961 Academy Awards, but Drury asked for, and won, an injunction preventing Columbia from opening the film before June 1962, when the production of the play based on the book was to finish its tour. Meanwhile, the film won some notoriety for its supposedly negative image of American government (Democratic senator Stephen M. Young of Ohio proclaimed the film "degrading of the

Senate" and tried to introduce a bill barring its distribution outside the United States).[25] Whereas, in general, the press had at least acknowledged that *Exodus* was a serious attempt at dramatizing recent history, reviewers approached *Advise & Consent* with skepticism. *Newsweek*, in one of the harshest reviews, judged it "one of the most reprehensibly sensational movies in years." In France, the film fared better; Jean-Louis Comolli wrote in *Cahiers du cinéma* that it was "Preminger's most complete film, and without doubt also his most terrifying."[26]

In *Anatomy of a Murder*, the main question confronting the jury and the film audience—whether Manion was insane when he shot Barney Quill—gets subordinated to a second question that is logically unrelated: whether Quill raped Laura. *Advise & Consent* performs a similar sleight of hand, by which one question is enfolded within another. What is ostensibly the main question of the film—whether Leffingwell is fit to be Secretary of State—gets subordinated to the question of whether he was once a member of a Communist cell. In a further movement, both questions get mixed up with Brig's suicide, which turns the senators' decision into a matter of individual conscience instead of political commitment. (No doubt it's no accident that both *The Cardinal* and *In Harm's Way* will take up again the theme of suicide, so closely linked to the question of freedom.)

The question posed at the beginning of *Advise & Consent* is not What is the truth? or What is right?, but What shall we do? The people who appeal to the concepts of truth and right, who seek to found their actions on these concepts, are shown to be out of step with the world of the Senate, which is the world of the film; and these people eliminate themselves or are eliminated: Brig, Van Ackerman, Gelman (who thought it was his "duty" to testify against Leffingwell).

The basis for a possible critique of the Senate, in *Advise & Consent*, lies here: those who are out of step must be eliminated. This body that praises itself for its "tolerance" must rigorously reject any claim made on behalf of a truth that brooks no compromise, that cannot be merely tolerated but must be obeyed unconditionally. Regarding such truths, the Senate is intolerant. If Brig commits suicide, the cause is not only his inability to face or forgive himself (although the film certainly shows this

inability as *a* cause); the cause is also the failure of the Senate to offer him a credible promise that he would still be accepted if the truth
about him were known. Similarly, Leffingwell finds himself *forced* to
lie to Brig's subcommittee. And though we may applaud the ostracism
of Van Ackerman at the end of the film, the thought is not dispelled
that the "peace" he poses as a transcendent goal is not, after all, an un-
worthy one.

Nevertheless, the film pointedly avoids filling out Van Ackerman's
concept of peace with any specific content. At Dolly's party, he rants un-
intelligibly to Orrin Knox: "You want to get us bombed out of existence
for some lousy two-bit country in Lower Slobovia that can't even feed itself?" The only thing that's clear about this remark is that Van Ackerman's notion of peace is fundamentally self-interested rather than
universalist. It's obvious that Van Ackerman is an idealist, but his ideal
remains, within the terms of the film, undefined. A certain vagueness
also characterizes the geopolitical discussion at the Senate subcommittee hearing. The characters speak in generalities, hypotheticals, and
metaphors. No one mentions the Soviet Union, or China; instead, the
senators and the nominee refer to "the Communists." The issues
raised—pride, compromise, concealment—thus appear in their general
applicability or in relation to Brig's personal conflicts (a relation that
would not be clear to a viewer unfamiliar with the plot of *Advise & Consent*, since at this point in the narrative Brig's conflicts have not
emerged).

Preminger said that *Advise & Consent* "is not about direct political issues; it is about moral issues." The clearest demonstration of this is the
final sequence. For Preminger, the Senate vote on Leffingwell's nomination becomes a complex symbol. This Senate session opens with a transcendence of both self-interest and practical advantage, as Cooley
admits that his opposition to Leffingwell was motivated partly by vindictiveness. He states the reasons, other than vindictive, that cause him to
oppose Leffingwell, and he concludes pointedly, "I ask no man to follow
me in this." Munson, though he supports Leffingwell, does follow Cooley, however, not just in speaking directly after him but in acknowledging
that because of the "tragic circumstances surrounding this nomination,"
the vote should be determined by individual conscience rather than by
political commitments. Accordingly, he announces, "all pledges made to

me are free to vote as they will." As the film goes on to show, Munson's gratuitous act leads to the defeat of the nomination, since Lafe Smith— who, early in the film, had promised Munson to vote for Leffingwell— now votes against him, so that at the end of the vote, the Senate is deadlocked. Preminger underlines Lafe's switch by dollying in, after the clerk calls his name, from a group shot of several senators, with Lafe in the middle ground, to a close shot of Lafe. Through this camera movement Preminger shows that freedom of choice exists and also affirms its importance. Had Preminger filmed the same scene—Lafe deep in thought, his hands in front of his face, pausing at length before voting no—with a stationary camera, the sense of the *responsibility* of choice would have been less urgent. Preminger's camera movement might be criticized as "heavy-handed" (an epithet that reviewers would apply with increasing frequency to his direction during the 1960s and 1970s), but in fact it does not determine our interpretation of Lafe's vote; it only, through its suspense, alerts us to the importance of the vote and, more generally, to the importance of the freedom to change. Lafe's vote is made to appear not merely as a random gesture but also as arising out of the accumulated spatial tensions of the sequence, now articulated through the forward dolly.

Lafe's is the third of the gratuitous acts in the sequence (following Cooley's and Munson's speeches)—the third change-for-its-own-sake by which an individual asserts his freedom. The last of these gratuitous acts is Harley's refusal to break the tie. As in Lafe's case, Harley's self-assertion takes the form of reneging on a promise previously made to Munson and puts into practice the release from political commitment that Munson has offered. The film poses Harley's announcement as the culmination of a series of changes. Since this culmination coincides with Harley's assumption of the presidential role, the structure of the narrative, in effect, anoints Harley as the ideal president, showing that executive power itself is the ultimate from of freedom of decision and passing to Harley the right to exercise this power.

The meaning of Harley's change has already been set up by his line in the shipboard scene: "The last night I saw Brig Anderson, I saw a man in terrible pain. I wonder if Leffingwell, or any one man, is worth all of this." Preminger links Harley's position here to his final refusal to vote through a complex relay of references. Before Harley's line, the President tells Munson, "You've got the votes committed, Bobby: use them." At this point the camera tracks forward slightly, seemingly to no purpose other than to reaffirm the existing, static composition, with Harley in the center of the frame in the middle ground between Munson at background left and the President at foreground right. The camera movement almost invisibly emphasizes Harley's centrality in relation to the Leffingwell vote and links Harley to Munson's future decision to release his committed votes. This link, rather than anything overtly stated in the dialogue (either in this scene or the subsequent Senate sequence), gives the film's answer to the President's curt dismissal of Harley: "Wondering doesn't run a government." For Preminger, wondering—when it forms a decision—*does* run a government. The point of the final Senate sequence is that freedom of conscience is a sort of miracle (as in *Anatomy of a Murder*, with Parnell's line, "God bless juries").

Harley's "I wonder" evokes Brig's speech at the subcommittee hearing, after Leffingwell trumps Cooley's "standing on my two hind legs" speech by characterizing it as exemplary of a nineteenth-century attitude, too dangerous in the age of nuclear weapons. Brig argues, "I wonder if there isn't a great deal of good sense in what Senator Cooley had to say. I wonder if we can't become too equivocal. I wonder if we can't reason away in the name of survival everything worth surviving for." Harley's "wondering" constitutes the link between Brig's own wondering and the Senate's final rejection of Leffingwell, which can be seen as vindicating Brig.

Advise & Consent is, like *Anatomy of a Murder*, a film about performance. Appropriately, the dialogue of *Advise & Consent* is filled with performatives. Senators say "I move," or "I yield," or "I ask," or "I suggest," or "I release," and their saying these things effectuates the things they say. The senators exercise power through their speech, and finally through their vote. The film is concerned with the value of speech ("your word isn't exactly the coin of the realm," Brig says bitterly to Leffingwell), with the identification of people with what they say. Brig's isolation, and his death, are figured appropriately in his refusal to talk to Harley on the plane, after he appears to be on the verge of unburdening himself. In contrast, Leffingwell is able to tell the truth to his son, Johnny, even though the latter, in one of the most telling gestures of the film, is prepared to let his father off the hook. Leffingwell, realizing that Johnny overheard Brig accusing him of lying, has no choice but to face his son, but at first he temporizes with "Well, I don't exactly know how to explain it," whereupon Johnny says, "Okay," turns, and starts to go (obviously what can't be explained is a familiar theme in the Leffingwell house).

The scenes in the Senate chamber juxtapose public and private speech. When the chaplain, in his opening prayer, prays for "strength and charity" in the Senate, "lest there slip into seats of power those who would misguide and mislead this great people," the camera, tracking slowly across the chamber, pauses in front of the Minority Leader as he whispers to a colleague, "Even the parson is getting into the Leffingwell act." Later in the same sequence, Orrin Knox's oration against Leffingwell is the occasion for an ironic aside by Stanley Danta and an encouraging one by Cooley, and during Cooley's interchange with Lafe Smith, Orrin crosses the aisle separating the two parties to share amused commentary with Brig.

Gelman's inadequate performance at the hearing introduces a striking contrast with the mastery displayed by most of the senators and by Leffingwell. Gelman speaks in a hesitant, uncertain voice, too quietly; he allows his excitement to distort his speech suddenly (when he first says that Leffingwell is a Communist). Rather than, as Cooley did in the Senate chamber, building dramatically, he changes his volume abruptly and jarringly.

Gelman's linguistic deficiencies point to a social isolation that links him with Van Ackerman, another figure whose speech style sets him sharply apart from the "orderly flow of legislative interchange" (Cooley's rhetorical term for what the Senate does). Both Gelman and Van Ackerman are zealots: just as Van Ackerman tries to justify his blackmail of Brig by telling Munson that he was motivated by "the good of my country," Gelman gives as his reason for testifying against Leffingwell that "I thought it was my duty to my country." The film makes it clear that both men's underlying motives are personal. Gelman bears a grudge against Leffingwell for having been fired and may have been obsessed with him for a longer period; Van Ackerman's envy of Brig becomes apparent at several points in the film, including the sequence of the subcommittee hearing, during which Van Ackerman uses his status as an outsider to criticize Brig.

Gelman and Ray are parallel characters: each reemerges from the past of a prominent man and threatens to discredit him. Each oscillates between loving and hating his intended victim. Gelman's vindictiveness against Leffingwell, with whom he has obviously long been obsessed, vanishes when he learns that Leffingwell smoothed the way for his position in the Treasury Department. (Drury is believed to have taken inspiration for Leffingwell and Gelman from Alger Hiss and Whittaker Chambers, who—during the period of intense public interest in them that followed Chambers's 1948 denunciation of former State Department official Hiss as a Communist—were rumored to have been romantically involved.) Both Gelman and Ray have personal problems that make them vulnerable to manipulation: Gelman has suffered from a nervous breakdown and shows signs of mental impairment; Ray is gay (obviously a "problem" in the context of the America of the film), impecunious, and given to drink. Ray becomes Van Ackerman's pawn, as Gelman becomes Cooley's.

As weak as Ray and Gelman are, they possess truth—or rather, they themselves, their bodies, are this truth that reaches out from the past to strike at Brig and Leffingwell in the present. Ray and Gelman represent the possibility for the body to become evidence, an object to be presented and used. Ray also happens to be, literally, a prostitute ("We've bought Ray," Ellen Anderson is told over the phone). Ray and Gelman thus make visible in the film a certain external constraint on individual action that contradicts the principle of free choice that the Senate stands for. (Leffingwell himself is a functionary: "I've put myself at [the president's] disposal," he tells Brig. "I'm waiting for him to tell me what he wants to do.")

Ray and Gelman are avatars of a key figure in the film, that of the functionary or staff member. This figure also assumes such incarnations as the Senate clerk who calls the roll; the female clerk at the subcommittee hearing who conveys Gelman's telegram to him for him to identify it (at the recess, after the senators and spectators leave, the camera lingers on this woman as she clears an ashtray from the table); the male stenographer who is seen in two-shots, first with Leffingwell and then with Gelman as he transcribes the hearing; and the Secret Service agents who enter the Senate chamber after the President's death. At the very end of the film, after the principals have left the stage under Preminger's high-angle long shot, the only people left on screen are such functionaries, picking up papers from the senators' desks.

Two other functionaries in the film are paired just as Ray and Gelman are paired: Manuel, Ray's pimp; and the eyeglasses-wearing member of Van Ackerman's "brain trust" who makes the anonymous call to Brig in the Senate cafeteria. Each functions as a communicator, a go-between. Each walks back and forth: the blackmailer crossing the cafeteria between his table and the pay phones, Manuel crossing the length of his apartment from the kitchen to the front room where he receives Brig. These back-and-forth movements parody Brig's futile round-trip to New York. The blackmailer's glasses, his thin and slight body, clean-shaven face, high forehead, and close-cropped hair all link him to the stenographer sitting beside Gelman at the hearing. Like the stenographer, the blackmailer works with signs, with the voice, but is never actually seen to speak: he makes the phone call offscreen (although, on returning to the table from the phone booth, he whistles a tune). His visual muteness makes the blackmailer's literally "a secret voice," in the words of the Frank Sinatra song (written for the film by Fielding and Ned Washington) heard emanating from the jukebox at Club 602, where Brig is directed to go in search of Ray.

The scene at Club 602 remains one of the most often cited scenes in all Preminger's work; it is usually mentioned, for example, in short reviews or descriptions of *Advise & Consent* in film-program schedules and newspaper listings. In such contexts, the scene is regularly the focus of a certain ambivalence, with writers tending to assume an uneasy condescension toward it and hinting that the outdated aspects of the scene may endow the film with a certain camp value. Other commentators have been more forthright in attacking the scene and the apartment scene that precedes it. Drew Casper, in his audio commentary to the U.S. DVD of *Advise & Consent*, calls the handling of Brig's trip to New York "extremely heavy-handed, loaded, stereotypic, and, in the end, I think, homophobic."[27] For Vito Russo, "the film virtually canonizes Brig for his dislike of Ray's surroundings. Look how the two young American soldiers turned out, the film seems to say; the one who was really straight became a senator of the United States, and the one who was really gay became a seedy hustler, a barfly and a blackmailer."[28]

In his doctrinaire emphasis on the supposed homophobia of *Advise & Consent*, Russo seems to me to mistake both the real attitude of the film and the implications of Brig's behavior. Far from "really straight," Brig becomes aware of his own homosexual desires when he enters the club, and it is his attraction to, rather than his dislike of, the surroundings that causes him to flee in panic. As for Ray, Preminger goes out of his way to make the "seedy hustler" and "barfly" as positive a figure as possible: he is handsome, his dress and manner are simple and unaffected, his companions at the bar are not negatively characterized, and, most important, he is obviously happy to see Brig. The film does not "canonize" Brig (although Russo's word choice is unintentionally helpful inasmuch as it offers a clue to the links between Brig, Joan of Arc, and the hero of Preminger's next film, *The Cardinal*); it distances us from him. That this is the case may, however, be difficult to see because of the sensationalism projected by Fielding's score (in the scene with Manuel and the exterior shots of Brig arriving at and leaving the club), with its "sleazy" saxophone, Latin percussion, and queasy, insistent orchestral phrases. The music's implication of danger and debauchery might seem to prompt a negative reading of the scene; against this, however, we have the presentation of the interior of the club, whose patrons, some of whom (including the three who look Brig over as he comes in) are obviously stereotyped as gay and some of whom are not, are in no way threatening or repellent. Robin Wood's account of the sequence (written before Wood's own coming-out) is clearly right: "Both Manuel's flat and the homosexual club are presented in the same pattern: we are made to share Brig's first impression of sinister horror, and then we go on to modify our impression while seeing that Brig fails to modify his."[29]

The sound cut from Fielding's incidental music to Sinatra's song is crucial. The melody of the song is recognizable from the film's main theme, and the instrumentation is recognizably in the composer's style. Even if we read the club denizens' appropriation of Sinatra as intentionally subversive or parodic, the Sinatra song thus tells us, without insisting on it, that Club 602 is part of the film's world and not an alien planet. Fielding's "sleazy" scoring of the other parts of the New York section of the film thus can be heard as reflecting Brig's attitude rather than imposing the viewpoint of the film. The sensationalism that is undeniably part of the sequence (Wendell Mayes said, "It was somewhat sensational in 1961, to be so open about a closed subject, and candidly, I suppose I dramatized it the way I did for its sensational impact")[30] is thus placed in the film as a tone associated with Brig, signifying his rejection of his own homosexuality; it cannot be taken as the film's authorial tone.

Advise & Consent is the most tightly and intricately structured of Preminger's narratives. Each of a large number of characters influences the narrative by his actions, and the entire film is, at every moment, both the detailed description of the situation formed by these actions and the image of the change in this situation in their consequence. Preminger's staging of scenes contains many concrete examples of the co-presence of these two schemes in the film. One example, banal on the surface, is deeply revelatory of Preminger's view of the world. At certain points in the film, two characters who are both in motion change their motion and turn toward each other. On the lawn in front of the Washington Monument, Cooley and Hardiman Fletcher both stop and turn toward each other at the moment when Cooley accuses Fletcher of being "James Morton," a member of Leffingwell's Communist cell. At the end of the film, as Harley passes Munson on the way out of the Senate chamber, the two men turn toward each other at the same time, before exchanging parting words. Preminger stages both these incidents as interlocking movements rather than as an initiatory or leading movement followed by a response. The effect is subtly paradoxical: as if two movements anticipated each other, neither seeking precedence. It is a way for temporal progression to remain the description of a situation, a coiled compromise between action and stasis.

For all the movement in *Advise & Consent*—and this is a film, as much as any of Preminger's, in constant and exciting movement— the viewer has the impression that in some sense, nothing happens in the film, nothing changes, so densely and completely is every element in the film counterbalanced by some other. ("The film is as well provided with checks and balances as the Constitution," Penelope Houston noted drily.)[31] For every character there is an opposing or equivalent character; for every action, a counteraction; for every line of dialogue there is a later line of dialogue that retrospectively justifies, or interprets, the earlier one.

Advise & Consent is one of Preminger's most exhilarating and sensuous films, marshaling camera movement and character movement with an unflagging energy and complexity and placing both types of movement in relation to the fixed points of reality provided by the Washington locations in order to provide that heightened sense of real space and time that is as important to Preminger's cinema as it is to, say, Tarkovsky's (to name a director who in other respects is antipodal to Preminger). The atmospheric night-for-night shot in which, leaving Dolly's party, Van Ackerman walks away from the house (the camera tracking back before him) and beckons toward his offscreen driver with a distinctive gesture (raising his hand and flapping its fingers in unison) shows Preminger's characteristic interest in what is left over, left behind, excluded—an interest that inverts the film, concentrating our attention momentarily on the other side of a scene, the outside of a narrative. (The fluidity of the dissolve of this night shot—the camera, the actor, and the background music from the party all still in motion as the scene slowly dies and gives way to the next—suggests that Preminger's cinema lost something essential when he renounced the dissolve with *Bunny Lake Is Missing* and *Hurry Sundown*.)

In one of the most memorable shots of the film, Brig, declining Harley's offer of a ride home and ignoring his concern over Brig's well-being, walks away toward the parking lot at Washington National Airport. The camera, at a slightly high angle, pans to follow Brig and tracks forward, at a distance, behind him as he walks away into the dark, vast space of the screen, his path intersecting the broken line of painted white rectangles that marks a pathway across the space. Stretching across the lower half of the screen, its lateral movement accentuated by the camera's rightward pan to follow Brig, the line of rectangles echoes the airport's long colonnade, which stretches across the upper half of the screen in the background. The impersonal geometry of this eloquent composition, the sharp contrast between the black expanse spreading away from the airport and the definite white shapes of the rectangles and of the colonnade, the drifting movement of the camera as it lets Brig increase the distance between him and us—all pronounce upon Brig's isolation and make it definitive.

28

A Certain Weakness

The Cardinal, a novel by the poet, editor, Joyce scholar, and general-purpose writer Henry Morton Robinson, was a bestseller in 1950. The long book relates the rise of Stephen Fermoyle, son of Irish immigrants living in Boston. Ordained a priest in 1915, Fermoyle quickly attracts his superiors' attention for his rare combination of scholarship, diplomatic ability, and energy. He becomes the secretary of Boston's Cardinal Glennon, then is appointed to the Vatican diplomatic staff. Distracted by a beautiful Italian countess who falls in love with him, Fermoyle suffers a crisis of faith, but he rebounds and, in 1939, is made cardinal.

In 1955 Louis de Rochemont announced plans to film *The Cardinal* for Columbia.[1] Whether because of behind-the-scenes opposition from the Church—Robinson's book was widely thought to be a disguised account of the life of Cardinal Spellman—or for some other reason, de Rochemont dropped his plans. On August 2, 1961, while Preminger was casting *Advise & Consent*, he announced his intention to film *The Cardinal*.

Preminger traced back his interest in the Catholic Church, under-standable in someone raised within a largely Catholic society, to the last play he directed before leaving Vienna, *The First Legion*. (Cardinal Innitzer, who would later become infamous for publicly endorsing the Anschluss and trying to reach an understanding with Hitler, attended the premiere of that production. The introduction of Innitzer as a character in *The Cardinal* is one of Preminger's most decisive changes to Robinson's book.) Robinson presents Stephen as a largely admirable figure, uniting "American" vigor and straightforwardness with "European" intellectualism, glibness, and appreciation of ceremony, but Preminger saw the ambiguity in such a figure, too.

After false starts with two screenwriters, James Lee and Dan Taradash, Preminger started working on the script in June 1962 with Robert Dozier, the son of Screen Gems executive William Dozier. Preminger and Dozier made substantial changes to the novel. Preminger has little interest in Stephen's parents, who are prominent in the book. On the other hand, Preminger and Dozier build up the character of Stephen's sister, Mona. A confession scene that, in the novel, involves an anonymous woman is rewritten for Mona. In both novel and film, Stephen refuses to allow doctors to kill Mona's unborn child in order to save her life; his refusal, a minor incident in the novel, becomes central in the film, leading directly to his questioning his vocation and taking a leave of absence from the priesthood.

The episodic nature of the film, in which Stephen figures as a kind of superpriest who travels around the world to take part in various adventures—including an encounter with the Ku Klux Klan in the southern United States—comes from the novel. Taking the opportunity afforded by this structure and the time frame of the narrative to depict the Austrian Anschluss, Preminger replaces Robinson's Italian countess with Annemarie, a Viennese woman who momentarily tempts Stephen. In Dozier's early drafts, Annemarie is Stephen's secretary in Vienna. In September and October 1962, Preminger put Gore Vidal to work revising Dozier's script. Vidal provided improvements throughout the script, notably in the Vienna section, in which Annemarie turns out to be the niece of the pro-Nazi state councillor Arthur Seyss-Inquart. It wasn't until later in the scripting that Annemarie, and her subplot, assumed the forms they would take in the finished film, in which she studies English with Stephen during his leave of absence from the church. When he returns to Vienna on church business several years later, she has married a wealthy businessman and is sympathetic to Hitler, an attitude she changes, too late, after her half-Jewish husband commits suicide.

In the fall of 1962 Hugh O'Brian and Stuart Whitman were mentioned as possibilities for Stephen. Preminger tested several actors in early November, including Cliff Robertson, Bradford Dillman, and Tom Tryon, whom he had seen in *Moon Pilot* and a TV adaptation of *Wuthering Heights* (in which Tryon played Heathcliff). In mid-November, Preminger announced that he had cast Tryon. The actor later reported, "There were a lot of big name actors who either wanted to do it or were under consideration, Peck, Finney, and O'Toole."[2] Tryon was thirty-four when Preminger signed him to a five-picture contract.[3]

Preminger's treatment of Tryon during production would contrast sharply with their warm initial meetings before the start of production. "I can remember sitting with this man and finding him charming and erudite, intelligent, and there was some sort of response there. And later on he reminded me of that time . . . During the test—I never saw him like that again—but he would come to me and he'd say, 'Now, Tom, I want you to . . . ,' and he would pull things out of me. And it was all very quiet, he never raised his voice on the set that day."[4]

At the same time that Preminger cast Tryon, he also cast Carol Lynley as Mona. Lynley signed a five-picture deal with Preminger, who also persuaded John Huston to take the part of Cardinal Glennon. "He didn't want to act and it took me several hours to convince him to do it," said Preminger.[5]

On January 28, 1963, Preminger submitted the script to Geoffrey Shurlock, who, with a few minor quibbles, found it acceptable. Preminger did not, and he continued to work on the script in February, now with another writer—Ring Lardner, Jr. In November 1962 Preminger had announced that he had hired Lardner to write the screenplay for *Genius*, a satirical novel by Patrick Dennis about the misadventures of a Hollywood film director in Mexico. The film, which would have marked Lardner's return from imposed pseudonymity, was eventually abandoned.[6] Instead, Preminger put Lardner to work on *The Cardinal*. "Otto, who was making a largely sympathetic portrayal of a Catholic prelate, knew I was an agnostic," recalled Lardner, "and he had read my satirical novel *The Ecstasy of Owen Muir* about Roman Catholicism in America. But he also knew I was very well informed about Catholic rituals and practices. I rewrote many scenes to achieve what he wanted, and wrote them in a way I would never have done under my own name." Lardner worked on the script with Preminger in New York, then accompanied him to Boston. He would go on to travel with the production to Vienna and then Rome.[7] Though, like Vidal, Lardner would receive no screen credit, his work on *The Cardinal* was substantial. He was probably responsible not only for the definitive version of the character of Annemarie but also for the overall structure of the film, with the narrative told in flashbacks from the ceremony in which Stephen is made cardinal.

Preminger and Eva Monley surveyed locations in Vienna from January 12 to 14. Otto Niedermoser, who had worked with Preminger as set designer at the Theater in der Josefstadt, was recruited to help line up locations in and around Vienna.

Despite Cardinal Spellman's opposition, Preminger obtained permission to shoot in St. John's Church in Stamford, Connecticut. The bishop of Bridgeport, Connecticut, Walter W. Curtis, visited St. John's on the first day of shooting to give his blessing. That first day—February 6, 1963—marked the beginning of a season in hell for Tom Tryon. Years later, Tryon said of Preminger, "He was a tyrant who ruled by terror. He tied me up in knots. He screamed at me. He called me names. He said I was lazy. He said I was a fool. He never cursed me. His insults were far more personal. The first day's shooting of the movie resulted in Preminger firing me. My parents were there on the set. He did it in front of them. I had garbled a line. Preminger told me I was stupid and unprofessional. I planned to go home with my parents. In an hour, he rehired me."[8]

First assistant director Gerry O'Hara (who had fulfilled the same function on *Exodus*) said that Preminger "literally destroyed Tom Tryon. And Tom was a very sweet guy. He was very modest, he was no great shakes as an actor, that's for sure . . . I don't know quite why Otto treated him so badly. Maybe he was trying to put a poker up his backside, and get a bigger performance."[9]

Tryon felt that Preminger's vindictiveness toward him was undeserved. "If I had been some arrogant bastard and misbehaving on the set and needed chastisement, that would have been one thing. But I'm a very agreeable guy. I don't make waves, and I never did. Very seldom did I show temperament on the set, and certainly never on his set."[10] Tryon, who was gay and an alcoholic, was temperamentally unable to stand up to Preminger's abuse, which continued throughout the long production. "I was so frightened he was going to scream that I didn't give a shit about what my acting was like. I simply wanted to get through the take and get a print. I wanted the experience to end."[11]

Stanley Kauffmann visited the shoot in the Boston area and noted, "Poor Tryon was sweating hard, trying to come up to Huston's level in a quarrel scene between them. Over and over Preminger made them do the scene, Tryon laboring weakly, Huston quietly roaring. Finally Preminger yelled at Tryon: 'Why don't you give it some gots?' He gestured at Huston. 'This man has *gots*. Why don't you give it some *gots* like him?' "[12] According to Bob Vietro, the second assistant director in New England, the shooting of the scene in which Stephen tells Glennon that he has come to question his vocation began one afternoon around 1:00 p.m., continued until seven or eight that evening, then resumed the next morning and went on until 2:00 p.m. "Tom came out of that in tears. We did something like 78 takes. Preminger wasn't getting what he wanted. It wasn't technical, it was purely Tom's performance. That means Huston does 78 takes also. And without a whimper."[13]

In an interview in 1970 with French critics Olivier Eyquem and Olivier Comte, Preminger made some comments that are highly revealing of his attitude toward both Tryon and toward Stephen Fermoyle. The interviewers have just asked Preminger about the "masochism" of several of the characters in *The Cardinal*.

I believe that the character of Tom Tryon—and therefore I probably chose him, without deliberation, because he *is* weak—the character of Tom Tryon *is* weak. I personally, for instance, feel, as long as we discuss it, though I don't like to discuss it, if I personally had been Tom Tryon, and my sister would have come to me, and I would have this dilemma between being a priest and being a brother, I would have chosen to be the brother. No matter what. In other words, to me, no law, no rule of an institution, whatever it is, would stop me from helping my sister. If I could save her life, or save the life of the child, even if I were a Catholic priest, I would save her life and leave the Church, because my personal opinions in my life would always prevail. I couldn't work against my brain, and my heart, I could not take a rule which is in my opinion at least antiquated, and put the whole responsibility on the Church . . . In order to save my sister, I would even kill people, particularly an unborn child. I do believe that this character is masochistic, if you want to call it, or weak. I do believe that the reason that he really never succeeds in the film is in a certain weakness in his character. On the other hand, if you want to belong to the Church, you have to submit to these rules. Drama is conflict. I'm quite sure, and I hope that many people who see it,

while they have compassion for him and understand him, that
they also feel that he shouldn't do it this way . . . Deep down,
I like him. I have compassion for him. But he never does what I
would think is right.[14]

"He wants to get out, but he's not strong enough to get out." Preminger, speaking of Stephen and the Church, could also have been speaking of Tryon and the film. "He fails because when you become a priest
you substitute your own judgment and your own feelings for the law of
the Church . . . The big decisions are made for him . . . When he leaves
the Church, he's trying to liberate himself, but he can't do it because he
is too involved, he believes in it." Preminger compared Fermoyle to
Glennon (just as, in directing the two actors, he set Tryon against Huston). "The character that John Huston plays, which is a much stronger
character, looks upon these things almost in a cynical way, in terms,
let's say, of a government rather than of a holy thing, and he wants
to preserve Tryon, because he thought he was a good servant of this
government."[15]

In mid-March, after five weeks of shooting in New England, the production crossed the Atlantic and arrived in Vienna. At the Hotel Imper-
ial, Preminger asked for and got the same suite Hitler stayed in when he
visited the city. "He was chortling like mad," recalled Columbia executive Syd Mirkin. "In many ways, he's like a little child, chortling over
some crazy things."[16]

Preminger later said, "The person who was then minister of education [Heinrich Drimmel] tried to stop me from shooting certain scenes.
He wanted everyone to forget that the Viennese had been Nazis. I was
given authorization to shoot in the National Library of Vienna, which is
one of the most beautiful monuments of the city, but the minister inter-
vened. I attacked him in the newspapers. He wanted that period to be
forgotten, but if one forgets it, it could repeat itself. I love Berlin and
Northern Germany: I think that they have truly forgotten Nazism, but
I'm not sure that the South, Bavaria, and Austria are completely cured
of it."[17]

Preminger had received permission from Cardinal Koenig of Vienna
to shoot in St. Stephen's Cathedral and in the cardinal's palace. A government minister barred Preminger from using some government build-

ings, partly on the grounds that Curt Jurgens, cast as Innitzer, was divorced. Citing a play commitment, Jurgens, conveniently for the production, bowed out of the cast of *The Cardinal*, and Preminger replaced him with Josef Meinrad, one of Austria's best-known character actors. The casting of Meinrad proved a masterstroke, for his performance is one of the best in the film, so good that it's hard to believe—yet, apparently, true—that Meinrad did not understand English and learned all his dialogue phonetically in sessions with Max Slater.

Ring Lardner, Jr., recalled, "I accompanied [Preminger] to Vienna and then to Rome, ostensibly to confer about *Genius*, but in reality so I could edit what he was going to film the next day. In Rome I discovered that he also had Gore Vidal writing parts of the picture . . . I don't know whether Otto realized that both Gore and I were atheists. Another thing we had in common, and which we jointly communicated to him, was our verdict that he had fallen into the habit of buying the movie rights to some of the worst-written best-sellers on the market."[18]

Photos taken during the shooting suggest that Romy Schneider and Preminger had real affection for each other. And cinematographer Leon Shamroy, according to Martin Schute (who had taken over as production manager for the European shoot), "fell madly in love with Romy Schneider. I have never seen Romy Schneider look so beautiful as when she was photographed by Leon Shamroy. It was a real work of love and art for him."[19] Perhaps it was to Schneider's benign presence that Tryon owed a letup in Preminger's oppressive handling. The actor recalled, "The only fun I ever had on *The Cardinal* was a scene I did with Romy. It was a big ballroom scene. I was in fish-and-soup and she was in a beautiful Donald Brooks gown. He called us over to the camera, and he was standing there, and he said, 'Now, in this scene, I want you should—,' and he looked at us, and he said, 'You know what to do.' So we went and we danced and we talked and we had a ball, it was terrific. And you can see the difference in the scene!"[20]

Observing the last three days of the production in Vienna, critic Jean Douchet saw Preminger erupt in "short but violent Germanic angers . . . They were always justified. Equipped with an admirable knowledge of his profession, he pardons no professional fault. But I saw him almost always, once the work was done, go excuse himself for his outburst to the still shaken (even if the dressing-down took place three hours before) person. It's true that everyone is terrified. Romy Schneider herself confirmed it to me. But all recognize the well-foundedness of the Premingerian demands." Schneider told Douchet, "Preminger taught me an important thing: work fast. It's true that it greatly helps our acting. Each of his directions, whether of gesture or of intonation, is precise and correct. Even better: it's the only one possible."[21]

Douchet watched Preminger direct the scene in Cardinal Innitzer's residence in which Fermoyle reproaches Innitzer for his public support of Hitler, and Innitzer shows him a photograph of Fermoyle and Annemarie. In rehearsal, which lasted an hour and a half, Preminger at first paid little attention to the actors' line readings, concentrating mainly on their postures and gestures. For Douchet, Preminger brought to mind Bresson directing *Journal d'un curé de campagne*: both directors devoted "the same passionate attention to the interior movement that is betrayed by every posture. But where there [with Bresson] was nothing but endless hesitations, reticences, scruples, here I see precision, certitude, perfection." Preminger demonstrated "a dozen times" the movement with which he wanted Meinrad to produce the police report, holding it between thumb and index finger, "as naturally as a very careful businessman removes a price quotation from a dossier, a gesture whose everyday simplicity must, in such a situation, give an unnerving quality and a greater force to the blackmail . . . Meinrad doesn't isolate it enough. He links it to the general movement, he takes away its dry quality. The way Preminger plays it is better. Nevertheless, he doesn't insist. With Meinrad, this gesture becomes softer, slyer. It matches his physique and his voice. Preminger—far from trying to break the actor—seeks to bend him to his direction, but never contradicts his temperament."[22]

Preminger realized during the rehearsal that instead of shooting the scene in a single take, he would have to make some cutaways to Fermoyle. Douchet comments, "The position of the camera, with the orientation of the dolly, is decided in a second (in the fifteen shots made before me by the great Otto, I never saw him, not even for a moment, hesitate over the placement of his camera; and, each time, I noticed that it was the simplest, the most natural, and dramatically the best)."[23]

After Shamroy set his lights, Preminger ran another rehearsal and then shot the scene. Twenty takes were needed, wrote Douchet. "Each phrase, each word, each syllable are minutely weighed. Preminger hates nothing as much as an intonation that pushes or insists. Everything must slide in a neutral manner, as in an amiable salon conversation, but with just that small intensity that betrays, beneath the disengaged tone, how much each character feels involved."[24] "He was a great director, but also very strict," Josef Meinrad later said of Preminger.[25]

While in Austria, the company shot at the monastery in Dürnstein. Gerry O'Hara remembered answering a summons to Tryon's dressing room to find the star in tears. "He was standing in front of a roaring fire, literally shivering! And he said, 'Gerry, I can't do it, I can't take it any more.'" O'Hara returned to Preminger to inform him, gently, that he had "overdone it this time." Preminger replied, "Go back to Tom and tell him I will not shout at him today. I will be very kind to him today. All day I will not raise my voice." O'Hara coaxed Tryon back onto the set, where for the next few hours at least Preminger was as good as his word.[26]

After four and a half weeks in Austria, the production finished in Schönbrunn Park on Saturday, April 13, and moved to Rome. There, Preminger shot at Saint Peter's Square, inside Saint Peter's Cathedral, and in the Santa Maria sopra Minerva church. Raf Vallone, cast as a bishop, appreciated the presence of actual priests and monks as extras in scenes of church ceremonies. "I gave a benediction," he said, "and when I saw the expressions of the priests I knew that for them it was real, and it became real for me." For one scene, Vallone recalled, Preminger called for "75 takes! For a scene where Tryon is walking. Finally he is getting the idea of his monologue. All *I* have to do is agree once. And I think, my God, now *I'll* start to make mistakes."[27]

In Italy, Tryon collapsed. By then he was taking vitamin injections by day and sleeping pills at night. An Italian doctor diagnosed his condition as nervous exhaustion and prescribed two days of rest. "How does he know?" Preminger was heard to object. "Someone get the American doctor and let's see what he has to say." Nevertheless, after this incident, according to Gerry O'Hara, Preminger eased up somewhat on Tryon.[28]

Ossie Davis, who started work on the film in Rome, liked Preminger, with whom he developed "a marvelous relationship."

During the filming, I met actors whom Otto liked, I met actors that had no relationship or no feelings one way or the other, and I met actors who were almost absolutely destroyed. They really almost literally were in panic because of Otto Preminger . . . Otto, it seemed to me, was always looking for a spark in whomever he met. And he never stopped looking. Whether you had the spark or not didn't matter, he was going to find it and even put it in you. He would pull aside whoever you were, your identity, your persona, and, move that nonsense, and—give me some fire, give me something. Evidently, what I had as a performer, as a person, satisfied Otto's need for that spark.[29]

Having shot in and around Rome for two and a half weeks, the production returned to Hollywood at the beginning of May. Here the Georgia scenes were shot on parts of the Universal back lot that had recently been used for *To Kill a Mockingbird*. Grady Sutton (who had appeared in *A Royal Scandal*) was engaged to play the southern Catholic priest. Tryon recalled, "I walked in and Otto was screaming and Grady was shaking like a leaf; his voice had gone real high. We were in this little room and by ten o'clock it was sweltering. We got up to lunch and they dismissed us. An hour later they came around and said, 'You can take some extra time for lunch. We won't be shooting until two.' I came back on the set to finish the scene and there was Chill Wills in a clerical collar. I said, 'Good God! What are you doing here?' He said, 'They let Grady go.' "[30]

For the scene in which Stephen is whipped by Ku Klux Klan members, Tryon claimed, "They literally flayed the skin off my back and shoulders. Otto kept saying, 'He's got enough skin left. Ve do one more take!' "[31]

Patrick O'Neal, cast as the apparent leader of the southern racists, had a better experience with Preminger. "When I began work on *The Cardinal*," the actor said, "sure I was nervous and scared, so Otto started out on me, but I stood my ground. I would not take it from him. Afterwards he gave me a lift back to Hollywood in his limousine and we drove around in the hills and ended up talking till dawn."[32] Preminger hired O'Neal again for *In Harm's Way*.

The Cardinal was edited at Shepperton. Postproduction was completed in August. The PCA approved the film on September 23.

Tryon recalled, "After the Paris premiere of *The Cardinal*, the whole cast went to Maxim's to celebrate. I happened to be sitting in the bar with Jean Seberg. Preminger had hurt her, too. We were commiserating with each other. He followed us to the bar and screamed: 'I know you're talking about me. Get back to the party.' "[33]

After *The Cardinal*, Tryon later recalled, "I was feeling a great malaise, a great dissatisfaction. I had done *The Cardinal*. Finally, I was in a position of being able to pick my roles. But I didn't like the movie. I didn't like me in the movie. To this day, I cannot look at that film . . . About four years later, after more of Preminger [on *In Harm's Way*], I shut the door on acting and started writing . . . When I became a successful writer, Preminger went to a party and said to mutual friends: 'I'm responsible for Tom Tryon's success. I was so mean that he had to give up acting. He owes me. He should say "thank you." ' It took me years to forgive him. I could only forgive him when I saw the humor of his arrogance."[34]

The Cardinal opened in the United States in December 1963 and received lukewarm reviews, many of them criticizing Tryon's acting. Yet Tryon's performance, so often criticized as wooden and inadequate, seems to me ideal. If *The Cardinal* is one of Preminger's greatest films, it is also, inevitably, one of his most underappreciated, since the same things that make it great also make it resist appreciation. Much of the tension of *The Cardinal* comes from the mystery of its central character—a mystery that also involves Preminger's view of the character and his relationship with his actor. Guarded rather than extroverted or emotionally compelling, Tryon comes off as uncomfortable and stiff, without by any means achieving the withdrawn and sharply edged elegance of a Bressonian model. Tryon conveys above all a certain inability to inhabit the film that, if one rises above standard dismissals of "bad acting," is an eloquent way of articulating Stephen's dilemma. As Preminger said to Eyquem and Comte, "I do believe that the reason that he really never succeeds in the film is in a certain weakness in his character." The "he" of whom Preminger speaks could be either Tom Tryon or Stephen Fermoyle; and the film only really makes sense once we perceive that it is, in fact, both: that Tryon *is* Fermoyle and that Preminger's direction of Tryon was driven, perhaps unconsciously, by the fusion of the two figures in his mind into a single embodiment of male inadequacy.

The film is highly critical of Stephen when he refuses to permit the doctor to save Mona's life, as it is critical of him in the other key scene

with his sister, the scene of her confession. In both scenes, Stephen
refers a decision affecting his sister's life to Church dogma in order to
avoid having to make a personal moral decision. In view of this abdication, his later statement to Cardinal Glennon that he wishes to avoid
responsibility over life and death betrays an immense lack of self-
knowledge. In fact, he has never exercised responsibility over life and
death; he has refused it, and that, for the film, for Preminger, is Stephen's sin.

Yet the film undercuts its own criticism of Stephen by making the
disapproval of the doctor and the nurse so stark. By showing the doctor's
contempt for Stephen and the fierce anger in the nurse's look as she
closes the double doors in his face while wheeling Mona in to surgery,
Preminger makes it more difficult for us simply to reject Stephen's
stance. The stylized performance of the actor playing the doctor, raising
an eyebrow as he says coolly, "I take it this is some kind of religious scru-
ple," distances his attitude from us.

Conversely, although the survival of Mona's baby daughter might
have served as a retrospective justification of Stephen, the character
later functions merely as a symbolic compensation, and the lines of dialogue devoted to considering her (at the New York pier, in a brief transitional scene between Stephen's departure from Rome and his arrival in
Georgia) are utterly conventional and handled without flair or conviction. Thus Preminger alludes to, but makes it difficult to assent to, a
possible vision of the case that would uphold Stephen's sacrifice of
Mona to Catholic dogma on the ground that it resulted in a new human
life. "Having her around has made it easier for me to accept God's will,"
says Stephen's mother. He chimes in, "Seeing her now has made it easier for me." Preminger clearly does not expect these lines, which are spoken blandly in one of the film's typical medium shots as a perfunctory
way of wrapping up a short transition scene, to convince us. Nor is the
irony of the scene meant to be contemptuous of the characters. Rather,
a purely formal mechanism, arising out of Preminger's relative uninvolvement with the characters at this point in the script, further distances Stephen from the audience and marks the passage of time in a
way that could not be more economical and brutal. At the end of the
film, Regina is merely one of the unnamed family members lined up to
screen left of Stephen's mother, all tiny, mute figures in long shot, to witness Stephen's apotheosis. (Given Preminger's well-known frugality, his

insistence on flying his American actors to Rome just for this is reveal-ing: it shows the importance he attached to the embodiment of history, of the past of the film, that the mere physical presence of the actors is able and sufficient to bring.)

The fear of responsibility, as dramatized for him by Mona's death, drives Stephen to seek to leave the priesthood. "I don't challenge the rules," he tells Glennon. "I just don't want to be the one to enforce them. Not for anybody's sister. I don't want the power over other people's lives. I can't face the responsibility, that's what it really comes down to. I sit in the confessional, listening to someone tell his sins, and I'm the one who's trembling in terror." Power is again, as with *Advise & Consent*, the main theme of the film: power, openly exercised or held in check (the functioning of power in the Church is illuminated when Innitzer, resist-ing to the end Stephen's diplomatic efforts to get him to cease his public support for Hitler, asks for a direct order from the pope on the matter). For Stephen, all personal problems are inevitably unresolvable; he can act confidently only on the large stage of mass movements. The first half of the film is meant not to show, but to hide—not to explain, but to ren-der mysterious.

Stephen is an empty sign, a medium, a commutator, representing no fixed value and standing for no determinate content. He is in the process of becoming, yet for us he never goes through this process but appears to leap over it, reappearing on the other side. The dissolves back and forth between Stephen's investiture and the flashbacks stand for this mysterious process in which nothing is seen to happen. The dissolves don't so much evoke time in its passage as destroy time, deprive the viewer of it, accentuating the hero's movement away from the viewer.

Appropriately, the dissolve takes on its highest importance in Prem-inger's cinema at the moment when it is about to disappear from that cinema entirely. (*In Harm's Way* still has numerous dissolves, but as a structural device the dissolve is diminished in importance; in *Bunny Lake Is Missing* and *Hurry Sundown* there are no dissolves.) Saul Bass's titles sequence for *The Cardinal*, with its multitudinous dissolves, cre-ates an effect of veils and veils of time dissolving, immersing us in a past neither remote nor close, but rather, set adrift, without reference to a specific historical moment (until, after the end of the credits, graffiti on a wall make it clear that we are in Fascist Italy).

Though the narrative structure of *The Cardinal* imposes a horizon of consciousness—Stephen's, during the ceremony in which he is made cardinal—that encompasses the events of the past, Preminger's cinema is one of ceaseless flow and alteration. The past is seen not as irreversible, but as always coming into being; the return to the present is not a sinking into finality, just as the reemergence of the past is not a repetition of the already finished; past and present are reversible and are in constant communication with each other.

The Cardinal is a film of displacement and transition. Throughout the film, Stephen is sent, or undertakes to go, from one place to another, and in his constant peregrinations he becomes a split person: he always has the alibi of somewhere else to go, something else to do. He himself characterizes this condition as a split between "priest" and "man." Two of the key scenes in the film—Mona's confession and Stephen's visit to Annemarie in the Nazi jail—reveal in a particularly stark way how Stephen switches to his priest role at the moment when a woman he loves, and who loves him, most needs him to be a "man."

In the scene of Mona's confession, she is in a truer position than Stephen. She is in tight close-up, he in medium close-up; her shots are held longer; her face is askew in the frame while his is upright; Lynley's acting is emotionally expressive, Tryon's restrained. Stephen's adoption of his "priest" role is unmistakably harsh. His voice is cruel and bitter as he instructs his sister: "Hard as it may be, you must give him up . . . You must stop these illicit relations immediately . . . What you've done is immoral, it's cheap." When she protests, "Steve!" he corrects her: "Father."

He finally relents before her pathetic "Help me, please help me," only to assume a worldly cynicism that is shockingly ill judged: he recites the Italian catchphrase *"L'amore fa passare il tempo, il tempo fa passare l'amore."* (Love makes time pass, time makes love pass.) As he speaks, Preminger cuts to a tight close-up of Mona's staring face. The shot underlines and criticizes Stephen's culture and intellectuality, which have been shown up before, though in a lighter manner, throughout the scenes with Monsignor Monaghan. Mona gives Stephen's banter the reply it deserves by reproducing the rote formula "For these and all other sins that I have committed I ask forgiveness" in a dulled and zombified manner that anticipates her final mimicry of Stephen from the hospital stretcher.

At the end of the film, Stephen's self-concealment before Annemarie's last vision of him is exactly comparable to his treatment of Mona in the confession booth. When Annemarie wants his love, Stephen switches to oratory, informing her that she is "not an ant in a totalitarian anthill but a human being, an individual, with a God-given soul of your own." As in the confession sequence, his speech is played over a close-up of Annemarie that enables us to register the inappropriateness of Stephen's discourse: he is not speaking to her, he is speaking over her (over her image), and her expression reflects the distance between them. Annemarie reacts as Mona did, following Stephen's lead by switching to a conventional, impersonal mode—"Thank you, Your Excellency, and goodbye"—but her last look at him, as she is being prodded from behind by the Gestapo guard, is filled with anger and reproach.

The two Vienna sections of the film constitute a peak in Preminger's cinema. The intensity of their realization undoubtedly reflects his personal involvement and his decision to make of *The Cardinal* an opportunity to come to terms with his Viennese past. Earlier in the film, the unsuccessful attempt to convert Benny, a Jew, to Catholicism has already made a clear reference to Preminger's biography. The first Vienna section takes place in 1924, as a superimposed title lets us know: that was the year of Preminger's first steps in the theater. In depicting the tragedy of Kurt and Annemarie von Hartmann, Preminger drew on the stories of people he knew, including philosopher (and, briefly, Reinhardt actor) Egon Friedell, who committed suicide for the same reason and in the same manner Kurt does, by jumping out a window when the Gestapo comes knocking at his door.

During the first Vienna section, a motif of windows and mirrors articulates the changing relationships among Stephen, Annemarie, and the camera. On their first outing together, the traveling camera remains outside a café as Stephen and Annemarie go inside: the camera moves to frame a large window, through which we see the two sit down. This section of the film concludes with Annemarie returning to the same café and looking through the same window at Stephen in his priest's costume, rising from a chair as he notices her. The window serves as a screen (as does the dissolve): we have direct access to Annemarie's face (Preminger cuts to a close-up of her reaction), but Stephen is visible only imperfectly, through the window. After she turns and walks away, Preminger cuts to a close shot of Stephen, the camera now inside the café with him.

In the ballroom scene, the out-of-focus reflection of the dance floor in a large, ornate mirror (out of focus because the focus is set for Stephen's entrance into the shot), a flow of liquid colors and forms filling the screen, ideally registers Stephen's alienation in this worldly environment as a visual dissonance: he literally cannot see the scene before him. Later, returning to his room, his view of himself in a mirror, dressed in top hat and cape, seems to arrest him. It is the incongruousness of this vision that causes him to remove his priest's suit from the wardrobe and drape it over the mirror, largely covering it. The covering-over of the mirror echoes what Stephen has said earlier: "I'm a priest, Annemarie, but I'm also a man. Men can show their feelings, but a priest has to learn how to hide them." The mirror represents the visible show of feelings—not directly, but by reflecting the situation of people in the world and placing this world against them (as does the mirror in the ballroom behind Stephen). Stephen's decision to withdraw from this state of visibility is registered in the next scene in his retreat behind the glass window of the café.

The beautiful shot of Stephen and Annemarie dancing away from the camera to become absorbed among the couples on the dance floor is the complement to the shot of Stephen emerging from the deep background at St. John's Church to preside over the crowd at the miracle of the leaking pipe. Later, Annemarie repeats the movement away from the camera—but this time she is alone—when she turns and walks away through the outdoor tables of the café. Always, what's crucial to Preminger is the time the movement takes—just as, in the Georgia sequence, the slow emergence of the black people into the wide frame—which has been left empty by the Klan's kidnapping of Stephen—registers not merely as a proscenium stage–like effect, but more precisely as the use of the film frame in a proscenium-like manner in order to convey a particular clash of rhythms and a sense of delay.

In the scene of Stephen's final meeting with Annemarie, who is now a prisoner of the Nazis, the force of the cut to a tight close-up of her face between two prison bars ("No, let me speak, please") underlines the terrible urgency and impersonality of the rush of time—a movement that now becomes the dominant fact of the film (just as, at the end of *Exodus*, there is no time to properly bury and mourn Taha and Karen). With her unceremonious "Goodbye," the dissolve that takes Annemarie away from Stephen and from us starts already, removing her face from the screen more quickly than we expect and returning us to the ritual of Stephen's becoming cardinal.

The use of the Panavision screen in *The Cardinal* is magnificent. In the scene in which Stephen tells Cardinal Glennon that he has decided to leave the priesthood, the low angle initially frames Stephen so that his head is at the juncture of two walls and a ceiling, expressing the crisis at which he finds himself, which his decision is an attempt to resolve, while his shadow is projected on a dark wood door at the right of the frame, tensely balancing his figure (at left). As he goes on to explain his decision, he paces back and forth, and in the same low-angle shot, the dark wood molding between the white ceiling and the white wall creates a bold line stretching across the middle of the screen behind Stephen's head, delineating his internal conflict. Finally, he sits tensely on a bench at the left edge of the frame, as if, since he can't vanish from the space altogether, the next best thing were to take up as little room in it as possible.

Live sound also plays a highly effective role in *The Cardinal*. In the hospital sequence, the insistence of natural sounds enforces an awareness of intractable and dismal physical reality while also contributing to the sense that Stephen has entered into a space where he is an outsider. During the encounter of Stephen, Frank, and Benny with the doctor in the reception room, the regular sound of typing continues throughout. Then, as Stephen tries to lead Mona in prayer before her surgery, we hear a random clatter of metal and glass objects, dull thuds, water running, voices, the whole culminating in the bang of a reflector lamp being switched on in the operating room in the background of the shot.

Though Andrew Sarris's characterization of Preminger as "a director who sees all problems and issues as a single-take two shot"[35] has been widely accepted as definitive, much of *The Cardinal* in fact consists of dialogue between two people filmed in shot/reverse shot. In the first sequence with Cardinal Glennon, a lengthy dialogue takes place between Glennon and Stephen across the cardinal's desk; Preminger films the two in separate frontal shots. Then, when Glennon rises and walks around the desk toward Stephen—a movement that coincides with the growing pointedness with which Glennon questions Stephen's motives—the camera pulls back, and a long take (about two and a half minutes) ensues. Here, the shot and reverse-shot technique is used when the situation is relatively conventional and comfortable for Stephen; the long take is a crucible of tension, culminating in Glennon's forcing Stephen to admit that he thinks "there is more in [himself] than being a mere parish priest."

The world revealed by *The Cardinal* contains heterogeneous and discordant elements: Preminger does not attempt to resolve all these elements in a unity but wants some of them to stick out, to remain inharmonious and irrecuperable. Responding to the mise-en-scène of Catholicism, Preminger's own mise-en-scène shows the constructed nature of a reality from which only its victims can escape by being destroyed. The alienness of Bobby and His Adora-Belles (the singing and dancing group whose boisterous performance of "They Haven't Got the Girls in the U.S.A." Stephen endures while searching for Mona) is this film's equivalent to the sudden eruption of the Zombies into the world of *Bunny Lake Is Missing*: in both scenes, the discordant musical element is introduced by a camera that travels forward, leaving behind the main characters and their narrative. Mona's emotion at the confessional pierces through the film, just as her screams pierce Stephen's mind when he finds her in labor in the boardinghouse and when she is wheeled away from him into the hospital operating room. Kurt's suicide—as stunning a moment as any Preminger ever staged—is an irrecuperable moment par excellence: an act performed with a perfect, premeditated smoothness, consistent with the fluidity and superficiality of the social world Preminger depicts, yet, by its finality, constituting a rupture within this world and exposing (this is its meaning and purpose) the rupture at the heart of reality that anti-Semitism represents.

29

Never Give Up

When the Japanese attacked Pearl Harbor, journalist James Bassett was serving as a lieutenant in the navy. During the war, he became public relations officer for Admiral William F. "Bull" Halsey's Third Fleet. Like Allen Drury, Bassett was a right-wing Republican; he worked for Richard Nixon during the 1950s and was planning director for Nixon's 1960 presidential campaign. For his novel *Harm's Way*, a fictionalized account of the Pacific war, Bassett drew on some of his own experiences and based his main character, Rockwell Torrey, on Admiral Halsey. The book was sent to Preminger in manuscript. Preminger announced his purchase of the rights in October 1962.

Bassett's *Harm's Way* resembles Drury's *Advise and Consent*: another long novel with many characters and subplots, through which the author analyzes the inner workings of a large and powerful institution. At the start of the narrative, Torrey, a career navy officer with the rank of captain, is commanding a cruiser near Pearl Harbor. When the Japanese attack, Torrey obeys an order to seek and engage the enemy, but his cruiser is torpedoed, and he is forced to return to base. Relieved of command after the disaster, Torrey is assigned to staff duty, during which he becomes romantically involved with a navy nurse, Lieutenant Maggie Haynes. Recognizing Torrey's qualities, the new commander in chief of the Pacific Fleet (CINCPAC) promotes him to rear admiral and puts him in command of a stalled operation to seize some strategically important islands held by the Japanese. After the first phase of Torrey's operation meets with success, he turns his attention to the operation's main target, the heavily fortified island of Levu-Vana. Torrey's chief of staff, Commander Paul Eddington, whose inner demons and troubled relationships with women have fueled a subplot, determines during a suicidal reconnaissance flight that a Japanese flotilla including the dreaded battleship *Yamato* is headed toward Levu-Vana. Torrey engages the Japanese and suffers heavy losses, but the *Yamato* turns back, and Torrey's operation is deemed a decisive victory.

Explaining his attraction to the material, Preminger articulated a point to which he would return ten years later with *Rosebud*: "So many movies made recently have a terribly pessimistic outlook on our future. It seems that the only way out for us is to give in to almost any kind of demand, or blackmail, or whatever you want to call it . . . Perhaps this story of an attack—we are attacked, we are unprepared in every way, and manage by sheer guts, character, and resourcefulness to start to work out of it—should remind us and perhaps other people that there is never any reason to give up or to give in to anything that is not right or dignified."[1]

Preminger hired Wendell Mayes to write the script. "I wrote the first screenplay, when Otto was in Europe, without him at all," Mayes said, "and then I went to London and started to do a rewrite, and Otto shelved the project. And then I believe it was about maybe two years later that the picture began and [I] had a fresher point of view and did many things that were not in the book at all. And I think we improved it for that reason, since we had quite forgotten the novel."[2] During the hiatus between Mayes's first draft and his return to the project, another writer, Richard Jessup, also worked on the project, but the final screenplay is entirely Mayes's. The work was more exacting than on Mayes and Preminger's previous collaborations, *Anatomy of a Murder* and *Advise & Consent*. "Particularly on this picture," Preminger said, "we sat together and worked almost every line over." They developed the character of Jere, Torrey's estranged son, a figure "which didn't really exist in the book. He was a completely innocuous boy, who just met the father and they immediately became friends; he had no feelings about the fact that his father had left his mother 18 years ago, and we changed that in the script."[3]

Casting Torrey posed no problems. "I never offered the part to anybody else" but John Wayne, Preminger said, although, according to Mayes, the script had been written without any actor in mind.[4] Nevertheless, Wayne's casting ought to have been easy to predict from Bassett's story: Torrey's estrangement from his wife and their son's surprise enlistment in the navy against his mother's wishes are precise recollections of John Ford's *Rio Grande* (1950), which starred Wayne as a cavalry colonel. Preminger sent Wayne an incomplete draft of the script, and Wayne phoned to accept the part. His casting was announced in February 1964. "I think because it has passive elements that a strong actor like Wayne is ideally cast," said Preminger.[5] Wayne got $500,000 to do the film.

Originally, the film was to be made at Columbia, but on January 10, 1964, Preminger signed a seven-film contract with Paramount and took *Harm's Way* with him as the first film in the deal. Preminger renamed it *In Harm's Way*, strengthening the link to John Paul Jones's famous phrase, "I wish to have no connection with any ship that does not sail fast, for I intend to go in harm's way." Mayes's first full script was ready by mid-March 1964. Preminger lined up the rest of his stars: Kirk Douglas in the secondary but rewarding part of Eddington; Patricia Neal as Maggie; Dana Andrews (working again with Preminger for the first time since *Where the Sidewalk Ends*) as the indecisive Admiral Broderick; Burgess Meredith and Franchot Tone as officers; Stanley Holloway as an Australian coastwatcher. To play Mac and Bev, a young married couple who are the protagonists of another subplot, Preminger exercised his option on Tom Tryon and signed Paula Prentiss. Carol Lynley was announced as the ill-fated Ensign Annalee Dorne, who commits suicide after becoming pregnant from her rape by Eddington, but the role would go to another Preminger alumna and contractee, Jill Haworth. Preminger sought Keir Dullea for Jere, but the actor turned down the part,[6] and Brandon de Wilde took the role.

From April 21 to 23, 1964, Preminger surveyed locations in Hawaii with art director Lyle Wheeler, director of photography Loyal Griggs, location manager Eva Monley, assistant director Daniel McCauley, and set decorator Richard Mansfield. Before leaving on this trip, Preminger was mentioned as one of six directors commissioned to do a series of ninety-minute TV specials dramatizing the work of the United Nations. Peter Stone was to write the script for Preminger's episode, "a light treatment of the language problem at the U.N." The other directors named were Stanley Kubrick, Robert Rossen, Joseph L. Mankiewicz, Peter Glenville, and Fred Zinnemann.[7]

Preminger decided to shoot *In Harm's Way* in black and white. "A picture like this has much more impact and you can create more of the feeling, the illusion of reality, than when you shoot it in color."[8] Since no ships that were afloat in 1941 were available, the production used newer ships and dressed them with false gun mounts.

On June 11 Geoffrey Shurlock gave the okay to the script, objecting only to some dialogue, including excessive "hells," a "son of a bitch," and the phrases "screw the captain" and "blew his ass off." Preminger removed "blew his ass off" but kept "screw the captain," spoken by Tom Tryon early in the film. The line became a sticking point when the finished film was submitted for the Seal, and on February 8, 1965, the PCA withheld its approval pending removal of the line. Preminger remained firm, and on March 9 the Seal was granted.

On June 18, 1964, Preminger and his staff took over the second floor of the new Ilikai Hotel in the Waikiki yacht harbor. Shooting started on Makapuu Beach on June 23 with scenes of Eddington's wife, Liz (newcomer Barbara Bouchet) and her lover, an air force officer played by Hugh O'Brian. The fact that Bouchet was topless (though photographed from behind) during one of the scenes enabled Preminger to secure coverage from *Playboy*, which published a color pictorial on the scene in its May 1965 issue. (Bouchet's stunning looks—later to grace many Italian genre movies—would be a major theme of the film's publicity campaign.)

At the end of the first week, on June 28, Ted Masters reported to Frank Caffey at Paramount that during the night-for-night shooting, drivers repeatedly got lost and were late getting to locations. "Transportation costs are fantastic." As shooting continued, more problems developed. On July 9 Masters notified Caffey, "Hear rumors that 10 days have been dropped from schedule. Understand he is on schedule but he has to be over budget due to the long hours, extra local help, crews working Sundays. Cannot find in the budget any allowances for that kind of conditions." Masters noted that a second unit had twice failed to get a shot of a car going over a cliff, that a second-unit shot of a marine landing was spoiled by water on the lens (the marine landing was eventually omitted from the film), and that Preminger had twice failed (because of technical difficulties) to get a "mystic-hour shot" of a plane ready for takeoff.[9]

On July 21 Preminger made the first attempt at one of the most spectacular shots in the film—a sedan carrying an admiral (played elsewhere in the film by Franchot Tone, though this particular shot surely used a stand-in) weaving down a street as bombs explode around. Because the camera truck delayed too long at one point, Preminger ordered the scene redone.

A writer working on a Preminger profile for *McCall's* visited the evening shoot of the aftermath of an air raid and watched as Preminger exploded at an assistant director. Seeing the writer staring, Preminger turned to him and said, in a normal voice, "Did I yell loud enough? I did it all for you." Preminger proceeded to badger the same assistant director, as well as others in the crew and the bit players and extras appearing in the scene. "As Otto made them do the scene over and over again, the feeling of panic came close to the surface. Perhaps that was what he wanted." As was his custom, Preminger rehearsed the actors before each scene "as long as necessary. There is no limit. Time is expensive and naturally in the back of one's mind; one cannot completely eliminate it, but I've educated myself just to forget it. Otherwise the whole thing becomes hurried and silly. I could make every picture ten days shorter if I slough it. Some actors just need more time and more rehearsal and some don't."[10]

Preminger found Wayne "the most cooperative actor, willing to rehearse, willing to do anything as long as anybody. I was surprised really how disciplined a professional Wayne is, and he liked this particular part very much." According to Max Slater (working as usual as Preminger's dialogue director), Wayne "never argued with Preminger. He took correction and direction. He listened to Otto's suggestions and followed them." Years later, Wayne had praise for Preminger. "He had my respect and I had his respect. He is terribly hard on the crew, and he's terribly hard on people that he thinks are sloughing. But this is a thing that I can understand because I've been there and I know that if a fellow comes on and he's careless and he hasn't thought at all about his . . . I come ready and that he appreciated. I was usually there ahead of him on the set, and he couldn't believe that. So we really had a nice relationship."[11]

Though the star had been pronounced fit at his medical checkup before the start of production, many on the film perceived that there was clearly something wrong with his health. "He *looked* ill," said Tom Tryon. "He was coughing badly. I mean, *really* awful. It was painful to see and hear, so God knows what it was like for him. He'd begin coughing and he wouldn't stop, and it sounded just horrendous. He'd begin coughing in the middle of a scene and Preminger would have to stop filming. If it was anyone else, Preminger would have yelled some kind of abuse at him, but he never yelled at Duke."[12] Pilar Wayne, who accompanied her husband to Hawaii, recalled that Wayne's coughing "began to interrupt the shooting, and soon everyone was aware of his deteriorating health— everyone but him. He refused to see a doctor while we were on the island."[13]

Kirk Douglas recalled, "[Preminger] never treated me badly on the set, and he didn't treat Wayne badly, but he was cruel to Tom Tryon. Just unendingly cruel. He would come right up to Tom and scream until he was spitting saliva."[14] Once, Douglas recalled, Preminger's cruelty to Tryon was so extreme that Douglas walked off the set. Douglas advised Tryon to yell back at Preminger and tell him he could fire him if he chose ("he's got to finish the picture"), but Tryon, just as on *The Cardinal*, was incapable of standing up to the director. Douglas said, "I never liked Otto after that. Once, he raised his voice in a nasty way toward me. I walked over to him, nose to nose. In a very low voice, I said, 'Are you talking to me?' That was the end of it. He never insulted me again . . . I didn't think Otto was a very good director."[15] Larry Hagman said that Preminger "made everyone so overwrought and anxious they screwed up, including me."[16]

Cast as the repellent Commander Owynn, Patrick O'Neal, on his second film for Preminger, defended the director to his detractors. "I remember in Hawaii, Jill Haworth and Tom [Tryon] and Paula Prentiss would huddle together on the set, yakking about how terrible Otto was. It got to be a big bore. They'd ask me, 'How is *he* today?' and to bug them I'd say '*Who?*' Once I told them, 'If your life means anything to you, you'll stand up to him once and find out he's a human being.' "[17]

Henry Fonda was a last-minute replacement for Chill Wills in the role of "CINCPAC II," a part equivalent to Admiral Chester W. Nimitz, who was put in command of the Pacific Fleet after Pearl Harbor. According to Tryon, "Preminger was at his absolute worst" in directing Wills, who tried to keep his dignity: "Mr. Preminger, my name is Chill Wills and I'm an actor. I've been in 144 movies; I have been acting for 42 years, and you are making me shake." Preminger fired Wills on the spot, Tryon said, and brought in Fonda the next morning.[18]

According to Tryon, Preminger "started on Paula Prentiss during *In Harm's Way* and got her screaming" and out of anger at the actress, he finished with her earlier than anticipated, eliminating her unshot scenes.[19] Examination of the final shooting script shows that only one short scene involving Prentiss's character failed to make it into the finished film. In that scene, Mac returns home after the attack on Pearl Harbor to find Bev searching dazedly through the rubble of their bungalow for the set of china her mother gave them. Interviewed for this book, Prentiss had nothing but praise for Preminger, whom she recalled as "absolutely wonderful to work with. For a scene to work, tension needs to be put into the scene. There have to be genuine efforts to make the scene work. And Preminger understood this, and was able to get so much conflict and tension into the scenes . . . He was very powerful and very gentle, no matter what anyone said. He had a mask." Asked for an example of his gentleness, Prentiss said, "I was supposed to tell Tom I was pregnant. [In fact, the scene called for Prentiss's character to ask her husband to make her pregnant.] Preminger told me about his wife's pregnancy; she'd been pregnant with twins. And that was so human, and that was all I needed to play the scene."[20]

On August 8 the unit left for Seattle. On August 10 they boarded the USS *St. Paul* (representing the *Columbia*) for five days of shooting at sea, accompanied by the admiral whose flagship it was. For Kirk Douglas, the trip was "the most exciting thing about the production . . . There was Otto Preminger . . . treating the personnel like his own personal crew, the boat like a prop, yelling to the captain, in his German accent, 'Push the boat the other vey, so ve get the sunlight!' "[21] Navy brass involved with the production took to calling the director Admiral Preminger. The *Los Angeles Times* reported that "for one key scene three destroyers and a cruiser were assigned to ride at anchor as background. They were 500 yards apart but Preminger wanted them closer. Navy personnel objected that they would collide but Otto insisted and the ships were moved closer."[22]

The cruiser arrived in Pearl Harbor on August 15. On August 20 Preminger finished in Hawaii—seventeen days ahead of the proposed schedule from May—and went with Wayne to Los Angeles. On August 24 the company started several days of shooting in the studio on sets representing a ship's bridge, the interiors of airplanes, and a chart room. Preminger found time to shoot an introduction to a seven-minute featurette intended for Paramount's international sales, merchandising, and marketing executives. (The scene shows Preminger addressing the executives from the engine room of a burning ship.) After Wayne finished work on the film on August 31, Pilar persuaded him to get another checkup. This time, doctors detected lung cancer and removed his left lung. Wayne recovered and lived another fifteen years. Preminger boasted that his efficiency in shooting *In Harm's Way* may have saved Wayne's life, and in fact, Wayne's contract for the film ran to September 23, three weeks later than he was actually last used.

As of October 8, Paramount's cost on the film was $5,436,423—higher than the approved budget limit of $5 million. Process shots (of a PT boat and an airplane cockpit) were done in November. Preminger had larger-than-usual miniatures—35 to 55 feet long—built for the battle scenes. The miniatures were shot on a lake in Mexico and in the Laguna de Términos, a shallow bay on the Gulf of Mexico. "I needed the real horizon, you know, and I think that makes a lot of difference."[23] *Life* reported that it took one month to shoot the Battle of Leyte Gulf, at a cost of $1 million.[24] Wayne liked the film, especially his love scene with Neal ("I just thought that was great"), but he objected strongly to the miniatures and later felt they hurt the film with audiences. "There was no way to tell him . . . goddamn, he wanted to have his picture taken on all those miniatures."[25]

Editing and scoring took place in November and December. In March 1965 Preminger hosted five preview screenings of *In Harm's Way* for military personnel and others in Honolulu. At a reception at Camp Smith, he told the officers and journalists present, "*In Harm's Way* is not a war picture. It is a picture about people who are trapped in a war." He called it a film with a message: "Whatever the weapons that we are attacked with, there is always a way to defend yourself. The same ingenuity, the same human mind that invents these weapons must also be able to defend."[26]

In Harm's Way was released in the United States in April 1965. The largely negative critical reaction followed the lead of Bosley Crowther, who pronounced the film "cliché-crowded melodrama."[27] An unexpected defense came from *The New Yorker*'s Brendan Gill, who wrote, "The things that Mr. Preminger can do well (the suave convincingness of the settings and technical backgrounds, the zestful, hard-driving elucidation of complicated plots) he has never done better than in *In Harm's Way*, and the things he does badly (the manipulation of characters who feel things about as deeply as the Rover Boys, the immediate vulgarization of any idea that happens to smuggle its way into a script) have never mattered less."[28]

In Harm's Way was not a success. In 1973 a *Variety* article reported the film's domestic rentals at $3,850,000.[29] *Cahiers du cinéma*, which had championed the director since the early 1950s, got off Preminger's train at *In Harm's Way*, its largely negative review (by Jean-Louis Comolli) of the film apparently prompting the director to remark at Cannes (as *Cahiers* itself reported), "These young French critics praised me to the skies when I made bad films and won't have anything to do with me now that I make good ones."[30]

Indeed, *In Harm's Way* is one of Preminger's greatest achievements: a film of continual vivid excitement, a film in which one discovers a world. With *Exodus*, it is perhaps the Preminger film that has the most to communicate about the exhilaration of this discovery, the film that is most involved with movement and physicality, the encounter and resistance of objects in space. The camera movements, appropriate for surveying a wasteland or a world about to become one, are magisterial. The film's abstract, chilling beauty is more overpowering than even the mood of *Angel Face* or *Bonjour Tristesse*.

Throughout *In Harm's Way* what seems to make sense turns out to be contradictory and unclear. Torrey's decision to forgo evasive action and engage the attacking Japanese, seemingly a correct interpretation of his orders, leads to his being removed from command. Eddington's rape of Annalee is completely unexpected. Part of what makes *In Harm's Way* a film of its time is Preminger's refusal to mitigate the sense of violent contradiction. The mise-en-scène supports Preminger's tolerant, practical point of view, his acceptance of illogicality and chaos.

The film's exceptionally rich cast of stars of the past, present, and future is nothing but a fragmented and dispersed body that stands in for ours and that experiences, in our place, terrible destruction. This aspect of the film's corporeality is echoed in its emphasis on geography, e.g., the repeated image of a map of a handful of islands scattered in the Pacific Ocean.

The second section of the film, devoted to the period of inaction that the first CINCPAC describes as "the vacuum between a peacetime navy and a wartime navy," is characterized by the separation of Torrey, reduced to an office post in Hawaii, and Eddington, consigned to a small "filling station" on the island of Toulebonne. A turning point is the reuniting of Torrey and Eddington, a scene Preminger treats as a complex and self-contained mini-operation in itself. Eddington is driven in a jeep between two rows of men. Arriving at a pier, he boards a motorized launch that takes him to an amphibious plane, from which Torrey emerges to join him in the launch. The launch then changes direction and returns to the pier, where Torrey and Eddington are met by the marine paratroop commander Gregory (George Kennedy): the three get into the jeep, which drives away between the rows of men. It is a tremendous scene, completely without dialogue (Torrey and Eddington converse inaudibly, observed at a distance by the camera, which is mounted on its own boat). The meanings of the scene are conveyed visually (supported by Jerry Goldsmith's magnificent score). Preminger emphasizes the use of vehicles of three different types, not just to put movement on the screen for its own sake, but to detail how the navy technology functions to reunite two separated friends—also the two main stars of the film (thus their meeting fulfills a wish of the narrative and a wish that may be called inherent in the star system: the pleasure of seeing a film with John Wayne and Kirk Douglas comes partly from seeing them *together*)—in order to participate in the impending military operation. (The scene complements the earlier one of the two men's separation, Eddington being carried away on a barge while Torrey walks away on a pier, and momentarily resolves the tension of loss that was then created.) In showing the conquest of space by technology, the scene functions as a metaphor for cinema and as an emblem for the film *In Harm's Way*, whose narrative spans disparate locations that are linked through cutting.

The functioning of technology also serves the verisimilitude of the film, contributing to a dense and intricate impression of reality. Much of this comes from the sound track. When "general quarters" is called on *Old Swayback* after the first sighting of Japanese planes, the ensuing rush by the crew to their battle stations is accompanied by a variety of sounds: bugle, sirens, whistles, bells, beeps.

Certain shots devoted to the complex coordination of movements are as brilliant and exciting as anything in Preminger's work. During the Pearl Harbor attack, the shots of the first CINCPAC's sedan speeding through the streets and arriving at the base, as chaos erupts on all sides, are magnificent. The great nighttime crane shot of Torrey, his arm in a sling, disembarking from *Old Swayback* on a stairway, while men repair the ship with soldering tools that send sparks flying in the background of the shot, is perhaps the most beautiful of the film's many beautiful shots: Wayne's solitary descent has a Fordian nobility and grace (though there's no warrant for assuming that when he conceived of this shot, Preminger was thinking specifically of *The Wings of Eagles*), but the workers' indifference to Torrey's departure creates a purely Premingerian effect of destinies detaching from each other in an unfolding space.

The shot of Torrey leaving the ship expresses both an authorial attitude and the attitude of the character. The authorial attitude may be summed up in the idea "it continues"—the ship is being repaired, it will sail again under a new captain, while Torrey (whose departure is unnoticed by the work crew) will move on to other responsibilities and an independent fate. The attitude of the character is one of resignation and self-abnegation in the face of his superiors' edict: the visible tension in the relationship between the figure and the background expresses Torrey's denial of emotion. This purely visual dynamic becomes ascribed to the character as an emotional-psychological quality; we perceive the tension as belonging to Torrey as part of his experience of the event.

The impression of reality that *In Harm's Way* achieves with such dexterity and control is compromised by a reliance (greater than in any other Preminger film except *Skidoo*) on special effects. In some shots of *Old Swayback* sustaining attack, smoke is obviously superimposed on the image; finally, there are the miniatures to which John Wayne objected, clearly identifiable as miniatures from the scale of the ships to the waves. The sense of unreality introduced by the superimposed smoke actually adds to the chaotic, unpredictable, threatening quality of the battle scenes. As for the miniatures, Preminger uses them mainly as poetic images rather than seeking to compel belief in them. The lap dissolves of ships sliding slowly forward through fog seem suspended in timelessness rather than forming part of the diegetic reality of the film; they belong to an alternate, symbolic space, and thus they resemble the magisterial end-credits sequence, an abstract visual poem not controlled by the narrative. Yet the ships are not cartoons. They are real ships, though clearly less than full size, and thus they belong to the photographic realism of the film.

In *In Harm's Way*, a certain compression in the handling of the narrative becomes apparent: Preminger and Mayes (following, to some extent, Bassett) contrive to meet the requirements of their multiple plots with a screenwriting economy that is dangerously close to being transparent. (The same could be said of the moment in *Advise & Consent* when the President dies in the middle of the Senate confirmation vote.) Yet they also use the overriding and impersonal imperative of the war effort to justify their economy, which thus serves as an element of verisimilitude as well as a formal and structural element. After breaking the news of Annalee's suicide to Jere, Torrey tries hesitantly to affirm the bond between him and his son: "This may not be the right time, but, somehow it seems that between—well, there ought to be some, uh . . ." Jere replies, "I know what you mean, sir. I wouldn't know how to say it myself. But I know what you mean." The introduction of the father-son theme at the very moment when the Jere-Annalee story reaches its climax may seem rather bald, but Preminger and Mayes get away with it by baring the device with Torrey's words, "This may not be the right time."

Timeliness and untimeliness are major concerns of the film. Broderick's delay on Gavabutu erodes the "element of surprise" that is the U.S. Navy's potential advantage over the Japanese. Maggie warns Annalee, "It gets late fast in these times." Meeting Torrey again on Gavabutu after a period of separation, Maggie asks, "Will there be time for us out here?" and he replies, "We'll make time, Maggie." The pacing of the film, driven by the editing, reflects the concern with time: much of the film is characterized by a leisurely flow of scenes linked by dissolves, or by fades out and in; in the later sections of the film, straight cuts join scenes unceremoniously and urgently, telescoping time (as in the scenes devoted to the revelation of Annalee's suicide and Eddington's suicide mission).

In Harm's Way is notable for the most positive view of love in any Preminger film. The honesty, maturity, and humor Torrey and Maggie display as they become involved with each other are admirable; one feels that Preminger's respect and affection for these two people are unclouded. Already, with Munson and Dolly in *Advise & Consent*, Preminger had offered a glimpse of the kind of model middle-aged couple formed in *In Harm's Way*. Mac and Bev provide another, less striking, example of love and loyalty and of how they are strengthened by the terrors and pressures of war.

"The absence of God helps man." Preminger's films bear out Hölderlin's dictum, and Preminger's optimism is a sensibility capable of taking the measure of such help. The pull toward consensus that can be felt in *Exodus*, *Advise & Consent*, *In Harm's Way*, and *Hurry Sundown* is the phenomenon of this absence in its positive, humanistic aspect; the images of dispersion, destruction, and absolute otherness in these films are its negative aspect. In no other Preminger film is the negative so shattering as in *In Harm's Way*, but in no other film is the positive so reassuring.

30

Organized Agitation

Of all Preminger's films, except perhaps *Saint Joan, Bunny Lake Is Missing* had the longest gestation period. After buying the rights to the novel by Merriam Modell (who published it under the pseudonym Evelyn Piper), Preminger announced the film for production in early 1959. At that time he planned to follow the novel in setting the story in New York, where he intended to shoot the film.

The story is a variation on the old Paris Exposition plot, in which a person reports the disappearance of another person, whose existence proves, on investigation, impossible to establish. Hitchcock's *The Lady Vanishes* used such a plot, and it appeared in something close to its pure form in the 1950 film *So Long at the Fair*, directed by Terence Fisher. The heroine of Modell's novel is Blanche Lake, a young woman who, on coming to pick up her three-year-old daughter, Bunny, from her first day at nursery school, finds that the girl has disappeared without a trace. Blanche goes to the police, who start inquiries, but her story is not believed: no one at the school can be found who ever saw Bunny, and the girl's name is not on the enrollment list. Blanche is unable to provide any evidence that Bunny even exists, and Blanche's erratic behavior calls her sanity into question. A psychiatrist, Newhouse, and his friend Wilson take an interest in the attractive Blanche and try to help her. It turns out that Bunny was kidnapped by a former teacher at the school who, childless and suffering from "menopausal psychosis," targeted the vulnerable Blanche and her daughter.

Ira Levin (whose psychological thriller *A Kiss Before Dying*, another story involving an out-of-wedlock pregnancy, Preminger had considered as a project for Fox in 1953) wrote the first script for *Bunny Lake Is Missing*, which was "very much like the book," Preminger said, but *Exodus* edged out *Bunny Lake* in Preminger's schedule. The main cause of Preminger's dissatisfaction with Levin's script lay in its fidelity to the novel's denouement. "The original book has a very weak solution," Preminger said. "The solution is OK, but the character who commits the crime is very weak and uninteresting."

Preminger turned to Dalton Trumbo for a fresh approach. The writer completed a draft of a screenplay in New York in early 1961. In Trumbo's script, the villain is a wealthy woman who, unable to have a child of her own and judged morally unfit to adopt, arranges with the school to kidnap Bunny. This version was "very theatrical and wrong," said Preminger,[1] and Trumbo concluded that his participation in the project was "a total disaster."[2] In May 1962 Preminger announced that he had contracted Arthur Kopit to write a new screenplay for *Bunny Lake*. This initiative seems to have led nowhere.

Preminger's persistence is all the more remarkable given that the very premise of the story gave him doubts. "I almost gave up *Bunny Lake* because while working on the script I realized that women would not like the film, because they'd be afraid, they are afraid of all situations in which a child is in danger."[3] Realizing that "the further away from home the mother who loses the child is, the more real the story seems," Preminger considered transplanting the story to Paris, "but this problem seemed almost insurmountable because then the police would have to ask everything through an interpreter." Preminger decided instead to take the story to London. He sent the novel to British novelist Penelope Mortimer, who agreed to work on a new script with her husband, John. "She came to New York for conferences," said Preminger, "and came up with a wonderful character, I think, of a heavy, which gave the whole picture a new dimension. That made me pick it up again."[4]

On June 15, 1964, shortly before the start of production on *In Harm's Way*, the Mortimers handed in a 158-page treatment. Though different in dialogue and situations from what was eventually shot, the treatment lays out the new plot that Preminger would use for the film. The main character, still named Blanche in this treatment, now has a brother, Steven. Americans, they have come to London with Blanche's daughter, Bunny. Newhouse is now a police inspector, and Wilson is the Lakes' drunken, *Duchess of Malfi*–quoting landlord. At the climax, Blanche realizes that the insane Steven, who has been possessive of his sister since childhood, has kidnapped Bunny and plans to kill her. After humoring her brother by pretending to play a game with him, Blanche retrieves her daughter as the police close in. A curious element in the treatment was that at the beginning of the film, in scenes at Kensington Gardens, in their flat, and at the school, Blanche and Steven would be shown behaving as if Bunny were there, but the child would remain silent and the compositions would keep her offscreen. Since both the narrative strategy and this way of using the camera are thoroughly uncharacteristic of Preminger, it is not surprising that this opening was discarded.[5]

Preminger flew the Mortimers to Honolulu to work with him on the script at night during the shooting of *In Harm's Way*. According to Martin Schute, who served as associate producer on *Bunny Lake*, "Otto was busy directing *In Harm's Way* and didn't really have the time to discuss the screenplay. And Penelope went mad. Absolutely furious. We came back. She almost, I think, bowed out, then. The final screenplay of *Bunny Lake* was written by John."[6]

While he was still working on *In Harm's Way*, Preminger felt confident enough to announce that he would shoot *Bunny Lake* in England in 1965. At a press conference in November 1964 to announce that he had bought the rights to *Hurry Sundown*, Preminger claimed he had hoped merely to produce *Bunny Lake*, but that Columbia insisted he also direct it.[7] This statement is surprising, since Preminger's long-held determination to film *Bunny Lake* suggests an exceptional level of personal involvement with the story. Perhaps the desire to disavow this involvement suggested to Preminger the idea of entrusting the direction of the film to someone else.

By the time he shot *Bunny Lake*, the modesty and intimacy of this suspense story made a sharp contrast with the general trend of his recent work. On the other hand, he held that the heroine's status as an unmarried mother gave *Bunny Lake* a social theme. "If you do not live in our society in a conformist manner, the law doesn't protect you: that is, if you like, the moral of the story, even though it is only a very small aspect of the film." Preminger's main concern in *Bunny Lake* lay elsewhere. "What interests me most of all is to show a woman alone in a big city. I'll put my camera in the middle of the street, as in *À bout de souffle*, which I saw and which I like a lot, for its way of showing Paris, and also because it proves that Jean Seberg wasn't as bad an actress as all that."[8] Preminger made these comments in 1961; in 1965, his direction of *Bunny Lake* remained faithful to the impulse that drew him to the story—and even, in the sequence of Ann's journey to the doll hospital, to his liking for Godard's mise-en-scène of the city in *À bout de souffle*. (Although he didn't mention it, Preminger could not have failed to notice the explicit reference in Godard's film to *Whirlpool*—the Preminger work to which *Bunny Lake Is Missing* is most closely linked.)

In February of 1965, Preminger and Eva Monley lined up locations. For the Lakes' flat and Wilson's flat, Monley and Preminger chose Carlton Terrace Mews, off Trafalgar Square, a former stables that art director Don Ashton transformed into a complex including both sets and production offices. An actual school at House on the Hill in Hampstead became the nursery. The Lakes' house in Frogmore End was in London's Camden borough.

In the three key roles, Preminger cast Laurence Olivier, Carol Lynley, and Keir Dullea. Colorful supporting parts of eccentrics went to Preminger veteran Martita Hunt (*The Fan, Bonjour Tristesse*) as Miss Ford, the retired cofounder of the school; Finlay Currie as a kindly mender of broken dolls; and Noël Coward as the flamboyant Wilson. Preminger had courted Coward for *Exodus* in January 1960, presumably for the role of Sutherland, but Coward turned down that offer.[9] Less showy parts were filled by other excellent English actors, including Anna Massey, Clive Revill, the ubiquitous Richard Wattis, and two veterans of Preminger's previous British productions, Victor Maddern (*Saint Joan*) and David Oxley (*Saint Joan* and *Bonjour Tristesse*).

The shooting script, dated April 1, differs from both the previous version and the final film in a crucial way: the script begins by establishing unequivocally the existence of Bunny, who is seen playing on a swing ("Higher! Make me go higher!") in the very first shot. The finished film would eliminate all the early scenes in which Bunny appears, making it possible for the audience to share Newhouse's doubt as to the child's existence. Nevertheless, one detail remains of the scripted scheme: as she moves into their new apartment, Ann places a cup containing Bunny's toothbrush on a shelf in the bathroom. (Steven's retrieval of a doll from the lawn in the opening shot already provides evidence of Bunny's existence.)

Preminger spent April 9 and 10 in a TV studio, where he filmed scenes of a news announcer and a performance by the pop group the Zombies, to be shown on a television in the pub where Newhouse takes Ann. On Monday, April 19, Preminger worked with Carol Lynley and Keir Dullea in a hotel suite he had made his office. During their read-through of the script, Preminger interrupted with corrections, explanations, and statements of principle. When Lynley and Dullea spoke a few lines quickly and in a uniform tone, Preminger launched into a fifteen-minute discourse, filled with recollections of greats he had worked with, from Albert Bassermann and John Barrymore to John Wayne, to underline the need for actors to use "a slow, thoughtful diction, in which each word spoken is lived and thought over again, instead of being a weakened echo of a text learned by heart," in the words of critic Jacques Lourcelles, who was present. Lourcelles's impression was that "Preminger put everyone at ease and we didn't feel the time pass."[10]

April 20 was spent on tests and camera rehearsals at the Hampstead school. Watching Preminger, Lourcelles was struck above all by the impression of "a contented man," contented with his family (his children, Mark and Victoria, now four years old, visited the set each day), with his script, "and with all this organized agitation around him, from which a new film was going to be born. It's the contentment of a man who is active and in his rightful place, absolutely without vanity and well made to prove what Amiel said, that 'true humility is contentment.'" Lourcelles also saw many examples of the famous Preminger wrath, aimed at people who failed to do their work correctly. Their negligence, Lourcelles believed, caused Preminger not only irritation but real regret: "a depressing anomaly in the harmony of the production, which must thus be pitilessly eliminated—and forgotten."[11]

Principal photography started on April 21 in the nursery, with scenes of Newhouse's investigation. Preminger had spent the morning looking at rushes from the test day. He told the lab technicians to make the blacks blacker and the whites whiter (Preminger's taste for a very high-contrast black and white dated back to his work with Joseph LaShelle on *Laura* and was apparent as recently as *Advise & Consent* and *In Harm's Way*) and instructed director of photography Denys Coop (camera operator on *Saint Joan* and *Bonjour Tristesse*) to do nothing to enhance Carol Lynley's beauty: instead, "You have to deepen her features, bring out her emotions."[12]

On the nursery set, it took eighteen takes to get the first shot, a lengthy tracking shot starting on a group of noisy children in a classroom and continuing to follow Newhouse and school administrator Miss Smollett (Anna Massey) across the hall. The second shot was New-house's interview with Ann in the small office of the school director. Olivier had trouble with the phrase "a revoltingly coy name for it" (spo-ken of the school's "first-day room"), which, after some polite discussion between the actor and the director, Preminger let him omit. Lynley proved able to convey her character's anger but appeared to have diffi-culty expressing the pain and sorrow of a mother who has lost her child. Preminger directed her to forget about the other subtexts of the scene and play only "the moment." After eleven takes of the lengthy scene, the shooting day ended without a good take having been achieved.[13]

Eva Monley recalled that a scene between Olivier and Lynley— probably the same one Lourcelles watched being shot—was not going well, and after fourteen takes, Lynley fled from the set. Dispatched to bring her back, Monley found the actress sobbing and protesting that she couldn't do the scene again. Preminger came, hugged Lynley, and told her that he was demanding retakes not because of her performance, but because Olivier was doing "a stage performance." With this reassur-ance, Lynley returned to the set, and the next take was perfect.[14]

Olivier later wrote, "I played a rather little man in *Bunny Lake Is Miss-ing*, probably bullied onto me by Otto Preminger—a real bully, who never let up. Noël Coward and I didn't like the man much. Almost put me off his *Carmen Jones*, which I thought an inspired piece of work. I have a taste for mixing forms, for experiment, and *Carmen Jones* was an innova-tive film. It's a miracle it came from such a heavy-handed egotist."[15] Yet Coward noted in his diary, a few days after finishing work on the film, "I found Otto P. an excellent director and I think I am good in it."[16]

A UPI correspondent who visited the set described Olivier as "clutching the script he studies constantly." In early May, another jour-nalist watched Preminger work with Coward and Lynley at Carlton Mews. "Carol appears with sulky look and a pink raincoat and recites the words in a breathy monotone. Preminger listens, then interrupts. He begins to give her line readings, he tries to show her how a particular word should be stressed, how a question should be inflected. Finally in exasperation he rushes over and plays Carol Lynley the way he thinks she should be played." In repeated takes of the scene, while leaving Coward alone, Preminger continues to goad Lynley, criticizing her performance: "Have you such a short memory? I want you to mean what you say." Soon Lynley is "sobbing uncontrollably," the journalist noted. "When she is completely hysterical, he shoots the closeup."[17]

For no one was *Bunny Lake Is Missing* a harder experience than Keir Dullea.

> Although I knew the reputation of Otto, I had the attitude of, "I'm a nice guy, it won't be that way with me." Well, it was just like so many actors. He would humililate, he would scream at you. I think humiliation was almost worse than being screamed at . . . I was so stressed from the way he treated Carol and myself, that even on a day that was kind of okay, I was still filled with, "Okay, when he is going to blow now?"
>
> His dripping sarcasm was the worst part of it. I can remember one day, for example. It was a very simple scene. I was very prepared in terms of knowing my lines. I mean, I always studied very hard, I always do. But the stress—I kept going up on my lines, or if not, there was some action where I was supposed to put a glass down, or pick up a glass, and he said, "Well, Mr. Dullea, I don't understand it. I hired you because you won this award for being the most promising actor of the year 1963, and what is this? I find this actor can't even remember a line, and if he remembers a line, he can't remember an action. What, you can't do these two things at the same time? What is it with you?" It was rough . . .
>
> Somebody heard Laurence Olivier quietly go up to Preminger at some point and say, "Otto, dear boy, I really wish you wouldn't scream at the children."[18]

Late in the production, Dullea found a way out of his hell. Inspired by a suggestion from his friend, director Irvin Kershner, Dullea decided to "create a mad scene" during the shooting of the scene in which Steven commits his sister to a hospital.

> In the middle of a take, I stopped. And he said, "Cut! What is wrong?" And I mumbled something so quietly, he couldn't hear

me. He says, "What?", and I mumbled again. He says, "What did you say?" And I mumbled again. He said, "Turn off the generator, I can't hear Mr. Dullea. What is it you're trying to say?" I said [mumbling], "I don't feel very well." "You don't what?" "I don't feel—" It probably wasn't until the eighth or ninth time that I said it, that he could hear it, and what I said was, "I don't feel very well." And he said, "Well, what can we do? Turn the lights off! You want water?" "No, water won't help." By this time, he was very concerned. I said, "It's not physical." "What do you mean?" "Because you scare the shit out of me." I had everything planned that I was going to say. And I, out of the blue, went bananas. I went more insane in volume, way beyond anything I did in the mad scenes [in the film].

I got done, and he said, "We're going to take a half-hour break. We don't want to scare you, that's not what we're here for. You take your time, and when you're ready, we'll go." We finally started shooting again, and he was very quiet. He never apologized, but what did change, was that he never screamed at me again.[19]

The hospital scenes were scheduled for almost the very end of the production, in early June. The film's scheduled end was the night of June 8, at the dolls' hospital (Barry Elder's Doll Museum in Hammersmith).

The PCA approved the film on September 7, 1965. In October the film went into release in the United States and the United Kingdom. Reviews were mixed, some reviewers harping on the alleged faults of logic in the plot, others praising the film as an engrossing thriller or a stylistic exercise.

Preminger is sometimes said to remove himself from his movies, and his detractors have accused him of having no personal viewpoint or style. In *Bunny Lake Is Missing*, however, the centrality of the director's point of view is established as early as Saul Bass's titles, which end with a hand (Preminger's title trademark since *The Man with the Golden Arm*) ripping away the black background on which Preminger's credit has just appeared, revealing in an extraordinary wipe the opening shot of the

film—Steven crossing a courtyard. At the end of the film, the hand will
return to fold back the cutout paper shape of a doll over the image of
Ann carrying Bunny. Thus the credits say that the activity of the film director is to tear away for a short time a small piece of darkness and reveal images, and they assign to this activity a reparative, restorative
function that it can, however, fulfill only at the price of giving way to
darkness again.

Within the narrative, Superintendent Newhouse serves a similar
function. Newhouse is the film's good father, in opposition to the perverse father Wilson. These two figures carry out a subtextual duel in the
absence of Bunny's father.

The distance installed at the heart of the film by the figure of Newhouse is crucial to the tone of *Bunny Lake Is Missing*. His reserve and
discretion—his habitual and rigorous refusal to pronounce on reality, to
give a verdict on appearances—make him a quintessential Preminger
figure. Again and again, confronted with testimony or pieces of evidence,
Newhouse will commit himself no further than to say that a certain hy-
pothesis is "possible." He embodies a disenchantment in the face of the
real (necessarily a disenchantment also with the fictional, in this film in
which so much, indeed, almost all, of the real proves fictional) that
seems close to the attitude of the author himself before the ruses of his
characters. This closeness makes Newhouse a limit character in Preminger's work. His detachment, and his equally fundamental commitment, are those of a professional (in this he resembles Munson in *Advise
& Consent* and Torrey in *In Harm's Way*). His apparent abdication (after
nearly being attacked by Steven in the pub, when Ann asks him, "What
are you going to do?" he snaps, "Go home!") proves to be a ruse: he does
not give up on the case. His obstinate persistence matches that of the
director. Both are signs of a certain faith in the permeability of surfaces,
the emergence of a meaning, and the inevitability that the narrative will
yield to the pressure of time ("What are we doing?" Ann asks impa-
tiently; "Waiting," Newhouse replies, "for something to happen").

Newhouse's distance subtly decenters the narrative by depriving the
other characters of their hold on reality and invalidating their claim to a
first-degree, present-time existence. If the narrative, for Ann, becomes
a kind of race to reenter the present, a metaphorical escape from the
prison of childhood (represented in turn by the school, the doll hospital,

and most decisively by the real hospital where Steven places her), the doubt offered by Newhouse is the more immediate impetus for this action than Bunny's disappearance.

If the audience shares Newhouse's skeptical point of view, it does so only to a certain extent. The special tension of *Bunny Lake Is Missing* comes from the discrepancy among points of view: that of Newhouse, that of Steven, that of Ann, that of Preminger. The film creates a montage among these points of view, not for the purpose of establishing some kind of whole; instead, Preminger's style expresses the impossibility of achieving a coherent, seamless, comprehensive picture of reality, and viewpoints clash all through the film.

From the beginning, the film engages the audience in questioning the appearance of the relationship between Ann and Steven. In the opening scenes, the audience is made to assume (not through any misdirection but simply through the absence of contrary indications, as Lourcelles points out) that the two are the married parents of Bunny; not until their first meeting with Miss Ford, during their search for Bunny, is it disclosed that the two are, in fact, brother and sister ("Curiouser and curiouser," comments Miss Ford). Here, Preminger plays on the assumptions of the viewer in order to expose the social logic behind those assumptions and to lead the viewer to question, with as much relentlessness as the film, the appearances of the logical, the normal, and the reasonable. A crucial two-shot shows Steven trying to console Ann after the discovery that Bunny's things have been removed from the apartment. He points out that the absence of these things proves that the person responsible wants Bunny to be comfortable. Ann is in deep shadow, and Steven is so brightly lit that the pores of his face are plainly visible. They are indeed a couple: each is dependent on the other and each is the necessary complement to the other. Ann's emotionality demands Steven's rationality. The irony of the shot is that, as Miss Ford will say of another discourse of Steven's, "it's *not* reasonable": his rationality is a surface, a mask, without any grounding in the secret, entirely irrational truth that both he and Ann refuse to confront.

In *Bunny Lake Is Missing*, Preminger—without timidity—confronts modernity. The mode of this confrontation is revealing. The narrative establishes that Ann has been in London for only a few days and that the city is foreign to her. All she knows are the isolated worlds of Frogmore

End and the nursery school. The narrative encourages the viewer to share Ann's point of view when Newhouse takes her to a pub for a sandwich and a drink. The two poles of the scene are comfort and alienation. Ann is not quite willing to accept the consolation Newhouse appears to offer, because she thinks he is trying to trap her, but she also depends on him as her surest link to the world outside her relationship with Steven. Preminger's camera is drawn irresistibly to the pole of alienation: there is a special relationship, a magnetic attraction, between the camera and disorder, an attraction revealed when the camera dollies toward the TV set during the news broadcast about the search for Bunny, whereupon the barman's hand reaches into the shot to switch the channel to a performance by the Zombies. It is a shockingly direct way for the film to deny the central stake of its own narrative—not by placing Bunny's disappearance in a larger social context, but by demonstrating the failure of her disappearance to find any signification within a social context that itself is absent (as Newhouse hints with his ironic remark about "merrie olde England"), having been replaced by the general discontinuity of television.

Later in the same scene, Newhouse goes to the bar to refill Ann's glass, and the camera waits with him at the bar as the Zombies continue to play on the TV. Though the choice of this band for the scene may well have been dictated by factors having nothing to do with their musical aesthetic, the Zombies are, in fact, an ideal choice for *Bunny Lake Is Missing* (as, say, the Rolling Stones or the Who would not have been) because their tense coolness and mannered detachment matches Preminger's. Their music embodies the tension between engagement and dissolution of self that is at the heart of the film.

One of the several contradictions on which Preminger plays in this sequence is that between the three-dimensionality of the pub space, emphasized by the camera's physical traversing of the space to approach the TV, and the flatness of the TV image. The shallow focus of the shots of the Zombies emphasize cutout body parts and isolated, abstracted faces that seem to cry out mutely *that* they signify, *that* they have depth, even as they are recuperated immediately as surfaces in a visual regime of surfaces. Similarly, the tightly compressed quality of the Zombies' music contrasts sharply with the spaciousness of the recording and mixing of the dialogue and diegetic sounds in the film (a contrast that is heightened in the scene of Ann's escape from the hospital later in the film, when one of the Zombies' songs, "Just Out of Reach," is heard again, this time over a watchman's tinny transistor radio).

The difference, or the discordance, introduced by the Zombies' pop songs in the sound track of the film highlights the concerted use of disparate, heterogeneous elements throughout the film. Paul Glass's score is already based on an opposition between a lyrical theme and largely athematic, atonal, and heavily percussive music, an opposition that underscores the increasingly frequent eruptions of anomalous or threatening elements in the narrative and the visual field of the film. Some of these elements are living beings, like the policemen and their German shepherds, scouring the school grounds. Some of the discordant elements are objects, like the African mask Wilson places on Ann's bed for her housewarming, and which Preminger's camera twice gestures toward, as though intuiting a relationship between this seemingly irrelevant image (told that it is a fertility symbol, Ann replies drily, "that doesn't seem to be my problem") and the mainsprings of the narrative.

The world of children is itself an alien world—to which the film introduces us, at one point, with a literal clash: the clash of cymbals, produced by a boy playing with his mates. The clash of this alienness is a crucial theme in the film: it signals the presence, in the same field of reality (of narrative), of two different and irreconcilable worldviews. The final sequence at Frogmore End is built entirely on this juxtaposition, as Ann, to distract Steven and save Bunny, enters into the childhood mode of play with her brother. ("I want to touch the sky!" she cries to Steven—echoing Laura Manion's "I'm waiting to be kicked to kingdom come" in *Anatomy of a Murder*.) What manifests itself in Steven as a retreat into fantasy is, for the children, a "very sensible" (Miss Ford's words) use of fantasy to block out potentially traumatic experiences, just as Ann sensibly simulates fantasy in order to cope with a real danger.

Bunny Lake carries us to the outer limits of Premingerian classicism and confirms how inadequate and deceptive a term "classicism" is, as applied to Preminger's work. Classicism implies the triumph of reason, but the ending of *Bunny Lake* shows not reason triumphant, but love. In everything that transpires before this ending, madness, a form of love, clearly holds sway, as Miss Ford observes in a line that gives a key to Preminger's work: overhearing Ann's exclamation to her brother, "This woman's mad!" Miss Ford asks, "Don't you think we all are, to one degree or other?" In this remark—which echoes Biegler's credo in *Anatomy of a Murder*, "Everybody loves something or someone"—Miss Ford suggests that the source of all narrative is madness: a projection of fantasy onto the world, or the world's replacement by fantasy. Though Preminger has confronted the excitement and danger of such a move before, especially in *Laura* and *Whirlpool* (two films in which—like Miss Ford with her recordings of children recounting their fantasies—characters use recording technology to create a doubled world), with *Bunny Lake Is Missing* he goes further and accepts a world that has gone mad, a regime of private desires and delusions that spill into and saturate public space. The only possible responses to this development are withdrawal (like Ann's, carrying Bunny, in the beautiful final shot) or the ironic but merciful detachment—seeking to adjust and restore things where it can— that belongs to Newhouse, and also to Preminger.

31

How Do You Know I've Never Been Black?

For the second film under his Paramount contract (*Bunny Lake Is Missing* was distributed by Columbia), Preminger secured the rights, prepublication, to *Hurry Sundown*, a mammoth novel written by Bert and Katya Gilden under the pseudonym K. B. Gilden. Preminger announced the purchase in a press conference in New York on November 17, 1964 (just before returning to Hollywood to shoot the miniatures in *In Harm's Way*). In its treatment of black-white relations in the post–World War II South, it would be, he said, "a very fair picture that shows the problems of all peoples." During production of *Hurry Sundown*, Preminger would tell the press, "I do not have any message. I give the facts and I leave people to draw their own conclusions. Of course, as a Jew, I do not like segregation."[1]

Established as a specialist in southern subjects from his plays and his Oscar-winning script for *To Kill a Mockingbird*, Horton Foote was an all but inevitable choice as screenwriter. "I worked with [Preminger] for six months on *Hurry Sundown*," the writer later recalled. "And he was wonderful."[2] Foote's December 28, 1965, script contains the basic plot and framework for the film that was made, showing that the important decisions on condensing the huge source novel had been reached.

The story is set in a small southern town shortly after World War II. Henry Warren, an ambitious schemer, hopes to sell to a northern development company a large piece of property belonging to his wife, Julie. To close the deal, Henry must also secure smaller farms belonging to his cousin, war veteran Rad McDowell, and a black woman, Rose Scott, who was Julie's wet nurse. At Rose's death, her land passes to her son, Reeve. Refusing to sell, Reeve and Rad instead team up to improve their property. Henry persuades Julie to contest Reeve's ownership of his land in court, but when Julie learns that Henry covered up his responsibility for an injury to their autistic son, Coley, she withdraws her claim to the land and breaks up with her husband. The vindictive Henry and a group of racist whites dynamite Rad's property, inadvertently killing Rad's oldest son, Charles, with whom Henry had a surrogate father-son relationship. Joined by their black neighbors, Reeve helps Rad rebuild his farm.

In dialogue and details Foote's script is far from what was eventually shot. According to Foote, "finally, we didn't agree about the screenplay so he hired another writer."[3] This was Thomas C. Ryan, who had worked for Preminger for years and had been responsible for a short promotional film on the making of *Saint Joan* and a souvenir program–type book on the making of *Exodus*. Ryan's *Hurry Sundown* shooting script would be finalized on May 27, 1966. Before then, Preminger got into the news over a dispute concerning a book he tried, but failed, to acquire. While dining with Hope at the "21" Club, Preminger saw literary agent Irving "Swifty" Lazar and accused him of having reneged on his promise to give Preminger first crack at the rights to Truman Capote's *In Cold Blood*. The ensuing argument led to Lazar's hitting Preminger over the head with a glass, causing a wound that needed fifty stitches.

For the main parts of Henry and Julie, Preminger cast Michael Caine and Candice Bergen. When Bergen dropped out of the cast, Jane Fonda took her place. Worried about Preminger's reputation, Caine forestalled his director by telling him before the start of shooting that if Preminger ever yelled at him, he would go into his dressing room for the day. Preminger paused, seemingly taken aback, and then replied, smiling, "I would never shout at Alfie." According to Caine, "that was the key to the long friendship I subsequently enjoyed with this unpopular man. Like many other men I have met, he secretly saw himself as another Alfie, and as far as he was concerned, so did I. That was it—I never got a cross word from him during the whole picture."[4]

Preminger saw Faye Dunaway in William Alfred's *Hogan's Goat* on Broadway, screen-tested her, and signed her to a six-picture contract, starting with the role of Lou, Rad's wife, in *Hurry Sundown*. (Just before making *Hurry Sundown*, she appeared in her first film, *The Happening*.) Preminger offered the part of Reeve to Sidney Poitier, who turned it down.[5] Instead, Robert Hooks took the role.

Preminger signed John Phillip Law, who had lately been noticed for his role in *The Russians Are Coming, The Russians Are Coming*, to a three-option contract. In *Hurry Sundown*, Preminger cast Law as Rad. Though Preminger would be merciless with him on the two films they would make together, Law liked Preminger and believed that the director liked him, too. "Otto liked the fact that I was interested in European culture and other filmmakers. [But] we didn't have too many in-depths. That wasn't his thing. He was intimidating enough that he wasn't a guy I would seek out for a conversation."[6]

Diahann Carroll was cast as Vivian, a northern-educated woman who returns to teach in the black school; Burgess Meredith as the bigoted Judge Purcell; and Beah Richards as Rose.

Variety reported that Preminger had hoped to shoot in Georgia, but union demands there prompted the decision to base the film in and around Baton Rouge, Louisiana. Production designer Gene Callahan (a set decorator on *The Cardinal*) was a native of Baton Rouge; his connections in the area helped smooth the way for some locations, including, perhaps, the Baton Rouge residence that was used for Henry and Julie's house. Rad's and Reeve's farms and the Riverside development site were built on land owned by the state prison farm at St. Gabriel. The courthouse was that of St. Francisville, which also provided the hardware store, Judge Purcell's house, Professor Thurlow's house, and some exteriors for the town. The black school was a school in Liverpool; the black church was in Bains; the white church was in Hammond.

The company arrived in Louisiana on June 1, 1966. The sprawling Bellemont Motor Hotel in Baton Rouge provided production headquarters and lodging for the company. The first few days were devoted to rehearsals, tests, and composer Hugo Montenegro's recording of a choral rendition of the film's title song. The first day of production, June 6, was devoted to scenes of Rad's return to town.

Everyone was shocked by the racism the production revealed. For some, it was their first experience of the Deep South. "You can cut the hostility here with a knife," Diahann Carroll said. "I'm not a fighter. I usually smile and then go into my room and cry my eyes out. But down here the terror has killed my taste for going anywhere." Robert Hooks noted the absence of onlookers during the exterior scenes: "You never see anybody, man. You can feel the eyes watching you behind lace curtains, though. Like they could cut your heart out."[7]

"We had this swimming pool at the motel," said Fonda, "and I'll never forget the first day one of the Negro actors jumped into it. There were reverberations all the way to New Orleans. People just stood and stared like they expected the water to turn black!"[8] John Phillip Law confirmed: "When we were first in the motel, we were in the swimming pool, and boy, the locals were hanging over the fence, just sitting there, 'Look at that, you ever see anything like that in your life?' Finally it became an issue. Otto solved the problem by just renting the entire motel, so it was no longer a motel we were sharing with other travelers. They put up a bunch of barricades, and that was that. There were still people who would try to shoot the tires out on the trucks going to work and stuff like that."[9]

A homemade bomb exploded in the swimming pool one night, causing minor damage. Later during the production, members of the cast found their dressing trailers shot with bullet holes.

Perhaps because of the tension around them, Preminger was at his most irascible during the production of *Hurry Sundown*. One day when they were shooting in a hospital ("People kept on running through with bottles of real blood," recalled Jane Fonda, "and in the next room people kept throwing up. I loved it"),[10] the heat, augmented by the soundman's request to turn off the air-conditioning, set off the automatic sprinkler system, drenching the cast, the crew, and the equipment. Caine recalled, "Otto exploded. I have never seen anyone so near apoplexy. His eyes bulged out of his head with fury and his vocal cords were torn in his throat as he spat curses on everyone in earshot. I had never witnessed anger like this. Eventually, having exhausted all of us and at last himself, he stalked out for the rest of the day."[11]

For Faye Dunaway, the shooting of *Hurry Sundown* "became like a psychodrama." A native southerner, she found in the role of Lou resonances with her own life that made the film important for her: "I was a dirt farmer's wife waiting for my husband to come back from World War II, just as my mother had waited for my father."[12] She found the experience of being "absolutely caught in this time warp from my past" anguishing. Preminger probably knew nothing and cared less about the actress's internal conflicts. "Otto knew from the first day of shooting what he wanted *Hurry Sundown* to be," recalled Dunaway. "He had a very tightly conceived notion of things and tended to work at imposing his idea of how a performance should be done on the actor or actress . . . Otto was one of those directors you can't listen to because he doesn't know anything at all about the process of acting. I didn't think he was ever right." For all her misgivings about Preminger, she thought that he was making a film that "dissected all the notions of race relations in changing times, in a way that I felt was brutally honest."[13]

While shooting the scene of Rad's homecoming, Preminger, dissatisfied with Law's performance, "went after John, tearing him apart, and the words were stinging," said Dunaway. Preminger next turned his wrath on hairdresser Freddy Jones, and then, when she tried to defend Jones, on Dunaway. "Otto turned on me like a mad dog and went at me. His face turned red, his eyes were bulging, and with his shaved head, the effect was extraordinary. I didn't say anything; I just watched him. Watched while his eyes glazed over, the saliva gathering in the corners of his mouth. His hands squeezed into fists so tight that the knuckles turned white. He was no longer focusing on me or anybody else. I think it was the only time I've really looked full in the face at somebody who's gone into that sort of complete state of rage, unblinking and refusing to react. I just froze."[14]

According to Dunaway, she told Preminger, "I don't want to work with you if you're going to behave like this," and he replied that it would be fine with him if she never worked for him again. Dunaway would make this statement the basis for her claim that Preminger had legally released her from her contract with him. The claim was not upheld in court; Dunaway wound up having to pay what she called "a lot of money" to get out of the contract. For the rest of the *Hurry Sundown* shoot, as Michael Caine confirmed, Dunaway was Preminger's "whipping boy."[15]

John Phillip Law remembered Preminger's direction of his love scene with Dunaway (of which, the editor's assembly sheet records, the director printed takes 15 and 16).[16]

Otto's looking through the camera, and he comes storming out from behind the camera, and he says, "You don't know how to kiss a girl?" I said, "What?" He took Faye Dunaway and he grabbed the back of her head and grabbed the back of mine and he banged our faces together. She got kind of a fat lip, I don't know if she cut her lip or something, because he just banged, and she was just livid, you know. She just went berserk . . . I was livid too. I was just gritting my teeth, because if you added fuel to the fire, then he would blow, he'd throw the camera at you before he would stop.[17]

Despite everything, Law found that Preminger could be a helpful director. "He would push me in directions, giving me clues, like 'don't bend down to the woman, bring the woman up to you,' or 'don't move so fast.' He would give me these little technical cues." One day, he paid Law the ultimate compliment by telling the actor he reminded him of Gary Cooper.[18]

Beah Richards, too, came to appreciate and like Preminger. One day she objected to a scene that she was supposed to do, saying she didn't think it was truthful to the experience of black people. When Preminger disagreed, Richards pointed out that he had never been black. To this seemingly unanswerable argument, Preminger had a ready reply: "How do you know I've never been black?" Faced with such self-assurance, Richards could only relent, and she did the scene as written.[19]

The call sheets for *Hurry Sundown* show that Loyal Griggs worked on the film as director of photography for the first twenty days, mainly on the locations for Rad's and Reeve's houses (he also shot all the scenes at the black church and school). Starting on June 29, Milton Krasner's name appears on the call sheets as director of photography; he went on to work for the remaining thirty-nine days of the schedule, which included all the scenes at Henry and Julie's house, the judge's house, and the courthouse, as well as all the Riverside scenes and further scenes at Rad's and Reeve's houses. Rex Reed, who visited the production in mid-July, reported in *The New York Times* that Griggs had been fired. This statement prompted Mortie Guterman, Grigg's agent, to write in a rebuttal letter that was published in the newspaper, "Mr. Griggs had hurt his back on the picture, and neither did he wish to leave the picture nor did Mr. Preminger wish to lose his valuable services. They both tried to continue and it was with great reluctance that Mr. Griggs asked to be replaced. The statement that he was fired is in error."[20] Griggs and Krasner would share director of photography credit for *Hurry Sundown*.

The editor's assembly sheet for *Hurry Sundown* shows that many shots required numerous takes before Preminger was satisfied. On June 14 he printed take 29 of the scene in which Rad and Lou find the sheriff (George Kennedy) in a diner and report that Charles has disappeared. On June 21, the scene in which Vivian and Reeve kiss went to twenty takes. In a scene among Thurlow (Rex Ingram), Reeve, and Vivian (June 25), Preminger printed takes 14, 15, and 21. On July 11 Preminger made twenty-three takes of a very long scene with Henry, Judge Purcell, and Sukie at the judge's house, printing takes 12, 14, and 23. (The script supervisor's notes show that many takes were declared no good because of Burgess Meredith's line readings.) Incidentally, the printed takes were timed at 3'35", 3'37", and 3'35"—an indication of the actors' professionalism and Preminger's meticulousness.

Production closed on August 13. Preminger used MGM facilities for the postproduction, during which (at the urging of his twins) he found time to guest star as the villainous Mr. Freeze in a two-part episode of the popular *Batman* series, under George Waggner's direction, an experience he seems to have enjoyed, though star Adam West disliked him intensely.[21]

Released in February 1967, *Hurry Sundown* was greeted by the worst critical reception ever yet accorded a Preminger film. In vehemence and derisiveness, the reviews of *Hurry Sundown* surpassed those of *Saint Joan*. Wilfred Sheed wrote in *Esquire* that "to criticize it would be like tripping a dwarf."[22] Brendan Gill, in *The New Yorker*, thought that Preminger's major failing was that he "refuses to distinguish between a good screenplay and a bad one. *Hurry Sundown* . . . is meretricious nonsense from start to finish, but Mr. Preminger seems not to have noticed."[23] This remark is at least suggestive. Most reviews merely treated the film as an occasion for jeering.

In *Hurry Sundown*, the major hallmarks of Preminger's cinema since *Exodus*—Panavision, a lengthy running time, a narrative that sets up a relay among various characters with competing or diverging interests, an attempt to define the figures by their places in a social, political, or institutional system—are vividly, triumphantly present. At the same time, the film reveals an undeniable coarsening of style in comparison with Preminger's previous films. Preminger is happy to have individuals inhabit his world, but he is satisfied with caricatures. In scenes such as the passage involving Beah Richards's Rose, Preminger comes closer than he has

ever come before to a certain kind of melodrama that, in American culture at least since the 1930s, has been generally disparaged and seen as
dated. Throughout *Hurry Sundown*, Preminger is more willing than ever
to allow his characters to become dispersed, lost in the pattern that contains them. The most telling shot of the film shows Henry's brigade of
dynamiters motionless on the ground in the lower half of the screen, as
Rad, Lou, and their children return home in their jalopy in the top half.
This is Preminger at his most formalist, his most schematic: it is a magnificent shot, achieving clarity on a large scale, but it is extremely abstract, and the clarity comes at the expense of any subtle or complex
engagement with the characters.

Hugo Montenegro's score is another kind of symptom. Its brassy
1960s pop sound is blatantly inappropriate for the period in which the
film is set, but it serves as a bridge instantly connecting the sixties audience to that time. It establishes *Hurry Sundown* as a pop film—a film in
which certain values are sacrificed to the demands of immediate clarity
and understanding.

Some of these values never mattered to Preminger. In *The Man with
the Golden Arm*, he threw out Algren's Dickensian-Dostoyevskian expansiveness and in their place erected something concise and hard. The
values of naturalism are superficially present in, but fundamentally
irrelevant to, *Anatomy of a Murder* and *Exodus*. Though with *Hurry Sundown*, Preminger would go farther away from naturalism than he had
done since *Porgy and Bess*, this movement was by no means an aberra-
tion in his work.

Hurry Sundown is above all an attempt to give simplified and bold
form, in a popular entertainment, to the mass consciousness of a social
crisis; it is a mythic retelling of postwar American social history, as *Exodus* is the mythic retelling of the formation of Israel. If *Hurry Sundown*
lacks subtlety, it is because subtlety is of no use to it. Poised uneasily
between institutionalized social consciousness and hyperbolic psychodrama, *Hurry Sundown* articulates and holds somewhat in reserve the
tensions that are released in Preminger's later films.

The narrative compression that results from Preminger's insistence
on simplification is more extreme in *Hurry Sundown* than in any other
film. In *In Harm's Way*, the great compression (visible above all in the
handling of Annalee's suicide and Jere's reaction to it) is justified by the

war situation. In *Hurry Sundown*, the condensation of interchange, the overloading of narrative information, the insistence on economy appear less well motivated and sometimes result in a severe flatness. In the classroom scene between Reeve and Vivian, the dialogue covers Rose's death, her real age (emphasizing the toil of her life), Reeve and Vivian's aborted romance, Vivian's move to New York. The abundance of overdetermined information leaves little room for any development of character, for any real sense of the relationship between the two characters. The film contains much expository dialogue and dialogue whose all too apparent function is to set up plot points for future payoffs. The early scene of Henry giving Rad a lift in his car contains several examples of these. Rad, ironically admiring Henry's car, remarks, "A lot different from the old days on the shrimp boats, huh?" The conversation shifts to Rad's oldest son, Charles, of whom Henry says, "Spittin' image of me when I was his age. Seems more like my son than my cousin."

The baldness with which the film plants its significant points is disconcerting; in these scenes, Preminger makes no effort to compensate for the perfunctory quality of the script but is content to allow the scenes to hurtle past. In other parts of the film, Preminger brings a more nuanced approach to the script. In her scene at Rose's house, Julie has a speech in which she reveals her deep motivation: "If Henry can make good at this, maybe he'll settle down. We might even have more children." Preminger stages the scene as a progressive revelation, having Julie step between the camera and the screen door in the background, pausing in her movement and silhouetting herself, and then, after she says "We might even have more children," continuing the movement and finally turning to present her frontally lit face to the offscreen Rose and to the camera. The lighting and the performance give a hesitation and a sense of struggle to the frank speech, so that the character appears to be discovering her inner conflict and her longing gradually and at the same time as she voices it.

Since the only characters in *Hurry Sundown* who are developed to any degree of complexity are Henry and Julie, the viewer comes to care about the rest only in an abstract way, more in a general spirit of attending to principles than anything else, and this is probably just as Preminger intended, but this means also that in a strictly aesthetic sense, it doesn't matter who is on-screen. Everybody is viewed in the same way,

without shadows and with no more right to the viewer's interest than is
conferred by the fact of being on-screen at a particular moment—which
is an immense value and, at heart, the only fundamental value expressed
by the film, other than the monumental quality of Preminger's images, in
which some trace remains, perhaps, of the early architectural style of
Lubitsch (who had also worked for Reinhardt).

The sweep of the movement in the early scenes is joyous and capti-
vating: the cut from Elwell's helicopter leaving to Rad's bus arriving; the
tracking shot that follows Rad walking through the small town, then
pushes forward, letting him go out of frame, to watch Dolph go into the
hardware store and make a phone call (we see him from outside,
through the window); the traveling shot alongside Henry's car as he gives
Rad a ride home. The narrative movement, indomitable, triumphs over
spatial dislocation with straight cuts: the cutting from the Warrens'
house to Rad and Lou's house, for example. Even more than in *Bunny
Lake Is Missing* (in which the exclusive use of straight cuts for temporal
transitions is less striking because of the limited real time of the story),
the use of straight cuts as scene transitions in *Hurry Sundown* creates an
exhilarating sense of ubiquity and mastery, all space becoming potentially intelligible, unfolding in logical sequence for the viewer.

Throughout the early scenes, the camera repeatedly tracks forward,
introducing the main objects of the film: Rad's house as he returns home
and looks for Lou; Rose in bed. This style is presentational; it also suggests that the camera is drawn to certain things, that it has its predilections, its interests.

Then, a slight, unexplained shift of perspective as the camera zooms
in on a close two-shot of Henry and Julie sitting in a pew of Clem's
church and looking at each other. This, the first zoom of the film, is followed by others: a zoom-in on Charles at the table as his father says
grace; a zoom-in on Julie lifting Coley in her arms after Henry roughly
takes the saxophone away from him; a zoom-in on Henry lifting Julie as
they kiss in a chair, followed, in the same shot, by a zoom-out as Julie
gets up to take care of Coley. The shot in the church establishes a link
between the zoom and sexuality that, though it is not maintained systematically, continues throughout the film. Preminger integrates the
zoom into his usual style perfectly: the variable focal length brings a
floating, hesitant, uncertain quality, an unpredictable element. In *Hurry*

Sundown, the zoom is used to continue a movement already entrusted to the crane toward an object of interest—to isolate the object, lifting it out of its position in real space while preserving that position, giving the object a momentary optical existence, as if the object belonged to two realities: the real space charted by the film, and a mental space created by the film. Preminger's main allegiance is always to the real space, whose continuity he restores by canceling the zoom, either by reversing it (as when the zoom-in on Henry and Julie in the chair is followed by a zoom-out) or by cutting.

The Cardinal is centrally concerned with displacement and distance (cf. Cardinal Glennon's anxiety over reaching Rome in time to vote in the papal election), *In Harm's Way* with dispersion, *Hurry Sundown* with man's claim to the right to occupy space. All these themes are encapsulated in *Exodus*. All four films, significantly, are set in the past, three of them in the 1940s—the last period before the technologies of instantaneity and ubiquity caused the collapse of space into time—thus a determinate period for the condition of the viewer who encounters, fascinated, in these films the narration of his/her own prehistory. In *Hurry Sundown*, this prehistory takes the form of a struggle for possession of land—that is, a struggle to hold on to the world before it slips away into the Heideggerian condition "in which everything is neither far nor near . . . uniform distancelessness."[24] Haunted by a sense of their own rootlessness, the characters try to exorcise it by laying claim to the earth. The contested relationship between man and the earth is both a historical and an existential metaphor (it is also a sexual metaphor, as is clear from the film's preoccupation with dynamite—its degree of potency and freshness, Rad's questioned ability to use it, the two series of explosions). Through this metaphor, *Hurry Sundown* takes on a quality both pathetic and hyperbolic.

32

If We Must Be Prisoners

In January 1966 Preminger bought the rights to John Hersey's novel *Too Far to Walk*, a contemporary story of college students, and announced it as his next production for Paramount. This project, which occupied Preminger's attention throughout much of 1967, would give him considerable trouble. Nelson Gidding wrote a script that Preminger found unsuitable; he then turned to a succession of other writers, including Venable Herndon, Robert Schlitt, Richard Jessup, and William Goodheart.

During the development of *Too Far to Walk*, Preminger learned that Erik Kirkland, his son by Gypsy Rose Lee, had been told the truth about his paternity. Preminger asked for, and was given, Lee's permission to get in touch with Erik, who was then serving in the army and stationed in Germany. The two met in Paris early in 1967. The two men—one over sixty, the other twenty-two—walked together through wintry Paris streets. Preminger recounted his brief relationship with Erik's mother, his early visits to New York after Erik's birth, their discontinuance at Lee's request. Erik wrote, "I was . . . tense and nervous, but Otto's unequivocal acceptance was very gradually getting to me."[1]

After Erik's discharge from the army, in July 1967, he started working for his father. "More than anything in my life, I wanted to find out what it was like to have a real father," Erik wrote.[2] Out of deference to Gypsy Rose Lee's wishes, the two men kept their relationship secret, and Erik continued to use the name Kirkland. The physical resemblance between them must have given rise to much speculation. Erik's ostensible main duty was as casting director for *Too Far to Walk*, but he quickly found himself pulled into other areas of his father's work, including script conferences for the film. In these sessions, Erik saw his father straining to stay contemporary, to keep up with a volatile culture—that of American college students—that was constantly yielding new forms of protest that

Preminger wanted to incorporate into the film. The difficulties with the script drove Preminger to increase his vodka consumption. "Otto was drinking quite a bit in those days," recalled Erik. "He started drinking actually quite a bit during the script conferences for *Too Far to Walk*, because he was so frustrated by them."[3]

Though alcohol was Preminger's drug of choice, it was not the only one he dabbled in during that period. Throwing himself with zeal into the research for *Too Far to Walk*, he took LSD (under Timothy Leary's supervision) to get experience with the drug, which figured in Hersey's story. Erik recounted:

> He threw Timothy Leary out of the house and managed to go through this event on his own. Given his passion for art and given his surroundings of all this wonderful modern art, I gather for him it was a pretty wonderful experience. He had a Matisse collage across from his bed, and he said when he looked at it, he could see the spine in the figure, and he could see the whole way it was created. Hope was on the phone with Nat Rudich throughout the next day, quite nervous about what was going on. But Otto never much cared about that, he came in the next day, full of new stories, smiling, and very proud of himself.

Preminger's psychedelic experience would create part of the background for the film that replaced *Too Far to Walk* on his schedule and emerged instead as his next project. The only one of Preminger's independent productions to be based on an original script rather than on a literary work that had been published in another form, *Skidoo* was originally written by Doran William Cannon in late 1966. Cannon's story involved Tony, a gangster who represents white middle-class America with its conservatism and patriotism. Accepting an assignment from a mob boss named God, Tony goes into prison to kill a former associate who has turned state's evidence against the mob. Unaware that the stationery of his draft dodger cellmate, Fred, is soaked with LSD, Tony accidentally ingests the drug by licking an envelope. He goes on a euphoric trip, and upon coming down from it he finds that he can no longer kill. Tony and Fred escape from prison in a balloon, having dosed the guards and inmates with LSD in order to facilitate their flight.

Cannon's agent submitted his name to Preminger for consideration

as a possible writer for the adaptation of *Too Far to Walk*. To show his
client's qualifications for a project concerning young people and drugs,
the agent sent two original scripts by Cannon: *Brewster McCloud* and
Skidoo. "*Brewster McCloud* I think he read like five pages of," recalled
Erik Preminger; "it was totally unlike anything Otto could process." But
he liked *Skidoo* and bought it in October 1967.

Preminger was under time pressure because the terms of his contract
with Paramount obliged him to deliver a film for 1968 release. After Gulf
& Western acquired Paramount in 1966, one of new movie mogul
Charles Bluhdorn's first moves was to renegotiate the studio's agree-
ments with its contract producers. According to Erik, "Otto—he used to
love to tell this story—said: 'What's to renegotiate? I have a contract, I'm
very happy with the contract, I'm sure you'll abide by the contract.' But
of course what Otto could not afford to do was breach so much as a
comma or a period in that contract . . . So he was running out of time to
deliver a picture. He would not have been able to deliver *Too Far to Walk*
within the time limit. He read *Skidoo*, and thought, 'I can do this within
the time required.' "

Skidoo became the next production on Preminger's schedule. The
third film under his Paramount contract, it was the first to be made under the new regime at the studio. Robert Evans, whom Bluhdorn had recently hired as head of production, tried to talk Preminger out of the
project. "Otto, we need bigger canvas films from you. Distribution is desperate for a Preminger Christmas film." According to Evans, Preminger's
response was an enraged "Who do you think you're talking to?" Evans
saw to it that Bluhdorn's negative opinion of the project was relayed to
Preminger. "It was a big mistake," Evans wrote in his autobiography. "He
retaliated by accelerating the starting date of *Skidoo*." (Evans also believed that Preminger's casting of Jaik Rosenstein, publisher of the scandal sheet *Hollywood Close-Up*, in a small role was a deliberate affront to
Bluhdorn and himself: Rosenstein, in reporting the hiring of Evans, had
used the headline "Bluhdorn's Blow Job." Preminger's support of Rosenstein would later drive a wedge between Preminger and his longtime
friend Billy Wilder, who refused to speak with Preminger after the latter
testified as a character witness for the defense in a libel suit against the
much-disliked scandal-sheet writer.)[4]

Under Preminger's Paramount contract, which spanned seven films, he had the right to make two that were "non-approved" by the studio: *Skidoo* became the first of these. The contract was eventually renegotiated: instead of seven films, two of which could be non-approved, Preminger settled for five films, including three non-approved. The two approved films had already been made: *In Harm's Way* and *Hurry Sundown*. With this renegotiation, in exchange for the right to make one additional film (over the originally contracted two) without the studio's story approval, Preminger conceded his right (and canceled his obligation) to make three more films that Paramount wanted to make.

Preminger worked with Cannon on revising the screenplay. The tape recordings of their story conferences, which have been preserved, reveal much about Preminger's work methods and about his convictions and intuitions about dramaturgy and filmmaking. Again and again over the sessions, his theme is that the humor will be funnier and the audience will identify more with the story if the situations are based in a credible, logically consistent reality. He is also concerned with creating well-developed and believable characters.

In Cannon's original script, Tony's doubt about the paternity of his daughter, Darlene, was briefly alluded to in an early scene and then dropped. Preminger would make Tony's suspicion an obsessive theme. "A man should be big enough to forget it at least if he's not sure. But this is Tony's weakness. This is why it is funny, this is why it is comedy, that he can't forget it. And this is why it adds tremendously to the picture that the trip makes him change his mind, that the trip makes him say, 'What difference.' Because that is the hippie philosophy."[5] In the story conferences Preminger suggests that Flo nurtures Tony's doubts in order to maintain control over her husband. (This is the exact reverse of the relationship in the original script, in which Darlene says to her father, "You just wanted Mommy to think you had doubts, to keep her faithful to you," and Tony agrees.)[6] Preminger also suggests that Tony doesn't want sex as much as Flo does, so she gets sex by making him mad so that he feels he must prove his virility. "I don't say that we should put all this in. But I want to build the human relationship as real as possible to serve comedy purposes."

Cannon seeks to make satirical points through stylization, but Preminger insists on not "preaching," on not sacrificing character consistency for the sake of a laugh, and on treating everything before the camera as belonging to the same order of reality. Whereas Cannon's script calls for titles resembling a 1930s gangster movie, Preminger objects that it's unnecessary to allude to the 1930s in representing the gangsters in *Skidoo*, since in 1967 the Mafia is "more alive than ever . . . Frankly, if this would be a picture about the Mafia, and the Mafia didn't exist, they've all been cleaned out, I wouldn't make it. What interests me is that the Mafia not only exists, but the Mafia is powerful, is underground, has gotten hold of legitimate business, that it is possible what you say there, that this ship where God [the mob boss] lives, is not a fantasy, that it is possible that he has the ship." If anything, Preminger is more disabused a critic of American society than Cannon. Cannon thinks that God's boat should be more than twelve miles offshore because then it's in international waters and the authorities can't touch him. Preminger replies, "No. God is untouchable by the American authorities anyway because he controls them."

Over the course of the discussions, Preminger becomes firmer and more impatient, whereas Cannon sounds defensive. Preminger objects to the "vacillation" of the script and insists, "it must be definite, it must be consistent." The format of their meetings turns into a relentless flow of dictation by Preminger. His emphasis is now not at all on humor, but on narrative consistency—one thing leading to another—and clarity of characterization. "There ought to be a human element in everybody," he says.

Preminger and Cannon finished a second draft of the script on November 6. "Preminger's style and mine so clashed," Cannon concluded, "that [the process] really represented the disintegration of a very good first draft into a miserable movie script." Erik observed that Cannon's *Skidoo* "was fanciful, and Otto was not fanciful. Otto insisted on bringing a certain logic to what was basically an illogical script." Austin Pendleton, who would play Fred in the film on Cannon's recommendation, echoed this assessment: "I just thought he didn't understand the music of it . . . What that script had, as did *Brewster McCloud*, was a tone that was very much happening . . . [Cannon] actually wrote these scripts before it had become so much a part of the counterculture, this tone that I'm about to describe. It was very offhanded. Kind of drifts along. Otto did not know offhanded, he just didn't understand that . . . Otto was very much into point-making in scenes. The idea of behavior just having its own expressiveness without making any points was utterly alien to him."[7]

Looking for a new writer, Preminger interviewed Mel Brooks but (fearing, as he told Cannon, that "between him and you, I will go crazy"[8]) instead hired Bernie Orenstein and Saul Turtletaub, then, in January 1968, turned to Elliot Baker, author of the novel *A Fine Madness*. Cannon observed that Baker "was giving Preminger exactly what he wanted and I had refused to give him." Erik thought that Baker's contribution lay in "normalizing the script. Taking the flightiness out of it." In March, as production was getting under way, Preminger asked Cannon to come back and help with the script. Cannon contributed some comments and suggestions but confessed, "Basically, the new directions the script has taken go beyond my own understanding of the story. My value to you therefore is now limited."[9]

Although Cannon's story and general structure were more or less retained in the film that Preminger eventually made, the situations and dialogue were completely overhauled. Only a few details remain from Cannon's first script: the TV-channel changing at the beginning; the line "If you don't dig nothing you can't dig anything. Dig?"; Tony and Fred's tense dialogue about Fred's draft dodging; Tony talking to his prospective victim via radios in their cells; a dosed guard having a vision of something that "wants" and "loves" him (in the first script, it was a flower; in the film it is a "big beautiful blob of nothing").

The scripting of Tony's acid trip underwent considerable revision from Cannon's first draft to his second, indicating that Preminger, armed with his personal experience, influenced its new content (as he would influence the realization of the special effects during postproduction). The first draft calls for a distorted image, from Tony's point of view, of the bedsprings of the bunk above him expanding and contracting. Then Tony would appear as a disembodied head on a limbo set, followed by a tearful Darlene, also in limbo. Tony would imagine himself lying in a coffin that moves through the void; Fred would speak in God's voice ("Die Tony"); Darlene would offer Tony a flower. Some of these elements, notably the wavering bedsprings and the offered flower, would remain in the finished film. The second draft brings the trip sequence closer to what was filmed: Fred and Leech now get smaller, the bedsprings turn into floating triangles, numbers join them, and Tony exclaims, "Mathematics! I see mathematics." God's head appears on the head of a screw; Tony looks for himself in the water. This version also includes some ideas that were later abandoned, including a hallucination of the Statue of Liberty and "a sensational kaleidoscope of multicolored images accompanied by music and voices."[10]

In the opinion of Ronald James Policy, who followed the production of *Skidoo* as a research project for his Ph.D. thesis, Preminger rushed the film into production before the script was ready. Preminger was under all the more pressure because the film's non-approved status meant, under his contract, that Paramount could take the film away from him if he exceeded the budget. According to Policy, "This stipulation caused some inconvenience late in the shooting schedule," when Preminger was forced to simplify and eliminate scripted scenes in order to finish.[11]

Preminger assembled his cast. "Otto really, really, really wanted" Jackie Gleason, said Erik, and used all his charm to persuade the star to play Tony. Carol Channing agreed to play Flo. Cesar Romero (whom Preminger had directed in *That Lady in Ermine*) and Frankie Avalon signed on in gangster roles, and Arnold Stang (from *The Man with the Golden Arm*) was cast as Tony's ill-fated sidekick, Harry. Exercising his rights under his contract with Faye Dunaway, Preminger demanded that she appear in *Skidoo* as Elizabeth, God's mistress. She refused, and on January 11, 1968, Preminger filed suit against her in the New York Supreme Court for breach of contract. Eventually an out-of-court settlement freed Dunaway in return for an undisclosed sum (which, according to one source, took the form of a portion of her pay for each of her five subsequent films).[12] Another Preminger contractee and *Hurry Sundown* veteran, John Phillip Law, a self-described "closet hippie," took the part of Stash, the main hippie in *Skidoo*. "It was such an abrupt change from *Too Far to Walk* to *Skidoo*," Law recalled. "Everyone who read the script said, 'My God, where did this come from?'"[13] Alexandra Hay, then performing in the Warner Playhouse production of Michael McClure's *The Beard*, for which she was repeatedly arrested for "indecent behavior," was cast as Darlene.

For the part he had originally intended for Dunaway, Preminger cast Detroit-born model Donyale Luna, whom he had met at a New York party for another model, Twiggy. Luna had appeared in one of Andy Warhol's *Screen Tests* in 1964 (Wayne Koestenbaum, in *Artforum*, described her appearance in the Warhol film as "pure diva, presenting a delicious mobile excess of mannerism"),[14] and Preminger invited her and Warhol to his office to screen the film for him. The next morning, Luna asked Preminger to lunch and asked if he would like to finance a Warhol film. Preminger told her, "I don't finance films, I direct them." She said, "Oh, you *direct* too." Preminger was amused. He remembered Luna later when casting *Skidoo*. The choice of a woman of color to play the part was not significant, he told a reporter. "The color doesn't mean anything. Call a character God and everything becomes a little unreal."[15]

Preminger hired Leon Shamroy as director of photography, ensuring for *Skidoo* a glossy look seemingly at odds with the script's countercultural aspects. To compose the score for the film, Preminger first sought the Jefferson Airplane but instead hired Harry Nilsson (whose contribution would prove an important asset). Defying the Directors Guild of America (DGA), Preminger hired non-guild member Steven North as second assistant director.

On March 11 Preminger held a first read-through of the (still unfinished) script. Policy recounted, "Preminger makes no attempt to supply motivations or modify characterizations of the readers. He interrupts only occasionally to describe a piece of business in greater detail or make a minor line change . . . Far from being a session with dynamic interchange between director and actors, it was rather solemn and perfunctory, marked with a ceremonial quality which may, after all, have been its prime value."[16]

Policy's presence during production meant that we have an unusually detailed record, take by take, of Preminger at work. (As we will see, documentation of nearly comparable extensiveness also exists for one other Preminger film, *Rosebud*. This means that Preminger's two most reviled films are those about whose productions the most is known.) Shooting began on March 12 with night-for-night shots of a flashback to Tony's theft of a file cabinet from the FBI. Policy observed, "Although the action is broadly comic, almost slapstick, Preminger insists that it appear plausible and well motivated." Policy caught a revealing moment when Preminger raged at Stang for failing to deliver a line during a take the actor assumed had already been spoiled. Policy recorded, "Preminger's face is a brilliant red, the veins at his temples distended. He storms over to Nat Rudich standing on the sidelines and, in an instant, his face relaxes. He whispers something to Rudich and both men laugh heartily."[17]

Preminger took pains with performance. When Tony discovers

Harry's body, Preminger objected "to Gleason's reaction of wide-eyed shock and coaxe[d] from him a smaller, grimmer sort of response." Later, in San Francisco, where the opening scenes in Tony's house were shot, Preminger became increasingly impatient with Stang's work ("Don't shout, Mr. Stang, we have microphones") and lectured the actor: "Screen acting must not appear to be acting. It must be real, otherwise it looks phony."[18]

Directing the interior house scene early in the film in which Tony and Stash criticize what each perceives to be the other's values, Preminger became "impatient and harsh, and an atmosphere of dejection and tension is mounting." Preminger shouted at Stang for being off his mark and at makeup man Web Overlander for letting Hay wear nail polish. Preminger rehearsed the actors repeatedly and told John Phillip Law exactly how to sit on a sofa. At one point Preminger cut in mid-take: "Mr. Law, we are not trying to delve into the mysteries of the hippies; we are making fun of them." Meanwhile, Preminger "remained genial and courtly" toward Channing and handled Gleason with tact.[19]

Doran William Cannon had seen Austin Pendleton acting onstage in New York and wrote the part of Fred for the actor. On Cannon's recommendation, Preminger brought Pendleton to San Francisco, ostensibly intending to shoot a screen test of him during production. While driving together to the location, they discussed the political situation in America. "It was an amazing time," Pendleton recalled. "It's almost impossible to communicate now. The air that spring was heavy with political importance in a way that I don't remember before or since." On arriving at the location, Preminger told the driver to take Pendleton to the airport. "We're not going to test?" asked the actor. Preminger replied, "You don't need to test. I like talking to you. You have the part."

Pendleton, who was and is on the left, later explained, "I think the thing Otto responded to most in the script was the character I played. Which may be why after a political discussion about the part, [he decided to cast me] . . . He wanted to know what my values were. I didn't realize it; I thought we were just having a talk on the way to a screen test, but the talk was the audition. He wanted to know where I was coming from with regard to all these things." After starting work on *Skidoo*, the actor continued his discussions with Preminger. "At the end of the day's shoot, a group of us would go to Otto's office at Paramount and drink vodka. He would talk primarily about politics and what was going on. He was a brilliant man. He could have written a column about politics that would have been interesting and valid."

After finishing in San Francisco ahead of schedule (a feat Preminger belittled with a typical remark: "Who knows about ahead of schedule? If I'm . . . ahead, there's something wrong with the schedule"),[20] the company moved to the Paramount studios for the scenes in the elaborately remote-controlled bachelor pad of Angie (Avalon), which was furnished with transparent Plexiglas furniture similar to that in Preminger's New York house. Policy appreciated Preminger's expertise at work during the scene of Angie receiving an unwanted visit from Flo: "On each successive take, Preminger works at refining the action, making it flow more smoothly."[21]

The next location was the Lincoln Heights Jail, an unused facility in downtown Los Angeles. Appearing in his first scene, "Austin Pendleton appears quite nervous," Policy observed, "and Preminger, during the rehearsal, is exceptionally gentle and patient with him." On the other hand, Michael Constantine, playing Tony's other cellmate, Leech, quickly became another of Preminger's whipping boys. Rehearsing the first cell scene, "Preminger again demonstrates his directorial preference for unobtrusive, understated acting by carrying on a running criticism of Michael Constantine's performance. Constantine, at this point still interpreting his Leech character quite broadly, seems unable or unwilling to tone down his characterization. Preminger says, 'you will see yourself on the screen and you will see that your personality comes across much better if you don't *act*.' "[22]

The next day, Preminger and Gleason tried to lighten the mood of the shoot, which had become "grindingly depressing," with "a running banter of mutual insult, Gleason ribbing Preminger about shouting tantrums, Preminger teasing him about his weight."[23] But it was to little avail. For Austin Pendleton, the predominant mood on the set was "sort of a let's-get-through-this type of despair. Otto would scream at everybody. Otto, in the past, would scream at people and results would happen. But here people were getting the screaming without it leading to anything that was working." Intimidated by Preminger's autocratic manner, Pendleton also felt that Preminger was ruining Cannon's script. "Day by day on the set, I thought scenes that were just fine in conception just got hammered into something very flat. Otto directed everything very strictly."

At one point about a week into the jail shoot, Preminger berated Pendleton for being off his mark, yelling, "You're an amateur!" The actor recalled:

> I just said, totally sincerely, "I know. I know I am." He turned on a dime. "No, you're not an amateur! Of course you're not!" It was at that point that our relationship changed. Gradually he began to encourage me. Jackie Gleason wouldn't rehearse, and all of my scenes were with Jackie Gleason. So, while the shot was being set up, we would just wait for Jackie, and Otto began to teach me about film acting. I learned almost everything I know about film acting from that shoot. He'd go over the scenes, and he'd talk about film acting as opposed to theater acting. He knew I had worked almost exclusively for theater, and he said, "Every take is like opening night." Because you never know which one is going to be printed and used. He talked about how truthful behavior is what the camera likes. He would talk to me about what he thought the scenes were about and what the relationships were about. It was direction of a kind that I've only had a few times since in film . . . Otto kept me so concentrated on the scenes. And the combination of being really concentrated on the scenes and really frightened has a lot of—there's something that film reacts well to, in that.

Pendleton credits Preminger with highlighting and humanizing the Tony-Fred relationship: "I think in that one respect, he may have gone a little bit beyond Bill Cannon. To Bill Cannon, that was all just kind of funny, that this kind of LSD guy of the time would give advice to a guy in the Mafia about LSD, but Otto saw [other] possibilities. Otto made a real point of that, with me and with Jackie." Though Gleason "was in a massive depression during the making of that film," according to Pendleton, "he was very generous to me. Very thoughtful, very aware that I was nervous. Very gentlemanly. So we had this relationship, and—I really learned this on this film—that stuff reads on film. What's going on actually between the people, the actors, reads on film. Jackie was a very complex man, and that shows up on film. There's a great sadness in him, which is always very powerful. And Otto realized this. That's why Otto didn't really get angry at Jackie for not coming out to rehearse. Otto knows when somebody is bringing their life onto the screen with them. And he likes that. What Otto hated was plastic acting."

After *Skidoo* had completed its disastrous commercial run, Preminger, conceding the film's failure, speculated that it suffered from the "wall" between him and his star. "While I could not argue with Gleason about what he was doing—it was all *correct*—it still did not really—I mean, there is such a difference between us—in the texture of our characters—and if he should read this he would probably say he's very happy about the difference. There's a different attitude toward life, toward our profession, toward men, toward women, toward friendship, toward love, toward war, toward peace, toward politics, toward *everything*. This made it impossible to project the meaning which I felt lay *underneath* the comedy. That's why for me the picture is not really successful."[24]

Preminger directed the beginning of Gleason's acid trip by talking to the actor while the camera was rolling, reading Pendleton's off-camera lines "and, at the same time, talking to Gleason, coaxing the reactions from him."[25] Recounting his own experience with acid, Preminger later told columnist Sheilah Graham, "I directed [Gleason] to be completely aware of what was going on. It's not like drinking, which dulls the senses. Everything is sharper."[26]

On April 22 *Skidoo* moved to San Pedro harbor, where the scenes set on God's yacht (actually John Wayne's yacht, the *Wild Goose*) were shot. The casting of Groucho Marx as God had apparently been settled only days before he started work (those who had turned down the part included Frank Sinatra, Rod Steiger, Zero Mostel, Anthony Quinn, Alfred Hitchcock, and Senator Everett Dirksen).[27] The scenes aboard the yacht, which had lately been rewritten, were further simplified during shooting, as Preminger quickly realized that Luna was incapable of delivering the dialogue to his satisfaction.

Most of the yacht interiors were filmed at Paramount in the final phase of production, starting April 29. If the previous weeks had been full of troubles, the last weeks brought new ones in the form of Groucho Marx's difficulties with his lines. On May 3 Policy noted the start of "a continual verbal jousting between Preminger and Marx." As Preminger became increasingly irritable during repeated takes of the scene of Stash using God's phone to send his fellow hippies a coded plea for help, Marx remarked, "We used to have fun when we made movies. The pictures were lousy, but we had fun." Policy observed, "It becomes increasingly clear that Preminger is disappointed in Marx's performance, but rather than confront him directly, he employs a scapegoat tactic, using Law or Luna to stop the take and then making a gentle suggestion to Marx." Luna's inability to keep still while standing behind Marx's chair drove Preminger to a fury (eventually he solved the problem by having her cross to the background). He took out some of his frustrations on Paramount studio manager Russ Brown, berating him for providing a "shamefully outdated" sound playback machine and yelling, "I'm not going to pay for today! You can sue me if you want to."[28] Preminger's treatment of Brown shows that the producer-director was not afraid of making himself unpopular at Paramount.

A scene of God and his mistress shooting pool required fourteen takes. According to Policy, "Luna is a source of difficulty, but in nearly every case the main problem would be Marx's inability, even with a teleprompter, to get through his lines. Little by little, Preminger deleted lines, cutting the scene down to the barest essentials." The next morning, Marx, who permitted himself the observation that "the script stinks," complained privately to Preminger about the lack of humor on the set. Preminger made some effort to lighten the mood, but the combination of Marx's failings and Preminger's reluctance to compromise could only be unpleasant. After take 14 of one scene, Preminger objected that Marx said "knock me off" instead of "bump me off." Marx cried, "Christ, do you consider that a mistake? Otto, they won't stay out of the theater because of that. They may, however, stay out for other reasons."[29]

When principal photography ended, on May 8, Policy wrote, "there [were] no cheers, no celebration." Summing up his experience on the set, Policy evaluated Preminger's shows of temper: "It may indeed be an efficient manner of dealing with people and obtaining instant obedience, but (and there were numerous instances of this within the ranks of the *Skidoo* crew) a man who wishes to avoid the humiliation of a dressing down in public is likely to do only what is demanded of him and nothing more. He is less likely to extend himself, to volunteer a contribution, to go beyond what is precisely demanded for fear of being wrong and, in so doing, bring down a wrathful response . . . If only from a standpoint of morale, the negative side-effects of Preminger's method of personnel manipulation were counter-productive."[30]

The postproduction of *Skidoo* took about four months. Editor George Rohrs took the place of Louis Loeffler, whose failing eyesight had forced his retirement. Rohrs found the ballet sequence frustrating. "Preminger's angles are so similar that they just don't cut together," he told Policy. "I always have to cut away to Fred Clark and then back to the ballet. It's shot too easily. Almost like he was afraid to get involved with the details of the choreography."[31] The obvious reply would be that Preminger wanted the scene to play from the point of view of the tower guards who are hallucinating the ballet.

Skidoo was the first Preminger film to be rated under the MPAA's rating system—a system that he had long advocated. It got an M ("suggested for mature audiences"—a category later rechristened GP and then PG).

The film premiered in Miami (Gleason's hometown) on December 19. Austin Pendleton attended. "We all sat in the back row of an orchestra section of this big theater in Miami, Otto and Hope, his wife, and Jackie Gleason and whoever he was with, and a couple of other people from the film. And from around a half an hour into the film we all just sat there and watched all these people walking up the aisle and walking out." Carol Channing later claimed that Gleason himself was among the walkouts.[32] The reception afterward, said Pendleton, "was one of those premiere parties where everyone there will talk about anything but the film, because it was such an evident disaster."

Skidoo went into general release the following week. Reviews were dismal. Some of them singled out Preminger, proving that the director's public visibility had once again (as with *Saint Joan* and *Hurry Sundown*) become a liability. This tendency reached its apotheosis with the review in *The New York Times* by Vincent Canby, who devoted his first three paragraphs to a discussion of Preminger's career and personality ("he is witty, but without much sense of humor; a man of charm who can be appallingly rude") and the remaining four to a pan of the film ("something only for Preminger-watchers, or for people whose minds need pressing by a heavy, flat object").[33]

A review that at least took the film seriously was Martin Lenine's in *The Washington Post*. Lenine found in the film "indications that Preminger is uneasy, perhaps not entirely consciously, about American society." When he suggested that a slow-motion shot during the sequence of the prisonwide LSD trip might have been a deliberate homage to Jean Vigo's *Zéro de conduite*,[34] the reviewer could not, presumably, have known that Doran William Cannon's first-draft script contained an epigraph from Vigo: "If we must be prisoners, at least let us choose our own prison and create there pleasure and joy so we'll want to live there all our lives."

Skidoo did poor business. Paramount didn't even bother to open the film in New York until March 1969, when it played on a double bill with Jules Dassin's *Up Tight!* The studio's treatment of the film was still a sore point with Preminger a year later, when *Variety* reported that he was "displeased with Paramount's handling of his last film, *Skidoo*, and said that if he were 'more greedy' he'd have done something about it. He still may."[35]

Skidoo is a deeply contradictory film. As personal as any Preminger film, it inaugurates a new phase in his work, one in which the author openly addresses his public and speaks as "I" about his own concerns. Preminger based Tony's acid trip on his own experience with the drug, and the director's voice is heard over a freeze-frame at the end of the film, telling the audience not to leave the theater before the end credits. Metaphorically, we can already hear Preminger speaking to us as early as the first scene of the film (almost its first line of dialogue), when, during Harry's channel-surfing, the Banks's TV set displays a shot from *In Harm's Way* (cropped from Panavision), and Flo protests, "No, Harry, I don't like movies on TV. They always cut them to pieces"—a complaint that links the narrative to Preminger's well-publicized battles over the TV broadcasting of his films. (In 1965 he had filed suit, unsuccessfully, to keep *Anatomy of a Murder* from being cut for TV and interrupted by commercials.)

Skidoo is also a negative film. From the prison observation tower (a privileged viewpoint in the film), the guard played by Fred Clark sees Tony and Fred's balloon as "a big beautiful blob of nothing" that "wants" and "loves" him. This perception is the converse of Stash's telling Darlene that he wants to be nothing (which he follows with the quip, "If you can't dig nothing, you can't dig anything, dig?"). The characters of *Skidoo* seek their own annihilation and that of everything around them, and Preminger is delighted to oblige them. The world *Skidoo* negates so effortlessly is a vacuous mediascape of stereotypical, repetitive, worn-out signs, as the casting of the film tells us at once. It's no accident that the gangsters are played by "celebrities" whom the film audience of 1968 might have encountered any night as a guest on a talk show, a performer in Las Vegas, or the star of an old movie on TV. The world of the gangsters in *Skidoo* is the world of American mass entertainment—a mass hallucination whose medium is television.

TV sets and monitors figure throughout the film, dissolving presence and enforcing a tense, nervous regime of surveillance and mediation. The opening shot of *Skidoo* tracks back to reveal that the cartooned microcosm of the opening title is enclosed within the frame of the Banks's TV set. God locks himself in his stateroom, away from contact with an outside world that he monitors via television and telephone. The sudden intrusion of Tony's remote voice in the vast space of Packard's luxurious prison cell disorients Packard and causes him to retreat in the medium-shot frame.

The television images that pervade the film are part of a wider pattern of the disintegration of the film frame. Preminger shows the flashback of Tony's burglary of an FBI office in a split-screen collage that juxtaposes the scene with a present-time medium shot of Tony, Flo, Hechy, and Angie in the Banks house—past and present changing places and entering into various configurations. (This treatment of space and time is an analogue of the quick, unceremonious, unexplained shuffling of styles and worldviews that occurs throughout the film—culminating in the final sequence's non-sequitur couplings: Angie and Elizabeth, God and Fred.) The trip sequence involves a variety of multi-image effects: God's head whirling on the head of a screw; Darlene's possible fathers swimming in a pool of orange, blue, and red light. The Panavision frame becomes a crucible of impermanence and fragmentation in which the phenomenal world is broken down. The screen is treated as a flat surface: a bright yellow billboard-size poster bearing the slogan BEAUTIFY AMERICA: GET A HAIRCUT fills the screen at the beginning of the scene in the mayor's office.

An important part of the strategy of *Skidoo* is to show both the Establishment and the hippies from each other's points of view, as broad caricatures embodying stereotypical attitudes and values. By the very terms in which he poses the cultural and ideological conflict that underpins the narrative, Preminger forecloses any possibility of a meaningful debate between the two sides. He offers instead a clash of empty signs.

Preminger's decision to train his camera on this degraded, flattened world is a logical step from the comic-book mode of *Hurry Sundown*. Yet he still means for us to take the characters seriously: we're still dealing, in *Skidoo*, with people we might ourselves be or know and with relationships we might be involved in. The opening sequence is acted "straight"; the situation is odd rather than funny, and only the score hints that we are watching a comedy. Gleason and Preminger play Tony's obsession over Darlene's biological paternity realistically: that the obsession never figures as a mainspring in the plot makes it all the more an element of realism—that is, of a social portrayal. Fred's mentoring of Tony becomes quite touching, Pendleton's natural compassion bringing out the vulnerability that lies just under Gleason's glum, wary surface.

Despite the impulse toward disintegration so apparent in much of the film, Preminger's visual control is fully evident throughout *Skidoo*. The elaborate traveling shot in the scene at the car wash, where Tony finds Harry's corpse in a car on a conveyor belt, is striking. More magisterial still is the single-take shot at the terminus where prisoners on their way to the penitentiary are allowed a restroom visit: Tony emerges from one of the stalls in place of the prisoner who just entered it, and the camera pans and tracks to follow him and the other prisoners as they are marched aboard a waiting launch, the camera relentlessly pushing forward toward the water. Several shots in the prison are small models of fluidity and precision in their staging, blocking, and integration of camera movement. The offhand, off-balance realism of the scenes of the hippies milling through the Banks home (they resemble the zombies taking over the farmhouse near the end of George Romero's *Night of the Living Dead*, made the same year) checks our impulse to laugh. Here, as in his great films, Preminger refuses to telegraph his intentions and dictate how the scene should be read.

Because Preminger doesn't pretend to depict a first-order contemporary reality in *Skidoo*, chortling attacks on the director for being "out of it" are beside the point. It's entirely legitimate for Preminger to dramatize the polarized culture of 1968 America in the stylized terms of *Ski-doo*. The success of this effort is certainly open to criticism, but criticism should at least recognize the nature of what it is criticizing.

During one of his appearances on the TV show *Laugh-In*, Preminger stared fixedly into the camera and intoned, "No . . . no . . . no . . . no," while making various hand gestures. It's as if he were rejecting everything before his gaze. The same intention animates *Skidoo*, a film that looks at the world around it and proclaims repeatedly that it sees "nothing."

33

The Love-In

Preminger bought the rights to Marjorie Kellogg's first novel, *Tell Me That You Love Me, Junie Moon*, in July 1968, before its publication. He also hired Kellogg, a forty-six-year-old hospital social worker, to write the script for the film.

In its simplicity and brevity, Kellogg's touching novel is the opposite of behemoths like Drury's *Advise and Consent* and Bassett's *Harm's Way*. The story of *Tell Me That You Love Me, Junie Moon* is ideally summarized in the novel's first paragraphs:

> Once there were three patients who met in the hospital and decided to live together. They arrived at this decision because they had no place to go when they were discharged.
>
> Despite the fact that these patients often quarreled and nagged each other, and had, so far as they knew, nothing in common, they formed an odd balance—like three pawnshop balls.[1]

The three are Junie Moon, a young woman whose face has been scarred from an acid attack by a deranged date; Arthur, a young man who has suffered since childhood from an undiagnosed progressive neurological disease; and Warren, a gay man who was left paraplegic by an accidental gunshot. The three rent a dilapidated house in a small town and, despite hostile neighbors and their own infirmities and insecurities, make a go of the arrangement. Arthur falls in love with Junie Moon, but his condition worsens and he dies in her arms underneath the banyan tree in their yard.

Kellogg, recalling her first meeting with Preminger, said, "He did all the talking. He'd read the book, and it was as though he were telling me about the book. It was interesting what he had to say about it . . . He said, 'These people have a lot of strength.' He admired strength in any form . . . I think he liked to see a situation that looked shaky or impossible and get into it and find out these things and find the strength of people."[2]

Work on the script took several months, first in Hollywood, where Preminger installed Kellogg in an office near the postproduction facilities he was using for *Skidoo*, then in New York, where he gave her a room in his office suite. "We both agreed to what needed to be done before we set out," said Kellogg. "That didn't take too long. He was very supportive. What he had to say was sometimes a little flamboyant, but it was always on the mark." Erik Preminger attributed his father's good relationship with Kellogg to his "basic chivalry" and her "incredible kindness and her professionalism . . . I wouldn't say that his direction of her was that much different from his direction of other actors or other writers. It was, 'Darling, you must understand that we must do it this way.' And she would do it this way, and there were very few times when she and Otto would not see eye to eye. I remember the ending was one. I remember that I was on her side, and Otto did it her way."[3]

At first Preminger anticipated making *Junie Moon* right after *Too Far to Walk*, which he now projected for a winter production on a New England campus. Late in 1968 he postponed *Too Far to Walk* and made *Junie Moon* the fourth film on his Paramount contract and the second "unapproved" one.

Junie Moon was the first Preminger film since *In the Meantime, Darling* to feature no established stars. He had at first sought to interest Mia Farrow in the part of Junie Moon, but eventually he cast Liza Minnelli, whom he had seen in a supporting part in *Charlie Bubbles*; her first film in a lead role, in Alan Pakula's *The Sterile Cuckoo*, would not be released until after *Junie Moon* finished production. Preminger saw a work print of the Pakula film and, responding to the "strange, Chaplinesque humor that comes through her body and eyes," decided to cast her.[4] He wanted to put her under a long-term contract, but she resisted.

In 1968, while *Skidoo* was in postproduction, Preminger considered having Austin Pendleton play Arthur, then announced John Phillip Law for the part. Finally, he chose Ken Howard, who had scored a success in *1776* on Broadway, and signed him to an extended contract. Robert

Moore, a successful stage director in New York (*Promises, Promises*; *The Boys in the Band*), went to see Preminger and asked if he could play a small part for him in order to watch him direct. "While we talked, I began to think that he might be able to play [Warren] in *Junie Moon*. We made a test and I signed him."[5] James Coco had played small roles in a few films but was mainly known as a New York stage actor. Preminger thought him "very much in the style of French comedians, very human, like in Marcel Pagnol's *Marius*,"[6] and cast him as Mario, a lonely fish seller who befriends the three heroes. When Coco's assurance that he could drive a car proved false, Preminger astonished the rest of the company. Instead of getting angry at the actor, he laughed "like it was one on him" (Ken Howard's words)[7] and simply arranged for Coco to take driving lessons. "Jimmy Coco could always make [Preminger] laugh," remembered Kellogg. "He was worth a billion dollars to him on that shoot."

Many of the supporting players had had little or no previous film experience. Fred Williamson, who had just done *M*A*S*H*, produced by Ingo Preminger, was cast as Beach Boy, an easygoing and entrepreneurial employee of the resort hotel where the three protagonists vacation. Kay Thompson, Minnelli's godmother and a renowned singer and vocal arranger, had appeared in only two previous films (the most recent being 1957's *Funny Face*): she took the part of Miss Gregory, the trio's eccentric landlady. The one true veteran in the cast, Anne Revere (from *Fallen Angel, Forever Amber,* and the ill-fated *Four Twelves Are 48*), had been blacklisted in 1951 (named by Lee J. Cobb) and had not made a film since. Cast as Miss Farber, a sympathetic hospital staffer, Revere later summed up her experience on *Junie Moon*: "It's only a tiny part, but, after all those years, God, I loved doing it."[8] Preminger secured the services of Boris Kaufman as cinematographer, a choice that suggested an intention of making *Junie Moon* into a prototypical non-Hollywood film: Kaufman, Jean Vigo's cinematographer, had won an Oscar for shooting Elia Kazan's *On the Waterfront* (1954) and had since worked on other Kazan films and become Sidney Lumet's regular cinematographer.

Kellogg completed a script on May 1, 1969, which, with a few changes, is close to what Preminger shot. It set off alarm bells at Paramount. A memo from Peter Bart, then the studio's vice president of production, to Robert Evans, dated May 12, complains—in terms that hint at the low esteem in which Preminger was held by both men—that the story "is intrinsically downbeat and depressing," that "the script is too long (184 pages)," and that some of the smaller parts "tend to be cardboard . . . Otto's heavy hand is at work here." A month later, from Bart's point of view, the situation had not improved. He sent a telex to Charles Bluhdorn on June 19, apparently hoping Bluhdorn would approach Preminger directly: "My rereading *Junie Moon* only reinforces earlier apprehensions about project. Very tough to advance constructive suggestions to Preminger since only total rewrite would ameliorate problems and there's no time." Bart recommends cutting the flashbacks to the central trio's pasts ("Believe contemporary audience hip enough to understand characters without flashbacks") and the death of Minnie, a hospital roommate of the central trio. He also felt that the scene of Miss Gregory trying to get Warren to walk "presently plays like parody of scenes we have seen in dozens of movies." Bart concludes, "Final point to Otto is that Junie Moon should not be made so grotesque that it would be agony to look at her for two hours. Story sufficiently uncommercial without Junie wearing Frankenstein mask. Could advance many other suggestions but feel would be unrealistic at this late date."[9]

Preminger ignored every one of Bart's suggestions.

Shooting began on July 9 at Salem Hospital on the North Shore of Massachusetts. Preminger sponsored a contest among local filmmakers, offering a $1,000 prize for the best short documentary on the making of *Junie Moon*. Deac Rossell, film critic for *Boston After Dark* and coordinator of the documentary contest, was impressed by Preminger's control of the production and his predilection for posing challenges to himself and his company by setting up complicated shots. "He was like a Byzantine patriarch, making decisions on the past, present, and future status of his company almost simultaneously." Rossell found that Preminger's behavior both confirmed and belied his reputation as a tyrant: "He is arbitrary and demanding on the set, flaring up in an instant at the first glimpse of incompetence. He has an iron will, and everyone around him is drawn into what *he* wants to talk about. He works harder than anyone on the set, and his moods change with the intensity and quickness of a pulsing strobe light. Yet he is rarely unfair, and often shows remarkable patience."[10]

Rossell watched Preminger shoot thirteen takes of a scene with Warren and a group of doctors in the hospital ward: the director, sweating under the hot lights, didn't blow up at the actors who were missing their cues, but merely told them, "Look, I know it is difficult. Will you please *concentrate* on your parts." During the shooting of the scene in the hospital recreation room, a technician pointed out a microphone shadow beneath a vase of flowers over the mantel. Repositioning the microphone would have required a distracting expense of time. Preminger looked at the shadow and concluded, "If anyone recognizes that as a mike shadow, they do not deserve this wonderful little film. Are we moving the mike?" The crew shouted, "No," and Preminger shot the scene, giving evidence of both his good mood and his continual tolerance of shadows cast by film equipment.

Ken Howard appreciated Preminger. In a scene between Arthur and Junie Moon, Preminger advised Howard, "Speak to Liza so that only she can hear you," which helped. Howard noticed, however, that Preminger's approach could backfire with certain actors. "He could be a little too abrupt. I think he knew it when he had it; I don't think he knew how to get it sometimes. I think he had a very good eye for good acting and simple acting, in kind of the European sense—not all this extra hoopla. But I don't think he had any sense of how to get that out of an actor. And quite frankly, I don't think that should be a director's job . . . Even though I was young, I got along with [Preminger]. I wasn't looking for that other kind of guidance. He was very good to me. He didn't abuse the contractual control that he had, and he was encouraging."[11]

Marjorie Kellogg, whom Preminger invited to accompany the production, confirmed that "there was a good deal of camaraderie on the set. We felt like a group of gypsies. The cast got to know each other in quite a different way." According to Kellogg, the actors, especially Moore, felt encouraged to ad-lib. Preminger "did what a good director should do. If he didn't like what he saw, he would say why he didn't like it, and they would talk about it. It was never an argument, it was just something that they had to clarify." Preminger kept Kellogg involved in the production, making her feel needed. "He never made even the smallest change without talking to me about it." Later, he brought Kellogg along to Cannes for the film's premiere (in competition) in May 1970.

Preminger no doubt saw a strategic advantage in portraying the making of *Junie Moon* as a "love-in" (journalist William Wolf's term). While the film was in release, he said of the production, "We became all one small family and the making of the film was a really warm, human experience . . . I hope (I cannot judge) this shows on the screen. We felt during the making of the film such friendship for each other that there was really never a problem that couldn't be solved."[12]

There was more to it. Although the two never clashed, Preminger's direction did not always sit well with Minnelli. She later said, "His theory is that the actor is hired to act, and he must be ready at all times. He wants the work immediately—and perfectly. You get the impression with Otto that you don't have time to ask questions, and you come in and don't ask. If you do it wrong, you get yelled at. It's like teachers. There are some who correct you by saying, 'It would be better this way,' and others just say, 'That's wrong!' Otto is the latter." Her disagreement with her director didn't prevent her from giving her all to the part. "For the duration of the film, Junie Moon and I were the same person. I felt what she felt; but I felt it as Junie Moon, not as Liza Minnelli, the actress."[13]

Ken Howard watched Preminger coach Minnelli through a take of the scene in which Junie Moon sees her disfigured face in a mirror. "Now you look up, see yourself, and realize—and now cry. [Pause.] Both eyes."[14] Luckily for her, Minnelli's tears flowed more easily than had Jean Seberg's in *her* mirror shot at the end of *Bonjour Tristesse*.

From Salem the company moved to nearby Manchester to shoot the scenes at the house where Junie, Arthur, and Warren take up residence. The Hammond Museum in Magnolia stood in for Miss Gregory's house; and Preminger also shot on locations in Rockport and elsewhere.

In August, after finishing the Boston-area scenes, the unit moved to Naples, Florida, to shoot the scenes in which Junie Moon, Arthur, and Warren take a vacation trip together. In Florida, the film ran into trouble when Preminger was told by a representative of the Chicago office of IATSE (the International Alliance of Theatrical Stage Employees) that he needed to augment his camera crew with five local members. On the second day of shooting in Florida, Preminger shut down the production and went to Los Angeles to search for a substitute location. He fumed to the press that IATSE was behaving "like the Mafia," that closed shops would lead to obsolescence by keeping out young talent, and that "by forcing more employment, the unions are making fewer jobs available." There was more to Preminger's decision to move the production than the union troubles, Erik Preminger revealed. "Otto didn't like Florida. It was hot. He didn't like where he was shooting, everything about it. He really used the union problems to cause a force majeure which allowed him to move to California without having to spend any money doing so, because the insurance company covered the lost time and the lost money. There's no overestimating his abilities as a producer."[15]

Boris Kaufman fell ill during shooting one night, and another great cameraman, Stanley Cortez, whose career had foundered since the days of *The Magnificent Ambersons* (1942) and *Night of the Hunter* (1955), stepped in at a moment's notice to shoot the scene on the pier of Arthur's epileptic seizure. *Junie Moon* wrapped in La Jolla in mid-September.

Preminger asked folk songwriter/singer Pete Seeger to write a song for the film and perform it in the under-the-titles sequences. (Previously, Preminger had screened the film for Bob Dylan, who had no interest in contributing a song to it but found Preminger's house interesting enough to ask for a second screening with his wife present.)[16] Seeger came up with the song "Old Devil Time," which Preminger filmed him singing in Sequoia National Park.

The film was released in July 1970. Though many of the reviews were dubious, they were the best Preminger had had since *Bunny Lake Is Missing*. Jonas Mekas, in his *Village Voice* column, praised *Junie Moon* for its "very curious (and complex) 'jagged' rhythm" and for Preminger's ability to convey through movement, pacing, and composition "that state of suffering, that state of anguish, angry persistence, creepy violence—all kinds of things that are not easy to name here, but which make up the real content of the movie."[17]

The film did poor business.

Tell Me That You Love Me, Junie Moon is in a place by itself in Preminger's oeuvre. The third of his confrontations with the altered society and culture of the 1960s, *Junie Moon* is the most direct in its affirmation of at least some of the values that had come to be associated with the word "counterculture." Whereas in *Skidoo*, "hippies" and "the Establishment" prove to be each other's mirror images and absorb each other, the countercultural figures of *Junie Moon* have no use for the Establishment, nor it for them. The film charts not so much a mutual rejection as a mutual obliviousness. Because of their disabilities, Junie, Arthur, and Warren have no place to go except outside the normal world, which in turn has no interest in them. On the other hand, *Junie Moon* goes further than *Skidoo* in refusing to grant any inherent value or significance to unconventionality: the figure in the film who most defies convention, Miss Gregory, is shown to be inhuman, whereas representatives of bureaucracy, normality, and entrepreneurism—Mario, Miss Farber, and Beach Boy—prove compassionate.

Junie Moon is the first of Preminger's films since *Anatomy of a Murder* not to be shot in a 2.35:1 aspect ratio. The scaling down represents a deliberate choice in favor of intimacy and a deference to the disempowerment of the three main characters. The Panavision screen (or its equivalent in screen proportions) lent itself to processes, to the functioning of power, to tracking groups of people through alien spaces, and to exploring these spaces with the people. With *Junie Moon*, there is a change in emphasis, also a change in point of view. The environment and its effect on the main characters do not cease to be important to Preminger. The house where Junie, Arthur, and Warren live and the seaside resort where they go on vacation are spaces whose opportunities for isolation or for reconciliation are of interest to Preminger. The state institution of Arthur's flashback is an alien environment as hostile and threatening as the hospital in *Bunny Lake* and the prison in *Skidoo*. By shooting with a normal lens (though, to be sure, Arthur's flashback is filmed anamorphically and printed squeezed), Preminger claims, however, that these spaces will not divert him from his main task, which is to concentrate on how the people react to the spaces, what they make of them, how they dwell in them or escape from them.

Tell Me That You Love Me, Junie Moon starts and ends under the sign of a generalized displaced address—that of Pete Seeger ("Old Devil Time")—the functional obscurity of which quickly acts on the viewer as a threat and lessens in advance the possibility of a coherent response to the drama that is to unfold. Preminger proceeds to thwart the formulation of such a response by any means necessary, in reckless apparent disregard of form and good taste. Like its central trio of characters, the film turns its abjection into the basis for an existential position and a political practice.

Preminger's approach to the narrative of *Junie Moon* remains to some extent consistent with his approach in his earlier films—though it is certainly not without its new, aberrant features. After a credits sequence that in itself constitutes one of these features, *Junie Moon* begins outside the story: a convertible Volkswagen Beetle pulls up in front of a hospital; the camera zooms in; a man gets out and goes into the building. This man will be introduced to us shortly as Dr. Miller, one of the hospital's resident physicians. Preminger enters the narrative in an arbitrary way, from the outside, and also in a way that is somewhat deceptive, since the character with whom we start will prove to have a minor role in the story. Preminger insists from the beginning on exterior movement, on a frame (the shot in front of the hospital performs this function), on an envelope: so, at the end of the film (just before the end-credits sequence, itself part of a larger and looser frame), Mario's truck takes Junie Moon and Warren away from the cemetery.

Inside the hospital, a phalanx of doctors and nurses charges down the corridor toward the camera—an inexorable movement that anticipates other movements to come, such as the propulsive dolly shot that accompanies/drives Junie Moon from her hospital bed to the mirror, where she inspects her scarred face. In the flashback to Junie Moon's ill-fated date with Jesse, a high-angle crane shot drives forward behind the couple as they make their way through a crowd to enter a waterfront discotheque. The same fluid and inexorable movement of the camera loses the pair, to proceed with a group of men who suddenly, for no apparent reason, pick up another man by his arms and legs, carry him to the back of the set, and throw him into the water. This bravura Premingerian shot stands out, as does the beautiful night shot in which the camera travels alongside Beach Boy's yellow jeep as he drives Warren and their two girlfriends past the row of waterfront amusement places.

Preminger retains his inclination to stage scenes in two-shots and fairly extended takes. A lengthy scene of Arthur and Junie Moon on their hotel-room balcony at night is staged as a single take, finishing on a dog walking up to a door that has just been closed (a remarkable bit of risk taking even for Preminger). A long take of Arthur's epileptic fit on the boardwalk at night is also extremely impressive and, like the best moments of the film, evocative. Staggering, Arthur retreats into a narrow walkway between two buildings and falls on the ground in shadow; then, the fit passing, he reemerges into the artificial light and rejoins the milling crowd. The episode has been purely private, unacknowledged by the world.

The zoom in *Junie Moon* takes on greater autonomy than in *Hurry Sundown* and *Skidoo*. Preminger uses zooms to denote a shift in levels of consciousness, or to suggest psychological crisis. The rigid, mechanical zoom-ins and -outs in the cafeteria scene emphasize in a rather abstract and schematic way the isolation and anguish of Arthur. An extraordinary shot follows Junie Moon walking down a street at night and then picks out Arthur in the background and zooms in on him as children from his imagination rush toward him. Here the zoom combines with an unnaturalistic use of color to create an unexpected sense of incursion and violation: Arthur, wearing a yellow-and-red-stripe T-shirt, exists in an objective reality that he shares with Junie Moon, but the children, in monochrome, belong to his fantasy and to his past.

The zoom is one of a barrage of techniques Preminger uses to delineate a distorted, personalized, subjective experience. In the flashback to the waterfront dance club, the camera tracks alternately toward and away from Jesse, stressing his disorientation. In the cemetery flashback, punchy big-band jazz alternates with a baroque organ piece over Jesse's inaudible, perhaps unarticulated words as he watches Junie Moon strip. At one point Preminger also adds Junie Moon's thought voice ("Run, why don't you run?"). The onset of Arthur's fit is heralded by strange, high-pitched sounds.

In the flashbacks to Arthur's institution in *Junie Moon*, Preminger uses the anamorphic lens but leaves the images squeezed—a deformation of the image that is the equivalent, in this film, of the matte shots and optical special effects of the LSD sequence in *Skidoo*. Preminger seeks again to violate the image, to attack its claim to objective truth, to rebel against its impersonality and inhumanity. (The fish-eye shots in *Such Good Friends* will present a minor variation on this theme.)

Preminger's decision to find a different, distorting style for each of the flashback sequences (farce for Warren, melodrama/psychodrama for Junie Moon, expressionism for Arthur) tends to distance these scenes, isolating the present-time characters from their pasts. As a result, the difficulty each character has in accepting, or even recalling, his or her past becomes unreal and abstract. We do not participate in the struggle of the characters to overcome their pasts, because we feel that their pasts are not integrated into their present experience. It is as if Preminger himself didn't believe in the past.

Preminger juxtaposes scenes of subjective experience, fantasy, and memory—whose subjective character is strongly marked by unusual aural and visual devices—with objective scenes. Thus, Arthur's epileptic fit on the floor of his room is intercut with a shot of Junie Moon knocking at his door. Later, the flashbacks to Arthur's ordeal at the institution are intercut with scenes of Junie Moon and Mario searching through town for him. A similar juxtaposition can also take place within a single shot, like the one mentioned earlier of Junie Moon, Arthur, and the monochrome boys at night. In these scenes, and in the discotheque and cemetery flashback, the effect achieved is of a violent collision of elements, a montage or collage effect quite different from the relativization of genres, consciousnesses, and modes of experience characteristic of Preminger's earlier works—though such a collision is anticipated in *In Harm's Way* and *Bunny Lake Is Missing*.

The element of caricature, so strong a feature of Preminger's work in *Hurry Sundown* and *Skidoo*, persists in *Junie Moon*. Junie's mother, the three heroes' suspicious and malicious neighbor, and Warren's potential fathers are broad caricatures; Miss Gregory is a grotesque; and Minnie is a kind of "folk" character from a tradition of African American earth wisdom (linking the film back to *Porgy and Bess* and *Hurry Sundown*). One effect of the flattening of these minor figures is to highlight the humanity and complexity of the three central characters. That Preminger is willing to sacrifice background complexity in favor of his foreground should neither surprise nor dismay, but it must be conceded that *Junie Moon* represents an advance in this tendency, even over his two previous films—another symptom of the narrowing of scope evident in Preminger's choice of a standard aspect ratio.

Along with an occasional self-consciousness and awkwardness in flaunting the success of the three main characters at forming their band apart, *Junie Moon* is distinguished by scenes of real warmth and sensitivity. Arthur and Junie Moon's postcoital dance in the hotel suite is graced by the unforced intimacy of the actors and the strange, harsh yet tender, shadow-filled lighting. The absence of music registers strongly here (particularly since the score throughout the film is such a strange grab bag of undistinguished rock, lounge, and orchestral music); instead we hear the sound of waves. Liza Minnelli's performance is very successful. Her non-reaction when Mario tenderly explores the scarred side of her face with the back of his hand (during their search for Arthur) is beautifully judged: neither frozen in tension nor registering obvious surprise, aware that she has permitted him to cross a boundary of privateness but not sure how to respond. It is an acting moment that Preminger must have prized, and that he either knew how to bring out or knew better than to interfere with. The penultimate scene in the yard, done in one extremely long take with a beautiful camera movement gliding around the tree, is very affecting: Junie Moon's screaming at the sky fiercely asserts the tragic sense that the film has been at pains to suppress.

Despite its strengths, *Tell Me That You Love Me, Junie Moon* is not fully satisfying. The theme of the story is the problem of accepting love—above all of accepting the self as worthy of love (this is made especially clear in the characterization of Mario, but it is expressed through all the principal characters). Perhaps, for all his compassion and goodwill, this problem does not fully engage Preminger; he does not fully believe in it. Yet *Fallen Angel* treats the same theme, and it is a superior film—moreover, one made without compassion, which even regards the compassion of its heroine (another June) with some irony.

In *Junie Moon*, Preminger fails to follow the lines of the story to their ends: his attitude remains ambivalent. He refuses to portray Junie Moon, Arthur, and Warren either as rebels or as victims ("I hate self-pity," he told Peter Bogdanovich).[18] Rather, he shows them as accommodators, people trying to adjust to the conditions of their life. It is a strength of the film that it does not "dramatize" their situation in a straightforward manner, but it is also a problem, since Preminger must find a different way of formulating their dilemma. Arthur, who demands unconditional love, is the most challenging of the trio, and he (like Plato in Nicholas Ray's *Rebel Without a Cause*) is killed. In a way, the problem of *Junie Moon* repeats the problem of *Saint Joan*, in which Preminger appears not to know what to do with the heroine after she has fulfilled her heroic mission, and, like the Dauphin and the court, he seems embarrassed by her continuing presence. In a way, too, these problems are inherent in the source material: neither Shaw's play nor Kellogg's novel states clearly how we are to conceive of the central characters and their story, what frame we are to place them in. It is essential to Preminger's conception of cinema and the world to deny us a frame, to play on its absence, but most of his films before *Junie Moon* offer at least the lure or the possibility of a frame. The Preminger films that borrow the frame of melodrama—*Fallen Angel, Where the Sidewalk Ends, Carmen Jones, The Man with the Golden Arm, Porgy and Bess, Advise & Consent, Hurry Sundown* among them—force us to question the frame, to look beyond or around it. The denial of melodrama in *Junie Moon* is a bold move, but Preminger's success in posing an alternate structure is only partial.

34

A Very Unpleasant Set

Preminger got into the news in early 1970 as one of several prominent guests at a cocktail party given by conductor Leonard Bernstein's wife as a benefit for the Black Panther Party. Preminger contributed to the Panthers' defense fund but got into an argument with a Panther at the party. The event was immortalized by Tom Wolfe in a satirical *New York* magazine article later included in his book *Radical Chic & MauMauing the Flak Catchers*.

Through Erik, who was then working as his story editor, Preminger had been tipped off while it was still in manuscript that Lois Gould's *Such Good Friends*, a novel about the sexual lives of a group of well-to-do Manhattanites, would be a hot book. Outbidding other parties, Preminger secured the film rights from Gould for a $200,000 guarantee in February 1970, well before its May 1970 publication.[1]

Gould's *Such Good Friends* is a brilliant novel, one of the best Preminger filmed. Like *The Man with the Golden Arm* (and unlike either *Tell Me That You Love Me, Junie Moon* or *The Human Factor*), it needed to be dismantled and put together again before it could become a movie. The novel is narrated in stream-of-consciousness mode by Julie Messinger, a housewife and mother of two. Her husband, Richard, a magazine art director and children's book illustrator, after undergoing surgery for the removal of a mole, has a bad reaction to the anesthetic and falls into a coma. The Messingers' friend, Cal, tells Julie that Richard has been having an affair with Cal's girlfriend, Miranda; and Julie determines that a mysterious diary she has found in Richard's files contains coded data on his numerous extramarital affairs. Stunned and confused, Julie engages in momentary flings with Cal and with Richard's doctor, Timmy. Richard's death leaves Julie trying to sort out her feelings about him and their marriage and facing the future with their children.

Work on the screenplay of *Such Good Friends* seems to have been more difficult than usual for Preminger, at least as measured by the number of writers gone through. At successive stages, Preminger worked with Joan Micklin Silver, David Slavitt, Joan Didion and John Gregory Dunne, and David Shaber, none of whom was able to complete a satisfactory draft. Silver, one of the first writers, was, Erik recalled, "just not right for Otto. She was a little more psychologically attuned to the character than Otto really cared to be, and probably a little bit more of a feminist than Otto cared to be."[2] The collaboration with Didion and Dunne lasted longest: he hired them in August and, in October, told an interviewer that he was working eight to ten hours a day with the couple. According to Dunne, Preminger tried to stop him and Didion from going home for Christmas. Finally, in early 1971, Preminger managed to secure the services of Elaine May. His original choice for the project, May had been unavailable when he first sought her.

The two finished the script in ten weeks. "I think that what Elaine gave him was, she kept him out of it," recalled Erik Preminger. "He was spared the frustration of having to develop a script." According to Erik, after each story conference with his father, May would disappear for two weeks, during which she couldn't be reached by phone. She would then resurface with a third of the script written. Preminger would work with her on a few pages, making minor changes, before she disappeared again. In this way, May completed a final script, which, according to Erik, was shot basically as written. May's name would not appear on the credits; instead, she substituted the pseudonym Esther Dale, the name of a Hollywood character actress who usually played matrons and maids. Erik said that May insisted from the beginning on not being credited, on a general principle of refusing credit on projects that were not her own. According to Erik, May was upset with his father for allowing her involvement to be publicized: "She felt he was more honorable than that."[3] (The following year, Erik would serve as associate producer of May's *The Heartbreak Kid*, in which he would also play a waiter.)

Preminger also went public with another kind of involvement during the preproduction of *Such Good Friends*. On February 5, 1971, he disclosed to the press that Erik was his son and that he had begun the formal process of adoption. He praised Gypsy Rose Lee (who had died in

April 1970). "She was only interested in having the baby. She was a very independent woman, way ahead of her time."[4]

Such Good Friends became the final film under Preminger's Paramount contract. Like *Skidoo* and *Tell Me That You Love Me, Junie Moon*, it was an unapproved project under the contract's terms. Paramount would have preferred that Preminger make something else, and in fact, the studio offered him the chance to produce and direct Mario Puzo's *The Godfather*. Preminger's reaction, according to Erik, was, "It's just another gangster movie, and the only way I would make it is if I could get Sinatra to play the Godfather."[5] Preminger offered the role to Sinatra, who turned it down, whereupon Preminger told Paramount he would pass on the project (and the rest, as they say, is history).

Dyan Cannon, who, since her success in Paul Mazursky's *Bob & Carol & Ted & Alice*, had floundered through several undemanding parts, liked Gould's novel but thought May's script was "different from the book. It's better. It's brilliant."[6] Casting proceeded through April, May, June, and July. Preminger exercised his option on Ken Howard to cast the actor as Cal and brought back James Coco as Timmy. Preminger cast Jennifer O'Neill, whom he had met on *The Joe Franklin Show*, as Miranda. For smaller roles, Preminger turned to old friends: Burgess Meredith, who agreed to do what amounted to a cameo, and a very strange one; Nancy Guild, a Twentieth Century-Fox contract starlet during Preminger's years there; and Sam Levene, who starred in the Broadway production of *Margin for Error*.

The production commandeered numerous locations in Manhattan, including the Flower-Fifth Avenue Hospital, the Guggenheim Museum, Central Park, and the Elizabeth Arden beauty salon on Fifth Avenue. Photographer Bert Stern's studio was used for Cal's studio. For the scene in which Julie nearly causes a traffic accident, the production closed down part of Seventh Avenue. The Central Park West apartment of a neighbor of Ingo's daughter Eve became the set for the Messingers' apartment.

Shooting started in late June 1971 and was, from the beginning, marked by an extremely bad relationship between the director and his star. Assistant director Charles Okun told the story this way: "We were shooting at Elizabeth Arden's. It was quite early in the shoot. [This location was, in fact, the very first on the schedule; the unit shot there on

June 29 and 30.] One of the rooms was made into a dressing room. Dyan was in there, and I guess wardrobe gave her an outfit to put on, and she didn't like it. She wasn't going to wear it, and she wasn't coming out. Otto went in there—who I never called Otto, it was Mr. Preminger—and I hear all this screaming in there. She was ranting, and he yelled back at her, and he walks out, and she's hysterical in there." Okun finally had to go in and persuade her to come out of the dressing room to work.[7] Erik Preminger saw the incident as a replay of the moment, big in his father's legend, when he let Lana Turner leave *Anatomy of a Murder* rather than allow her to choose her own costumes. "Here's what happened. Hope, who is his wife and whom he is extremely loyal to, has picked out the costumes for Dyan to wear. Dyan does not like one of them and says to Hope that she doesn't want to wear it. Hope tells Otto that Dyan doesn't want to wear this. That's it. She will wear it, and from that point on it was open warfare."[8]

Hope Preminger recalled that Cannon "seemed very unprofessional to us. She'd be late, and she wasn't very nice to the little guys, you know, to the runners and to the wardrobe man, and I finally blew up at her." Cannon annoyed Hope by making disparaging remarks about Otto in her presence.[9] According to Otto Preminger, "She wanted to play star. She came late, then left the stage for new makeup. I only get mad when someone doesn't know their lines, or is late. To keep 120 people waiting is unforgivable. And in rather bad taste, I think."[10]

Willi Frischauer visited the set midway through production in August and observed that "when not actually before the cameras, Dyan Cannon keeps as far away from him as possible. No private word passes between director and star."[11] Barrett Rudich, Nat's son, who worked as a still photographer on *Such Good Friends*, saw Cannon walk off the set. "I know it was an emotional scene they were working on . . . He was probably pressuring her just a little too much; she felt vulnerable. I got the impression she was really trying very hard. He got very upset about her walking off. I remember him saying something like, 'We have a contract with her.' He was outraged."[12]

Ken Howard recounted an incident when "he really just ripped into her, and incorrectly. She had a moment where she's dealing with the fact that her husband's dying, and she went through this whole emotional thing, but there was a laugh at one point, one of those ironic things, and he got all angry at her, like she wasn't really in the scene, and missed the point—'cause he could be a little blunt—that it was part of one other level of crazy emotion that one might go through in a situation like that."[13]

Before the film was released, Cannon, speaking more diplomatically than she later would about her director, described working with Preminger as *"different*. Sometimes he could be a joy. And then the next minute—Un-rea-son-able. You could not reason with him. His attitude toward you changed every day. It didn't matter *who* you were. You never knew . . . It's not what he [Preminger] says. It's the *way* in which he says it. And it comes so suddenly—without warning—that it hits you like an avalanche. You know, it's like walking down a street and having eighty tons fall right in front of you and seeing a great big hole and realizing— Some people work better under tension. I don't."[14]

By keeping Cannon on edge, Preminger elicited unrehearsed effects from her on camera, which surprised her costars. Nina Foch, who played Julie's mother, recalled, "I would do my part of the scene, and then he would make Dyan Cannon cry so hard that she would play her part of the scene in a way that completely surprised me. If I'd known she was going to play it that way, I wouldn't have played my part the way I did."[15] Normally Preminger could have been expected to oppose such improvisations, but at the moments in question he must have been satisfied with Cannon's acting.

Preminger almost drove Jennifer O'Neill to tears by yelling at her for moving her head during one scene. While the film was still in production, O'Neill said, "It's just like a whole atmosphere blows up and settles down, and blows up and settles down, and then you can't remember what it's all about. I don't understand it at all . . . why he's that way."[16] Preminger asked Ken Howard to work with O'Neill, and Howard advised Preminger to let her modify her dialogue slightly to make it more comfortable for her. Though in similar situations throughout his career and as recently as *Skidoo* he had insisted on the lines being spoken exactly as in the script, Preminger took Howard's advice.[17]

Howard recalled an example of what seemed to him Preminger's perversity—in setting up the scene in which Cal reveals to Julie that Miranda and Richard have been having an affair. The scene, set in a restaurant, is filmed largely in two setups, one on Julie, one on Cal. The dialogue was filmed in continuous takes of their conversation, which is interrupted periodically by a waiter. After repeated takes, the actors' energy came to focus less on their situation than on whether the actor playing the waiter would be able to get through his lines without making a mistake. "That was a perfect example of, Jesus, Otto, shoot it so you're shooting yourself in the foot! It became about the waiter. Dyan and I would look at each other like, 'I can't believe this.'"[18]

Preminger occasionally became annoyed with his cinematographer, Gayne Rescher. According to Barrett Rudich, "Preminger could get impatient with this guy's fussing with the lighting at the last minute. He made some comment like 'Who do you think you are, Leon Shamroy?'"[19] On the other hand, first assistant Charles Okun enjoyed "a great relationship with Preminger. Even though he was a tyrant, I thought he was a fair guy. I did my job, I knew my job; the key thing was, I did whatever he told me to do. I would never question it with him, but when I did, I would be 150 percent right."[20]

Laurence Luckinbill, who played Richard, respected Preminger. "He's ruled by his instincts—right or wrong. On some scenes he'd say, 'Print' after the first take."[21] Nina Foch gave Preminger a mixed review:

> Basically, he's a fine craftsman. He's so good at his own work. But the way he goes about getting his results! He knows when he comes in exactly how he will shoot; where you are going to stand; where you are going to go and how you are going to get there. But he doesn't give you a chance to probe, to define, to explore . . . I don't think Preminger casts well. He traps himself. Then he is forced to tell everybody what he expects of them to the smallest detail. Of course, for the actor it is much more productive to be allowed to feel out the part . . . to have options open.
>
> Ingmar Bergman speaks of working in an atmosphere of love. Otto Preminger, yelling and screaming, sets up an atmosphere under which most people don't work well at all. To hear him scream at this eight-year-old kid was almost too much.[22]

Erik Preminger recalled, "It was a very, very, very unpleasant set. How the movie even got made is amazing, it was so unpleasant."[23] Shooting ended in early September, and Preminger rushed through post-production with his usual alacrity.

Two years after the film was released and disappeared, Cannon had not got over Preminger: "Elaine May wrote a great screenplay. *Brilliant* humor. He took a piece of beauty and screwed it up. It was an incredible part. I was in *every* frame of that film—except for one short scene— and he destroyed it. I have been the victim of some killers in my time. He's one of the biggest. He's a *horrible* man. That was a very painful period in my life. I was a wreck. I was absolutely destroyed by that man. *Phew!* But who ever hears of him anymore? Is he still alive?"[24]

Ken Howard summed up *Such Good Friends*: "I think in someone else's hands that movie could have been really good. I just thought he was too heavy-handed and not right . . . He was trying to be hip, and he didn't have whatever that feeling is. If Paul Mazursky or some director like that had had *Such Good Friends* and done it, I think it would have been a whole other kind of thing. But Preminger took on things that a lot of people would avoid. He wasn't afraid of controversial material or difficult material that was a little bit off the beaten path. So you can't say, well, somebody else should have directed it, because who else was going to take a shot?"[25]

The film was released to mixed reviews and weak business (by the end of 1972 it had earned $1.75 million in domestic rentals, slightly less than American International's *Frogs*). One of the most interesting notices came from Clive Barnes, who wrote, "Preminger loves New York not because he likes it, but because it amuses him. The outrageousness of its extravagance appeals to his apparently byzantine mind . . . The novel was full of cleverly feminine insights. The film observes those insights with a bleak and masculine amusement." Barnes concludes by recommending *Such Good Friends* "as a film that while not perhaps giving a picture of the real New York, at least gives a most comprehensive overview of a New York that many real New Yorkers regard as real."[26]

Of Preminger's last four films—from *Tell Me That You Love Me, Junie Moon* to *The Human Factor*—*Such Good Friends* is the best. Each of these late films instills a certain discomfort in the viewer, a discomfort that Preminger's detractors have ascribed to his failing directorial powers and fading contact with the world he is depicting, but which repays consideration in more positive terms. The critique of modernity in these films becomes progressively more stringent from *Such Good Friends* to *The Human Factor*. It's in *Such Good Friends* that Preminger achieves the most complex and satisfying balance between his fundamental humanism and the pessimism that appears to be his reflexive, but also considered, response to the world of the 1970s.

This isn't to say that *Such Good Friends* is a total success; it is, in fact, the most uneven of the four late films. Its very unevenness is a mark of its author. Like many of Preminger's films, including the three that preceded it, *Such Good Friends* starts without preliminaries, in a clipped, abrupt manner. The film is already in a rush, with Julie, whom we meet in her apartment as she is preparing to go to a reception for Richard. Starting like this makes it difficult for the film to establish a point of view and a pace. We seem to have to rush to keep up with Julie's real life, when Preminger is already disrupting the film with flashes of her fantasy life and with grotesque touches that seem to correspond to no point of view (the wide-angle extreme close-up of the doorman, eyes bulging, gazing at Julie's exposed breasts).

Burgess Meredith's nude scene, one of the film's obvious lapses, can be explained partly as Preminger's ironic reaction to the contemporary vogue for nudity in American film—a trend for which, as a public opponent of censorship and a producer whose challenges to the Production Code helped lead to the MPAA's adoption of the rating system, he might have taken some credit, but from which he refrained from drawing much benefit in his films. (Angelique Pettyjohn's brief romp in *Junie Moon* and the chaste and embarrassed nudity in *Rosebud* hardly qualify as plunges into prurience; the strip show in *The Human Factor* is something else again.) Unclothing Meredith is Preminger's way of making fun of his audience for expecting nudity; it also relieves the erotic pressure on the film, letting it be about something besides eroticism. Later, the insert of the developed Polaroid of the topless Julie functions as both a sop and a chastisement to viewers who crave titillation; that the photo is an obvious composite (Cannon refused to bare her breasts for the film) only strengthens its inherent antipornography.

Such Good Friends is another example—and the last—of the perennial problem Preminger had with comedy, as early as *A Royal Scandal*. The dialogue sometimes comes off as overemphatic and strained in its attempt at urban sophistication, notably in the scene of the magazine art department meeting. Lines that are supposed to be funny rarely land that way—the misunderstanding about the doctor's "slides," for instance. The actors often throw away their funnier lines, as if expecting the humor to take care of itself. At the same time, they seem conscious that the lines are intended to be funny, and the combination of self-consciousness and underplaying produces a weird, hollow effect. It's as if Preminger's instinct for representing the reality that the script is parodying prevents him from letting the parody be stronger than the reality (which it would have to be in order to be funny); to compensate (since he knows the film is supposed to be funny), he directs the actors to announce that what they are doing is funny. The extremely detailed and realistic portrayal of the hospital staff's attempts to revive the comatose Richard is strikingly out of place in a comedy, even one from a period that also saw *M*A*S*H* and *The Hospital* (already, in *Skidoo*, Preminger had used a hospital for uncomfortable dark comedy).

Except for some brief intimate passages between Richard and Julie, the restaurant scene between Cal and Julie is the first scene in the movie that really works. From this point on, *Such Good Friends* takes off and achieves and sustains the tone I think Preminger wanted for the film, both grave and compassionate.

Such Good Friends is a film on two parallel planes: one plane is a documentation of a society, of a way of life, and the characteristic mode Preminger brings to this aspect of the film is the wide-angle group shot. Such a shot occurs in the first sequence, when five actors are wedged into Julie's kitchen during the chaos preceding her departure for Richard's roof-garden reception. Subsequently, a lengthy take of a conversation at Cal's party for Richard keeps six people in frame. Finally, there is a remarkable shot in the hospital waiting room of Julie realizing that her husband is dying, while a large number of relatives, friends, and onlookers stand motionless behind and around her: the only movement is Timmy's entrance from offscreen right to bring, silently, the news that Richard has died. In such shots, Preminger's theatrical sensibility is fully evident. He stylizes the scenes, producing something that announces itself as an image of reality.

The other plane is the personal, hallucinatory, imaginary plane, where, for moments scattered persistently throughout the film, Julie is alone, face to face with herself. The film introduces this plane early, with the shot of Julie, having taken off her bra, looking at herself in a full-length mirror ("Take a good look, Tom, this is what I am, do you still want me for your wife?"). The shot recalls the shot of Junie Moon dressing for her ill-fated date with Jesse. As in *Tell Me That You Love Me, Junie Moon*, the mirror is the link between consciousness and visibility, between the present and the past.

Dyan Cannon felt that "Julie's big problem was that she tried to please all those people and ended up pleasing nobody, herself included. Finally she learns that there's something positive in being selfish. For the first time, she starts to think about herself and what she wants to do with her life."[27] Yet Preminger's handling of Julie's development is more ambiguous, more fretful than Cannon's account of the character.

The remote, placid medium shot in which Julie berates the comatose Richard and breaks down sobbing is a moral statement by Preminger. The camera refuses to pity her; it is there only to record her; its deepest commitment is to the objective reality of a subjective process. Finally, there is the expansiveness of the backward tracking shot of Julie leaving the building with her two children and taking them into Central Park. This unexpected and haunting shot summarizes the movement of the whole film. The character emerges (literally), becomes real, takes responsibility for her life, but the camera movement that celebrates this step is able to follow her only a short way before letting her go, both respectful of a dignity that is not to be penetrated (Preminger is acutely aware, in *Such Good Friends*, of the difficulty in the position of a man making a film about a woman) and acknowledging that the fate of a person thus liberated or reborn is unknowable.

Cannon's performance is strange and difficult to evaluate: quiet, restrained, holding herself back, she appears conscious of herself at all times. Attacked by her director, Cannon may have felt herself alone on the set, and in the film, Julie does appear at times to be a woman alone. (Among the notable exceptions are some scenes with Richard, in which Cannon is natural and convincing and in which she gets Luckinbill, whose performance elsewhere is a little mannered, to relax.) Her dazed moments are among her most successful, as when, arriving at the hospital, she murmurs, "How do I look?" (to Timmy's objection—"Julie, he's unconscious"—she replies in the same deadpan tone, "I know, but I want to look nice": it is the kind of anesthetized acting later perfected by Louise Lasser on the TV show *Mary Hartman, Mary Hartman*; Lasser, incidentally, plays, very well, a small part in *Such Good Friends*), or when she reacts to Cal's revelation of Richard's infidelity by murmuring, "Oh my God, the eggs will get cold." At one point in Lois Gould's novel, the narrator describes herself as a person waiting for her "internal Novocain" to wear off.[28] Cannon gives an ideal portrayal of this person.

As played by Cannon, Julie never coheres as a character, never becomes synopsizable, and this is the great success of the performance. Julie always remains removed from the audience, never graspable; we sense that she is removed from herself, and this aspect of Cannon's performance becomes an important device for representing the character's story. The circumstances of her life have long allowed her to remain concealed, to live through an image; and suddenly she is deprived of the image. Julie's estrangement from herself, her failure to be fully present at the unfolding of her own destiny, and her eventual self-realization make her a close cousin of Preminger's previous heroines.

35

Before the Doors Close on This Whole World

Such Good Friends ended Preminger's Paramount contract. Thirty-five years after first reporting for work at Twentieth Century-Fox, he closed down his last office in Hollywood.

After that, he worked on several projects. One real-life story that was close to his heart was the 1953 trial of Julius and Ethel Rosenberg, who were convicted of passing atomic secrets to the Soviets and were subsequently executed. Preminger had first announced his intention to make a film of the Rosenbergs' trial in July 1969, during production of *Tell Me That You Love Me, Junie Moon*. At that time, the film was to be called *Open Question*. Two years later, during production of *Such Good Friends*, the project was reannounced, this time as a two-hour TV movie for ABC, with a script by Louis Nizer. In March 1972 the project was being called *Implosion*.

In 1970, after Frank Sinatra had turned down Preminger's proposal of playing the lead in *The Godfather*, Preminger came up with another project for the star, Dorothy Salisbury Davis's mystery novel *Where the Dark Streets Go*, about a New York City Catholic priest who becomes involved in the investigation of the murder of an artist. Said Erik, Preminger "was looking for projects that he could leverage his past relationships and involvements with. He had a good relationship with Sinatra, Sinatra was bankable, and he liked working with Sinatra." *Where the Dark Streets Go* was announced as an independent production by Sinatra and Preminger. Plans for the project fell apart over a contretemps between Preminger and Sinatra's manager, Milton "Mickey" Rudin. Erik recalled, "It was in California. Nat Rudich was there, and I was with Nat. Suddenly we heard Otto absolutely over-the-top screaming. Screamed him [Rudin] out of the office. That was the end of the project and the end of his relationship with Sinatra."[1] This incident can be seen as emblematic of Preminger's last decade of filmmaking.

In 1973 he staged Erich Maria Remarque's play *Die letzte Station* (*The Last Station*), adapted by Peter Stone and retitled *Full Circle*. The cast included Bibi Andersson, whose performance in English in Ingmar Bergman's *The Touch* he had admired, and Leonard Nimoy. The play closed quickly.

In September 1973 Preminger bought the rights to *Rosebud*, a political thriller by Paul Bonnecarrère and Joan Hemingway. Originally published in French, the novel concerns the kidnapping of five girls while they are vacationing in the Mediterranean on a luxury yacht, the *Rosebud*. The girls are daughters of powerful political and business leaders in the West; the kidnappers are Palestinians who offer, through the Western media, to release the girls one by one if a series of escalating demands are met. French, Israeli, and German secret agents collaborate to find the Corsica farm where the girls are being held, release the girls, and capture the terrorist leader at his stronghold in Lebanon.

On the dual strength of the book and Preminger's proven ability to bring in economical superproductions (a skill that was still considered, at least by some, as potentially outweighing his late string of commercial failures), and partly, no doubt, in recognition of the successes his films had scored for the company in the past, United Artists agreed to finance and distribute *Rosebud*. Otto asked Erik to write the script. According to Hope Preminger, "Otto really wanted to do something for Erik, and so he allowed him to write it. I think he was trying to encourage him to any kind of career, because by this time he was thirty-something-odd years old [in fact, twenty-nine], and he hadn't stuck with anything."[2]

At around the time Erik was finishing his first draft of the script, in early February 1974, reality gave the material an uncanny stamp of approval when nineteen-year-old heiress Patricia Hearst was kidnapped by an obscure terrorist group, the Symbionese Liberation Army. Her grandfather, publisher William Randolph Hearst, had provided the model for Orson Welles's *Citizen Kane*, to which the title *Rosebud* pays tribute.

Otto later said that he thought *Rosebud* was in his usual tradition of fairness to both parties in a conflict. "When the spokesman of the Arab terrorists who have kidnapped a group of girls tells about the Arabs' plight, I let him do this in a very honest, straightforward way because I wanted to give them a chance to show their side."[3] But taking the Palestinian political position seriously "was not even on the table," said Erik. His father "was willing to make the actual terrorists sympathetic as people, but only to a point . . . By this point, Otto was very black and white, I felt. It wasn't that he was anti-Palestinian, it was that he absolutely, fervently, loved Israel."[4]

The making of *Rosebud* is recounted in the book *Soon to Be a Major Motion Picture*, by Ted Gershuny (director of several low-budget films and former husband of Andy Warhol star Mary Woronov), whose subtitle calls the film "an all-star, big-budget, multimillion-dollar disaster." The book is something to treasure: less for its nuanced, complex, and not unsympathetic view of Preminger himself than for its account of the endlessness of the numbing, bantering, desperate, sometimes exhilarating life going on in the trenches, among a crew of volunteers in the "foreign legion for creative nomads" who made possible the international coproductions of the 1960s and 1970s. Gershuny is interested in *Rosebud* for how it reveals "the larger confusion—the dizzy uncertainty—of all movie life."[5]

In March, Eva Monley, whom Preminger had hired as production manager, became, for once in her career, the victim of this uncertainty. Preminger was "destroying [her] with condescension,"[6] she felt, doubting her cost estimates and raging at her when she said she needed more time to prepare a reliable budget. Monley gave Preminger her notice, with sadness, but she did not abandon the film without lining up and breaking in her replacement, Graham Cottle.

Following Preminger and Cottle from the French Riviera to Corsica to Israel to Germany as they scouted locations, Gershuny thought the director insensible to, or at least unwilling to be inspired by, his locations: "The demands of time, money, and his impatience separated him from the landscape, forcing him to superimpose *his* need on the settings rather than be stimulated by them." (Another version of Dyan Cannon's complaint: "How can a director who has no feeling make a movie about a feeling woman?") Gershuny also thought that Preminger "catered to the tourist instinct in his audience. The director craved 'true' places— reality—preferably with 'beauty.' If he had a choice of locations, he took the more picturesque." Yet Denys Coop, once again Preminger's director of photography (as he had been on *Bunny Lake Is Missing* as well as a camera operator on *Saint Joan* and *Bonjour Tristesse*), explained to Gershuny that Preminger wanted *Rosebud* to look "not documentary, but not pretty. Not false. If a scene is lit by one light, then it's lit by one light."[7] Coop's cinematography would be one of *Rosebud*'s undeniable saving graces, giving the film both roughness and splendor.

The script was a source of mounting consternation. "My father wants everyone to be a character," Erik said, but the characters never emerged through yards of excessively plot-oriented dialogue. Though they signed on, Robert Mitchum (cast in the lead role of American secret agent Martin—in the book, the character was French) and Cliff Gorman (cast as Hamlekh, the main Israeli agent) both did so expressing misgivings about the script. Preminger, who told everyone that the script was just temporary, confided to Graham Cottle in March that he, too, had "questions about the dialogue, the characters"—especially the girls and the main villain, Sloat, a pro-Palestinian Englishman (in the novel the equivalent character was an anti-Israel Jew).[8] Hope Preminger recalled, "Otto was disappointed, but he didn't ever say anything about it to anybody outside the family. He wanted to help him, to his own detriment, because he insisted on using Erik."[9]

Erik recognized that the collaboration was not working and tried at one point to get out. He recounted: "[Otto] read some pages and in his own inimitable fashion was saying what he thought, and I said, 'Otto, you'd better get somebody else to do this, I can't do this.' He said, 'Nonsense, we'll make this work, we'll make a great picture together.' And like an idiot I stayed. It was a terrible mistake, and one that I regret. I don't regret much in my life but I do regret that. Because of the result, because of the tension that it put on my relationship with him."[10]

Preminger brought in Marjorie Kellogg to help with the script: she arrived in Nice in late April, about a month before *Rosebud* was due to start shooting on May 29, and spent a few weeks huddled with the Premingers. Kellogg, who had become friendly with Erik while working on *Junie Moon*, recalled, "I only went because Erik wanted me to come and give him a little hand. He was in trouble with his father . . . His father was driving him into the ground. He told me the problems on the script. We did it together. I had no desire to have any credit at all on this."[11] In the end, she received none. Kellogg tried to give the kidnap victims indi-

vidual personalities but had no chance to tell the story that really interested her, about the girls' experience in captivity. "It's a long film already,"
Otto must have firmly impressed on her.[12]

Preminger spent two weeks in Juan-les-Pins rehearsing the five
girls—Isabelle Huppert (whom Preminger told, when he first interviewed her in his production office, that she reminded him of Marion
Mill),[13] Lalla Ward, Barbara Emerson, Kim Cattrall, and Debra Berger.
Gershuny watched them run dialogue in the hotel coffee shop: "Preminger was clearly not an acting teacher. He simply told what results he
wanted. *How* they were achieved concerned him as little as how Denys
powered his lights . . . Criticism was sharp and specific." Lalla Ward was
impressed: "So accurate . . . He says 'It's so *simple*,' and he's right." (She
could not have known that she was echoing Romy Schneider.) Preminger brought out charm and humor in Huppert, who remained impervi-
ous to his temper even while she struggled with the English dialogue.
Nevertheless, the work was far from smooth, especially for Barbara
Emerson, whose tortured Method emoting proved resistant to Preminger's entreaties, threats, and resolute straightforwardness ("Just visualize
yourself in the situation, and say the line . . . Don't put it in a category").
Three days before the start of shooting, Preminger sent her packing and
replaced her with Brigitte Ariel.[14]

Gershuny's general impression was that "on *Rosebud*, Preminger can
make right choices, wrong choices, any choices. Things simply *will not
work*." Shooting started on May 28 with an easy scene, newsman Julian
Pettifer's report, and then proceeded in earnest on May 29, Preminger
working with the girls on the yacht. The combination of the actresses' inexperience, the French actors' difficulties with English, and the cramped
shooting conditions meant that "every take had a problem," wrote Gershuny. The next day, a scene between Sabine (Ariel) and her lover,
Patrice (Yves Beneyton), in bed ran to twenty-six takes, the actors unable to believably suggest intimacy in English. On June 1 Beneyton either quit or was fired, to be replaced by Georges Beller, with whom
Preminger now had to retake the scenes already done with Beneyton.
Behind schedule and faced with his actors' impenetrable difficulties
with their lines, Preminger cut more and more dialogue, sacrificing nu-
ances he had before insisted on. He told Kim Cattrall ungallantly, "You
run a close second to Kim Novak and Marilyn Monroe. Not in attrac-

tiveness but in number of takes!"[15] (Before leaving for Europe, she had been warned by well-wishers, "Don't cry in front of him!" Now people on the film were encouraging her to look to the future: "Don't worry, movies aren't like this." Preminger's unpredictable changes between kindness and yelling bewildered the seventeen-year-old: "I can't hate him and I can't love him," she said when it was over.)[16]

Preminger persevered, trying to shape the movements of his actors into a whole. Critic Olivier Eyquem, who followed the entire production and kept a detailed journal, watched Preminger set up a scene aboard the yacht as a sequence of complementary movement-events. "All his effort," Eyquem noted, "aims at a greater fluidity in the succession of these given elements and toward eliminating the superfluous."[17] Preminger impressed Eyquem with his minutely detailed attempt to turn the script's schematic dinner-table confrontation between the wealthy Fargeau (Claude Dauphin) and the radical intellectual Patrice into a tense and subtle "close combat." But Beller's difficulties with the English dialogue forced Preminger to break up the scene into short shots.

After finishing on the yacht, a day over schedule, Preminger shot with Mitchum in Juan-les-Pins and Corsica. At first, Eyquem found in Mitchum "a total mastery" and foresaw how the character of Martin, and the film, might benefit from "the irony that he conveys without effort in his smallest gesture." As the afternoon of Mitchum's first day on the film wore on, the actor's behavior became more disruptive: he interrupted Preminger, patronized Huppert, clowned, and left the set, only to return "after a certain delay, in a state obviously unfavorable for the improvement of his performance."[18]

Different versions have been given of Mitchum's departure. Gershuny's account is the most detailed. On June 24, he reported, the star was drinking heavily and became "clearly irritated" when Preminger, leaving the set to attend a ceremony at which he was made an honorary citizen of L'Île Rousse, entrusted to assistant director Wolfgang Glattes a shot of Mitchum driving away in a car. Early the next morning, Mitchum, arriving at the farm location, berated Preminger for dragging him out of bed to find the crew still laying dolly track. "As quiet and firm as I have ever seen him," in Gershuny's words, Preminger told Mitchum, "Bob, we cannot go on this way," and pointed out that Mitchum's drinking was costing them time and hurting the film. "Yeah! Right!" Mitchum replied, "Say it to me! Shake hands!" Preminger: "Bob, I won't shake your hand. If I let you go, I'll have to sue you for every cent—" Mitchum: "You want me to go, huh? Okay! I'm going. That's it!" And he had his driver take him back to the hotel.[19] Eyquem wrote that afterward, "O.P. remains in an astonishing calm, taking his star's defection with serenity, as if relieved by the sudden clarification of the situation. Extreme difficulty seems to reassure him, and it's with a smile that he characterizes the situation as 'dramatic.' "[20]

Within two days Preminger had found Mitchum's replacement in Peter O'Toole—another actor with a drinking problem and a reputation for hell-raising ("Hell, that's like replacing Ray Charles with Helen Keller," Mitchum remarked). O'Toole arrived in Corsica to begin retaking the scenes that had been done with Mitchum. The casting change necessitated script revisions—by a new writer, Roy Clarke—to make Martin sound British. To support his characterization, O'Toole also wanted Clarke to put more humor in the part. Preminger acquiesced in this effort to an extent ("it's a role that can exist only on the basis of what the actor brings to it of his own personality," as he admitted),[21] though he balked occasionally. In every scene, O'Toole wore or had within reach an Irish tweed hat: "It's my whole performance," he said.[22] Eyquem saw that the detachment the actor brought to Martin (a reluctant participant in the crisis) made a "curious parallel" with O'Toole's relationship to the film: "not to say that he plays *against* the film, but it seems evident that he seeks to involve himself in it as little as possible, building on the basis of his character a series of protective idiosyncracies."[23] O'Toole later spoke with affection of Preminger, praising his "total, complete integrity to his will and purpose."[24]

In early July, *Rosebud* moved to Paris, where Preminger worked with (and got the film's biggest publicity boost from) former New York mayor John Lindsay, cast in the small role of a U.S. senator, father of one of the hostages. (Two other fathers were played by Preminger veterans Raf Vallone and Peter Lawford.) By now the grips had a board displayed in their truck, listing odds on who would be the nineteenth person fired from the film. After finishing his first day's work in Paris, O'Toole had to be rushed to the hospital with acute stomach pains; his hospitalization shut the production down for ten days. Preminger took advantage of the downtime to work with editor Peter Thornton on assembling the film: already he was making decisions to tighten the early scenes and drop footage in order to conceal the inadequacies of the actors.

When shooting could resume, Preminger had Coop leave the zoom lens permanently mounted on the camera (Coop had also brought along several prime lenses) in order to save time in reframing. Gershuny saw in Preminger (and this was Ronald James Policy's impression during the last weeks of shooting on *Skidoo*) "a director driven by a producer's need to hurry, to finish with economy—to avoid the least taint of creative self-indulgence." Josef Shiloah wanted to try to make his character, the terrorist Hacam, a tragic figure, but he felt discouraged by his director. The problems besetting the production meant that as much as on any film he had ever done, Preminger needed to keep things hard and practical: in Gershuny's words, "never experiment, never improvise." When Cliff Gorman asked for a "moment" when he first sees the liberated Hélène (Huppert) in Martin's apartment, Preminger refused. "He likes everything to move," said Gorman.[25] There was an ideological element to Preminger's relentlessness. Roy Clarke came up with a scene in which Sloat comforts a Palestinian terrorist as the young man dies in his arms. Enthusiastic, Erik showed the pages to his father, who, after reading them, said angrily, "United Artists would rather burn the film than release it with this scene in it."[26]

In August the company shot the Hamburg and Berlin scenes at such speed that sound engineer Robin Gregory likened the work to "computerized filming."[27] Preminger still had enough sense of detail to insist that the window of the Berlin camera shop (in real life, a candy store, which Preminger had chosen for its location near the Kaiser-Wilhelm-Gedächtnis-Kirche on the Kurfürstendamm) be re-dressed when he noticed that the art department had decorated it using only products from a single brand.

Klaus Löwitsch, who played Schloss, the German agent, later remembered *Rosebud* as the worst experience of his career. Löwitsch had the impression that Preminger came to Germany "prepared to find National Socialism" and singled him out for abuse because he was German. "The only German he could get was me. He shouted at me, screamed at me, roared at me. 'Faster, faster, faster.' 'Slow it down.' We did a five-minute crane shot with me and Peter O'Toole. Three pages of dialogue.

He said to me, 'Stop your bloody German acting! It's not Goethe.' " At the end of this shot (in a museum of primitive art, where Schloss demonstrates to Martin a complicated surveillance apparatus), a technician, played by a local actor whom Löwitsch had recommended, had to say one line. Take after take, the terrified actor froze, unable to get the line out. "The whole building was shaking" as Preminger berated both Germans. Yet when they were alone, he said to Löwitsch, "You know something, you're a really good actor."[28] Preminger acknowledged in his autobiography that "in the northern part of Germany, Berlin and Hamburg, where I worked several weeks in 1974 during the filming of *Rosebud*, I could detect no remnants of the Nazi period."[29] O'Toole later recalled Preminger's behavior during this phase of the production as strange. "In Germany, Otto stumbled along in a sort of mad apoplexy most of the time, saying: 'Ze real Nazis are Austrians. I know, I am an Austrian!' One scene he directed from a car. He just rolled down the window: 'Action! Cut!' "[30]

Israel brought Preminger and the harassed crew a new crop of problems: the Arab extras recruited to play Sloat's soldiers proved incompetent, forcing Preminger to drop a scene of their unsuccessful attempt to stop the Israeli commandos from abducting Sloat. For the shot of a parachute drop, the crew, on the ground, found themselves without radio contact with the plane and unable to anticipate where the parachutists would jump or land. That day, said Gershuny, marked "the only time I have seen [Preminger] sit down during a filming session."[31]

For the scene in which Sloat betrays himself, Preminger tried to get Richard Attenborough (a late addition to the cast as Sloat) to come down a bit: "Dickie, why are you so dramatic? It's like you're doing Shakespeare!" (Preminger's dig at Löwitsch about Goethe might have sounded less anti-German to Löwitsch if he had heard him reproach Attenborough with Shakespeare.) "But then he said later I was wonderful," Attenborough said. "Shouting or not, it's an extraordinary experience!"[32]

By the time the company returned to Juan-les-Pins, Preminger was "sick, exhausted, struggling to finish," in Gershuny's words. Here Preminger finished the retakes necessitated by the replacement of Mitchum. On September 4, for the last shot of both the production and the film, Preminger added a scene not in the original script: Martin takes a phone call, is told that a plane has been hijacked (the hijackers demanding the release of Hacam), and turns down the mission of handling the crisis. "As he walked away, one could visualize the end credits," marveled Gershuny.[33] (Preminger dropped the scene in editing, preferring to end with a frisson aboard the hijacked plane.)

Among those for whom the production of *Rosebud* was a crucible, Erik, for whom it may have first seemed like a golden opportunity, no doubt suffered the most. Marjorie Kellogg thought that Erik "was afraid of his father. His father really wasn't nice to him. And Erik reflected that. It wasn't a good, strong father-son relationship."[34] Kim Cattrall told of Erik's saying, in Paris, that if he had it all to do over again, he would never go through the experience.[35] At the very beginning, in New York, when Gershuny had got the go-ahead to write his book on the production, Erik told him, "I don't care what you write about me, but if you do anything to hurt my relationship with my father, I'll sue you for every cent."[36] The insecurity this remark revealed could only have been aggravated by the problems on the production. Erik recalled:

We had a cast party at the Hotel du Cap in Cap d'Antibes. I remember thanking Peter O'Toole, who had been wonderful, and the various actors who had all been most kind and the people that I worked with, and saying goodbye to Otto, and going back to my hotel room and literally crying hysterically in relief that it was over, and in sadness, all night long. I was still crying the next morning when I got in my car and left for Le Havre; I had booked passage on one of the last crossings of the French Line, which I remembered from when I was a child, and that was my present to myself, and of course they blockaded the port so I never got to take it. But I was still crying when I loaded up my car and left. I could cry now thinking about it.[37]

Rosebud was released in March 1975 to the worst reviews of Preminger's career and very poor business.

The weaknesses of the film have most often been attributed to Erik Preminger's script, and though these weaknesses are severe, it is worth acknowledging what the script is trying to do. Above all, it places a strong emphasis on technology and on *how* things are done or known. That this theme (which culminates in the betrayal of Sloat by recording technology) is often highlighted at the expense of characterization and dramatic momentum is apparent. Starting with a long speech informing us of how an anonymous character knows where the girls' yacht was abandoned, detailed discussions of processes and procedures fill up the film. An exchange between Martin and Schloss perhaps inadvertently sums up this aspect of *Rosebud* and its numbing effect on the film's pace and mood: Martin admiringly says of an elaborate surveillance apparatus, "It's like precision engineering"; Schloss replies: "I thought you would like it. Now all we do is wait for something to happen." In his on-screen bit as a computer operator working for the Israelis, Erik Preminger states his attitude toward technology: "The machinery is irrelevant. It's the information inside that counts." This line has a perhaps unintended irony, since amid the film's detailed and prolonged examination of machinery, the information gets lost. For long stretches, *Rosebud* seems to be about nothing but the machinery. The high point or nadir is reached in the sequence in which a technician (played by Ted Gershuny) tells his colleagues about the water supply to the Tardets farm: every imaginable detail, it seems, is asked about and explained.

The severest limitation the script imposes comes from its superficial cynicism, its refusal to allow any empathy for any of the characters to develop. Martin is the film's hero by default because his cynicism matches that of the film; his sarcasm is so indiscriminate that it destroys the possibility for the emergence of any strong value, any basis for action. The kidnapped girls would seem automatic beneficiaries of audience sympathy, but the flat performances by most of them and the inane dialogue they're given (sometimes with a pointedly critical or deflating intention, as when, as they languish in their cell, one of them is heard to ask for a nail file) ensure that, with the exception of Huppert's Hélène, they remain obnoxious ciphers.

The enormous flaws of the film are evident, and *Rosebud* is without doubt the hardest of Preminger's films to defend; making a case for *Hurry Sundown* or *Skidoo* is relatively simple. Still, the potential fascination of *Rosebud* lies in the same qualities that make it "bad" and "boring." These negative qualities are of a piece with those aspects of the film that even its severest detractors might be persuaded to acknowledge as successful—especially its intermittent, usually nocturnal visual grandeur, notable in the shot of Fargeau's helicopter taking off against a brilliant midnight blue sky or in the scene of Martin's dinner with Mr. and Mrs. Nikolaos, the Eiffel Tower visible in the background against another beautiful night sky. (The scene was shot in director Anatole Litvak's penthouse apartment.) Preminger incorporates visual beauty in the field of the film; he accepts beauty. But the beauty is always fleeting; there is no one within the film to comment on it or to be solicited by it.

Preminger's career-long preoccupation with external movement reaches its extreme in *Rosebud*. Shots of cars pulling up in front of buildings were a Preminger trademark since *In the Meantime, Darling*: he was always attracted to vehicular movement as part of the trappings of modernity. In *Rosebud*, the preoccupation with movement for its own sake seems to be his response to a new, technological modernity, for which he feels little sympathy and in which he finds little cause for hope. Abandoning concern for people, the film concentrates on the fates of things and their containers. The German section of *Rosebud*, which, by the way, adds nothing to the main plot, is particularly notable for its obsession with things inside things (the van, the car, the package, the photo shop), with delivering things (the woman courier). The limit is reached with the shots of Volkswagen vans driving off a transport ship in preparation for the raid on the Tardets farm: boxes emerging from inside bigger boxes in order to move people to different boxes.

The camera's way of recording all this movement is not without a self-conscious intended irony, apparent in the sequence in which the kidnappers fool the blindfolded Hélène into thinking that she is being taken on a long journey over land and through the air. A high-angle long shot pans over a landscape to find a white truck driving around and around randomly in a parody of the urgent transnational displacements of the film's many cars, boats, planes, helicopters, and other vehicles. The flight simulator on which the terrorists take Hélène becomes one of the film's central metaphors, reminding us that cinema itself is a simulation, a copy of experience, intended to deceive a bewildered and sensation-deprived viewer (or to train for experience a purposeful and attentive viewer).

For all the turmoil (mostly merely alluded to rather than shown) lying behind it and around it, *Rosebud* is a strangely peaceful film. It is also bitterly sad. In the pitiful and derisory pointlessness of the Berlin scenes, the film reaches its heart of darkness, conveying the senses of both cosmic joke and historical twilight. As German location manager Rudolph Hertzog said to Gershuny at the end of the recces, it's "like going to the museum . . . before the doors close on this whole world."[38] Almost nothing human is left here—a dereliction for which Preminger would atone in his next film.

36

The Human Factor

After the debacle of *Rosebud*, Preminger may have been relieved to turn to a project he could control: his autobiography. Ken McCormick, an editor in chief at Doubleday, approached him with the idea, and a large advance was negotiated. Preminger was given the services of June Callwood, a longtime ghostwriter for the publisher. Callwood remembered that when she was presented to Preminger, "he was visibly distressed that it was a woman. He was a very chauvinistic guy." Over several months in 1975 and 1976, Callwood interviewed Preminger in his office whenever he slotted her into his schedule between his normal business. At first Callwood found him difficult to work with and uncooperative, but over time his attitude changed and he became friendly. She realized that he was "deeply sentimental." One thing that changed little over the period was his bad memory. Callwood marveled, "He was *proud* of his memory deficits! He didn't think it was a valuable thing to have a good memory."[1] Adamant that no other witnesses to his life should be called on to fill the gaps, he refused to put Callwood in touch with anyone.

The book that emerged was a collection of Preminger's tried-and-true stories, less an autobiography than an anthology of routines. "I think everybody who knew Otto heard those stories many, many times before they saw the book between covers," said Erik Preminger.[2] His old enemy, Nelson Algren, reviewed the book for the *Los Angeles Times* (calling it, not inaptly, "an innocuous little memoir") and used the occasion to air his old grievances with the director of *The Man with the Golden Arm*.[3]

"That was a terrible time for him, terrible," Erik recalled. "Because it was a very real critique of where he was in his career, that nobody would finance his pictures."[4] Even if his recent pictures had made money, Preminger would have found the late 1970s an inauspicious time for his kind of filmmaking. For some time, he tried to develop a film based on the life of Dr. Norman Bethune, a Canadian physician who became the chief medical officer of Mao Tse-tung's Red Army during its struggle against the Japanese. Preminger had had the Bethune film on his plate since 1972 and had gone through several writers with it. Eventually he told the press that restrictions placed by the Chinese government on his shooting the film in China had led him to cancel the project.

In 1975, a Preminger film about Supreme Court justice Hugo Black was announced as a forthcoming TV film for CBS. Preminger worked on the script with Max Lerner, then with Jerome Charyn, who recalled, "He hired me—you can see what despair he was in, because I had no film credits whatsoever. He didn't know who I was, he had never read a word I'd written, but he hired me immediately because he was so desperate. I found him to be a wonderful, enchanting man. He had married, perhaps for the third time, and had a son and daughter, twins about twelve years old. And I was absolutely amazed to see what a wonderful father he was. He was totally delighted with these kids, and at the same time, he was the image of Otto Preminger the ogre . . . It was sad, because he was a multimillionaire with his own film company, but he couldn't get anyone to buy his work." Eventually Charyn asked to be released from the assignment. "He was completely shattered, not because anything had happened, but because having a writer gave him the sense that something was in process."[5]

One of Preminger's biggest disappointments—and the most telling in the pattern of his personal history—was his inability to set up a production in Israel. Not only did he have strong sentimental ties to the country, but thanks to *Exodus* he could also claim to be one of Israel's biggest supporters. During the production of *Rosebud*, he had made a new friend in the young Israeli production manager Yoram Ben-Ami (to whom he confided that he was taking rejuvenation shots in Europe). In 1976, Ben-Ami, whose own career as a producer was on the rise, visited Preminger in New York. "Yoram, you have to help me out," Preminger appealed. "They don't want to give me the rights to make the movie on the Entebbe raid. How can you help me? How can we get to [Prime Minister Yitzhak] Rabin?" According to Ben-Ami, "I already realized that he was not focused, and he didn't have a chance to get it. Although when we were [in Israel], the army people loved him. But the government wouldn't let him do it. And it hurt him." Preminger also talked of doing a film version of Moshe Dayan's autobiography, but this, too, came to nothing.[6]

Preminger also wanted to film Graham Greene's *A Burnt-Out Case*, to which he had owned the rights since 1967 and for which Eleanor Perry wrote a first-draft script. In March 1978 Preminger bought the rights to another Greene novel, *The Human Factor*, a few weeks before its publication, and he announced that it would replace the Moshe Dayan story as his next production. According to *Publishers Weekly*, the deal required Preminger to make "a large down payment against a substantial six-figure price."[7]

Preminger first asked Greene to write the screenplay, but the writer declined. Preminger turned to Tom Stoppard, whose screenplay would be remarkably faithful to the novel. "I was much more nervous of displeasing Graham Greene than I was of displeasing Otto," Stoppard said later.[8] The writer turned in a first draft on August 1, 1978, then a second on August 25. Preminger sought both Richard Burton and Michael Caine for the central role of Castle, a low-level functionary in the British Foreign Office who, out of loyalty to the Communist who helped Castle's black South African wife elude imprisonment in that country, assumes a quiet double life as a Soviet spy. Burton and Caine both declined the part, which Nicol Williamson eventually accepted.

To finance the film, Preminger turned to Paul Crosfield, a man with little film-production experience but seemingly solid connections. Through Crosfield, Preminger met Valerie (Val) Robins, who was initially hired to help set up the production and who then stayed on as production manager. Preminger lined up the distinguished trio of Richard Attenborough, Robert Morley, and John Gielgud to play Castle's superiors in the British agency, and Derek Jacobi took the part of Castle's unfortunate colleague, Davis, on whom suspicion first falls when it is discovered that there is a leak to the Soviets from Castle's office. Preminger chose the Somali-born model Iman as Castle's wife. Before production, the Rank Organisation bought distribution rights for the United Kingdom, Australia, New Zealand, South Africa, the Netherlands, and Portugal. MGM would later buy the rights for the United States and Canada.

Shooting began on May 30, 1979, in England. Greene had made his own birthplace—the village of Berkhamsted, Hertfordshire, an hour

northeast of London—his hero's residence, and Preminger was faithful
to this choice. The many scenes at Castle's house were shot at a house
the production rented in the town. For the London scenes, Preminger
got access to a soon-to-be-demolished Victorian house. A pheasant shoot
was filmed at a Shropshire estate. The final sequence, with its back-
projection view of Moscow, was done at Shepperton. "For political reasons," the film's pressbook recounted, "Preminger decided against
location filming in the story's true settings in South Africa, but felt he
could obtain equally convincing backgrounds in Kenya."

Preminger and Nicol Williamson clashed early in the production—
the actor walking off the set after Preminger upbraided him for blowing
his lines—and developed what seems to have been at best a professional
relationship. Hope Preminger recalled that Williamson "behaved badly,
was so sarcastic, had the crew all upset, and was snarling at everybody."[9]

The director of photography, Australian-born Mike Molloy, found
Preminger insistent on visual homogeneity. "I started out trying to light it
with a bit of mood to it and a bit of contrast, and he had an apoplexy at
the first batch of rushes." Preminger complained of not being able to see
the actors' eyes; from then on, he made Molloy light everything very
flatly and directly. Camera placement was simple: typically, scenes were
shot with a 20 mm lens, with the camera in the corner of a room. "For
somebody who had made some wonderfully visual pictures," Molloy
said, "there was a complete lack of interest in the visual side of it." The
cameraman saw that it would be futile to argue. "He was totally autocratic. It would have been completely wasted time to say, 'Why don't you
do the shot over here,' or, 'What about over here?', like you would normally with the director. I can't remember discussing anything [with Prem-
inger] other than he wanted things to be done as quickly as possible . . .
I got along with him quite well in a funny kind of way. But to me he really was past his prime, putting it politely."[10]

Val Robins found Preminger a determined and efficient director. "He
knew what he wanted; he would shoot until he got it, whether it was one
take or thirty. He would not waste film; he would not shoot extra takes,
he would move on. There were many times we would wrap early. He
would shoot very quickly. We were nearly always ahead of schedule. I
think we finished in England a week before we were scheduled to."
Preminger lived up to his legend for toughness. "If he saw that you were

a little weak," said Robins, "he did tend to jump on it a little bit. If you knew what you were doing and stood your ground, he had a great deal of respect for that. If you did not, and sort of meekly went on by, then he would jump on that too. There were two or three members of our crew and cast that he did indeed bring to tears, not that he meant to, but that's just the way he is. He will have an argument and turn around and walk away, and it's all finished, and it's been done, it's said, it's forgotten, and on we go. Unfortunately other people couldn't quite forget it as easily as Otto could."[11]

Like many screenwriters before him, Stoppard found Preminger scrupulous in respecting the script. "Say what you will about Otto, he would never make a change in the script without consulting the writer first." He also found that the director still enjoyed playing the demonic "Otto Preminger" for his guests. One day, Stoppard visited the production with his wife and two young children. "Otto was charming to them," the writer recalled. "I said something like, 'He has a reputation for a bad temper and rudeness but obviously he has been misunderstood, he's so kind . . . etc.' The next moment a second assistant or someone said to the D.P. something like 'Should we break for lunch, sir?', and Otto instantly blew his top—'Who are you? Who asked you?!'—and sacked the man on the spot."[12]

Robert Morley's account of the production confirms that despite his age, Preminger had not mellowed. Morley recalled him berating Richard Attenborough for not coming to the set when called. When Attenborough protested, "I was just outside the door," Preminger replied, "Outside the door is no good for me." Delighted to glimpse, behind Preminger's "stern, sometimes forbidding exterior . . . genuine irresponsibility," Morley commented, "His approach to actors is uncompromising, either they know the lines or they don't. Where other directors chop and change Otto sets up the camera and presses forward. Artistes who expect to cover their mistakes in close-ups are usually disappointed. He is the only director I ever worked with who tires of the scene before the actor does."[13]

Mike Molloy recalled, "The actors were petrified of him. He would scream and shout and do all the stuff that he was famous for. I can't actually specifically remember him giving them any directions except sort of barking orders at them." On the other hand, Molloy thought that Preminger "was rather good with [Iman]. He didn't bully her around. I think he was understanding of the fact that she was inexperienced. He was quite good with the little boy [Gary Forbes, who played the Castles' young son, Sam]."[14] Val Robins, too, remembered Preminger's patience with Iman. "He was very gentle with Iman . . . He worked with her and tried to get it out of her. As opposed to, in some cases, if it's an actor who's been around the block, if they didn't get it, he could be seen to lose his temper." One sequence with Williamson and Iman, at the Castles' house, went on until late into the night because of problems that, Robins recalled, had partly to do with Iman's performance.

On the surface, *The Human Factor* may have resembled a typical Preminger production. Behind the scenes, the film—and Preminger— were in trouble. On the assumption that Crosfield's funding, which had not yet arrived, would soon come through, Preminger had used his own money to start shooting. After the company moved to Nairobi at the end of July, payroll checks began to bounce. According to Hope Preminger, "Crosfield didn't know what he was doing, and his friends didn't back him." On August 16 the *Los Angeles Times* reported, "Some checks have not been met, but Preminger, who says he put $1 million of his own into the picture, says it has all been a misunderstanding." Val Robins recalled, "The crew to all intents and purposes went on strike . . . The end result was that Otto yet again provided his personal finances to cover the costs."[15] To hurry up and get out of Africa, Preminger made cuts in the script.

Hope Preminger summed up *The Human Factor* as "a tough picture to make. It was Otto's last picture, and he was failing a little bit, and it was hard . . . At his age, it was a tough picture to do physically. I remember one set in Africa where he had to climb up on a rocky hill to show the cameraman a setup. [Assistant director] Kip [Gowans] had to help him up the rocky hill. It was the first time I'd ever seen him having to be helped up a piece of terrain."[16] Mike Molloy thought that Preminger "was not bad for somebody that age. I think he was still pretty sharp . . . Once we knocked him over by accident. He was trying to walk behind the Steadicam and couldn't get backwards quickly enough. Poor old thing, he collapsed on the ground with everybody on top of him. And for that, he thought that was rather funny, he didn't fly off the handle at all."[17]

After wrapping in Kenya, Preminger, back in London, gave a press conference on August 21, admitting that members of the cast and crew were still owed $500,000 and that finishing costs had not yet been met. He blamed three European financiers for failing to meet their obligation to the production. Breaking his long-held rule of never discussing the budget or cost of one of his films, Preminger disclosed that the total production cost would be about $5,500,000 and that he himself had contributed more than $2,500,000 to the production. Later news articles changed the figure to $2 million. Whatever the true figure, Val Robins was certain that "every penny that was spent on the production was Otto's personal money."[18]

On October 24 it was revealed in the press that Preminger was putting pieces from his art collection on the market in order to raise funds to cover the costs of *The Human Factor*. Later accounts disclosed that in order to raise money for the production, he sold his house in the South of France and two paintings by Matisse. "It's the first time in my career that I tried to make a picture with private financing," he admitted to journalist Roderick Mann. "I did it out of greed, I admit, because you get a better deal if it works. In my case, it didn't. The only good thing is that now I have no partners at all, so once all the actors are paid and the film starts to make money, it all goes to me."[19] Preminger's optimism about the commercial prospects of *The Human Factor* was ill founded.

On December 13, the London *Times* reported that with Williamson, Morley, and others still owed £150,000 (then about $330,000), the actors' union, British Equity, had agreed to distribution of the film (which they had blocked) under an arrangement whereby all revenue from it would be put into a creditors' fund until the creditors had been paid. "This agreement is actually written in such a way that Otto Preminger could actually be sent to prison, by either the London or the New York courts, if it is broken."[20] Morley was eventually paid, though not without what his son called a long fight.[21]

In January 1984 *Screen International* reported that Preminger still owed £500,000 (about $700,000) to various creditors, including the London firm Lee Electric (Lighting), which sued Preminger and Sigma. The suit was later settled out of court.

When the film was released, in early 1980 (after a brief run in Los Angeles in December to qualify for the 1979 Oscars), reviews were mixed. A number of American critics saw *The Human Factor* as a return to form for the director. On the other hand, David Robinson, in the London *Times*, pointed out that "Preminger has no success at all in making either actress or character out of the spectacularly beautiful Iman; and since the pivot of Castle's tragedy is his relationship with his wife, this leaves a rather devastating lacuna in the middle of the story."[22] Iman was the last in a long line of Preminger-cast novices whose inexperience made them an obvious target for reviewers.

The Human Factor is in many ways an uncharacteristic work of its director. It looks like no other Preminger film: it gives the impression of being mainly a succession of interior dialogue scenes in which most of what little movement occurs involves getting the actors to their seats and then up again. Most scenes are covered with a wide-angle lens that, while stretching the evidently compact dimensions of the rooms, emphasizes their blandness. In the scene in Castle's hotel room in Pretoria, the camera operator hand-holds the camera, at one point following Castle unsteadily from the bedroom to the bathroom, where he goes to add water to Sarah's whiskey (the movement, and the shot, are designed so as to catch Castle checking his appearance in the mirror before returning). The shot would be unexceptional in most commercial features made since about 1976, but for Preminger it is aberrant. Though he had used a handheld camera before (notably in *Bunny Lake Is Missing*), camera movement through space throughout his work required a fluidity and a transhuman dimension that the crane, track, or dolly are ideally suited to provide. Handheld movement through space carries entirely different connotations and calls attention to itself in a way that more fluid camera work does not.

The single flourish of "Premingerian" camera movement in *The Human Factor* comes late in the film and appears irrelevant to its main concerns: the shot in the Sheraton Skyline Hotel at Heathrow Airport that follows Castle across the lobby and then loses him as it tracks onto a patio and pans across a swimming pool, ending up on a steel band. (Mike Molloy recalled that, exceptionally, Preminger ordered this scene reshot after viewing the rushes. "He didn't like what I did with that, so we went back and reshot that." "It surprised us all," said Val Robins, "because we never expected him to do things like that. He didn't like the feel, he wanted it done again, and we went back, and we shot it again. I'm really not sure [what was wrong].")[23]

The restraint of the mise-en-scène is, no doubt, appropriate to the subject of the film, though it is impossible to avoid the feeling that the Preminger of 1969, to say nothing of 1949, would have got more movement into it. That the Preminger who made *The Human Factor* was physically tired, more aware of his limits than his old self, and less willing to test them is obvious. Still, the sense of tiredness, of going through the motions, that pervades much of *The Human Factor* proves appropriate to the slack and static atmosphere in which Greene's story is set and that gives it its special mood. And no one can say whether Preminger chose this manner of directing *The Human Factor* because he was too old and tired to do anything else, or whether he chose *The Human Factor* as material because it suited his condition and his inclinations.

Greene's metaphor of people living in boxes (explained by Dr. Percival in the novel with reference to a room decorated with Ben Nicholson lithographs; the film substitutes Mondrian for Nicholson) becomes the controlling visual idea of the film. Percival articulates to Daintry nothing less than a worldview: "Boxes. All part of the same picture. Each one separate, but held in perfect balance. Everyone to his own box, you in yours, I in mine. No responsibility for the next man's box." The box metaphor takes on a sinister resonance with the South African government's secret plan to use tactical nuclear weapons to create an "invisible wall" to seal off their country from the north. (In *Bonjour Tristesse*, Cécile spoke of being surrounded by "an invisible wall made of memories I can't lose.") The film's last box is Castle's Moscow apartment, a studio set whose unconvincing view of a Moscow skyline through a window makes the room's desolation and isolation more inescapable. Throughout *The Human Factor*, characters are imprisoned and pinned to precise areas of the screen: Sarah between a lamp and a TV set while talking on the phone with Castle; Castle shot through a pane of glass in a phone box. In one of the most striking shots of the film, Daintry, calling Percival from a pub to inform the doctor that he killed the wrong man, is framed in a small window in the background behind the L-shaped bar as the camera slowly zooms in on him from the other side of the bar.

The bland intimacy of the film, with its elaborate insistence on banal details (the Maltesers—malted chocolate balls—that Daintry brings to Hargreaves's country house; the baby-powder advertising slogan invented by Daintry's future son-in-law), pays off in the few visual explosions, such as the violent cut from Castle and Sarah kissing to the photographer shooting them from the window of an apartment in a neighboring building. On the other hand, the typical visual style of the film is so undistinguished that Preminger is able to make a point of it. The first South African flashback is triggered in an unceremonious manner: Castle enters Hargreaves's office; the camera zooms in on Castle as he recognizes Muller, the third man in the room; on the sound track, a kalimba plays; the shot dissolves quickly to another drab and featureless office, this time Muller's, where Castle is again standing before two seated men.

The story of *The Human Factor* is built around romantic love and requires that we accept love as the primary force in its hero's life. ("We have our own country: you and I and Sam," Sarah says to Castle.) A central weakness of the film is that, as David Robinson perceived, the woman Castle loves is never fully compelling. Iman brings dignity but little passion to the part of Sarah. On the other hand, little in the film indicates that Preminger helped her by devising movement and business that would give her performance rhythmic form. In the scene in which Castle packs Sarah and Sam into a cab—a moment that, we are to believe, both Castle and Sarah realize could be their last moment together—the perfunctory direction allows for no nuance from Sarah and no sense that she wishes to cling to her home and her husband. The hollowness of her characterization means that the love between her and Castle has to be largely conveyed through Nicol Williamson's (excellent) performance and, for the rest, accepted by the viewer as an unproved premise. The restraint of *The Human Factor* is, then, both a virtue and a failing.

After *The Human Factor*, Preminger continued to work on the Hugo Black story. He read the trade papers every day. By this time he had closed his offices on Fifth Avenue and was working in a section of his town house on East Sixty-fourth Street. According to Val Robins, who, after *The Human Factor*, had come on board as Preminger's assistant, "he seemed frustrated, but not discouraged" by his inability to find financing for the Black film or for other films he wanted to make.[24]

One day a few months after the release of *The Human Factor*, Preminger was walking from the St. Regis Hotel, where he had just finished his routine of a manicure and haircut (still not entirely bald, he had long kept his head shaved in the back), toward the restaurant La Caravelle, just across Fifth Avenue on Fifty-fifth Street. According to Hope Preminger, "he was walking with the light, it was a sunny day, about 12:30, and this cab driver came careening around the corner and hit him. Otto bounced onto the hood of the cab, and the cab never stopped. He kept going from 55th Street all the way to the other side of Saks on 49th. The people on the street were saying, 'Stop, stop!' It turned out later he was drunk. Finally he came to a halt. He slammed on his brakes, and Otto went crashing off, and that's when he hit his head on the ground."[25] Though bruised and shaken, he felt well enough to walk back to La Caravelle. Later, it was found that he had suffered a trauma to the head, the effects of which were rapid and devastating.

Though he continued to go through the motions of working, "all of us knew that it was more for show than anything else," recalled Val Robins. "It got to a point that he wasn't really working on writing a project or developing a project . . . He never meant to retire, and officially he never did. He just wouldn't. But those of us who knew him knew that he would not make another film."

Preminger's symptoms were similar to those of Alzheimer's disease, which was, at that time, beginning to be better understood by the general public. By the mid-1980s, newspapers were reporting that he had Alzheimer's.

Old acquaintances, meeting him by chance, found him confused, unable to recognize them, and afraid. Peter Bogdanovich, whom Otto had befriended when the younger man's career was taking an upswing in the late 1960s, visited the Premingers one afternoon.

He was in a cardigan sweater and appeared shrunken, bent over slightly; he had always stood very straight and tall. It had been a joke with Preminger for as long as I knew him that the problem with our relationship was that I had all the questions but that he couldn't give proper answers because he didn't remember the pictures well enough; he loved to say that I knew his films better than he did. That afternoon, as we sat around, he joked again, but it was a dark joke because of the Alzheimer's that had already made itself felt. Yes, Hope said, Otto never could remember much about his old pictures. "Now," Otto said quietly, "I *really* can't." "But you never could, darling," Hope said. Otto smiled but his eyes looked sad and somewhat confused.[27]

Hope Preminger later denied that her husband had Alzheimer's, and since no autopsy was performed, it is impossible to know. Up until the accident, she said, he had been "as clear as a bell." In any case, as she said, "he didn't die from that. He faded and faded and faded. Then he had pain in his stomach, and we took him to the hospital, and it took them three weeks to find out he had colon cancer. And they operated, and there was nothing they could do."[28] Preminger died four weeks later, on April 23, 1986.

Austin Pendleton, a New Yorker, was another of the old friends who met Preminger during his decline. At their occasional meetings over the preceding years, "he was always telling me I would be in his next film," Pendleton recalled. "In 1980, I was out in Hollywood. I went to see what became his last film, *The Human Factor*, which had gotten pretty good reviews. The theater was empty. I thought it was really good. It was up there with some of his best films, I thought. I was really impressed with that. Then soon after that I was back in New York, and I ran into him on Third Avenue. And he looked sad. I think he might just recently have been diagnosed with Alzheimer's, but I didn't know that. 'Otto, I saw *The Human Factor*, and I just thought it was great.' He looked infinitely sad and troubled, and he said, 'You will be in my next film.' And walked away on Third Avenue."[29]

Afterword

During his lifetime, and in the more than two decades since his death, Otto Preminger's critical reputation has had many ups and downs. As of this writing, his reputation is evidently rising, for reasons that no doubt have as much to do with the increased distance of the period of his celebrity and with changes in the ways older films are perceived and consumed as with the prestige of certain genres (in particular, film noir).

Still, it's not, I think, generally recognized that Preminger is one of the filmmakers who created worlds. It is one of the great things a filmmaker can do. Not all of them do it; not all try to do it. You can look again at *Anatomy of a Murder*, *Exodus*, and *In Harm's Way* and see it at once: it's not just a film, it's a world.

In this book I've occasionally referred to "the world of the film," as if Preminger's films possessed—or were themselves—worlds. The phrase has two different senses. On the one hand, I've called the time-space unity formed by a film the film's "world." The fact that this unity exists, and the surprise and pleasure of its discovery, happen to be unusually strong elements in Preminger's films, much stronger than in most. This is because of his embrace of the reality that stands before the camera and his insistence on enhancing the value of this reality for the viewer, through long takes, camera movement, and a range of other strategies and approaches that I've tried to describe and analyze.

On the other hand, I've designated by the "world" of a film the society that the film depicts and in which its characters move, a society that (in many cases) Preminger and his privileged heroes come to reject as corrupt. This rejection is as crucial a Premingerian gesture as the other one, that of embracing wholeness.

The questions that Preminger's films invite us to explore—questions of reality, unity, and integrity, of the isolated individual, of perception and value, of the links between one world and the other one—are not the only questions of cinema, but they're some of the essential ones. In their fascination, and in the contradictory and forbidding personality of the artist himself, lies the continuing fascination of Preminger.

Notes

Introduction

1. Ian Cameron, Mark Shivas, Paul Mayersberg, "Interview with Otto Preminger," *Movie* 13 (Summer 1965), pp. 15–16.
2. Otto Preminger, "Propos," *Positif* 128 (June 1971), pp. 17–18.
3. *New York Herald Tribune*, October 17, 1965, p. 55.
4. Helga Cranston (Keller), interview with the author, Herzliyya, Israel, October 7, 2004.
5. Theodore Gershuny, *Soon to Be a Major Motion Picture: The Anatomy of an All-Star, Big-Budget, Multimillion-Dollar Disaster* (New York: Holt, Rinehart and Winston, 1980), pp. 176–77.
6. Mark Shivas, "Interview with Otto Preminger," *Movie* 4 (November 1962), p. 20.

1. Breaking the Lightning

1. Otto Preminger, *Preminger: An Autobiography* (New York: Doubleday and Co., 1977), p. 27.
2. William O. McCagg, Jr., *A History of Habsburg Jews, 1670–1918* (Bloomington: Indiana University Press, 1989), pp. 172–73; 219.
3. *Preminger: An Autobiography*, pp. 28–29.
4. Norbert Grob, Rolf Aurich, Wolfgang Jacobsen, *Otto Preminger* (Berlin: Stiftung Deutsche Kinemathek and Jovis Verlagsbüro, 1999), p. 163.
5. *Preminger: An Autobiography*, pp. 29–30.
6. Willi Frischauer, *Behind the Scenes of Otto Preminger: An Unauthorized Biography* (New York: William Morrow & Company, 1974), p. 28.
7. Ingo Preminger, interview with the author, Pacific Palisades, California, May 22, 2002. All subsequent quotations from Ingo Preminger in this chapter are from this interview.
8. Quoted in Robert S. Wistrich, *The Jews of Vienna in the Age of Franz Joseph* (Oxford: Oxford University Press, 1989), p. 595.
9. Dwight Pickard, "Preminger," *Moderator* (December 1969), p. 12.
10. Gottfried Reinhardt, *The Genius: A Memoir of Max Reinhardt* (New York: Alfred A. Knopf, 1979) pp. 373–74.
11. *Preminger: An Autobiography*, p. 36.
12. Erik Preminger, interview with the author, April 5, 2006.
13. Samuel L. Leiter, *From Stanislavsky to Barrault: Representative Directors of the Euro-*

pean Stage (Contributions in Drama and Theatre Studies, Number 34) (New York: Greenwood Press, 1991), p. 85.

14. Peter Bogdanovich, "Peter Bogdanovich Interviews Otto Preminger," *On Film*, vol. 1, no. 0 (1970), p. 38.

15. George E. Wellwarth and Alfred G. Brooks, eds., *Max Reinhardt 1873–1973: A Centennial Festschrift of Memorial Essays and Interviews on the One Hundredth Anniversary of His Birth* (Binghamton, N.Y.: Max Reinhardt Archive, 1973), pp. 110–11.

16. Excerpt from "Living Space and the Theatre," in Oliver M. Sayler, ed., *Max Reinhardt and His Theatre* (New York: Benjamin Blom, 1968), p. 338.

17. *Preminger: An Autobiography*, p. 41.

18. Eileen Creelman, "Picture Plays and Players," *New York Sun*, August 26, 1943.

19. Grob et al., *Otto Preminger*, p. 167.

20. W. E. Yates, *Theatre in Vienna: A Critical History, 1776–1995* (Cambridge: Cambridge University Press, 1996), p. 211.

21. *Die Stunde*, April 12, 1930, cited in Grob et al., *Otto Preminger*, p. 170.

22. Grob et al., *Otto Preminger*, p. 170.

23. Ibid., p. 150.

24. Ibid.

25. Jacques Doniol-Valcroze and Eric Rohmer, "Entretien avec Otto Preminger," *Cahiers du cinéma* 21:121 (July 1961), p. 10.

26. See Robert von Dassanowsky, *Austrian Cinema: A History* (Jefferson, North Carolina: McFarland & Company, 2005), Chapter 2.

27. Marion Mill Preminger, *All I Want Is Everything* (New York: Funk & Wagnalls, 1957), pp. 113, 142.

28. *Preminger: An Autobiography*, p. 51.

29. Judy Bachrach, "Otto Preminger: 'Full Circle,'" *Washington Post*, September 27, 1973, p. B14.

30. Bruce F. Pauley, *From Prejudice to Persecution: A History of Austrian Anti-Semitism* (Chapel Hill: University of North Carolina Press, 1992), p. 270.

31. Eileen Creelman, "Picture Plays and Players," *New York Sun*, August 26, 1943.

2. It's the Artistic Side That's Questionable

1. *Preminger: An Autobiography*, p. 7.

2. Edith J. R. Isaacs, *Theatre Arts*, February 1936, p. 105.

3. Grob et al., *Otto Preminger*, p. 7.

4. *Preminger: An Autobiography*, p. 54.

5. *Preminger: An Autobiography*, pp. 16–17.

6. *Variety*, November 18, 1936.

7. *Preminger: An Autobiography*, pp. 17–18.

8. Leonard Mosley, *Zanuck: The Rise and Fall of Hollywood's Last Tycoon* (Boston: Little, Brown and Company, 1984), p. 181.

9. Clipping in New York Public Library of Performing Arts, source unidentified, dated April 7, 1938.

10. *Time*, November 15, 1937, p. 42.

11. Gerald Pratley, *The Cinema of Otto Preminger* (New York: A. S. Barnes, 1971), p. 48.

12. Ibid.

3. Cues for Passion

1. *Preminger: An Autobiography*, p. 55.
2. Reinhardt, *The Genius*, pp. 339–40.
3. Ingo Preminger, interview with the author, May 22, 2002, Pacific Palisades.
4. *Preminger: An Autobiography*, pp. 56–57.
5. Interview with the author, May 22, 2002, Pacific Palisades.
6. FBI documents obtained under FOIPA.
7. Leon Askin and C. Melvin Davidson, *Quietude and Quest: Protagonists and Antagonists in the Theatre, on and off Stage as Seen through the Eyes of Leon Askin* (California: Ariadne Press, 1989), p. 159.
8. *Preminger: An Autobiography*, p. 65.
9. Marguerite Courtney, *Laurette* (New York: Rinehart and Company, 1955), pp. 378–79.
10. *New York Times*, January 15, 1939.
11. Alfred G. Brooks and Oscar B. Goodman, eds., *Theater Symposium II—The Director and the Actor, October 16–17, 1968* (Binghamton, N.Y.: The Max Reinhardt Archive, 1970), pp. 30–31.
12. *Preminger: An Autobiography*, p. 62.
13. Alma Power-Waters, *John Barrymore: The Legend and the Man* (New York: Julian Messner, Inc., 1941), pp. 229, 231.
14. Ibid., p. 236.
15. John Kobler, *Damned in Paradise: The Life of John Barrymore* (New York: Atheneum, 1977), p. 332.
16. *Preminger: An Autobiography*, p. 68.
17. Kobler, *Damned in Paradise*, p. 334.
18. Burns Mantle, ed., *The Best Plays of 1939–40 and the Year Book of the Drama in America* (New York: Dodd, Mead, 1940), p. 322.
19. Michael Mok, *New York Post*, November 29, 1939.
20. Otto L. Preminger file, Yale School of Drama records.
21. Brooks and Goodman, *Theater Symposium II—The Director and the Actor*, p. 34.
22. Brooks Atkinson, *New York Times*, November 8, 1940, 24:2.
23. Lucius Beebe, "Stage Asides," *New York Herald Tribune*, August 31, 1941.
24. Atkinson, *New York Times*, December 29, 1941, 20:2; Watts, *New York Herald Tribune*, December 29, 1941; Lockridge, *New York Sun*, December 29, 1941; Brown, *New York World Telegram*, December 29, 1941; *Preminger: An Autobiography*, p. 81.

4. Second Apprenticeship

1. Grob et al., *Preminger*, p. 179.
2. Reinhardt, *The Genius*, p. 299.
3. Preminger, *All I Want Is Everything*, p. 200.
4. Reinhardt, *The Genius*, p. 304.
5. Ronald James Policy, *Otto Preminger's Skidoo: Biography of a Motion Picture* (University of Wisconsin, Ph.D. thesis, 1973), p. 25.
6. *Preminger: An Autobiography*, pp. 82, 83.
7. Samuel Fuller, interview with Olivier Eyquem and Michael Henry Wilson, October 26, 1974, Paris.

8. *Preminger: An Autobiography*, p. 83.

9. Ibid.

10. Christian Cargnelli and Michael Omasta, eds., *Aufbruch ins Ungewisse*, t. 1 (Vienna: Wespennest, 1993), pp. 219–20.

11. *Variety*, January 13, 1943.

12. FBI documents obtained under FOIPA.

13. Ring Lardner, Jr., *I'd Hate Myself in the Morning: A Memoir* (New York: Thunder's Mouth Press, 2000), p. 106.

14. Kenneth Geist, "The Films of Ring Lardner Jr.," *Film Comment* Vol. 6, No. 4 (Winter 1970–71), p. 46.

15. Peter Bogdanovich, "The Making of *Laura* by Otto Preminger as Told to Peter Bogdanovich," *On Film* vol. 1, no. 0 (1970), p. 49. Cf. Pratley, *Cinema of Otto Preminger*, p. 9; *Preminger: An Autobiography*, p. 85.

16. Henry Ephron, *We Thought We Could Do Anything: The Life of Screenwriters Phoebe and Henry Ephron* (New York: W. W. Norton & Company, 1977), pp. 30–31.

17. Lardner, *I'd Hate Myself in the Morning*, p. 106.

18. Otto Preminger, interview with Olivier Eyquem and Olivier Comte, May 1970, Paris. Parts of this interview were published in French translation in *Positif* 554 (April 2007).

19. Jacques Rivette, "Rencontre avec Otto Preminger," *Cahiers du cinéma* 5:29 (December 1953), p. 9.

20. Paul Mayersberg, *Hollywood: The Haunted House* (Harmondsworth, England: Penguin Books, 1967), p. 32.

21. All quotations from PCA correspondence in this and subsequent chapters are from the files on the respective films in the Academy of Motion Pictures Arts and Sciences (AMPAS) Library, Motion Picture Association of America Production Code Administration Records.

22. Pratley, *Cinema of Otto Preminger*, p. 70.

23. *Preminger: An Autobiography*, p. 101.

5. If You Can Find Something Different

1. Preminger, *All I Want Is Everything*, pp. 185–88.

2. *Preminger: An Autobiography*, p. 54.

3. Ibid., p. 97.

4. *Preminger, All I Want Is Everything*, p. 212.

5. *Preminger: An Autobiography*, pp. 95–96.

6. Erik Lee Preminger, *Gypsy & Me: At Home and on the Road with Gypsy Rose Lee* (Boston: Little, Brown and Company, 1984), p. 258.

7. Bogdanovich, "Peter Bogdanovich Interviews Otto Preminger," p. 37.

8. Robert Porfirio, Alain Silver, and James Ursini, eds., *Film Noir Reader 3: Interviews with Filmmakers of the Classic Noir Period* (New York: Limelight Editions, 2002), p. 92.

9. Vera Caspary, "My 'Laura' and Otto's," *Saturday Review* 54:26 (June 26, 1971), p. 37.

10. All quotations from Zanuck story-conference notes and memos in this and subsequent chapters are from the files on the respective films in the UCLA Arts Library–Special Collections, Twentieth Century-Fox Produced Scripts Collection.

11. Bogdanovich, "The Making of *Laura*," pp. 49–50.
12. *Preminger: An Autobiography*, p. 85.
13. Gene Tierney, with Mickey Herskowitz, *Self-Portrait* (Wyden Books, 1979), pp. 132–33.
14. Bogdanovich, "The Making of *Laura*," p. 50.
15. Caspary, "My 'Laura' and Otto's," p. 36.
16. Bogdanovich, "The Making of *Laura*," pp. 50–51.
17. Preminger, "Propos," p. 17.
18. Bogdanovich, "The Making of *Laura*," p. 51.
19. "Dana Andrews Oral History," interview with Joan and Robert Franklin, Columbia University Oral History Research Office (1958).
20. *Preminger: An Autobiography*, p. 90; Bogdanovich, "The Making of *Laura*," p. 51.
21. *Preminger: An Autobiography*, p. 90.
22. "Dana Andrews Oral History."
23. Bogdanovich, "The Making of *Laura*," p. 51.
24. Rudy Behlmer, *America's Favorite Movies* (New York: Ungar Publishing Company, 1982), pp. 190–91.
25. Gregory J. M. Catsos, "Priceless: A Farewell Interview with Vincent Price," *Filmfax* 42 (December 1993/January 1994), p. 46.
26. Behlmer, *America's Favorite Movies*, p. 191.
27. Tierney, *Self-Portrait*, p. 135.
28. Ibid., pp. 135–36.
29. Caspary, "My 'Laura' and Otto's," p. 37.
30. Behlmer, *America's Favorite Movies*, p. 192.
31. Bogdanovich, "The Making of *Laura*," p. 51.
32. Catsos, "Farewell Interview with Vincent Price," p. 46.
33. Leonard Maltin, *The Art of the Cinematographer: A Survey and Interview with Five Masters* (New York: Dover Publications, 1978, p. 110; Jacques Lourcelles, "Laura: Scénario d'un scénario," *L'Avant-Scène Cinéma* 211–12 (July–September 1978), p. 8.
34. Bogdanovich, "The Making of *Laura*," p. 52.
35. David Raksin, interview with the author, September 27, 1994, Boston.
36. Ibid.
37. Aubrey Solomon, *Twentieth Century-Fox: A Corporate and Financial History* (Metuchen, N.J.: The Scarecrow Press, 1988), pp. 220, 242.
38. Tierney, *Self-Portrait*, p. 136.
39. Charles Baudelaire, *Les Paradis artificiels* (Paris: Garnier-Flammarion, 1966), p. 25.

6. The Lubitsch Touch

1. Pratley, *Cinema of Otto Preminger*, p. 70.
2. Andrew Sarris, *The American Cinema: Directors and Directions 1929–1968* (New York: E. P. Dutton & Co., 1968), p. 106.
3. Tallulah Bankhead, *Tallulah: My Autobiography* (New York: Harper and Brothers, 1952), p. 270.
4. John Kobal, *People Will Talk* (New York: Alfred A. Knopf, 1985), p. 667.
5. Scott Eyman, *Ernst Lubitsch, Laughter in Paradise* (New York: Simon & Schuster, 1993), p. 334.

6. Bogdanovich, "Peter Bogdanovich Interviews Otto Preminger," p. 38.
7. *Preminger: An Autobiography*, p. 106.
8. Kobal, *People Will Talk*, p. 665.
9. *New York Times*, October 8, 1944.
10. Kobal, *People Will Talk*, p. 667.
11. Rivette, "Rencontre avec Otto Preminger," p. 8.
12. Kobal, *People Will Talk*, p. 667.
13. *Preminger: An Autobiography*, p. 107.
14. Solomon, *Twentieth Century-Fox*, pp. 220, 242.
15. *Preminger: An Autobiography*, pp. 107–108.

7. Obsession

1. *New York Sun*, February 6, 1946.
2. *Fallen Angel* file, Twentieth Century-Fox collection, USC Cinematic Arts Library.
3. Louella Parsons, *Los Angeles Examiner*, April 5, 1945.
4. *New York Sun*, February 6, 1946.
5. "Dana Andrews Oral History."
6. David Raksin, interview with the author, Boston, September 27, 1994.
7. Doug McClelland, *Forties Film Talk: Oral Histories of Hollywood* (Jefferson, N.C.: McFarland & Co., 1992), p. 59.
8. Ronald L. Davis, *Hollywood Beauty: Linda Darnell and the American Dream* (Norman, Ok.: University of Oklahoma Press, 1991), p. 100.
9. James Robert Parish, *The Fox Girls* (New Rochelle, N.Y.: Arlington House, 1971), p. 301.
10. Allen Eyles, "Dana Andrews," *Focus on Film* 26 (1977), p. 16.
11. Patrick McGilligan, ed., *Backstory 2: Interviews with Screenwriters of the 1940s and 1950s* (Berkeley: University of California Press, 1991), pp. 234–35.
12. *Preminger: An Autobiography*, p. 121.
13. Raksin, interview with the author.
14. Pratley, *Cinema of Otto Preminger*, p. 76.

8. A Bucket of Ashes

1. Script conference memo, January 24, 1944, in *Centennial Summer* file, Twentieth Century-Fox collection, USC Cinematic Arts Library.
2. Bogdanovich, "Peter Bogdanovich Interviews Otto Preminger," p. 39.
3. Kobal, *People Will Talk*, p. 44.
4. Undated press release in AMPAS Library *Centennial Summer* clippings file.
5. Stuart Oderman, *Lillian Gish: A Life on Stage and Screen* (Jefferson, N.C.: McFarland & Company, 2000), p. 259.
6. Davis, *Hollywood Beauty*, p. 100.
7. McClelland, *Forties Film Talk*, p. 190.
8. Undated press release in AMPAS Library *Centennial Summer* clippings file.
9. Philip Dunne, *Take Two* (New York: McGraw-Hill Book Company, 1980), pp. 55–56.
10. *New York Times*, July 18, 1946, p. 78.

9. The Limbo of Movies

1. *Newsweek*, April 8, 1957.
2. Dunne, *Take Two*, p. 185.
3. Ibid., pp. 183, 184.
4. Zanuck to Perlberg and Dunne, October 16, 1945, in UCLA Arts Library Special Collections, Twentieth Century-Fox Legal Records; Breen memo to files, October 16, 1945, in AMPAS Library, MPAA-PCA Records, *Forever Amber* file.
5. Fred Stanley, "'Amber' in Hollywood," *New York Times*, March 10, 1946, p. X1.
6. Dunne, *Take Two*, p. 184.
7. Thomas F. Brady, "'Amber' in Hollywood," *New York Times*, Nov. 3, 1946, p. 65; *Los Angeles Times*, July 25, 1946.
8. *New York Times*, May 2, 1946, p. 27.
9. "'Forever Amber' or 'Crime Doesn't Pay,'" *New York Times*, Aug. 4, 1946, p. 93.
10. Davis, *Hollywood Beauty*, pp. 96–97.
11. Pratley, *Cinema of Otto Preminger*, p. 63.
12. Samuel Fuller, interview with Olivier Eyquem and Michael Henry Wilson, October 26, 1974, Paris.
13. *Preminger: An Autobiography*, p. 127.
14. *Preminger: An Autobiography*, pp. 126–27; Pratley, *Cinema of Otto Preminger*, p. 63.
15. Lardner, *I'd Hate Myself in the Morning*, p. 117.
16. Dunne, *Take Two*, p. 184.
17. Brady, "'Amber' in Hollywood," p. 65.
18. Davis, *Hollywood Beauty*, pp. 98, 99.
19. Brady, "'Amber' in Hollywood," p. 65.
20. *Preminger: An Autobiography*, p. 128.
21. Herb A. Lightman, "*Forever Amber*: Tapestry in Technicolor," *American Cinematographer* 29:1 (January 1948), pp. 8–9.
22. Solomon, *Twentieth Century-Fox*, p. 243.
23. "Perlberg Says Fox Won't Change 'Amber,'" *New York Times*, October 24, 1947, p. 19.
24. *Preminger: An Autobiography*, pp. 128–29.
25. Frank Walsh, *Sin and Censorship: The Catholic Church and the Motion Picture Industry* (New Haven: Yale University Press, 1996), pp. 212–13.
26. Walsh, *Sin and Censorship*, p. 214; Rudy Behlmer, *Memo from Darryl F. Zanuck: The Golden Years at Twentieth Century-Fox* (New York: Grove Press, 1993), pp. 202–203.

10. A Search for Lucidity

1. Charles Castle, *Joan Crawford: The Raging Star* (London: New English Library, 1977), p. 122; "Dana Andrews Oral History"; Bob Thomas, *Joan Crawford: A Biography* (New York: Simon & Schuster, 1978), p. 158.
2. Castle, *Joan Crawford*, p. 122.
3. *Preminger: An Autobiography*, p. 123.
4. Lawrence J. Quirk and William Schoell, *Joan Crawford: The Essential Biography* (Lexington: The University Press of Kentucky, 2002), p. 146; Roy Newquist, *Conversations with Joan Crawford* (Secaucus, N.J.: Citadel Press, 1980), p. 160.
5. David Raksin, interview with the author, September 27, 1994, Boston.

11. Hollywood Crossroads

1. Herman G. Weinberg, *The Lubitsch Touch: A Critical Study* (New York: Dover Publications, 1977), p. 226.
2. Weinberg, *The Lubitsch Touch*, p. 307.
3. Pratley, *Cinema of Otto Preminger*, p. 72.
4. Eyman, *Ernst Lubitsch*, p. 359; *Variety*, December 17, 1947, p. 2.
5. Lardner, *I'd Hate Myself in the Morning*, p. 124.
6. FBI documents obtained under FOIPA. See also Patrick McGilligan, *Fritz Lang: The Nature of the Beast* (New York: St. Martin's Press, 1997), pp. 257–59 and 377–78; Anthony Heilbut, *Exiled in Paradise: German Refugee Artists and Intellectuals in America from the 1930s to the Present* (Berkeley: University of California Press, 1983), pp. 101–16.
7. Tom McGee, *The Girl with the Million Dollar Legs* (Vestal, N.Y.: Vestal Press, 1995), p. 148.
8. Eyman, *Ernst Lubitsch*, pp. 364–65.
9. Brooks and Goodman, eds., *Theater Symposium II—The Director and the Actor*, p. 23.
10. Eyman, *Ernst Lubitsch*, p. 365.
11. Ronald L. Davis, Oral History Collection 280 (Douglas Fairbanks, Jr.), DeGolyer Library, Southern Methodist University.
12. Louella Parsons, *Los Angeles Examiner*, January 13, 1948.
13. Unidentified newspaper clipping, January 13, 1948, Otto Preminger clippings file, AMPAS Library.
14. *Preminger: An Autobiography*, p. 124.

12. Sick Children

1. McGilligan, *Backstory 2*, p. 235.
2. Bogdanovich, "Peter Bogdanovich Interviews Otto Preminger," p. 40.
3. Rivette, "Rencontre avec Otto Preminger," p. 10.
4. Alain Bergala, ed., *Jean-Luc Godard par Jean-Luc Godard* (Paris: Éditions de l'Étoile, 1985), p. 224.
5. E. J. Strong, " 'Lady Windermere's Fan' Made Modern for Film," *Los Angeles Times*, August 29, 1948.
6. Paul Kohner Agency Files, Filmmuseum Berlin.
7. McGilligan, *Backstory 2*, p. 235.
8. Bosley Crowther, *New York Times*, April 2, 1949, p. 12.

13. From Self to Self

1. *Preminger: An Autobiography*, p. 101.
2. George F. Custen, *Twentieth Century's Fox: Darryl F. Zanuck and the Culture of Hollywood* (New York: Basic Books, 1997), p. 334.
3. *New York Times*, February 28, 1949 and March 24, 1949; Philip Dunne, *Take Two*, pp. 224–29.
4. Ben Hecht, *A Child of the Century* (New York: Simon and Schuster, 1954), p. 482.
5. David Raksin, interview with the author, September 27, 1994, Boston.

6. *Los Angeles Times*, August 11, 1949; *Los Angeles Examiner*, August 26, 1949.
7. Preminger, *All I Want Is Everything*, pp. 210–11.
8. Ibid., p. 165.
9. *Los Angeles Examiner*, September 1, 1949.
10. Louella Parsons, *Los Angeles Examiner*, September 22, 1949.
11. Gérard Legrand, "Un miroir si fidèle: *Whirlpool*," *Positif* 310 (décembre 1986), p. 69.
12. Odile Bächler, *Laura* (Paris: Éditions Nathan, 1995), p. 115.
13. Legrand writes that "*Whirlpool* appears as a 'parody' of *Laura*" ("Un miroir si fidèle," p. 70). Cf. Jacques Lourcelles, *Otto Preminger* (Paris: Éditions Seghers, 1965), pp. 41–42. Giulia Carluccio and Linda Cena offer further points of comparison between *Whirlpool* and *Laura* in *Otto Preminger* (Rome: La Nuova Italia, 1991), pp. 60–61.

14. The Unseeing Witness

1. Gary Merrill, *Bette, Rita, and the Rest of My Life* (New York: Berkley Books, 1990), p. 74.
2. Rui Nogueira, "Voyage au centre du monde (du cinéma) en compagnie d'Otto Preminger," *Cinéma 71* number 155 (April 1971), p. 52.
3. Karl Malden, with Carla Malden, *When Do I Start? A Memoir* (New York: Simon and Schuster, 1997), pp. 220–21.
4. Philip T. Hartung, *Commonweal*, July 21, 1950, p. 368.
5. *Skidoo* story conferences, audio recordings in Doran William Cannon Collection, AMPAS Library.

15. Private Arrangements

1. Rivette, "Rencontre avec Otto Preminger," p. 10.
2. *The 13th Letter* file, Twentieth-Century Fox collection, USC Cinematic Arts Library.
3. Howard Koch, *As Time Goes By: Memoirs of a Writer in Hollywood, New York and Europe* (New York: Harcourt Brace Jovanovich, 1979), p. 176.
4. *New York Times*, July 28, 1950, p. 13; August 17, 1950, p. 24; August 19, 1950, p. 21; August 23, 1950, p. 35; August 28, 1950, p. 13; September 2, 1950, p. 22.
5. *Preminger: An Autobiography*, p. 146.

16. What the Jury Decides

1. Otto Preminger Legal File, Twentieth Century-Fox Legal Files collection, UCLA Arts Library; *Los Angeles Examiner*, August 11, 1950; February 5, 1951; April 2, 1951.
2. Philip K. Scheuer, "Bilingual Filming of 'The Moon' Makes It Either Blue or Blau," *Los Angeles Times* (January 18, 1953), p. 3.
3. Robert Horton, ed., *Billy Wilder: Interviews* (Jackson: University Press of Mississippi, 2001), p. 106.
4. Philip K. Scheuer, *Los Angeles Times*, February 5, 1953, p. A9.
5. Alain Archambault, Jacques Lourcelles, and Michel Mourlet, "Entretien avec Otto Preminger," *Présence du cinéma* 11 (February 1962), p. 16.

6. William MacAdams, *Ben Hecht: The Man Behind the Legend* (New York: Charles Scribner's Sons, 1990), p. 260.
7. *Los Angeles Times*, August 10, 1952, p. 3.
8. *Angel Face* file, Motion Picture Association of America Production Code Administration Records, AMPAS Library.
9. Stewart Granger, *Sparks Fly Upward* (London: Granada Publishing, 1981), p. 262.
10. Jerry Roberts, ed., *Mitchum—In His Own Words: Interviews with Robert Mitchum* (New York: Proscenium Publishers, 2000), p. 69.
11. Lourcelles, *Otto Preminger*, p. 34.
12. Reynold Humphries, "Entre anges et démons: des femmes trop fatales (psychanalyse, film noir et désir spectatoriel)," in *Les cahiers du CIRCAV* 9 (1997) pp. 85–86.

17. The Accepted or Common Thing

1. Ronald L. Davis, Oral History Collection 363 (Barry Nelson), DeGolyer Library, Southern Methodist University.
2. Louis Sheaffer, "Curtain Time," *Brooklyn Eagle*, July 17, 1951, p. 4.
3. Wambly Bald, "Your Play Opening? Get Drunk," *New York Post*, April 15, 1951.
4. Ben Hecht, Introduction to *The Moon Is Blue*, by F. Hugh Herbert (New York: Random House, 1951), pp. ix–xi.
5. Brooks Atkinson, *New York Times*, March 9, 1951.
6. Martin Schute, interview with the author, June 13, 2002, Saltash, England; Eva Monley, interview with the author, June 12, 2002, London.
7. *New York Times*, Oct. 21, 1951, p. 101.
8. *The Moon Is Blue* file, United Artists collection, Wisconsin Center for Film and Theater Research. See also *New York Times*, May 9, 1952, p. 20.
9. Gershuny, *Soon to Be a Major Motion Picture*, p. 276.
10. Otto Preminger, interview with Eyquern and Comte.
11. David Niven, *The Moon's a Balloon and Bring On the Empty Horses* (London: Octopus Books, 1984), p. 256.
12. Peter Haining, *The Last Gentleman: A Tribute to David Niven* (London: W. H. Allen, 1984), p. 78.
13. See Grob et al., *Otto Preminger*, p. 179.
14. Scheuer, "Bilingual Filming of 'The Moon,'" p. 3; *New York Herald Tribune*, February 1, 1953.
15. Letter to Edward Small, December 23, 1952, *The Moon Is Blue* file, United Artists collection, Wisconsin Center for Film and Theater Research.
16. Kenneth Clark to Joseph L. Breen, August 10, 1954, *The Moon Is Blue* file, Motion Picture Association of America Production Code Administration Records, AMPAS Library.
17. Jack Vizzard, *See No Evil: Life Inside a Hollywood Censor* (New York: Simon and Schuster, 1970), pp. 152–53.
18. Ibid., p. 153–55.
19. "G.M.S. [Geoffrey Shurlock]," Memo for files, January 6, 1953, *The Moon Is Blue* file, Motion Picture Association of America Production Code Administration Records, AMPAS Library.

20. Vizzard, *See No Evil*, p. 155.
21. Leonard J. Leff and Jerold L. Simmons, *The Dame in the Kimono: Hollywood, Censorship, and the Production Code*, second edition (Lexington: The University Press of Kentucky, 2001), p. 199.
22. Alain Archambault et al., "Entretien avec Otto Preminger," p. 16.
23. *Variety*, June 10, 1953, p. 3.
24. Leff and Simmons, *Dame in the Kimono*, p. 202.
25. Michael Conant, *Antitrust in the Motion Picture Industry: Economic and Legal Analysis* (Berkeley: University of California Press, 1960), pp. 41–42.
26. *Variety*, June 30, 1953, p. 1.
27. *The Nation*, July 4, 1953, p. 18.
28. Howard Thompson, "Random Observations on Pictures and People," *New York Times*, August 9, 1953.
29. Max E. Youngstein to George Schaefer, June 5, 1953, *The Moon Is Blue* file, United Artists collection, Wisconsin Center for Film and Theater Research.
30. See Myer P. Beck to Max E. Youngstein, September 21, 1953, *The Moon Is Blue* file, United Artists collection, Wisconsin Center for Film and Theater Research.
31. Youngstein to Krim, September 24, 1953, *The Moon Is Blue* file, United Artists collection, Wisconsin Center for Film and Theater Research.

18. All Things Are in Process, and Nothing Stays Still

1. Stanley Rubin, interview with the author, April 18, 2006.
2. *Preminger: An Autobiography*, p. 153.
3. Pratley, *Cinema of Otto Preminger*, p. 109; Bogdanovich, "Peter Bogdanovich Interviews Otto Preminger," p. 41.
4. Rubin, interview with the author, April 18, 2006.
5. Rivette, "Rencontre avec Otto Preminger," p. 12.
6. "Peter Bogdanovich Interviews Otto Preminger," p. 41; Preminger, "Propos," p. 21.
7. Rubin, interview with the author, April 18, 2006.
8. Paul A. Helmick, *Cut, Print, and That's a Wrap!* (Jefferson, N.C.: McFarland & Company, 2001), pp. 54–55.
9. Donald Spoto, *Marilyn Monroe: The Biography* (New York: HarperCollins, 1993), p. 244.
10. *Preminger: An Autobiography*, p. 154.
11. Barbara Leaming, *Marilyn Monroe* (New York: Crown Publishers, 1998), p. 91.
12. Helmick, *Cut, Print, and That's a Wrap!*, p. 56.
13. Rubin, interview with the author, April 18, 2006.
14. Shelley Winters, *Shelley: Also Known as Shirley* (New York: William Morrow and Company, 1980), p. 453.
15. Helmick, *Cut, Print, and That's a Wrap!*, pp. 56–57; Shivas, "Interview with Otto Preminger," p. 20.
16. Rubin, interview with the author, April 18, 2006.
17. Ibid.
18. Ibid.
19. *Time*, November 2, 1953, p. 87.
20. Leaming, *Marilyn Monroe*, p. 93.

21. Preminger interview with Olivier Eyquem and Olivier Comte.
22. André Bazin, "Évolution du Western," in *Qu'est-ce que le cinéma?* (Paris: Éditions du Cerf, 1985), p. 238.
23. V. F. Perkins, *Film as Film: Understanding and Judging Movies* (Harmondsworth, England: Penguin Books, 1972), pp. 128–29.
24. "Why Preminger?" in Ian Cameron, ed., *Movie Reader* (New York: Praeger Publishers, 1972), p. 43.
25. David Bordwell, "Widescreen Aesthetics and Mise en Scene Criticism," *The Velvet Light Trap* 21 (Summer 1985), pp. 22–23.

19. Taboo

1. Dictaphone transcription of phone conversation, July 28, 1953, in Irene Mayer Selznick Collection, Boston University Special Collections.
2. *Preminger: An Autobiography*, pp. 159–60; *Carmen Jones* file, Twentieth Century-Fox Legal Files, UCLA Arts Library Special Collections.
3. Donald Bogle, *Dorothy Dandridge* (New York: Amistad Press, 1997), p. 271.
4. Ibid., p. 273.
5. Earl Mills, *Dorothy Dandridge* (Los Angeles: Holloway House, 1991), p. 174.
6. Ibid., p. 178.
7. Dorothy Dandridge and Earl Conrad, *Everything and Nothing: The Dorothy Dandridge Tragedy* (New York: Abelard-Schuman, 1970), pp. 160–62.
8. Bogle, *Dandridge*, p. 277.
9. Ibid., p. 278.
10. Ibid., p. 284.
11. Ibid., p. 286; Diahann Carroll with Ross Firestone, *Diahann: An Autobiography* (Boston: Little, Brown & Co., 1986), p. 48.
12. Bogle, *Dandridge*, pp. 284–85.
13. Brock Peters, interview with the author, May 11, 2004.
14. Bogle, *Dandridge*, p. 285.
15. Carroll, *Diahann*, p. 49.
16. American Television Interview with Diahann Carroll, Academy of Television Arts & Sciences Foundation, March 2, 1994, Roll 3.
17. Carroll, *Diahann*, pp. 47–48.
18. Peters, interview with the author, May 11, 2004.
19. Ginger Rogers, *Ginger: My Story* (New York: HarperCollins Publishers, 1991), p. 334.
20. For a discussion of these themes as they function in Bizet's opera and its French cultural context, see Susan McClary, *Georges Bizet: Carmen* (Cambridge: Cambridge University Press, 1992), especially Chapter Three.
21. McClary, *Georges Bizet: Carmen*, p. 132.
22. James Baldwin, *Notes of a Native Son* (Boston: Beacon Press, 1955), pp. 48, 49–50, 52–53.
23. Pratley, *Cinema of Otto Preminger*, pp. 110–11.
24. Dandridge and Conrad, *Everything and Nothing*, pp. 171, 173.
25. Bogle, *Dandridge*, p. 333.
26. Ibid., p. 290.
27. Dandridge and Conrad, *Everything and Nothing*, p. 171.

28. Ibid., pp. 180, 183.
29. Bogle, *Dandridge*, p. 340.
30. Dandridge and Conrad, *Everything and Nothing*, p. 168.
31. Mills, *Dandridge*, p. 194.
32. Dandridge and Conrad, *Everything and Nothing*, pp. 182–83.
33. Bogle, *Dandridge*, pp. 342, 376. See *Preminger: An Autobiography*, p. 166.
34. Bogle, *Dandridge*, p. 377.
35. Dandridge and Conrad, *Everything and Nothing*, pp. 189–90.
36. Geri Branton recalled, "She would go with him once a year to Paris and London for clothes." Bogle, *Dandridge*, pp. 339–40.

20. A Conservative Liberal

1. *Arts*, 1955.
2. *The Court-Martial of Billy Mitchell* file, Warner Bros. Archives, USC Cinematic Arts Library.
3. Don Kranze, interview with the author, May 1, 2004, Beverly Hills.
4. Porfirio et al., *Film Noir Reader 3*, p. 95.
5. Kranze, interview with the author.
6. Cf. MacAdams, *Ben Hecht: The Man Behind the Legend*, p. 271.
7. Bogdanovich, "Peter Bogdanovich Interviews Otto Preminger," p. 41.
8. Gregory Walcott, *Hollywood Adventures: The Gregory Walcott Story* (Wilson, N.C.: The Wilson Daily Times, 2003), pp. 86–87.

21. Hooked

1. Breen to Roberts, March 7, 1950; memo to file from E.G.D., March 23, 1950; Breen to Roberts, June 21, 1950, *The Man with the Golden Arm* file, PCA files, AMPAS Library.
2. Interview with Ingo Preminger for the documentary *Otto Preminger: Ein Portrait* (Stiftung Deutsche Kinemathek/Arte) by Wolfgang Jacobsen, Martin Koerber, and René Perraudin, 1999.
3. United Artists collection, Wisconsin Center for Film and Theater Research. See Proposed Agreement re *The Man with the Golden Arm*, November 8, 1954; letter, Leonard S. Picker to Edwin Van Pelt, August 25, 1955; Financing Agreement, December 20, 1954.
4. Bettina Drew, *Nelson Algren: A Life on the Wild Side* (New York: G. P. Putnam's Sons, 1989), pp. 260, 264.
5. See Nelson Algren, "Otto Preminger's Strange Suspenjers," in *The Last Carousel* (New York: G. P. Putnam's Sons, 1973), pp. 21–36; Nelson Algren, "Otto Preminger: Man with the Golden Prerogative," *Los Angeles Times*, May 15, 1977.
6. H. E. F. Donohue and Nelson Algren, *Conversations with Nelson Algren* (New York: Berkley, 1965), pp. 104, 106, 121.
7. Ibid., p. 107.
8. Drew, *Nelson Algren*, p. 261; Algren to Maxwell Geismar, February 10, 1955, Maxwell Geismar Collection, Howard Gotlieb Archival Research Center, Boston University.
9. *Preminger: An Autobiography*, pp. 135, 136.

10. Algren, "Otto Preminger: Man with the Golden Prerogative."
11. Rui Nogueira, "Interview with Walter Newman," *Focus on Film* 11 (Autumn 1972), p. 40.
12. Nogueira, ibid.; A. H. Weiler, "By Way of Report," *New York Times*, March 13, 1955, p. X5.
13. Nogueira, "Interview with Walter Newman," p. 40.
14. Pratley, *Cinema of Otto Preminger*, pp. 113–14.
15. Nelson Algren, *The Man with the Golden Arm* (Garden City, New York: Doubleday & Company, 1949), p. 17.
16. Cf. Richard Davenport-Hines, *The Pursuit of Oblivion: A Global History of Narcotics* (New York: W. W. Norton & Company, 2002), p. 353.
17. Nogueira, "Interview with Walter Newman," pp. 41–42.
18. Memo from Robert S. Picker to Seymour Peyser, May 2, 1955, United Artists collection, Wisconsin Center for Film and Theater Research.
19. *The Man with the Golden Arm* file, MPAA PCA Records, AMPAS Library.
20. Jerold Simmons, "Challenging the Production Code: *The Man with the Golden Arm*," *Journal of Popular Film and Television* 33:1 (Spring 2005), p. 41.
21. Alain Archambault et al., "Entretien avec Otto Preminger," p. 11.
22. "Ottocrat of the Silver Screen: Preminger Still Takes the Direct Approach," *Washington Post*, April 10, 1980, p. F1.
23. Larry Kleno, *Kim Novak on Camera* (San Diego: A. S. Barnes & Company, 1980), p. 73.
24. Evelyn Harvey, "The Man Who Changed the Moral Code," *Pageant* (September 1956), pp. 99, 100.
25. Nogueira, "Interview with Walter Newman," p. 42.
26. Sammy Davis, Jr., *Hollywood in a Suitcase* (New York: William Morrow and Company, 1980), p. 116.
27. Bob Willoughby, *The Star Makers: On Set with Hollywood's Greatest Directors* (London: Merrell Publishers, 2003), p. 38.
28. See Davenport-Hines, *The Pursuit of Oblivion*.
29. Oscar Godbout, "Hollywood Scene: Preminger Presents Case for His 'Man with the Golden Arm,'" *New York Times*, October 2, 1955, p. X7.
30. *Variety*, November 15, 1955; "Preminger, Wald Let Potshots Fly," *Variety*, December 28, 1955.
31. *Variety*, November 9, 1955; November 15, 1955.
32. "Amendment of Code Sure," *Variety*, December 14, 1955, p. 27.
33. Ibid.
34. *Variety*, December 28, 1955, p. 13.
35. *Variety*, December 14, 1955, p. 4.
36. Louella Parsons, *Los Angeles Herald-Examiner*, December 30, 1955.
37. Liner notes, *Music from the Sound Track of "The Man with the Golden Arm"* (Decca Records LP, 1955).
38. Proposed Agreement, November 8, 1954, United Artists collection, Wisconsin Center for Film and Theater Research.
39. All comments by Bass in this chapter are from an interview conducted by Valerie Robins for her film *Preminger: Anatomy of a Filmmaker* (Otto Preminger Films, 1991).

40. *Hollywood Reporter*, April 24, 1956.

41. Drew, *Nelson Algren*, pp. 274, 285.

42. Val Adams, "Preminger Gets No-Cut Pact for 'Golden Arm' on TV," *New York Times*, December 28, 1966.

22. Too Much Reason

1. Archambault et al., "Entretien avec Otto Preminger," p. 16.

2. Memo from Arthur B. Krim to Seymour M. Peyser, March 22, 1956, United Artists collection, Wisconsin Center for Film and Theater Research.

3. *Preminger: An Autobiography*, pp. 182–83.

4. *New York Times*, February 17, 1957.

5. Pratley, *Cinema of Otto Preminger*, p. 118.

6. Letter, August 17, 1956, United Artists collection, Wisconsin Center for Film and Theater Research.

7. *New York Times*, September 2, 1956.

8. Richard Widmark, interviewed at the National Film Theatre, London, July 14, 2002, by Adrian Wooton, www.bfi.org.uk/showing/nft/interviews/widmark/tyrants.html.

9. Art Buchwald, *New York Herald Tribune*, March 10, 1957, p. B-5.

10. *Life*, October 24, 1956.

11. Donald W. LaBadie, "Everybody's Galatea: For Jean Seberg, Nothing Has Succeeded Like Failure," *Show* 3:8 (August 1963), p. 77.

12. David Richards, *Played Out: The Jean Seberg Story* (New York: Random House, 1981), p. 37.

13. *Los Angeles Examiner*, December 10, 1957.

14. Richards, *Played Out*, p. 66.

15. *New York Times*, October 22, 1956, p. 24.

16. Memo from Max E. Youngstein to Arthur Krim et al., March 21, 1957, United Artists collection, Wisconsin Center for Film and Theater Research.

17. *New York Times*, October 9, 1956, p. 31.

18. Sir John Gielgud, *A Life in Letters*, edited by Richard Mangan (New York: Arcade Publishing, 2004), p. 199.

19. Helga Cranston (Keller), interview with the author, Herzliyya, Israel, October 7, 2004.

20. Pratley, *Cinema of Otto Preminger*, p. 119.

21. LaBadie, "Everybody's Galatea," p. 77.

22. Cranston, interview with the author, Herzliyya, Israel, October 7, 2004.

23. Richards, *Played Out*, p. 44.

24. Stephen Watts, "Screening Shaw's 'Saint Joan' on Schedule," *New York Times*, February 17, 1957; Richards, "Played Out," pp. 48, 49.

25. Interview with the author, June 14, 2002, London.

26. Sheridan Morley, *John Gielgud: The Authorized Biography* (New York: Simon & Schuster, 2002), p. 312.

27. Marianne Ruuth, *Cruel City: The Dark Side of Hollywood's Rich and Famous* (Malibu, Calif.: Roundtable, 1991), p. 85.

28. Richard Widmark, "Lettre à Elia Kazan sur mon expérience avec certains de mes metteurs en scène," *Positif* 519 (2004), p. 45.

29. Cranston, interview with the author.

30. Richards, *Played Out*, p. 50.

31. Gerlinde Waz and Ronny Loewy, " 'Very easy to cut my films . . .': Gespräch mit Helga Cranston," *FilmGeschichte* 13 (June 1999), p. 62.

32. Ingo Preminger, interview with the author, Pacific Palisades, California, May 22, 2002.

33. Shivas, "Interview with Otto Preminger," p. 20; Otto Plaschkes, interview with the author, June 14, 2002, London.

34. *Newsweek*, April 8, 1957.

35. Plaschkes, interview with the author, June 14, 2002, London.

36. Ibid.

37. Gilbert Millstein, *New York Times*, April 7, 1957.

38. Waz and Loewy, " 'Very easy . . . ,' " p. 62.

39. Plaschkes, interview with the author, November 12, 2000 (by telephone).

40. Plaschkes, interview with the author, June 14, 2002, London.

41. Richards, *Played Out*, p. 51.

42. *Newsweek*, April 8, 1957.

43. Cranston, interview with the author.

44. Waz and Loewy, " 'Very Easy . . . ,' " p. 63.

45. Plaschkes, interview with the author, June 14, 2002, London.

46. Waz and Loewy, " 'Very Easy . . . ,' " p. 63.

47. *Time*, July 1, 1957.

48. Archambault et al., "Entretien avec Otto Preminger," p. 17.

49. London *Times*, November 22, 1962.

50. Bogdanovich, "Peter Bogdanovich Interviews Otto Preminger," p. 42.

51. George Bernard Shaw, *Nine Plays* (New York: Dodd, Mead & Company, 1947), p. 1094.

23. An Invisible Wall

1. Harvey, "The Man Who Changed the Moral Code," p. 101.

2. McGilligan, *Backstory 2: Interviews with Screenwriters of the 1940s and 1950s*, pp. 150–51.

3. Hope Preminger, interview with the author, September 14, 2000, New York.

4. Martin Schute, interview with the author, June 13, 2002, Saltash, England.

5. Serge Friedman, interview with Olivier Eyquem, March 1972; Martin Schute, interview with the author, June 13, 2002, Saltash, England; Haining, *The Last Gentleman: A Tribute to David Niven*, p. 78.

6. Friedman, interview with Eyquem, March 1972.

7. Richards, *Played Out*, p. 54.

8. Friedman, interview with Eyquem.

9. Richards, *Played Out*, p. 66.

10. Frischauer, *Behind the Scenes*, p. 162; Mylène Demongeot, *Tiroirs secrets* (Paris: Le Pré aux clercs, 2001), p. 171.

11. Richards, *Played Out*, pp. 63, 64, 69.

12. Demongeot, *Tiroirs secrets*, pp. 169–70.

13. Ibid., pp. 166–67, 171.

14. Schute, interview with the author, June 13, 2002, Saltash, England.

15. Friedman, interview with Eyquem.

16. Mylène Demongeot, interview with the author, June 22, 2002, Paris.

17. Schute, interview with the author, June 13, 2002, Saltash, England.

18. Waz and Loewy, " 'Very easy . . . ,' " pp. 63–64.

19. Helga Cranston, interview with the author, Herzliyya, Israel, October 7, 2004.

20. Cranston, interview with the author.

21. Demongeot, *Tiroirs secrets*, p. 173.

22. Cranston, interview with the author.

23. *Los Angeles Examiner*, December 6, 1957.

24. *Commonweal*, January 31, 1958, p. 458; *Saturday Review*, February 15, 1958, p. 30; *Time*, January 20, 1958.

25. Richards, *Played Out*, p. 74.

26. Ibid., p. 83.

27. Gregg Kilday, "Otto-matic," *Los-Angeles Herald-Examiner*, December 17, 1979.

28. G. Cabrera Infante, *A Twentieth Century Job*, trans. Kenneth Hall (London: Faber and Faber, 1991), p. 241.

24. Plenty of Nothing

1. Sidney Poitier, *This Life* (New York: Alfred A. Knopf, 1980), p. 205.

2. Hollis Alpert, *The Life and Times of Porgy and Bess: The Story of an American Classic* (New York: Alfred A. Knopf, 1990), p. 263.

3. Brock Peters, interview with the author, May 11, 2004.

4. *Variety*, July 28, 1958, p. 1; A. Scott Berg, *Goldwyn: A Biography* (New York: Alfred A. Knopt, 1989), p. 485.

5. Bogle, *Dorothy Dandridge*, p. 410.

6. " 'Porgy-Bess' Battle Blazing: Goldwyn Forces Counter Whipper Jab at Preminger with Bailey-Davis Support," *Hollywood Reporter*, August 7, 1958; "Racial Bias Thrown into 'Porgy' Fight; Stars Backing Preminger," *Daily Variety*, August 7, 1958; "Directors Guild Board Burns Midnite Oil on 'Porgy' Issue," *Hollywood Reporter*, August 8, 1958.

7. Dandridge and Conrad, *Everything and Nothing*, p. 190.

8. Ibid.

9. Shivas, "Interview with Otto Preminger," p. 18.

10. Carol Easton, *The Search for Sam Goldwyn: A Biography* (New York: William Morrow and Company, 1976), pp. 278–79.

11. Peters, interview with the author, May 11, 2004.

12. *Preminger: An Autobiography*, p. 163.

13. Peters, interview with the author, May 11, 2004.

14. Shivas, "Interview with Otto Preminger," p. 18.

15. Poitier, *This Life*, pp. 220–21.

16. Sammy Davis, Jr., *Hollywood in a Suitcase*, p. 57; *Porgy and Bess* pressbook.

17. Dandridge and Conrad, *Everything and Nothing*, p. 189.

18. Peters, interview with the author, May 11, 2004.

19. Poitier, *This Life*, p. 221.

20. Bogle, *Dandridge*, pp. 414, 420

21. Poitier, *This Life*, pp. 222–24.
22. Pearl Bailey, *Between You and Me* (New York: Doubleday, 1989), p. 185.
23. Davis, *Hollywood in a Suitcase*, pp. 54, 55
24. Ibid., p. 57.
25. Pratley, *Cinema of Otto Preminger*, p. 125.
26. Helmick, *Cut, Print, and That's a Wrap!*, p. 129.
27. Easton, *Search for Sam Goldwyn*, p. 281.
28. London *Times*, June 19, 1974.
29. Peters, interview with the author.
30. *Porgy and Bess* files, N. Richard Nash Papers, Wisconsin Center for Film and Theater Research.
31. Alpert, *Life and Times of Porgy and Bess*, p. 278.
32. *Variety*, May 27, 1959.
33. *Time*, July 6, 1959, p. 57.
34. Berg, *Goldwyn*, p. 487.
35. *Los Angeles Times*, January 5, 1960, p. B6.
36. *Los Angeles Times*, April 10, 1959, p. A8.
37. Archambault et al., "Entretien avec Otto Preminger," p. 21.
38. David Gritten, "Gershwins Were No Fans of Preminger's 'Porgy'," *Los Angeles Times*, January 19, 1993, p. F5.
39. Michael Marcel, "Otto Preminger on Black Movies," *Encore* (August 1973), p. 57.

25. Man's Disorganized Soul

1. Richard D. Shaul, "Backwoods Barrister," *Michigan History* (November/December 2001), pp. 84–85; Shirley J. Bergman, "The Real Trial," *Michigan History* (November/December 2001), pp. 90–91.
2. Archambault et al., "Entretien avec Otto Preminger," p. 4.
3. Maurice Zolotow, *Billy Wilder in Hollywood*, (New York: G. P. Putnam's Sons, 1977), p. 195.
4. Rui Nogueira, "Wendell Mayes: The Jobs Poured Over Me," in Pat McGilligan, ed., *Backstory 3: Interviews with Hollywood Screenwriters of the 1960s* (Berkeley: University of California Press, 1997), p. 263.
5. Robert Traver, *Anatomy of a Murder* (New York: Dell Publishing, 1959), p. 329.
6. Joseph Wershba, "Anatomy of a Producer," *New York Post*, July 12, 1959, p. M2.
7. *Preminger: An Autobiography*, p. 185.
8. Lana Turner, *Lana: The Lady, the Legend, the Truth* (New York: E. P. Dutton, Inc., 1982), p. 263.
9. Wershba, "Anatomy of a Producer," p. M2.
10. *Los Angeles Examiner*, June 10, 1958.
11. *Los Angeles Examiner*, June 19, 1958.
12. *Los Angeles Herald*, March 11, 1959.
13. *Preminger: An Autobiography*, p. 186.
14. Hope Preminger, interview with the author, New York, June 17, 2004.
15. Otto Preminger, "Your Taste, My Taste . . . and the Censors," *Films and Filming* 6:2 (November 1959), p. 7.
16. Preminger, "Your Taste, My Taste," p. 7.

17. Bogdanovich, "Peter Bogdanovich Interviews Otto Preminger," p. 43.
18. Archambault et al., "Entretien avec Otto Preminger," p. 18.
19. James W. Merrick, *New York Times*, April 12, 1959, p. X7.
20. *Preminger: An Autobiography*, p. 186.
21. David Hajdu, *Lush Life: A Biography of Billy Strayhorn* (New York: Farrar Strauss Giroux, 1996), p. 189.
22. Gary Fishgall, *Pieces of Time: The Life of James Stewart* (New York: Lisa Drew Book, 1997), pp. 272–74.
23. Lee Remick, interview with Olivier Eyquem.
24. Ben Gazzara, telephone interview with the author, May 25, 2005.
25. Ben Gazzara, *In the Moment: My Life as an Actor* (New York: Carroll & Graf Publishers, 2004), p. 102.
26. Gazzara, telephone interview with the author, May 25, 2005.
27. Joan G. Hansen, *Anatomy of "Anatomy": The Making of a Movie* (Ishpeming, Mich.: Globe Printing, 1997), p. 51.
28. *Penthouse*, May 1973.
29. Hope Preminger, interview with the author, New York, June 17, 2004.
30. Hansen, *Anatomy of "Anatomy*," p. 39.
31. *Preminger: An Autobiography*, p. 184.
32. Lawrence J. Quirk, *James Stewart: Behind the Scenes of a Wonderful Life* (New York: Applause, 1997), p. 248.
33. Eve Arden, *Three Phases of Eve* (New York: St. Martin's Press, 1985), p. 133.
34. Fishgall, *Pieces of Time*, p. 274.
35. Lee Remick, interview with Eyquem.
36. Preminger, "Your Taste, My Taste," p. 7.
37. Archambault et al., "Entretien avec *Otto Preminger*," p. 6.
38. Krin Gabbard, *Jammin' at the Margins: Jazz and the American Cinema* (Chicago: University of Chicago Press, 1996), pp. 188–92.
39. Pratley, *Cinema of Otto Preminger*, p. 150.

26. Make Them All Brilliant and I Will Direct Unevenly

1. *Preminger: An Autobiography*, 196–97.
2. *New York Times*, August 21, 1950, p. 15; *Los Angeles Times*, September 13, 1950, p. B10.
3. Hope Preminger, interview with the author, September 14, 2000, New York.
4. Arthur B. Krim to Robert S. Benjamin, May 16, 1958, United Artists collection, Wisconsin Center for Film and Theater Research.
5. United Artists collection, Wisconsin Center for Film and Theater Research.
6. Arthur B. Krim to Robert S. Benjamin, May 16, 1958; Krim to I. H. Prinzmetal, February 18, 1960, United Artists collection, Wisconsin Center for Film and Theater Research.
7. Pratley, *Cinema of Otto Preminger*, p. 135; see also "*Exodus* Production Notes" in United Artists collection, Wisconsin Center for Film and Theater Research.
8. *Exodus* files, Albert Maltz collection, Wisconsin Center for Film and Theater Research.
9. Ilan Hartuv, interview with the author, November 26, 2000.

10. Meyer Weisgal, *Meyer Weisgal . . . So Far: An Autobiography* (New York: Random House, 1971), p. 314.
11. *Jerusalem Post*, May 5, 1960.
12. *Exodus* file, Albert Maltz collection, Howard Gotlieb Archival Research Center, Boston University.
13. *Rolling Stone*, July 5, 1973.
14. Eva Marie Saint, interview with the author, March 31, 2006.
15. James Spada, *Peter Lawford: The Man Who Kept the Secrets* (New York: Bantam Books, 1991), p. 222.
16. *New York Post*, January 8, 1961, p. 25; *Jerusalem Post*, June 22, 1960, p. 2.
17. Eva Monley, interview with the author, November 6, 2000.
18. *Preminger: An Autobiography*, p. 199.
19. Ingo Preminger, interview with the author, May 22, 2002.
20. Bruce Cook, *Dalton Trumbo* (New York: Charles Scribner's Sons, 1977), p. 274; *Preminger: An Autobiography*, p. 199.
21. *New York Post*, November 29, 1961, p. 41; Dalton Trumbo, *Additional Dialogue: Letters of Dalton Trumbo, 1942–1962*, edited by Helen Manfull (New York: M. Evans & Company, 1970), pp. 528–30.
22. A. H. Weiler, *New York Times*, January 20, 1960; Tom Ryan, *Otto Preminger Films Exodus: A Report* (Random House, 1960), pp. 10–11.
23. Trumbo, *Additional Dialogue*, p. 528.
24. Abraham Polonsky, "How the Blacklist Worked in Hollywood," *Film Culture* 50–51 (Fall–Winter 1970), p. 46.
25. Jeffrey P. Smith, " 'A Good Business Proposition': Dalton Trumbo, *Spartacus*, and the End of the Blacklist," *The Velvet Light Trap* 23 (Spring 1989), p. 90.
26. Joe Morgenstern, *New York Herald Tribune*, January 21, 1960, Section 4, p. 4.
27. "Random Notes to O.P.," in *Exodus* files, Dalton Trumbo collection, Wisconsin Center for Film and Theater Research.
28. Ibid.
29. "Notes on the Re-writes," *Exodus* files, Dalton Trumbo collection, Wisconsin Center for Film and Television Research.
30. Otto Plaschkes, interview with the author, November 12, 2000.
31. Hope Preminger, interview with the author, September 14, 2000, New York; Weisgal, *So Far*, p. 314.
32. *Jerusalem Post*, June 5, 1960, p. 3; Martin Schute, interview with the author, November 6, 2000; *Daily Variety*, October 20, 1970, p. 3.
33. Hartuv, interview with the author, November 26, 2000; Larry Frisch, interview with the author, October 3, 2004.
34. Paul Kohn, *Jerusalem Post*, April 22, 1960.
35. Eva Monley, interview with the author, November 6, 2000.
36. Wagner, "Pendant le tournage d'*Exodus*," *Présence du cinema* 11 (February 1962), p. 29.
37. Ilan Eldad, interview with the author, October 7, 2004, Tel Aviv; Martin Schure, interview with the author, November 6, 2000; Kohn, *Jerusalem Post*, April 22, 1960; Wagner, "Pendant le tournage d'*Exodus*," p. 30.
38. Saint, interview with the author, March 31, 2006; Plaschkes, interview with the author, June 14, 2002, London.

39. Otto Plaschkes, interview with the author, November 12, 2000; Boze Hadleigh, *Conversations with My Elders* (New York: St. Martin's Press, 1986).

40. Plaschkes, interview with the author, November 12, 2000; Yoel Zilberg, interview with the author, October 5, 2004, Tel Aviv.

41. *Jerusalem Post*, May 9, 1960, p. 4; Weisgal, *So Far*, pp. 315–16; Yoel Zilberg, interview with the author, October 5, 2004, Tel Aviv.

42. Plaschkes, interview with the author, June 14, 2002, London.

43. Hope Preminger, interview with the author, September 14, 2000, New York.

44. Eddie Hodges, e-mail interview with the author, August 14, August 20, September 3, 2004.

45. *Variety*, December 14, 1960.

46. Memo, Arthur B. Krim to Arnold Picker, August 3, 1962, *Exodus* files, United Artists collection, Wisconsin Center for Film and Theater Research.

47. Philip T. Hartung, *The Commonweal* 73:12 (December 16, 1960), p. 317.

48. Pratley, *Cinema of Otto Preminger*, p. 133.

49. Hartuv, interview with the author, November 26, 2000.

27. Gratuitous Acts

1. *Hollywood Reporter*, November 11, 1959; Memo, Seymour M. Peyser to Arthur B. Krim, November 10, 1959, United Artists collection, Wisconsin Center for Film and Theater Research.

2. Otto Preminger, "The Cardinal and I," *Films and Filming* 10: (November 1963), p. 12.

3. Nogueira, "Wendell Mayes: The Jobs Poured Over Me," in McGilligan, *Backstory 3*, p. 264.

4. Raymond Durgnat, *Films and Feelings* (Cambridge: M.I.T. Press, 1971), p. 84.

5. Allen Drury, *Advise and Consent* (New York: Pocket Books, 1961), p. 734.

6. Mark Shivas, "Preminger on *Advise and Consent*," *Movie* 4 (November 1962), pp. 26–27.

7. Ronald L. Davis, Oral History Collection 454 (Don Murray), DeGolyer Library, Southern Methodist University.

8. Walter Kerr, *New York Herald Tribune*, December 15, 1960.

9. Vito Russo, *The Celluloid Closet*, revised edition (New York: Harper & Row, 1987), pp. 121–22.

10. Jean Domarchi, "Voyage à Washington," *Cahiers du cinéma* 22: 128 (February 1962), p. 30.

11. Ronald L. Davis, Oral History: Don Murray.

12. George Grizzard, interview with the author, April 4, 2006.

13. Ronald L. Davis, Oral History: Don Murray.

14. Grizzard, interview with the author, April 4, 2006.

15. Ibid.

16. Don Kranze, interview with the author, May 1, 2004, Beverly Hills.

17. Eddie Hodges, interview with the author, by e-mail, September 1, 2004.

18. Leonard Maltin, "*Film Fan Monthly* Interviews Burgess Meredith," in Leonard Maltin, ed., *Hollywood: The Movie Factory* (New York: Popular Library, 1976), p. 221.

19. Jean Domarchi, "Voyage à Washington," pp. 26, 27, 28.
20. *Los Angeles Times*, October 21, 1961.
21. *Los Angeles Times*, October 28, 1961.
22. James Bacon, "Film Maker Finishes Up His Memoirs," *Los Angeles Herald-Examiner*, February 9, 1976; Yoram Ben-Ami, interview with the author, October 5, 2004, Tel Aviv; Don Kranze, interview with the author, May 1, 2004, Beverly Hills.
23. *Daily Variety*, June 11, 1962, pp. 1, 10.
24. Don Kranze, interview with the author, May 1, 2004, Beverly Hills.
25. *Daily Variety*, April 12, 1962.
26. Jean-Louis Comolli, "La mort blanche," *Cahiers du cinéma* 23:137 (November 1962), p. 47.
27. *Advise & Consent*, Warner Home Video, 2005.
28. Russo, *Celluloid Closet*, p. 143.
29. Robin Wood, "Attitudes in *Advise and Consent*," *Movie Reader*, edited by Ian Cameron (New York: Praeger Publishers, 1972), p. 55.
30. Russo, *Celluloid Closet*, p. 143.
31. Quoted in Jonathan Rosenbaum, "Otto Preminger," in *Cinema: A Critical Dictionary, The Major Film-makers*, edited by Richard Roud, vol. 2 (New York: Viking Press, 1980), p. 797.

28. A Certain Weakness

1. *Daily Variety*, August 10, 1955.
2. *Newark Evening News*, March 8, 1964.
3. *New York Times*, November 25, 1962, p. 165.
4. Tom Tryon interview in Robins, *Preminger: Anatomy of a Filmmaker*.
5. Gene D. Phillips, "Both Sides of the Question: Otto Preminger," *Focus on Film* 33 (August 1979), pp. 25–26.
6. Lardner, *I'd Hate Myself in the Morning*, p. 154.
7. McGilligan, *Backstory* 3, p. 221.
8. Marian Christy, "The Flamboyant Tom Tyron," *Boston Globe*, November 2, 1986, p. C25.
9. Gerry O'Hara, telephone interview with the author, May 22, 2004.
10. Tryon interview in Robins, *Preminger: Anatomy of a Filmmaker*.
11. David Galligan, "Tom Tryon: 'All That Glitters,'" *Drama-Logue*, January 29–February 4, 1987, p. 4.
12. Stanley Kauffmann, *New Republic*, July 20, 1974.
13. Bob Vietro, interview with the author, Rowayton, Connecticut, June 14, 2004.
14. Preminger interview with Eyquem and Comte.
15. Ibid.
16. November 5, 1963, wire transcript in Charles Champlin collection ("Payne Showbiz Preminger"), AMPAS Library.
17. Preminger, "Propos," p. 20.
18. Lardner, *I'd Hate Myself in the Morning*, pp. 154–55.
19. Interview for Jacobsen et al., *Otto Preminger: Ein Portrait*.
20. Interview in Robins, *Preminger: Anatomy of a Filmmaker*.
21. Jean Douchet, "Vienne année Otto," *Cahiers du cinéma* 145 (July 1963), p. 18.

22. Ibid., p. 20.

23. Ibid.

24. Ibid.

25. Interview in Robins, *Preminger: Anatomy of a Filmmaker*.

26. O'Hara, telephone interview with the author, May 22, 2004.

27. *New York Herald Tribune*, May 5, 1963; Gershuny, *Soon to Be a Major Motion Picture*, p. 105.

28. "Payne Showbiz Preminger," Charles Champlin collection, AMPAS Library; Gerry O'Hara, telephone interview with the author, May 22, 2004.

29. Interview in Robins, *Preminger: Anatomy of a Filmmaker*.

30. Galligan, "Tom Tryon," p. 4.

31. Ibid., p. 22.

32. *New York Herald Tribune*, October 17, 1965, p. 55.

33. Christy, "The Flamboyant Tom Tryon."

34. Ibid.

35. Sarris, *The American Cinema*, p. 106.

29. Never Give Up

1. Cameron et al., "Interview with Otto Preminger," p. 14.

2. Nogueira, "Wendell Mayes: The Jobs Poured Over Me," in McGilligan, *Backstory 3*, p. 266.

3. Cameron et al., "Interview with Otto Preminger," pp. 14, 15.

4. Nogueira, "Wendell Mayes: The Jobs Poured Over Me," in McGilligan, *Backstory 3*, p. 265.

5. Otto Preminger, "Keeping Out of Harm's Way," *Films and Filming* v. 11, n. 9 (June 1965), p. 6.

6. Keir Dullea, interview with the author, February 3, 2006.

7. *Newsweek* 63:16 (April 20, 1964).

8. Cameron et al., "Interview with Otto Preminger," p. 15.

9. *In Harm's Way* file, Paramount Pictures production files, AMPAS Library.

10. *McCall's*, March 1965, p. 177; Cameron et al., "Interview with Otto Preminger," p. 16.

11. Maurice Zolotow, *Shooting Star: A Biography of John Wayne* (New York: Simon & Schuster, 1974), pp. 361–62; Tony Macklin and Nick Pici, eds., *Voices from the Set: The* Film Heritage *Interviews*. (Lanham, Maryland: The Scarecrow Press, 2000), p. 145.

12. Michael Munn, *John Wayne: The Man Behind the Myth* (London: Robson Books, 2003), pp. 254–55.

13. Pilar Wayne with Alex Thorleifson, *John Wayne: My Life with the Duke* (New York: McGraw-Hill Book Company, 1987), p. 176.

14. Munn, *John Wayne*, p. 255.

15. Kirk Douglas, *The Ragman's Son: An Autobiography* (New York: Simon & Schuster, 1988), pp. 380–81.

16. Larry Hagman, with Todd Gold, *Hello Darlin': Tall (and Absolutely True) Tales About My Life* (New York: Simon & Schuster, 2001), pp. 119, 120.

17. *New York Herald Tribune*, October 17, 1965, p. 55.

18. Galligan, "Tom Tryon, 'All That Glitters,' " p. 4.
19. Ibid., pp. 4, 22.
20. Paula Prentiss, interview with the author, March 25, 2004.
21. Douglas, *The Ragman's Son*, p. 378.
22. George H. Jackson, "Movie War Is Gigantic Task," *Los Angeles Times*, March 27, 1965.
23. Cameron et al., "Interview with Otto Preminger," p. 15.
24. *Life*, March 5, 1965.
25. Macklin and Pici, *Voices from the Sets*, p. 145.
26. *Honolulu Star-Bulletin*, March 3, 1965, p. C1.
27. Bosley Crowther, *New York Times*, April 7, 1965.
28. Brendan Gill, *The New Yorker*, April 17, 1965, p. 158.
29. *Daily Variety*, October 9, 1973.
30. Antoine de Baecque, *Les Cahiers du cinéma, Histoire d'une revue; Tome 2: Cinéma, tours détours 1959–1981* (Paris: Cahiers du cinéma, 1991), p. 148, n. 51.

30. Organized Agitation

1. Cameron et al., "Interview with Otto Preminger," p. 16.
2. Dalton Trumbo collection, Wisconsin Center for Film and Theater Research.
3. Preminger, "Propos," p. 18.
4. Cameron et al., "Interview with Otto Preminger," p. 16.
5. Penelope Mortimer Collection, Special Collections, Howard Gotlieb Archival Research Center, Boston University.
6. Martin Schute, interview with the author, June 13, 2002, Saltash, England.
7. "Preminger Gets Rights to 'Hurry Sundown,' " *Boxoffice*, November 23, 1964.
8. Doniol-Valcroze and Rohmer, "Entretien avec Otto Preminger," p. 8.
9. Graham Payn and Sheridan Morley, eds., *The Noël Coward Diaries* (London: George Weidenfeld and Nicolson, 1982), pp. 427–28.
10. Jacques Lourcelles, *Otto Preminger*, pp. 124, 125.
11. Ibid., p. 126.
12. Ibid., p. 128.
13. Ibid., p. 132.
14. Eva Monley, telephone interview with the author, November 7, 2000.
15. Laurence Olivier, *On Acting* (New York: Simon & Schuster, 1986), p. 325.
16. Payn and Morley, *Noël Coward Diaries*, p. 599.
17. *New York Herald Tribune*, October 17, 1965, p. 55.
18. Keir Dullea, interview with the author, February 3, 2006.
19. Dullea, interview with the author, February 3, 2006.

31. How Do You Know I've Never Been Black?

1. "Preminger Buys 'Sundown' Novel," *Film Daily*, November 18, 1964, p. 3; Gerard Garrett, "Picture of a Lad from the Elephant getting down to work in the Deep South," *Evening Standard* (London), July 29, 1966.
2. "Conversation with Horton Foote and John Guare," *On Writing* 15 (Writers Guild of America, East, May 2002), p. 3.

3. Ibid.
4. Michael Caine, *What's It All About?: An Autobiography* (New York: Turtle Bay Books, 1992), p. 262.
5. Aram Goudsouzian, *Sidney Poitier: Man, Actor, Icon* (Chapel Hill: University of North Carolina Press, 2004), p. 251.
6. John Phillip Law, interview with the author, July 10, 2005.
7. Rex Reed, " 'Like They Could Cut Your Heart Out,' " *New York Times*, August 21, 1966.
8. Thomas Kiernan, *Jane: An Intimate Biography of Jane Fonda* (New York: G. P. Putnam's Sons, 1973), p. 200.
9. Law, interview with the author, July 10, 2005.
10. Garrett, "Picture of a Lad."
11. Caine, *What's It All About?*, p. 265.
12. Faye Dunaway, with Betsy Sharkey, *Looking for Gatsby: My Life* (New York: Simon & Schuster, 1995), p. 28.
13. Ibid., pp. 109, 111–12.
14. Ibid., p. 114.
15. Ibid., p. 115; Caine, *What's It All About?*, p. 262.
16. Otto Preminger collection, Wisconsin Center for Film and Theater Research.
17. Law, interview with the author, July 10, 2005.
18. Ibid.
19. Austin Pendleton, interview with the author, October 6, 2000, Newton, Massachusetts.
20. Reed, " 'Like They Could Cut Your Heart Out,' "; Letters, *New York Times*, September 11, 1966.
21. Adam West with Jeff Rovin, *Back to the Batcave* (New York: Berkley Books, 1994), pp. 144–45.
22. Wilfred Sheed, *Esquire* (September 1967), p. 24.
23. Brendan Gill, *The New Yorker* (April 8, 1967), p. 145.
24. Martin Heidegger, "The Thing," *Poetry, Language, Thought*, trans. by Albert Hofstadter (New York: Harper & Row, 1971), p. 166.

32. If We Must Be Prisoners

1. Erik Preminger, *Gypsy & Me*, p. 259.
2. Ibid., p. 259.
3. Erik Preminger, interview with the author, June 11, 2005. All subsequent quotations from Erik Preminger in this chapter are from this interview.
4. Robert Evans, *The Kid Stays in the Picture* (New York: Hyperion, 1994), pp. 122–23; Maurice Zolotow, *Billy Wilder in Hollywood*, pp. 188–89.
5. This and subsequent quotations from the *Skidoo* story conferences are from audio recordings in the Doran William Cannon Collection, AMPAS Library.
6. *Skidoo*, first draft script (May 1967), p. 20. In Otto Preminger collection, Wisconsin Center for Film and Theater Research.
7. Austin Pendleton, interview with the author, October 6, 2000, Newton, Massachusetts. All subsequent quotations from Austin Pendleton in this chapter are from this interview.

8. Doran William Cannon, May 31, 1991, note regarding *Skidoo* in Cannon collection, AMPAS Library.

9. Cannon to Preminger, March 18, 1968, in *Skidoo* file, Otto Preminger collection, Wisconsin Center for Film and Theater Research.

10. *Skidoo*, second draft script, (November 6, 1967), Otto Preminger collection, Wisconsin Center for Film and Theater Research.

11. Policy, *Preminger's Skidoo*, p. 545.

12. Ibid., p. 128.

13. John Phillip Law, interview with the author, July 10, 2005.

14. Wayne Koestenbaum, "'Andy Warhol: Screen Tests,'" *Artforum*, October 2003.

15. Judy Stone, "Luna, Who Dreamed of Being Snow White," *New York Times*, May 19, 1968, p. D19.

16. Policy, *Preminger's Skidoo*, pp. 143, 145.

17. Ibid., pp. 156, 168.

18. Ibid., pp. 165, 194, 196, 204.

19. Ibid., pp. 204–205, 208–209.

20. *Film and Television Daily*, April 2, 1968, p. 4.

21. Policy, *Preminger's Skidoo*, p. 273.

22. Ibid., pp. 288, 292.

23. Ibid., p. 302.

24. Bogdanovich, "Peter Bogdanovich Interviews Otto Preminger," p. 47.

25. Policy, *Preminger's Skidoo*, p. 319.

26. Sheilah Graham, "LSD Experiment Enough for Otto," *Hollywood Citizen-News*, February 3, 1969.

27. *Daily Variety*, April 10, 1968, p. 2; *Cincinatti Enquirer*, April 14, 1968.

28. Policy, *Preminger's Skidoo*, pp. 374, 378.

29. Ibid., pp. 379–80, 390.

30. Ibid., pp. 396, 575–76.

31. Ibid., pp. 430–31.

32. Judy Klemesrud, "Dolly Levi Says Hello to Broadway Again," *New York Times*, March 5, 1978, p. D4.

33. Vincent Canby, *New York Times*, March 6, 1969, p. 36.

34. Martin Lenine, *Washington Post*, December 26, 1968, p. F9.

35. *Daily Variety*, June 30, 1970, p. 8.

33. The Love-In

1. Marjorie Kellogg, *Tell Me That You Love Me, Junie Moon* (New York: Popular Library, 1968), p. 7.

2. Marjorie Kellogg, interview with the author, June 1, 2002, Santa Barbara, California. All subsequent quotations from Marjorie Kellogg in this chapter are from this interview.

3. Erik Preminger, interview with the author, June 11, 2005.

4. Preminger interview with Eyquem and Comte; William Wolf, *Los Angeles Times*, August 17, 1969; Alan W. Petrucelli, *Liza! Liza! An Unauthorized Biography of Liza Minnelli* (New York: Karz-Cohl, 1983), p. 76.

5. *Preminger: An Autobiography*, p. 191.

6. Preminger interview with Eyquem and Comte.

7. Ken Howard, interview with the author, May 12, 2004.

8. Robert Frey, "Anne Revere Begins Again: The Interrupted Career of a 'Featured Player,'" *After Dark* (December 1970), p. 32.

9. *Tell Me That You Love Me, Junie Moon* file, Paramount Pictures production files, AMPAS Library.

10. Deac Rossell, "Toscanini of Hollywood: Master of Detail," *Boston After Dark* (August 13, 1969), pp. 1, 13.

11. Ken Howard, interviews with the author, May 5, 2004, and May 12, 2004.

12. Pratley, *Cinema of Otto Preminger*, p. 167.

13. Petrucelli, *Liza! Liza!*, pp. 76, 81.

14. Howard, interview with the author, May 5, 2004.

15. Erik Preminger, interview with the author, June 11, 2005.

16. Howard Sounes, *Down the Highway: The Life of Bob Dylan* (New York: Grove Press, 2001), p. 237.

17. Jonas Mekas, "Movie Journal," *Village Voice* (July 30, 1970), p. 42.

18. Bogdanovich, "Peter Bogdanovich Interviews Otto Preminger," p. 47.

34. A Very Unpleasant Set

1. *New York Times*, July 31, 1971, p. 12; *Daily Variety*, February 3, 1970.

2. Erik Preminger, interview with the author, June 11, 2005.

3. Erik Preminger, interview with the author, May 16, 2005.

4. *Time*, February 15, 1971.

5. Erik Preminger, interview with the author, June 11, 2005.

6. David Johnson, "Preminger Made Her Cry But 'Such Good Friends' Should Make Her Crow," *Show* (February 1972), p. 33.

7. Charles Okun, interview with the author, June 10, 2004.

8. Erik Preminger, interview with the author, June 11, 2005.

9. Hope Preminger, interview with the author, June 17, 2005.

10. Paul Rosenfield, "Anatomy of a Reputation: Preminger Tells Less Than All," *Los Angeles Times*, May 5, 1977.

11. Frischauer, *Behind the Scenes of Otto Preminger*, p. 241 (See Chapter 1, note 6).

12. Barrett Rudich, interview with the author, June 19, 2004.

13. Ken Howard, interview with the author, May 12, 2004.

14. Johnson, "Preminger Made Her Cry," p. 35.

15. Donald Chase, *Filmmaking: The Collaborative Art* (Boston: Little, Brown and Company, 1975), p. 94.

16. *New York Times*, September 5, 1971, p. D7.

17. Howard, interview with the author, May 12, 2004.

18. Ibid.

19. Barrett Rudich, interview with the author, June 19, 2004.

20. Charles Okun, interview with the author, June 10, 2004.

21. Bernard Carragher, "The Entertaining Larry Luckinbill, the Man with 'Such Good Friends'," *Show* (February 1972), p. 40.

22. Chase, *Filmmaking*, pp. 93–94.

23. Erik Preminger, interview with the author, June 11, 2005.

24. David Johnson, "Dyan Cannon—Broadside!" *After Dark* (October 1974), p. 59.
25. Howard, interview with the author, May 12, 2004.
26. London *Times*, January 15, 1972, p. 13.
27. Johnson, "Preminger Made Her Cry," p. 33.
28. Lois Gould, *Such Good Friends* (New York: Dell Publishing, 1971), p. 150.

35. Before the Doors Close on This Whole World

1. Erik Preminger, interview with the author, June 11, 2005.
2. Hope Preminger, interview with the author, New York, June 18, 2004.
3. Gene D. Phillips, "Both Sides of the Question: Otto Preminger," *Focus on Film* 33 (August 79), p. 26.
4. Erik Preminger, interview with the author, June 11, 2005.
5. Gershuny, *Soon to Be a Major Motion Picture*, p. 164.
6. Ibid., p. 58.
7. Ibid., pp. 92, 107, 172.
8. Ibid., p. 93.
9. Hope Preminger, interview with the author, New York, June 18, 2004.
10. Erik Preminger, interview with the author, June 11, 2005.
11. Marjorie Kellogg, interview with the author, June 1, 2002, Santa Barbara, California.
12. Gershuny, *Soon to Be a Major Motion Picture*, p. 159.
13. Isabelle Huppert, interview with Olivier Eyquem, 1974.
14. Gershuny, *Major Motion Picture*, pp. 174–80.
15. Ibid., pp. 180, 216, 233.
16. Kim Cattrall, interview with Olivier Eyquem and Jean-Marie Pélissié, Paris, July 1974.
17. Eyquem, "Souvenirs de tournage de 'Rosebud,'" *L'Avant-Scène Cinéma* 211/12 (July–September 1978), p. 83.
18. Ibid., pp. 85, 86.
19. Gershuny, *Major Motion Picture*, pp. 269–70.
20. Eyquem, "Souvenirs de tournage de 'Rosebud,'" p. 87.
21. Ibid., p. 89.
22. Gershuny, *Major Motion Picture*, p. 303.
23. Eyquem, "Souvenirs de tournage de 'Rosebud,'" p. 89.
24. Interview with Gregory J. M. Catsos, January 26, 1978, www.members.tripod.com/peter_otoole/id148.htm.
25. Gershuny, *Major Motion Picture*, pp. 254, 307, 333.
26. Erik Preminger, interview with the author, June 11, 2005.
27. Gershuny, *Major Motion Picture*, p. 313.
28. Klaus Löwitsch, interview with the author, Berlin, October 25, 2002.
29. *Preminger: An Autobiography*, p. 219.
30. Nicholas Wapshott, *Peter O'Toole: A Biography* (New York: Beaufort Books, 1983), pp. 175–76.
31. Gershuny, *Major Motion Picture*, p. 321.
32. Ibid., p. 327.
33. Ibid., pp. 331, 333.
34. Kellogg, interview with the author, June 1, 2002, Santa Barbara, California.

35. Kim Cattrall, interview with Olivier Eyquem and Jean-Marie Pélissié, Paris, July 1974.
36. Gershuny, *Major Motion Picture*, p. 8.
37. Erik Preminger, interview with the author, June 11, 2005. In September 1974, the craw of the luxury passenger ship *France* mutinied to protest the French government's termination of its subsidy of the ship. The authorities responded by blockading the *France* in the navigation channel leading into the port of Le Havre.
38. Gershuny, *Major Motion Picture*, p. 153.

36. The Human Factor

1. June Callwood, telephone interview with the author, April 16, 2002.
2. Erik Preminger, interview with the author, April 5, 2006.
3. Nelson Algren, "Otto Preminger: Man with the Golden Prerogative."
4. Erik Preminger, interview with the author, April 5, 2006.
5. Frederic Tuten, "An Interview with Jerome Charyn," *Review of Contemporary Fiction* 12:2 (Summer 1992).
6. Yoram Ben-Ami, interview with the author, October 5, 2004, Tel Aviv.
7. *Publishers Weekly*, March 27, 1978.
8. Ira B. Nadel, "Stoppard and Film," in Katherine E. Kelly, ed., *The Cambridge Companion to Tom Stoppard* (Cambridge: Cambridge University Press, 2001).
9. Hope Preminger, interview with the author, June 17, 2004, New York.
10. Mike Molloy, interview with the author, July 19, 2005.
11. Val Robins, interview with the author, March 3, 2006.
12. Nadel, "Stoppard and Film, p. 93; Tom Stoppard, e-mail to the author, June 2, 2006.
13. Robert Morley, *Morley Matters* (London: Robson Books, 1980), pp. 135–36.
14. Molloy, interview with the author, July 19, 2005.
15. Robins, interview with the author, March 3, 2006.
16. Hope Preminger, interview with the author, June 17, 2004, New York.
17. Mike Malloy, interview with the author, July 19, 2005.
18. Val Robins, interview with the author, March 3, 2006.
19. Roderick Mann, *Los Angeles Times*, December 13, 1979.
20. London *Times*, December 13, 1979, p. 12.
21. Sheridan Morley, *Robert My Father* (London: Weidenfeld and Nicolson, 1993), p. 206.
22. David Robinson, London *Times*, February 1, 1980, p. 13.
23. Robins, interview with the author, March 3, 2006.
24. Ibid., March 3, 2006.
25. Hope Preminger, interview with the author, June 17, 2004, New York.
26. Robins, interview with the author, March 3, 2006.
27. Bogdanovich, *Who the Devil Made It* (New York: Ballantine Books, 1997), pp. 610–11.
28. Hope Preminger, interview with the author, June 17, 2004, New York.
29. Austin Pendleton, interview with the author, October 6, 2000, Newton, Massachusetts.

Films Directed by Otto Preminger

When two years are given, the first is the year of the completion of production, the second the year of theatrical release. When two company names appear after the year, the first is that of the production company, the second that of the U.S. distributor. The positions of key production personnel are abbreviated as follows: Dir[ector], Prod[ucer], Scr[eenplay], D[irector of] P[hotography], Sets [art director or production designer], Ed[itor]. Where no producer's name is given, Otto Preminger is the producer.

Die grosse Liebe (1931, Allianz-Film). Prod: Emmerich Taussig. Scr: Siegfried Bernfeld, Artur Berger. DP: Hans Theyer. Sets: Artur Berger. Music: Walter Landauer. Ed: Paul Falkenberg. Cast: Hansi Niese, Attila Hörbiger, Ferdinand Maierhofer, Maria Waldner, Betty Bird, Hugo Thimig, Adrienne Gessner.

Under Your Spell (1936, Twentieth Century-Fox). Associate prod: John Stone. Scr: Frances Hyland, Saul Elkins, based on a story by Bernice Mason (adapted by Sy Bartlett). DP: Sidney Wagner. Sets: Duncan Cramer. Music: Arthur Lange. Songs: Arthur Schwartz, Howard Dietz. Ed: Fred Allen. Cast: Lawrence Tibbett, Wendy Barrie, Gregory Ratoff, Arthur Treacher, Gregory Gaye, Berton Churchill, Jed Prouty, Claudia Coleman.

Danger—Love at Work (1937, Twentieth Century-Fox). Associate prod: Harold Wilson. Scr: James Edward Grant, Ben Markson, B.G. DeSylva, based on a story by James Edward Grant. DP: Virgil Miller. Sets: Duncan Cramer. Music: David Buttolph. Ed: Jack Murray. Cast: Ann Sothern, Jack Haley, Mary Boland, Edward Everett Horton, John Carradine, Walter Catlett, Bennie Bartlett, Maurice Cass, Alan Dinehart, Etienne Girardot, E. E. Clive.

Margin for Error (1943, Twentieth Century-Fox). Prod: Ralph Dietrich. Scr: Lillie Hayward (and Samuel Fuller, uncredited), based on the play by Clare Boothe. DP: Edward Cronjager. Sets: Richard Day, Lewis Creber. Music: Leigh Harline. Ed: Louis Loeffler. Cast: Joan Bennett, Milton Berle, Otto Preminger, Carl Esmond, Howard Freeman, Poldy Dur, Clyde Fillmore.

In the Meantime, Darling (1944, Twentieth Century-Fox). Scr: Arthur Kober, Michael Uris. DP: Joe MacDonald. Sets: James Basevi, John Ewing. Music: Cyril J. Mockridge. Ed: Louis Loeffler. Cast: Jeanne Crain, Frank Latimore, Stanley Prager, Gale Robbins, Jane Randolph, Eugene Pallette, Mary Nash, Doris Merrick.

Laura (1944, Twentieth Century-Fox). Scr: Jay Dratler, Samuel Hoffenstein, Betty Reinhardt (and Jerome Cady and Ring Lardner, Jr., uncredited), based on the novel by Vera Caspary. DP: Joseph LaShelle. Sets: Lyle Wheeler, Leland Fuller. Music: David Raksin. Ed: Louis Loeffler. Cast: Gene Tierney, Dana Andrews, Clifton Webb, Vincent Price, Judith Anderson, Dorothy Adams, Ralph Dunn, James Flavin.

A Royal Scandal (1945, Twentieth Century-Fox). Prod: Ernst Lubitsch. Scr: Edwin Justus Mayer, based on the play *Die Zarin* by Lajos Biro and Melchior Lengyel (adapted by Bruno Frank). DP: Arthur Miller. Sets: Lyle Wheeler, Mark-Lee Kirk. Music: Alfred Newman. Ed: Dorothy Spencer. Cast: Tallulah Bankhead, Anne Baxter, William Eythe, Charles Coburn, Vincent Price, Mischa Auer, Sig Ruman, Vladimir Sokoloff, Mikhail Rasumny, Grady Sutton, Eva Gabor.

Fallen Angel (1945, Twentieth Century-Fox). Scr: Harry Kleiner, based on the novel by Marty (Mary) Holland. DP: Joseph LaShelle. Sets: Lyle Wheeler; Leland Fuller. Music: David Raksin. Ed: Harry Reynolds. Cast: Dana Andrews, Alice Faye, Linda Darnell, Charles Bickford, Anne Revere, Bruce Cabot, John Carradine, Percy Kilbride, Olin Howlin, Jimmy Conlin, Dorothy Adams.

Centennial Summer (1946, Twentieth Century-Fox). Scr: Michael Kanin, based on the novel by Albert E. Idell. DP: Ernest Palmer (Technicolor). Sets: Lyle Wheeler, Lee Fuller. Music: Alfred Newman. Songs: Jerome Kern, Leo Robin, Oscar Hammerstein II, E. Y. Harburg. Ed: Harry Reynolds. Cast: Jeanne Crain, Cornel Wilde, Linda Darnell, William Eythe, Walter Brennan, Constance Bennett, Dorothy Gish, Barbara Whiting, Buddy Swan.

Forever Amber (1947, Twentieth Century-Fox). Prod: William Perlberg. Scr: Philip Dunne, Ring Lardner, Jr., based on the novel by Kathleen Winsor (adapted by Jerome Cady). DP: Leon Shamroy (Technicolor). Sets: Lyle Wheeler, Richard Day. Music: David Raksin. Ed: Louis Loeffler. Cast: Linda Darnell, Cornel Wilde, Richard Greene, George Sanders, Glenn Langan, Richard Haydn, Jessica Tandy, Anne Revere, John Russell, Jane Ball, Robert Coote, Leo G. Carroll, Natalie Draper, Margaret Wycherly.

Daisy Kenyon (1947, Twentieth Century-Fox). Scr: David Hertz, based on the novel by Elizabeth Janeway. DP: Leon Shamroy. Sets: Lyle Wheeler, George Davis. Music: David Raksin. Ed: Louis Loeffler. Cast: Joan Crawford, Dana Andrews, Henry Fonda, Ruth Warrick, Martha Stewart, Peggy Ann Garner, Connie Marshall, Nicholas Joy, Art Baker.

That Lady in Ermine (1948, Twentieth Century-Fox). Dir and Prod: Ernst Lubitsch and (uncredited) Otto Preminger. Scr: Samson Raphaelson, based on the operetta *Die Frau im Hermelin* (book by Rudolf Schanzer and Ernst Welisch). DP: Leon Shamroy (Technicolor). Sets: Lyle Wheeler, J. Russell Spencer. Music: Alfred Newman. Songs: Frederick Hollander, Leo Robin. Ed: Dorothy Spencer. Cast: Betty Grable, Douglas Fairbanks, Jr., Cesar Romero, Walter Abel, Reginald Gardiner, Harry Davenport.

The Fan (1948/1949, Twentieth Century-Fox). Scr: Walter Reisch, Dorothy Parker, Ross Evans, based on the play by Oscar Wilde. DP: Joseph LaShelle. Sets: Lyle Wheeler, Leland Fuller. Music: Daniele Amfitheatrof. Ed: Louis Loeffler. Cast: Jeanne Crain, Madeleine Carroll, George Sanders, Richard Greene, Martita Hunt, John Sutton, Hugh Dempster, Richard Ney, Virginia McDowall.

Whirlpool (1949/1950, Twentieth Century-Fox). Scr: Ben Hecht, Andrew Solt, based on the novel *Methinks the Lady . . .* by Guy Endore. DP: Arthur Miller. Sets: Lyle Wheeler, Leland Fuller. Music: David Raksin. Ed: Louis Loeffler. Cast: Gene Tierney, Richard Conte, José Ferrer, Charles Bickford, Barbara O'Neil, Eduard Franz, Constance Collier, Fortunio Bonanova.

Where the Sidewalk Ends (1950, Twentieth Century-Fox). Scr: Ben Hecht, based on the novel *Night Cry* by William L. Stuart (adapted by Victor Trivas, Frank P. Rosenberg, and Robert E. Kent). DP: Joseph LaShelle. Sets: Lyle Wheeler, J. Russell Spencer. Music: Cyril Mockridge. Ed: Louis Loeffler. Cast: Dana Andrews, Gene Tierney, Gary Merrill, Bert Freed, Karl Malden, Tom Tully, Ruth Donnelly, Craig Stevens, Robert Simon, Harry von Zell, Don Appell, Neville Brand, Grace Mills, Oleg Cassini.

The 13th Letter (1951, Twentieth Century-Fox). Scr: Howard Koch, based on the story and screenplay by Louis Chavance and Henri-Georges Clouzot for Clouzot's film *Le Corbeau*. DP: Joseph LaShelle. Sets: Lyle Wheeler, Maurice Ransford. Music: Alex North. Ed: Louis Loeffler. Cast: Michael Rennie, Charles Boyer, Constance Smith, Linda Darnell, Françoise Rosay, Judith Evelyn, Guy Sorel, June Hedin.

Angel Face (1952/1953, RKO). Scr: Frank Nugent, Oscar Millard, based on a story by Chester Erskine. DP: Harry Stradling. Sets: Albert S. D'Agostino, Carroll Clark. Music: Dimitri Tiomkin. Ed: Frederic Knudtson. Cast: Robert Mitchum, Jean Simmons, Mona Freeman, Herbert Marshall, Leon Ames, Barbara O'Neil, Kenneth Tobey, Raymond Greenleaf, Jim Backus, Robert Gist, Frank Kumagai, May Takasugi.

The Moon Is Blue (1952/1953, Holmby Productions/United Artists). Scr: F. Hugh Herbert, based on his play. DP: Ernest Laszlo. Sets: Nicolai Remisoff. Music: Herschel Burke Gilbert. Ed: Otto Ludwig. Cast: Maggie McNamara, William Holden, David Niven, Dawn Addams, Tom Tully, Fortunio Bonanova, Gregory Ratoff.

Die Jungfrau auf dem Dach (1952/1953, Holmby Productions/United Artists). Scr: F. Hugh Herbert, based on his play *The Moon Is Blue*. German dialogue: Carl Zuckmayer. DP: Ernest Laszlo. Sets: Nicolai Remisoff. Music: Herschel Burke Gilbert. Ed: Otto Ludwig. Cast: Hardy Krüger, Johanna Matz, Johannes Heesters, Dawn Addams, Sig Ruman, Gregory Ratoff.

River of No Return (1953/1954, Twentieth Century-Fox). Dir: Otto Preminger (and Jean Negulesco, uncredited). Prod: Stanley Rubin. Scr: Frank Fenton, based on a story by Louis Lantz. DP: Joseph LaShelle (Technicolor, CinemaScope). Sets: Lyle Wheeler, Addison Hehr. Music: Cyril Mockridge. Songs: Lionel Newman, Ken Darby. Ed: Louis Loeffler. Cast: Robert Mitchum, Marilyn Monroe, Rory Calhoun, Tommy Rettig, Murvyn Vye, Douglas Spencer, Don Beddoe, Arthur Shields.

Carmen Jones (1954, Carlyle Productions/Twentieth Century-Fox). Scr: Harry Kleiner, based on the musical (book by Oscar Hammerstein II), the opera *Carmen* (libretto by Henri Meilhac and Ludovic Halévy), and the novella *Carmen* by Prosper Mérimée. DP: Sam Leavitt (Technicolor, CinemaScope). Sets: Edward L. Ilou. Music: Georges Bizet. Music Director: Herschel Burke Gilbert. Ed: Louis Loeffler. Cast: Dorothy Dandridge, Harry Belafonte, Pearl Bailey, Olga James, Joe Adams, Brock Peters, Diahann Carroll.

The Court-Martial of Billy Mitchell (1955, United States Pictures/Warner Bros.). Prod: Milton Sperling. Scr: Milton Sperling, Emmet Lavery (and Ben Hecht, uncredited). DP: Sam Leavitt (WarnerColor, CinemaScope). Sets: Malcolm Bert. Music: Dimitri Tiomkin. Ed: Folmar Blangsted. Cast: Gary Cooper, Charles Bickford, Ralph Bellamy, Rod Steiger, Elizabeth Montgomery, Fred Clark, James Daly, Jack Lord, Peter Graves, Darren McGavin, Robert Simon.

The Man with the Golden Arm (1955, Carlyle Productions/United Artists). Scr: Walter Newman, Lewis Meltzer (and Ben Hecht, uncredited), based on the novel by Nelson Algren. DP: Sam Leavitt. Sets: Joe Wright. Music: Elmer Bernstein. Ed: Louis R. Loeffler. Cast: Frank Sinatra, Eleanor Parker, Kim Novak, Arnold Stang, Darren McGavin, Robert Strauss, John Conte, Doro Merande, George E. Stone, George Mathews, Leonid Kinskey, Emile Meyer, Shorty Rogers, Will Wright.

Saint Joan (1957, Wheel Productions/United Artists). Scr: Graham Greene, based on the play by George Bernard Shaw. DP: Georges Périnal. Sets: Roger Furse. Music: Mischa Spoliansky. Ed: Helga Cranston. Cast: Jean Seberg, Richard Widmark, Richard Todd, John Gielgud, Anton Walbrook, Felix Aylmer, Harry Andrews, Barry Jones, Kenneth Haigh, Finlay Currie, Bernard Miles, Victor Maddern.

Bonjour Tristesse (1958, Wheel Productions/Columbia). Scr: Arthur Laurents, based on the novel by Françoise Sagan. DP: Georges Périnal (Technicolor, CinemaScope). Sets: Roger Furse. Music: Georges Auric. Ed: Helga Cranston. Cast: Jean Seberg, David Niven, Deborah Kerr, Mylène Demongeot, Geoffrey Horne, Walter Chiari, Martita Hunt, Juliette Gréco.

Porgy and Bess (1958/1959, Samuel Goldwyn Productions/Columbia). Prod: Samuel Goldwyn. Scr: N. Richard Nash, based on the opera (libretto by DuBose Heyward) and the play *Porgy* by DuBose and Dorothy Heyward. DP: Leon Shamroy (Technicolor, Todd-AO). Sets: Oliver Smith. Music: George Gershwin, Ken Darby. Music supervisor: André Previn. Ed: Daniel Mandell. Cast: Sidney Poitier, Dorothy Dandridge, Sammy Davis, Jr., Pearl Bailey, Brock Peters, Diahann Carroll, Leslie Scott, Ruth Attaway.

Anatomy of a Murder (1959, Carlyle Productions/Columbia). Scr: Wendell Mayes, based on the novel by Robert Traver (John Voelker). DP: Sam Leavitt. Sets: Boris Leven. Music: Duke Ellington. Ed: Louis R. Loeffler. Cast: James Stewart, Lee Remick, Ben Gazzara, Arthur O'Connell, Eve Arden, George C. Scott, Joseph Welch, Kathryn Grant, Murray Hamilton, Brooks West.

Exodus (1960, Carlyle-Alpina Productions/United Artists). Scr: Dalton Trumbo, based on the novel by Leon Uris. DP: Sam Leavitt (Technicolor, Super Panavision 70). Sets: Richard Day. Music: Ernest Gold. Ed: Louis R. Loeffler. Cast: Paul Newman, Eva Marie Saint, Sal Mineo, Jill Haworth, Ralph Richardson, Peter Lawford, Lee J. Cobb, David Opatoshu, John Derek, Felix Aylmer, Hugh Griffith, Gregory Ratoff, Michael Wager, Alexandra Stewart.

Advise & Consent (1961/1962, Alpha-Alpina Productions/Columbia). Scr: Wendell Mayes, based on the novel by Allen Drury. DP: Sam Leavitt (Panavision). Sets: Lyle Wheeler. Music: Jerry Fielding. Ed: Louis R. Loeffler. Cast: Don Murray, Walter Pidgeon, Henry Fonda, Charles Laughton, Franchot Tone, Lew Ayres, George Grizzard, Inga Swenson, Peter Lawford, Gene Tierney, Burgess Meredith, Eddie Hodges, Paul Ford.

The Cardinal (1963, Gamma Productions/Columbia). Scr: Robert Dozier (and Ring Lardner, Jr., and Gore Vidal, uncredited), based on the novel by Henry Morton Robinson. DP: Leon Shamroy (Technicolor, Panavision). Sets: Lyle Wheeler, Otto Niedermoser. Music: Jerome Moross. Ed: Louis R. Loeffler. Cast: Tom Tryon, Romy Schneider, Carol Lynley, John Huston, Josef Meinrad, Burgess Meredith, Jill Haworth, Raf Vallone, John Saxon, Tullio Carminati, Ossie Davis, Dorothy Gish, Maggie McNamara, Robert Morse.

In Harm's Way (1964/1965, Sigma Productions/Paramount). Scr: Wendell Mayes, based on the novel Harm's Way by James Bassett. DP: Loyal Griggs (Panavision). Sets: Lyle Wheeler. Music: Jerry Goldsmith. Ed: George Tomasini, Hugh S. Fowler. Cast: John Wayne, Kirk Douglas, Patricia Neal, Tom Tryon, Paula Prentiss, Brandon de Wilde, Jill Haworth, Burgess Meredith, Dana Andrews, Stanley Holloway, Franchot Tone, Patrick O'Neal, Carroll O'Connor, George Kennedy, Barbara Bouchet, Henry Fonda.

Bunny Lake Is Missing (1965, Wheel Productions/Columbia). Scr: John and Penelope Mortimer, based on the novel by Evelyn Piper (Merriam Modell). DP: Denys Coop (Panavision). Sets: Don Ashton. Music: Paul Glass. Ed: Peter Thornton. Cast: Carol Lynley, Keir Dullea, Laurence Olivier, Noël Coward, Anna Massey, Martita Hunt, Clive Revill, Lucie Mannheim, the Zombies, Finlay Currie.

Hurry Sundown (1966/1967, Sigma Productions/Paramount). Scr: Thomas C. Ryan, Horton Foote, based on the novel by K. B. Gilden (Bert and Katya Gilden). DP: Milton Krasner, Loyal Griggs (Technicolor, Panavision). Music: Hugo Montenegro. Ed: Louis R. Loeffler, James Wells. Cast: Michael Caine, Jane Fonda, John Phillip Law, Diahann Carroll, Robert Hooks, Faye Dunaway, Burgess Meredith, George Kennedy, Beah Richards, Rex Ingram, Robert Reed, Jim Backus, Doro Merande.

Skidoo (1968, Sigma Productions/Paramount). Scr: Doran William Cannon (and Elliott Baker, uncredited). DP: Leon Shamroy (Technicolor, Panavision). Sets: Robert E. Smith. Music: Harry Nilsson. Ed: George Rohrs. Cast: Jackie Gleason, Carol Channing, John Phillip Law, Groucho Marx, Austin Pendleton, Alexandra Hay, Luna, Frankie Avalon, Fred Clark, Michael Constantine, Frank Gorshin, Peter Lawford, Burgess Meredith, George Raft, Cesar Romero, Mickey Rooney, Arnold Stang, Harry Nilsson.

Tell Me That You Love Me, Junie Moon (1969/1970, Sigma Productions/Paramount). Scr: Marjorie Kellogg, based on her novel. DP: Boris Kaufman, Stanley Cortez (Technicolor). Sets: Lyle Wheeler. Music: Philip Springer. Ed: Henry Berman, Dean O. Ball. Cast: Liza Minnelli, Ken Howard, Robert Moore, James Coco, Kay Thompson, Fred Williamson, Ben Piazza, Emily Yancy, Leonard Frey, Clarice Taylor, James Beard, Anne Revere, Pete Seeger.

Such Good Friends (1971, Sigma Productions/Paramount). Scr: Esther Dale (Elaine May), based on the novel by Lois Gould (adapted by David Shaber). DP: Gayne Rescher (Movielab Color). Sets: Rouben Ter-Arutunian. Music: Thomas Z. Shepard. Ed: Harry Howard. Cast: Dyan Cannon, Ken Howard, James Coco, Jennifer O'Neill, Laurence Luckinbill, Nina Foch, Louise Lasser, Burgess Meredith, Sam Levene, Rita Gam, Nancy Guild.

Rosebud (1974/1975, Sigma Productions/United Artists). Scr: Erik Lee Preminger (and Marjorie Kellogg and Roy Clarke, uncredited), based on the novel by Joan Hemingway and Paul Bonnecarrère. DP: Denys Coop (Eastmancolor, Panavision). Sets: Michael Seymour. Music: Laurent Petitgirard. Ed: Peter Thornton, Thom Noble. Cast: Peter O'Toole, Cliff Gorman, Richard Attenborough, Isabelle Huppert, Josef Shiloah, Amidou, Claude Dauphin, John V. Lindsay, Peter Lawford, Raf Vallone, Kim Cattrall.

The Human Factor (1979, Wheel Productions/MGM). Scr: Tom Stoppard, based on the novel by Graham Greene. DP: Mike Molloy (Technicolor). Sets: Ken Ryan. Music: Richard Logan, Gary Logan. Ed: Richard Trevor. Cast: Nicol Williamson, Iman, Richard Attenborough, Derek Jacobi, Robert Morley, Joop Doderer, John Gielgud, Ann Todd, Richard Vernon.

Acknowledgments

I owe an unpayable debt to the many people (some of them now departed) who were so kind and generous as to share with me their memories of Otto Preminger and their thoughts about his films: Jared Barclay, Yoram Ben-Ami, Peter Bogdanovich, June Callwood, Pat Crowley, Elfi von Dassanowsky, Michael Daves, Mylène Demongeot, Keir Dullea, Ilan Eldad, Larry Frisch, Ben Gazzara, George Grizzard, Ilan Hartuv, Eddie Hodges, Ken Howard, Helga Keller (Cranston), Marjorie Kellogg, Don Kranze, John Phillip Law, Klaus Löwitsch, Mike Molloy, Eva Monley, Rui Nogueira, Gerry O'Hara, Charles Okun, Austin Pendleton, Brock Peters, Otto Plaschkes, Larry Powell, Erik Lee Preminger, Hope Preminger, Ingo Preminger, Victoria Preminger, Paula Prentiss, David Raksin, Val Robins, Stanley Rubin, Barrett Rudich, Glynn Rudich, Eva Marie Saint, Martin and Pat Schute, Tom Stoppard, Bertrand Tavernier, Bob Vietro, and Yoel Zilberg.

I am in great debt to the many people at archives, libraries, and research institutions who made it possible for me to view prints of Preminger films and consult manuscripts and rare printed materials. These institutions included the Austrian Film Museum (Alex Horwath); the British Film Institute; the Cinémathèque française (Laure Bouissou); the Filmarchiv Austria; the Filmmuseum Berlin—Stiftung Deutsche Kinemathek (Rolf Aurich, Wolfgang Jacobsen, Hans Helmut Prinzler, Gerrit Thies); the Howard Gotlieb Archival Research Center, Boston University; the Harvard Film Archive (Julie Buck, Steve Livernash, Clayton Mattos) and Houghton Library, Harvard University; the Margaret Herrick Library, Academy of Motion Picture Arts and Sciences; the Library of Congress (Madeline Matz); the New York Public Library for the Performing Arts; New York State Archives; Paramount Pictures

(Barry Allen); the Harry Ransom Humanities Research Center, University of Texas at Austin; the Theater in der Josefstadt; UCLA Arts Library Special Collections (Lauren Buisson); the UCLA Film and Television Archive; the Cinema/Television Library (Ned Comstock) and the Warner Bros. Archives at the University of Southern California; Wesleyan Cinema Archives, Wesleyan University; the Wisconsin Center for Film and Theater Research; and Yale University Library Manuscripts and Archives.

Special thanks to Larry Chadbourne and Gregg Rickman for providing tapes; Mattias Frey, Gretchen Hachmeister, and Ria You for translating German texts; Monica Garrido and Liz Murphy for research assistance; Claudia Hahn-Raabe for making it possible for me to learn a little German at the Goethe-Institut in Berlin and Boston; A. S. Hamrah and Miguel Marías for their comments on the manuscript of the book; Rachel Innerarity for transcribing interviews; Ken Kramer for showing me his beautiful print of *Porgy and Bess*; Denise Oswald, my editor; John Thornton, my agent; and Ran Blake, David Bordwell, Paul Buhle, Robert von Dassanowsky, Frank Lafond, Bill Krohn, Blake Lucas, Herbert Poetzl, Dana Polan, Pierre Rissient, Phil Schaap, David Shalit, Yehuda Stav, Dede Tryon, Walter van de Leur, Dave Wagner, Sachiko Watanabe, and Michael Henry Wilson. Extra special thanks to Olivier Eyquem, a consummate Premingerian, for sharing with me audio interviews, photographs, and nuggets from his extensive research.

Index